THE SPEECHES OF AESCHINES

106

THE SPEECHES OF AESCHINES

WITH AN ENGLISH TRANSLATION BY
CHARLES DARWIN ADAMS, Ph.D.
LAWRENCE PROFESSOR OF GREEK IN DARTMOUTH COLLEGE

AGAINST TIMARCHUS

ON THE EMBASSY

AGAINST CTESIPHON

CAMBRIDGE MASSACHUSETTS
HARVARD UNIVERSITY PRESS
LONDON
WILLIAM HEINEMANN LTD
MCMLXXXVIII

American ISBN 0-674-99118-4
British ISBN 0 434 99106 6

First printed 1919
Reprinted 1948, 1958, 1968, 1988

*Printed in Great Britain by
Richard Clay Ltd, Bungay, Suffolk*

CONTENTS

INTRODUCTION

THE LIFE OF AESCHINES

OUR knowledge of the family and life of Aeschines comes from his own speeches and those of Demosthenes. The brief biographies which have come down to us are late and untrustworthy. At the time of the speech *On the Embassy* we hear of Aeschines' father as an old man of ninety-four years. He was in the court-room, and Demosthenes, speaking to a jury some of whom, at least, were likely to know something of the family, and speaking subject to contradiction by Aeschines, whose plea was to follow his, makes no serious charge against Aeschines' family. He speaks contemptuously of the poverty of the schoolmaster-father (xix. 249) and sarcastically of the mother's " harvest " from the property of the people who resorted to her " initiations and purifications " (xix. 199, 249, 281). But in the speech *On the Crown*, delivered thirteen years later, when the father was no longer alive and few of the hearers would remember the family, and when, moreover, Demosthenes, as the last speaker in the case, was not subject to contradiction by Aeschines, he gives free rein to a malignant imagination, and paints a picture of a slave-schoolmaster and a shameless harlot mother, which deserves no serious attention. From the uncontradicted statements of both orators in their speeches *On the Embassy* we gather the following facts.

Aeschines was born about 390 B.C. His father, Atrometus, had already lost his property in the Peloponnesian war, had been exiled with the rest of the democrats by the Thirty Tyrants, and had shared in the glorious enterprise of the democratic " return." The mother, Glaucothea, was sister of a successful general, Cleobulus. The children of such parents had a right to be proud both of the purity of their blood and the patriotic achievements of father and uncle. But the losses by war and exile forced the father to take up the little honoured profession of schoolmaster, while the mother, we may perhaps believe, contributed something to the support of the family by service as a priestess in some one of the secret religious cults.

We hear of three sons in the schoolmaster's family, all reaching positions of some honour in the public service. The eldest, Philochares, served under the famous Iphicrates, and was himself in 343 serving his third successive term as general. The third son, Aphobetus, had in the same year already made a record for himself as an ambassador to Persia, and had received the high honour of election as a special Commissioner of Finance.

Aeschines, the second son, was performing the regular services of an Athenian young man as cadet when the battle of Leuctra plunged Greece into the nine years' Theban wars. He won the praise of his commander in an expedition for the relief of Phlius in 366, and served in other Athenian expeditions, at last taking part in the battle of Mantinea. All this was in his early manhood. In subsequent years we find him serving in the successful expedition for the relief of Eretria in Euboea, hastily organized under the enthusiasm aroused by Timotheus (357 B.C.), and in the Euboean expedition of 348. In the latter, Aeschines' bravery at the battle of Tamynae was so distinguished that he received a wreath of honour from his commanding officers, and was appointed one of the two messengers to carry the news of the victory to Athens, where he was again crowned as the bringer of good news (Aeschines *On the Embassy*, §§ 167 ff.).

In the earlier years of his citizenship Aeschines was employed with his younger brother as a clerk in the civil service. But military service and clerical employment were only incidental or temporary occupations for the gifted young man. His early profession became that of tragic actor. The organization of the Athenian stage was such that a group of three men naturally formed a " company." Aeschines became the third member of a company of which the two most famous actors of the time, Theodorus and Aristodemus, were the chiefs. We conclude that as an actor he fell just short of the highest attainments. The sneers with which

INTRODUCTION

Demosthenes in his speech *On the Crown* refers to his efforts on the stage are in flat contradiction to Demosthenes' own testimony in the earlier speech that he was associated with actors of such rank. It appears from Demosthenes xix. 337 that by the year 343 Aeschines had left the stage.

We cannot trace the steps by which Aeschines made his way to political influence. We hear only of his holding an elective clerkship, probably that of reader of documents to senate and assembly, a position for which he was well fitted by his stage training in elocution. But when in 348 Philip of Macedon had destroyed Olynthus and seized the whole Chalcidic peninsula, Aeschines took an active part in arousing Athens to meet the danger which was threatening her interests. And when, on motion of Eubulus, it was voted to send ambassadors to the Greek states to invite them to a congress for concerted action toward Macedon — whether for war or peace — Aeschines was sent on one of the most important missions, that to Arcadia. Two facts are evident here : that Aeschines was now, at the age forty-two, already a man of influence in political affairs, and that he was a supporter of Eubulus, the great leader of the conservatives. When, shortly after this, Aeschines' former associate on the stage, Aristodemus, had unofficially opened the way for peace negotiations with Philip, it was natural that Aeschines, both as his personal friend and a man already active in anti-Macedonian preparations, should

be made one of the ten ambassadors to treat with
Philip. Here he came into intimate relations with
Demosthenes, who had already come to the front,
during Philip's movement against Olynthus, as the
ablest of the radical leaders. The part which Aeschines and Demosthenes each played in this embassy
to Macedonia, in the deliberations at Athens with the
ambassadors whom Philip sent in his turn, in the
negotiations of the second embassy (for the ratification
of the peace of Philocrates, which Philip's ambassadors
had negotiated at Athens), and in the final report at
Athens, is discussed by both orators in great detail
and with irreconcilable contradictions in the speeches
On the Embassy and *On the Crown*. It seems to the
writer probable that Aeschines worked honourably
on the first embassy, though with less effect than his
vanity led him to think ; that he agreed with Demosthenes in at first opposing the terms proposed by
Philocrates, but joined Demosthenes the next day in
accepting them as the best to which Philip's
ambassadors would consent; that he went on the
second embassy believing that he could persuade
Philip to interpret the peace in a way more favourable to Athens than the literal terms of the treaty
demanded, and that he returned to Athens convinced
that he had succeeded and that Philip was about to
humble Thebes. In all this he had been completely
deceived by the astute Macedonian, and by his report
to the people he prevented any attempt on the part
of Athens to interfere before Philip could come down

and take possession of Phocis. Of course in all this Demosthenes saw sheer bribery. He was probably honest in his conviction that Aeschines had, after the first embassy, gone over to the paid service of Philip. Of this there is no proof whatever; the conduct of Aeschines is entirely explicable as that of a man of only mediocre political ability, flattered by his success as a public speaker and his rapid advance as a diplomat, and shrewdly used by Philip, the master of diplomacy.

On receipt of the news of the surrender of the Phocians, ambassadors were appointed to go to Philip for the protection of Athenian interests. They found Philip and his Thessalian and Theban allies deliberating with the Amphictyonic Council (in a special session, to which Athens had refused to send delegates) as to the fate of the Phocians. Aeschines, though properly having no voice in the Council, appeared before them and pleaded successfully for a mitigation of the severe penalty that some of the delegates were urging.

After the decision of the Amphictyonic Council as to the fate of the Phocians, and the reorganization of the Council, Philip held a thanksgiving feast, in which Aeschines and the other Athenian ambassadors took part.

On his return to Athens Aeschines found himself under grave suspicion. The peace was now detested by the whole people, and all who had urged it were suspected of having acted as agents of Macedon.

INTRODUCTION

Meanwhile Demosthenes, whether from an honest conviction that Aeschines had been playing the traitor, or in order to turn the anger of the people from himself as one of the authors of the peace, made haste to bring indictment against Aeschines on the charge of treason in the second embassy. In this proceeding Demosthenes was joined by Timarchus, a prominent politician of the anti-Macedonian group, and an associate of Demosthenes in the senate the year before. Aeschines was in extreme peril. His first move was to secure delay until popular excitement should have time to abate, and to discredit the prosecution, by bringing a counter indictment against Timarchus. It was notorious that Timarchus had in his earlier life been a spendthrift and a libertine. Aeschines now attacked him in the courts under a law which excluded from the platform of the Athenian assembly any man found to have prostituted his person or squandered his patrimony. Aeschines won his case, thus ridding himself of one of his prosecutors, and prejudicing Demosthenes' suit.

Demosthenes nevertheless persisted in the prosecution, and in 343 the case against Aeschines came to trial. The speeches of both prosecutor and defendant are preserved. Both show how deadly the hatred between the two men had become. Demosthenes failed to secure conviction in the court, but the effect of the attack must have been to shake the confidence of the people in Aeschines' loyalty, while it made Demosthenes still more prominent as the head of the anti-Macedonian movement.

In the following years it is evident that both men were constantly on the watch for opportunities for personal attack, but Aeschines seems to have taken no prominent part in public affairs. Demosthenes was steadily growing in influence, arousing the anti-Macedonian feeling in Athens, and building up an alliance with other states against Philip. He had finally succeeded in bringing Athens to an open break with Philip, and in checking his advance to the Euxine by the rescue of Perinthus and Byzantium, when in 339 his enemy Aeschines quite unexpectedly found himself in a position which seemed to promise the recovery of his own prestige and his return to influence in international affairs. The occasion was a meeting of the Amphictyonic Council at Delphi. Aeschines was one of the Athenian delegation, though not one of the two voting members. A sharp dispute having arisen between the representatives of the little state Amphissa and the Athenian representatives, Aeschines took the lead in proposing the proclamation of a holy war against the Amphissians, on the ground that they had transgressed ancient decrees setting aside certain territory close to Delphi as consecrated to Apollo. Returning to Athens, elated at the prominence that he had attained in the Amphictyonic proceedings, Aeschines tried to persuade the people to endorse his holy war. In this he met the determined opposition of Demosthenes, who succeeded in convincing the people that a war of this sort would, like the late Phocian war, give to Philip precisely the opportunity he was waiting for—to come down into central Greece as champion of one section against another, and so to gain control of both. The other Amphictyonic states voted for the war, but Athens and Thebes held aloof, and together stood against Philip when, under the opportunity offered by the war, he came down with his allies. (A full account of the whole affair is given in the speech of Aeschines *Against Ctesiphon*, §§ 106 ff., and that of Demosthenes *On the Crown*, §§ 145 ff.) In all this Amphictyonic proceeding Aeschines had shown himself zealous and eloquent, nor is there any reason for believing Demosthenes' charge that he had been hired by Philip to stir up an Amphictyonic war. The only criticism that can be made as to his motives is that perhaps he was actuated in part by ambition to secure personal and party advantage over Demosthenes. But he was fatally short-sighted. The one disaster against which any public man in Athens should have been on his guard at just that time was any disturbance among the Greek states that could give Philip a pretext for intervention.

After the defeat of Athens and her allies at Chaeronea in 338, Aeschines was one of the ambassadors sent by Athens to open negotiations for peace, a service to which he was naturally called both because of his cordial relations with Philip on the two earlier embassies, and because of his opposition to the war party of Demosthenes.

We have no further mention of definite political activity of Aeschines until the year 336, when Ctesiphon made his motion that the city should confer a golden crown on Demosthenes in recognition of his lifelong patriotic service. Aeschines now saw his opportunity for revenge for the savage attack that Demosthenes had made on him seven years before. He instituted suit against Ctesiphon as having made an illegal motion. For reasons that are wholly unknown to us the trial of the case was delayed for six years. When at last the trial came, Aeschines was overwhelmingly defeated. His humiliation was such that he left the city. He is said to have gone to Ephesus, thence to Rhodes, where he became a teacher of rhetoric, and finally to have removed to Samos, where he died at the age of seventy-five.

A review of Aeschines' political career shows that he was not, like Demosthenes, a great party leader, nor does he seem to have been constantly active in public affairs (*cp.* Demosthenes *On the Crown,* §§ 307 ff.). Only on special occasions did he come into prominence. He was a steady supporter of Eubulus and Phocion, the great conservatives, who after the establishment of Philip's power in the north believed in a policy of peace with him. There

is no doubt that Aeschines was a friend of both
Philip and Alexander, but there is no proof that he
was ever in their pay; there was no need of bribery
with a man whose limited understanding and un-
limited vanity made him so easy a tool.

In the two speeches of Aeschines in which we
should expect a review of the whole field of international relations during the critical period of the
rise of the Macedonian power, we find nowhere any
large grasp of the situation, no broad view of either
Athenian or Hellenic interests, nothing statesman-
like in the discussion of policies. This is the fundamental defect that places him on a plane entirely
below that of Demosthenes. Both men indulge in
all possible accusations and slanders, both carry
personal attack beyond the bounds of decency;
but in Demosthenes these personal features are subordinate; the final impression, in the case of
Demosthenes' speech *On the Crown*, at least, is one
of broad statesmanship. To this height Aeschines
cannot rise.

We know nothing of Aeschines' training for
public speaking. The brief biographies which have
come down to us connect him with some of the
rhetorical teachers of the time, but these accounts
are late and untrustworthy. His training for the
stage and his experience there gave him a refined
literary taste, and a wide and excellent vocabulary,
together with thorough discipline in elocution and
gesture. Moreover the current rhetorical devices,

the "figures" of speech and rhetoric, all the superficial tricks of the trade, were so generally "in the air" in the time of Aeschines' youth, that he required no special training of the schools to give him the mastery of them which his speeches show. He never, however, attained full command of the condensed, rounded rhetorical period, which is the consummate product of the art of rhetoric. He is at his best in clear narrative and vivid description. Perhaps it was his early service in clerical offices which gave him his facility in expounding legal documents. In the higher forms of reasoning he is less successful. Personal feeling and prejudice are so constantly evident, and so often lead to exaggerated assertion and unfair inference, that he fails to carry conviction. His style passes readily from exposition and argument to the emotional, where he knows how to inspire the real tragic feeling of his earlier profession. Aeschines has the art of putting himself readily upon the most familiar terms with his audience ; he likes to talk the matter over with them rather than to declaim to them ; his only fault here is a tendency to assume something of the didactic tone of the schoolmaster. He has the pride in exhibiting his knowledge of history and in quotation of poetry that is apt to mark the self-made man, and his vanity in his influence as statesman and orator is unconcealed. He often assumes the high moral and patriotic tone, but somehow his moral indignation seldom rings true.

INTRODUCTION

This is perhaps in part due to the difficulty of his situation. Assuming that he was honourably convinced that the best interests of Athens demanded that she keep the friendship of Philip and Alexander, we can see how impossible it was for him to speak out candidly in defence of this conviction. Even after Philip's unexpectedly mild treatment of Athens when the battle of Chaeronea had left her helpless in his hands, the mass of the people looked upon the Macedonian as a deadly foe, and hated the position of dependence into which he had brought their city. Many modern students can and do argue persuasively for the benefits that came to Greece through the extension of the power of Macedon and her world conquest; perhaps Aeschines believed in them, but he could not say so in the Athenian assembly or before an Athenian jury. This fact made it impossible for him to reach the heights of impassioned eloquence that were open to Demosthenes, whose words expressed the deepest convictions of his soul.

BIBLIOGRAPHY

The *Editio Princeps* of the speeches of Aeschines was the Aldus of 1513. Successive stages in the establishment of the text are marked by the editions of Reiske, 1771; Bremi, 1823; Bekker, 1824; Dindorf, 1824; Baiter and Sauppe, 1840; Franke,

INTRODUCTION

1851, 1860 ; Schultz, 1865 ; Weidner, 1872 ; Blass, 1896, 1908.

The speech *Against Ctesiphon* has been edited with explanatory notes by Sommer, Paris, 1842 ; Bremi, Gotha, 1845 ; Champlin, London, 1851 ; G. A. and W. H. Simcox (*The Orations of Demosthenes and Aeschines On the Crown*), Oxford, 1872 ; Weidner, Berlin, 1878 ; Richardson (on the basis of Weidner's edition), Boston, 1889 ; Gwatkin and Shuckburgh, London, 1890.

The speech *On the Embassy* has been edited with explanatory notes by Julien and Péréra, Paris, 1902.

We have a complete *Index Aeschineus* by Preuss, Leipzig, 1896 (bound also with the *editio major* of Blass' Teubner text).

Translations of the speeches are :—

Demosthenes und Aeschines Reden verdeutscht, Reiske, 1764–68.

Aeschines der Redner übersetzt, Bremi, 1828.

Aeschines Reden, Griechisch und Deutsch, übersetzt und erklärt, Benseler, 1855--60.

The Two Orations On the Crown, Biddle, Philadelphia, 1881.

Chefs d'oeuvre de Démosthène et d'Eschine, Stiévenart, 1842, 1889.

Aeschines Rede gegen Ktesiphon, übersetzt, eingel. u erläut., Reeb, 1894.

A translation of Aeschines *Against Ctesiphon* is included in Westermann's translation of *Demosthenes*

INTRODUCTION

Ausgewählte Reden, 1856–73, 1905, and in Leland's translation of selected speeches of Demosthenes (1819).

The most critical and complete account of events involved in the speeches of Aeschines is to be found in Schaefer, *Demosthenes und seine Zeit*. The life and works of Aeschines are discussed in detail by Blass, *Die attische Beredsamkeit*, III. ii.

The events in the contest with Philip are accurately treated in Pickard-Cambridge's *Demosthenes* (1914).

A full account of recent (1886–1912) literature for Aeschines is given by Kurt Emminger in Bursian's *Jahresbericht über die Fortschritte der klassischen Altertumswissenschaft*, Bd. CLXI. (1913), 214–240.

We now have:—

Discours I. *Contre Timarque.* Sur l'embassade infidèle. Ed. and French translation by V. Martin and G. de Budé. Paris. Budé, 1927.

Discours II. *Contre Ctesiphon. Lettres.* Ed. and French translation by V. Martin and G. de Budé. Paris. Budé, 1928.

THE TEXT

The three speeches of Aeschines have come down to us in manuscripts which date from the tenth to the sixteenth century. Twenty-six manuscripts have been collated by successive editors. No one

5

manuscript has commanding superiority. All go back to a common archetype. Editors divide them into three (some into four) groups, and differ in opinion as to the superior value of one or another group.

Twelve letters have come down under the name of Aeschines, but scholars are agreed in denying their genuineness. Certain affidavits and citations of laws contained in the MSS. of the speech *Against Timarchus* are also generally rejected as spurious.

Editors of Aeschines' speeches agree that our manuscripts have been seriously contaminated by numerous marginal notes of ancient editors, which have crept into the text. We constantly find words and phrases which are needless in the context, or inappropriate to it, but which serve to explain some expression or allusion of the orator. Not infrequently these words and phrases bear the external marks of the gloss: variation in position, or inclusion in only a part of the manuscripts. Cobet pointed out many of these glosses; Weidner went to the extreme in rejecting suspicious words and phrases; Blass in his Teubner text rejected some of the same expressions, and bracketed many.

In considering the evidence for or against an expression which is not absolutely necessary to the meaning, and which has something of the appearance of an editor's note, it is to be remembered that in an oral argument before a jury, people of only ordinary intelligence, the speaker himself feels

INTRODUCTION

the need of more detailed explanation and more
repetition of words than would be required in an
argument composed primarily to be read. Moreover,
Aeschines is in general by no means as terse and
vigorous as Demosthenes; the modern critic is in
some danger of making the orator's style better than
it really was. The force of the external signs of the
gloss may also be overrated, for variation in position
in the case of necessary words is not uncommon in
our manuscripts of Aeschines.

In this edition the critical notes record all readings accepted by the editor without manuscript
authority. In matters of orthography Blass' Teubner
text has been followed without note.

BIBLIOGRAPHICAL ADDENDUM (1988)

Editions:

Eschine, Discours (Budé edition by G. de Budé
and V. Martin), Paris 1927 and 1928

Translations:

Demosthenes and Aeschines, trans. by Arnold N.
W. Saunders (Penguin Classics), Harmonds-
worth 1970

General:

G. Kennedy: *The Art of Persuasion in Greece*,
Princeton 1963

L. Pearson: *The Art of Demosthenes*, Meisenheim
1976 (repr. Chico 1981)

THE
SPEECHES OF AESCHINES
I.—AGAINST TIMARCHUS

THE SPEECHES OF AESCHINES

I.—AGAINST TIMARCHUS

345 B.C.

INTRODUCTION

AESCHINES and Demosthenes had served together
on the embassy which had been sent to Macedon [1] to
receive from Philip and his allies their ratification of
the Peace of Philocrates. Soon after their return
Demosthenes, supported by Timarchus, a prominent
politician, who had served with Demosthenes in the
senate the previous year, brought formal charge of
treason against Aeschines. As a counter attack, intended to delay the impending trial, to prejudice the
case of the prosecution, and to rid himself of one of
his prosecutors, Aeschines brought indictment against
Timarchus, declaring that in his earlier life he had
been addicted to personal vices which by law should
for ever exclude him from the platform of the
Athenian assembly. We learn the contents of this
law from §§ 28 ff. A conviction under this law
would not technically exclude Timarchus from prosecuting a case in the courts, but it would so discredit him in popular opinion that it would be fatal
to any case to have him as an advocate. More-

[1] In 346 B.C.

over, Aeschines introduces in his plea another law, which would exclude a man of the lewd life with which he charges Timarchus, not only from the courts, but from all public and religious functions (§§ 19 ff.). In the case of Timarchus, conviction under the first law would be a virtual, though not a technical, conviction under the second.

It was understood that Demosthenes would speak in defence of Timarchus, but we have no knowledge of his speech. Possibly no attempt at defence was made. Aeschines won his case, and Demosthenes was left without help in the prosecution of his case against Aeschines in the matter of the embassy.

I.—ΚΑΤΑ ΤΙΜΑΡΧΟΥ

Οὐδένα πώποτε τῶν πολιτῶν, ὦ ἄνδρες Ἀθηναῖοι, οὔτε γραφὴν γραψάμενος οὔτ' ἐν εὐθύναις λυπήσας, ἀλλ' ὡς ἔγωγε νομίζω μέτριον ἐμαυτὸν πρὸς ἔκαστα τούτων παρεσχηκώς, ὁρῶν δὲ τήν τε πόλιν μεγάλα βλαπτομένην ὑπὸ Τιμάρχου τουτουὶ δημηγοροῦντος παρὰ τοὺς νόμους, καὶ αὐτὸς ἰδίᾳ συκοφαντούμενος (ὃν δὲ τρόπον, προϊ-
2 όντος ἐπιδείξω τοῦ λόγου), ἔν τι τῶν αἰσχίστων ἡγησάμην εἶναι μὴ βοηθῆσαι τῇ τε πόλει πάσῃ καὶ τοῖς νόμοις καὶ ὑμῖν καὶ ἐμαυτῷ· εἰδὼς δ' αὐτὸν ἔνοχον ὄντα οἷς ὀλίγῳ πρότερον ἠκούσατε ἀναγιγνώσκοντος τοῦ γραμματέως, ἐπήγγειλα αὐτῷ τὴν δοκιμασίαν ταυτηνί. καὶ ὡς ἔοικεν, ὦ ἄνδρες Ἀθηναῖοι, οἱ εἰωθότες λόγοι λέγεσθαι ἐπὶ τοῖς δημοσίοις ἀγῶσιν οὐκ εἰσὶ ψευδεῖς· αἱ γὰρ ἴδιαι ἔχθραι πολλὰ πάνυ τῶν κοινῶν ἐπανορθοῦσι.
3 Τοῦ μὲν οὖν ὅλου ἀγῶνος φανήσεται οὔθ' ἡ πόλις αἰτία οὖσα Τιμάρχῳ οὔθ' οἱ νόμοι οὔθ'

---

[1] The Athenian Constitution provided for rigid auditing of the accounts of all officials at the close of their year of office, and gave full opportunity to any citizen to bring charges against any act of their administration. Such opportunity might easily be used for malicious or blackmailing attack.

I.—AGAINST TIMARCHUS

I HAVE never, fellow citizens, brought indictment against any Athenian, nor vexed any man when he was rendering account of his office [1]; but in all such matters I have, as I believe, shown myself a quiet and modest man. [2] But when I saw that the city was being seriously injured by the defendant, Timarchus, who, though disqualified by law, was speaking in your assemblies, [3] and when I myself was made a victim of his blackmailing attack—the nature of the attack I will show in the course of my speech—I decided that it would be a most shameful thing if I failed to come to the defence of the whole city and its laws, and to your defence and my own; and knowing that he was liable to the accusations that you heard read a moment ago by the clerk of the court, I instituted this suit, challenging him to official scrutiny. Thus it appears, fellow citizens, that what is so frequently said of public suits is no mistake, namely, that very often private enmities correct public abuses.

You will see, then, that Timarchus cannot blame the city for any part of this prosecution, nor can he

[2] A quiet citizen, as distinguished from the professional political blackmailer, συκοφάντης.
[3] As the speech proceeds we shall see that Aeschines declares that Timarchus was guilty of immoral practices that disqualified him from speaking before the people.

ὑμεῖς οὔτ' ἐγώ, ἀλλ' αὐτὸς οὗτος ἑαυτῷ. οἱ μὲν
γὰρ νόμοι προεῖπον αὐτῷ αἰσχρῶς βεβιωκότι
μὴ δημηγορεῖν, ἐπίταγμα, ὥς γε δὴ ἐγὼ κρίνω,
οὐ χαλεπὸν ἐπιτάξαντες, ἀλλὰ καὶ πάνυ ῥάδιον·
ἐμὲ δ' ἐξῆν αὐτῷ, εἰ ἐσωφρόνει, μὴ συκοφαντεῖν.
περὶ μὲν οὖν τούτων μετρίως ἐλπίζω μοι προ-
ειρῆσθαι.

4   Οὐκ ἀγνοῶ δέ, ὦ ἄνδρες Ἀθηναῖοι, ἃ μέλλω ἐν
πρώτοις λέγειν, ὅτι φανεῖσθε καὶ ἑτέρων πρότερον
ἀκηκοότες· ἀλλά μοι δοκεῖ καιρὸς εἶναι καὶ ἐμὲ
νῦν πρὸς ὑμᾶς τῷ αὐτῷ λόγῳ χρήσασθαι. ὁμο-
λογοῦνται γὰρ τρεῖς εἶναι πολιτεῖαι παρὰ πᾶσιν
ἀνθρώποις, τυραννὶς καὶ ὀλιγαρχία καὶ δημο-
κρατία· διοικοῦνται δ' αἱ μὲν τυραννίδες καὶ
ὀλιγαρχίαι τοῖς τρόποις τῶν ἐφεστηκότων, αἱ
δὲ πόλεις αἱ δημοκρατούμεναι τοῖς νόμοις τοῖς
5   κειμένοις. εὖ δ' ἴστε, ὦ ἄνδρες Ἀθηναῖοι, ὅτι
τὰ μὲν τῶν δημοκρατουμένων σώματα καὶ τὴν
πολιτείαν οἱ νόμοι σῴζουσι, τὰ δὲ τῶν τυράννων καὶ ὀλιγαρχικῶν[1] ἀπιστία καὶ ἡ μετὰ
τῶν ὅπλων φρουρά. φυλακτέον δὴ τοῖς μὲν
ὀλιγαρχικοῖς καὶ τοῖς τὴν ἄνισον πολιτείαν
πολιτευομένοις τοὺς ἐν χειρῶν νόμῳ τὰς πολιτείας καταλύοντας, ὑμῖν δὲ τοῖς τὴν ἴσην
καὶ ἔννομον πολιτείαν ἔχουσι τοὺς παρὰ τοὺς
νόμους ἢ λέγοντας ἢ βεβιωκότας· ἐντεῦθεν γὰρ
ἰσχύσετε, ὅταν εὐνομῆσθε καὶ μὴ καταλύησθε
6   ὑπὸ τῶν παρανομούντων. προσήκειν δὲ ἔγωγε
νομίζω, ὅταν μὲν νομοθετῶμεν, τοῦθ' ἡμᾶς σκοπεῖν, ὅπως καλῶς ἔχοντας καὶ συμφέροντας

---

[1] ὀλιγαρχικῶν Taylor : ὀλιγαρχιῶν MSS.

blame the laws, nor you, nor me, but only himself. For because of his shameful private life the laws forbade him to speak before the people, laying on him an injunction not difficult, in my opinion, to obey—nay, most easy; and had he been wise, he need not have made his slanderous attack upon me. I hope, therefore, that in this introduction I have spoken as a quiet and modest citizen ought to speak.

I am aware, fellow citizens, that the statement which I am about to make first is something that you will undoubtedly have heard from other men on other occasions; but I think the same thought is especially timely on this occasion, and from me. It is acknowledged, namely, that there are in the world three forms of government, autocracy, oligarchy, and democracy: autocracies and oligarchies are administered according to the tempers of their lords, but democratic states according to established laws. And be assured, fellow citizens, that in a democracy it is the laws that guard the person of the citizen and the constitution of the state, whereas the despot and the oligarch find their protection in suspicion and in armed guards. Men, therefore, who administer an oligarchy, or any government based upon inequality, must be on their guard against those who attempt revolution by the law of force; but you, who have a government based upon equality and law, must guard against those whose words violate the laws or whose lives have defied them; for then only will you be strong, when you cherish the laws, and when the revolutionary attempts of lawless men shall have ceased. And it behooves us, I think, not only when we are enacting laws, to consider always how the laws that we make may be

νόμους τῇ πολιτείᾳ θησόμεθα, ἐπειδὰν δὲ νομο-
θετήσωμεν, τοῖς νόμοις τοῖς κειμένοις πείθεσθαι,
τοὺς δὲ μὴ πειθομένους κολάζειν, εἰ δεῖ τὰ τῆς
πόλεως καλῶς ἔχειν.

Σκέψασθε γάρ, ὦ ἄνδρες Ἀθηναῖοι, ὅσην
πρόνοιαν περὶ σωφροσύνης ἐποιήσατο ὁ Σόλων
ἐκεῖνος, ὁ παλαιὸς νομοθέτης, καὶ ὁ Δράκων καὶ
7 οἱ κατὰ τοὺς χρόνους ἐκείνους νομοθέται. πρῶτον
μὲν γὰρ περὶ τῆς σωφροσύνης τῶν παίδων τῶν
ἡμετέρων ἐνομοθέτησαν, καὶ διαρρήδην ἀπέδειξαν,
ἃ χρὴ τὸν παῖδα τὸν ἐλεύθερον ἐπιτηδεύειν, καὶ
ὡς δεῖ αὐτὸν τραφῆναι, ἔπειτα δεύτερον περὶ τῶν
μειρακίων, τρίτον δ' ἐφεξῆς περὶ τῶν ἄλλων
ἡλικιῶν, οὐ μόνον περὶ τῶν ἰδιωτῶν, ἀλλὰ καὶ
περὶ τῶν ῥητόρων. καὶ τούτους τοὺς νόμους
ἀναγράψαντες ὑμῖν παρακατέθεντο, καὶ ὑμᾶς
αὐτῶν ἐπέστησαν φύλακας.

8 Βούλομαι δὴ καὶ ἐγὼ νυνὶ πρὸς ὑμᾶς τὸν αὐτὸν
τρόπον χρήσασθαι τῷ λόγῳ ὅνπερ τοῖς νόμοις ὁ
νομοθέτης. πρῶτον μὲν γὰρ διέξειμι πρὸς ὑμᾶς
τοὺς νόμους οἳ κεῖνται περὶ τῆς εὐκοσμίας τῶν
παίδων τῶν ὑμετέρων, ἔπειτα δεύτερον τοὺς περὶ
τῶν μειρακίων, τρίτον δ' ἐφεξῆς τοὺς περὶ τῶν
ἄλλων ἡλικιῶν, οὐ μόνον περὶ τῶν ἰδιωτῶν, ἀλλὰ
καὶ περὶ τῶν ῥητόρων· οὕτω γὰρ ἄν μοι μάλιστα
ὑπολαμβάνω τοὺς λόγους εὐμαθεῖς γενέσθαι.
ἅμα δὲ καὶ βούλομαι, ὦ ἄνδρες Ἀθηναῖοι, διεξελθεῖν πρῶτον πρὸς ὑμᾶς, ὡς ἔχουσιν οἱ νόμοι οἱ
τῆς πόλεως,[1] πάλιν δὲ μετὰ τοῦτο ἀντεξετάσαι
τοὺς τρόπους τοὺς Τιμάρχου· εὑρήσετε γὰρ αὐτὸν
ἐναντίως ἅπασι τοῖς νόμοις βεβιωκότα.

---

[1] οἱ τῆς πόλεως H. Wolf : περὶ τῆς πόλεως MSS.

good and advantageous to the democracy, but when once we have enacted them, it equally behooves us, if all is to be well with the state, to obey the laws that we have enacted, and to punish those who do not obey them.

Consider, fellow citizens, how much attention that ancient lawgiver, Solon, gave to morality, as did Draco and the other lawgivers of those days. First, you recall, they laid down laws to protect the morals of our children, and they expressly prescribed what were to be the habits of the freeborn boy, and how he was to be brought up; then they legislated for the lads, and next for the other age-groups in succession, including in their provision, not only private citizens, but also the public men. And when they had inscribed these laws, they gave them to you in trust, and made you their guardians.

Now it is my desire, in addressing you on this occasion, to follow in my speech the same order which the lawgiver followed in his laws. For you shall hear first a review of the laws that have been laid down to govern the orderly conduct of your children, then the laws concerning the lads, and next those concerning the other ages in succession, including not only private citizens, but the public men as well. For so, I think, my argument will most easily be followed. And at the same time I wish, fellow citizens, first to describe to you in detail the laws of the state, and then in contrast with the laws to examine the character and habits of Timarchus. For you will find that the life he has lived has been contrary to all the laws.

9 Ὁ γὰρ νομοθέτης πρῶτον μὲν τοῖς διδασκάλοις, οἷς ἐξ ἀνάγκης παρακατατιθέμεθα τοὺς
ἡμετέρους αὐτῶν παῖδας, οἷς ἐστιν ὁ μὲν βίος
ἀπὸ τοῦ σωφρονεῖν, ἡ δ᾽ ἀπορία ἐκ τῶν ἐναντίων,
ὅμως ἀπιστῶν φαίνεται, καὶ διαρρήδην ἀπο-
δείκνυσι, πρῶτον μὲν ἣν ὥραν προσήκει ἰέναι
τὸν παῖδα τὸν ἐλεύθερον εἰς τὸ διδασκαλεῖον,
ἔπειτα μετὰ πόσων παίδων εἰσιέναι, καὶ πηνίκα
10 ἀπιέναι, καὶ τοὺς διδασκάλους τὰ διδασκαλεῖα
καὶ τοὺς παιδοτρίβας τὰς παλαίστρας ἀνοίγειν
μὲν ἀπαγορεύει μὴ πρότερον πρὶν ἂν ἥλιος ἀνίσχῃ,
κλῄειν δὲ προστάττει πρὸ ἡλίου δεδυκότος, τὰς
ἐρημίας καὶ τὸ σκότος ἐν πλείστῃ ὑποψίᾳ ποιού-
μενος· καὶ τοὺς νεανίσκους τοὺς εἰσφοιτῶντας
οὕς τινας δεῖ εἶναι καὶ ἅς τινας ἡλικίας ἔχοντας,
καὶ ἀρχὴν ἥτις ἔσται ἡ τούτων ἐπιμελησομένη,
καὶ περὶ παιδαγωγῶν ἐπιμελείας καὶ περὶ Μου-
σείων ἐν τοῖς διδασκαλείοις καὶ περὶ Ἑρμαίων ἐν
ταῖς παλαίστραις, καὶ τὸ τελευταῖον περὶ τῆς
συμφοιτήσεως τῶν παίδων καὶ τῶν χορῶν τῶν
11 κυκλίων.[1] κελεύει γὰρ τὸν χορηγὸν τὸν μέλλοντα
τὴν οὐσίαν τὴν ἑαυτοῦ εἰς ὑμᾶς ἀναλίσκειν ὑπὲρ
τετταράκοντα ἔτη γεγονότα τοῦτο πράττειν, ἵν᾽
ἤδη ἐν τῇ σωφρονεστάτῃ αὐτοῦ ἡλικίᾳ ὤν, οὕτως
ἐντυγχάνῃ τοῖς ὑμετέροις παισίν.

Ἀναγνώσεται οὖν ὑμῖν τούτους τοὺς νόμους,
ἵν᾽ εἰδῆτε ὅτι ὁ νομοθέτης ἡγήσατο τὸν καλῶς

---

[1] κυκλίων Franke : ἐγκυκλίων MSS.

In the first place, consider the case of the teachers. Although the very livelihood of these men, to whom we necessarily entrust our own children, depends on their good character, while the opposite conduct on their part would mean poverty, yet it is plain that the lawgiver distrusts them; for he expressly prescribes, first, at what time of day the free-born boy is to go to the school-room; next, how many other boys may go there with him, and when he is to go home. He forbids the teacher to open the school-room, or the gymnastic trainer the wrestling school, before sunrise, and he commands them to close the doors before sunset; for he is exceeding suspicious of their being alone with a boy, or in the dark with him. He prescribes what children are to be admitted as pupils, and their age at admission. He provides for a public official who shall superintend them, and for the oversight of slave-attendants of school-boys. He regulates the festivals of the Muses in the school-rooms, and of Hermes in the wrestling-schools. Finally, he regulates the companionships that the boys may form at school, and their cyclic dances.[1] He prescribes, namely, that the choregus, a man who is going to spend his own money for your entertainment, shall be a man of more than forty years of age when he performs this service, in order that he may have reached the most temperate time of life before he comes into contact with your children.

These laws, then, shall be read to you, to prove that the lawgiver believed that it is the boy who has

---

[1] Dances by specially trained groups of boys, often competitive between tribes, were popular features of many of the Greek festivals. Those dances which were arranged for a circular dancing-ground were called "cyclic."

τραφέντα παῖδα ἄνδρα γενόμενον χρήσιμον ἔσεσθαι τῇ πόλει· ὅταν δ᾽ ἡ φύσις τοῦ ἀνθρώπου
εὐθὺς πονηρὰν τὴν ἀρχὴν λάβῃ τῆς παιδείας, ἐκ
τῶν κακῶς τεθραμμένων παίδων παραπλησίους
ἡγήσατο πολίτας ἔσεσθαι Τιμάρχῳ τουτῳί. λέγε
αὐτοῖς τοὺς νόμους τούτους.

NOMOI

12   [Οἱ δὲ τῶν παίδων διδάσκαλοι ἀνοιγέτωσαν
μὲν τὰ διδασκαλεῖα μὴ πρότερον ἡλίου ἀνιόντος, κλειέτωσαν δὲ πρὸ ἡλίου δύνοντος. καὶ
μὴ ἐξέστω τοῖς ὑπὲρ τὴν τῶν παίδων ἡλικίαν
οὖσιν εἰσιέναι τῶν παίδων ἔνδον ὄντων, ἐὰν
μὴ υἱὸς διδασκάλου ἢ ἀδελφὸς ἢ θυγατρὸς
ἀνήρ· ἐὰν δέ τις παρὰ ταῦτ᾽ εἰσίῃ, θανάτῳ
ζημιούσθω. καὶ οἱ γυμνασιάρχαι τοῖς Ἑρ-
μαίοις μὴ ἐάτωσαν συγκαθιέναι μηδένα τῶν
ἐν ἡλικίᾳ τρόπῳ μηδενί· ἐὰν δὲ ἐπιτρέπῃ
καὶ μὴ ἐξείργῃ τοῦ γυμνασίου, ἔνοχος ἔστω
ὁ γυμνασιάρχης τῷ τῆς ἐλευθέρων φθορᾶς
νόμῳ. οἱ δὲ χορηγοὶ οἱ καθιστάμενοι ὑπὸ τοῦ
δήμου ἔστωσαν τὴν ἡλικίαν ὑπὲρ τετταράκοντα ἔτη.] [1]

13   Μετὰ ταῦτα τοίνυν, ὦ ἄνδρες Ἀθηναῖοι, νομο-
θετεῖ περὶ ἀδικημάτων μεγάλων μέν, γιγνομένων
δ᾽ οἶμαι ἐν τῇ πόλει· ἐκ γὰρ τοῦ πράττεσθαί τιν᾽

---

[1] The documents which Aeschines placed in the hands of
the Clerk of the Court, to be read to the jury as the speech
proceeded, seem not to have been published by the author
with the text of his speeches. The " laws," etc., which are

been well brought up that will be a useful citizen when he becomes a man. But when a boy's natural disposition is subjected at the very outset to vicious training, the product of such wrong nurture will be, as he believed, a citizen like this man Timarchus. (*To the Clerk of the Court.*) Read these laws to the jury.

LAWS

[The teachers of the boys shall open the school-rooms not earlier than sunrise, and they shall close them before sunset. No person who is older than the boys shall be permitted to enter the room while they are there, unless he be a son of the teacher, a brother, or a daughter's husband. If any one enter in violation of this prohibition, he shall be punished with death. The superintendents of the gymnasia shall under no conditions allow any one who has reached the age of manhood to enter the contests of Hermes together with the boys. A gymnasiarch who does permit this and fails to keep such a person out of the gymnasium, shall be liable to the penalties prescribed for the seduction of free-born youth. Every choregus who is appointed by the people shall be more than forty years of age.]

Now after this, fellow citizens, he lays down laws regarding crimes which, great as they undoubtedly are, do actually occur, I believe, in the city. For the very fact that certain unbecoming things were being

---

found in our MSS. were probably composed by an ancient editor.

ὧν οὐ προσῆκεν, ἐκ τούτου τοὺς νόμους ἔθεντο
οἱ παλαιοί.   διαρρήδην γοῦν λέγει ὁ νόμος, ἐάν
τινα ἐκμισθώσῃ ἑταιρεῖν πατὴρ ἢ ἀδελφὸς ἢ
θεῖος ἢ ἐπίτροπος ἢ ὅλως τῶν κυρίων τις, κατ᾽
αὐτοῦ μὲν τοῦ παιδὸς οὐκ ἐᾷ γραφὴν εἶναι, κατὰ
δὲ τοῦ μισθώσαντος καὶ τοῦ μισθωσαμένου, τοῦ
μὲν ὅτι ἐξεμίσθωσε, τοῦ δὲ ὅτι, φησίν, ἐμισθώσατο.   καὶ ἴσα τὰ ἐπιτίμια ἑκατέρῳ πεποίηκε,
καὶ μὴ ἐπάναγκες εἶναι τῷ παιδὶ ἡβήσαντι τρέφειν τὸν πατέρα μηδὲ οἴκησιν παρέχειν, ὃς ἂν
ἐκμισθωθῇ ἑταιρεῖν· ἀποθανόντα δὲ θαπτέτω καὶ
14 τἆλλα ποιείτω τὰ νομιζόμενα.   σκέψασθε δή,
ὡς καλῶς, ὦ ἄνδρες Ἀθηναῖοι.   ζῶντος μὲν αὐτοῦ
ἀφαιρεῖται τὴν ὄνησιν τῆς παιδοποιίας, ὥσπερ
ἐκεῖνος ἐκείνου τὴν παρρησίαν, τελευτήσαντα δὲ
αὐτόν, ἡνίκα ὁ μὲν εὐεργετούμενος οὐκ αἰσθάνεται
ὧν εὖ πάσχει, τιμᾶται δὲ ὁ νόμος καὶ τὸ θεῖον,
θάπτειν ἤδη κελεύει καὶ τἆλλα ποιεῖν τὰ νομιζόμενα.

Καὶ τίνα ἕτερον νόμον ἔθηκε φύλακα τῶν
ὑμετέρων παίδων; τὸν τῆς προαγωγείας, τὰ
μέγιστα ἐπιτίμια ἐπιγράψας, ἐάν τις ἐλεύθερον
παῖδα ἢ γυναῖκα προαγωγεύῃ.

15 Καὶ ποῖον ἄλλον; τὸν τῆς ὕβρεως, ὃς ἐνὶ κεφαλαίῳ ἅπαντα τὰ τοιαῦτα συλλαβὼν ἔχει· ἐν
ᾧ διαρρήδην γέγραπται, ἐάν τις ὑβρίζῃ εἰς παῖδα

---

[1] The son, as one whose person had been prostituted, was
debarred from addressing the assembly of the people. *cp.* § 3.

14

done was the reason for the enactment of these laws by the men of old. At any rate the law says explicitly: if any boy is let out for hire as a prostitute, whether it be by father or brother or uncle or guardian, or by any one else who has control of him, prosecution is not to lie against the boy himself, but against the man who let him out for hire and the man who hired him; against the one because he let him out for hire, and against the other, it says, because he hired him. And the law has made the penalties for both offenders the same. Moreover the law frees a son, when he has become a man, from all obligation to support or to furnish a home to a father by whom he has been hired out for prostitution; but when the father is dead, the son is to bury him and perform the other customary rites. See, gentlemen, how admirably this legislation fits the case: so long as the father is alive he is deprived of all the benefits of fatherhood, precisely as he deprived his son of a citizen's right to speak;[1] but when he is dead, and unconscious of the service that is being rendered him, and when it is the law and religion that receive the honour, then at last the lawgiver commands the son to bury him and perform the other customary rites.

But what other law has been laid down for the protection of your children? The law against panders. For the lawgiver imposes the heaviest penalties if any person act as pander in the case of a free-born child or a free-born woman.

And what other law? The law against outrage, which includes all such conduct in one summary statement, wherein it stands expressly written: if

THE SPEECHES OF AESCHINES

(ὑβρίζει δὲ δή που ὁ μισθούμενος) ἢ ἄνδρα ἢ
γυναῖκα, ἢ τῶν ἐλευθέρων τινὰ ἢ τῶν δού/.ων, ἢ
ἐὰν παράνομόν τι ποιῇ εἰς τούτων τινά, γραφὰς
ὕβρεως εἶναι πεποίηκεν καὶ τίμημα ἐπέθηκεν, ὅ
τι χρὴ παθεῖν ἢ ἀποτεῖσαι. λέγε τὸν νόμον.

ΝΟΜΟΣ

16   [Ἄν τις Ἀθηναίων ἐλεύθερον παῖδα ὑβρίσῃ,
γραφέσθω ὁ κύριος τοῦ παιδὸς πρὸς τοὺς
θεσμοθέτας, τίμημα ἐπιγραψάμενος. οὗ δ'
ἂν¹ τὸ δικαστήριον καταψηφίσηται, παρα-
δοθεὶς τοῖς ἕνδεκα τεθνάτω αὐθημερόν. ἐὰν
δὲ εἰς ἀργύριον καταψηφισθῇ, ἀποτεισάτω ἐν
ἕνδεκα ἡμέραις μετὰ τὴν δίκην, ἐὰν μὴ παραχρῆμα δύνηται ἀποτίνειν· ἕως δὲ τοῦ ἀποτεῖσαι εἰρχθήτω. ἔνοχοι δὲ ἔστωσαν ταῖσδε
ταῖς αἰτίαις καὶ οἱ εἰς τὰ οἰκετικὰ σώματα
ἐξαμαρτάνοντες.]

17   Ἴσως ἂν οὖν τις θαυμάσειεν ἐξαίφνης ἀκούσας,
τί δή ποτ' ἐν τῷ νόμῳ τῷ τῆς ὕβρεως προσεγράφη
τοῦτο τὸ ῥῆμα, τὸ τῶν δούλων. τοῦτο δὲ ἐὰν
σκοπῆτε, ὦ ἄνδρες Ἀθηναῖοι, εὑρήσετε ὅτι πάντων ἄριστα ἔχει· οὐ γὰρ ὑπὲρ τῶν οἰκετῶν
ἐσπούδασεν ὁ νομοθέτης, ἀλλὰ βουλόμενος ὑμᾶς
ἐθίσαι πολὺ ἀπέχειν τῆς τῶν ἐλευθέρων ὕβρεως,
προσέγραψε μηδ᾽ εἰς τοὺς δούλους ὑβρίζειν. ὅλως
δὲ ἐν δημοκρατίᾳ τὸν εἰς ὁντινοῦν ὑβριστήν,
τοῦτον οὐκ ἐπιτήδειον ἡγήσατο εἶναι συμπολι-

---

¹ οὗ δ' ἂν Dobree : ᾧ ἂν (or οὗ ἂν) MSS.

any one outrage a child (and surely he who hires,
outrages) or a man or woman, or any one, free or
slave, or if he commit any unlawful act against
any one of these. Here the law provides prosecution for outrage, and it prescribes what bodily
penalty he shall suffer, or what fine he shall pay.
(*To the Clerk.*) Read the law.

LAW

[If any Athenian shall outrage a free-born
child, the parent or guardian of the child shall
prosecute him before the Thesmothetae, and
shall demand a specific penalty. If the court
condemn the accused to death, he shall be
delivered to the constables and be put to death
the same day. If he be condemned to pay a
fine, and be unable to pay the fine immediately,
he must pay within eleven days after the trial,
and he shall remain in prison until payment is
made. The same action shall hold against those
who abuse the persons of slaves.]

Now perhaps some one, on first hearing this law,
may wonder for what possible reason this word
"slaves" was added in the law against outrage.
But if you reflect on the matter, fellow citizens,
you will find this to be the best provision of all.
For it was not for the slaves that the lawgiver was
concerned, but he wished to accustom you to keep
a long distance away from the crime of outraging
free men, and so he added the prohibition against
the outraging even of slaves. In a word, he was
convinced that in a democracy that man is unfit for
citizenship who outrages any person whatsoever.

18 τεύεσθαι. κἀκεῖνο δέ μοι συνδιαμνημονεύσατε,
ὦ ἄνδρες Ἀθηναῖοι, ὅτι ἔνταῦθ' ὁ νομοθέτης οὔπω
διαλέγεται αὐτῷ τῷ σώματι τοῦ παιδός, ἀλλὰ
τοῖς περὶ τὸν παῖδα, πατρί, ἀδελφῷ, ἐπιτρόπῳ,
διδασκάλοις, καὶ ὅλως τοῖς κυρίοις· ἐπειδὰν δ'
ἐγγραφῇ τις εἰς τὸ ληξιαρχικὸν γραμματεῖον, καὶ
τοὺς νόμους εἰδῇ τοὺς τῆς πόλεως, καὶ ἤδη δύνηται
διαλογίζεσθαι τὰ καλὰ καὶ τὰ μή, οὐκέτι ἑτέρῳ
19 διαλέγεται, ἀλλ' ἤδη αὐτῷ, ὦ Τίμαρχε. καὶ πῶς
λέγει; ἄν τις Ἀθηναίων, φησίν, ἑταιρήσῃ, μὴ
ἐξέστω αὐτῷ τῶν ἐννέα ἀρχόντων γενέσθαι, ὅτι
οἶμαι στεφανηφόρος ἡ ἀρχή, μηδ' ἱερωσύνην
ἱερώσασθαι, ὡς οὐδὲ καθαρεύοντι[1] τῷ σώματι,
μηδὲ συνδικησάτω, φησί, τῷ δημοσίῳ, μηδὲ ἀρ-
ξάτω ἀρχὴν μηδεμίαν μηδέποτε, μήτ' ἔνδημον
μήτε ὑπερόριον, μήτε κληρωτὴν μήτε χειροτονη-
20 τήν· μηδὲ κηρυκευσάτω, μηδὲ πρεσβευσάτω, μηδὲ
τοὺς πρεσβεύσαντας κρινέτω, μηδὲ συκοφαντείτω
μισθωθείς, μηδὲ γνώμην εἰπάτω μηδέποτε μήτε
ἐν τῇ βουλῇ μήτε ἐν τῷ δήμῳ, μηδ' ἂν δεινότατος
ᾖ λέγειν Ἀθηναίων. ἐὰν δέ τις παρὰ ταῦτα
πράττῃ, γραφὰς ἑταιρήσεως πεποίηκε καὶ τὰ
μέγιστα ἐπιτίμια ἐπέθηκεν. λέγε αὐτοῖς καὶ
τοῦτον τὸν νόμον, ἵν' εἰδῆτε οἵων νόμων ὑμῖν
κειμένων, ὡς καλῶν καὶ σωφρόνων, τετόλμηκε
Τίμαρχος δημηγορεῖν, ὁ τοιοῦτος τὸν τρόπον οἷον
ὑμεῖς ἐπίστασθε.

[1] καθαρεύοντι Franke : καθαρῷ διαλέγεται MSS.

And I beg you, fellow citizens, to remember this
also, that here the lawgiver is not yet addressing
the person of the boy himself, but those who are
near him, father, brother, guardian, teachers, and
in general those who have control of him. But
as soon as the young man has been registered in
the list of citizens, and knows the laws of the state,
and is now able to distinguish between right and
wrong, the lawgiver no longer addresses another,
Timarchus, but now the man himself. And what
does he say? "If any Athenian," he says, "shall
have prostituted his person, he shall not be permitted to become one of the nine archons," because, no doubt, that official wears the wreath;[1]
"nor to discharge the office of priest," as being
not even clean of body; "nor shall he act as an
advocate for the state," he says, "nor shall he
ever hold any office whatsoever, at home or abroad,
whether filled by lot or by election; nor shall he
be a herald or an ambassador"—nor shall he prosecute men who have served as ambassadors, nor
shall he be a hired slanderer—"nor ever address
senate or assembly," not even though he be the
most eloquent orator in Athens. And if any one
act contrary to these prohibitions, the lawgiver has
provided for criminal process on the charge of prostitution, and has prescribed the heaviest penalties
therefor. (*To the Clerk.*) Read to the jury this law
also, that you may know, gentlemen, in the face of
what established laws of yours, so good and so moral,
Timarchus has had the effrontery to speak before the
people—a man whose character is so notorious.

---

[1] The myrtle wreath was worn as sign of the sacred character of the office, and it protected the person from assault.

THE SPEECHES OF AESCHINES

21 [Ἐάν τις Ἀθηναῖος ἑταιρήσῃ, μὴ ἐξέστω
αὐτῷ τῶν ἐννέα ἀρχόντων γενέσθαι, μηδ᾽
ἱερωσύνην ἱερώσασθαι, μηδὲ συνδικῆσαι τῷ
δήμῳ, μηδὲ ἀρχὴν ἀρχέτω μηδεμίαν, μήτε
ἔνδημον μήτε ὑπερόριον, μήτε κληρωτὴν μήτε
χειροτονητήν, μηδ᾽ ἐπὶ κηρυκείαν ἀποστελ-
λέσθω, μηδὲ γνώμην λεγέτω, μηδ᾽ εἰς τὰ
δημοτελῆ ἱερὰ εἰσίτω, μηδ᾽ ἐν ταῖς κοιναῖς
στεφανηφορίαις στεφανούσθω, μηδ᾽ ἐντὸς τῆς
ἀγορᾶς τῶν περιρραντηρίων πορευέσθω. ἐὰν
δέ τις παρὰ¹ ταῦτα ποιῇ, καταγνωσθέντος
αὐτοῦ ἑταιρεῖν, θανάτῳ ζημιούσθω.]

22 Τοῦτον μὲν τὸν νόμον ἔθηκε περὶ τῶν μειρακίων
τῶν προχείρως εἰς τὰ ἑαυτῶν σώματα ἐξαμαρτα-
νόντων· οὓς δὲ ὀλίγῳ πρότερον ὑμῖν ἀνέγνω, περὶ
τῶν παίδων· οὓς δὲ νυνὶ μέλλω λέγειν, περὶ τῶν
ἄλλων Ἀθηναίων. ἀπαλλαγεὶς γὰρ τῶν νόμων
τούτων ἐσκέψατο, τίνα χρὴ τρόπον συλλεγομένους
ἡμᾶς εἰς τὰς ἐκκλησίας βουλεύεσθαι περὶ τῶν
σπουδαιοτάτων πραγμάτων. καὶ πόθεν ἄρχεται;
" Νόμοι," φησί, " περὶ εὐκοσμίας." ἀπὸ σωφροσύνης πρῶτον ἤρξατο,² ὡς, ὅπου πλείστη εὐ-
κοσμία ἐστί, ταύτην ἄριστα τὴν πόλιν οἰκησομέ-
23 νην. καὶ πῶς κελεύει τοὺς προέδρους χρηματίζειν;

---

¹ παρὰ added by Reiske.
² Sakorraphos considers the words ἀπὸ ... ἤρξατο an
unquestionable interpolation.

THE LAW

[If any Athenian shall have prostituted his person, he shall not be permitted to become one of the nine archons, nor to discharge the office of priest, nor to act as an advocate for the state, nor shall he hold any office whatsoever, at home or abroad, whether filled by lot or by election; he shall not be sent as a herald; he shall not take part in debate, nor be present at the public sacrifices; when the citizens are wearing garlands, he shall wear none; and he shall not enter within the limits of the place that has been purified for the assembling of the people. If any man who has been convicted of prostitution act contrary to these prohibitions, he shall be put to death.]

This law was enacted concerning youths who recklessly sin against their own bodies. The laws relating to boys are those read to you a moment ago; but I am going to cite now laws that have to do with the citizens at large. For when the lawgiver had finished with these laws, he next turned to the question of the proper manner of conducting our deliberations concerning the most important matters, when we are met in public assembly. How does he begin? "Laws," he says, "concerning orderly conduct." He began with morality, thinking that that state will be best administered in which orderly conduct is most common. And how does he command the presiding officers to proceed? After the purifying

THE SPEECHES OF AESCHINES

ἐπειδὰν τὸ καθάρσιον περιενεχθῇ καὶ ὁ κῆρυξ
τὰς πατρίους εὐχὰς εὔξηται, προχειροτονεῖν κελεύει τοὺς προέδρους περὶ ἱερῶν τῶν πατρίων καὶ
κήρυξι καὶ πρεσβείαις καὶ ὁσίων, καὶ μετὰ ταῦτα
ἐπερωτᾷ ὁ κῆρυξ· " Τίς ἀγορεύειν βούλεται τῶν
ὑπὲρ πεντήκοντα ἔτη γεγονότων;" ἐπειδὰν δὲ
οὗτοι πάντες εἴπωσι, τότ' ἤδη κελεύει λέγειν
τῶν ἄλλων Ἀθηναίων τὸν βουλόμενον, οἷς ἔξεστιν.

24 σκέψασθε δὴ ὡς καλῶς, ὦ ἄνδρες Ἀθηναῖοι.
οὐκ ἠγνόει οἶμαι ὁ νομοθέτης ὅτι οἱ πρεσβύτεροι
τῷ μὲν εὖ φρονεῖν ἀκμάζουσιν, ἡ δὲ τόλμα ἤδη
αὐτοὺς ἄρχεται ἐπιλείπειν διὰ τὴν ἐμπειρίαν τῶν
πραγμάτων. βουλόμενος δὴ συνεθίσαι τοὺς ἄριστα
φρονοῦντας, τούτους ἐπάναγκες περὶ τῶν πραγμάτων λέγειν, ἐπειδὴ ὀνομαστὶ[1] αὐτῶν ἕνα ἕκαστον
ἀπορεῖ προσειπεῖν, τῇ ἐπωνυμίᾳ[2] τῆς ὅλης ἡλικίας
περιλαβὼν[3] παρακαλεῖ ἐπὶ τὸ βῆμα καὶ προ-
τρέπει δημηγορεῖν. ἅμα δὲ καὶ τοὺς νεωτέρους
διδάσκει αἰσχύνεσθαι τοὺς πρεσβυτέρους, καὶ
πάνθ' ὕστερον πράττειν, καὶ τιμᾶν τὸ γῆρας, εἰς

25 ὃ πάντες ἀφιξόμεθα, ἐὰν ἄρα διαγενώμεθα. καὶ
οὕτως ἦσαν σώφρονες οἱ ἀρχαῖοι ἐκεῖνοι ῥήτορες,

---

[1] ὀνομαστὶ Reiske : ὀνόματι MSS.
[2] τῇ ἐπωνυμίᾳ Blass : τὴν (or τὴν κοινὴν) ἐπωνυμίαν MSS.
[3] περιλαβὼν Blass (Emperius) : ὑπολαβὼν (or ἀπο-) MSS.

---

[1] " It was the custom at Athens to purify the ecclesia, the
theatres, and the gatherings of the people in general by the
sacrifice of very small pigs, which they named καθάρσια."—
Harpocration.
[2] The above interpretation is confirmed by Aristotle, *Constitution of Athens*, xliii. 1, 29 f., where we find the same
phraseology, evidently that of the law itself. Heralds,

sacrifice has been carried round[1] and the herald has offered the traditional prayers, the presiding officers are commanded to declare to be next in order the discussion of matters pertaining to the national religion, the reception of heralds and ambassadors, and the discussion of secular matters.[2] The herald then asks, " Who of those above fifty years of age wishes to address the assembly ? " When all these have spoken, he then invites any other Athenian to speak who wishes (provided such privilege belongs to him).[3] Consider, fellow citizens, the wisdom of this regulation. The lawgiver does not forget, I think, that the older men are at their best in the matter of judgment, but that courage is now beginning to fail them as a result of their experience of the vicissitudes of life. So, wishing to accustom those who are the wisest to speak on public affairs, and to make this obligatory upon them, since he cannot call on each one of them by name, he comprehends them all under the designation of the age-group as a whole, invites them to the platform, and urges them to address the people. At the same time he teaches the younger men to respect their elders, to yield precedence to them in every act, and to honour that old age to which we shall all come if our lives are spared. And so decorous were those public men of old, Pericles,

whose person was inviolate even in time of war, were often sent to carry messages from one state to another. They frequently prepared the way for negotiations to be conducted by ambassadors, appointed for the special occasion.

[3] That is, any citizen who is not disqualified by some loss of civic privilege inflicted as a penalty. Aeschines has in mind the fact that a man like Timarchus would not have the privilege.

ὁ Περικλῆς καὶ ὁ Θεμιστοκλῆς καὶ ὁ Ἀριστείδης,
ὁ τὴν ἀνόμοιον ἔχων ἐπωνυμίαν Τιμάρχῳ τουτῳί,[1]
ὥστε ὃ νυνὶ πάντες ἐν ἔθει πράττομεν, τὸ τὴν
χεῖρα ἔξω ἔχοντες λέγειν, τότε τοῦτο θρασύ τι
ἐδόκει εἶναι, καὶ εὐλαβοῦντο αὐτὸ πράττειν. μέγα
δὲ πάνυ τούτου σημεῖον ἔργῳ ὑμῖν οἶμαι ἐπιδείξειν.
εὖ γὰρ οἶδ' ὅτι πάντες ἐκπεπλεύκατε εἰς Σαλαμῖνα
καὶ τεθεωρήκατε τὴν Σόλωνος εἰκόνα, καὶ αὐτοὶ
μαρτυρήσαιτ' ἂν ὅτι ἐν τῇ ἀγορᾷ τῇ Σαλαμινίων
ἀνάκειται ὁ Σόλων ἐντὸς τὴν χεῖρα ἔχων. τοῦτο
δ'[2] ἐστίν, ὦ ἄνδρες Ἀθηναῖοι, ὑπόμνημα καὶ
μίμημα τοῦ Σόλωνος σχήματος, ὃν τρόπον ἔχων
αὐτὸς διελέγετο τῷ δήμῳ τῶν Ἀθηναίων.

26 Σκέψασθε δή, ὦ ἄνδρες Ἀθηναῖοι, ὅσον διαφέρει ὁ Σόλων Τιμάρχου καὶ οἱ ἄνδρες ἐκεῖνοι
ὧν ὀλίγῳ πρότερον ἐπεμνήσθην. ἐκεῖνοι μέν γε
ᾐσχύνοντο ἔξω τὴν χεῖρα ἔχοντες λέγειν, οὑτοσὶ
δὲ οὐ πάλαι, ἀλλὰ πρώην ποτὲ ῥίψας θοἰμάτιον
γυμνὸς ἐπαγκρατίαζεν ἐν τῇ ἐκκλησίᾳ, οὕτω
κακῶς καὶ αἰσχρῶς διακείμενος τὸ σῶμα ὑπὸ
μέθης καὶ βδελυρίας, ὥστε τούς γε εὖ φρονοῦντας
ἐγκαλύψασθαι, αἰσχυνθέντας ὑπὲρ τῆς πόλεως,
27 εἰ τοιούτοις συμβούλοις χρώμεθα. ἃ συνιδὼν ὁ
νομοθέτης διαρρήδην ἀπέδειξεν οὓς χρὴ δημη-

---

[1] The MSS. have ὁ δίκαιος ἐπικαλούμενος (who was called The
Just) before ὥστε. Blass brackets, after Scheibe. The phrase
ὁ τὴν . . . τουτῳί may also be an interpolation, both phrases
being perhaps adapted on the model of iii. 181.
[2] τοῦτο δ' Blass, after an ancient quotation : τοῦτο MSS.

Themistocles, and Aristeides (who was called by a name most unlike that by which Timarchus here is called), that to speak with the arm outside the cloak, as we all do nowadays as a matter of course, was regarded then as an ill-mannered thing, and they carefully refrained from doing it. And I can point to a piece of evidence which seems to me very weighty and tangible. I am sure you have all sailed over to Salamis, and have seen the statue of Solon there. You can therefore yourselves bear witness that in the statue that is set up in the Salaminian market-place Solon stands with his arm inside his cloak. Now this is a reminiscence, fellow citizens, and an imitation of the posture of Solon, showing his customary bearing as he used to address the people of Athens.[1]

See now, fellow citizens, how unlike to Timarchus were Solon and those men of old whom I mentioned a moment ago. They were too modest to speak with the arm outside the cloak, but this man not long ago, yes, only the other day, in an assembly of the people threw off his cloak and leaped about like a gymnast, half naked, his body so reduced and befouled through drunkenness and lewdness that right-minded men, at least, covered their eyes, being ashamed for the city, that we should let such men as he be our advisers. It was with such conduct as this in view that the lawgiver expressly prescribed who were to address the assembly, and

---

[1] Aristotle (*Constitution of Athens*, xxviii. 3) says of Cleon : "He was the first to use unseemly shouting and coarse abuse on the Bema, and to harangue the people with his cloak girt up short about him, whereas all his predecessors had spoken decently and in order." (Kenyon's trans.)

γορεῖν καὶ οὓς οὐ δεῖ λέγειν ἐν τῷ δήμῳ. καὶ οὐκ
ἀπελαύνει ἀπὸ τοῦ βήματος, εἴ τις μὴ προγόνων
ἐστὶν ἐστρατηγηκότων,[1] οὐδέ γε εἰ τέχνην τινὰ
ἐργάζεται ἐπικουρῶν τῇ ἀναγκαίᾳ τροφῇ, ἀλλὰ
τούτους καὶ μάλιστα ἀσπάζεται, καὶ διὰ τοῦτο
πολλάκις ἐπερωτᾷ, τίς ἀγορεύειν βούλεται.

28 Τίνας δ᾽ οὐκ ᾤετο δεῖν λέγειν; τοὺς αἰσχρῶς
βεβιωκότας· τούτους οὐκ ἐᾷ δημηγορεῖν. καὶ
ποῦ τοῦτο δηλοῖ; "Δοκιμασία," φησί, "ῥητόρων·
ἐάν τις λέγῃ ἐν τῷ δήμῳ τὸν πατέρα τύπτων ἢ
τὴν μητέρα, ἢ μὴ τρέφων, ἢ μὴ παρέχων οἴκησιν"
τοῦτον οὐκ ἐᾷ λέγειν. νὴ Δία καλῶς γε, ὡς
ἔγωγέ φημι. διὰ τί; ὅτι εἴ τις, οὓς ἐξ ἴσου δεῖ
τιμᾶν τοῖς θεοῖς, εἰς τούτους ἐστὶ φαῦλος, τί ποτε,
φησίν, ὑπ᾽ αὐτοῦ πείσονται οἱ ἀλλότριοι καὶ ἡ
πόλις ὅλη; καὶ τίσι δεύτερον ἀπεῖπε μὴ λέγειν;

29 "Ἢ τὰς στρατείας," φησί, "μὴ ἐστρατευμένος,
ὅσαι ἂν αὐτῷ προσταχθῶσιν, ἢ τὴν ἀσπίδα
ἀποβεβληκώς," δίκαια λέγων. τί δή ποτε; ἄν-
θρωπε, τῇ πόλει, ὑπὲρ ἧς τὰ ὅπλα μὴ τίθεσαι ἢ
διὰ δειλίαν μὴ δυνατὸς εἶ ἐπαμῦναι, μηδὲ συμ-

---

[1] ἐστρατηγηκότων Baiter : ἐστρατηγηκότων υἱός MSS.

---

[1] The Athenian ῥήτωρ was both public speaker and political
leader. The profession was definite and well recognised.
No one English word covers both the political and the
oratorical activity of the profession.

All public officials were required to submit to a formal
scrutiny (δοκιμασία) before taking office. The examining

who were not to be permitted to speak before
the people. He does not exclude from the platform
the man whose ancestors have not held a general's
office, nor even the man who earns his daily bread by
working at a trade; nay, these men he most heartily
welcomes, and for this reason he repeats again and
again the invitation, "Who wishes to address the
assembly?"

Who then are they who in the lawgiver's opinion
are not to be permitted to speak? Those who have
lived a shameful life; these men he forbids to address
the people. Where does he show this? Under the
heading "Scrutiny of public men"[1] he says, "If any
one attempts to speak before the people who beats
his father or mother, or fails to support them or to
provide a home for them." Such a man, then, he forbids to speak. And right he is, by Zeus, say I! Why?
Because if a man is mean toward those whom he
ought to honour as the gods, how, pray, he asks,
will such a man treat the members of another household, and how will he treat the whole city? Whom
did he, in the second place, forbid to speak? "Or
the man who has failed to perform all the military
service demanded of him, or who has thrown away
his shield." And he is right. Why? Man, if
you fail to take up arms in behalf of the state,
or if you are such a coward that you are unable
to defend her, you must not claim the right to

body was usually a law-court; in the case of the archons it
was a court, after a preliminary hearing by the senate;
senators elect appeared before the outgoing senate. From
our passage it appears that a sort of "scrutiny" might
be applied to the men who made politics their profession, without regard to any office for which they might be
candidates.

βουλεύειν ἀξίου. τρίτον τίσι διαλέγεται; "Ἢ
πεπορνευμένος," φησίν, "ἢ ἡταιρηκώς·" τὸν γὰρ
τὸ σῶμα τὸ ἑαυτοῦ ἐφ᾽ ὕβρει πεπρακότα, καὶ τὰ
κοινὰ τῆς πόλεως ῥᾳδίως ἡγήσατο ἀποδώσεσθαι.
30 τέταρτον τίσι διαλέγεται; "Ἢ τὰ πατρῷα,"
φησί, " κατεδηδοκώς, ἢ ὧν ἂν κληρονόμος γένη-
ται·" τὸν γὰρ τὴν ἰδίαν οἰκίαν κακῶς οἰκήσαντα,
καὶ τὰ κοινὰ τῆς πόλεως παραπλησίως ἡγήσατο
διαθήσειν, καὶ οὐκ ἐδόκει οἷόν τ᾽ εἶναι τῷ νομοθέτῃ τὸν αὐτὸν ἄνθρωπον ἰδίᾳ μὲν εἶναι πονηρόν,
δημοσίᾳ δὲ χρηστόν, οὐδ᾽ ᾤετο δεῖν[1] τὸν ῥήτορα
ἥκειν ἐπὶ τὸ βῆμα τῶν λόγων ἐπιμεληθέντα πρό-
31 τερον, ἀλλ᾽ οὐ τοῦ βίου. καὶ παρὰ μὲν ἀνδρὸς
καλοῦ καὶ ἀγαθοῦ, κἂν πάνυ κακῶς καὶ ἁπλῶς
ῥηθῇ,[2] χρήσιμα τὰ λεγόμενα ἡγήσατο εἶναι τοῖς
ἀκούουσι· παρὰ δὲ ἀνθρώπου βδελυροῦ, καὶ
καταγελάστως μὲν κεχρημένου τῷ ἑαυτοῦ σώματι, αἰσχρῶς δὲ τὴν πατρῷαν οὐσίαν κατεδηδο-
κότος, οὐδ᾽ ἂν εὖ πάνυ λεχθῇ συνοίσειν ἡγήσατο
32 τοῖς ἀκούουσι. τούτους οὖν ἐξείργει ἀπὸ τοῦ
βήματος, τούτους ἀπαγορεύει μὴ δημηγορεῖν. ἐὰν
δέ τις παρὰ ταῦτα μὴ μόνον λέγῃ, ἀλλὰ καὶ
συκοφαντῇ καὶ ἀσελγαίνῃ, καὶ μηκέτι τὸν τοιοῦτον ἄνθρωπον δύναται φέρειν ἡ πόλις, " Δοκιμασίαν μέν," φησίν, " ἐπαγγειλάτω Ἀθηναίων ὁ
βουλόμενος, οἷς ἔξεστιν," ὑμᾶς δ᾽ ἤδη κελεύει

---

[1] δεῖν Baiter : δεῖν ὁ νομοθέτης MSS.
[2] ῥηθῇ Bekker : ῥηθῇ ὁ λόγος MSS.

advise her, either. Whom does he specify in the third place? "Or the man," he says, "who has debauched or prostituted himself." For the man who has made traffic of the shame of his own body, he thought would be ready to sell the common interests of the city also. But whom does he specify in the fourth place? "Or the man," he says, "who has squandered his patrimony or other inheritance." For he believed that the man who has mismanaged his own household will handle the affairs of the city in like manner; and to the lawgiver it did not seem possible that the same man could be a rascal in private life, and in public life a good and useful citizen; and he believed that the public man who comes to the platform ought to come prepared, not merely in words, but, before all else, in life. And he was of the opinion that the advice of a good and upright man, however simple and even awkward the words in which it is given, is profitable to the hearers; but the words of a shameless man, who has treated his own body with scorn, and disgracefully squandered his patrimony—the words of such a man the lawgiver believed could never benefit the hearers, however eloquently they might be spoken. These men, therefore, he debars from the speaker's platform, these he forbids to address the people. But if any one, in violation of these prohibitions, not only speaks, but is guilty of blackmail and wanton scurrility, and if the city is no longer able to put up with such a man, "Let any citizen who chooses," he says, "and is competent thereto,[1] challenge him to a suit of scrutiny;" and

[1] That is, any man who is not debarred, by crimes of his own, from the ordinary privileges of the courts.

περὶ τούτων ἐν τῷ δικαστηρίῳ διαγιγνώσκειν· καὶ
νῦν ἐγὼ κατὰ τούτου τὸν νόμον ἥκω πρὸς ὑμᾶς.

33 Ταῦτα μὲν οὖν πάλαι νενομοθέτηται· ὑμεῖς δ'
ἔτι προσέθεσθε καινὸν νόμον μετὰ τὸ καλὸν παγκράτιον, ὃ οὗτος ἐπαγκρατίασεν ἐν τῇ ἐκκλησίᾳ,
ὑπεραισχυνθέντες ἐπὶ τῷ πράγματι, καθ' ἑκάστην
ἐκκλησίαν ἀποκληροῦν φυλὴν ἐπὶ τὸ βῆμα, ἥτις
προεδρεύσει. καὶ τί προσέταξεν ὁ τιθεὶς τὸν
νόμον; καθῆσθαι κελεύει τοὺς φυλέτας βοη-
θοῦντας τοῖς νόμοις καὶ τῇ δημοκρατίᾳ, ὡς εἰ μὴ
βοήθειάν ποθεν μεταπεμψόμεθα ἐπὶ τοὺς οὕτω
βεβιωκότας, οὐδὲ βουλεύεσθαι δυνησομένους ἡμᾶς
34 περὶ τῶν σπουδαιοτάτων πραγμάτων. ἔστι δ'
οὐδὲν ὄφελος, ὦ ἄνδρες Ἀθηναῖοι, ζητεῖν τοὺς
τοιούτους ἀνθρώπους ἀπελαύνειν ἀπὸ τοῦ βήματος ταῖς κραυγαῖς· οὐ γὰρ αἰσχύνονται· ἀλλὰ
τιμωρίαις τούτους ἀπεθίζειν χρή· μόνως γὰρ ἂν
οὕτως ἀνεκτοὶ γένοιντο.

Ἀναγνώσεται οὖν ὑμῖν τοὺς νόμους τοὺς περὶ
τῆς εὐκοσμίας κειμένους τῶν ῥητόρων. τὸν γὰρ
περὶ τῆς προεδρίας τῶν φυλῶν νόμον Τίμαρχος
οὑτοσὶ καὶ ἕτεροι τοιοῦτοι ῥήτορες συνελθόντες

---

[1] You, the people as jurymen.   [2] See § 26.

[3] We can only conjecture that the members of this tribe
were given the block of seats immediately in front of the
platform, and were expected to enforce the commands of
the presiding officers, the nine πρόεδροι.

[4] By "orderly conduct" Aeschines means orderly conduct

then he commands you[1] to render decision on the case in a court of justice. This is the law under authority of which I now appear before you.

Now these regulations of the law have long been in force; but you went further and added a new law, after that charming gymnastic exhibition which Timarchus gave in an assembly of the people[2]; for you were exceedingly ashamed of the affair. By the new law, for every meeting of the assembly one tribe is to be chosen by lot to have charge of the speaker's platform, and to preside.[3] And what did the proposer of the law prescribe? That the members of the tribe should sit as defenders of the laws and of the democracy; for he believed that unless we should summon help from some quarter against men who have lived such a life, we should not be able even to deliberate on matters of supreme importance. For there is no use in attempting, fellow citizens, to drive such men from the platform by shouting at them, for they have no sense of shame. We must try, rather, to break them of their habits by pains and penalties; for so only can they be made endurable.

The clerk shall therefore read to you the laws that are in force to secure orderly conduct[4] on the part of our public men. For the law that introduced the presidency of a tribe[5] has been attacked in the courts by Timarchus here, in conspiracy with other men like himself, as being

in private life. The editor who composed (or compiled) the law given in § 35 understood him to be speaking of conduct on the platform. The law that Aeschines caused to be read would contain the prohibitions that he has been discussing in §§ 28-32. [5] The new law described in § 33.

γεγραμμένοι εἰσὶ μὴ ἐπιτήδειον εἶναι, ἵν' ἐξῇ
αὐτοῖς καὶ ζῆν καὶ λέγειν ὡς αὐτοὶ βούλονται.

NOMOI

35 [Τῶν ῥητόρων ἐάν τις λέγῃ ἐν τῇ[1] βουλῇ
ἢ ἐν τῷ δήμῳ μὴ[2] περὶ τοῦ εἰσφερομένου,
ἢ μὴ χωρὶς περὶ ἑκάστου, ἢ δὶς περὶ τοῦ
αὐτοῦ ὁ αὐτὸς τῆς αὐτῆς, ἢ λοιδορῆται, ἢ
κακῶς ἀγορεύῃ τινά, ἢ ὑποκρούῃ, ἢ χρηματι-
ζόντων μεταξὺ ἀνεστηκὼς λέγῃ περὶ του μὴ
ἐπὶ τοῦ βήματος, ἢ παρακελεύηται, ἢ ἕλκῃ
τὸν ἐπιστάτην, ἀφειμένης τῆς ἐκκλησίας ἢ
τῆς βουλῆς κυριευέτωσαν οἱ πρόεδροι μέχρι
πεντήκοντα δραχμῶν καθ' ἕκαστον ἀδίκημα
ἐγγράφειν[3] τοῖς πράκτορσιν. ἐὰν δὲ πλέονος
ἄξιος ᾖ ζημίας, ἐπιβαλόντες μέχρι πεντήκοντα δραχμῶν εἰσφερέτωσαν εἰς τὴν βουλὴν
ἢ εἰς τὴν πρώτην ἐκκλησίαν.[4] ὅταν δ' ἐξίωσιν
αἱ[5] κλήσεις, κρινάτωσαν· καὶ ἐὰν κατα-
γνωσθῇ αὐτοῦ κρύβδην ψηφιζομένων, ἐγγρα-
ψάτωσαν οἱ πρόεδροι τοῖς πράκτορσιν.]

36 Τῶν μὲν οὖν νόμων ἀκηκόατε, ὦ ἄνδρες Ἀθηναῖοι, καὶ εὖ οἶδ' ὅτι δοκοῦσιν ὑμῖν καλῶς ἔχειν.
τούτους μέντοι τοὺς νόμους εἶναι χρησίμους ἢ
ἀχρήστους ἐφ' ὑμῖν ἐστιν· ἐὰν μὲν γὰρ κολάζητε
τοὺς ἀδικοῦντας, ἔσονται ὑμῖν οἱ νόμοι καλοὶ καὶ
κύριοι, ἐὰν δ' ἀφιῆτε, καλοὶ μέν, κύριοι δὲ οὐκέτι.

---

[1] τῇ added by Bake.   [2] μὴ added by Schoemann.
[3] ἐγγράφειν Taylor : ἐπιγράφειν MSS.
[4] ἐκκλησίαν Baiter and Sauppe : ἐκκλησίαν ἐν τῷ βουλευτηρίῳ MSS.   [5] αἱ added by Matthiae.

inexpedient, their object being to have license to speak, as well as to behave, as they choose.

LAWS

[If any public man, speaking in the senate or in the assembly of the people, shall not speak on the subject which is before the house, or shall fail to speak on each proposition separately, or shall speak twice on the same subject in one day, or if he shall speak abusively or slanderously, or shall interrupt the proceedings, or in the midst of the deliberations shall get up and speak on anything that is not in order, or shall shout approval, or shall lay hands on the presiding officer, on adjournment of the assembly or the senate the board of presidents are authorized to report his name to the collectors, with a fine of not more than 50 drachmas for each offence. But if he be deserving of heavier penalty, they shall impose a fine of not more than 50 drachmas, and refer the case to the senate or to the next meeting of the assembly. After due summons that body shall pass judgment; the vote shall be secret, and if he be condemned, the presiding officers shall certify the result to the collectors.]

You have heard the laws, fellow citizens, and I am sure that you approve of them. But whether these laws are to be of use or not, rests with you. For if you punish the wrong-doers, your laws will be good and valid; but if you let them go, the laws will still be good, indeed, but valid no longer.

37 Βούλομαι δέ, ὥσπερ ὑπεθέμην,[1] ἐπειδὴ περὶ τῶν
νόμων εἴρηκα, πάλιν τὸ μετὰ τοῦτο ἀντεξετάσαι τοὺς τρόπους τοὺς Τιμάρχου, ἵν᾽ εἰδῆτε ὅσον
διαφέρουσι τῶν νόμων τῶν ὑμετέρων. δέομαι δ᾽
ὑμῶν, ὦ ἄνδρες Ἀθηναῖοι, συγγνώμην ἔχειν, ἐὰν
ἀναγκαζόμενος λέγειν περὶ ἐπιτηδευμάτων φύσει
μὲν μὴ καλῶν, τούτῳ δὲ πεπραγμένων, ἐξαχθῶ τι
ῥῆμα εἰπεῖν ὅ ἐστιν ὅμοιον τοῖς ἔργοις τοῖς
38 Τιμάρχου. οὐδὲ γὰρ ἂν δικαίως ἐμοὶ ἐπιτιμή-
σαιτε, εἴ τι σαφῶς εἴποιμι διδάσκειν ὑμᾶς βουλόμενος, ἀλλὰ πολὺ μᾶλλον τούτῳ, εἰ αἰσχρῶς
οὕτω τυγχάνει βεβιωκώς, ὥστε τὸν τὰ τούτῳ
πεπραγμένα διεξιόντα ἀδύνατον εἶναι εἰπεῖν ὡς
αὐτὸς βούλεται, ἐὰν μή τι καὶ τῶν τοιούτων
φθέγξηται ῥημάτων. εὐλαβήσομαι δ᾽ αὐτὸ ποιεῖν
ὡς ἂν δύνωμαι μάλιστα.

39 Σκέψασθε δέ, ὦ ἄνδρες Ἀθηναῖοι, ὡς μετρίως
μέλλω προσφέρεσθαι Τιμάρχῳ τουτῳί. ἐγὼ γάρ,
ὅσα μὲν παῖς ὢν εἰς τὸ σῶμα τὸ ἑαυτοῦ ἡμάρ-
τηκεν, ἀφίημι, καὶ ἔστω ταῦτα ὥσπερ τὰ ἐπὶ τῶν
τριάκοντα ἢ τὰ πρὸ Εὐκλείδου, ἢ εἴ τις ἄλλη
πώποτε τοιαύτη ἐγένετο προθεσμία· ἃ δὲ ἤδη
φρονῶν καὶ μειράκιον ὢν καὶ τοὺς νόμους ἐπι-
στάμενος τοὺς τῆς πόλεως διαπέπρακται, περὶ
τούτων ἐγώ τε[2] τὰς κατηγορίας ποιήσομαι, καὶ
ὑμᾶς ἐπ᾽ αὐτοῖς ἀξιῶ σπουδάζειν.

40 Οὗτος γὰρ πάντων μὲν πρῶτον, ἐπειδὴ ἀπηλλάγη ἐκ παίδων, ἐκάθητο ἐν Πειραιεῖ ἐπὶ τοῦ
Εὐθυδίκου ἰατρείου, προφάσει μὲν τῆς τέχνης

---

[1] ὑπεθέμην Weidner : the MSS. have ἀρχόμενος τοῦ λόγου
before or after ὑπεθέμην.
[2] ἐγώ τε Emperius : ἐγώ γε MSS.

Now that I have finished with the laws, I wish next, as I proposed at the outset, to inquire into the character of Timarchus, that you may know how completely at variance it is with your laws. And I beg you to pardon me, fellow citizens, if, compelled to speak about habits which by nature are, indeed, unclean, but are nevertheless his, I be led to use some expression that is as bad as Timarchus' deeds. For it would not be right for you to blame me, if now and again I use plain language in my desire to inform you; the blame should rather be his, if it is a fact that his life has been so shameful that a man who is describing his behaviour is unable to say what he wishes without sometimes using expressions that are likewise shameful. But I will try my best to avoid doing this.

See, fellow citizens, with what moderation I am going to deal with Timarchus here. For I remit all the sins that as a boy he committed against his own body; let all this be treated as were the acts committed in the days of the Thirty, or before the year of Eucleides,[1] or whenever else a similar statute of limitations has been passed. But what he is guilty of having done after he had reached years of discretion, when he was already a youth, and knew the laws of the state, that I will make the object of my accusation, and to that I call upon you to give serious attention.

First of all, as soon as he was past boyhood he settled down in the Peiraeus at the establishment of Euthydicus the physician, pretending to be a

---

[1] That is, "forgiven and forgotten," as were the crimes of the supporters of the Thirty Tyrants after the restoration of the democracy, in the archonship of Eucleides, 403/2.

μαθητής, τῇ δ᾽ ἀληθείᾳ πωλεῖν αὑτὸν προῃρη-
μένος, ὡς αὐτὸ τοὖργον ἔδειξεν. ὅσοι μὲν οὖν
τῶν ἐμπόρων ἢ τῶν ἄλλων ξένων ἢ τῶν πολιτῶν
τῶν ἡμετέρων κατ᾽ ἐκείνους τοὺς χρόνους ἐχρήσαντο τῷ σώματι τῷ[1] Τιμάρχου, ἑκὼν καὶ τούτους ὑπερβήσομαι, ἵνα μή τις εἴπῃ ὡς ἄρα λίαν
ἀκριβολογοῦμαι ἅπαντα· ὧν δ᾽ ἐν ταῖς οἰκίαις
γέγονε καταισχύνων τὸ σῶμα τὸ ἑαυτοῦ καὶ τὴν
πόλιν, μισθαρνῶν ἐπ᾽ αὐτῷ τούτῳ ὃ ἀπαγορεύει ὁ
νόμος μὴ πράττειν ἢ μηδὲ δημηγορεῖν, περὶ τούτων ποιήσομαι τοὺς λόγους.

41 Μισγόλας ἔστι τις Ναυκράτους, ὦ ἄνδρες Ἀθηναῖοι, Κολλυτεύς, ἀνὴρ τὰ μὲν ἄλλα καλὸς κἀγα-
θός, καὶ οὐδαμῇ ἄν τις αὐτὸν μέμψαιτο, περὶ δὲ
τὸ πρᾶγμα τοῦτο δαιμονίως ἐσπουδακώς, καὶ ἀεί
τινας ἔχειν εἰωθὼς περὶ αὑτὸν κιθαρῳδοὺς ἢ κιθα-
ριστάς. ταυτὶ δὲ λέγω οὐ τοῦ φορτικοῦ ἕνεκα,
ἀλλ᾽ ἵνα γνωρίσητε αὐτὸν ὅστις ἐστίν. οὗτος,
αἰσθόμενος ὧν ἕνεκα τὰς διατριβὰς ἐποιεῖτο Τίμαρχος οὑτοσὶ ἐπὶ τοῦ ἰατρείου, ἀργύριόν τι
προαναλώσας ἀνέστησεν αὐτὸν καὶ ἔσχε παρ᾽
ἑαυτῷ, εὔσαρκον ὄντα καὶ νέον καὶ βδελυρὸν καὶ
ἐπιτήδειον πρὸς τὸ πρᾶγμα ὃ προῃρεῖτο ἐκεῖνος
42 μὲν πράττειν, οὗτος δὲ πάσχειν. καὶ ταῦτα οὐκ
ὤκνησεν, ἀλλ᾽ ὑπέστη Τίμαρχος οὑτοσί, οὐδενὸς
ὢν τῶν μετρίων ἐνδεής· πολλὴν γὰρ πάνυ κατέλιπεν ὁ πατὴρ αὐτῷ οὐσίαν, ἣν οὗτος κατεδήδοκεν,
ὡς ἐγὼ προϊόντος ἐπιδείξω τοῦ λόγου· ἀλλ᾽
ἔπραξε ταῦτα δουλεύων ταῖς αἰσχίσταις ἡδοναῖς,
ὀψοφαγίᾳ καὶ πολυτελείᾳ δείπνων καὶ αὐλητρίσι
καὶ ἑταίραις καὶ κύβοις καὶ τοῖς ἄλλοις, ὑφ᾽ ὧν

[1] τῷ added by Blass.

student of medicine, but in fact deliberately offering himself for sale, as the event proved. The names of the merchants or other foreigners, or of our own citizens, who enjoyed the person of Timarchus in those days I will pass over willingly, that no one may say that I am over particular to state every petty detail. But in whose houses he has lived to the shame of his own body and of the city, earning wages by precisely that thing which the law forbids, under penalty of losing the privilege of public speech, of this I will speak.

Fellow citizens, there is one Misgolas, son of Naucrates, of the deme Collytus, a man otherwise honourable, and beyond reproach save in this, that he is bent on that sort of thing like one possessed, and is accustomed always to have about him singers or cithara-players. I say this, not from any liking for indecent talk, but that you may know what sort of man Misgolas is. Now this Misgolas, perceiving Timarchus' motive in staying at the house of the physician, paid him a sum of money in advance and caused him to change his lodgings, and got him into his own home; for Timarchus was well developed, young, and lewd, just the person for the thing that Misgolas wanted to do, and Timarchus wanted to have done. Timarchus did not hesitate, but submitted to it all, though he had income enough to satisfy all reasonable desires. For his father had left him a very large property, which he has squandered, as I will show in the course of my speech. But he behaved as he did because he was a slave to the most shameful lusts, to gluttony and extravagance at table, to flute-girls and harlots, to dice, and to all those other things

οὐδενὸς χρὴ κρατεῖσθαι τὸν γενναῖον καὶ ἐλεύθερον. καὶ οὐκ ᾐσχύνθη ὁ μιαρὸς οὗτος ἐκλιπὼν
μὲν τὴν πατρῴαν οἰκίαν, διαιτώμενος δὲ παρὰ
Μισγόλᾳ, οὔτε πατρικῷ ὄντι φίλῳ οὔθ᾽ ἡλικιώτῃ,[1]
ἀλλὰ παρ᾽ ἀλλοτρίῳ καὶ πρεσβυτέρῳ ἑαυτοῦ, καὶ
παρ᾽ ἀκολάστῳ περὶ ταῦτα ὡραῖος ὤν.

43   Πολλὰ μὲν οὖν καὶ ἄλλα καταγέλαστα πέπρακται Τιμάρχῳ κατ᾽ ἐκείνους τοὺς χρόνους, ἓν δὲ
ὃ καὶ διηγήσασθαι ὑμῖν βούλομαι. ἦν μὲν Διονυσίων τῶν ἐν ἄστει ἡ[2] πομπή, ἐπόμπευον δ᾽ ἐν
ταὐτῷ ὅ τε Μισγόλας ὁ τούτου ἀνειληφὼς καὶ
Φαῖδρος Καλλίου Σφήττιος. συνθεμένου δ᾽ αὐτοῖς
συμπομπεύειν Τιμάρχου τουτουί, οἱ μὲν περὶ
τὴν ἄλλην παρασκευὴν διέτριβον, οὗτος δὲ οὐκ
ἐπανῆκε. παρωξυμμένος δὲ πρὸς τὸ πρᾶγμα ὁ
Μισγόλας ζήτησιν αὐτοῦ ἐποιεῖτο μετὰ τοῦ Φαίδρου, ἐξαγγελθέντος δ᾽ αὐτοῖς εὑρίσκουσι τοῦτον
ἐν συνοικίᾳ μετὰ ξένων τινῶν συναριστῶντα.
διαπειλησαμένου δὲ τοῦ Μισγόλα καὶ τοῦ Φαίδρου τοῖς ξένοις, καὶ κελευόντων ἤδη ἀκολουθεῖν
εἰς τὸ δεσμωτήριον, ὅτι μειράκιον ἐλεύθερον διέφθειραν, φοβηθέντες οἱ ξένοι ᾤχοντο[3] καταλι-
πόντες τὰ παρεσκευασμένα.

44   Καὶ ταῦθ᾽ ὅτι ἀληθῆ λέγω, πάντες, ὅσοι κατ᾽
ἐκείνους τοὺς χρόνους ἐγίγνωσκον Μισγόλαν καὶ
Τίμαρχον, ἴσασιν. ᾗ δὴ καὶ πάνυ χαίρω, ὅτι μοι
γέγονεν ἡ δίκη πρὸς ἄνθρωπον οὐκ ἠγνοημένον ὑφ᾽
ὑμῶν, οὐδ᾽ ἀπ᾽ ἄλλου γιγνωσκόμενον οὐδενός, ἢ ἀπ᾽

---

[1] Weidner deletes οὔτε παρ᾽ ἐπιτρόπῳ which the MSS. have
after ἡλικιώτῃ.

[2] ἡ added by Sauppe.

[3] Weidner deletes φεύγοντες which the MSS. have before
or after ᾤχοντο.

no one of which ought to have the mastery over a man who is well-born and free. And this wretch was not ashamed to abandon his father's house and live with Misgolas, a man who was not a friend of his father's, nor a person of his own age, but a stranger, and older than himself, a man who knew no restraint in such matters, while Timarchus himself was in the bloom of youth.

Among the many ridiculous things which Timarchus did in those days was one which I wish to relate to you. The occasion was the procession at the City Dionysia. Misgolas, who had taken possession of him, and Phaedrus, son of Callias, of the deme Sphettus, were to march in the procession together. Now Timarchus here had agreed to join them in the procession, but they were busy with their general preparations, and he failed to come back. Misgolas, provoked at the thing, proceeded to make search for him in company with Phaedrus. They got word of him and found him at lunch with some foreigners in a lodging-house. Misgolas and Phaedrus threatened the foreigners and ordered them to follow straight to the lock-up for having corrupted a free youth. The foreigners were so scared that they dropped everything and ran away as fast as they could go.

The truth of this story is known to everybody who knew Misgolas and Timarchus in those days. Indeed, I am very glad that the suit that I am prosecuting is against a man not unknown to you, and known for no other thing than precisely that

39

αὐτοῦ τοῦ ἐπιτηδεύματος περὶ οὗ καὶ τὴν ψῆφον
μέλλετε φέρειν. περὶ μὲν γὰρ τῶν ἀγνοουμένων
σαφεῖς ἴσως προσήκει τὰς ἀποδείξεις ποιεῖσθαι
τὸν κατήγορον, περὶ δὲ τῶν ὁμολογουμένων οὐ λίαν
ἔγωγε μέγα ἔργον εἶναι νομίζω τὸ κατηγορεῖν·
ἀναμνῆσαι γὰρ μόνον προσήκει τοὺς ἀκούοντας.
45 ἐγὼ τοίνυν καίπερ ὁμολογουμένου τοῦ πράγματος,
ἐπειδὴ ἐν δικαστηρίῳ ἐσμέν, γέγραφα μαρτυρίαν
τῷ Μισγόλᾳ ἀληθῆ μέν, οὐκ ἀπαίδευτον δέ, ὥς γ᾽[1]
ἐμαυτὸν πείθω. αὐτὸ μὲν γὰρ τοὔνομα τοῦ ἔργου
ὃ ἔπραττε πρὸς τοῦτον, οὐκ ἐγγράφω, οὐδ᾽ ἄλλο
γέγραφα οὐδὲν ὃ ἐπιζήμιόν ἐστιν ἐκ τῶν νόμων τῷ
τἀληθῆ μαρτυρήσαντι· ἃ δέ ἐστιν ὑμῖν τε ἀκοῦσαι
γνώριμα, ἀκίνδυνά τε[2] τῷ μαρτυροῦντι καὶ μὴ
αἰσχρά, ταῦτα γέγραφα.
46 Ἐὰν μὲν οὖν ἐθελήσῃ ὁ Μισγόλας δεῦρο
παρελθὼν τἀληθῆ μαρτυρεῖν, τὰ δίκαια ποιή-
σει· ἐὰν δὲ προαιρῆται ἐκκλητευθῆναι μᾶλλον
ἢ τἀληθῆ μαρτυρεῖν, ὑμεῖς τὸ ὅλον πρᾶγμα
συνίδετε. εἰ γὰρ ὁ μὲν πράξας αἰσχυνεῖται καὶ
προαιρήσεται χιλίας μᾶλλον δραχμὰς ἀποτεῖσαι
τῷ δημοσίῳ, ὥστε μὴ δεῖξαι τὸ πρόσωπον τὸ
ἑαυτοῦ ὑμῖν, ὁ δὲ πεπονθὼς δημηγορήσει, σοφὸς
ὁ νομοθέτης ὁ τοὺς οὕτω βδελυροὺς ἐξείργων
47 ἀπὸ τοῦ βήματος. ἐὰν δ᾽ ἄρα ὑπακούσῃ μέν,
τράπηται δὲ ἐπὶ τὸ ἀναιδέστατον, ἐπὶ τὸ ἐξό-

---

[1] ὥς γ᾽ Sakorraphos : ὡς ἐγὼ MSS.
[2] ἀκίνδυνά τε Blass : ἀκίνδυνα δὲ MSS.

practice as to which you are going to render your verdict. For in the case of facts which are not generally known, the accuser is bound, I suppose, to make his proofs explicit; but where the facts are notorious, I think it is no very difficult matter to conduct the prosecution, for one has only to appeal to the recollection of his hearers. However, although the fact in this case is acknowledged, I remember that we are in court, and so I have drafted an affidavit for Misgolas, true and not indelicate in its phrasing, as I flatter myself. For I do not set down the actual name of the thing that Misgolas used to do to him, nor have I written anything else that would legally incriminate a man who has testified to the truth.[1] But I have set down what will be no news for you to hear, and will involve the witness in no danger nor disgrace.

If therefore Misgolas is willing to come forward here and testify to the truth, he will be doing what is right; but if he prefers to refuse the summons rather than testify to the truth, the whole business will be made clear to you. For if the man who did the thing is going to be ashamed of it and choose to pay a thousand drachmas into the treasury rather than show his face before you,[2] while the man to whom it has been done is to be a speaker in your assembly, then wise indeed was the lawgiver who excluded such disgusting creatures from the platform. But if Misgolas does indeed answer the summons, but resorts to the most shameless course, denial of

[1] That is, Misgolas can testify to the truth of the affidavit without thereby testifying to any criminal act of his own.

[2] It is evident from this that when a formal summons to testify in court was refused, a definite fine was inflicted.

μνυσθαι τὰς ἀληθείας, ὡς Τιμάρχῳ μὲν χάριτας
ἀποδιδούς, ἑτέροις δ' ἐπίδειξιν ποιούμενος ὡς εὖ
ἐπίσταται τὰ τοιαῦτα συγκρύπτειν, πρῶτον μὲν εἰς
ἑαυτὸν ἐξαμαρτήσεται, ἔπειτα οὐδὲν ἔσται [1] πλέον.
ἑτέραν γὰρ ἐγὼ γέγραφα μαρτυρίαν τοῖς εἰδόσι
Τίμαρχον τουτονὶ καταλιπόντα τὴν πατρῴαν
οἰκίαν καὶ διαιτώμενον παρὰ Μισγόλᾳ, πρᾶγμα
οἶμαι χαλεπὸν ἐξεργάσασθαι ἐπιχειρῶν· οὔτε γάρ
με δεῖ τοὺς ἐμαυτοῦ φίλους μάρτυρας παρασχέσθαι, οὔτε τοὺς τούτων ἐχθρούς, οὔτε τοὺς μηδε-
τέρους ἡμῶν γιγνώσκοντας, ἀλλὰ τοὺς τούτων
48 φίλους. ἂν δ' ἄρα καὶ τούτους πείσωσι μὴ
μαρτυρεῖν, ὡς οὐκ οἴομαι· εἰ δὲ μή, ἀλλ' οὐχ
ἅπαντάς γε·[2] ἐκεῖνό γε οὐ μήποτε δυνήσονται,[3]
ἀφελέσθαι τὴν ἀλήθειαν, οὐδὲ τὴν ἐν τῇ πόλει
περὶ Τιμάρχου φήμην, ἣν οὐκ ἐγὼ τούτῳ παρε-
σκεύασα, ἀλλ' αὐτὸς οὗτος ἑαυτῷ. οὕτω γὰρ
χρὴ καθαρὸν εἶναι τὸν βίον τοῦ σώφρονος ἀνδρός,
ὥστε μηδ' ἐπιδέχεσθαι δόξαν αἰτίας πονηρᾶς.

49 Βούλομαι δὲ κἀκεῖνο προειπεῖν, ἐὰν ἄρα ὑπακούσῃ ὁ Μισγόλας τοῖς νόμοις καὶ ὑμῖν. εἰσὶ
φύσεις ἀνθρώπων πολὺ διαφέρουσαι ὀφθῆναι τῶν
ἄλλων τὰ περὶ τὴν ἡλικίαν· ἔνιοι μὲν γὰρ νέοι
ὄντες προφερεῖς καὶ πρεσβύτεροι φαίνονται,
ἕτεροι δέ, πολὺν ἀριθμὸν χρόνου γεγονότες, παντ-
άπασι νέοι. τούτων δ' ἐστὶ τῶν ἀνδρῶν ὁ
Μισγόλας. τυγχάνει μὲν γὰρ ἡλικιώτης ὢν ἐμὸς

---

[1] ἔσται Weidner : ἔστ' αὐτῷ or αὐτῷ ἔσται MSS.
[2] ἅπαντάς γε Blass, transposing γε, which some MSS. have
after οἴομαι.
[3] οὐ μήποτε δυνήσονται Emperius : οὐδὲ μήποτε δύνωνται (or
δυνήσονται) or οὐδέποτε δυνήσονται MSS.

the truth under oath, as a grateful return to Timarchus, and a demonstration to the rest of them that he well knows how to help cover up such conduct, in the first place he will damage himself, and in the second place he will gain nothing by it. For I have prepared another affidavit for those who know that this man Timarchus left his father's house and lived with Misgolas, though it is a difficult thing, no doubt, that I am undertaking. For I have to present as my witnesses, not friends of mine nor enemies of theirs, nor those who are strangers to both of us, but their friends. But even if they do persuade these men also not to testify—I do not expect they will, at any rate not all of them—one thing at least they will never succeed in accomplishing : they will never hush up the truth, nor blot out Timarchus' reputation among his fellow citizens—a reputation which he owes to no act of mine, but to his own conduct. For the life of a virtuous man ought to be so clean that it will not admit even of a suspicion of wrongdoing.

But I wish to say another thing in anticipation, in case Misgolas shall answer before the laws and before you. There are men who by nature differ widely from the rest of us as to their apparent age. For some men, young in years, seem mature and older than they are ; others, old by count of years, seem to be mere youths. Misgolas is such a man. He happens, indeed, to be of my own age, and was

καὶ συνέφηβος, καὶ ἔστιν ἡμῖν τουτὶ πέμπτον καὶ
τετταρακοστὸν ἔτος· καὶ ἐγὼ μὲν τοσαυτασὶ
πολιὰς ἔχω ὅσας ὑμεῖς ὁρᾶτε, ἀλλ' οὐκ ἐκεῖνος.
διὰ τί οὖν ταῦτα προλέγω; ἵνα μὴ ἐξαίφνης αὐτὸν
ἰδόντες θαυμάσητε καὶ τοιοῦτόν τι τῇ διανοίᾳ
ὑπολάβητε· "Ὦ Ἡράκλεις, ἀλλ' οὗτός γε τούτου
οὐ πολὺ διαφέρει." ἅμα μὲν γὰρ ἡ φύσις ἐστὶ
τοιαύτη τοῦ ἀνδρός, ἅμα δὲ ἤδη μειρακίῳ ὄντι
αὐτῷ ἐπλησίαζεν.

50 Ἵνα δὲ μὴ διατρίβω, πρῶτον μὲν κάλει μοι
τοὺς εἰδότας Τίμαρχον τουτονὶ διαιτώμενον ἐν τῇ
Μισγόλα οἰκίᾳ, ἔπειτα τὴν Φαίδρου μαρτυρίαν
ἀναγίγνωσκε, τελευταίαν δέ μοι λαβὲ τὴν αὐτοῦ
Μισγόλα μαρτυρίαν, ἐὰν ἄρα[1] καὶ τοὺς θεοὺς
δεδιὼς καὶ τοὺς συνειδότας αἰσχυνόμενος καὶ τοὺς
ἄλλους πολίτας καὶ ὑμᾶς τοὺς δικαστὰς ἐθελήσῃ
τἀληθῆ μαρτυρεῖν.

ΜΑΡΤΥΡΙΑΙ

[Μισγόλας Νικίου Πειραιεὺς μαρτυρεῖ. ἐμοὶ
ἐγένετο ἐν συνηθείᾳ Τίμαρχος ὁ ἐπὶ τοῦ Εὐθυδίκου ἰατρείου ποτὲ καθεζόμενος, καὶ κατὰ
τὴν γνῶσίν μου[2] τὴν πρότερον[3] αὐτὸν πολυω-
ρῶν εἰς τὴν νῦν οὐ διέλιπον.]

51 Εἰ μὲν τοίνυν, ὦ ἄνδρες Ἀθηναῖοι, Τίμαρχος
οὑτοσὶ διέμεινε παρὰ τῷ Μισγόλα καὶ μηκέτι ὡς
ἄλλον ἧκε, μετριώτερ' ἂν διεπέπρακτο, εἰ δή

---

[1] ἐὰν ἄρα Dahms : ἵνα MSS.   [2] μου Bernardi : μοι MSS.
[3] πρότερον Emperius : πρὸς MSS.

---

[1] All Athenian young men were required to undergo military training during the two years following their eighteenth

in the cadet corps with me;[1] we are now in our forty-fifth year. I am quite gray, as you see, but not he. Why do I speak of this? Because I fear that, seeing him for the first time, you may be surprised, and some such thought as this may occur to you: "Heracles! This man is not much older than Timarchus." For not only is this youthful appearance characteristic of the man, but moreover Timarchus was already past boyhood when he used to be in his company.

But, not to delay, (*to the Clerk of the Court*) call first, if you please, those who know that Timarchus here lived in the house of Misgolas, then read the testimony of Phaedrus, and, finally, please take the affidavit of Misgolas himself, in case fear of the gods, and respect for those who know the facts as well as he does, and for the citizens at large and for you the jurors, shall persuade him to testify to the truth.

TESTIMONY

[Misgolas, son of Nicias, of Piraeus, testifies. Timarchus, who once used to stay at the house of Euthydicus the physician, became intimate with me, and I hold him to-day in the same esteem as in all my past acquaintance with him.]

Now, fellow citizens, if Timarchus here had remained with Misgolas and never gone to another man's house, his conduct would have been more

birthday. The first year they were in garrison at the Piraeus. At the close of the year, after a public exhibition of their military attainments, they received a shield and spear from the state, and then were sent out for another year to garrison the forts and patrol the borders.

τι τῶν τοιούτων ἐστὶ μέτριον, καὶ ἔγωγε οὐκ
ἂν ἐτόλμησα[1] αὐτὸν οὐδὲν αἰτιᾶσθαι ἀλλ᾽[2] ἢ
ὅπερ ὁ νομοθέτης παρρησιάζεται, ἡταιρηκέναι
μόνον· ὁ γὰρ πρὸς ἕνα τοῦτο πράττων, ἐπὶ μισθῷ
δὲ τὴν πρᾶξιν ποιούμενος, αὐτῷ μοι δοκεῖ τούτῳ
52 ἔνοχος εἶναι. ἐὰν δ᾽ ὑμᾶς ἀναμνήσας ἐπιδείξω,
ὑπερβαίνων τούσδε τοὺς ἀγρίους, Κηδωνίδην
καὶ Αὐτοκλείδην καὶ Θέρσανδρον, αὐτοὺς δὲ[3]
λέγων ὧν ἐν ταῖς οἰκίαις ἀνειλημμένος γέγονε,
μὴ[4] μόνον παρὰ τῷ Μισγόλᾳ μεμισθαρνηκότα
αὐτὸν ἐπὶ τῷ σώματι, ἀλλὰ καὶ παρ᾽ ἑτέρῳ καὶ
πάλιν παρ᾽ ἄλλῳ, καὶ παρὰ τούτου ὡς ἕτερον
ἐληλυθότα, οὐκέτι δήπου φανεῖται[5] μόνον ἡταιρη-
κώς, ἀλλὰ (μὰ τὸν Διόνυσον οὐκ οἶδ᾽ ὅπως δυνή-
σομαι περιπλέκειν ὅλην τὴν ἡμέραν) καὶ πεπορ-
νευμένος· ὁ γὰρ εἰκῆ τοῦτο καὶ πρὸς πολλοὺς
πράττων καὶ μισθοῦ, αὐτῷ μοι δοκεῖ τούτῳ
ἔνοχος εἶναι.

53 Ἐπειδὴ τοίνυν ὁ Μισγόλας τῇ τε δαπάνῃ
ἀπεῖπε καὶ τοῦτον ἐξέπεμψε παρ᾽ ἑαυτοῦ, μετὰ
τοῦτο[6] ἀναλαμβάνει αὐτὸν Ἀντικλῆς Καλλίου
Εὐωνυμεύς. οὗτος μὲν οὖν ἄπεστιν ἐν Σάμῳ
μετὰ τῶν κληρούχων· ἀλλὰ τὰ μετὰ ταῦτα ἐρῶ.
ὡς γὰρ ἀπηλλάγη παρὰ τοῦ Ἀντικλέους καὶ τοῦ
Μισγόλα Τίμαρχος οὑτοσί, οὐκ ἐνουθέτησεν ἑαυτόν, οὐδὲ βελτιόνων διατριβῶν ἥψατο, ἀλλὰ

---

[1] ἐτόλμησα Reiske : ὤκνησα MSS.
[2] ἀλλ᾽ added by Sakorraphos.
[3] αὐτοὺς δὲ added by Sakorraphos : καὶ ἐπιδείξω αὐτοὺς MSS.
[4] μὴ Blass, following an ancient quotation : καὶ μὴ MSS.
[5] φανεῖται Cobet : φαίνεται MSS.
[6] μετὰ τοῦτο Blass, first ed. (Blass brackets in second ed):
μετὰ τοῦτον MSS.

decent—if really any such conduct is "decent"—
and I should not have ventured to bring any other
charge against him than that which the lawgiver
describes in plain words, simply that he was a
kept man. For the man who practises this thing
with one person, and practises it for pay, seems to
me to be liable to precisely this charge. But if, saying nothing about these bestial fellows, Cedonides,
Autocleides, and Thersandrus, and simply telling
the names of those in whose houses he has been
an inmate, I refresh your memories and show that he
is guilty of selling his person not only in Misgolas'
house, but in the house of another man also, and
again of another, and that from this last he went
to still another, surely you will no longer look upon
him as one who has merely been a kept man, but—
by Dionysus, I don't know how I can keep glossing
the thing over all day long—as a common prostitute.
For the man who follows these practices recklessly
and with many men and for pay seems to me to
be chargeable with precisely this.

Well, when now Misgolas found him too expensive and dismissed him, next Anticles, son of Callias,
of the deme Euonymon, took him up. Anticles,
however, is absent in Samos as a member of the
new colony, so I will pass on to the next incident.
For after this man Timarchus had left Anticles and
Misgolas, he did not repent or reform his way of
life, but spent his days in the gambling-place, where

47

διημέρευεν ἐν τῷ κυβείῳ, οὗ ἡ τηλία τίθεται καὶ
τοὺς ἀλεκτρυόνας συμβάλλουσιν καὶ κυβεύουσιν·
ἤδη γὰρ οἶμαί τινας ὑμῶν ἑωρακέναι, εἰ δὲ μή,
54 ἀλλ᾽ ἀκηκοέναι γε. τῶν δὲ ἐκ τῆς διατριβῆς
ταύτης ἐστί τις Πιττάλακος, ἄνθρωπος δημόσιος
οἰκέτης τῆς πόλεως. οὗτος εὐπορῶν ἀργυρίου καὶ
ἰδὼν τοῦτον ἐν τῇ διατριβῇ, ἀνέλαβεν αὐτὸν καὶ
ἔσχε παρ᾽ ἑαυτῷ. καὶ ταῦτ᾽ οὐκ ἐδυσχέρανεν[1]
ὁ μιαρὸς οὑτοσί, μέλλων ἑαυτὸν καταισχύνειν
πρὸς ἄνθρωπον δημόσιον οἰκέτην τῆς πόλεως·
ἀλλ᾽ εἰ λήψεται χορηγὸν τῇ βδελυρίᾳ τῇ ἑαυτοῦ,
τοῦτο μόνον ἐσκέψατο, τῶν δὲ καλῶν ἢ τῶν
αἰσχίστων οὐδεμίαν πώποτε πρόνοιαν ἐποιήσατο.

55 Καὶ τοιαῦτα ἁμαρτήματα καὶ τοιαύτας ὕβρεις
ἐγὼ ἀκήκοα γεγονέναι ὑπὸ τοῦ ἀνθρώπου τούτου
εἰς τὸ σῶμα τὸ Τιμάρχου, οἵας ἐγὼ μὰ τὸν Δία
τὸν Ὀλύμπιον οὐκ ἂν τολμήσαιμι πρὸς ὑμᾶς
εἰπεῖν· ἃ γὰρ οὑτοσὶ ἔργῳ πράττων οὐκ ᾐσχύνετο,
ταῦτ᾽ ἐγὼ λόγῳ σαφῶς ἐν ὑμῖν εἰπὼν οὐκ ἂν
δεξαίμην[2] ζῆν. ὑπὸ δὲ τοὺς αὐτοὺς χρόνους τούτους ἐν οἷς οὗτος ἦν παρὰ τῷ Πιτταλάκῳ, κατα-
πλεῖ δεῦρο ἐξ Ἑλλησπόντου Ἡγήσανδρος, περὶ
οὗ πάλαι εὖ οἶδ᾽ ὅτι θαυμάζετε διότι οὐ μέμνημαι·
οὕτως ἐναργές ἐστιν ὃ ἐρῶ.

56 Οὗτος ὁ Ἡγήσανδρος ἀφικνεῖται, ὃν ὑμεῖς ἴστε
κάλλιον ἢ ἐγώ. ἔτυχε δὲ τότε συμπλεύσας εἰς
Ἑλλήσποντον ταμίας Τιμομάχῳ τῷ Ἀχαρνεῖ τῷ
στρατηγήσαντι, καὶ ἧκε δεῦρο ἀπολελαυκώς, ὡς
λέγεται, τῆς ἐκείνου εὐηθείας, ἔχων οὐκ ἐλάττους
ὀγδοήκοντα μνᾶς ἀργυρίου· καὶ τρόπον τινὰ οὐχ

---

[1] ἐδυσχέρανεν Blass : ἐδυσχέραινεν MSS.
[2] δεξαίμην Cobet : ἐδεξάμην MSS.

the gaming-table is set, and cock-fighting and dice-throwing are the regular occupations. I imagine some of you have seen the place; at any rate you have heard of it. Among the men who spend their time there is one Pittalacus, a public slave who is the property of the city. He had plenty of money, and seeing Timarchus spending his time thus he took him and kept him in his own house. This foul wretch here was not disturbed by the fact that he was going to defile himself with a public slave, but thought of one thing only, of getting him to be paymaster for his own disgusting lusts; to the question of virtue or of shame he never gave a thought.

Now the sins of this Pittalacus against the person of Timarchus, and his abuse of him, as they have come to my ears, are such that, by the Olympian Zeus, I should not dare to repeat them to you. For the things that he was not ashamed to do in deed, I had rather die than describe to you in words. But about the same time, while, as I have said, he was staying with Pittalacus, here comes Hegesandrus, back again from the Hellespont. I know you are surprised that I have not mentioned him long before this, so notorious is what I am going to relate.

This Hegesandrus, whom you know better than I, arrives. It happened that he had at that time sailed to the Hellespont as treasurer to the general Timomachus, of the deme Acharnae; and he returned, having made the most, it is said, of the simple-mindedness of the general, for he had in his possession no less than eighty minas of silver. Indeed, he proved to be, in a way, largely responsible

49

ἥκιστα αἴτιος ἐγένετο Τιμομάχῳ τῆς συμφορᾶς.
57 ὧν δ' ἐν τοιαύτῃ ἀφθονίᾳ καὶ εἰσφοιτῶν ὡς τὸν
Πιττάλακον συγκυβευτὴν ὄντα, καὶ τοῦτον ἐκεῖ
πρῶτον ἰδών, ἥσθη τε καὶ ἐπεθύμησε καὶ ἐβουλή-
θη ὡς αὐτὸν ἀναλαβεῖν, καί πως [1] ἡγήσατο αὐτὸν
ἐγγὺς εἶναι τῆς αὐτοῦ φύσεως. πρῶτον μὲν οὖν
τῷ Πιτταλάκῳ διελέχθη δεόμενος παραδοῦναι
τοῦτον· ὡς δ' οὐκ ἔπειθεν, αὐτῷ τούτῳ προσβάλ-
λει, καὶ οὐ πολὺν ἀνήλωσε λόγον, ἀλλ' εὐθὺς
ἐπεπείκει· καὶ γὰρ εἰς αὐτὸ τὸ πρᾶγμα δεινὴ ἡ
ἀκακία καὶ εὐπείστία,[2] ὥστε καὶ ἐξ αὐτῶν τούτων
εἰκότως ἂν μισοῖτο.
58   Ὡς δ' ἀπήλλακτο μὲν παρὰ τοῦ Πιτταλάκου,
ἀνείληπτο δὲ ὑπὸ τοῦ Ἡγησάνδρου, ὠδυνᾶτο,
οἶμαι, ὁ Πιττάλακος, μάτην, ὥς γ' ᾤετο, τοσοῦτον
ἀργύριον ἀνηλωκώς, καὶ ἐζηλοτύπει τὰ γιγνόμενα.
καὶ ἐφοίτα ἐπὶ τὴν οἰκίαν. ὅτε [3] δὲ αὐτοῖς ἠνώ-
χλει, σκέψασθε μεγάλην ῥώμην Ἡγησάνδρου καὶ
Τιμάρχου· μεθυσθέντες γάρ ποτε καὶ αὐτοὶ καὶ
ἄλλοι τινές, ὧν οὐ βούλομαι τὰ ὀνόματα λέγειν,
59 εἰσπηδήσαντες νύκτωρ εἰς τὴν οἰκίαν οὗ ᾤκει ὁ
Πιττάλακος, πρῶτον μὲν συνέτριβον τὰ σκευάρια
καὶ διερρίπτουν εἰς τὴν ὁδόν, ἀστραγάλους τέ
τινας διασείστους καὶ φιμοὺς καὶ κυβευτικὰ ἕτερα
ὄργανα, καὶ τοὺς ὄρτυγας καὶ τοὺς ἀλεκτρυόνας,

---

[1] πως Cobet : πως ἴσως MSS.
[2] εὐπειστία Reiske : εὐπιστία or ἀπιστία MSS.
[3] ὅτε Taylor : ὅτι MSS.

---

[1] Between 363 and 359 one Athenian general after another
was condemned to death or heavily fined for lack of success
in the North.   Timomachus was sent into banishment.

for the fate of Timomachus.[1] Hegesandrus, being so
well supplied with money, resorted to the house of
Pittalacus, who gambled with him; there he first saw
this man Timarchus; he was pleased with him, lusted
after him, and wanted to take him to his own house,
thinking, doubtless, that here was a man of his own
kidney. So he first had a talk with Pittalacus,
asking him to turn Timarchus over to him. Failing
to persuade him, he appealed to the man himself.
He did not spend many words; the man was
instantly persuaded. For when it is a question
of the business itself, Timarchus shows an open-
mindedness and a spirit of accommodation that
are truly wonderful; indeed, that is one of the very
reasons why he ought to be an object of loathing.

When now he had left Pittalacus' house and been
taken up by Hegesandrus, Pittalacus was enraged,
I fancy, at having wasted, as he considered it, so
much money, and, jealous at what was going on,
he kept visiting the house. When he was getting
to be a nuisance, behold, a mighty stroke on the
part of Hegesandrus and Timarchus! One night
when they were drunk they, with certain others,
whose names I do not care to mention, burst into
the house where Pittalacus was living. First they
smashed the implements of his trade and tossed
them into the street—sundry dice[2] and dice-boxes,
and his gaming utensils in general; they killed the

---

[2] Probably the scholiast is right in explaining ἀστραγάλους
διασείστους "shaken astragali," as the gamester's name for a
sort of dice. Perhaps the hearers would understand that
they were loaded dice. Benseler, however, approves Dor-
ville's explanation, that these dice had been many a time
before now "shaken" between Pittalacus and the rascals
who are now tossing them into the street.

οὓς ἠγάπα ὁ τρισκακοδαίμων ἄνθρωπος, ἀπέκτειναν, τὸ δὲ τελευταῖον δήσαντες πρὸς τὸν κίονα
αὐτὸν τὸν Πιττάλακον ἐμαστίγουν τὰς ἐξ ἀνθρώπων πληγὰς οὕτω πολὺν χρόνον, ὥστε καὶ τοὺς
γείτονας αἰσθέσθαι τῆς κραυγῆς.

60   Τῇ δ' ὑστεραίᾳ ὑπεραγανακτήσας τῷ πράγματι
ὁ Πιττάλακος ἔρχεται γυμνὸς εἰς τὴν ἀγοράν, καὶ
καθίζει ἐπὶ τὸν βωμὸν τὸν τῆς μητρὸς τῶν θεῶν.
ὄχλου δὲ συνδραμόντος, οἷον εἴωθε γίγνεσθαι,
φοβηθέντες ὅ τε Ἡγήσανδρος καὶ ὁ Τίμαρχος μὴ
ἀνακηρυχθῇ αὐτῶν ἡ βδελυρία εἰς πᾶσαν τὴν
πόλιν (ἐπῄει δὲ ἐκκλησία), θέουσι πρὸς τὸν βω-
61   μὸν καὶ αὐτοὶ καὶ τῶν συγκυβευτῶν τινες, καὶ
περιστάντες ἐδέοντο τοῦ Πιτταλάκου ἀναστῆναι,
λέγοντες ὅτι τὸ ὅλον πρᾶγμα παροινία γέγονεν,
καὶ αὐτὸς οὗτος, οὔπω μὰ Δία ὥσπερ νῦν ἀργα-
λέος ὢν τὴν ὄψιν, ἀλλ' ἔτι χρήσιμος, ὑπογενειά-
ζων τὸν ἄνθρωπον καὶ πάντα φάσκων πράξειν ἃ
ἂν ἐκείνῳ συνδοκῇ. πέρας πείθουσιν ἀναστῆναι
ἀπὸ τοῦ βωμοῦ,[1] ὡς τευξόμενόν τινος τῶν δικαίων.
ὡς δ' ἀπῆλθεν ἐκ τῆς ἀγορᾶς, οὐκέτι προσεῖχον
62   αὐτῷ τὸν νοῦν. βαρέως δὲ φέρων τὴν ὕβριν
αὐτῶν ὁ ἄνθρωπος, δίκην ἑκατέρῳ αὐτῶν λαγχάνει.

Ὅτε δ' ἐδικάζετο, ἄλλην[2] σκέψασθε μεγάλην
ῥώμην Ἡγησάνδρου· ἄνθρωπον οὐδὲν αὐτὸν ἠδικη-
κότα, ἀλλὰ τὸ ἐναντίον ἠδικημένον, οὐδὲ προσήκοντα

---

[1] Blass brackets τὸν ἄνθρωπον which the MSS. have before
or after ἀπὸ τοῦ βωμοῦ.   [2] ἄλλην added by the editor.

quails and cocks, so well beloved by the miserable man; and finally they tied Pittalacus himself to the pillar and gave him an inhuman whipping, which lasted until even the neighbours heard the uproar.

The next day Pittalacus, exceeding angry over the affair, comes without his cloak to the market-place and seats himself at the altar of the Mother of the Gods. And when, as always happens, a crowd of people had come running up, Hegesandrus and Timarchus, afraid that their disgusting vices were going to be published to the whole town— a meeting of the assembly was about to be held —hurried up to the altar themselves, and some of their gaming-companions with them, and surrounding Pittalacus begged him to get up, saying that the whole thing was only a drunken frolic; and this man himself, not yet, by Zeus, repulsive to the sight as he is now, but still usable, begged, touching the fellow's chin, and saying he would do anything Pittalacus pleased. At last they persuaded him to get up from the altar, believing that he was going to receive some measure of justice. But as soon as he had left the market-place, they paid no more attention to him. The fellow, angry at their insolent treatment, brings a suit against each of them.[1]

When now the case was coming to trial, behold, another mighty stroke on the part of Hegesandrus! Here was a man who had done him no wrong, but, quite the opposite, had been wronged by him, a man

---

[1] Proceedings in court in behalf of an ordinary slave would be conducted by his master in his own name; but Pittalacus was a state slave (§ 54). Probably he would have to bring suit under the name of some citizen as his protector ($\pi\rho o\sigma\tau\acute{a}\tau\eta s$).

αὐτῷ, ἀλλὰ δημόσιον οἰκέτην τῆς πόλεως, ἦγεν
εἰς δουλείαν φάσκων ἑαυτοῦ εἶναι.[1] ἐν παντὶ δὲ
κακοῦ[2] γενόμενος ὁ Πιττάλακος προσπίπτει ἀνδρὶ
καὶ μάλα χρηστῷ. ἔστι τις Γλαύκων Χολαργεύς·
63 οὗτος αὐτὸν ἀφαιρεῖται εἰς ἐλευθερίαν. τὸ δὲ
μετὰ τοῦτο δικῶν λήξεις ἐποιήσαντο. προϊόντος
δὲ τοῦ χρόνου ἐπέτρεψαν διαγνῶναι τὸ πρᾶγμα
Διοπείθει τῷ Σουνιεῖ, δημότῃ τε ὄντι τοῦ Ἡγησάνδρου, καὶ ἤδη ποτὲ καὶ χρησαμένῳ, ὅτ᾽ ἦν
ἐν ἡλικίᾳ· παραλαβὼν δὲ τὸ πρᾶγμα ὁ Διοπείθης
ἀνεβάλλετο χαριζόμενος τούτοις χρόνους ἐκ χρό-
64 νων. ὡς δὲ παρῄει ἐπὶ τὸ βῆμα τὸ ὑμέτερον ὁ
Ἡγήσανδρος, ὅτε καὶ προσεπολέμει Ἀριστοφῶντι
τῷ Ἀζηνιεῖ, πρὶν αὐτῷ τὴν αὐτὴν ταύτην ἐν τῷ
δήμῳ ἠπείλησεν ἐπαγγελίαν ἐπαγγελεῖν[3] ἥνπερ
ἐγὼ Τιμάρχῳ, καὶ ἐπειδὴ Κρωβύλος ὁ ἀδελφὸς
αὐτοῦ ἐδημηγόρει, καὶ ὅλως ἀπετόλμων ὑμῖν
οὗτοι περὶ τῶν Ἑλληνικῶν συμβουλεύειν, ἐνταῦθα
ἤδη καταμεμψάμενος ἑαυτὸν ὁ Πιττάλακος, καὶ
ἐκλογισάμενος ὅστις ὢν πρὸς οὕστινας ἐπολέμει
εὖ ἐβουλεύσατο (δεῖ γὰρ τἀληθὲς λέγειν)· ἡσυχίαν ἔσχεν, καὶ ἠγάπησεν εἴ τι μὴ προσλάβοι
καινὸν κακόν.

Ἐνταῦθα δὴ τὴν καλὴν ταύτην νίκην νενικηκὼς
ὁ Ἡγήσανδρος ἀκονιτί, εἶχε παρ᾽ ἑαυτῷ Τίμαρχον

---

[1] εἶναι Sakorraphos : εἶναι δοῦλον MSS.
[2] κακοῦ Blomfield : κακῷ MSS.
[3] ἐπαγγελεῖν Blass : the MSS. omit or have ἐπαγγέλλει.

---

[1] Suits between Glaucon and Hegesandrus, who claimed
that Pittalacus was a slave of his.

on whom he had no claim, in fact, a slave belonging to the city; this man he attempted to enslave to himself, alleging that he was his owner. Now Pittalacus, reduced to desperate straits, falls in with a man—a very good man he is—one Glaucon of the deme Cholargus; he attempts to rescue Pittalacus and secure his freedom. Law-suits were next begun.[1] As time went on they submitted the matter to the arbitration of Diopeithes of Sunium, a man of Hegesandrus' own deme and one with whom he had had dealings in his younger years. Diopeithes undertook the case, but put it off again and again in order to favour these parties. But when now Hegesandrus was coming before you as a public speaker, being at the same time engaged in his attack on Aristophon of Azenia, an attack which he kept up until Aristophon threatened to institute against him before the people the same process that I have instituted against Timarchus, and when Hegesandrus' brother Crobylus[2] was coming forward as a public man, when, in short, these men had the effrontery to advise you as to international questions, then at last Pittalacus, losing confidence in himself and asking himself who he was that he should attempt to fight against such men as these, came to a wise decision—for I must speak the truth: he gave up, and considered himself lucky if his ill-treatment should stop there.

So now when Hegesandrus had won this glorious victory—without a fight!—he kept possession of the

[2] Crobylus, "Top-knot," was the nickname of Hegesippus, as associate of Demosthenes in the anti-Macedonian agitation. He owed his name to his old-fashioned way of wearing his hair.

65 τουτονί. καὶ ταῦτα ὅτι ἀληθῆ λέγω, πάντες ἴστε·
τίς γὰρ ὑμῶν πώποτε [1] εἰς τοὔψον ἀφῖκται καὶ
τὰς δαπάνας τὰς τούτων οὐ τεθεώρηκεν; ἢ τίς
τοῖς τούτων κώμοις καὶ μάχαις [2] περιτυχὼν οὐκ
ἠχθέσθη ὑπὲρ τῆς πόλεως; ὅμως δέ, ἐπειδήπερ ἐν
δικαστηρίῳ ἐσμέν, κάλει μοι Γλαύκωνα Χολαργέα
τὸν ἀφελόμενον εἰς ἐλευθερίαν τὸν Πιττάλακον,
καὶ τὰς ἑτέρας μαρτυρίας ἀναγίγνωσκε.

MAPTYPIAI

66 [Μαρτυρεῖ Γλαύκων Τιμαίου Χολαργεύς.
ἐγὼ ἀγόμενον εἰς δουλείαν ὑπὸ Ἡγησάνδρου
Πιττάλακον ἀφειλόμην εἰς ἐλευθερίαν. χρόνῳ
δ' ὕστερον ἐλθὼν πρὸς ἐμὲ Πιττάλακος ἔφη
βούλεσθαι διαλυθῆναι τὰ πρὸς Ἡγήσανδρον
προσπέμψας [3] αὐτῷ, ὥστε ἄρασθαι τὰς δίκας, [4]
ἥν τε αὐτὸς ἐνεκαλέσατο Ἡγησάνδρῳ καὶ
Τιμάρχῳ, [5] καὶ ἣν Ἡγήσανδρος τῆς δουλείας
αὐτῷ· καὶ διελύθησαν.
Ὡσαύτως Ἀμφισθένης [6] μαρτυρεῖ. ἐγὼ
ἀγόμενον εἰς δουλείαν ὑπὸ Ἡγησάνδρου Πιττάλακον ἀφειλόμην εἰς ἐλευθερίαν, καὶ τὰ
ἑξῆς.]

67 Οὐκοῦν καὶ αὐτὸν ὑμῖν καλῶ τὸν Ἡγήσανδρον.
γέγραφα δ' αὐτῷ μαρτυρίαν κοσμιωτέραν μὲν ἢ
κατ' ἐκεῖνον, μικρῷ δὲ σαφεστέραν ἢ τῷ Μισγόλᾳ.

---

[1] The MSS. have ὃς οὐ or οὗτος ὃς οὐ or οὐ before πώποτε :
Blass deletes.   [2] μάχαις Hamaker : μοιχείαις MSS.
[3] προσπέμψας Reiske : προπέψας or προπέμψαι MSS.
[4] ὥστε ἄρασθαι τὰς δίκας Blass : ἄρασθαι or ἄρασθαι τῆς
δίκης MSS.

defendant, Timarchus. That this is true you all know. For who of you that has ever gone to the stalls where dainty foods are sold has not observed the lavish expenditures of these men? Or who that has happened to encounter their revels and brawls has not been indignant in behalf of the city? However, since we are in court, call, if you please, Glaucon of Cholargus, who restored Pittalacus to freedom,[1] and read his affidavit and the others.

AFFIDAVITS

[Glaucon, son of Timaeus, of Cholargus, testifies. I rescued Pittalacus and secured his freedom, when Hegesandrus was attempting to make him his slave. Some time after this, Pittalacus came to me and said that he wished to send to Hegesandrus and come to such settlement with him that the suits should be dropped, both his own suit against Hegesandrus and Timarchus, and the suit of Hegesandrus for his enslavement. And they came to a settlement.

Amphisthenes testifies to the same effect. " I rescued Pittalacus and secured his freedom, when Hegesandrus was attempting to make him his slave," and so forth.]

Now I will summon Hegesandrus himself for you. I have written out for him an affidavit that is too respectable for a man of his character, but a little more explicit than the one I wrote for Misgolas. I am

---

[1] The comparative freedom of a state-slave in place of the slavery that Hegesandrus had attempted to impose on him.

ª Ἡγησάνδρῳ . . . Τιμάρχῳ Franke : MSS. have the accus.

ᵇ Weidner deletes ΜΑΡΤΥΡΙΑ before Ἀμφισθένης.

57

οὐκ ἀγνοῶ δ' ὅτι ἀπομεῖται καὶ ἐπιορκήσει. διὰ
τί οὖν καλῶ[1] ἐπὶ τὴν μαρτυρίαν; ἵν' ὑμῖν ἐπιδείξω
οἵους ἀπεργάζεται ἀνθρώπους τὸ ἐπιτήδευμα
τοῦτο, ὡς καταφρονοῦντας μὲν τῶν θεῶν, ὑπερο-
ρῶντας δὲ τοὺς νόμους, ὀλιγώρως δὲ ἔχοντας πρὸς
ἅπασαν αἰσχύνην. κάλει μοι τὸν Ἡγήσανδρον.

MARTYRIA

68   [Ἡγήσανδρος Διφίλου Στειριεὺς μαρτυρεῖ.
ὅτε κατέπλευσα ἐξ Ἑλλησπόντου, κατέλαβον
παρὰ Πιτταλάκῳ τῷ κυβευτῇ διατρίβοντα
Τίμαρχον τὸν Ἀριζήλου, καὶ ἐξ ἐκείνης τῆς
γνώσεως ἐχρησάμην Τιμάρχῳ ὁμιλῶν τῇ αὐτῇ
χρήσει[2] ᾗ καὶ τὸ πρότερον Λεωδάμαντι.]

69   Οὐκ ἠγνόουν ὅτι ὑπερόψεται τὸν ὅρκον, ὦ
ἄνδρες Ἀθηναῖοι, ἀλλὰ καὶ προεῖπον ὑμῖν. κἀ-
κεῖνό γε πρόδηλόν ἐστιν, ὅτι ἐπειδὴ νῦν οὐκ ἐθέ-
λει μαρτυρεῖν, αὐτίκα πάρεισιν ἐν τῇ ἀπολογίᾳ.
καὶ οὐδὲν μὰ Δία θαυμαστόν· ἀναβήσεται γὰρ
οἶμαι δεῦρο πιστεύων τῷ ἑαυτοῦ βίῳ ἀνὴρ καλὸς
κἀγαθὸς καὶ μισοπόνηρος, καὶ τὸν Λεωδάμαντα
ὅστις ἦν οὐ γιγνώσκων, ἐφ' ᾧ ὑμεῖς ἐθορυβήσατε
τῆς μαρτυρίας ἀναγιγνωσκομένης.

70   Ἆρά γε ἐξαχθήσομαί τι σαφέστερον εἰπεῖν ἢ
κατὰ τὴν ἐμαυτοῦ φύσιν; εἴπατέ μοι πρὸς τοῦ
Διὸς καὶ τῶν ἄλλων θεῶν, ὦ ἄνδρες Ἀθηναῖοι,

---

[1] Weidner deletes αὐτὸν which the MSS. have before or
after καλῶ
[2] χρήσει Wolf : ἄρσει MSS.

perfectly aware that he will refuse to swear to it, and presently will perjure himself. Why then do I call him to testify? That I may demonstrate to you what sort of man this kind of life produces—how regardless of the gods, how contemptuous of the laws, how indifferent to all disgrace. Please call Hegesandrus.[1]

AFFIDAVIT

[Hegesandrus, son of Diphilus, of Steiria testifies. When I returned from my voyage to the Hellespont, I found Timarchus, son of Arizelus, staying at the house of Pittalacus, the gambler. As a result of this acquaintance I enjoyed the same intimacy with Timarchus as with Leodamas previously.]

I was sure, fellow citizens, that Hegesandrus would disdain the oath, and I told you so in advance. This too is plain at once, that since he is not willing to testify now, he will presently appear for the defence. And no wonder, by Zeus! For he will come up here to the witness stand, I suppose, trusting in his record, honourable and upright man that he is, an enemy of all evil-doing, a man who does not know who Leodamas was—Leodamas, at whose name you yourselves raised a shout as the affidavit was being read.

Shall I yield to the temptation to use language somewhat more explicit than my own self-respect allows? Tell me, fellow citizens, in the name of Zeus and the other gods, when a man has defiled

[1] The Clerk of the Court now reads the affidavit, and calls on Hegesandrus to swear to it. He refuses.

THE SPEECHES OF AESCHINES

ὅστις αὐτὸν κατήσχυνε πρὸς Ἡγήσανδρον, οὐ
δοκεῖ ὑμῖν πρὸς τὸν πόρνον πεπορνεῦσθαι; ἢ
τίνας αὐτοὺς οὐκ οἰόμεθ᾽ ὑπερβολὰς ποιεῖσθαι
βδελυρίας παροινοῦντας καὶ μονουμένους; οὐκ
οἴεσθε τὸν Ἡγήσανδρον ἀπολυόμενον[1] τὰς πρὸς
τὸν Λεωδάμαντα πράξεις τὰς περιβοήτους, ἃς
ὑμεῖς ἅπαντες σύνιστε, ὑπερήφανα ἐπιτάγματα
ἐπιτάττειν, ὡς ταῖς τούτου ὑπερβολαῖς αὐτὸν
δόξοντα μέτρια διαπεπρᾶχθαι;

71 Ἀλλ᾽ ὅμως ὄψεσθε ὅτι καὶ μάλα ἐπιστρεφῶς
καὶ ῥητορικῶς αὐτὸς καὶ ὁ ἀδελφὸς αὐτοῦ Κρωβύλος αὐτίκα μάλα δεῦρο ἀναπηδήσαντες ταῦτα
μὲν εἶναι πολλῆς ἀβελτερίας φήσουσιν, ἃ ἐγὼ
λέγω, ἀξιώσουσι δέ με μάρτυρας παρασχέσθαι
διαρρήδην μαρτυροῦντας, ὅπου ἔπραττεν, ὅπως
ἐποίει, ἢ τίς εἶδεν, ἢ τίς ἦν ὁ τρόπος, πρᾶγμα
72 οἶμαι ἀναιδὲς λέγοντες. οὐ γὰρ ἔγωγε ὑπολαμβάνω οὕτως ὑμᾶς ἐπιλήσμονας εἶναι, ὥστε ἀμνη-
μονεῖν ὧν ὀλίγῳ πρότερον ἠκούσατε ἀναγιγνωσκο-
μένων νόμων,[2] ἐν οἷς γέγραπται, ἐάν τις μισθώσηταί τινα Ἀθηναίων ἐπὶ ταύτην τὴν πρᾶξιν, ἢ
ἐάν τις ἑαυτὸν μισθώσῃ, ἔνοχον εἶναι τοῖς μεγίστοις καὶ τοῖς ἴσοις ἐπιτιμίοις. τίς οὖν οὕτω
ταλαίπωρός ἐστιν ἄνθρωπος, ὅστις ἂν ἐθελήσειε
σαφῶς τοιαύτην μαρτυρίαν μαρτυρῆσαι, ἐξ ἧς
ὑπάρχει αὐτῷ, ἐὰν τἀληθῆ μαρτυρήσῃ, ἐπιδεικνύναι ἔνοχον ὄντα ἑαυτὸν τοῖς ἐσχάτοις ἐπιτιμί-
73 οις; οὐκοῦν ὑπόλοιπόν ἐστι τὸν πεπονθότα
ὁμολογεῖν. ἀλλὰ διὰ τοῦτο κρίνεται, ὅτι ταῦτα
πράξας παρὰ τοὺς νόμους δημηγορεῖ.[3] βούλεσθε

[1] ἀπολυόμενον Sakorraphos : ἀπολογούμενον MSS.
[2] νόμων Cobet : τῶν νόμων MSS.
[3] δημηγορεῖ Cobet : ἐδημηγόρει MSS.

60

himself with Hegesandrus, does not that man seem
to you to have prostituted himself to a prostitute?
In what excesses of bestiality are we not to imagine
them to have indulged when they were drunken and
alone! Don't you suppose that Hegesandrus, in his
desire to wipe out his own notorious practices with
Leodamas, which are known to all of you, made
extravagant demands on the defendant, hoping to
make Timarchus' conduct so exceedingly bad that
his own earlier behaviour would seem to have been
modest indeed?

And yet you will presently see Hegesandrus and
his brother Crobylus leaping to the platform here
and most vehemently and eloquently declaring that
what I say is all nonsense. They will demand that
I present witnesses to testify explicitly where he did
it, how he did it, or who saw him do it, or what sort
of an act it was—a shameless demand, I think. For
I do not believe your memory is so short that you
have forgotten the laws that you heard read a few
moments ago, in which it stands written that if any
one hires any Athenian for this act, or if any one
lets himself out for hire, he is liable to the most
severe penalties, and the same penalties for both
offences. Now what man is so reckless that he would
be willing to give in plain words testimony which, if
the testimony be true, would inevitably amount to information against himself, as liable to extreme punishment? Only one alternative then remains: that the
man who submitted to the act shall acknowledge it.
But he is on trial on precisely this charge, that after
such conduct as this, he breaks the laws by speaking
before the assembly. Shall we, then, drop the whole

οὖν τὸ ὅλον πρᾶγμα ἀφῶμεν καὶ μὴ ζητῶμεν; νὴ
τὸν Ποσειδῶ καλῶς ἄρα τὴν πόλιν οἰκήσομεν, εἰ
ἃ αὐτοὶ ἔργῳ ἴσμεν γιγνόμενα, ταῦτα ἐὰν μή τις
ἡμῖν δεῦρο παρελθὼν σαφῶς ἅμα καὶ ἀναισχύν-
τως μαρτυρήσῃ, διὰ τοῦτο ἐπιλησόμεθα.

74 Σκέψασθε δὲ καὶ ἐκ παραδειγμάτων· ἀνάγκη δ'
ἴσως ἔσται παραπλήσια τὰ παραδείγματα εἶναι
τοῖς τρόποις τοῖς Τιμάρχου. ὁρᾶτε τουτουσὶ
τοὺς ἐπὶ τῶν οἰκημάτων καθημένους, τοὺς ὁμολογουμένως τὴν πρᾶξιν πράττοντας. οὗτοι μέντοι
ὅταν πρὸς τῇ ἀνάγκῃ ταύτῃ γίγνωνται, ὅμως πρό
γε τῆς αἰσχύνης προβάλλονταί τι καὶ συγκλῄ-
ουσι τὰς θύρας. εἰ δή τις ὑμᾶς ἔροιτο τοὺς ὁδῷ
πορευομένους, τί νῦν ὁ ἄνθρωπος [1] πράττει, εὐθὺς
ἂν εἴποιτε τοῦ ἔργου τοὔνομα, οὐχ ὁρῶντες, οὐδ'
εἰδότες [2] τὸν εἰσεληλυθότα ὅστις ἦν, ἀλλὰ τὴν
προαίρεσιν τῆς ἐργασίας τοῦ ἀνθρώπου συνειδό-
75 τες, καὶ τὸ πρᾶγμα γνωρίζετε. οὐκοῦν τὸν αὐτὸν τρόπον προσήκει ὑμᾶς καὶ περὶ Τιμάρχου
ἐξετάζειν, καὶ μὴ σκοπεῖν εἴ τις εἶδεν, ἀλλ' εἰ
πέπρακται τούτῳ ἡ πρᾶξις. ἐπεὶ πρὸς θεῶν τί
χρὴ λέγειν, Τίμαρχε; τί ἂν εἴποις αὐτὸς περὶ
ἑτέρου ἀνθρώπου ἐπὶ τῇ αἰτίᾳ ταύτῃ κρινομένου;
ἢ τί χρὴ λέγειν, ὅταν μειράκιον νέον, καταλιπὸν
τὴν πατρῴαν οἰκίαν, ἐν ἀλλοτρίαις οἰκίαις νυκτε-
ρεύῃ, τὴν ὄψιν ἑτέρων διαφέρον, καὶ πολυτελῆ
δεῖπνα δειπνῇ ἀσύμβολον, καὶ αὐλητρίδας ἔχῃ
καὶ ἑταίρας τὰς πολυτελεστάτας, καὶ κυβεύῃ, καὶ

---

[1] ὁ ἄνθρωπος Weidner : οὗτος ὁ ἄνθρωπος or ὁ ἄνθρωπος οὗτος
MSS.
[2] οὐδ' εἰδότες Herwerden : the MSS. have οὐχ ὁρῶντες τὸν
or οὐκ εἰδότες τόν.

affair, and make no further inquiry? By Poseidon, a fine home this city will be for us, if when we ourselves know that a thing has been done in fact, we are to ignore it unless some man come forward here and testify to the act in words as explicit as they must be shameless.

But pray consider the case with the help of illustrations; and naturally the illustrations will have to be like the pursuits of Timarchus. You see the men over yonder who sit in the bawdy-houses, men who confessedly pursue the profession. Yet these persons, brought to such straits as that, do nevertheless make some attempt to cover their shame: they shut their doors. Now if, as you are passing along the street, any one should ask you, "Pray, what is the fellow doing at this moment?" you would instantly name the act, though you do not see it done, and do not know who it was that entered the house; knowing the profession of the man, you know his act also. In the same way, therefore, you ought to judge the case of Timarchus, and not to ask whether anyone saw, but whether he has done the deed. For by heaven, Timarchus, what shall a man say? What would you say yourself about another man on trial on this charge? What shall we say when a young man leaves his father's house and spends his nights in other people's houses, a conspicuously handsome young man? When he enjoys costly suppers without paying for them, and keeps the most expensive flute-girls and harlots? When he gambles and pays

76 μηδὲν ἐκτίνῃ αὐτός, ἀλλ' ἕτερος ὑπὲρ ἐκείνου; ἔτι
ταῦτα μαντείας προσδεῖται; οὐκ εὔδηλον ὅτι
πᾶσα ἀνάγκη τὸν τὰ τηλικαῦτα ἐπιτάγματά
τισιν ἐπιτάττοντα καὶ αὐτὸν ἀντὶ τούτων ἡδονάς
τινας παρασκευάζειν τοῖς τὸ ἀργύριον προαναλί-
σκουσιν; οὐ γὰρ ἔχω, μὰ τὸν Δία τὸν Ὀλύμπιον,
τίνα τρόπον εὐφημότερον μνησθῶ τῶν σοὶ καταγελάστως πεπραγμένων ἔργων.

77 Θεωρήσατε δέ, εἰ βούλεσθε, τὸ πρᾶγμα καὶ ἐκ
πολιτικῶν τινων παραδειγμάτων, καὶ μάλιστα ἐκ
τούτων ἃ νυνὶ μετὰ χεῖρας ἔχετε. γεγόνασι διαψηφίσεις ἐν τοῖς δήμοις, καὶ ἕκαστος ἡμῶν ψῆφον
δέδωκε περὶ τοῦ σώματος, ὅστις Ἀθηναῖος ὄντως
ἐστὶ καὶ ὅστις μή. καὶ ἔγωγε, ἐπειδὰν προσστῶ
πρὸς τὸ δικαστήριον καὶ ἀκροάσωμαι τῶν ἀγωνι-
ζομένων, ὁρῶ ὅτι ἀεὶ τὸ αὐτὸ παρ' ὑμῖν ἰσχύει.

78 ἐπειδὰν γὰρ εἴπῃ ὁ κατήγορος· "Ἄνδρες δικασταί,
τουτουὶ κατεψηφίσαντο οἱ δημόται ὀμόσαντες,
οὐδενὸς ἀνθρώπων οὔτε κατηγορήσαντος οὔτε
καταμαρτυρήσαντος, ἀλλ' αὐτοὶ συνειδότες," εὐθὺς θορυβεῖτε ὑμεῖς ὡς οὐ μετὸν τῷ κρινομένῳ τῆς
πόλεως· οὐδὲν γὰρ οἶμαι δοκεῖ προσδεῖσθαι ὑμῖν
λόγου οὐδὲ μαρτυρίας, ὅσα τις σαφῶς οἶδεν αὐτός.

79 Φέρε δὴ πρὸς τοῦ Διός, εἰ, ὥσπερ περὶ τοῦ
γένους, οὕτω καὶ περὶ τοῦ ἐπιτηδεύματος τούτου
ἐδέησε δοῦναι ψῆφον Τίμαρχον, εἴτ' ἔνοχός ἐστιν
εἴτε μή, ἐκρίνετο δὲ τὸ πρᾶγμα ἐν τῷ δικαστηρίῳ,

nothing himself, but another man always pays for him? Does it take a wizard to explain all that? Is it not perfectly plain that the man who makes such demands must himself necessarily be furnishing in return certain pleasures to the men who are spending their money on him? I say "furnishing pleasures," because, by the Olympian Zeus, I don't know how I can use more euphemistic language than that in referring to your contemptible conduct.

But also look at the case, if you please, with the help of certain illustrations taken from the field of politics, especially matters which you have in hand just now. We have been having revisions of the citizen-lists in the demes, and each one of us has submitted to a vote regarding himself, to determine whether he is a genuine citizen or not. Now whenever I am in the court-room listening to the pleas,[1] I see that the same argument always prevails with you: when the prosecutor says "Gentlemen of the jury, the men of the deme have under oath excluded this man on their own personal knowledge, although nobody brought accusation or gave testimony against him," you immediately applaud, assuming that the man who is before the court has no claim to citizenship. For I suppose you are of the opinion that when one knows a thing perfectly of his own knowledge, he does not need argument or testimony in addition.

Come now, in God's name! if, as on the question of birth, so on the question of these personal habits, Timarchus had to submit to a vote as to whether he is guilty of the charge or not, and the case were

---

[1] A person whose name was thrown out by the decision of the members of the deme had an appeal to the courts.

εἰσήγετο δ᾽ εἰς ὑμᾶς ὥσπερ νυνί, μὴ ἐξῆν δ᾽ ἐκ
τοῦ νόμου ἢ τοῦ ψηφίσματος μήτε ἐμοὶ κατηγορεῖν μήτε τούτῳ ἀπολογεῖσθαι, ὁ δὲ κῆρυξ
οὑτοσὶ ὁ νυνὶ παρεστηκὼς ἐμοὶ ἐπηρώτα ὑμᾶς τὸ
ἐκ τοῦ νόμου κήρυγμα· "Τῶν ψήφων ἡ τετρυπη-
μένη, ὅτῳ δοκεῖ πεπορνεῦσθαι Τίμαρχος, ἡ δὲ
πλήρης, ὅτῳ μή," τί ἂν ἐψηφίσασθε; ἀκριβῶς
80 οἶδ᾽ ὅτι κατέγνωτ᾽ ἂν αὐτοῦ. εἰ δή τις με ἔροιτο
ὑμῶν· "Σὺ δὲ τί οἶσθα, εἰ ἡμεῖς ἂν τούτου κατε-
ψηφισάμεθα;" εἴποιμ᾽ ἂν "Διότι πεπαρρησίασθέ[1]
μοι καὶ διείλεχθε." καὶ ὁπότε καὶ ὅπου ἕκαστος,
ἐγὼ ὑμᾶς ὑπομνήσω· ὅταν οὗτος[2] ἀναβῇ ἐπὶ τὸ
βῆμα·[3] καὶ ἡ βουλή, ὅτε ἐβούλευε[4] πέρυσιν. εἰ
γὰρ μνησθείη[5] τειχῶν ἐπισκευῆς ἢ πύργου, ἢ
ὡς ἀπήγετό ποι[6] τις, εὐθὺς ἐβοᾶτε καὶ ἐγελᾶτε,
καὶ αὐτοὶ ἐλέγετε τὴν ἐπωνυμίαν τῶν ἔργων ὧν
81 σύνιστε αὐτῷ. καὶ τὰ μὲν πολλὰ καὶ παλαιὰ
ἐάσω, τὰ δὲ ἐν αὐτῇ τῇ ἐκκλησίᾳ γενόμενα, ὅτε

---

[1] πεπαρρησίασθε Blass : ἐπαρρησίασθε MSS.
[2] οὗτος Blass : οὑτοσί MSS.
[3] Weidner deletes ἐν τῷ δήμῳ given by the MSS. before or
after ἐπὶ τὸ βῆμα.
[4] ἐβούλευε Emperius : ἐβούλευσε MSS.
[5] εἰ γὰρ μνησθείη Blass : ὅταν μνησθῇ or ὅταν ἐμνήσθη or ἢ
ἐὰν μνησθῇ MSS.   [6] ποι Reiske : που MSS.

---

[1] Each juror was provided with two small disks, one with
a solid stem through the middle, the other with a hollow
stem. The juror who wished to vote for conviction cast the
disk with the hollow stem, and *vice versa*. The unused

being tried in court and were being brought before
you as now, except that it were not permitted by
constitution or statute either for me to accuse or for
him to defend himself, and if this crier who is now
standing at my side were putting the question to
you in the formula prescribed by law, "The hollow
ballot for the juror who believes that Timarchus has
been a prostitute, the solid ballot for the juror who
does not,"[1] what would be your vote? I am absolutely sure that you would decide against him. Now
if one of you should ask me, "How do you know
that we would vote against him?" I should answer,
"Because you have spoken out and told me." And
I will remind you when and where each man of you
speaks and tells me : it is every time that Timarchus
mounts the platform in the assembly ; and the senate
spoke out, when last year he was a member of the
senate. For every time he used such words as
"walls" or "tower" that needed repairing, or told
how so-and-so had been "taken off" somewhere, you
immediately laughed and shouted, and yourselves
spoke the words that belong to those exploits of
which he, to your knowledge, is guilty.[2] I will
pass over most of these incidents and those which
happened long ago, but I do wish to remind you of

ballot was dropped into another urn. As the juror came
forward with the two disks, one in each hand, the ends of
the stem pressed between thumb and forefinger, even the
nearest bystander could not see which disk he cast to be
counted, and which he discarded.

[2] Fortunately the modern reader is spared a knowledge of
the *double entente* that made the vulgar listeners laugh when
a man like Timarchus used the words τεῖχος, πύργος, and
ἀπάγειν. Probably πύργος suggested the women's apartments,
and ἀπάγειν may have suggested seduction.

ἐγὼ τὴν ἐπαγγελίαν ταύτην Τιμάρχῳ ἐπήγγειλα,
ταῦθ᾽ ὑμᾶς ἀναμνῆσαι βούλομαι.

Τῆς γὰρ βουλῆς τῆς ἐν Ἀρείῳ πάγῳ πρόσοδον
ποιουμένης πρὸς τὸν δῆμον κατὰ τὸ ψήφισμα, ὃ
οὗτος εἰρήκει περὶ τῶν οἰκήσεων τῶν ἐν τῇ Πυκνί,
ἦν μὲν ὁ τὸν λόγον λέγων ἐκ τῶν Ἀρεοπαγιτῶν
Αὐτόλυκος, καλῶς νὴ τὸν Δία καὶ τὸν Ἀπόλλω
καὶ σεμνῶς καὶ ἀξίως ἐκείνου τοῦ συνεδρίου βε-
82 βιωκώς· ἐπειδὴ δέ που προϊόντος τοῦ λόγου εἶπεν
ὅτι τό γε εἰσήγημα τὸ Τιμάρχου ἀποδοκιμάζει ἡ
βουλή, "Καὶ περὶ τῆς ἐρημίας ταύτης καὶ τοῦ
τόπου τοῦ ἐν τῇ Πυκνὶ μὴ θαυμάσητε, ὦ ἄνδρες
Ἀθηναῖοι, εἰ Τίμαρχος ἐμπειροτέρως ἔχει τῆς
βουλῆς τῆς ἐξ Ἀρείου πάγου," ἀνεθορυβήσατε
ὑμεῖς ἐνταῦθα καὶ ἔφατε τὸν Αὐτόλυκον ἀληθῆ
83 λέγειν· εἶναι γὰρ αὐτὸν ἔμπειρον. ἀγνοήσας δ᾽
ὑμῶν τὸν θόρυβον, ὁ Αὐτόλυκος μάλα σκυθρωπάσας καὶ διαλιπὼν εἶπεν· "Ἡμεῖς μέντοι, ὦ ἄνδρες
Ἀθηναῖοι, οἱ Ἀρεοπαγῖται οὔτε κατηγοροῦμεν
οὔτε ἀπολογούμεθα, οὐ γὰρ ἡμῖν πάτριόν ἐστιν,
ἔχομεν δὲ τοιαύτην τινὰ συγγνώμην Τιμάρχῳ·
οὗτος ἴσως," ἔφη, "ᾠήθη ἐν τῇ ἡσυχίᾳ ταύτῃ
μικρὸν ὑμῶν ἑκάστῳ ἀνάλωμα γίγνεσθαι." πάλιν
ἐπὶ τῇ ἡσυχίᾳ καὶ τῷ μικρῷ ἀναλώματι μείζων
84 ἀπήντα παρ᾽ ὑμῶν μετὰ γέλωτος θόρυβος. ὡς δ᾽
ἐπεμνήσθη τῶν οἰκοπέδων καὶ τῶν λάκκων, οὐδ᾽

---

[1] The first step in the process was for Aeschines, at a
meeting of the assembly, formally to summon Timarchus to
legal scrutiny (δοκιμασία) of his right to speak before the
people.

[2] Evidently the region was a disreputable one, and the
houses known as cheap places of ill repute.

what took place at the very assembly in which I instituted this process against Timarchus.[1]

The Senate of the Areopagus appeared before the people in accordance with the resolution that Timarchus had introduced in the matter of the dwelling-houses on the Pnyx. The member of the Areopagus who spoke was Autolycus, a man whose life has been good and pious, by Zeus and Apollo, and worthy of that body. Now when in the course of his speech he declared that the Areopagus disapproved the proposition of Timarchus, and said, "You must not be surprised, fellow citizens, it Timarchus is better acquainted than the Senate of the Areopagus with this lonely spot and the region of the Pnyx," then you applauded and said Autolycus was right, for Timarchus was indeed acquainted with it.[2] Autolycus, however, did not catch the point of your uproar; he frowned and stopped a moment; then he went on: "But, fellow citizens, we members of the Areopagus neither accuse nor defend, for such is not our tradition, but we do make some such allowance as this for Timarchus: he perhaps," said he, "thought that where everything is so quiet, there will be but little expense for each of you." Again, at the words "quiet" and "little expense," he encountered still greater laughter and shouting from you.[3] And when he spoke of the "house sites" and the "tanks" you simply couldn't

___

[3] Apparently the speaker meant that Timarchus thought that in this time of peace, with its small demands on the treasury, only a light burden would fall on each citizen, if the state should carry out the local improvements proposed, perhaps the clearing away of the disreputable houses from the slope of the hill.

ἀναλαβεῖν αὐτοὺς ἐδύνασθε. ἔνθα δὴ καὶ παρ-
έρχεται Πύρρανδρος ἐπιτιμήσων ὑμῖν, καὶ ἤρετο
τὸν δῆμον, εἰ οὐκ αἰσχύνοιντο γελῶντες παρούσης
τῆς βουλῆς τῆς ἐξ Ἀρείου πάγου. ὑμεῖς δ᾽ ἐξεβάλλετε αὐτὸν ὑπολαμβάνοντες· "Ἴσμεν, ὦ Πύρ-
ρανδρε, ὅτι οὐ δεῖ γελᾶν τούτων ἐναντίον· ἀλλ᾽
οὕτως ἰσχυρόν ἐστιν ἡ ἀλήθεια, ὥστε πάντων
85 ἐπικρατεῖν τῶν ἀνθρωπίνων λογισμῶν." ταύτην
ἐγὼ ὑπολαμβάνω μαρτυρίαν μεμαρτυρῆσθαι ὑμῖν
ὑπὸ τοῦ δήμου τοῦ Ἀθηναίων, ὃν[1] ἁλῶναι ψευ-
δομαρτυρίων οὐ καλῶς ἔχει. οὐκοῦν ἄτοπον, ὦ
ἄνδρες Ἀθηναῖοι, εἰ μηδὲν μὲν ἐμοῦ λέγοντος
αὐτοὶ βοᾶτε τὴν ἐπωνυμίαν τῶν ἔργων ὧν σύνιστε
τούτῳ, ἐμοῦ δὲ λέγοντος ἐπιλέλησθε, καὶ μὴ γενομένης μὲν κρίσεως περὶ τοῦ πράγματος ἑάλω ἄν,
γεγονότος δὲ ἐλέγχου ἀποφεύξεται.

86 Ἐπεὶ δὲ ἐμνήσθην τῶν διαψηφίσεων καὶ τῶν
Δημοφίλου πολιτευμάτων, βούλομαί τι καὶ ἄλλο
παράδειγμα περὶ τούτων εἰπεῖν. ὁ γὰρ αὐτὸς
οὗτος ἀνὴρ καὶ πρότερόν τι τοιοῦτον πολίτευμα
ἐπολιτεύσατο. ᾐτιάσατό τινας εἶναι οἳ ἄρα ἐνεχείρουν συνδεκάζειν τὴν ἐκκλησίαν καὶ τἆλλα
δικαστήρια, ὥσπερ καὶ νυνὶ Νικόστρατος· καὶ
περὶ τούτων κρίσεις αἱ μὲν γεγόνασιν,[2] αἱ δὲ
87 ἐνεστᾶσιν ἔτι.[3] φέρε δὴ πρὸς τοῦ Διὸς καὶ θεῶν,

---

[1] ὃν Franke : ἣν MSS.

[2] γεγόνασιν Weidner : πάλαι γεγόνασιν or ἐγένοντο πάλαι
MSS.

[3] αἱ δὲ ἐνεστᾶσιν ἔτι Weidner : MSS. have αἱ δὲ νεωστὶ νῦν
ἔτ᾽ εἰσί or αἱ δὲ νῦν ἐνεστάσιν ἔτι.

restrain yourselves.[1] Thereupon Pyrrandrus came
forward to censure you, and he asked the people if
they were not ashamed of themselves for laughing
in the presence of the Senate of the Areopagus.
But you drove him off the platform, replying, " We
know, Pyrrandrus, that we ought not to laugh in
their presence, but so strong is the truth that it
prevails—over all the calculations of men." This,
then, I understand to be the testimony that has
been offered you by the people of Athens, and
it would not be proper that they should be convicted of giving false testimony. When I, fellow
citizens, say not a word, you of yourselves shout the
name of the acts of which you know he is guilty;
strange, then, it would be if, when I name them,
you cannot remember them ; even had there been
no trial of this case, he would have been convicted ;
strange indeed then if, when the charge has been
proved, he is to be acquitted !

But since I have mentioned the revision of the
lists and the measures proposed by Demophilus,[2] I
wish to cite a certain other illustration in this connection. For this Demophilus had previously brought
in a measure of the following sort : he declared that
there were certain men who were attempting to
bribe the members of the popular assembly and the
courts as well—the same assertion that Nicostratus
also has made very recently. Some cases under this
charge have been in the courts, others are still
pending. Come now, in the name of Zeus and

[1] It is not unlikely that the vulgar crowd made merry
over the word οἰκοπέδων as sounding like ὀρχιπέδων (testicles),
and λάκκων like λακκοπέδων (scrota).
[2] Demophilus was the author of the proposition to revise
the citizen lists.

εἰ ἐπὶ τὴν αὐτὴν ἐτράποντο ἀπολογίαν ἥνπερ
Τίμαρχος νυνὶ καὶ οἱ συναγορεύοντες αὐτῷ, καὶ
ἠξίουν διαρρήδην τινὰ μαρτυρεῖν περὶ τῆς αἰτίας ἢ
τοὺς δικαστὰς μὴ πιστεύειν· πᾶσα δήπου ἀνάγκη
ἦν ἐκ τοῦ λόγου τούτου μαρτυρεῖν τὸν μέν, ὡς
ἐδέκαζε, τὸν δέ, ὡς ἐδεκάζετο, προκειμένης ἑκατέρῳ ζημίας ἐκ τοῦ νόμου θανάτου, ὥσπερ ἐνθάδε,
ἐάν τις μισθώσηταί τινα Ἀθηναίων ἐφ᾽ ὕβρει, καὶ
πάλιν ἐάν τις Ἀθηναίων ἐπὶ τῇ τοῦ σώματος
88 αἰσχύνῃ ἑκὼν μισθαρνῇ. ἔστιν οὖν ὅστις ἂν
ἐμαρτύρησεν, ἢ κατήγορος ὃς ἐνεχείρησ᾽ ἂν [1]
τοιαύτην ποιεῖσθαι τὴν ἀπόδειξιν τοῦ πράγματος;
οὐ δῆτα. τί οὖν; ἀπέφυγον οἱ κρινόμενοι; μὰ
τὸν Ἡρακλέα, ἐπεὶ θανάτῳ ἐζημιώθησαν, πολὺ
νὴ τὸν Δία καὶ τὸν Ἀπόλλω ἔλαττον ἁμάρτημα
ἡμαρτηκότες τουτουὶ τοῦ ἀνθρώπου· ἐκεῖνοι μέν
γε οἱ ταλαίπωροι οὐ δυνάμενοι γῆρας ἅμα καὶ
πενίαν ἀμύνεσθαι, τὰ μέγιστα τῶν ἐν ἀνθρώποις
κακῶν, ταύταις ἐχρήσαντο ταῖς συμφοραῖς, οὗτος
δ᾽ οὐκ ἐθέλων τὴν ἑαυτοῦ βδελυρίαν κατέχειν.

89   Εἰ μὲν τοίνυν ἦν ὁ ἀγὼν οὑτοσὶ ἐν πόλει ἐκ-
κλήτῳ, ὑμᾶς ἂν ἔγωγε ἠξίωσα μάρτυράς μοι γενέσθαι, τοὺς ἄριστα εἰδότας ὅτι ἀληθῆ λέγω· εἰ δ᾽
ὁ μὲν ἀγών ἐστιν Ἀθήνησιν, οἱ δ᾽ αὐτοὶ δικασταί
μοι καὶ μάρτυρές ἐστε τῶν λόγων, ἐμοὶ μὲν ἀναμι-
μνήσκειν προσήκει, ὑμᾶς δέ μοι μὴ ἀπιστεῖν. καὶ
γὰρ ἔμοιγε δοκεῖ Τίμαρχος οὑτοσί, ὦ ἄνδρες Ἀθηναῖοι, οὐχ ὑπὲρ αὑτοῦ μόνον ἐσπουδακέναι, ἀλλὰ
καὶ περὶ τῶν ἄλλων τῶν ταὐτὰ διαπεπραγμένων

---

[1] ἂν is inserted by the editor. Some MSS. omit the ἂν of
the first clause.

the gods, if they had resorted to the same defence
that Timarchus and his advocates now offer, and
demanded that someone should testify explicitly
to the crime, or else that the jurors should refuse
to believe the charge, surely according to that
demand it would have been absolutely necessary
for the one man to testify that he gave a bribe,
the other, that he took a bribe, though the law
threatens each of them with death, precisely as
in this case if anyone hires an Athenian for a disgraceful purpose, and again if any Athenian voluntarily hires himself out to the shame of his body.
Is there any man who would have testified, or
any prosecutor who would have undertaken to
present such proof of the act? Surely not. What
then? Were the accused acquitted? No, by
Heracles! They were punished with death, though
their crime was far less, by Zeus and Apollo, than
that of this defendant; those poor wretches met
such a fate because they were unable to defend
themselves against old age and poverty together,
the greatest of human misfortunes; the defendant
should suffer it because he is unwilling to restrain
his own lewdness.

Now if this trial were taking place in another
city, and that city were the referee, I should have
demanded that you should be my witnesses, you who
best know that I am speaking the truth. But since
the trial is at Athens, and you are at the same
time judges and witnesses of the truth of what
I say, it is my place to refresh your memory, and
yours not to disbelieve me. For I think Timarchus'
anxiety is not for himself alone, fellow citizens,
but for all the others also whose practices have

90 αὐτῷ. εἰ γὰρ ἡ μὲν πρᾶξις αὕτη ἔσται, ὥσπερ
εἴωθε γίγνεσθαι, λάθρᾳ καὶ ἐν ἐρημίαις καὶ ἐν
ἰδίαις οἰκίαις, ὁ δὲ ἄριστα μὲν εἰδώς, καταισχύνας
δέ τινα τῶν πολιτῶν, ἐὰν τἀληθῆ μαρτυρήσῃ,
ἔνοχος ἔσται τοῖς μεγίστοις ἐπιτιμίοις, ὁ δὲ κρινόμενος καταμεμαρτυρημένος ὑπὸ τοῦ ἑαυτοῦ βίου
καὶ τῆς ἀληθείας ἀξιώσει μὴ ἐξ ὧν γιγνώσκεται,
ἀλλ' ἐκ τῶν μαρτυριῶν κρίνεσθαι, ἀνῄρηται ὁ
νόμος καὶ ἡ ἀλήθεια, καὶ δέδεικται φανερὰ ὁδός,
δι' ἧς οἱ τὰ μέγιστα κακουργοῦντες ἀποφεύξονται.

91 τίς γὰρ ἢ τῶν λωποδυτῶν ἢ τῶν μοιχῶν ἢ τῶν
ἀνδροφόνων, ἢ τῶν τὰ μέγιστα μὲν ἀδικούντων,
λάθρᾳ δὲ τοῦτο πραττόντων, δώσει δίκην; καὶ
γὰρ τούτων οἱ μὲν ἐπ' αὐτοφώρῳ ἁλόντες, ἐὰν
ὁμολογῶσι, παραχρῆμα θανάτῳ ζημιοῦνται, οἱ δὲ
λαθόντες καὶ ἔξαρνοι γιγνόμενοι κρίνονται ἐν τοῖς
δικαστηρίοις, εὑρίσκεται δὲ ἡ ἀλήθεια ἐκ τῶν
εἰκότων.

92   Χρήσασθε δὴ παραδείγματι τῇ βουλῇ τῇ ἐξ
Ἀρείου πάγου, τῷ ἀκριβεστάτῳ συνεδρίῳ τῶν ἐν
τῇ πόλει. πολλοὺς γὰρ ἤδη ἔγωγε τεθεώρηκα
ἐν τῷ βουλευτηρίῳ τούτῳ εὖ πάνυ εἰπόντας καὶ
μάρτυρας πορισαμένους ἁλόντας· ἤδη δέ τινας
κακῶς πάνυ διαλεχθέντας καὶ πρᾶγμα ἀμάρτυρον
ἔχοντας οἶδα νικήσαντας. οὐ γὰρ ἐκ τοῦ λόγου
μόνον οὐδ' ἐκ τῶν μαρτυριῶν, ἀλλ' ἐξ ὧν αὐτοὶ
συνίσασι καὶ ἐξητάκασι, τὴν ψῆφον φέρουσι.

been the same as his. For if in the future, as always in the past, this practice is going to be carried on in secret, and in lonely places and in private houses, and if the man who best knows the facts, but has defiled one of his fellow citizens, is to be liable to the severest punishment if he testifies to the truth, while the man on trial, who has been denounced by the testimony of his own life and of the truth, is to demand that he be judged, not by the facts that are notorious, but by the testimony of witnesses, then the law is done away with, and so is the truth, while a plain path is marked out by which the worst wrongdoers may escape. For what foot-pad or adulterer or assassin, or what man who has committed the greatest crimes, but has done it secretly, will be brought to justice? For whereas such of these criminals as are caught in the act are instantly punished with death, if they acknowledge the crime, those who have done the act secretly and deny their guilt, are tried in the courts, and the truth can be determined by circumstantial evidence only.

Take the example of the Senate of the Areopagus, the most scrupulous tribunal in the city. I myself have before now seen many men convicted before this tribunal, though they spoke most eloquently, and presented witnesses; and I know that before now certain men have won their case, although they spoke most feebly, and although no witnesses testified for them. For it is not on the strength of the pleading alone, nor of the testimony alone, that the members of the court give their verdict, but on the strength of their own knowledge and their own investigations. And this is the reason

τοιγάρτοι διατελεῖ τοῦτο τὸ συνέδριον εὐδοκιμοῦν
93 ἐν τῇ πόλει. τὸν αὐτὸν τοίνυν τρόπον, ὦ ἄνδρες
Ἀθηναῖοι, καὶ ὑμεῖς τὴν κρίσιν ταύτην ποιήσασθε.
πρῶτον μὲν μηδὲν ὑμῖν ἔστω πιστότερον ὧν αὐτοὶ
σύνιστε καὶ πέπεισθε περὶ Τιμάρχου τουτουί,[1]
ἔπειτα τὸ πρᾶγμα θεωρεῖτε μὴ ἐκ τοῦ παρόντος,
ἀλλ' ἐκ τοῦ παρεληλυθότος χρόνου. οἱ μὲν γὰρ
ἐν τῷ παρεληλυθότι χρόνῳ λόγοι λεγόμενοι περὶ
Τιμάρχου καὶ τῶν τούτου ἐπιτηδευμάτων διὰ τὴν
ἀλήθειαν ἐλέγοντο, οἱ δ' ἐν τῇδε τῇ ἡμέρᾳ ῥηθησό-
μενοι διὰ τὴν κρίσιν τῆς ὑμετέρας ἀπάτης ἕνεκα.
ἀπόδοτε οὖν τὴν ψῆφον τῷ πλείονι χρόνῳ καὶ
τῇ ἀληθείᾳ καὶ οἷς αὐτοὶ σύνιστε.

94 Καίτοι λογογράφος γέ τις φησίν, ὁ μηχανώ-
μενος αὐτῷ[2] τὴν ἀπολογίαν, ἐναντία με λέγειν
ἐμαυτῷ. οὐ γὰρ δὴ δοκεῖν[3] εἶναι αὐτῷ δυνατὸν
τὸν αὐτὸν ἄνθρωπον πεπορνεῦσθαι καὶ τὰ πατρῷα
κατεδηδοκέναι· τὸ μὲν γὰρ ἡμαρτηκέναι τι περὶ
τὸ σῶμα παιδὸς εἶναί φησι, τὸ δὲ τὰ πατρῷα
κατεδηδοκέναι ἀνδρός. ἔτι δὲ τοὺς καταισχύ-
νοντας αὑτοὺς μισθοὺς φησι πράττεσθαι τοῦ
πράγματος· ἀποθαυμάζων οὖν περιέρχεται καὶ
τερατευόμενος κατὰ τὴν ἀγοράν, εἰ ὁ αὐτὸς πεπόρ-
νευταί τε καὶ τὰ πατρῷα κατεδήδοκεν.

95 Εἰ δέ τις ἀγνοεῖ ταῦθ' ὅπως ἔχει, ἐγὼ σαφέστερον αὐτὰ πειράσομαι διορίσαι τῷ λόγῳ. ἕως
μὲν γὰρ ἀντήρκει ἡ τῆς ἐπικλήρου οὐσία ἣν
Ἡγήσανδρος ὁ τοῦτον ἔχων ἔγημε, καὶ τὸ ἀργύριον ὃ ἦλθεν ἔχων ἐκ τῆς μετὰ Τιμομάχου ἀπο-

---

[1] τουτουί Bake : τούτου MSS.
[2] αὐτῷ Sauppe : αὐτοῖς MSS.
[3] δοκεῖν Cobet : δοκεῖ MSS.

why that tribunal maintains its high repute in the city. Therefore, my fellow citizens, I call upon you to make your decision in this case in the same manner. In the first place, let nothing be more credible in your eyes than your own knowledge and conviction regarding this man Timarchus. In the second place, look at the case in the light, not of the present moment, but of the time that is past. For the words spoken before to-day about Timarchus and his practices were spoken because they were true; but what will be said to-day will be spoken because of the trial, and with intent to deceive you. Give, therefore, the verdict that is demanded by the longer time, and the truth, and your own knowledge.

And yet a certain speech-writer who is concocting his defence [1] says that I contradict myself; since it seems to him impossible, he says, for the same man to have been a prostitute and to have consumed his patrimony. For, he says, to have sinned against one's own body is the act of a boy, but to have consumed one's patrimony is that of a man. And furthermore he says that those who defile themselves exact pay for it. He therefore goes up and down the market-place expressing his wonder and amazement that one and the same man should have prostituted himself and also have consumed his patrimony.

Now if anyone does not understand the facts of the case, I will try to explain them more clearly. Hegesandrus, who kept Timarchus, had married an heiress. So long as her inheritance held out, and the money that Hegesandrus had brought back with

---

[1] Aeschines names this speech-writer in § 119.

THE SPEECHES OF AESCHINES

δημίας, ἦσαν ἐπὶ πολλῆς ἀσελγείας καὶ ἀφθονίας·
ἐπειδὴ δὲ ταῦτα μὲν ἀπωλώλει καὶ κατεκεκύβευτο
καὶ κατωψοφάγητο, οὑτοσὶ δ' ἔξωρος ἐγένετο,
ἐδίδου δ' εἰκότως οὐδεὶς ἔτι οὐδέν, ἡ δὲ βδελυρὰ
φύσις καὶ ἀνόσιος ἀεὶ¹ τῶν αὐτῶν ἐπεθύμει, καὶ
καθ' ὑπερβολὴν ἀκρασίας ἕτερον ἐφ' ἑτέρῳ ἐπί-
96 ταγμα ἐπέταττε, καὶ ἀπεφέρετο εἰς τὸ καθ' ἡμέραν
ἔθος, ἐνταῦθα ἤδη ἐτράπετο ἐπὶ τὸ καταφαγεῖν
τὴν πατρῴαν οὐσίαν. καὶ οὐ μόνον κατέφαγεν,
ἀλλ' εἰ οἷόν τ' ἐστὶν εἰπεῖν, καὶ κατέπιεν. καὶ
γὰρ οὐδὲ τῆς ἀξίας ἕκαστον τῶν κτημάτων ἀπέδοτο, οὐδ' ἐδύνατ' ἀναμένειν τὸ πλέον οὐδὲ τὸ
λυσιτελοῦν, ἀλλὰ τοῦ ἤδη εὑρίσκοντος ἀπεδίδοτο·
οὕτως ἠπείγετο σφόδρα πρὸς τὰς ἡδονάς.
97 Τούτῳ γὰρ κατέλιπεν ὁ πατὴρ οὐσίαν, ἀφ' ἧς
ἕτερος μὲν κἂν² ἐλῃτούργει, οὗτος δὲ οὐδ' αὑτῷ
διαφυλάξαι ἐδυνήθη· οἰκίαν μὲν ὄπισθεν τῆς πόλεως, ἐσχατιὰν δὲ Σφηττοῖ, Ἀλωπεκῆσι δ' ἕτερον
χωρίον, χωρὶς δὲ οἰκέτας δημιουργοὺς τῆς σκυτο-
τομικῆς τέχνης ἐννέα ἢ δέκα, ὧν ἕκαστος τούτῳ
δύ' ὀβολοὺς ἀποφορὰν ἔφερε τῆς ἡμέρας, ὁ δ'
ἡγεμὼν τοῦ ἐργαστηρίου τριώβολον· ἔτι δὲ πρὸς
τούτοις γυναῖκα ἀμόργινα ἐπισταμένην ἐργάζεσθαι
καὶ ἔργα λεπτὰ εἰς τὴν ἀγορὰν ἐκφέρουσαν,
καὶ ἄνδρα ποικιλτήν, καὶ ὀφείλοντάς τινας αὐτῷ
ἀργύριον, καὶ ἔπιπλα.

¹ ἀεὶ Weidner : ἀεὶ τούτου or ἡ τούτου ἀεὶ MSS.
² κἂν Cobet : ἂν καὶ or ἂν MSS.

---

¹ Such a fortune would have been enough to enable the
ordinary man to perform the special honourable services
demanded of rich citizens, to be trierarch, choregus, etc.

him from his voyage with Timomachus, they lived
in all luxury and lewdness. But when these resources had been wasted and gambled away and
eaten up, and this defendant had lost his youthful
charm, and, as you would expect, no one would
any longer give him anything, while his lewd and
depraved nature constantly craved the same indul-
gences, and with excessive incontinence kept making
demand after demand upon him, then, at last, in-
cessantly drawn back to his old habits, he resorted
to the devouring of his patrimony. And not only
did he eat it up, but, if one may so say, he also
drank it up! He sold one piece of property after
another, not for what it was worth—he couldn't
wait for a higher offer nor even for the bare value,
but let it go for what it would fetch on the instant,
so urgently did he hasten to gratify his lusts.

His father left him a fortune which another man
would have found sufficient for the service of the state
also.[1] But Timarchus was not able even to preserve
it for himself. There was a house south of the Acropolis, a suburban estate at Sphettus, another piece of
land at Alopeke, and besides there were nine or ten
slaves who were skilled shoemakers, each of whom
paid him a fee of two obols a day, and the superintendent of the shop three obols.[2] Besides these
there was a woman skilled in flax-working, who
produced fine goods for the market, and there was a
man skilled in embroidery. Certain men also owed
him money, and there were house furnishings.

[2] Masters sometimes allowed their slaves to buy their
time at so much per day ; this fee was called ἀποφορά. Such
slaves could do business for themselves, or hire themselves
out to manufacturers, contractors, etc. Much of the skilled
labour of the city was performed by slaves.

98 Καὶ ὅτι ταῦτ' ἀληθῆ λέγω, ἐνταῦθα μέντοι νὴ
Δία σαφῶς πάνυ καὶ διαρρήδην ἐγὼ μαρτυροῦντας
ὑμῖν τοὺς μάρτυρας παρέξομαι· οὐδεὶς γὰρ κίνδυνος, ὥσπερ ἐκεῖ, οὐδ' αἰσχύνη πρόσεστιν οὐδεμία τῷ τἀληθῆ μαρτυροῦντι. τὴν μὲν γὰρ
οἰκίαν τὴν ἐν ἄστει ἀπέδοθ' οὗτος Ναυσικράτει
τῷ κωμικῷ ποιητῇ, ὕστερον δ' αὐτὴν ἐπρίατο
παρὰ τοῦ Ναυσικράτους εἴκοσι μνῶν Κλεαίνετος
ὁ χοροδιδάσκαλος· τὴν δ' ἐσχατιὰν ἐπρίατο παρ'
αὐτοῦ Μνησίθεος ὁ Μυρρινούσιος, τόπον μὲν
99 πολύν, δεινῶς δ' ἐξηγριωμένον ὑπὸ τούτου· τὸ δ'
Ἀλωπεκῆσι χωρίον, ὃ ἦν ἄπωθεν τοῦ τείχους
ἕνδεκα ἢ δώδεκα στάδια, ἱκετευούσης καὶ ἀντι-
βολούσης τῆς μητρός, ὡς ἐγὼ πυνθάνομαι, ἐᾶσαι
καὶ μὴ ἀποδόσθαι, ἀλλ' εἰ μή τι ἄλλο, ἐνταφῆναί
γ' [1] ὑπολιπεῖν αὐτῇ, οὐδὲ τούτου τοῦ χωρίου
ἀπέσχετο, ἀλλὰ καὶ τοῦτ' ἀπέδοτο δισχιλίων
δραχμῶν. καὶ τῶν θεραπαινῶν καὶ τῶν οἰκετῶν
οὐδένα κατέλιπεν, ἀλλ' ἅπαντας πέπρακε. καὶ
ταῦθ' ὅτι οὐ ψεύδομαι, ἐγὼ μέν, ὡς κατέλιπεν
αὐτῷ ὁ πατήρ, μαρτυρίας παρέξομαι, οὗτος δέ, εἰ
μή φησι πεπρακέναι, τὰ σώματα τῶν οἰκετῶν
100 ἐμφανῆ παρασχέτω. ὡς δὲ καὶ ἀργύριόν τισιν
ἐδάνεισεν, ὃ κομισάμενος οὗτος ἀνήλωκε, μάρτυρα
παρέξομαι Μεταγένην ὑμῖν τὸν Σφήττιον, ὃς ὠφεί-
λησε μὲν ἐκείνῳ πλείους ἢ τριάκοντα μνᾶς, ὃ δ'
ἦν ὑπόλοιπον τελευτήσαντος τοῦ πατρός, τούτῳ
ἀπέδωκεν ἑπτὰ μνᾶς. [2] καί μοι κάλει Μεταγένην

---

[1] γ' added by Reiske.
[2] μνᾶς Franke : μνᾶς Τιμάρχῳ MSS.

Here, at any rate, by Zeus, I will present my
witnesses to prove the truth of what I say, and
they will testify most clearly and explicitly; for
there is no danger, as there was the other time,
to the man who testifies to the truth, nor any
disgrace either. The city residence he sold to
Nausicrates, the comic poet;[1] afterward Cleaenetus, the chorus-master, bought it of Nausicrates
for twenty minas. The suburban estate Mnesitheus
of Myrrinoussa bought of him, a large tract, but
wretchedly run down by his neglect. The place
at Alopeke, distant eleven or twelve furlongs from
the city-wall, his mother begged and besought
him, as I have heard, to spare and not to sell,
or, if he would do nothing more, at least to leave
her there a place to be buried in. But even
from this spot he did not withhold his hand;
this too he sold, for 2,000 drachmas. Of the
slaves, men and women, he left not one; he has
sold them all. To prove that I am not lying, I
will produce witness that his father left the slaves;
but if he denies that he has sold them, let him produce their persons in court. But to prove, further,
that his father had lent money to certain men, and
that Timarchus collected and has spent it, I will
call as witnesses for you Metagenes of Sphettus,
who owed more than thirty minas, and paid to the
defendant what was still due at his father's death,
seven minas. Please call Metagenes of Sphettus.

---

[1] The MSS. vary between the readings ποιητῇ *poet* and
ὑποκριτῇ *actor*. Suidas attests the name Nausicrates as that
of a comic poet, and mentions two of his comedies. The
name occurs in an Attic inscription (*I.G.* ii. 977) in a list of
comic poets, but the same inscription gives the name in a list
of comic actors also.

Σφήττιον.[1] πασῶν δὲ πρώτην ἀνάγνωθι τὴν
Ναυσικράτους μαρτυρίαν τοῦ τὴν οἰκίαν πρια-
μένου· καὶ τὰς ἄλλας ἁπάσας λαβὲ περὶ ὧν
ἐμνήσθην ἐν τῷ αὐτῷ.[2]

MARTΥΡΙΑΙ

101   Ὡς τοίνυν ἐκέκτητο ὁ πατὴρ αὐτοῦ ἀργύριον
οὐκ ὀλίγον, ὃ οὗτος ἠφάνικε, τοῦθ᾿ ὑμῖν ἐπιδείξω.
φοβηθεὶς γὰρ τὰς λῃτουργίας ἀπέδοτο ἃ ἦν αὐτῷ
κτήματα ἄνευ τῶν ἀρτίως εἰρημένων, χωρίον
Κηφισιᾶσιν, ἕτερον[3] Ἀμφιτροπῆσιν, ἐργαστήρια
δύο ἐν τοῖς ἀργυρείοις, ἓν μὲν ἐν Αὐλῶνι, ἕτερον
δ᾿ ἐπὶ Θρασύλλῳ.

102   Ὅθεν δὲ ταῦτ᾿ ηὐπόρησεν, ἐγὼ ἐρῶ. ἦσαν
οὗτοι τρεῖς ἀδελφοί, Εὐπόλεμός τε ὁ παιδοτρίβης
καὶ Ἀρίζηλος ὁ τούτου πατὴρ καὶ Ἀρίγνωτος,
ὃς ἔτι καὶ νῦν ἔστι, πρεσβύτης διεφθαρμένος τοὺς
ὀφθαλμούς. τούτων πρῶτος ἐτελεύτησεν Εὐ-
πόλεμος, ἀνεμήτου τῆς οὐσίας οὔσης, δεύτερος δ᾿
Ἀρίζηλος ὁ Τιμάρχου πατήρ· ὅτε δ᾿ ἔζη, πᾶσαν
τὴν οὐσίαν διεχείριζε διὰ τὴν ἀσθένειαν καὶ τὴν
συμφορὰν τὴν περὶ τὰ ὄμματα τοῦ Ἀριγνώτου
καὶ διὰ τὸ τετελευτηκέναι τὸν Εὐπόλεμον, καί τι
καὶ εἰς τροφὴν συνταξάμενος ἐδίδου τῷ Ἀριγνώτῳ.

103   ἐπεὶ δὲ καὶ ὁ Ἀρίζηλος ἐτελεύτησεν ὁ Τιμάρχου
τουτουὶ πατήρ, τοὺς μὲν πρώτους χρόνους, ἕως
παῖς ἦν οὗτος, ἅπαντα τὰ μέτρια ἐγίγνετο παρὰ

---

[1] Σφήττιον Blass : τὸν Σφήττιον MSS.
[2] τῷ αὐτῷ Sakorraphos : τῷ αὐτῷ λόγῳ MSS.
[3] ἕτερον Cobet : ἕτερον ἀγρὸν MSS.

---

[1] The special demands made by the state on the rich
citizens, like the trierarchy, choregia, etc.

But first of all read the testimony of Nausicrates, who bought the house, and take all the other depositions that I mentioned in the same connection.

I will now show you that his father had not a little ready money, which the defendant has squandered. For the father, afraid of the special services to which he would be liable,[1] sold the property that he owned (with the exception of the items I have mentioned)—a piece of land in Cephisia, another in Amphitrope, and two workshops at the silver mines, one of them in Aulon, the other near the tomb of Thrasyllus.

How it was that the father became so well-to-do I will tell you. There were three brothers in this family, Eupolemus, the gymnastic trainer, Arizelus, the father of the defendant, and Arignotus, who is still living, an old man now, and blind. Of these, Eupolemus was the first to die, before the estate had been divided; next, Arizelus, the father of Timarchus. So long as Arizelus lived, he managed the whole estate, because of the ill-health of Arignotus and the trouble with his eyes, and because Eupolemus was dead. By agreement with Arignotus he regularly gave him a sum of money for his support. Then Arizelus, the father of the defendant Timarchus, died also. In the first years thereafter, so long as the defendant was a child, Arignotus received from the guardians[2] all that one could

---

[2] The same men would act as administrators of the undivided estate and as guardians of the boy during his minority.

τῶν ἐπιτρόπων τῷ Ἀριγνώτῳ· ἐπειδὴ δ᾽ ἐνεγράφη
Τίμαρχος εἰς τὸ ληξιαρχικὸν γραμματεῖον καὶ
κύριος ἐγένετο τῆς οὐσίας, παρωσάμενος ἄνδρα
πρεσβύτην καὶ ἠτυχηκότα, θεῖον ἑαυτοῦ, τήν τε
οὐσίαν ἠφάνισε, καὶ τῶν ἐπιτηδείων οὐδὲν ἐδίδου
τῷ Ἀριγνώτῳ, ἀλλὰ περιεῖδεν ἐκ τοσαύτης οὐσίας
104 ἐν τοῖς ἀδυνάτοις μισθοφοροῦντα. καὶ τὸ τελευταῖον, ὃ καὶ δεινότατον, ἀπολειφθέντος τοῦ
πρεσβύτου τῆς γιγνομένης τοῖς ἀδυνάτοις δοκιμασίας, καὶ[1] ἱκετηρίαν θέντος εἰς τὴν βουλὴν
ὑπὲρ τοῦ μισθοῦ, βουλευτὴς ὢν καὶ προεδρεύων
ἐκείνην τὴν ἡμέραν, οὐκ ἠξίωσεν αὐτῷ συνειπεῖν,
ἀλλὰ περιεῖδεν ἀπολέσαντα τὸν τῆς πρυτανείας
μισθόν. ὅτι δ᾽ ἀληθῆ λέγω, κάλει μοι Ἀρίγνωτον
Σφήττιον, καὶ τὴν μαρτυρίαν ἀναγίγνωσκε.

ΜΑΡΤΥΡΙΑ

105 Ἀλλ᾽ ἴσως ἄν τις εἴποι, ὡς ἀποδόμενος τὴι
πατρῴαν οἰκίαν ἑτέραν ἄλλοθί που τοῦ ἄστεως
ἐκτήσατο, ἀντὶ δὲ τῆς ἐσχατιᾶς καὶ τοῦ χωρίου
τοῦ Ἀλωπεκῆσι καὶ τῶν δημιουργῶν καὶ τῶν
ἄλλων εἰς τἀργύρειά τι κατεσκευάσατο, ὥσπερ
καὶ ὁ πατὴρ αὐτοῦ πρότερον. ἀλλ᾽ οὐκ ἔστι
τούτῳ λοιπὸν οὐδέν, οὐκ οἰκία, οὐ συνοικία, οὐ
χωρίον, οὐκ οἰκέται, οὐ δάνεισμα, οὐκ ἄλλ᾽ οὐδὲν
ἀφ᾽ ὧν ἄνθρωποι μὴ κακοῦργοι ζῶσιν. ἀλλὰ

---

[1] καὶ added by Franke.

---

[1] "The Senate also examines the infirm paupers. For
there is a law that provides that persons who have property
of less than three minas and are so infirm of body as to be
unable to do any work, are to be examined by the Senate,

ask. But after Timarchus was enrolled in the citizens' list, and had come into control of the estate, he thrust aside this old and unfortunate man, his own uncle, and made way with the estate. He gave nothing to Arignotus for his support, but was content to see him, fallen from such wealth, now receiving the alms that the city gives to disabled paupers.[1] Finally—and most shameful of all—when the old man's name had been omitted at a revision of the list of pauper-pensioners, and he had laid a petition before the senate to have his dole restored, the defendant, who was a member of the senate, and one of the presiding officers that day, did not deign to speak for him, but let him lose his monthly pension.[2] To prove the truth of what I say, call, if you please, Arignotus of Sphettus, and read his affidavit.

AFFIDAVIT

But perhaps someone may say that after selling his father's house he bought another one somewhere else in the city, and that in place of the suburban estate and the land at Alopeke, and the slaves and the rest, he made investments in connection with the silver mines, as his father had done before him. No, he has nothing left, not a house, not an apartment, not a piece of ground, no slaves, no money at interest, nor anything else from which honest men get a living. On the contrary, in place

and to receive from the state two obols each per day for their support."—Aristotle, *Constitution of Athens*, xlix. (Kenyon's trans.).

[2] Aeschines calls it the "prytany payment." Probably the payment was made prytany by prytany, the prytany being one of the ten regular subdivisions of the civil year.

τούτῳ ἀντὶ τῶν πατρῴων περίεστι βδελυρία,
συκοφαντία, θράσος, τρυφή, δειλία, ἀναίδεια,
τὸ μὴ ἐπίστασθαι ἐρυθριᾶν ἐπὶ τοῖς αἰσχροῖς·
ἐξ ὧν ἂν ὁ κάκιστος καὶ ἀλυσιτελέστατος πολίτης
γένοιτο.

106 Οὐ τοίνυν μόνον τὰ πατρῷα κατεδήδοκεν, ἀλλὰ
καὶ τὰ κοινὰ τὰ ὑμέτερα, ὅσων πώποτε κύριος
γέγονεν. οὗτος γὰρ ταύτην τὴν ἡλικίαν ἔχων ἣν
ὑμεῖς ὁρᾶτε, οὐκ ἔστιν ἥντινα [1] οὐκ ἦρξεν ἀρχήν,
οὐδεμίαν λαχὼν οὐδὲ χειροτονηθείς, ἀλλὰ πάσας
παρὰ τοὺς νόμους πριάμενος. ὧν τὰς μὲν πλείστας
παρήσω, δυοῖν δ᾽ ἢ τριῶν μόνον μνησθήσομαι.

107 Λογιστὴς γὰρ γενόμενος πλεῖστα μὲν τὴν πόλιν
ἔβλαψε δῶρα λαμβάνων παρὰ τῶν μὴ [2] δικαίως
ἀρξάντων, μάλιστα δ᾽ ἐσυκοφάντησε τῶν ὑπευθύνων τοὺς μηδὲν ἠδικηκότας. ἦρξε δ᾽ ἐν Ἄνδρῳ
πριάμενος τριάκοντα μνῶν τὴν ἀρχήν, δανεισά-
μενος ἐπ᾽ ἐννέα ὀβολοῖς τὴν μνᾶν, εὐπορίαν τῇ
βδελυρίᾳ τῇ ἑαυτοῦ τοὺς συμμάχους τοὺς ὑμετέρους ποιούμενος· καὶ τοσαύτην ἀσέλγειαν ἐπεδείξατο εἰς ἐλευθέρων ἀνθρώπων γυναῖκας ἡλίκην
οὐδεὶς πώποθ᾽ ἕτερος. ὧν οὐδένα ἐγὼ παρακαλῶ
δεῦρο τὴν αὑτοῦ συμφοράν, ἣν εἵλετο σιγᾶν, εἰς
πολλοὺς ἐκμαρτυρήσοντα, ἀλλ᾽ ὑμῖν τοῦτο κατα-
108 λείπω σκοπεῖν. τί δὲ προσδοκᾶτε; τὸν Ἀθήνησιν ὑβριστὴν οὐκ εἰς τοὺς ἄλλους μόνον, ἀλλὰ

---

[1] ἥντινα Cobet : ἥντινα πώποτ᾽ MSS.
[2] μὴ Sauppe : οὐ MSS.

---

[1] The Athenian constitution provided for a rigorous
system of accounting by all public officers at the close of
their year of office. Not only their handling of public funds,
but every official act, was passed upon by a board of state

of his patrimony, the resources he has left are lewdness, calumny, impudence, wantonness, cowardice, effrontery, a face that knows not the blush of shame—all that would produce the lowest and most unprofitable citizen.

But it is not only his patrimony that he has wasted, but also the common possessions of the state, your possessions, so far as they have ever come under his control. You see for yourselves how young he is, and yet there is not a public office which he has not held, not one of them by lot or by election, but every one by purchase, in defiance of the laws. The most of them I will pass over, and mention two or three only.

He held the office of auditor, and did the state serious injury by taking bribes from office holders who had been dishonest,[1] though his specialty was the blackmailing of innocent men who were to appear before the auditing board. He held a magistracy in Andros, which he bought for thirty minas, borrowing the money at nine obols on the mina,[2] and thus he made your allies a ready source of supply for his own lusts. And in his treatment of the wives of free men he showed such licentiousness as no other man ever did. Of these men I call no one into court to testify publicly to his own misfortune, which he has chosen to cover in silence, but I leave it to you to investigate this matter. But what do you expect? If a man at Athens not only abuses other people, but even his

auditors (Λογισταί). The findings of the auditors were subject to review by a court.

[2] The 9 obols is the interest per month, 1½ drachmas on the hundred drachmas, or 18 per cent. per year. Ordinary interest rates ran from 12 per cent. to 18 per cent.

THE SPEECHES OF AESCHINES

καὶ εἰς τὸ σῶμα τὸ ἑαυτοῦ, νόμων ὄντων, ὑμῶν
ὁρώντων, ἐχθρῶν ἐφεστηκότων, τοῦτον τὸν[1]
αὐτὸν λαβόντα ἄδειαν καὶ ἐξουσίαν καὶ ἀρχήν,
τίς ἂν ἐλπίσειεν ἀπολελοιπέναι τι τῶν ἀσελ-
γεστάτων ἔργων; ἤδη νὴ τὸν Δία καὶ τὸν Ἀπόλλω
πολλάκις ἐνεθυμήθην τὴν εὐτυχίαν τὴν τῆς ὑμετέρας πόλεως, κατὰ πολλὰ μὲν καὶ ἄλλα, οὐχ
ἥκιστα δὲ καὶ κατὰ τοῦτο,[2] ὅτι κατ᾽ ἐκείνους
τοὺς χρόνους οὐδεὶς ἐγένετο τῆς Ἀνδρίων πόλεως
ὠνητής.

109 Ἀλλὰ καθ᾽ αὑτὸν μὲν ἄρχων φαῦλος ἦν, μετὰ
πλειόνων δὲ ἐπιεικής. πόθεν; οὗτος, ὦ ἄνδρες
Ἀθηναῖοι, βουλευτὴς ἐγένετο ἐπὶ ἄρχοντος Νικο-
φήμου. ἅπαντα μὲν οὖν διεξελθεῖν ἃ ἐν τούτῳ
τῷ ἐνιαυτῷ ἐκακούργησε, πρὸς μικρὸν μέρος
ἡμέρας οὐκ ἄξιον ἐπιχειρεῖν· ἃ δ᾽ ἐστὶν ἐγγυτάτω
τῆς αἰτίας καθ᾽ ἣν ἡ παροῦσα κρίσις ἐστί, ταῦτ᾽
110 ἐρῶ διὰ βραχέων. ἐπὶ τοίνυν τοῦ αὐτοῦ ἄρχοντος
ὅθ᾽ οὗτος ἐβούλευεν, ταμίας ἦν τῶν τῆς θεοῦ
Ἡγήσανδρος ὁ Κρωβύλου ἀδελφός, ἔκλεπτον δὲ
τῆς πόλεως κοινῇ καὶ μάλα φιλεταίρως χιλίας
δραχμάς. αἰσθόμενος δὲ τὸ πρᾶγμα ἀνὴρ ἐπιεικής, Πάμφιλος ὁ Ἀχερδούσιος, προσκρούσας τι
τούτῳ καὶ παροξυνθείς, ἐκκλησίας οὔσης εἶπεν
ἀναστάς· "Ὦ ἄνδρες Ἀθηναῖοι, κλέπτουσιν ὑμῶν

---

[1] τὸν added by Emperius.
[2] τοῦτο Cobet : ταῦτα MSS.

---

[1] The year 361/60 B.C.
[2] Ten treasurers, οἱ ταμίαι τῆς Ἀθηνᾶς, appointed annually
by lot, had the care of the treasures and revenues of the
Parthenon (Aristotle, *Constitution of Athens*, xlvii.). It

88

own body, here where there are laws, where you are
looking on, where his personal enemies are on the
watch, who would expect that same man, when he
had received impunity and authority and office, to
have placed any limit on his license? By Zeus and
Apollo, many a time before now have I marvelled at
the good fortune of your city, shown on many other
occasions, but not least in this, that in those days he
found nobody to whom he could sell the state of
Andros!

But, you say, although he was worthless when
he held office alone, yet when he was associated
with others he was all right! How so? This man,
fellow citizens, became a member of the senate in
the archonship of Nicophemus.[1] Now to recount
all the rascalities of which he was guilty in that
year would be too large an undertaking for the
small fraction of a day; but those which are most
germane to the charge that underlies the present
trial, I will relate in a few words. In the same year
in which Timarchus was a member of the senate,
Hegesandrus, the brother of Crobylus, was a
treasurer of the funds of the goddess,[2] and together, in right friendly comradeship, they were
in the act of stealing a thousand drachmas which
belonged to the city. But a reputable man, Pam-
philus of the deme Acherdous, who had had some
trouble with the defendant and was angry with
him, found out what was going on, and at a meeting
of the assembly arose and said, "Fellow citizens,
a man and a woman are conspiring to steal one

appears that they also had custody of any state funds that
were for the time being unappropriated, the Opisthodomos
of the Parthenon serving as their treasury.

111 ἀνὴρ καὶ γυνὴ κοινῇ χιλίας δραχμάς." θαυμα-
σάντων δ' ὑμῶν, πῶς ἀνὴρ καὶ γυνὴ καὶ τίς ὁ
λόγος, εἶπε μικρὸν διαλιπών· "'Αγνοεῖτε," ἔφη,
"ὅ τι λέγω; ὁ μὲν ἀνήρ ἐστιν Ἡγήσανδρος
ἐκεῖνος νυνί," ἔφη, "πρότερον δ' ἦν καὶ αὐτὸς
Λεωδάμαντος γυνή· ἡ δὲ γυνὴ Τίμαρχος οὑτοσί.
ὃν δὲ τρόπον κλέπτεται τὸ ἀργύριον, ἐγὼ ἐρῶ."
μετὰ ταῦτα ἤδη διεξῄει περὶ τοῦ πράγματος καὶ
μάλα εἰδότως καὶ σαφῶς. διδάξας δὲ ταῦτα,
"Τί οὖν ἐστιν," ἔφη, "ὦ ἄνδρες 'Αθηναῖοι, ἃ
συμβουλεύω ὑμῖν; ἐὰν μὲν ἡ βουλὴ καταγνοῦσα
τουτουὶ[1] καὶ ἐκφυλλοφορήσασα δικαστηρίῳ παραδῷ, δότε τὴν δωρεὰν αὐτοῖς, ἐὰν δὲ μὴ κολάσωσι,
μὴ δῶτε, ἀλλ' εἰς ἐκείνην αὐτοῖς τὴν ἡμέραν
112 ἀπομνημονεύσατε." μετὰ ταῦτα ὡς ἐπανῆλθεν
ἡ βουλὴ εἰς τὸ βουλευτήριον, ἐξεφυλλοφόρησε
μὲν αὐτόν, ἐν δὲ τῇ ψήφῳ κατεδέξατο. ὅτι δ' οὐ
παρέδωκε δικαστηρίῳ οὐδ' ἐξήλασεν ἐκ τοῦ βουλευτηρίου, ἄχθομαι μὲν λέγων, ἀνάγκη δ' ἐστὶν
εἰπεῖν, ὅτι τῆς δωρεᾶς ἀπέτυχε.[2] μὴ τοίνυν
φανῆτε, ὦ ἄνδρες 'Αθηναῖοι, τῇ μὲν βουλῇ χαλε-
πήναντες καὶ πεντακοσίους ἄνδρας τῶν πολιτῶν
ἀστεφανώτους ποιήσαντες, ὅτι τοῦτον οὐκ ἐτιμω-

---

[1] τουτουὶ Franke : τουτονὶ ἀδικεῖν MSS.
[2] ἀπέτυχε Weidner : οὐκ ἔτυχε or ἀπετύγχανε MSS.

---

[1] At the close of their year of office the senate had become
accustomed to expect a vote of the popular assembly bestowing a crown (garland) as a testimonial for their services.
[2] The senators had been sitting with the other citizens as

thousand drachmas of yours." When you in astonishment cried, " How 'a man and a woman,' what are you talking about?" after a little he went on : "Don't you understand," said he, "what I mean? The man is our friend Hegesandrus there, a man now, though he too used to be a woman, Laodamas's woman ; as for the woman, she is Timarchus yonder. How the money is being stolen I will tell you." He then proceeded to give a full account of the matter, and in a way that showed that there was no guesswork about it. After he had given you this information, "What is it, fellow citizens," said he, "that I advise? If the senate sustains the charge against this man and expels him, and then hands him over to the courts, give the senate the usual testimonial ;[1] but if they fail to punish him, refuse to give it, and lay up this thing against them for that day." After this, when the senate had returned to the senate chamber,[2] they expelled him on the preliminary ballot, but took him back on the final vote.[3] I must tell you, however unpleasant it is to mention it, that for their failure to hand him over to the courts, or even to expel him from the senate chamber, they failed to receive the usual testimonial. I beg you therefore, fellow citizens, not to present the spectacle of showing resentment toward the senate, and depriving five hundred citizens of a crown because they failed to punish the defendant, and then

members of the assembly. After the adjournment of the assembly, the senate resumed its session.

[3] It appears that on the question of the expulsion of a member there was a preliminary vote with leaves as ballots, and a final one with the ordinary ballots.

ρήσατο, αὐτοὶ δὲ ἀφῆτε, καὶ τὸν τῇ βουλῇ μὴ
συνενεγκόντα ῥήτορα, τοῦτον τῷ δήμῳ περι-
ποιήσητε.

113 Ἀλλὰ περὶ μὲν τὰς κληρωτὰς ἀρχάς ἐστι
τοιοῦτος, περὶ δὲ τὰς χειροτονητὰς βελτίων. καὶ
τίς ὑμῶν οὐκ οἶδεν ὡς περιβοήτως ἐξηλέγχθη
κλέπτης ὤν; πεμφθεὶς γὰρ ὑφ' ὑμῶν ἐξεταστὴς
τῶν ἐν Ἐρετρίᾳ ξένων, μόνος τῶν ἐξεταστῶν
ὡμολόγει λαβεῖν ἀργύριον, καὶ οὐ περὶ τοῦ πράγματος ἀπελογεῖτο, ἀλλ' εὐθὺς περὶ τοῦ τιμήματος
ἱκέτευεν ὁμολογῶν ἀδικεῖν. ὑμεῖς δὲ τοῖς μὲν
ἐξάρνοις ἐτιμήσατε ταλάντου ἑκάστῳ, τούτῳ δὲ
τριάκοντα μνῶν. οἱ δὲ νόμοι κελεύουσι τῶν κλε-
πτῶν τοὺς μὲν ὁμολογοῦντας θανάτῳ ζημιοῦσθαι,
τοὺς δ' ἀρνουμένους κρίνεσθαι.

114 Τοιγάρτοι οὕτως ὑμῶν κατεφρόνησεν, ὥστ' εὐθὺς ἐπὶ ταῖς[1] διαψηφίσεσι δισχιλίας δραχμὰς
ἔλαβε. φήσας γὰρ Φιλωτάδην τὸν Κυδαθηναιᾶ,
ἕνα τῶν πολιτῶν, ἀπελεύθερον εἶναι ἑαυτοῦ, καὶ
πείσας ἀποψηφίσασθαι τοὺς δημότας, ἐπιστὰς
τῇ κατηγορίᾳ ἐπὶ τοῦ δικαστηρίου, καὶ λαβὼν
εἰς τὴν ἑαυτοῦ χεῖρα τὰ ἱερά, καὶ ὀμόσας μὴ
λαβεῖν δῶρα μηδὲ λήψεσθαι, καὶ ἐπομόσας τοὺς

---

[1] ταῖς Sauppe : ταῖς ἐν τοῖς δήμοις or ταῖς δημοσίαις MSS.

---

[1] "All the magistrates that are concerned with the ordinary routine of administration are elected by lot, except the
Military Treasurer, the Commissioners of the Theoric Fund,
and the Superintendent of Springs. These are elected by
vote, and the magistrates thus elected hold office from one
Panathenaic festival to another. All military officers are

letting him go free yourselves; and I beg you not to preserve for the popular assembly a public man who has proved useless to the senate.

But, you say, though such is his record in the offices filled by lot, he has been a better man in the elective offices.[1] Why, who of you has not heard of his notorious conviction for stealing? You will recall that you sent him as an inspector of the mercenary troops in Eretria.[2] He and he only of the board of inspectors acknowledged that he had taken money, and made no defence against the charge, but immediately admitted his guilt, making his plea only as to the penalty. You punished those who denied their guilt with a fine of a talent apiece, but him with half a talent. Whereas the laws command that thieves who admit their guilt shall be punished with death; it is those who deny their guilt that are to be put on trial.

In consequence of this experience so great became his contempt for you that immediately, on the occasion of the revision of the citizen lists, he gathered in two thousand drachmas. For he asserted that Philotades of Cydathenaeon, a citizen, was a former slave of his own, and he persuaded the members of the deme to disfranchise him. He took charge of the prosecution in court,[3] and after he had taken the sacred offerings in his hand and sworn that he had not taken a bribe and would not, and

also elected by vote."—Aristotle, *Constitution of Athens*, xliii. (Kenyon's trans.).

[2] The handling of the funds for the payment of mercenary troops gave such opportunities for dishonesty, especially in the padding of the rolls, that inspectors were sent out to check the accounts on the spot.

[3] See on § 77.

115 ὁρκίους θεοὺς καὶ ἐξώλειαν[1] ἐπαρασάμενος ἑαυτῷ,
εἰληφὼς ἠλέγχθη παρὰ Λευκωνίδου τοῦ Φιλωτάδου κηδεστοῦ διὰ Φιλήμονος τοῦ ὑποκριτοῦ εἴκοσι
μνᾶς, ἃς ἐν ὀλίγῳ χρόνῳ πρὸς Φιλοξένην ἀνήλωσε
τὴν ἑταίραν, καὶ προὔδωκε τὸν ἀγῶνα, καὶ τὸν
ὅρκον ἐπιώρκησεν. ὅτι δ' ἀληθῆ λέγω, κάλει μοι
Φιλήμονα τὸν δόντα τὸ ἀργύριον[2] καὶ Λευκωνίδην
τὸν Φιλωτάδου κηδεστήν, καὶ τῶν συνθηκῶν ἀνάγνωθι τὰ ἀντίγραφα, καθ' ἃς τὴν πρᾶσιν ἐποιήσατο τοῦ ἀγῶνος.

MΑΡΤΥΡΙΑΙ. ΣΥΝΘΗΚΑΙ

116 Περὶ μὲν οὖν τοὺς πολίτας καὶ τοὺς οἰκείους
οἷος γεγένηται, καὶ τὴν πατρῴαν οὐσίαν ὡς αἰσχρῶς ἀνήλωκε, καὶ τὴν ὕβριν τὴν εἰς τὸ ἑαυτοῦ
σῶμα ὡς ὑπερεώρακε, συνῇστε[3] μὲν καὶ πρὶν ἐμὲ
λέγειν, ἱκανῶς δ' ὑμᾶς ὑπομέμνηκε[4] καὶ ὁ παρ'
ἐμοῦ λόγος· δύο δέ μοι τῆς κατηγορίας εἴδη λεί-
πεται, ἐφ' οἷς ἐμαυτόν τ' εἰπεῖν εὔχομαι τοῖς θεοῖς
πᾶσι καὶ πάσαις ὑπὲρ τῆς πόλεως ὡς προῄρημαι,
ὑμᾶς τε βουλοίμην ἂν οἷς ἐγὼ μέλλω λέγειν
προσέχειν[5] καὶ παρακολουθεῖν εὐμαθῶς.

117 Ἔστι δ' ὁ μὲν πρότερός μοι λόγος προδιήγησις
τῆς ἀπολογίας ἧς ἀκούω μέλλειν γίγνεσθαι, ἵνα
μὴ τοῦτο ἐμοῦ παραλιπόντος ὁ τὰς τῶν λόγων
τέχνας κατεπαγγελλόμενος τοὺς νέους διδάσκειν

---

[1] ἐξώλειαν Baiter: τὴν ἐξώλειαν MSS.
[2] Weidner deletes Τιμάρχῳ which the MSS. have before
or after τὸ ἀργύριον.   [3] συνῇστε Cobet: σύνιστε MSS.
[4] ὑπομέμνηκε Cobet: ὑπομιμνήσκει MSS.
[5] προσέχειν Weidner: προσέχειν τὸν νοῦν or προσέχειν τὴν
γνώμην MSS.

though he swore by the usual gods of oaths [1] and
called down destruction on his own head, yet it
has been proved that he received twenty minas
from Leuconides, the brother-in-law of Philotades,
at the hands of Philemon the actor, which money
he soon spent on his mistress Philoxene. And so
he broke his oath and abandoned the case. To
prove that I speak the truth please call Philemon,
who paid over the money, and Leuconides, the
brother-in-law of Philotades, and read the copy of
the agreement by which he effected the sale of
the case.

AFFIDAVITS.   AGREEMENT

Now what manner of man he has shown himself
to be in his dealings with his fellow citizens and his
own family, how shamefully he has wasted his patrimony, how he has submitted to the abuse of his
own body, all this you knew as well as I, before
ever I spoke, but my account of it has sufficiently
refreshed your memory. Two points of my plea
remain, and I pray to all the gods and goddesses
that I may be enabled to speak regarding them
as I have planned to do, for the public good; and
I should like you to give attention to what I am
about to say, and to follow me with willing mind.

The first of these points is an anticipation of the
defence which I hear he is about to offer, for I fear
that if I neglect this topic, that man who professes
to teach the young the tricks of speech [2] may mis-

---

[1] The scholiast tells us that these gods were Apollo,
Demeter, and Zeus.

[2] The reference is to Demosthenes, who, we must from
this statement conclude, was in his earlier years a professional teacher of rhetoric, as well as a lawyer and politician.

ἀπάτῃ τινὶ παραλογισάμενος ὑμᾶς ἀφέληται τὸ
τῆς πόλεως συμφέρον. ὁ δὲ δεύτερός ἐστί μοι
λόγος παράκλησις τῶν πολιτῶν πρὸς ἀρετήν. ὁρῶ
δὲ πολλοὺς μὲν τῶν νεωτέρων προσεστηκότας
πρὸς τῷ δικαστηρίῳ, πολλοὺς δὲ τῶν πρεσβυτέρων, οὐκ ἐλαχίστους δὲ ἐκ τῆς ἄλλης Ἑλλάδος
118 συνειλεγμένους ἐπὶ τὴν ἀκρόασιν· οὓς μὴ νομίζετ'
ἐμὲ θεωρήσοντας ἥκειν, ἀλλὰ πολὺ μᾶλλον ὑμᾶς
εἰσομένους, εἰ μὴ μόνον εὖ νομοθετεῖν ἐπίστασθε,
ἀλλὰ καὶ κρίνειν τὰ καλὰ καὶ τὰ μὴ καλὰ
δύνασθε, καὶ εἰ τιμᾶν ἐπίστασθε τοὺς ἀγαθοὺς
ἄνδρας, καὶ εἰ θέλετε κολάζειν τοὺς ὀνείδη τὸν
ἑαυτῶν βίον τῇ πόλει κατασκευάζοντας.[1] λέξω
δὲ πρῶτον πρὸς ὑμᾶς περὶ τῆς ἀπολογίας.

119 Ὁ γὰρ περιττὸς ἐν τοῖς λόγοις Δημοσθένης ἢ
τοὺς νόμους φησὶν ὑμᾶς ἐξαλείφειν δεῖν, ἢ τοῖς
ἐμοῖς λόγοις οὐκ εἶναι προσεκτέον. ἀποθαυμάζει
γάρ, εἰ μὴ πάντες μέμνησθ' ὅτι καθ' ἕκαστον
ἐνιαυτὸν ἡ βουλὴ πωλεῖ τὸ πορνικὸν τέλος· καὶ
τοὺς πριαμένους τὸ τέλος οὐκ εἰκάζειν, ἀλλ' ἀκριβῶς εἰδέναι τοὺς ταύτῃ χρωμένους τῇ ἐργασίᾳ.
ὁπότε δὴ οὖν τετόλμηκα ἀντιγράψασθαι πεπορ-
νευμένῳ Τιμάρχῳ μὴ ἐξεῖναι δημηγορεῖν, ἀπαι-
τεῖν φησι τὴν πρᾶξιν αὐτὴν οὐκ αἰτίαν κατηγόρου,
ἀλλὰ μαρτυρίαν τελώνου τοῦ παρὰ Τιμάρχου
τοῦτο ἐκλέξαντος τὸ τέλος.

120 Ἐγὼ δὲ πρὸς ταῦτα, ὦ ἄνδρες Ἀθηναῖοι, σκέ-
ψασθ' ἂν ἁπλοῦν ὑμῖν καὶ ἐλευθέριον δόξω λόγον
λέγειν. αἰσχύνομαι γὰρ ὑπὲρ τῆς πόλεως, εἰ
Τίμαρχος, ὁ τοῦ δήμου σύμβουλος καὶ τὰς εἰς τὴν
Ἑλλάδα τολμῶν πρεσβείας πρεσβεύειν, μὴ τὸ

---

[1] κατασκευάζοντας Blass : παρασκευάζοντας MSS.

lead you by some artifice, and so defraud the state. My second point is an exhortation of the citizens to virtue. And I see many young men present in court, and many of their elders, and not a few citizens of other states of Hellas, gathered here to listen. Do not imagine that they have come to look at me. Nay, rather have they come to find out about you, whether you not only know how to make good laws, but also are able to distinguish between good conduct and bad; whether you know how to honour good men; and whether you are willing to punish those who make their own life a reproach to the city. I will first speak to you about the defence.

The eminent orator Demosthenes says that you must either wipe out your laws, or else no attention must be paid to my words. For he is amazed, he says, if you do not all remember that every single year the senate farms out the tax on prostitutes, and that the men who buy this tax do not guess, but know precisely, who they are that follow this profession. When, therefore, I have dared to bring impeachment against Timarchus for having prostituted himself, in order that I may deprive him of the right to address the people in assembly, Demosthenes says that the very act complained of calls, not for an accuser's arraignment, but for the testimony of the tax-gatherer who collected this tax from Timarchus.

Now, fellow citizens, see whether the reply that I make seems to you frank and straightforward. For I am ashamed in the city's behalf, if Timarchus, the counsellor of the people, the man who dares to go out into Hellas on their embassies, if this man,

πρᾶγμα ὅλον ἀποτρίψασθαι ἐπιχειρήσει, ἀλλὰ
τοὺς τόπους ἐπερωτήσει ὅπου ἐκαθέζετο, καὶ τοὺς
τελώνας, εἰ πώποτε παρ' αὐτοῦ τὸ πορνικὸν τέλος
121 εἰλήφασιν.   ταύτης μὲν οὖν τῆς ἀπολογίας ὑμῶν
ἔνεκα παραχωρησάτω· ἕτερον δ' ἐγώ σοι λόγον
ὑποβαλῶ καλὸν καὶ δίκαιον, ᾧ χρήσῃ, εἰ μηδὲν
αἰσχρὸν σαυτῷ σύνοισθα.   τόλμησον γὰρ εἰς τοὺς
δικαστὰς βλέψας εἰπεῖν ἃ προσήκει ἀνδρὶ σώφρονι τὰ περὶ τὴν ἡλικίαν· "'Άνδρες 'Αθηναῖοι,
τέθραμμαι μὲν ἐκ παιδὸς καὶ μειρακίου παρ' ὑμῖν,
οὐκ ἀφανεῖς δὲ διατριβὰς διατρίβω, ἀλλ' ἐν ταῖς
122 ἐκκλησίαις μεθ' ὑμῶν ὁρῶμαι.   οἶμαι δ' ἄν, εἰ
πρὸς ἄλλους τινὰς ἦν ὁ λόγος μοι περὶ τῆς αἰτίας
ἧς κρίνομαι, ταῖς ὑμετέραις μαρτυρίαις ῥᾳδίως ἂν
ἀπολύσασθαι τοὺς τοῦ κατηγόρου λόγους.   μὴ
γὰρ ὅτι, εἰ πέπρακταί μοι τι τούτων, ἀλλ' εἰ δοκῶ
ὑμῖν παραπλησίως βεβιωκέναι ταῖς λεγομέναις
ὑπὸ τούτου αἰτίαις, ἀβίωτον ἡγούμενος[1] ἐμαυτῷ
τὸν λοιπὸν βίον, παραδίδωμι τὴν εἰς ἐμαυτὸν
τιμωρίαν ἐναπολογήσασθαι τῇ πόλει πρὸς τοὺς
'Έλληνας, οὐδ' ἥκω παραιτησόμενος ὑμᾶς, ἀλλὰ
καταχράσθέ μοι, εἰ δοκῶ τοιοῦτος εἶναι."

Αὕτη μέν ἐστιν, ὦ Τίμαρχε, ἀνδρὸς ἀγαθοῦ καὶ
σώφρονος ἀπολογία, καὶ πεπιστευκότος τῷ βίῳ
καὶ καταφρονοῦντος εἰκότως ἁπάσης βλασφημίας·
123 ἃ δὲ πείθει σε Δημοσθένης,[2] οὐκ ἀνδρός ἐστιν
ἐλευθέρου, ἀλλὰ πόρνου περὶ τῶν τόπων διαφερο-
μένου.   ἐπειδὴ δ' εἰς τὰς ἐπωνυμίας τῶν οἰκήσεων

---

[1] Weidner deletes εἶναι, which the MSS. have before or
after ἡγούμενος.
[2] Weidner deletes λέγειν, which the MSS. have before or
after Δημοσθένης.

instead of undertaking to clear his record of the whole matter, shall ask us to specify the localities where he plied his trade, and to say whether the tax collectors have ever collected the prostitutes' licence from him. For your sakes pray let him give up such defence as that! But I myself will suggest to you, Timarchus, a different line of defence, which is honourable and fair, and you will adopt it, if you are conscious of having done nothing shameful. Come, dare to look the jury in the face and say that which a decent man ought to say of his youth: "Fellow citizens, I have been brought up as boy and youth among you; how I have spent my time is no secret to you, and you see me with you in your assemblies. Now if I were defending myself before any other set of men on the charge on which I stand accused, I think your testimony would readily suffice to refute the words of my accuser. For if any such act has been committed by me, nay rather if my life has exhibited to you even any resemblance to that of which he accuses me, I feel that the rest of my life is not worth living; I freely concede you my punishment, that the state may have therein a defence in the eyes of Hellas. I have not come here to beg for mercy from you; nay, do with me what you will, if you believe that I am such a man as that."

This, Timarchus, is the defence of a good and decent man, a man who has confidence in his past life, and who with good reason looks with contempt upon all efforts to slander him. But the defence which Demosthenes persuades you to make is not for a free man, but for a prostitute—quibbling about when and where! But since you do take refuge

καταφεύγεις, κατ' οἴκημα τὸ πρᾶγμα ἐξετάζεσθαι
ἀξιῶν ὅπου ἐκαθέζου, ἃ μέλλω λέγειν ἀκούσας
εἰσαῦθις οὐ χρήσῃ τοιούτῳ λόγῳ, ἐὰν σωφρονῇς.
οὐ γὰρ τὰ οἰκήματα οὐδ' αἱ οἰκήσεις τὰς ἐπωνυμίας τοῖς ἐνοικήσασι παρέχουσιν, ἀλλ' οἱ ἐνοική-
σαντες τὰς τῶν ἰδίων ἐπιτηδευμάτων ἐπωνυμίας
124 τοῖς τόποις παρασκευάζουσιν. ὅπου μὲν γὰρ
πολλοὶ μισθωσάμενοι μίαν οἴκησιν διελόμενοι
ἔχουσι, συνοικίαν καλοῦμεν, ὅπου δ' εἷς ἐνοικεῖ,
οἰκίαν. ἐὰν δ' εἰς ἓν δήπου τούτων τῶν ἐπὶ ταῖς
ὁδοῖς ἐργαστηρίων ἰατρὸς εἰσοικίσηται, ἰατρεῖον
καλεῖται· ἐὰν δ' ὁ μὲν ἐξοικίσηται, εἰς δὲ τὸ αὐτὸ
τοῦτο ἐργαστήριον χαλκεὺς εἰσοικίσηται, χαλ-
κεῖον ἐκλήθη, ἐὰν δὲ κναφεύς, κναφεῖον, ἐὰν δὲ
τέκτων, τεκτονεῖον· ἐὰν δὲ πορνοβοσκὸς καὶ πόρ-
ναι, ἀπὸ τῆς ἐργασίας αὐτῆς ἐκλήθη πορνεῖον.
ὥστε σὺ πολλὰ πορνεῖα τῇ τῆς πράξεως εὐχερείᾳ
πεποίηκας. μὴ οὖν, ὅπου ποτὲ ἔπραττες, ἐρώτα,
ἀλλ' ὡς οὐ πεποίηκας, τοῦτο[1] ἀπολογοῦ.
125 Ἥξει δ' ὡς ἔοικε καὶ ἕτερος λόγος τις ὑπὸ τοῦ
αὐτοῦ σοφιστοῦ συγκείμενος. λέγει γὰρ ὡς οὐδέν
ἐστιν ἀδικώτερον φήμης, ἀγοραῖα τεκμήρια καὶ
παντελῶς ἀκόλουθα τῷ αὐτοῦ βίῳ παρεχόμενος.
πρῶτον μὲν γὰρ τὴν ἐν Κολωνῷ συνοικίαν τὴν
Δήμωνος καλουμένην ψευδῆ φησι τὴν ἐπωνυμίαν
ἔχειν· οὐ γὰρ εἶναι Δήμωνος· ἔπειτα τὸν Ἑρμῆν

---

[1] οὐ πεποίηκας, τοῦτο Blass : τοῦτο οὐ πεποίηκας or οὐ τοῦτο
πεποίηκας or τοῦτο πεποίηκας MSS.

---

[1] Some of Aeschines' anticipations of the arguments of his
opponents would be possible in the preparation of his speech
for the court-room; others were probably added to the

in the names of the lodgings, demanding that in our proof we specify every single house where you plied your trade, to such an argument as that you will never again resort, if you are wise, when you have heard what I am about to say. For it is not the lodgings and the houses which give their names to the men who have lived in them, but it is the tenants who give to the places the names of their own pursuits. Where, for example, several men hire one house and occupy it, dividing it between them, we call it an "apartment house," but where one man only dwells, a "house." And if perchance a physician moves into one of these shops on the street, it is called a "surgery." But if he moves out and a smith moves into this same shop, it is called a "smithy"; if a fuller, a "laundry"; if a carpenter, a "carpenter's shop"; and if a pimp and his harlots, from the trade itself it gets its name of "brothel." So that you have made many a house a brothel by the facility with which you have plied your profession. Ask not, then, where it was that you practised it, but make this your defence, that you have never done the thing.

But it seems that we are to have another argument, too, concocted by the same sophist. For he says that nothing is more unjust than common report, and he goes to the market-place for his evidence, the sort of thing that is quite in harmony with his own life. He says first [1] that the apartment house in Colonus which is called Demon's is falsely named, for it does not belong to Demon. Again,

---

speech as prepared for publication, after the speeches for the defence had been heard. Probably some of these replies were given extempore in court.

126 τὸν Ἀνδοκίδου καλούμενον οὐκ Ἀνδοκίδου, ἀλλ᾽
Αἰγῆδος φυλῆς εἶναι ἀνάθημα. παραφέρει δ᾽ αὐτὸν ἐν σκώμματος μέρει, ὡς ἡδὺς ὢν [1] ἀνὴρ καὶ
περὶ τὰς ἰδίας διατριβὰς γελοῖος· “Εἰ μὴ καὶ ἐμὲ
δεῖ,” φησίν, “ὑπακούειν τοῖς ὄχλοις μὴ Δημοσθένην καλούμενον, ἀλλὰ Βάταλον, ὅτι ταύτην ἐξ
ὑποκορίσματος τίτθης τὴν ἐπωνυμίαν ἔχω.” εἰ
δὲ Τίμαρχος ὡραῖος ἐγένετο καὶ σκώπτεται τῇ
τοῦ πράγματος διαβολῇ καὶ μὴ τοῖς αὑτοῦ ἔργοις,
οὐ δήπου διὰ τοῦτ᾽ αὐτόν φησι δεῖν συμφορᾷ
περιπεσεῖν.

127 Ἐγὼ δέ, ὦ Δημόσθενες, περὶ μὲν τῶν ἀναθημά-
των καὶ τῶν οἰκιῶν καὶ τῶν κτημάτων καὶ πάντων
ὅλως τῶν ἀφώνων πολλοὺς καὶ παντοδαποὺς καὶ
οὐδέποτε τοὺς αὐτοὺς ἀκούω λόγους λεγομένους·
οὐ γάρ εἰσιν ἐν αὐτοῖς οὔτε καλαὶ οὔτε αἰσχραὶ
πράξεις, ἀλλ᾽ ὁ προσαψάμενος αὐτῶν καὶ παρα-
τυχών, ὅστις ἂν ᾖ, κατὰ τὸ μέγεθος τῆς αὑτοῦ
δόξης λόγον παρέχει· περὶ δὲ τὸν τῶν ἀνθρώπων
βίον καὶ τὰς πράξεις [2] ἀψευδής τις ἀπὸ ταὐτομά-
του πλανᾶται φήμη κατὰ τὴν πόλιν, καὶ διαγ-
γέλλει τοῖς πολλοῖς τὰς ἰδίας πράξεις, πολλὰ δὲ
128 καὶ μαντεύεται περὶ τῶν μελλόντων ἔσεσθαι. καὶ
οὕτως ἐναργές ἐστι καὶ οὐ πεπλασμένον ὃ λέγω,
ὥσθ᾽ εὑρήσετε καὶ τὴν πόλιν ἡμῶν καὶ τοὺς προγόνους φήμης ὡς θεοῦ μεγίστης βωμὸν ἱδρυμένους,

---

[1] ὢν added by Dobree.
[2] καὶ τὰς πράξεις Scheibe : καὶ λόγον (or τὸν λόγον) καὶ τὰς
πράξεις MSS.

---

[1] On the nickname, see Speech II, § 99.
[2] The scholiast tells us that this altar was dedicated to

that the herm called "the Herm of Andocides" is not that of Andocides, but a votive offering of the tribe Aegeïs. And Demosthenes by way of a jest presents himself as an example, for he poses as a man who knows how to indulge in pleasantries and to joke about his own manner of life. "Unless," he says, "I am to answer to the name when the crowd call me, not Demosthenes, but 'Batalus,' just because I got that nickname from my nurse, as my baby-name."[1] And he says that if Timarchus did develop into a handsome youth, and if he is jeered at through slanderous interpretation of that fact, and not because of his own actions, surely he ought not for that reason to fall into misfortune.

But, Demosthenes, in the case of votive offerings, houses, estates, and all dumb objects in general, I do indeed hear many names applied, ever changing, never twice the same; for in them are no actions good or bad, but the man who happens to have become connected with them, whoever he may be, gives them a name according to the greatness of his own reputation. But in the case of the life and conduct of men, a common report which is unerring does of itself spread abroad throughout the city; it causes the private deed to become matter of public knowledge, and many a time it even prophesies what is about to be. So manifest and so far from being fabricated is this statement of mine, that you will find that both our city and our forefathers dedicated an altar to Common Report, as one of the greatest gods;[2] and you

commemorate news of a victory of Cimon's in Pamphylia, received at Athens the day the battle was fought. Pausanias (I. xvii. 1) attests the existence of the altar.

καὶ τὸν Ὅμηρον πολλάκις ἐν τῇ Ἰλιάδι λέγοντα
πρὸ τοῦ τι τῶν μελλόντων γενέσθαι· "Φήμη δ'
εἰς στρατὸν ἦλθε," καὶ πάλιν τὸν Εὐριπίδην
ἀποφαινόμενον τὴν θεὸν ταύτην οὐ μόνον τοὺς
ζῶντας ἐμφανίζειν δυναμένην, ὁποῖοί τινες ἂν
τυγχάνωσιν ὄντες, ἀλλὰ καὶ τοὺς τετελευτηκότας,
ὅταν λέγῃ,

φήμη τὸν ἐσθλὸν κἂν μυχῷ δείκνυσι γῆς.

129 ὁ δ' Ἡσίοδος καὶ διαρρήδην θεὸν αὐτὴν ἀποδεί-
κνυσι, πάνυ σαφῶς φράζων τοῖς βουλομένοις
συνιέναι· λέγει γάρ,

φήμη δ' οὔτις πάμπαν ἀπόλλυται, ἥντινα λαοὶ
πολλοὶ φημίξωσι· θεός νύ τίς ἐστι καὶ αὐτή.

καὶ τούτων τῶν ποιημάτων τοὺς μὲν εὐσχημόνως
βεβιωκότας εὑρήσετε ἐπαινέτας ὄντας· πάντες
γὰρ οἱ δημοσίᾳ φιλότιμοι παρὰ τῆς ἀγαθῆς φήμης ἡγοῦνται τὴν δόξαν κομιεῖσθαι· οἷς δ' αἰ-
σχρός ἐστιν ὁ βίος, οὐ τιμῶσι τὴν θεὸν ταύτην·
κατήγορον γὰρ αὐτὴν ἀθάνατον ἔχειν ἡγοῦνται.
130 ἀναμνήσθητε οὖν, ὦ ἄνδρες, τίνι κέχρησθε φήμῃ
περὶ Τιμάρχου. οὐχ ἅμα τοὔνομα λέγεται καὶ
τὸ ἐρώτημα ἐρωτᾶτε· "Ποῖος Τίμαρχος; ὁ πόρ-
νος;" ἔπειτα εἰ μὲν μάρτυρας παρειχόμην περὶ
τινος, ἐπιστεύετ' ἄν μοι· εἰ δὲ τὴν θεὸν μάρτυρα
παρέχομαι, οὐ πιστεύσετε; ἢ οὐδὲ ψευδομαρ-
131 τυρίων θέμις ἐστὶν ἐπισκήψασθαι. ἐπεὶ καὶ περὶ
τῆς Δημοσθένους ἐπωνυμίας, οὐ κακῶς ὑπὸ τῆς

---

[1] The quotation from Hesiod is from *Works and Days*,
763 f.; that from Euripides is not found in any of the extant

will find that Homer again and again in the *Iliad*
says, of a thing that has not yet come to pass,
"Common Report came to the host;" and again
you will find Euripides declaring that this god is
able not only to make known the living, revealing
their true characters, but the dead as well, when
he says, "Common Report shows forth the good
man, even though he be in the bowels of the
earth;" and Hesiod expressly represents her as
a goddess, speaking in words that are very plain
to those who are willing to understand, for he says,
"But Common Report dies never, the voice that
tongues of many men do utter. She also is divine." [1]
You will find that all men whose lives have been
decorous praise these verses of the poets. For all who
are ambitious for honour from their fellows believe
that it is from good report that fame will come
to them. But men whose lives are shameful pay
no honour to this god, for they believe that in her
they have a deathless accuser. Call to mind, therefore, fellow citizens, what common report you have
been accustomed to hear in the case of Timarchus.
The instant the name is spoken you ask, do you not,
"What Timarchus do you mean? The prostitute?"
Furthermore, if I had presented witnesses concerning any matter, you would believe me; if then
I present the god as my witness, will you refuse
to believe? But she is a witness against whom
it would be impiety even to bring complaint of
false testimony. In the case of Demosthenes, too,
it was common report, and not his nurse, that

plays, nor do we find the Homeric phrase in the *Iliad*.
Indeed, the word φήμη does not occur in the *Iliad*, and it is
found only three times in the *Odyssey* (ii. 35 ; xx. 100, 105),
where it is used of words of ominous meaning.

φήμης, ἀλλ' οὐχ ὑπὸ τῆς τίτθης, Βάταλος προσα-
γορεύεται, ἐξ ἀνανδρίας καὶ κιναιδίας ἐνεγκάμενος
τοὔνομα. εἰ γάρ τίς σου τὰ κομψὰ ταῦτα
χλανίσκια περιελόμενος καὶ τοὺς μαλακοὺς χι-
τωνίσκους, ἐν οἷς τοὺς κατὰ τῶν φίλων λόγους
γράφεις, περιενέγκας δοίη εἰς τὰς χεῖρας τῶν
δικαστῶν, οἶμαι ἂν αὐτούς, εἴ τις μὴ προειπὼν
τοῦτο ποιήσειεν, ἀπορῆσαι εἴτε ἀνδρὸς εἴτε γυναι-
κὸς εἰλήφασιν ἐσθῆτα.

132   Ἀναβήσεται δ' ἐν τῇ ἀπολογίᾳ καὶ τῶν στρατηγῶν τις, ὡς ἀκούω, ὑπτιάζων καὶ κατασκοπού-
μενος ἑαυτόν, ὡς ἐν παλαίστραις καὶ διατριβαῖς
γεγονώς· ὃς ἐπιχειρήσει διασύρειν τὴν ὅλην ἔν-
στασιν τοῦ ἀγῶνος, οὐ κρίσιν ἐξευρηκέναι με φάσκων, ἀλλὰ δεινῆς ἀπαιδευσίας ἀρχήν, παραφέ-
ρων πρῶτον μὲν τοὺς εὐεργέτας τοὺς ὑμετέρους,
Ἁρμόδιον καὶ Ἀριστογείτονα, καὶ τὴν πρὸς ἀλλήλους πίστιν καὶ τὸ πρᾶγμα ὡς συνήνεγκε τῇ πόλει
133   διεξιών· οὐκ ἀφέξεται δέ, ὥς φασιν, οὐδὲ τῶν
Ὁμήρου ποιημάτων οὐδὲ τῶν ὀνομάτων τῶν ἡρωι-

---

1 Writing speeches against his former friends is as brave
an act as Demosthenes is capable of, and the only armour
that he knows or needs is his soft shirt! Aeschines is
smarting under the fact that Demosthenes, who, in the
beginning of the negotiations with Philip for peace, had
been on good terms with himself, has now caused his indictment for treason, and will shortly conduct the prosecution
in court.

gave him his nickname; and well did common report name him Batalus, for his effeminacy and lewdness! For, Demosthenes, if anyone should strip off those exquisite, pretty mantles of yours, and the soft, pretty shirts that you wear while you are writing your speeches against your friends,[1] and should pass them around among the jurors, I think, unless they were informed beforehand, they would be quite at a loss to say whether they had in their hands the clothing of a man or of a woman!

But in the course of the defence one of the generals will, as I am told, mount the platform, with head held high and a self-conscious air, as one who should say, Behold the graduate of the wrestling schools, and the student of philosophy! And he will undertake to throw ridicule upon the whole idea of the prosecution, asserting that this is no legal process that I have devised, but the first step in a dangerous decline in the culture of our youth.[2] He will cite first those benefactors of yours, Harmodius and Aristogeiton, describing their fidelity to one another, and telling how in their case this relationship proved the salvation of the state.[3] Indeed, they say he will not even spare the poems of Homer or the names of the heroes,

[2] Probably the hearers would be quick to catch the half-hidden thought suggested by the word ἀπαιδευσία. The Athenian gentlemen did indeed "cultivate" the handsome boys and young men, and for most immoral purposes. The culture that the boys received was too often not εὐπαιδευσία, but παιδεραστία.

[3] The story was that the tyrant Hipparchus sought to become the lover of Harmodius, who was loved by Aristogeiton, and that the jealousies of this παιδεραστία led to the liberation of the state.

κῶν, ἀλλὰ καὶ τὴν λεγομένην γενέσθαι φιλίαν δι'
ἔρωτα Πατρόκλου καὶ Ἀχιλλέως ὑμνήσει, καὶ
τὸ κάλλος, ὥσπερ οὐ πάλαι μακαριζόμενον, ἂν
τύχῃ σωφροσύνης, νῦν ἐγκωμιάσεται. εἰ γὰρ τὴν
τοῦ σώματος εὐπρέπειαν ταύτην τινὲς διαβάλ-
λοντες συμφορὰν τοῖς ἔχουσι καταστήσουσιν, οὐ
ταὐτὰ κοινῇ ψηφιεῖσθαί φησιν ὑμᾶς καὶ ἰδίᾳ
134 εὔχεσθαι· ἄτοπον γὰρ εἶναι δοκεῖν[1] αὐτῷ, εἰ τοὺς
μὲν υἱεῖς τοὺς μηδέπω γεγονότας ἅπαντες εὔχεσθε
οἱ μέλλοντες παιδοποιεῖσθαι καλοὺς κἀγαθοὺς
τὰς ἰδέας φῦναι καὶ τῆς πόλεως ἀξίους, τοὺς δ'
ἤδη γεγονότας, ἐφ' οἷς προσήκει σεμνύνεσθαι τὴν
πόλιν, ἐὰν κάλλει καὶ ὥρᾳ διενεγκόντες ἐκπλή-
ξωσί τινας καὶ περιμάχητοι ἐξ ἔρωτος γένωνται,
τούτους ὡς ἔοικεν Αἰσχίνῃ πεισθέντες ἀτιμώσετε.
135 Κἀνταῦθα δή τινα καταδρομήν, ὡς ἀκούω, μέλλει ποιεῖσθαι περὶ ἐμοῦ, ἐπερωτῶν εἰ οὐκ αἰσχύνομαι αὐτὸς μὲν ἐν τοῖς γυμνασίοις ὀχληρὸς ὢν
καὶ πλείστων ἐραστὴς γεγονώς, τὸ δὲ πρᾶγμα εἰς
ὄνειδος καὶ κινδύνους καθιστάς. καὶ τὸ τελευταῖον, ὡς ἀπαγγέλλουσί τινές μοι, εἰς γέλωτα καὶ
λῆρόν τινα προτρεπόμενος ὑμᾶς, ἐπιδείξεσθαί[2]
μου φησὶν ὅσα πεποίηκα ἐρωτικὰ εἴς τινας ποιήματα, καὶ λοιδοριῶν τινων καὶ πληγῶν ἐκ τοῦ
πράγματος, αἳ περὶ ἐμὲ γεγένηνται, μαρτυρίας
φησὶ παρέξεσθαι.

---

[1] δοκεῖν Baiter and Sauppe : δοκεῖ or ὡς δοκεῖ or ὡς δοκεῖν
MSS.   [2] ἐπιδείξεσθαι Wolf : ἐπιδείξασθαι MSS.

but will celebrate the friendship between Patroclus and Achilles, which, we are told, had its source in passion. And he will pronounce an encomium on beauty now, as though it were not recognised long since as a blessing, if haply it be united with morality. For he says that if certain men by slandering this beauty of body shall cause beauty to be a misfortune to those who possess it, then in your public verdict you will contradict your personal prayers. For you seem to him, he says, in danger of being strangely inconsistent; for when you are about to beget children, you pray one and all that your sons still unborn may be fair and beautiful in person, and worthy of the city; and yet when you have sons already born, of whom the city may well be proud, if by their surpassing beauty and youthful charm they infatuate one person or another, and become the subject of strife because of the passion they inspire, these sons, as it seems, you propose to deprive of civic rights—because Aeschines tells you to do it.

And just here I understand he is going to carry the war into my territory, and ask me if I am not ashamed on my own part, after having made a nuisance of myself in the gymnasia and having been many times a lover, now to be bringing the practice into reproach and danger. And finally— so I am told—in an attempt to raise a laugh and start silly talk among you, he says he is going to exhibit all the erotic poems I have ever addressed to one person or another, and he promises to call witnesses to certain quarrels and pommellings in which I have been involved in consequence of this habit.

136 Ἐγὼ δὲ οὔτε ἔρωτα δίκαιον ψέγω, οὔτε τοὺς
κάλλει διαφέροντάς φημι πεπορνεῦσθαι, οὔτ'
αὐτὸς ἐξαρνοῦμαι μὴ οὐ γεγονέναι τ' [1] ἐρωτικός,
καὶ ἔτι καὶ νῦν εἶναι, τάς τε ἐκ τοῦ πράγματος
γιγνομένας πρὸς ἑτέρους φιλονικίας καὶ μάχας
οὐκ ἀρνοῦμαι μὴ οὐχὶ συμβεβηκέναι μοι. περὶ
δὲ τῶν ποιημάτων ὧν φασιν οὗτοί με πεποιηκέναι,
τὰ μὲν ὁμολογῶ, τὰ δὲ ἐξαρνοῦμαι μὴ τοῦτον
ἔχειν τὸν τρόπον ὃν οὗτοι διαφθείροντες παρέξονται.

137 Ὁρίζομαι δ' εἶναι τὸ μὲν ἐρᾶν τῶν καλῶν καὶ
σωφρόνων φιλανθρώπου πάθος καὶ εὐγνώμονος
ψυχῆς, τὸ δὲ ἀσελγαίνειν ἀργυρίου τινὰ μισθού-
μενον ὑβριστοῦ καὶ ἀπαιδεύτου ἀνδρὸς ἔργον· [2] καὶ
τὸ μὲν ἀδιαφθόρως ἐρᾶσθαί φημι καλὸν εἶναι, τὸ
δ' ἐπαρθέντα μισθῷ πεπορνεῦσθαι αἰσχρόν. ὅσον
δ' ἑκάτερον τούτων ἀπ' ἀλλήλων διέστηκε καὶ ὡς
πολὺ διαφέρει, ἐν τοῖς ἐφεξῆς ὑμᾶς πειράσομαι
138 λόγοις διδάσκειν. οἱ γὰρ πατέρες ἡμῶν, ὅθ' ὑπὲρ
τῶν ἐπιτηδευμάτων καὶ τῶν ἐκ φύσεως ἀναγκαίων ἐνομοθέτουν, ἃ τοῖς ἐλευθέροις ἡγοῦντο
εἶναι πρακτέα, ταῦτα τοῖς δούλοις ἀπεῖπον μὴ
ποιεῖν. " Δοῦλον," φησὶν ὁ νόμος, " μὴ γυμνάζεσθαι μηδὲ ξηραλοιφεῖν ἐν ταῖς παλαίστραις."
καὶ οὐκέτι προσέγραψε· " Τὸν δ' ἐλεύθερον ἀλεί-
φεσθαι καὶ γυμνάζεσθαι." ὁπότε γὰρ οἱ νομοθέται τὸ καλὸν τὸ ἐκ τῶν γυμνασίων κατιδόντες
ἀπεῖπον τοῖς δούλοις μὴ μετέχειν, τῷ αὐτῷ [3]
ἡγοῦντο, ᾧ ἐκείνους ἐκώλυον, τοὺς ἐλευθέρους

---

[1] τ' added by Blass.
[2] ἔργον Sauppe : ἔργον εἶναι ἡγοῦμαι MSS.
[3] τῷ αὐτῷ Blass : τῷ αὐτῷ νόμῳ or τούτῳ αὐτῷ λόγῳ MSS.

Now as for me, I neither find fault with love that is honourable, nor do I say that those who surpass in beauty are prostitutes. I do not deny that I myself have been a lover and am a lover to this day, nor do I deny that the jealousies and quarrels that commonly arise from the practice have happened in my case. As to the poems which they say I have composed, some I acknowledge, but as to others I deny that they are of the character that these people will impute to them, for they will tamper with them.

The distinction which I draw is this : to be in love with those who are beautiful and chaste is the experience of a kind-hearted and generous soul; but to hire for money and to indulge in licentiousness is the act of a man who is wanton and illbred. And whereas it is an honour to be the object of a pure love, I declare that he who has played the prostitute by inducement of wages is disgraced. How wide indeed is the distinction between these two acts and how great the difference, I will try to show you in what I shall next say. Our fathers, when they were laying down laws to regulate the habits of men and those acts that inevitably flow from human nature, forbade slaves to do those things which they thought ought to be done by free men. "A slave," says the law, "shall not take exercise or anoint himself in the wrestlingschools." It did not go on to add, "But the free man shall anoint himself and take exercise;" for when, seeing the good that comes from gymnastics, the lawgivers forbade slaves to take part, they thought that in prohibiting them they were by

139 προτρέπειν.¹ πάλιν ὁ αὐτὸς εἶπε νομοθέτης·
"Δοῦλον ἐλευθέρου παιδὸς μήτ' ἐρᾶν μήτ' ἐπακολουθεῖν, ἢ τύπτεσθαι τῇ δημοσίᾳ μάστιγι
πεντήκοντα πληγάς." ἀλλ' οὐ τὸν ἐλεύθερον
ἐκώλυσεν ἐρᾶν καὶ ὁμιλεῖν καὶ ἀκολουθεῖν, οὐδὲ
βλάβην τῷ παιδί, ἀλλὰ μαρτυρίαν σωφροσύνης
ἡγήσατο συμβαίνειν. ἀκύρου δ' οἶμαι καὶ ἀδυνάτου ἔτι ὄντος κρῖναι τὸν ὄντως εὔνουν καὶ μή, τὸν
ἐρῶντα σωφρονίζει, καὶ τοὺς τῆς φιλίας λόγους
εἰς τὴν φρονοῦσαν καὶ πρεσβυτέραν ἡλικίαν ἀνα-
βάλλεται· τὸ δ' ἐπακολουθεῖν καὶ ἐφορᾶν φρουρὰν
καὶ φυλακὴν σωφροσύνης ἡγήσατο εἶναι μεγίστην.
140 τοιγάρτοι τοὺς τῆς πόλεως μὲν εὐεργέτας, ταῖς δ'
ἀρεταῖς ὑπερενηνοχότας, Ἁρμόδιον καὶ Ἀριστογείτονα, ὁ σώφρων καὶ ἔννομος, εἴτε ἔρωτα εἴτε
ὄντινα² τρόπον χρὴ προσειπεῖν, τοιούτους ἐπαί-
δευσεν, ὥστε τοὺς ἐπαινοῦντας τὰ ἐκείνων ἔργα
καταδεεστέρους δοκεῖν εἶναι ἐν τοῖς ἐγκωμίοις
τῶν ἐκείνοις πεπραγμένων.
141 Ἐπειδὴ δὲ Ἀχιλλέως καὶ Πατρόκλου μέμνησθε
καὶ Ὁμήρου καὶ ἑτέρων ποιητῶν, ὡς τῶν μὲν
δικαστῶν ἀνηκόων παιδείας ὄντων, ὑμεῖς δὲ εὐ-
σχήμονές τινες³ καὶ περιφρονοῦντες ἱστορίᾳ τὸν
δῆμον, ἵν' εἰδῆτε ὅτι καὶ ἡμεῖς τι ἤδη ἠκούσαμεν
καὶ ἐμάθομεν, λέξομέν τι καὶ⁴ περὶ τούτων.
ἐπειδὴ γὰρ ἐπιχειροῦσι φιλοσόφων ἀνδρῶν μεμνῆσθαι καὶ καταφεύγειν ἐπὶ τοὺς εἰρημένους ἐν τῷ
μέτρῳ λόγους, θεωρήσατε ἀποβλέψαντες, ὦ ἄνδρες

---

¹ προτρέπειν Cobet : προτρέπειν ἐπὶ τὰ γυμνάσια MSS.
² ὄντινα added by Baiter and Sauppe.
³ τινες Cobet : τινες προσποιεῖσθε εἶναι MSS.
⁴ καὶ Hamaker : καὶ ἡμεῖς MSS

the same words inviting the free. Again, the same lawgiver said, "A slave shall not be the lover of a free boy nor follow after him, or else he shall receive fifty blows of the public lash." But the free man was not forbidden to love a boy, and associate with him, and follow after him, nor did the lawgiver think that harm came to the boy thereby, but rather that such a thing was a testimony to his chastity. But, I think, so long as the boy is not his own master and is as yet unable to discern who is a genuine friend, and who is not, the law teaches the lover self-control, and makes him defer the words of friendship till the other is older and has reached years of discretion; but to follow after the boy and to watch over him the lawgiver regarded as the best possible safeguard and protection for chastity. And so it was that those benefactors of the state, Harmodius and Aristogeiton, men pre-eminent for their virtues, were so nurtured by that chaste and lawful love— or call it by some other name than love if you like— and so disciplined, that when we hear men praising what they did, we feel that words are inadequate to the eulogy of their deeds.

But since you make mention of Achilles and Patroclus, and of Homer and the other poets—as though the jury were men innocent of education, while you are people of a superior sort, who feel yourselves quite beyond common folks in learning— that you may know that we too have before now heard and learned a little something, we shall say a word about this also. For since they undertake to cite wise men, and to take refuge in sentiments expressed in poetic measures, look, fellow citizens,

Ἀθηναῖοι, εἰς τοὺς ὁμολογουμένως ἀγαθοὺς καὶ
χρηστοὺς ποιητάς, ὅσον κεχωρίσθαι ἐνόμισαν
τοὺς σώφρονας καὶ τῶν ὁμοίων ἐρῶντας, καὶ τοὺς
142 ἀκρατεῖς ὧν οὐ χρὴ καὶ τοὺς ὑβριστάς. λέξω δὲ
πρῶτον μὲν περὶ Ὁμήρου, ὃν ἐν τοῖς πρεσβυτάτοις
καὶ σοφωτάτοις τῶν ποιητῶν εἶναι τάττομεν.
ἐκεῖνος γὰρ πολλαχοῦ μεμνημένος περὶ Πατρόκλου καὶ Ἀχιλλέως, τὸν μὲν ἔρωτα καὶ τὴν
ἐπωνυμίαν αὐτῶν τῆς φιλίας ἀποκρύπτεται, ἡγούμενος τὰς τῆς εὐνοίας ὑπερβολὰς καταφανεῖς εἶναι
143 τοῖς πεπαιδευμένοις τῶν ἀκροατῶν. λέγει γάρ
που Ἀχιλλεὺς ὀδυρόμενος τὸν τοῦ Πατρόκλου
θάνατον, ὡς ἕν τι τοῦτο τῶν λυπηροτάτων ἀνα-
μιμνησκόμενος, ὅτι τὴν ὑπόσχεσιν τὴν πρὸς τὸν
πατέρα τὸν Πατρόκλου Μενοίτιον ἄκων ἐψεύσατο·
ἐπαγγείλασθαι γὰρ εἰς Ὀποῦντα σῶν ἀπάξειν, εἰ
συμπέμψειεν αὐτὸν εἰς τὴν Τροίαν καὶ παρα-
καταθεῖτο αὐτῷ. ᾧ καταφανής ἐστιν, ὡς δι'
144 ἔρωτα τὴν ἐπιμέλειαν αὐτοῦ παρέλαβεν. ἔστι δὲ
τὰ ἔπη ἃ ἐγὼ νυνὶ μέλλω λέγειν·

Ὦ πόποι, ἦ ῥ' ἅλιον ἔπος ἔκβαλον ἤματι κείνῳ
θαρσύνων ἥρωα Μενοίτιον ἐν μεγάροισιν.
φῆν δέ οἱ εἰς Ὀπόεντα περικλυτὸν υἱὸν ἀπάξειν,
Ἴλιον ἐκπέρσαντα λαχόντα τε ληίδος αἶσαν.
ἀλλ' οὐ Ζεὺς ἄνδρεσσι νοήματα πάντα τελευτᾷ·
ἄμφω γὰρ πέπρωται ὁμοίην γαῖαν ἐρεύθειν.

145 οὐ τοίνυν ἐνταῦθα μόνον σχετλιάζων φαίνεται,
ἀλλ' οὕτως αὐτὸν ἰσχυρῶς ἐπένθησεν, ὥστε παρὰ

into the works of those who are confessedly good
and helpful poets, and see how far apart they
considered chaste men, who love their like, and
men who are wanton and overcome by forbidden
lusts. I will speak first of Homer, whom we
rank among the oldest and wisest of the poets.
Although he speaks in many places of Patroclus
and Achilles, he hides their love and avoids giving
a name to their friendship, thinking that the
exceeding greatness of their affection is manifest
to such of his hearers as are educated men. For
Achilles says somewhere in the course of his lament
for the death of Patroclus, as recalling one of the
greatest of sorrows, that unwillingly he has broken
the promise he had given to Menoetius, the father
of Patroclus; for he had promised to bring his son
back safe to Opus, if he would send him along
with him to Troy, and entrust him to his care.
It is evident from this that it was because of love
that he undertook to take care of him. But the
verses, which I am about to recite, are these:[1]

" Ah me, I rashly spoke vain words that day
  When in his halls I cheered Menoetius.
  I told the hero I would surely bring
  His famous son to Opus back again,
  When he had ravaged Ilium, and won
  His share of spoil. But Zeus does not fulfil
  To men their every hope. For fate decrees
  That both of us make red one spot of earth."

And indeed not only here do we see his deep dis-
tress, but he mourned so sorely for him, that

---

[1] *Iliad*, xviii. 324–29.

Θέτιδος τῆς αὑτοῦ μητρὸς προακούσας ὅτι μὴ
μετελθὼν μὲν τοὺς ἐχθρούς, ἀλλ' ἐάσας ἀτιμώρη-
τον τὸν τοῦ Πατρόκλου θάνατον, ἐπανελθὼν οἴκαδε
γηραιὸς ἐν τῇ αὑτοῦ πατρίδι ἀποθανεῖται, τιμωρη-
σάμενος δὲ διὰ ταχέων μέλλοι τὸν βίον τελευτᾶν,
εἵλετο τὴν τοῦ τεθνεῶτος πίστιν μᾶλλον ἢ τὴν
σωτηρίαν. οὕτω δὲ μεγαλοψύχως ἠπείγετο τὸν
φονέα τὸν ἐκείνου τιμωρήσασθαι, ὥστε πάντων
αὐτὸν παραμυθουμένων καὶ κελευόντων λούσασθαι
καὶ σῖτον προσενέγκασθαι, ἀπόμνυσι μηδὲν τούτων πράξειν, πρὶν ἂν τὴν τοῦ Ἕκτορος κεφαλὴν
146 ἐπὶ τὸν τοῦ Πατρόκλου τάφον ἐνέγκῃ. καθεύ-
δοντος δ' αὐτοῦ ἐπὶ τῇ πυρᾷ, ὥς φησιν ὁ ποιητής,
εἴδωλον ἐφίσταται Πατρόκλου, καὶ τοιούτων ἐπεμνήσθη καὶ τοιαῦτα ἐπέσκηψε τῷ Ἀχιλλεῖ, ἐφ'
οἷς καὶ δακρῦσαι καὶ ζηλῶσαι τὴν ἀρετὴν καὶ τὴν
φιλίαν ἄξιον αὐτῶν ἐστιν. ἐπισκήπτει μὲν γὰρ
αὐτῷ, προειπὼν ὅτι οὐδὲ ἐκεῖνος ἀπέχει μακρὰν
τῆς τοῦ βίου τελευτῆς, εἴ πως εἴη δυνατόν, προ-
διοικήσασθαι, ὅπως τὸν αὐτὸν τρόπον, ὥσπερ καὶ
ἐτράφησαν καὶ ἐβίωσαν ἐν τῷ αὐτῷ, οὕτω καὶ
τελευτησάντων αὐτῶν τὰ ὀστᾶ ἐν τῇ αὐτῇ σορῷ
147 κείσεται· ὀδυρόμενος δὲ καὶ τὰς διατριβὰς διεξιὼν
ἃς μετ' ἀλλήλων ζῶντες διέτριβον, λέγει ὅτι "Οὐκέτι περὶ τῶν μεγίστων, ὥσπερ τὸ πρότερον,
καθεζόμενοι μετ' ἀλλήλων μόνοι ἄπωθεν τῶν
ἄλλων φίλων βουλευσόμεθα," τὴν πίστιν οἶμαι
καὶ τὴν εὔνοιαν ποθεινοτάτην ἡγούμενος εἶναι.
ἵνα δὲ καὶ διὰ τοῦ μέτρου τὰς γνώμας ἀκούσητε
τοῦ ποιητοῦ, ἀναγνώσεται ὑμῖν ὁ γραμματεὺς τὰ
148 ἔπη τὰ περὶ τούτων ἃ Ὅμηρος πεποίηκε. λέγε
πρῶτον τὰ περὶ τῆς Ἕκτορος τιμωρίας.

although his mother Thetis cautioned him and told him that if he would refrain from following up his enemies and leave the death of Patroclus unavenged, he should return to his home and die an old man in his own land, whereas if he should take vengeance, he should soon end his life, he chose fidelity to the dead rather than safety. And with such nobility of soul did he hasten to take vengeance on the man who slew his friend, that when all tried to comfort him and urged him to bathe and take food, he swore that he would do none of these things until he had brought the head of Hector to the grave of Patroclus. And when he was sleeping by the funeral pyre, as the poet says, the ghost of Patroclus stood before him, and stirred such memories and laid upon Achilles such injunctions, that one may well weep, and envy the virtue and the friendship of these men. He prophesies that Achilles too is not far from the end of life, and enjoins upon him, if it be in any wise possible, to make provision that even as they had grown up and lived together, even so when they are dead their bones may lie in the same coffer. Weeping, and recalling the pursuits which they had followed together in life, he says, " Never again shall we sit together alone as in the old days, apart from our other friends, and take high counsel," feeling, I believe, that this fidelity and affection were what they would long for most. But that you may hear the sentiments of the poet in verse also, the clerk shall read to you the verses on this theme which Homer composed. Read first the verses about the vengeance on Hector.[1]

---

[1] *Iliad*, xviii. 333-35.

'Αλλ' ἐπεὶ οὖν, φίλ' ἑταῖρε, σεῦ ὕστερος εἰμ' ὑπὸ
    γαῖαν,
οὔ σε πρὶν κτεριῶ, πρίν γ' Ἕκτορος ἐνθάδ'
    ἐνεῖκαι
τεύχεα καὶ κεφαλήν, μεγαθύμου σεῖο φονῆος.

149 ἀναγίγνωσκε δὴ ἃ περὶ τοῦ ὁμοτάφους αὐτοὺς
γενέσθαι λέγει ἐν τῷ ὕπνῳ ὁ Πάτροκλος, καὶ περὶ
τῶν διατριβῶν, ἃς συνδιέτριβον ἀλλήλοις.

Οὐ γὰρ ἔτι ζωοί γε φίλων ἀπάνευθεν ἑταίρων
βουλὰς ἑζόμενοι βουλεύσομεν· ἀλλ' ἐμὲ μὲν Κὴρ
ἀμφέχανε στυγερή, ἥπερ λάχε γεινόμενόν περ·
καὶ δὲ σοὶ αὐτῷ μοῖρα, θεοῖς ἐπιείκελ' Ἀχιλλεῦ,
τείχει ὕπο Τρώων εὐηγενέων ἀπολέσθαι,
μαρνάμενον δηίοις Ἑλένης ἕνεκ' ἠυκόμοιο.
ἄλλο δέ τοι ἐρέω, σὺ δ' ἐνὶ φρεσὶ βάλλεο σῇσιν·
μὴ ἐμὰ σῶν ἀπάνευθε τιθήμεναι ὀστέ', Ἀχιλλεῦ,
ἀλλ' ἵνα πέρ σε καὶ αὐτὸν ὁμοίη γαῖα κεκεύθῃ,
χρυσέῳ ἐν ἀμφιφορεῖ, τόν τοι πόρε πότνια
    μήτηρ,
ὡς ὁμοῦ ἐτράφεμέν περ ἐν ὑμετέροισι δόμοισιν,
εὐτέ με τυτθὸν ἐόντα Μενοίτιος ἐξ Ὀπόεντος
ἤγαγεν ὑμέτερόνδ' ἀνδροκτασίης ὕπο λυγρῆς,
ἤματι τῷ, ὅτε παῖδα κατέκτανον Ἀμφιδάμαντος,
νήπιος, οὐκ ἐθέλων, ἀμφ' ἀστραγάλοισι χολω-
    θείς·
ἔνθα με δεξάμενος ἐν δώμασιν ἱππότα Πηλεὺς
ἔτρεφέ τ' ἐνδυκέως καὶ σὸν θεράποντ' ὀνόμηνεν·
ὣς δὲ καὶ ὀστέα νῶιν ὁμὴ σορὸς ἀμφικαλύπτοι.

150 ὡς τοίνυν ἐξῆν αὐτῷ σωθῆναι μὴ τιμωρησαμένῳ
τὸν τοῦ Πατρόκλου θάνατον, ἀνάγνωθι ἃ λέγει ἡ
Θέτις.

" But since, dear comrade, after thee I go
  Beneath the earth, I will not bury thee
  Till here I bring thee Hector's head and arms,
  The spoils of that proud prince who took thy life."

Now read what Patroclus says in the dream about
their common burial and about the intercourse that
they once had with one another.[1]

" For we no longer as in life shall sit
  Apart in sweet communion.   Nay, the doom
  Appointed me at birth has yawned for me.
  And fate has destined thee, Achilles, peer
  Of gods, to die beneath the wall of Troy's
  Proud lords, fighting for fair-haired Helen's sake.
  More will I say to thee, pray heed it well :
  Let not my bones be laid apart from thine,
  Achilles, but that thou and I may lie
  In common earth, I beg that I may share
  That golden coffer which thy mother brought
  To be thine own, even as we in youth
  Grew up together in thy home.   My sire
  Menoetius brought me, a little lad, from home,
  From Opus, to your house, for sad bloodshed,
  That day, when, all unwitting, in childish wrath
  About the dice, I killed Amphidamas' son.
  The knightly Peleus took me to his home
  And kindly reared me, naming me thy squire.
  So let one common coffer hide our bones."

Now to show that it was possible for him to have
been saved had he refrained from avenging the
death of Patroclus, read what Thetis says.[2]

---

[1] *Iliad*, xxiii. 77 ff.   [2] *Iliad*, xviii. 95 ff.

'Ωκύμορος δή μοι τέκος ἔσσεαι, οἷ' ἀγορεύεις·
αὐτίκα γάρ τοι ἔπειτα μεθ' "Εκτορα πότμος
ἑτοῖμος.
τὴν δ' αὖτε προσέειπε ποδάρκης δῖος 'Αχιλλεύς·
αὐτίκα τεθναίην, ἐπεὶ οὐκ ἄρ' ἔμελλον ἑταίρῳ
κτεινομένῳ ἐπαμῦναι, ὅ μοι πολὺ φίλτατος
ἔσκεν.

151 Ὁ τοίνυν οὐδενὸς ἧττον σοφὸς τῶν ποιητῶν
Εὐριπίδης, ἔν τι τῶν καλλίστων ὑπολαμβάνων
εἶναι τὸ σωφρόνως ἐρᾶν, ἐν εὐχῆς μέρει τὸν ἔρωτα
ποιούμενος λέγει που·

Ὁ δ' εἰς τὸ σῶφρον ἐπ' ἀρετήν τ' ἄγων ἔρως
ζηλωτὸς ἀνθρώποισιν, ὧν εἴην ἐγώ.

152 πάλιν τοίνυν ὁ αὐτὸς ἐν τῷ Φοίνικι ἀποφαίνεται,
ὑπὲρ τῆς γεγενημένης αὐτῷ πρὸς τὸν πατέρα διαβολῆς ἀπολογούμενος, καὶ ἀπεθίζων τοὺς ἀνθρώπους μὴ ἐξ ὑποψίας μηδ' ἐκ διαβολῆς, ἀλλ' ἐκ
τοῦ βίου, τὰς κρίσεις ποιεῖσθαι·

"Ηδη δὲ πολλῶν ἠρέθην λόγων κριτής,
καὶ πόλλ' ἁμιλληθέντα μαρτύρων ὕπο
τἀναντί' ἔγνων συμφορᾶς μιᾶς πέρι.
κἀγὼ μὲν οὕτω, χὥστις ἔστ' ἀνὴρ σοφός,
λογίζομαι τἀληθές, εἰς ἀνδρὸς φύσιν
σκοπῶν δίαιτάν θ',[1] ἥντιν' ἡμερεύεται.[2]

[1] θ' added by Boissonade from an ancient quotation.
[2] ἡμερεύεται Gainsford : ἐμπορεύεται MSS.

---

[1] The above quotations from Homer show considerable
variations from our MSS. of the poet. It seems that
Aeschines was using a very corrupt text of Homer. In
Iliad, xviii. 324 ff., there is variation in one word : in xviii.
333–35, in two words ; the long passage from xxiii. has two

" Ah me, my son, swift fate indeed will fall
    On thee, if thou dost speak such words.   For know,
    Swift after Hector's death fate brings thine own.
    To her divine Achilles, swift of foot,
    In turn made answer.   Straightway let me die,
    For when my friend was slain, my dearest friend,
    It was not granted me to succour him." [1]

Again, Euripides, a poet than whom none is wiser,
considering chaste love to be one of the most beautiful things, says somewhere,[2] making love a thing
to be prayed for :

" There is a love that makes men virtuous
    And chaste, an envied gift.   Such love I crave."

Again the same poet, in the *Phoenix*,[3] expresses his
opinion, making defence against false charges brought
by the father, and trying to persuade men habitually
to judge, not under the influence of suspicion or of
slander, but by a man's life :

" Many a time ere now have I been made
    The judge in men's disputes, and oft have heard
    For one event conflicting witnesses.
    And so, to find the truth, I, as do all
    Wise men, look sharp to see the character
    That marks the daily life, and judge by that.

lines that are not found in our MSS. of the *Iliad*, one line
that is changed in position, and four that show verbal
changes.   The quotation from xviii. 95–99 shows a verbal
change in one line, and an entire change in the last half-line.
    That widely divergent texts of Homer were in circulation
as early as the time of Aeschines has been proved by the
papyrus fragments.
    [2] In the lost *Sthenoboea*, No. 672, Nauck.
    [3] No. 812, Nauck.

ὅστις δ' ὁμιλῶν ἥδεται κακοῖς ἀνήρ,
οὐ πώποτ' ἠρώτησα, γιγνώσκων ὅτι
τοιοῦτός ἐσθ' οἷοισπερ ἥδεται[1] ξυνών.

153 σκέψασθε δέ, ὦ ἄνδρες Ἀθηναῖοι, τὰς γνώμας ἃς
ἀποφαίνεται ὁ ποιητής. ἤδη δὲ πολλῶν πραγμάτων φησὶ γεγενῆσθαι κριτής, ὥσπερ νῦν ὑμεῖς
δικασταί, καὶ τὰς κρίσεις οὐκ ἐκ τῶν μαρτυριῶν,
ἀλλ' ἐκ τῶν ἐπιτηδευμάτων καὶ τῶν ὁμιλιῶν, φησι
ποιεῖσθαι, ἐκεῖσε ἀποβλέπων, πῶς τὸν καθ' ἡμέραν βίον ζῇ ὁ κρινόμενος, καὶ ὅντινα τρόπον διοικεῖ
τὴν ἑαυτοῦ οἰκίαν, ὡς παραπλησίως αὐτὸν καὶ τὰ
τῆς πόλεως διοικήσοντα· καὶ τίσι χαίρει πλησιά-
ζων· καὶ τελευτῶν οὐκ ὤκνησεν ἀποφήνασθαι
τοιοῦτον εἶναι οἷοισπερ[2] ἥδεται ξυνών. οὐκοῦν
δίκαιον καὶ περὶ Τιμάρχου τοῖς αὐτοῖς ὑμᾶς Εὐρι-
154 πίδῃ χρήσασθαι λογισμοῖς. πῶς διῴκηκε τὴν
ἑαυτοῦ οὐσίαν; κατεδήδοκε τὰ πατρῷα καὶ[3] μεμι-
σθαρνηκὼς τῷ σώματι καὶ δωροδοκῶν δημοσίᾳ
πάντ' ἠφάνικεν, ὥστε μηδὲν ἄλλ' ἢ τὰς αἰσχύνας
αὐτῷ περιεῖναι. χαίρει δὲ τῷ συνών; Ἡγησάνδρῳ.
ὁ δ' Ἡγήσανδρος ἐκ τίνων ἐστὶν ἐπιτηδευμάτων;
ἐκ τούτων ἃ τὸν πράξαντα οἱ νόμοι ἀπαγορεύουσι
μὴ δημηγορεῖν. ἐγὼ δὲ τί λέγω κατὰ Τιμάρχου,
καὶ τίνα ποτ' ἐστὶν ἃ ἀντιγέγραμμαι; δημηγορεῖν[4]
Τίμαρχον πεπορνευμένον καὶ τὴν πατρῴαν οὐσίαν
κατεδηδοκότα. ὑμεῖς δὲ τί ὀμωμόκατε; ὑπὲρ αὐτῶν ψηφιεῖσθαι ὧν ἂν ἡ δίωξις ᾖ.

---

[1] ἐσθ' οἷοισπερ ἥδεται H. Wolf : ἔστιν οἷσπερ ἥδεται or ἔστιν
ἕκαστος οἷσπερ ἥδεται MSS.
[2] οἷοισπερ Taylor : οἷσπερ MSS.
[3] καὶ Hamaker : καὶ τὰ τῶν φίλων MSS.
[4] The MSS. have μὴ δημηγορεῖν : Blass brackets μὴ.

The man who loves companionship of knaves
I care not to interrogate. What need
Is there? I know too well the man is such
As is the company he loves to keep."

Examine the sentiments, fellow citizens, which the
poet expresses. He says that before now he has
been made judge of many cases, as you to-day are
jurors; and he says that he makes his decisions, not
from what the witnesses say, but from the habits and
associations of the accused; he looks at this, how the
man who is on trial conducts his daily life, and in
what manner he administers his own house, believing that in like manner he will administer the affairs
of the state also; and he looks to see with whom
he likes to associate. And, finally, he does not
hesitate to express the opinion that a man is like
those whose " company he loves to keep." It is
right, therefore, that in judging Timarchus you follow
the reasoning of Euripides. How has he administered his own property? He has devoured his
patrimony, he has consumed all the wages of his
prostitution and all the fruits of his bribery, so
that he has nothing left but his shame. With
whom does he love to be? Hegesandrus! And
what are Hegesandrus' habits? The habits that
exclude a man by law from the privilege of addressing the people. What is it that I say against
Timarchus, and what is the charge that I have
brought? That Timarchus addresses the people,
a man who has made himself a prostitute and has
consumed his patrimony. And what is the oath
that you have taken? To give your verdict on the
precise charges that are presented by the prosecution.

155 Ἵνα δὲ μὴ μακρολογῶ περὶ τῶν ποιητῶν διεξιών, ἀνδρῶν ἐρῶ πρεσβυτέρων καὶ γνωρίμων
ὑμῖν ὀνόματα καὶ μειρακίων καὶ παίδων, ὧν τοῖς
μὲν διὰ τὴν εὐπρέπειαν πολλοὶ γεγόνασιν ἐρασταί,
ἐνίοις δὲ τῶν ἐν ἡλικίᾳ ἔτι καὶ νῦν εἰσίν, ὧν οὐδεὶς
πώποτ' εἰς τὰς αὐτὰς αἰτίας ἀφῖκται Τιμάρχῳ·
καὶ πάλιν ὑμῖν ἀντιδιέξειμι ἀνθρώπων πεπορνευ-
μένων αἰσχρῶς καὶ φανερῶς ὀνόματα, ἵνα ὑμεῖς
ἀναμνησθέντες κατανείμητε εἰς τὴν προσήκουσαν
156 τάξιν Τίμαρχον. πρῶτον δὲ λέξω τὰ τῶν ἐλευθερίως[1] καὶ καλῶς βεβιωκότων ὀνόματα. γιγνώ-
σκετε, ὦ ἄνδρες Ἀθηναῖοι, Κρίτωνα τὸν Ἀστυόχου
καὶ Περικλείδην τὸν Περιθοίδην καὶ Πολεμαγένην
καὶ Πανταλέοντα τὸν Κλεαγόρου καὶ Τιμησίθεον
τὸν δρομέα, καλλίστους οὐ μόνον τῶν πολιτῶν,
ἀλλὰ καὶ τῶν Ἑλλήνων γεγενημένους, καὶ πλείστων καὶ σωφρονεστάτων τυχόντας ἐραστῶν·
157 ἀλλ' ὅμως οὐδεὶς πώποτε αὐτοὺς ἔψεξε. πάλιν
ἐκ τῶν μειρακίων καὶ τῶν ἐν παισὶν ἔτι καὶ νῦν
ὄντων πρῶτον μὲν τὸν ἀδελφιδοῦν τὸν Ἰφικράτους, υἱὸν δὲ Τεισίου τοῦ Ῥαμνουσίου, ὁμώνυμον
δὲ τοῦ νυνὶ κρινομένου·[2] ὃς εὐπρεπὴς ὢν ἰδεῖν
τοσοῦτον ἀπέχει τῶν αἰσχρῶν, ὥστε πρῴην ἐν
τοῖς κατ' ἀγροὺς Διονυσίοις κωμῳδῶν ὄντων ἐν
Κολλυτῷ, καὶ Παρμένοντος τοῦ κωμικοῦ ὑποκριτοῦ εἰπόντος τι πρὸς τὸν χορὸν ἀνάπαιστον, ἐν
ᾧ ἦν εἶναί τινας πόρνους μεγάλους Τιμαρχώδεις,
οὐδεὶς ὑπελάμβανεν εἰς τὸ μειράκιον, ἀλλ' εἰς σὲ
πάντες· οὕτω κληρονόμος εἶ τοῦ ἐπιτηδεύματος.

---

[1] ἐλευθερίως Weidner : ἐλευθέρων MSS.
[2] κρινομένου Cobet : κρινομένου Τιμάρχου MSS.

But not to dwell too long on the poets, I will
recite to you the names of older and well-known
men, and of youths and boys, some of whom have
had many lovers because of their beauty, and some
of whom, still in their prime, have lovers to-day, but
not one of whom ever came under the same accusations as Timarchus. Again, I will tell over to you in
contrast men who have prostituted themselves shamefully and notoriously, in order that by calling these
to mind you may place Timarchus where he belongs.
First I will name those who have lived the life of
free and honourable men. You know, fellow citizens,
Crito, son of Astyochus, Pericleides of Perithoedae,
Polemagenes, Pantaleon, son of Cleagoras, and
Timesitheus the runner, men who were the most
beautiful, not only among their fellow citizens, but
in all Hellas, men who counted many a man of
eminent chastity as lover; yet no man ever censured
them. And again, among the youths and those who
are still boys, first, you know the nephew of Iphicrates, the son of Teisias of Rhamnos, of the same
name as the defendant. He, beautiful to look upon,
is so far from reproach, that the other day at the
rural Dionysia when the comedies were being played
in Collytus, and when Parmenon the comic actor
addressed a certain anapaestic verse to the chorus,
in which certain persons were referred to as " big
Timarchian prostitutes," nobody thought of it as
aimed at the youth, but, one and all, as meant for
you, so unquestioned is your title to the practice.

πάλιν Ἀντικλέα τὸν σταδιοδρόμον καὶ Φειδίαν
τὸν ἀδελφὸν τὸν¹ Μελησίου. ἔτι δὲ εἰπεῖν ἔχων
πολλοὺς παύσομαι, ἵνα μὴ δοκῶ τὸν ἔπαινον
θεραπείᾳ τινὶ κατ' αὐτῶν ποιεῖσθαι.

158 Περὶ δὲ τῶν ὁμοτρόπων τῶν Τιμάρχου, φεύγων
τὰς ἀπεχθείας, ὧν ἥκιστά μοι μέλει μνησθήσομαι.
τίς γὰρ ὑμῶν τὸν ὀρφανὸν καλούμενον Διόφαντον
οὐκ οἶδεν, ὃς τὸν ξένον πρὸς τὸν ἄρχοντα ἀπήγαγεν,
ᾧ παρήδρευεν Ἀριστοφῶν ὁ Ἀζηνιεύς, ἐπαιτιασά-
μενος τέτταρας δραχμὰς αὐτὸν ὑπὲρ τῆς πράξεως
ταύτης ἀπεστερηκέναι, καὶ τοὺς νόμους λέγων, οἳ
κελεύουσι τὸν ἄρχοντα τῶν ὀρφανῶν ἐπιμελεῖσθαι,
τοὺς ὑπὲρ τῆς σωφροσύνης κειμένους αὐτὸς² ὑπερ-
βεβηκώς; ἢ τίς τῶν πολιτῶν οὐκ ἐδυσχέρανε³
Κηφισόδωρον τὸν τοῦ Μόλωνος καλούμενον καλ-
λίστην ὥραν ὄψεως ἀκλεέστατα διεφθαρκότα; ἢ
Μνησίθεον τὸν τοῦ μαγείρου καλούμενον; ἢ πολ-
159 λοὺς ἑτέρους, ὧν ἑκὼν ἐπιλανθάνομαι; οὐ γὰρ
ἐπεξελθεῖν αὐτῶν ἕκαστον κατ' ὄνομα πικρῶς βούλομαι, ἀλλὰ μᾶλλον τῶν τοιούτων ἀπορεῖν ἂν
εὐξαίμην ἐν τῷ λόγῳ διὰ τὴν πρὸς τὴν πόλιν
εὔνοιαν. ἐπειδὴ δὲ ἑκατέρων προελόμενοί τινας
διεξεληλύθαμεν, χωρὶς μὲν τοὺς διὰ σωφροσύνης
ἐρωμένους, χωρὶς δὲ τοὺς εἰς ἑαυτοὺς ἐξαμαρτά-
νοντας, ὑμεῖς ἤδη τοῦτ' ἐρωτηθέντες ἀποκρίνασθε
πρὸς ἐμέ, εἰς ὁποτέραν τὴν⁴ τάξιν Τίμαρχον
κατανέμετε, πότερα εἰς τοὺς ἐρωμένους ἢ εἰς τοὺς
πεπορνευμένους. οὐκοῦν μὴ καταλιπὼν ἣν εἵλου

---

¹ τὸν Bekker : τοῦ MSS.
² αὐτὸς Bekker : the MSS. omit or have αὐτούς.
³ ἐδυσχέρανε Blass : ἐδυσχέραινε MSS.
⁴ τὴν added by Blass.

Again, Anticles, the stadium runner, and Pheidias, the brother of Melesias. Although I could name many others, I will stop, lest I seem to be in a way courting their favour by my praise.

But as to those men who are kindred spirits with Timarchus, for fear of arousing their enmity I will mention only those toward whom I am utterly in-different. Who of you does not know Diophantes, called "the orphan," who arrested the foreigner and brought him before the archon, whose associate on the bench was Aristophon of Azenia?[1] For Diophantes accused the foreigner of having cheated him out of four drachmas in connection with this practice, and he cited the laws that command the archon to protect orphans, when he himself had violated the laws that enjoin chastity. Or what Athenian was not indig-nant at Cephisodorus, called Molon's son, for having ruined his surpassing beauty by a most infamous life? Or Mnesitheus, known as the cook's son? Or many others, whose names I am willing to forget? For I have no desire to tell over the whole list of them one by one in a spirit of bitterness. Nay, rather I could wish that I might be at a loss for such examples in my speech, for I love my city. But since we have selected for special mention a few from each of the two classes, on the one side men who have been loved with a chaste love, and on the other men who sin against themselves, now let me ask you this question, and pray answer me: To which class do you assign Timarchus— to those who are loved, or to those who are prostitutes? [*Cries of "To the prostitutes."*] You see, Timarchus, you are

---

[1] The archon eponymus is meant. When sitting as presi-dent of a court he was assisted by two advisers, πάρεδροι.

συμμορίαν αὐτομολήσῃς εἰς τὰς τῶν ἐλευθέρων διατριβάς.

160 Ἐὰν δ' ἐπιχειρῶσι λέγειν, ὡς οὐχ ἡταίρηκεν ὅστις μὴ κατὰ συγγραφὰς ἐμισθώθη, καὶ γραμματεῖον καὶ μάρτυρας ἀξιῶσί με τούτων παρασχέσθαι, πρῶτον μὲν τοὺς περὶ τῆς ἑταιρήσεως νόμους μέμνησθε, ἐν οἷς οὐδαμοῦ μνείαν ὁ νομοθέτης περὶ συνθηκῶν πεποίηται. οὐ γάρ, εἰ κατὰ γραμματεῖόν τις ἑαυτὸν κατῄσχυνε, τοῦτ' ἐξήτασεν, ἀλλὰ παντελῶς, ὅπως ἂν ἡ πρᾶξις γένηται, τὸν πράξαντα κελεύει μὴ μετέχειν τῶν τῆς πόλεως κοινῶν. εἰκότως· ὅστις γὰρ νέος ὢν ἀπέστη δι' αἰσχρὰς ἡδονὰς τῆς εἰς τὰ καλὰ φιλοτιμίας, τοῦτον οὐκ ᾤήθη δεῖν πρεσβύτερον

161 γενόμενον[1] ἐπίτιμον εἶναι. ἔπειτα καὶ τὴν εὐήθειαν τοῦ λόγου τούτου ῥᾴδιόν ἐστιν ἐξετάσαι. πάντες γὰρ ἂν τοῦθ' ὁμολογήσαιμεν, ὅτι τὰς συνθήκας τῆς πρὸς ἀλλήλους ἀπιστίας ἕνεκα ποιούμεθα, ἵνα ὁ μὴ παραβὰς τὰ γεγραμμένα δίκην λάβῃ τῇ ψήφῳ παρὰ τοῦ παραβάντος. οὐκοῦν, εἴπερ τὸ πρᾶγμα δίκης προσδεῖται, τοῖς κατὰ γραμματεῖον ἡταιρηκόσιν, ἂν ἀδικῶνται, ἡ τῶν νόμων ὡς[2] οὗτοί φασιν ἐπικουρία καταλείπεται. καὶ τίς ἂν λόγος ἑκατέρου φανείη; μὴ γὰρ ὑπ' ἐμοῦ λεγόμενον, ἀλλὰ γιγνόμενον τὸ πρᾶγμα νομίσαθ' ὁρᾶν.

162 Ἔστω γὰρ ὁ μὲν μισθωσάμενος δίκαιος εἰς τὸ πρᾶγμα, ὁ δὲ μισθωθεὶς ἄδικος καὶ μὴ βέβαιος, ἢ

---

[1] γενόμενον Hamaker: γενόμενον ὁ τοὺς νόμους εἰσφέρων MSS.

[2] ὡς Bremi: ὧν MSS.

not to be permitted to desert the company which you have chosen and go over to the ways of free men.

But if they shall undertake to say that no man has been a prostitute unless he was hired under contract, and if they demand that I produce writings and witnesses, I ask you first to call to mind the laws concerning prostitution; in them the lawgiver has nowhere made mention of contracts, for he did not inquire whether it was by contract that a person had defiled himself, but in comprehensive terms, no matter how the deed is done, he commands that the man who did it shall take no part in public affairs. And he is right; for the man who in his youth was led by shameful indulgence to surrender honourable ambition, that man, he believed, ought not in later life to be possessed of the citizen's privileges. In the second place, it is easy to demonstrate the folly of this plea. For we should all acknowledge this, that we enter into contracts because we do not trust one another, the object being that the party who has not violated the written terms may receive satisfaction by verdict of the courts from the one who has. If, therefore, this business needs the help of the courts, those who have served as prostitutes by contract, in case they are wronged, have left them, according to the argument of the defendants, recourse to the protection of the laws. And what would be the plea that either side would advance? Imagine the case, not as something that I am telling you, but as going on before your eyes.

Assume that the man who hired the other is in the right as regards the fact, and the man who

πάλιν τοὐναντίον ὁ μὲν μισθωθεὶς μέτριος καὶ
ποιῶν τὰ ὡμολογημένα, ὁ δὲ τὴν ἡλικίαν προλαβὼν
καὶ μισθωσάμενος ἐψεύσθω· καὶ δικαστὰς ὑμᾶς
αὐτοὺς ὑπολάβετε καθῆσθαι. οὐκοῦν ὁ πρεσβύ-
τερος, ἀποδοθέντος τοῦ ὕδατος αὐτῷ καὶ λόγου,
κατηγορῶν[1] μετὰ σπουδῆς, βλέπων δηλονότι πρὸς
163 ὑμᾶς, λέξει· "'Εμισθωσάμην, ὦ ἄνδρες 'Αθηναῖοι,
Τίμαρχον ἑταιρεῖν ἐμαυτῷ κατὰ τὸ γραμματεῖον τὸ
παρὰ Δημοσθένει κείμενον·" οὐδὲν γὰρ κωλύει
οὕτως εἰρῆσθαι· "ὁ δ' οὐ ποιεῖ μοι τὰ ὡμολογημένα." καὶ ταῦτ' ἤδη διέξεισι δηλονότι πρὸς τοὺς
δικαστάς, λέγων ἃ χρὴ τὸν τοιοῦτον ποιεῖν. ἔπειτα
οὐ καταλευσθήσεται ὁ μισθούμενος τὸν 'Αθηναῖον
παρὰ τοὺς νόμους, καὶ προσοφλὼν ἄπεισιν ἐκ
τοῦ δικαστηρίου οὐ τὴν ἐπωβελίαν μόνον, ἀλλὰ
καὶ πολλὴν[2] ὕβριν;

164 'Αλλ' οὐχ οὗτος, ἀλλ' ὁ μισθωθεὶς δικάζεται.
λεγέτω δὴ παρελθών, ἢ[3] ὁ σοφὸς Βάταλος ὑπὲρ
αὐτοῦ, ἵν' εἰδῶμεν τί ποτ' ἐρεῖ. "'Άνδρες δικασταί,
ἐμισθώσατό με ἑταιρεῖν αὐτῷ ἀργυρίου ὁστισδη-
ποτοῦν" οὐδὲν γὰρ διαφέρει·[4] "κἀγὼ μὲν ἅπαντα
καὶ πεποίηκα καὶ ἔτι καὶ νῦν ποιῶ κατὰ τὸ γραμ

---

[1] κατηγορῶν Reiske : MSS. vary between κατηγορίαν, κατηγορίας, and κατηγοριῶν.
[2] πολλὴν Blass (Scholiast) : ἄλλην MSS.
[3] ἢ added by Blass.
[4] διαφέρει Hamaker : διαφέρει οὕτως εἰρῆσθαι MSS.

---

[1] Each speaker was given a definite time allowance,
measured by the water-clock ; hence the expression, ἀποδοθέντος τοῦ ὕδατος, *when the water is given him.*

was hired is in the wrong and has no ground to
stand on; or assume the opposite, that the man
who was hired is fair and fulfils his engagement,
but the man who has plucked the flower of his
youth and hired him has broken his word; then
imagine that you yourselves are sitting as jury.
Now the elder man, when his time allowance
and the right to speak are given him,[1] will press
his accusation vigorously, and looking, of course,
into your faces, he will say, "Fellow citizens,
I hired Timarchus to serve me as a prostitute according to the contract that is deposited with
Demosthenes"—there is no reason why that statement might not be made !—"but he fails to
carry out his engagement with me." And now,
of course, he proceeds to describe this engagement
to the jury, telling what it is that a man of that
sort is expected to do. Thereupon will not the
man be stoned who has hired an Athenian contrary
to the laws, and will he not leave the court-room
not only sentenced to pay his fine,[2] but also convicted of wanton outrage?

But suppose it is not this man, but the one who
was hired, that is bringing suit. Now let him come
forward and speak—or else let the wise Batalus
speak in his stead, that we may know what he will
find to say ! "Gentlemen of the jury, so-and-so"
—it does not matter who—"hired me to be his
prostitute for money, and I have done, and still
continue to do, according to the terms of the con-

[2] In certain classes of private suits, if the plaintiff failed
to receive one-fifth of the votes of the jury, he had to pay
to the defendant one-sixth of the sum for which he had
sued (one obol in the drachma (= six obols), hence the name
ἐπωβελία).

ματεῖον, ἃ χρὴ ποιεῖν τὸν ἑταιροῦντα· οὗτος δὲ
ὑπερβαίνει τὰς συνθήκας." ἔπειτ' οὐ πολλὴ
κραυγὴ παρὰ τῶν δικαστῶν αὐτῷ ἀπαντήσεται;
τίς γὰρ οὐκ ἐρεῖ· "'Επειτα ἐμβάλλεις [1] εἰς τὴν
ἀγοράν, ἢ στεφανοῖ, ἢ πράττεις τι τῶν αὐτῶν
ἡμῖν;" οὔκουν οὐδὲν ὄφελος τῆς συγγραφῆς.

165   Πόθεν οὖν ἴσχυκε καὶ σύνηθες γεγένηται λέγειν,
ὡς κατὰ γραμματεῖον ἤδη τινὲς ἡταίρησαν, ἐρῶ.[2]
ἀνὴρ εἷς τῶν πολιτῶν (τὸ δ' ὄνομα οὐ λέξω· τὰς
γὰρ ἀπεχθείας φεύγω) οὐδὲν προϊδόμενος ὧν ὀλίγῳ
πρότερον ἐγὼ διεξῆλθον πρὸς ὑμᾶς, λέγεται κατὰ
συνθήκας ἡταιρηκέναι τὰς παρ' 'Αντικλεῖ κει-
μένας· οὐκ ὢν δ' [3] ἰδιώτης, ἀλλὰ πρὸς τὰ κοινὰ
προσιὼν καὶ λοιδορίαις περιπίπτων, εἰς συνήθειαν
ἐποίησε τοῦ λόγου τούτου τὴν πόλιν καταστῆναι,
καὶ διὰ τοῦτο ἐρωτῶσί τινες, εἰ κατὰ γραμματεῖον
ἡ πρᾶξις γεγένηται.   ὁ δὲ νομοθέτης οὐχ ὅπως τὸ
πρᾶγμα γεγένηται ἐφρόντισεν, ἀλλ' ἐὰν ὁπωσοῦν
μίσθωσις γένηται, κατέγνωκε τοῦ πράξαντος
αἰσχύνην.

166   'Αλλ' ὅμως οὕτω σαφῶς τούτων διωρισμένων,
πολλαὶ παρεμβολαὶ λόγων ὑπὸ Δημοσθένους εὑρε-
θήσονται.   καὶ ταῖς μὲν ὑπὲρ [4] τοῦ πράγματος
κακοηθείαις λεγομέναις ἧττον ἄν τις ἀγανακτή-
σειεν· ἃ δὲ ἔξωθεν ἐπεισάξεται λυμαινόμενος τὰ
τῆς πόλεως δίκαια, ἐπὶ τούτοις ἄξιόν ἐστιν ὀργι-

---

[1] ἐμβάλλεις Bremi : ἐμβαλλεῖς, ἐμβαλεῖς, or ἐμβάλλῃ MSS.
[2] ἐρῶ Blass : ἤδη ἐρῶ MSS.   [3] δ' added by Bekker.
[4] ὑπὲρ H. Wolf : ὑπὸ MSS.

tract, all that a prostitute is under obligation to do; he, however, fails to fulfil the agreement." Will he not immediately have to face a loud protest from the jurors? For who will not say, "And then do you thrust yourself into the market-place, do you put on a garland,[1] do you attempt to do anything else that the rest of us do?" His contract, you see, is of no use to him.

Now let me tell you how it happens that it has become the prevailing custom to say, that persons have in the past become prostitutes "under written contract." One of our citizens (I will not name him, for I have no desire to make myself hated), foreseeing none of the consequences which I have just described to you, is said to have served as prostitute according to a contract deposited with Anticles. Now, since he was not a private citizen, but active in politics and subject to scurrilous attack, he caused the city to become accustomed to this expression, and that is the reason why some men ask whether in a given case the practice has been "by written contract." But the lawgiver did not care how the thing was brought about; on the contrary, if there is a letting for hire in any way whatsoever, the man who does the deed is condemned by him to disgrace.

But nevertheless, although all this is so plainly defined, many irrelevant arguments will be invented by Demosthenes. Possibly, when he sticks to his subject, we might be less indignant with him for the animosity he shows; but when, to the injury of our national rights, he foists in matters that do not belong to the case, then one may well be

---

[1] See the note on § 19.

σθῆναι. πολὺς μὲν γὰρ ὁ Φίλιππος ἔσται,
ἀναμειχθήσεται δὲ καὶ τὸ τοῦ παιδὸς ὄνομα Ἀλεξάνδρου. καὶ γὰρ πρὸς τοῖς ἄλλοις κακοῖς ἄμου-
σός τις οὗτος καὶ ἀπαίδευτος ἄνθρωπός ἐστι.

167 τὸ μὲν γὰρ εἰς τὸν Φίλιππον τῷ λόγῳ πλημμελεῖν
ἀμαθὲς μὲν καὶ ἄκαιρον, ἔλαττον δ᾽ οὐ μέλλω
λέγειν ἁμάρτημα· ὁμολογουμένως γὰρ εἰς ἄνδρα,
καίπερ οὐκ ὢν αὐτὸς ἀνήρ, τὰς βλασφημίας
ποιήσεται· ὅταν δὲ ταῖς εἰς τὸν παῖδα πεπρα-
γματευμέναις μεταφοραῖς ὀνομάτων αἰσχρὰς ὑποψίας παρεμβάλλῃ, καταγέλαστον τὴν πόλιν

168 ποιεῖ. ὡς γὰρ τὰς ἐμὰς εὐθύνας βλάπτων, ἃς
ὑπὲρ τῆς πρεσβείας μέλλω διδόναι, φησί με, ὅτ᾽
αὐτὸς πρώην ὑπὲρ τοῦ παιδὸς Ἀλεξάνδρου διεξῄει,
ὡς ἔν τῳ πότῳ ἡμῶν κιθαρίζοι καὶ λέγοι ῥήσεις
τινὰς καὶ ἀντικρούσεις πρὸς ἕτερον παῖδα, καὶ
περὶ τούτων ἃ δή ποτε αὐτὸς ἐτύγχανε γιγνώσκων
πρὸς τὴν βουλὴν ἀπεφήνατο, οὐχ ὡς συμπρεσβευ-
τήν, ἀλλ᾽ ὡς συγγενῆ τοῖς εἰς τὸν παῖδα σκώμ-

169 μασιν ἀγανακτῆσαι. ἐγὼ δ᾽ Ἀλεξάνδρῳ μὲν
εἰκότως διὰ τὴν ἡλικίαν οὐ διείλεγμαι, Φίλιππον
δὲ νῦν μὲν διὰ τὴν τῶν λόγων εὐφημίαν ἐπαινῶ· ἐὰν
δ᾽ ὁ αὐτὸς ἐν τοῖς πρὸς ἡμᾶς ἔργοις γένηται, οἷος
νῦν ἐστιν ἐν τοῖς ἐπαγγέλμασιν, ἀσφαλῆ καὶ
ῥάδιον τὸν καθ᾽ αὑτοῦ ποιήσεται ἔπαινον. ἐπετί-
μησα δ᾽ ἐν τῷ βουλευτηρίῳ Δημοσθένει οὐ τὸν

---

[1] See the Introduction to Speech II., p. 159.

angry. Philip will be largely in evidence, and the name of Philip's son Alexander is going to be mixed up in it. For in addition to all the rest that is bad in him, this Demosthenes is an ill-mannered and boorish sort of person. His offensive talk against Philip is foolish and out of place, but not so serious a mistake as that which I am about to mention. For confessedly he will be making his slanderous charges against a man—he who is himself no man. But when he insinuates shameful suspicions against the boy, by deliberately applying to him words of double meaning, he makes our city ridiculous. For, under the impression that he is hurting me with reference to the accounting which I am about to render for my service on the embassy,[1] he says that when the other day he himself was describing the boy Alexander, telling how at a certain banquet of ours he played the cithara, reciting certain passages in which there were thrusts at another boy, and when he reported to the senate what he himself happened to know about the incident, I got angry at his jests at the expense of the boy,[2] as though I were not merely a member of the embassy, but one of the boy's own family. Now I naturally have had no conversation with Alexander, because of his youth, but Philip I do praise now because of his auspicious words, and if in what he does toward us in the future he shall fulfil the promise of what he now says, he will make praise of him a safe and easy thing. I did, indeed, rebuke Demosthenes in the senate-chamber, not because

[2] The words of double meaning that Aeschines says Demosthenes applied to the boy Alexander would be connected with the story of this "playing" and "reciting."

παῖδα ἐκθεραπεύων, ἀλλ' ἐὰν τὰ τοιαῦτα ἀπο-
δέχησθε, ὁμοίαν νομίζων τὴν πόλιν φανήσεσθαι
τῇ τοῦ λέγοντος ἀκοσμίᾳ.

170   "Ολως δέ, ὦ ἄνδρες 'Αθηναῖοι, τὰς ἔξωθεν τοῦ
πράγματος ἀπολογίας μὴ προσδέχεσθε, πρῶτον
μὲν τῶν ὅρκων ἕνεκα οὓς ὠμόσατε, δεύτερον δὲ
ὑπὲρ τοῦ μὴ παρακρουσθῆναι ὑπὸ ἀνθρώπου
τεχνίτου λόγων. μικρὸν δ' ἄνωθεν ἄρξομαι
διδάσκειν ὑμᾶς. Δημοσθένης γάρ, ἐπειδὴ τὴν
πατρῴαν οὐσίαν ἀνήλωσε, περιῄει[1] τὴν πόλιν
θηρεύων νέους πλουσίους,[2] ὧν οἱ μὲν πατέρες
ἐτετελευτήκεσαν, αἱ δὲ μητέρες διῴκουν τὰς οὐσίας. πολλοὺς δ' ὑπερβὰς ἑνὸς τῶν δεινὰ πεπον-
171 θότων μνησθήσομαι. κατιδὼν γὰρ οἰκίαν πλουσίαν καὶ οὐκ εὐνομουμένην, ἧς ἡγεμὼν μὲν ἦν γυνὴ
μέγα φρονοῦσα καὶ νοῦν οὐκ ἔχουσα, νεανίσκος
δὲ ὀρφανὸς ἡμιμανὴς διεχείριζε τὴν οὐσίαν, 'Αρί-
σταρχος ὁ τοῦ Μόσχου, τούτου προσποιησάμενος
ἐραστὴς εἶναι, καὶ τὸ μειράκιον εἰς τὴν φιλανθρωπίαν ταύτην προκαλεσάμενος,[3] ἐλπίδων κενῶν
ἐμπλήσας, ὡς αὐτίκα δὴ μάλα τῶν ῥητόρων
172 πρωτεύσοντα, κατάλογον ἀποφαίνων, τοιούτων
εἰσηγητὴς αὐτῷ καὶ διδάσκαλος ἔργων ἐγένετο,
ἐξ ὧν ἐκεῖνος μὲν φεύγει τὴν πατρίδα, οὗτος δ'
αὐτοῦ τὰ τῆς φυγῆς ἐφόδια προλαβὼν τρία

[1] περιῄει περὶ MSS.: Blass brackets περὶ.
[2] πλουσίους Cobet : πλουσίους ὀρφανούς MSS.
[3] προκαλεσάμενος Linder : προσκαλεσάμενος MSS.

I was courting the favour of the boy, but because I felt that if you should listen to such words as his, the city would show itself as ill-behaved as the speaker.

But, fellow citizens, I beg you not to accept their irrelevant pleas at all, in the first place for the sake of the oaths which you have sworn, in the second place that you may not be misled by a fellow who makes a trade of the manipulation of words. But I will go back a little way for your instruction. Demosthenes, after he had spent his patrimony, went up and down the city, hunting rich young fellows whose fathers were dead, and whose mothers were administering their property. I will omit many instances, and will mention only one of those who were outrageously treated. He discovered a household that was rich and ill-managed, the head of which was a woman, proud and of poor judgment. A fatherless young man, half crazy, was managing the estate, Aristarchus, son of Moschus. Demosthenes, pretending to be a lover of his, invited the young man to this intimacy, filling him up with empty hopes, assuring him that without any delay whatever he should become the foremost man in public life, and he showed him a list of names.[1] So he became prompter and teacher of the young man in conduct which has made Aristarchus an exile from his fatherland, while Demosthenes, getting hold of the money that was to support him in his banishment, has cheated him out of three talents, and,

[1] Doubtless a list of young men who had studied oratory with Demosthenes and become successful public men. So the Scholiast.

τάλαντα ἀπεστέρηκε, Νικόδημος δ' ὁ ᾿Αφιδναῖος
ὑπ' ᾿Αριστάρχου τετελεύτηκε βιαίῳ θανάτῳ,
ἐκκοπεὶς ὁ δείλαιος ἀμφοτέρους τοὺς ὀφθαλμοὺς
καὶ τὴν γλῶτταν ἐκτμηθείς,¹ ᾗ ἐπαρρησιάζετο
πιστεύων τοῖς νόμοις καὶ ὑμῖν.

173 Ἔπειθ' ὑμεῖς, ὦ ἄνδρες ᾿Αθηναῖοι, Σωκράτην
μὲν τὸν σοφιστὴν ἀπεκτείνατε, ὅτι Κριτίαν ἐφάνη
πεπαιδευκώς, ἕνα τῶν τριάκοντα τῶν τὸν δῆμον
καταλυσάντων, Δημοσθένης δ' ὑμῖν ἑταίρους ἐξαιρήσεται,² ὁ τηλικαύτας τιμωρίας λαμβάνων παρὰ
τῶν ἰδιωτῶν καὶ δημοτικῶν ἀνθρώπων ὑπὲρ τῆς
ἰσηγορίας; ᾧ παρακεκλημένοι τινὲς τῶν μαθητῶν
ἥκουσιν ἐπὶ τὴν ἀκρόασιν· κατεπαγγέλλεται γὰρ
πρὸς αὐτούς, ἐργολαβῶν ἐφ' ὑμᾶς, ὡς ἐγὼ πυνθάνομαι, λήσειν μεταλλάξας τὸν ἀγῶνα καὶ τὴν
174 ὑμετέραν ἀκρόασιν, καὶ περιστήσειν τῷ μὲν φεύ-
γοντι³ θαρρεῖν, ὅταν αὐτὸς δεῦρο παρέλθῃ, ἐκπε-
πλῆχθαι δὲ τῷ κατηγόρῳ καὶ πεφοβῆσθαι περὶ
αὐτοῦ, τοσούτους δὲ καὶ τηλικούτους ἐκκαλεῖσθαι⁴
παρὰ τῶν δικαστῶν θορύβους, παρεμβάλλων τὰς
ἐμὰς δημηγορίας καὶ ψέγων τὴν εἰρήνην τὴν δι'
ἐμοῦ καὶ Φιλοκράτους γεγενημένην, ὥστ' οὐδὲ
ἀπαντήσεσθαί με ἐπὶ τὸ δικαστήριον ἀπολογησό-
μενον, ὅταν τῆς πρεσβείας τὰς εὐθύνας διδῶ, ἀλλ'

¹ ἐκτμηθείς Blass (Suidas under the word παρρησία):
ἀποτμηθείς MSS.
² ἐξαιρήσεται Blass' conjecture, confirmed by the Geneva
papyrus: ἐξαιτήσεται MSS.
³ φεύγοντι Blass (Suidas under the word δεῦρο): φυγόντι
MSS.
⁴ ἐκκαλεῖσθαι Cobet: ἐκκαλέσεσθαι or ἐκκαλέσασθαι MSS.

¹ The murdered man, Nicodemus, was a friend and supporter of Demosthenes' influential personal and political

at the hands of Aristarchus, Nicodemus of Aphidna
has met a violent death, poor man! after having
had both eyes knocked out, and that tongue cut
off with which he had been wont to speak out
freely, trusting in the laws and in you.[1]

Did you put to death Socrates the sophist, fellow citizens, because he was shown to have been
the teacher of Critias, one of the Thirty who put
down the democracy, and after that, shall Demosthenes succeed in snatching companions of his own
out of your hands, Demosthenes, who takes such
vengeance on private citizens and friends of the
people for their freedom of speech? At his invitation some of his pupils are here in court to listen
to him. For with an eye to business at your expense,[2] he promises them, as I understand, that he
will juggle the issue and cheat your ears, and you
will never know it; assuring them that, as soon as
he shall come forward to speak, the situation shall
be reversed, the defendant filled with confidence,
the plaintiff confounded, frightened for his own
safety; and that he will lug in my speeches, and
find fault with the peace which was brought about
through Philocrates and myself, until he shall call
out such bursts of applause from the jurors that
I will not even face him in the court-room to
defend myself when I render account of my service on the embassy, but will consider myself lucky

---

[1] enemies, Meidias and Eubulus, and had taken part in an
unsuccessful attempt to convict Demosthenes of desertion in
the Euboean campaign. When he was found murdered,
Meidias made repeated attempts to throw suspicion on
Demosthenes.

[2] Success in this case will increase Demosthenes' reputation, and bring him more pupils and tuition fees.

ἀγαπήσειν, ἐὰν μετρίῳ τιμήματι περιπέσω καὶ μὴ
175 θανάτῳ ζημιῶμαι. μηδενὶ δὴ τρόπῳ καθ᾽ ὑμῶν
αὐτῶν γέλωτα τῷ σοφιστῇ καὶ διατριβὴν παρά-
σχητε, ἀλλ᾽ ὑπολαμβάνεθ᾽ ὁρᾶν εἰσεληλυθότα ἀπὸ
τοῦ δικαστηρίου οἴκαδε καὶ σεμνυνόμενον ἐν τῇ
τῶν μειρακίων διατριβῇ, καὶ διεξιόντα, ὡς εὖ τὸ
πρᾶγμα ὑφείλετο τῶν δικαστῶν· "Ἀπαγαγὼν γὰρ
αὐτοὺς ἀπὸ τῶν περὶ Τίμαρχον αἰτιῶν, ἐπέστησα
φέρων ἐπὶ τὸν κατήγορον καὶ Φίλιππον καὶ Φωκέας, καὶ φόβους ἐπήρτησα τοῖς ἀκροωμένοις,
ὥσθ᾽ ὁ μὲν φεύγων κατηγόρει, ὁ δὲ κατηγορῶν
ἐκρίνετο, οἱ δὲ δικασταί, ὧν μὲν ἦσαν κριταί,[1]
ἐπελάθοντο, ὧν δ᾽ οὐκ ἦσαν,[2] περὶ τούτων ἤκουον."
176 ὑμέτερον δ᾽ ἐστὶν ἔργον πρὸς ταῦτα ἀντιτετάχθαι,
καὶ πανταχῇ παρακολουθοῦντας μηδαμῇ παρεκ-
κλίνειν αὐτὸν ἐᾶν, μηδὲ τοῖς ἐξαγωνίοις[3] λόγοις
διισχυρίζεσθαι· ἀλλ᾽ ὥσπερ ἐν ταῖς ἱπποδρομίαις
εἰς τὸν τοῦ πράγματος αὐτὸν δρόμον εἰσελαύνετε.
κἂν ταῦτα ποιῆτε, οὐ καταφρονηθήσεσθε, καὶ τὴν
αὐτὴν ἕξετε γνώμην νομοθετοῦντες καὶ δικάζοντες·
εἰ δὲ μή, δόξετε μελλόντων μὲν γίγνεσθαι τῶν
ἀδικημάτων προαισθάνεσθαι καὶ ὀργίζεσθαι, γεγονότων δὲ οὐκέτι φροντίζειν.
177 Ὡς δ᾽ ἐν κεφαλαίῳ εἰρῆσθαι, ἐὰν μὲν κολάζητε
τοὺς ἀδικοῦντας, ἔσονται ὑμῖν οἱ νόμοι καλοὶ καὶ
κύριοι, ἐὰν δ᾽ ἀφιῆτε, καλοὶ μέν, κύριοι δ᾽ οὐκέτι.
ὧν δ᾽ ἕνεκα ταῦτα λέγω, οὐκ ὀκνήσω πρὸς ὑμᾶς
παρρησιάσασθαι. ἔσται δ᾽ ὁ λόγος ἐπὶ παραδεί-
γματος. διὰ τί οἴεσθε, ὦ ἄνδρες Ἀθηναῖοι, τοὺς

---

[1] κριταί Herwerden : δικασταί MSS.
[2] ἦσαν Franke, Herwerden : ἦσαν κριταί MSS.
[3] ἐξαγωνίοις Blass (Suidas) : ἔξω τοῦ ἀγῶνος MSS.

if I get off with a moderate fine instead of being punished with death. So I do beg you by all means not to furnish this sophist with laughter and patronage at your expense. Imagine that you see him when he gets home from the court-room, putting on airs in his lectures to his young men, and telling how successfully he stole the case away from the jury. "I carried the jurors off bodily from the charges brought against Timarchus, and set them on the accuser, and Philip, and the Phocians, and I suspended such terrors before the eyes of the hearers that the defendant began to be the accuser, and the accuser to be on trial; and the jurors forgot what they were to judge; and what they were not to judge, to that they listened." But it is your business to take your stand against this sort of thing, and following close on his every step, to let him at no point turn aside nor persist in irrelevant talk; on the contrary, act as you do in a horse-race, make him keep to the track—of the matter at issue. If you do that, you will not fail of respect, and you will have the same sentiments when you are called to enforce laws that you had when you made them; but if you do otherwise, it will appear that when crimes are about to be committed, you foresee them and are angry, but after they have been committed, you no longer care.

To sum it all up, if you punish the wrongdoers, your laws will be good and valid; but if you let them go, good laws, indeed, but valid no longer. And I shall not hesitate to speak out and tell you why I say this. I will explain by means of an illustration. Why do you suppose it is, fellow

νόμους μὲν καλῶς κεῖσθαι, τὰ δὲ ψηφίσματα
εἶναι τὰ¹ τῆς πόλεως καταδεέστερα, καὶ τὰς
κρίσεις ἐνίοτε τὰς ἐν τοῖς δικαστηρίοις ἔχειν ἐπι-
178 πλήξεις; ἐγὼ τὰς τούτων αἰτίας ἐπιδείξω. ὅτι
τοὺς μὲν νόμους τίθεσθε ἐπὶ πᾶσι δικαίοις,² οὔτε
κέρδους ἔνεκ' ἀδίκου, οὔτε χάριτος οὔτ' ἔχθρας,
ἀλλὰ πρὸς αὐτὸ μόνον τὸ δίκαιον καὶ τὸ συμφέρον
ἀποβλέποντες· ἐπιδέξιοι δ' οἶμαι φύντες ἑτέρων
μᾶλλον, εἰκότως καλλίστους νόμους τίθεσθε. ἐν
δὲ ταῖς ἐκκλησίαις καὶ τοῖς δικαστηρίοις πολλάκις ἀφέμενοι τῶν εἰς αὐτὸ τὸ πρᾶγμα λόγων, ὑπὸ
τῆς ἀπάτης καὶ τῶν ἀλαζονευμάτων ὑπάγεσθε,
καὶ πάντων ἀδικώτατον ἔθος εἰς τοὺς ἀγῶνας
παραδέχεσθε· ἐᾶτε γὰρ τοὺς ἀπολογουμένους ἀν-
179 τικατηγορεῖν τῶν κατηγορούντων. ἐπειδὰν δ' ἀπὸ
τῆς ἀπολογίας ἀποσπασθῆτε καὶ τὰς ψυχὰς ἐφ'
ἑτέρων γένησθε, εἰς λήθην ἐμπεσόντες τῆς κατηγορίας, ἐξέρχεσθ' ἐκ τῶν δικαστηρίων, οὐδὲ παρ'
ἑτέρου δίκην εἰληφότες, οὔτε παρὰ τοῦ κατηγόρου,
ψῆφος γὰρ κατ' αὐτοῦ οὐ δίδοται, οὔτε παρὰ τοῦ
ἀπολογουμένου, ταῖς γὰρ ἀλλοτρίαις αἰτίαις ἀπο-
τριψάμενος τὰ ὑπάρχοντα αὐτῷ ἐγκλήματα ἐκ-
πέφευγεν ἐκ τοῦ δικαστηρίου· οἱ δὲ νόμοι κατα-
λύονται καὶ ἡ δημοκρατία διαφθείρεται καὶ τὸ
ἔθος ἐπὶ πολὺ προβαίνει· εὐχερῶς γὰρ ἐνίοτε
λόγον ἄνευ χρηστοῦ βίου προσδέχεσθε.

¹ τὰ added by Sauppe.
² δικαίοις Hillebrand, confirmed by the Geneva papyrus:
τοῖς δικαίοις MSS.

---

¹ A law (νόμος) could be enacted or amended only by a
special legislative commission, by an elaborate process, under

citizens, that the existing laws are good, but that the decrees of the city are inferior to them,[1] and that the verdicts rendered in the courts are sometimes open to censure? I will explain to you the reason. It is because you enact the laws with no other object than justice, not moved by unrighteous gain, or by either partiality or animosity, looking solely to what is just and for the common good. And because you are, as I think, naturally more clever than other men, it is not surprising that you pass most excellent laws. But in the meetings of the assembly and in the courts, you oftentimes lose all hold of the discussion of the matter in hand, and are led away by deceit and trickery; and you admit into your cases at law a custom that is utterly unjust, for you allow the defendants to bring counter accusations against the complainants. And when you have been drawn away from the defence itself, and your minds have become intent on other things, you forget the accusation entirely, and leave the court-room without having received satisfaction from either party—not from the complainant, for you are given no opportunity to vote with reference to him, and not from the defendant, for by his extraneous charges he has brushed aside the original complaints against himself, and gone out of court scot-free. Thus the laws are losing their force, the democracy is being undermined, and the custom is steadily gaining ground. For you sometimes thoughtlessly listen to mere talk that is unsupported by a good life.

careful precautions, at a fixed time in the civil year. A decree (ψήφισμα) could be passed any day by joint action of senate and assembly, and as easily amended or repealed.

180 Ἀλλ᾿ οὐ Λακεδαιμόνιοι· καλὸν δ᾿ ἐστὶ καὶ τὰς
ξενικὰς ἀρετὰς μιμεῖσθαι. δημηγοροῦντος γάρ
τινος ἐν τῇ τῶν Λακεδαιμονίων ἐκκλησίᾳ, ἀνδρὸς
βεβιωκότος μὲν αἰσχρῶς, λέγειν δ᾿ εἰς ὑπερβολὴν
δυνατοῦ, καὶ τῶν Λακεδαιμονίων, ὥς φασι, κατὰ
τὴν ἐκείνου γνώμην ψηφίζεσθαι μελλόντων, παρελθών τις τῶν γερόντων, οὓς ἐκεῖνοι καὶ αἰσχύ-
νονται καὶ δεδίασι, καὶ τὴν τῆς ἡλικίας αὐτῶν
ἐπωνυμίαν ἀρχὴν μεγίστην εἶναι νομίζουσι, καθιστᾶσι δ᾿ αὐτοὺς ἐκ τῶν ἐκ παιδὸς εἰς γῆρας
σωφρόνων, τούτων εἷς, ὡς λέγεται, παρελθὼν
ἰσχυρῶς ἐπέπληξε τοῖς Λακεδαιμονίοις, καί τι
τοιοῦτον κατ᾿ αὐτῶν ἐβλασφήμησεν, ὡς οὐ πολὺν
χρόνον τὴν Σπάρτην ἀπόρθητον οἰκήσουσι, τοιούτοις ἐν ταῖς ἐκκλησίαις συμβούλοις χρώμενοι.
181 ἅμα δὲ παρακαλέσας ἄλλον τινὰ τῶν Λακεδαιμονίων, ἄνδρα λέγειν μὲν οὐκ εὐφυᾶ, τὰ δὲ κατὰ
πόλεμον λαμπρὸν καὶ πρὸς δικαιοσύνην καὶ ἐγκρά-
τειαν διαφέροντα, ἐπέταξεν αὐτῷ τὰς αὐτὰς εἰπεῖν
γνώμας οὕτως ὅπως ἂν δύνηται, ἃς εἶπεν ὁ πρότερος ῥήτωρ, "Ἵνα," ἔφη, "οἱ Λακεδαιμόνιοι ἀνδρὸς
ἀγαθοῦ φθεγξαμένου ψηφίσωνται, τὰς δὲ τῶν
ἀποδεδειλιακότων[1] καὶ πονηρῶν ἀνθρώπων φωνὰς
μηδὲ τοῖς ὡσὶ προσδέχωνται." ταῦθ᾿ ὁ γέρων ὁ
ἐκ παιδὸς σεσωφρονηκὼς παρήνεσε τοῖς ἑαυτοῦ
πολίταις. ταχύ γ᾿ ἂν[2] Τίμαρχον ἢ τὸν κίναιδον
Δημοσθένην εἴασε πολιτεύεσθαι.

---

[1] ἀποδεδειλιακότων Wolf : ὑποδεδειλιακότων MSS.
[2] γ᾿ ἂν Porson : γὰρ or γε MSS.

Not so the Lacedaemonians (and it is well to imitate virtue even in a foreigner). For instance, when a certain man had spoken in the assembly of the Lacedaemonians, a man of shameful life but an exceedingly able speaker, and when, we are told, the Lacedaemonians were on the point of voting according to his advice, a man came forward from the Council of Elders [1]—a body of men whom they reverence and fear, whose age gives its name to that office which they consider the highest, and whom they appoint from among those who have been men of sobriety from boyhood to old age—one of these, it is said, came forward and vehemently rebuked the Lacedaemonians and denounced them in words like these: that the homes of Sparta would not long remain unravaged if the people followed such advisers in their assemblies. At the same time he called forward another of the Lacedaemonians, a certain man who was not gifted in speech, but brilliant in war and distinguished for justice and sobriety, and he ordered him to express as best he could the same sentiments that the former orator had uttered, "In order," he explained, "that a good man may speak before the Lacedaemonians vote, but that they may not even receive into their ears the voices of proven cowards and rascals." Such was the advice that the old man, who had lived a pure life from childhood, gave to his fellow citizens. He would have been quick, indeed, to allow Timarchus or the low-lived Demosthenes to take part in public affairs!

[1] The Council of Elders (Γέροντες) consisted of twenty-eight men, elected by the people from those nobles who had passed their sixtieth year; an elder thus elected held the office the rest of his life.

182 Ἵνα δὲ μὴ δοκῶ Λακεδαιμονίους θεραπεύειν, καὶ τῶν ἡμετέρων προγόνων μνησθήσομαι. οὕτω γὰρ ἦσαν πρὸς τὰς αἰσχύνας χαλεποί, καὶ περὶ πλείστου τῶν τέκνων τὴν σωφροσύνην ἐποιοῦντο, ὥστ᾽ ἀνὴρ εἷς τῶν πολιτῶν, εὑρὼν τὴν ἑαυτοῦ θυγατέρα διεφθαρμένην, καὶ τὴν ἡλικίαν οὐ καλῶς διαφυλάξασαν μέχρι γάμου, ἐγκατῳκοδόμησεν αὐτὴν μεθ᾽ ἵππου εἰς ἔρημον οἰκίαν, ὑφ᾽ οὗ προδήλως ἔμελλεν ἀπολεῖσθαι[1] συγκαθειργμένη. καὶ ἔτι καὶ νῦν τῆς οἰκίας ταύτης ἕστηκε τὰ οἰκόπεδα ἐν τῷ ὑμετέρῳ ἄστει, καὶ ὁ τόπος οὗτος καλεῖται

183 παρ᾽ ἵππον καὶ κόρην. ὁ δὲ Σόλων ὁ τῶν νομοθετῶν ἐνδοξότατος γέγραφεν ἀρχαίως καὶ σεμνῶς περὶ τῆς τῶν γυναικῶν εὐκοσμίας. τὴν γὰρ γυναῖκα ἐφ᾽ ᾗ ἂν ἁλῷ μοιχός, οὐκ ἐᾷ κοσμεῖσθαι, οὐδὲ εἰς τὰ δημοτελῆ ἱερὰ εἰσιέναι, ἵνα μὴ τὰς ἀναμαρτήτους τῶν γυναικῶν ἀναμειγνυμένη διαφθείρῃ· ἐὰν δ᾽ εἰσίῃ ἢ κοσμῆται, τὸν ἐντυχόντα κελεύει καταρρηγνύναι τὰ ἱμάτια καὶ τὸν κόσμον ἀφαιρεῖσθαι καὶ τύπτειν, εἰργόμενον θανάτου καὶ τοῦ ἀνάπηρον ποιῆσαι, ἀτιμῶν τὴν τοιαύτην γυναῖκα καὶ τὸν βίον ἀβίωτον αὐτῇ κατασκευάζων.

184 καὶ τὰς προαγωγοὺς καὶ τοὺς προαγωγοὺς γράφεσθαι κελεύει, κἂν ἁλῶσι, θανάτῳ ζημιοῦν, ὅτι τῶν ἐξαμαρτάνειν ἐπιθυμούντων ὀκνούντων καὶ αἰσχυνομένων ἀλλήλοις ἐντυγχάνειν, αὐτοὶ τὴν αὑτῶν ἀναίδειαν παρασχόντες ἐπὶ μισθῷ τὸ πρᾶγμα εἰς διάπειράν καὶ λόγον κατέστησαν.

185 Ἔπειθ᾽ οἱ μὲν πατέρες ὑμῶν οὕτω περὶ τῶν αἰσχρῶν καὶ καλῶν διεγίγνωσκον, ὑμεῖς δὲ Τίμαρχον τὸν τοῖς αἰσχίστοις ἐπιτηδεύμασιν ἔνοχον

---

[1] ἀπολεῖσθαι Dobree : ἀπολεῖσθαι διὰ λιμὸν MSS.

But that I may not seem to be flattering the Lacedaemonians, I will make mention of our ancestors also. For so stern were they toward all shameful conduct, and so precious did they hold the purity of their children, that when one of the citizens found that his daughter had been seduced, and that she had failed to guard well her chastity till the time of marriage, he walled her up in an empty house with a horse, which he knew would surely kill her, if she were shut in there with him. And to this day the foundations of that house stand in your city, and that spot is called "the place of the horse and the maid." And Solon, the most famous of lawgivers, has written in ancient and solemn manner concerning orderly conduct on the part of the women. For the woman who is taken in the act of adultery he does not allow to adorn herself, nor even to attend the public sacrifices, lest by mingling with innocent women she corrupt them. But if she does attend, or does adorn herself, he commands that any man who meets her shall tear off her garments, strip her of her ornaments, and beat her (only he may not kill or maim her); for the lawgiver seeks to disgrace such a woman and make her life not worth the living. And he commands that procurers, men and women, be indicted, and if they are convicted, be punished with death, because to people who lust after sin but hesitate and are ashamed to meet one another, the procurers offer their own shamelessness for pay, and make it possible to discuss the act and to accomplish it.

Such, then, was the judgment of your fathers concerning things shameful and things honourable; and shall their sons let Timarchus go free, a man chargeable with the most shameful practices, a creature

ἀφήσετε; τὸν ἄνδρα μὲν καὶ ἄρρενα τὸ σῶμα,
γυναικεῖα δὲ ἁμαρτήματα ἡμαρτηκότα; τίς οὖν
ὑμῶν γυναῖκα λαβὼν ἀδικοῦσαν τιμωρήσεται; ἢ
τίς οὐκ ἀπαίδευτος εἶναι δόξει τῇ μὲν κατὰ φύσιν
ἁμαρτανούσῃ χαλεπαίνων, τῷ δὲ παρὰ φύσιν
186 ἑαυτὸν ὑβρίσαντι συμβούλῳ χρώμενος; τίνα δ'
ἔχων ἕκαστος ὑμῶν γνώμην ἐπάνεισιν οἴκαδε ἐκ
τοῦ δικαστηρίου; οὔτε γὰρ ὁ κρινόμενος ἀφανής,
ἀλλὰ γνώριμος, οὔθ' ὁ νόμος ὁ περὶ τῆς τῶν
ῥητόρων δοκιμασίας φαῦλος, ἀλλὰ κάλλιστος, τό
τ' ἐρέσθαι τοῖς παισὶ καὶ τοῖς μειρακίοις τοὺς
ἑαυτῶν οἰκείους, ὅπως τὸ πρᾶγμα κέκριται, πρό-
187 χειρον. τί οὖν δὴ λέξετε οἱ τῆς ψήφου νυνὶ
γεγονότες κύριοι, ὅταν οἱ ὑμέτεροι παῖδες ὑμᾶς
ἔρωνται, εἰ κατεδικάσατε ἢ ἀπεψηφίσασθε; οὐχ
ἅμα Τίμαρχον ἀπολῦσαι ὁμολογήσετε, καὶ τὴν
κοινὴν παιδείαν ἀνατρέψετε; τί δ' ὄφελος παιδα-
γωγοὺς τρέφειν ἢ παιδοτρίβας καὶ διδασκάλους
τοῖς παισὶν ἐφιστάναι, ὅταν οἱ τὴν τῶν νόμων
παρακαταθήκην ἔχοντες πρὸς τὰς αἰσχύνας κατα-
κάμπτωνται;
188   Θαυμάζω δ' ὑμῶν, ὦ ἄνδρες Ἀθηναῖοι, κἀκεῖνο,
εἰ τοὺς μὲν πορνοβοσκοὺς μισεῖτε, τοὺς δ' ἑκόντας
πεπορνευμένους ἀφήσετε· καὶ ὡς ἔοικεν ὁ αὐτὸς
οὗτος ἀνὴρ ἱερωσύνην μὲν οὐδενὸς θεῶν κληρώ-
σεται, ὡς οὐκ ὢν ἐκ τῶν νόμων καθαρὸς τὸ σῶμα·
γράψει δ' ἐν τοῖς ψηφίσμασιν εὐχὰς ὑπὲρ τῆς

with the body of a man defiled with the sins of a woman? In that case, who of you will punish a woman if he finds her in wrong doing? Or what man will not be regarded as lacking intelligence who is angry with her who errs by an impulse of nature, while he treats as adviser [1] the man who in despite of nature has sinned against his own body? How will each man of you feel as he goes home from court? For the person who is on trial is no obscure man, but well known; the law governing the official scrutiny of public speakers is not a trivial law, but a most excellent one; and we must expect that the boys and young men will ask the members of their families how the case was decided. What then, pray, are you going to answer, you in whose hands the decision now rests, when your sons ask you whether you voted for conviction or acquittal? When you acknowledge that you set Timarchus free, will you not at the same time be overturning our whole system of training the youth? What use is there in keeping attendants for our children, or setting trainers and teachers over them, when those who have been entrusted with the laws allow themselves to be turned into crooked paths of shame?

I am also surprised, fellow citizens, that you who hate the brothel-keeper propose to let the willing prostitute go free. And it seems that a man who is not to be permitted to be a candidate for election by lot for the priesthood of any god, as being impure of body as that is defined by the laws, this same man is to write in our decrees prayers to the August

---

[1] The question at issue is whether Timarchus is to be allowed to continue to be an adviser of the city, by speaking in the assembly of the people.

πόλεως ταῖς σεμναῖς θεαῖς. εἶτα τί θαυμάζομεν
τὴν κοινὴν ἀπραξίαν, τοιούτων ῥητόρων ἐπὶ τὰς
τοῦ δήμου γνώμας ἐπιγραφομένων; καὶ τὸν αἰσχρῶς οἴκοι βεβιωκότα ἔξω τῆς πόλεως πρεσβευτὴν πέμψομεν, καὶ τούτῳ περὶ τῶν μεγίστων
διαπιστεύσομεν; τί δ' οὐκ ἂν ἀποδοῖτο ὁ τὴν τοῦ
σώματος ὕβριν πεπρακώς; τίνα δ' ἂν οὗτος ἐλεή-
σειεν ὁ αὑτὸν οὐκ ἐλεήσας;

189   Τίνι δ' ὑμῶν οὐκ εὔγνωστός ἐστιν ἡ Τιμάρχου
βδελυρία; ὥσπερ γὰρ τοὺς γυμναζομένους, κἂν
μὴ παρῶμεν ἐν τοῖς γυμνασίοις, εἰς τὰς εὐεξίας
αὐτῶν ἀποβλέποντες γιγνώσκομεν, οὕτω τοὺς
πεπορνευμένους, κἂν μὴ παρῶμεν αὐτῶν τοῖς
ἔργοις, ἐκ τῆς ἀναιδείας καὶ τοῦ θράσους καὶ τῶν
ἐπιτηδευμάτων γιγνώσκομεν. ὁ γὰρ ἐπὶ τῶν
μεγίστων τοὺς νόμους καὶ τὴν σωφροσύνην ὑπερ-
ιδών, ἔχει τινὰ ἕξιν τῆς ψυχῆς ἣ διάδηλος ἐκ τῆς
ἀκοσμίας τοῦ τρόπου γίγνεται.

190   Πλείστους δ' ἂν εὕροιτ' ἐκ τῶν τοιούτων ἀνθρώπων πόλεις ἀνατετροφότας καὶ ταῖς μεγίσταις
συμφοραῖς αὐτοὺς περιπεπτωκότας. μὴ γὰρ
οἴεσθε, ὦ ἄνδρες Ἀθηναῖοι,[1] τὰς τῶν ἀδικημάτων
ἀρχὰς ἀπὸ θεῶν, ἀλλ' οὐκ ἀπ'[2] ἀνθρώπων ἀσελγείας γίγνεσθαι, μηδὲ τοὺς ἠσεβηκότας, καθάπερ
ἐν ταῖς τραγῳδίαις, Ποινὰς ἐλαύνειν καὶ κολάζειν
191 δασὶν ἡμμέναις· ἀλλ' αἱ προπετεῖς τοῦ σώματος
ἡδοναὶ καὶ τὸ μηδὲν ἱκανὸν ἡγεῖσθαι, ταῦτα πλη-
ροῖ τὰ ληστήρια, ταῦτ' εἰς τὸν ἐπακτροκέλητα
ἐμβιβάζει, ταῦτά ἐστιν ἑκάστῳ Ποινή, ταῦτα

---

[1] ὦ ἄνδρες Ἀθηναῖοι Blass : ὦ Ἀθηναῖοι MSS.
[2] οὐκ ἀπ' Bremi : οὐχ ὑπ' MSS.

Goddesses[1] in behalf of the state. Why then do we wonder at the futility of our public acts, when the names of such public men as this stand at the head of the people's decrees? And shall we send abroad as ambassador a man who has lived shamefully at home, and shall we continue to trust that man in matters of the greatest moment? What would he not sell who has trafficked in the shame of his own body? Whom would he pity who has had no pity on himself?

To whom of you is not the bestiality of Timarchus well known? For just as we recognize the athlete, even without visiting the gymnasia, by looking at his bodily vigour, even so we recognize the prostitute, even without being present at his act, by his shamelessness, his effrontery, and his habits. For he who despises the laws and morality in matters of supreme importance, comes to be in a state of soul which is plainly revealed by his disorderly life.

Very many men of this sort you could find who have overthrown cities and have fallen into the greatest misfortunes themselves. For you must not imagine, fellow citizens, that the impulse to wrong doing is from the gods; nay, rather, it is from the wickedness of men; nor that ungodly men are, as in tragedy, driven and chastised by the Furies[2] with blazing torches in their hands. No, the impetuous lusts of the body and insatiate desire—these it is that fill the robbers' bands, that send men on board the pirates' boats; these are, for each man, his Fury,

---

[1] The Eumenides.

[2] The Furies (Poenae) are gods of punishment, more definitely personified in the Erinyes. The hearers would be reminded of the chasing of Orestes in the *Eumenides* of Aeschylus.

παρακελεύεται σφάττειν τοὺς πολίτας, ὑπηρετεῖν
τοῖς τυράννοις, συγκαταλύειν τὸν δῆμον. οὐ γὰρ
τὴν αἰσχύνην οὐδ᾽ ἃ πείσονται λογίζονται, ἀλλ᾽
ἐφ᾽ οἷς κατορθώσαντες εὐφρανθήσονται, τούτοις
κεκήληνται. ἐξαιρεῖτ᾽ οὖν, ὦ ἄνδρες Ἀθηναῖοι,
τὰς τοιαύτας φύσεις, καὶ τὰ τῶν νέων ζηλώματα
ἐπ᾽ ἀρετὴν προτρέψεσθε.[1]

192   Εὖ δ᾽ ἐπίστασθε, καί μοι σφόδρα τὸ μέλλον ῥηθήσεσθαι διαμνημονεύετε, εἰ μὲν δώσει τῶν ἐπιτηδευμάτων Τίμαρχος δίκην, ἀρχὴν εὐκοσμίας ἐν
τῇ πόλει κατασκευάσετε· εἰ δ᾽ ἀποφεύξεται, κρείτ-
των ἦν ὁ ἀγὼν μὴ γεγενημένος. πρὶν μὲν γὰρ εἰς
κρίσιν Τίμαρχον καταστῆναι, φόβον τισὶ παρεῖ-
χεν ὁ νόμος καὶ τὸ τῶν δικαστηρίων ὄνομα· εἰ δ᾽ ὁ
πρωτεύων βδελυρίᾳ καὶ γνωριμώτατος εἰσελθὼν
περιγενήσεται, πολλοὺς ἁμαρτάνειν ἐπαρεῖ, καὶ
τελευτῶν οὐχ ὁ λόγος, ἀλλ᾽ ὁ καιρὸς ὑμᾶς ἐξορ-
193   γιεῖ.   μὴ οὖν εἰς ἀθρόους, ἀλλ᾽ εἰς ἕνα ἀπο-
σκήψατε, καὶ τὴν παρασκευὴν καὶ τοὺς συνηγόρους αὐτῶν παρατηρεῖτε· ὧν οὐδενὸς ἐγὼ
ὀνομαστὶ μνησθήσομαι, ἵνα μὴ ταύτην ἀρχὴν τοῦ
λόγου ποιήσωνται, ὡς οὐκ ἂν παρῆλθον, εἰ μή τις
αὐτῶν ὀνομαστὶ ἐμνήσθη. ἀλλ᾽ ἐκεῖνο ποιήσω·
ἀφελὼν τὰ ὀνόματα, διεξιὼν δὲ τὰ ἐπιτηδεύματα,
καὶ τὰ σώματα αὐτῶν γνώριμα καταστήσω.
ἔσται δ᾽ αὐτὸς ἑαυτῷ ἕκαστος αἴτιος, ἐὰν δεῦρο
194   ἀναβῇ καὶ ἀναισχυντῇ.   τούτῳ γὰρ παρίασιν ἐκ
τριῶν εἰδῶν συνήγοροι, οἱ μὲν ταῖς καθ᾽ ἡμέραν

---

[1] προτρέψεσθε Cobet : προτρέψασθε MSS.

urging him to slay his fellow citizens, to serve the
tyrant, to help put down the democracy. For such
men reck not of disgrace, nor yet of punishment
to come, but are beguiled by the pleasures they
expect if they succeed. Therefore, fellow citizens,
remove from among us such natures, for so shall you
turn the aspirations of the young toward virtue.

And be assured—I earnestly beg of you to remember what I am about to say—be assured that
if Timarchus shall pay the penalty for his practices,
you will lay the foundation for orderly conduct in
this city; but if he shall be cleared, the case had
better never have been tried. For before Timarchus
came to trial, the law and the name of the courts
did cause some men to fear; but if the leader in
indecency and the most notorious man of all shall
once have been brought into court and then come
safely off, many will be induced to offend; and it
will finally be, not what is said, but the desperate
situation, that will arouse your anger. Therefore
punish one man, and do not wait till you have
a multitude to punish; and be on your guard
against their machinations and their advocates. I
will name no one of these, lest they make that
their excuse for speaking, saying that they would
not have come forward had not someone mentioned
them by name. But this I will do: I will omit
their names, but by describing their habits will make
known their persons also. And each man will
have only himself to blame if he comes up here
and displays his impudence. Three sorts of supporters, namely, are going to come into court to
help the defendant: firstly, men who have squandered

δαπάναις ἀνηλωκότες τὰς πατρῴας οὐσίας, οἱ δὲ
ταῖς ἡλικίαις καὶ τοῖς ἑαυτῶν σώμασιν οὐ καλῶς
κεχρημένοι, καὶ δεδιότες οὐ περὶ Τιμάρχου, ἀλλὰ
περὶ ἑαυτῶν καὶ τῶν ἐπιτηδευμάτων μή ποτε εἰς
κρίσιν καταστῶσιν· ἕτεροι δ' ἐκ τῶν ἀκολάστων
καὶ τῶν τοῖς τοιούτοις κεχρημένων ἀφθόνως, ἵνα
ταῖς βοηθείαις αὐτῶν πιστεύοντες ῥᾷόν τινες
195 ἐξαμαρτάνωσιν. ὧν πρὶν τῆς συνηγορίας ἀκοῦσαι τοὺς βίους ἀναμιμνήσκεσθε, καὶ τοὺς μὲν εἰς
τὰ σώματα ἡμαρτηκότας μὴ ὑμῖν ἐνοχλεῖν, ἀλλὰ
παύσασθαι δημηγοροῦντας κελεύετε· οὐδὲ γὰρ ὁ
νόμος τοὺς ἰδιωτεύοντας, ἀλλὰ τοὺς πολιτευομένους ἐξετάζει· τοὺς δὲ τὰ πατρῷα κατεδηδο-
κότας ἐργάζεσθαι καὶ ἑτέρωθεν κτᾶσθαι τὸν βίον
κελεύετε· τοὺς δὲ τῶν νέων, ὅσοι ῥᾳδίως ἁλίσκον-
ται, θηρευτὰς ὄντας εἰς τοὺς ξένους καὶ τοὺς
μετοίκους τρέπεσθαι κελεύετε, ἵνα μήτ' ἐκεῖνοι
τῆς προαιρέσεως ἀποστερῶνται μήθ' ὑμεῖς βλά-
πτησθε.

196   Τὰ μὲν οὖν παρ' ἐμοῦ δίκαια πάντα ἀπειλήφατε·
ἐδίδαξα τοὺς νόμους, ἐξήτασα τὸν βίον τοῦ κρινομένου. νῦν μὲν οὖν ὑμεῖς ἐστε τῶν ἐμῶν λόγων
κριταί, αὐτίκα δ' ὑμέτερος ἐγὼ θεατής· ἐν γὰρ
ταῖς ὑμετέραις γνώμαις ἡ πρᾶξις καταλείπεται.
εἰ οὖν βουλήσεσθε, τὰ δίκαια καὶ τὰ συμφέροντα
ὑμῶν ποιησάντων, φιλοτιμότερον ἡμεῖς ἕξομεν
τοὺς παρανομοῦντας ἐξετάζειν.[1]

[1] The last sentence, εἰ οὖν ... ἐξετάζειν, is found in a part
of the MSS. only.

their patrimony by the extravagance of their daily life; secondly, men who have abused their youth and their own bodies, and now are afraid, not for Timarchus, but for themselves and their own habits, lest they one day be called to account; and still others from the ranks of the licentious, and of those who have freely associated with licentious men; for they would have certain men rely on their aid, and thus be the more ready to indulge in wrong-doing. Before you hear the pleas of these men in his support, call to mind their lives, and bid those who have sinned against their own bodies to cease annoying you and to stop speaking before the people; for the law investigates, not men in private station, but those who are in public life. And tell those who have eaten up their patrimony to go to work, and find some new way to get their living. And as for the hunters of such young men as are easily trapped, command them to turn their attention to the foreigners and the resident aliens, that they may still indulge their predilection, but without injuring you.

And now I have fulfilled all my obligation to you: I have explained the laws, I have examined the life of the defendant. Now, therefore, you are judges of my words, and soon I shall be spectator of your acts, for the decision of the case is now left to your judgment. If, therefore, you do what is right and best, we on our part shall, if it be your wish, be able more zealously to call wrongdoers to account.

II.—ON THE EMBASSY

II.—THE SPEECH ON THE EMBASSY

343 B.C.

INTRODUCTION

AFTER Philip, by the seizure of the Athenian
colonial city Amphipolis, and the conquest of the
whole Chalcidic peninsula, had made himself the
most formidable power on the northern coasts, he
let it be known at Athens that he was disposed to
open negotiations for peace. The Athenians, discouraged by the failure of their weak attempts to
check his advance during the past ten years, sent
ten ambassadors to Macedonia. Demosthenes and
Aeschines were among them. When, on the return
of this embassy, ambassadors came from Philip, and
definite peace proposals were discussed in the Athenian assembly, Aeschines and Demosthenes both
took prominent part in the debates. The people
having voted the peace, the same ambassadors were
sent to Macedonia to receive the signatures of Philip
and his allies, and to attempt by further negotiations
with Philip himself to secure guarantees that had
not been included in the terms of the peace. The
signatures were given, after considerable delay, but
no concessions were obtained from Philip. On the
return of the embassy Demosthenes declared that
Philip's intentions and his immediate preparations
were all against the interests of Athens; that he
was preparing to intervene in the Phocian war, and

INTRODUCTION

unite with the Thebans in the control of central Greece. Aeschines, on the other hand, declared that Demosthenes knew nothing of the real state of the case; that he himself was fully in Philip's confidence, and that while he could not yet openly declare all Philip's plans, he could assure the people that in the end they would see precisely what they wished—the humiliation of Thebes, and all other conditions in central Greece made wholly favourable to Athens. Aeschines' hopeful view prevailed with the people, and Philip was left with a free hand. In less than ten days he had forced the surrender of the Phocians and was hastening to re-establish the rule of Thebes over all Boeotia. Athens found that the peace negotiations had served only to ratify Philip's claims to territory that he had taken in the north from her allies and from herself, to open the way for his unopposed control of central Greece in cooperation with Thessaly and Thebes, and to give him the commanding position in the Amphictyonic Council, thus putting an end to all treatment of him as a "barbarian."

By law the members of the late embassy were required to render account of their services to a standing board of review. On the occasion of this accounting, Demosthenes and Timarchus, a political associate of his, made formal charge that Aeschines had been guilty of treason on the second embassy to Philip. The case was set for trial in the courts. But Aeschines, by bringing a personal charge against Timarchus (see the introduction to the speech against Timarchus) succeeded in ridding himself of one of his prosecutors and in deferring the trial. The case finally came into court in the summer of 343, three years after the events. By this time Philocrates, the author of the peace treaty, had so shamelessly made it evident that he was in the paid service of Philip, that he had been forced to flee from the city in order to escape the death penalty.

In the prosecution of Aeschines, Demosthenes assumed that he had been the lieutenant of Philocrates, and charged him with a full share of the responsibility for all the evil results of the now detested peace. He asserted that whereas Aeschines had at first been one of the most vociferous opponents of Philip, and had on the first day of the peace discussions vigorously opposed the draft of a treaty of peace presented by Philocrates, he totally changed his position over-night, and helped Philocrates to carry his proposition on the second day of the deliberations, thereby excluding the Phocians from the protection of the peace, and preventing the inclusion of other Greek states who should have had time to join Athens and her allies in making it. He charged that when the second embassy had been appointed to secure the signatures of Philip and his allies to the treaty of peace, Aeschines was one of the men responsible for such delay on the journey that Philip was able to secure control of commanding positions on the Thracian coast ; that he made no attempt to secure from Philip the concessions that the people at home had understood were to be urged, and that on the return of the embassy to Athens, Aeschines joined Philocrates in hooting down Demosthenes at a meeting of the Assembly, when he attempted to tell them the truth as to Philip's plans and preparations. He charged that Aeschines gave to the people a false report of the intentions of Philip, assuring them that he was himself fully in the confidence of the king, and saying that while Philip could not openly declare his intentions, he could himself assure the Athenians that the real purpose of Philip was to humble Thebes, to protect the Phocians, and to enlarge the power of Athens. Demosthenes declared that in consequence of this false report to the Assembly, the Athenians were prevented from going out to resist Philip's entrance into central Greece (as they had so effectually done six years before), and that the Phocians were so discouraged at the report of the Athenian attitude that they made haste to give themselves into Philip's hands. He declared further that after these predictions of Aeschines had all proved to be false, and Philip had at every point shown himself to be the enemy of Athens, Aeschines had nevertheless joined in Philip's thanksgiving feast, and remained his constant supporter.

In his defence against these charges Aeschines could not deny the chief facts of the case; his main defence had to be a different interpretation of the facts. Of actual bribery by Philip, Demosthenes had, of course, been able to bring no specific proof, and it was in Aeschines' favour that the people had to some extent satisfied their resentment by the exile of Philocrates, and that now, three years after the events, their feelings were less hot than at first; Aeschines had also the powerful influence of his party chief, Eubulus, on his side.

Demosthenes failed to secure conviction, but he did succeed in leaving Aeschines under a cloud of popular suspicion.

II.—ΠΕΡΙ ΤΗΣ ΠΑΡΑΠΡΕΣΒΕΙΑΣ

Δέομαι ὑμῶν, ὦ ἄνδρες ᾿Αθηναῖοι, ἐθελῆσαί μου μετ᾽ εὐνοίας ἀκοῦσαι λέγοντος, ὑπολογιζομένους τό τε μέγεθος τοῦ κινδύνου καὶ τὸ πλῆθος τῶν αἰτιῶν πρὸς ἃς ἀπολογήσασθαί με δεῖ, καὶ τὰς τέχνας καὶ τὰς κατασκευὰς τοῦ κατηγόρου καὶ τὴν ὠμότητα, ὃς ἐτόλμησε παρακελεύσασθαι πρὸς ἄνδρας ὀμωμοκότας τῶν ἀντιδίκων ὁμοίως ἀμφοτέρων ἀκούσεσθαι τοῦ κινδυνεύοντος φωνὴν 2 μὴ ὑπομένειν. καὶ ταῦτ᾽ εἶπεν οὐ δι᾽ ὀργήν· οὐδεὶς γὰρ τῶν ψευδομένων τοῖς ἀδίκως διαβαλλομένοις ὀργίζεται, οὐδ᾽ οἱ τἀληθῆ λέγοντες κωλύουσι λόγου τυχεῖν τὸν φεύγοντα· οὐ γὰρ πρότερον ἡ κατηγορία παρὰ τοῖς ἀκούουσιν ἰσχύει, πρὶν ἂν ὁ φεύγων ἀπολογίας τυχὼν ἀδυνατήσῃ τὰς προ-3 ειρημένας αἰτίας ἀπολύσασθαι. ἀλλ᾽ οἶμαι Δημοσθένης οὐ χαίρει δικαίοις λόγοις, οὐδ᾽ οὕτω παρεσκεύασται, ἀλλὰ τὴν ὑμετέραν ὀργὴν ἐκκαλέσασθαι βεβούληται. καὶ κατηγόρηκε δωροδοκίας, ἀπίθανος ὢν πρὸς τὴν ὑποψίαν ταύτην· τὸν γὰρ ἐπὶ ταῖς δωροδοκίαις προτρεπόμενον[1] ὀργίζεσθαι, αὐτὸν χρὴ τῶν τοιούτων ἔργων ἀπέχεσθαι.[2] 4 ᾿Εμοὶ δέ, ὦ ἄνδρες ᾿Αθηναῖοι, συμβέβηκε τῆς Δημοσθένους ἀκούοντι κατηγορίας μήτε δεῖσαι

[1] Weidner omits τοὺς δικαστάς, which the MSS. have before or after προτρεπόμενον.
[2] Most MSS. add πολύ, but in varying position.

II.—ON THE EMBASSY

I BEG you, fellow citizens, to hear me with willing and friendly mind, remembering how great is my peril, and how many the charges against which I have to defend myself; remembering also the arts and devices of my accuser, and the cruelty of the man who, speaking to men who are under oath to give equal hearing to both parties, had the effrontery to urge you not to listen to the voice of the defendant. And it was not anger that made him say it; for no man who is lying is angry with the victim of his calumny, nor do men who are speaking the truth try to prevent the defendant from obtaining a hearing; for the prosecution does not find justification in the minds of the hearers until the defendant has had opportunity to plead for himself, and has proved unable to refute the charges that have been preferred. But Demosthenes, I think, is not fond of fair argument, nor is that the sort of preparation he has made. No, it is your anger that he is determined to call forth. And he has accused me of receiving bribes—he who would be the last man to make such suspicion credible! For the man who seeks to arouse the anger of his hearers over bribery must himself refrain from such conduct.

But, fellow citizens, as I have listened to Demosthenes' accusation, the effect upon my own mind has

πώποθ' οὕτως ὡς ἐν τῇδε τῇ ἡμέρᾳ, μήτ' ἀγανακτῆσαι μᾶλλον ἢ νῦν, μήτ' εἰς ὑπερβολὴν ὁμοίως
ἡσθῆναι. ἐφοβήθην μὲν γάρ, καὶ ἔτι καὶ νῦν
τεθορύβημαι, μή τινες ὑμῶν ἀγνοήσωσί με ψυχα-
γωγηθέντες τοῖς ἐπιβεβουλευμένοις καὶ κακοή-
θεσι τούτοις ἀντιθέτοις· ἐξέστην δ' ἐμαυτοῦ καὶ
τὴν αἰτίαν βαρέως ἤνεγκα, ὅθ' ὕβριν καὶ παρ-
οινίαν εἰς γυναῖκα ἐλευθέραν καὶ τὸ γένος Ὀλυνθίαν κατηγόρει· ἥσθην δέ, ὅτ' αὐτὸν ἐπὶ τῆς
αἰτίας ὄντα ταύτης ἐξεβάλλετε, καὶ τῶν σεσω-
φρονημένων ἐν τῷ βίῳ μοι χάριν ἀπειληφέναι
5 νομίζω. ὑμᾶς μὲν οὖν ἐπαινῶ καὶ διαφερόντως
ἀγαπῶ, ὅτι τῷ βίῳ μᾶλλον τῷ τῶν κρινομένων
πιστεύετε, ἢ ταῖς παρὰ τῶν ἐχθρῶν αἰτίαις· αὐτὸς
δ' οὐκ ἂν ἀποσταίην τῆς πρὸς ταῦτ' ἀπολογίας.
εἰ γάρ τις ἢ τῶν ἔξωθεν περιεστηκότων πέπεισται,
σχεδὸν δ' οἱ πλεῖστοι τῶν πολιτῶν πάρεισιν, ἢ
τῶν δικαζόντων ὑμῶν, ὡς ἐγὼ τοιοῦτόν τι διαπέ-
πραγμαι, μὴ μόνον εἰς ἐλεύθερον σῶμα, ἀλλὰ καὶ
εἰς τὸ τυχόν, ἀβίωτον εἶναί μοι τὸν λοιπὸν βίον
νομίζω· κἂν μὴ προϊούσης τῆς ἀπολογίας ἐξελέγξω καὶ τὴν αἰτίαν οὖσαν ψευδῆ, καὶ τὸν τολμή-
σαντ' εἰπεῖν ἀνόσιον καὶ συκοφάντην, κἂν τἆλλα
πάντα μηδὲν ἀδικῶν φαίνωμαι, θανάτου τιμῶμαι.
6   Παράδοξος δέ μοι κἀκεῖνος ὁ λόγος ἐφάνη καὶ
δεινῶς ἄδικος, ὅθ' ὑμᾶς ἐπηρώτα, εἰ οἷόν τ' ἐστὶν

been this: never have I been so apprehensive as on this day, nor ever more angry than now, nor so exceedingly rejoiced. I was frightened, and am still disturbed, lest some of you form a mistaken judgment of me, beguiled by those antitheses of his, conceived in deliberate malice. And I was indignant—fairly beside myself, at the charge, when he accused me of insolence and drunken violence towards a free woman of Olynthus.[1] But I was rejoiced when, as he was dwelling on this charge, you refused to listen to him. This I consider to be the reward that you bestow upon me for a chaste and temperate life. To you I do, indeed, give praise and high esteem for putting your faith in the life of those who are on trial, rather than in the accusations of their enemies; however, I would not myself shrink from defending myself against this charge. For if there is any man among those who are standing outside the bar—and almost the whole city is in the court—or if there is any man of you, the jurors, who is convinced that I have ever perpetrated such an act, not to say towards a free person, but towards any creature, I hold my life as no longer worth the living. And if as my defence proceeds I fail to prove that the accusation is false, and that the man who dared to utter it is an impious slanderer, then, even though it be clear that I am innocent of all the other charges, I declare myself worthy of death.

But strange indeed did that other argument of his seem to me, and outrageously unjust, when he asked

---

[1] Demosthenes in his speech (xix. 196 ff.) had told in detail the story of the abuse of a well-born Olynthian captive by Aeschines and others at a banquet in Macedonia.

ἐν τῇ αὐτῇ πόλει Φιλοκράτους μὲν θάνατον κατα-
ψηφίσασθαι, ὅτι καταγνοὺς ἑαυτοῦ ἀδικεῖν τὴν
κρίσιν οὐχ ὑπέμεινεν, ἐμοῦ δ᾽ ἀπογνῶναι. ἐγὼ δ᾽
ἐπ᾽ αὐτῷ τούτῳ δικαίως ἂν ὑπολαμβάνω μάλιστα
σῴζεσθαι· εἰ γὰρ ὁ καταγνοὺς ἑαυτοῦ καὶ μὴ
παρὼν ἀδικεῖ, ὅ γε ἀπογνοὺς καὶ τὸ σῶμα τοῖς
νόμοις καὶ τοῖς πολίταις παραδοὺς οὐκ ἀδικεῖ.

7 Περὶ δὲ τῆς ἄλλης κατηγορίας δέομαι ὑμῶν, ὦ
ἄνδρες Ἀθηναῖοι, ἐάν τι παραλίπω καὶ μὴ μνησθῶ, ἐπερωτᾶν με καὶ δηλοῦν ὅ τι ἂν ποθῆτε
ἀκοῦσαι, μηδὲν προκατεγνωκότας,[1] ἀλλ᾽ ἴσῃ τῇ
εὐνοίᾳ ἀκούοντας. ἀπορῶ δ᾽ ὁπόθεν χρὴ πρῶτον
ἄρξασθαι, διὰ τὴν ἀνωμαλίαν τῆς κατηγορίας.
σκέψασθε δ᾽ ἂν ὑμῖν εἰκός τι πρᾶγμα δόξω πά-
8 σχειν. εἰμὶ μὲν γὰρ ὁ κινδυνεύων ἐγὼ νυνὶ περὶ
τοῦ σώματος, τῆς δὲ κατηγορίας τὴν πλείστην
πεποίηται Φιλοκράτους καὶ Φρύνωνος καὶ τῶν
ἄλλων συμπρέσβεων, καὶ Φιλίππου καὶ τῆς εἰρήνης καὶ τῶν Εὐβούλου πολιτευμάτων, ἐν ἅπασι
δὲ τούτοις ἐγὼ τέταγμαι. μόνος δ᾽ ἐν τῷ λόγῳ
φαίνεται κηδεμὼν τῆς πόλεως Δημοσθένης, οἱ δ᾽
ἄλλοι προδόται· διατετέλεκε γὰρ εἰς ἡμᾶς ὑβρί-
ζων, καὶ λοιδορίας ψευδεῖς οὐκ ἐμοὶ μόνον λοιδο-
9 ρούμενος, ἀλλὰ καὶ τοῖς ἄλλοις. ὃν δ᾽ οὕτως
ἀτιμάζει, πάλιν ἐκ μεταβολῆς, ὅπου ἂν τύχῃ,[2]
ὥσπερ Ἀλκιβιάδην ἢ Θεμιστοκλέα κρίνων, οἳ
πλεῖστον τῶν Ἑλλήνων δόξῃ διήνεγκαν, ἀνῃρηκέ-
ναι μὲν αἰτιᾶται[3] τὰς ἐν Φωκεῦσι πόλεις, ἀπηλ-

---

[1] προκατεγνωκότας Hamaker : προκατεγνωκότας ὡς ἀδικῶ
MSS.

[2] ὅπου ἂν τύχῃ Scholiast : ὅπου τύχῃ or ὅπου τύχοι MSS.

[3] αἰτιᾶται Cobet : αἰτιᾶταί με MSS.

you whether it was possible in one and the same city to sentence Philocrates to death because he would not await trial and so condemned himself, and then to acquit me. But I think that on this very ground I ought most certainly to be cleared; for if the man who condemns himself by not awaiting trial is guilty, certainly he who denies the charge and submits his person to the laws and to his fellow citizens is not guilty.

Now, fellow citizens, as regards the rest of his accusations, if I pass over any point and fail to mention it, I beg of you to question me and let me know what it is that you wish to hear about, and to refrain from forming any judgment in advance, but to listen with impartial goodwill. I do not know where I ought to begin, so inconsistent are his accusations. See whether you think I am being treated in a reasonable way. It is I who am now on trial, and that too for my life; and yet the greater part of his accusation has been directed against Philocrates and Phrynon and the other members of the embassy, against Philip and the peace and the policies of Eubulus; it is only as one among all these that he gives me a place. But when it is a question of solicitude for the interests of the state, one solitary man stands out in all his speech— Demosthenes; all the rest are traitors! For he has unceasingly insulted us and poured out his slanderous lies, not upon me alone, but upon all the rest as well. And after treating a man with such contempt, later, when it suits his whim, he turns about, and as though he were accusing an Alcibiades or a Themistocles, the most famous men among all the Greeks, he proceeds to charge that same man with having

λοτριωκέναι δ' ὑμῶν τὸν ἐπὶ Θράκης τόπον, ἐκ-
βεβληκέναι δὲ τῆς ἀρχῆς Κερσοβλέπτην, ἄνδρα
10 φίλον καὶ σύμμαχον τῆς πόλεως. ἐνεχείρησε δ'
ἀπεικάζειν με Διονυσίῳ τῷ Σικελίας τυράννῳ, καὶ
μετὰ σπουδῆς καὶ κραυγῆς πολλῆς παρεκελεύσαθ'
ὑμῖν φυλάξασθαι, καὶ τὸ τῆς ἱερείας ἐνύπνιον τῆς
ἐν Σικελίᾳ διηγήσατο. οὕτω δ' ἄνω τὸ πρᾶγμα
ἐξάρας, ἐφθόνησέ μου ταῖς διαβολαῖς, τὰς αἰτίας
ἀνατιθεὶς τῶν πεπραγμένων οὐ τοῖς ἐμοῖς λόγοις,
ἀλλὰ τοῖς ὅπλοις τοῖς Φιλίππου.

11 Πρὸς δὴ τοσαύτην τόλμαν καὶ τερατείαν ἀνθρώπου χαλεπὸν καὶ διαμνημονεῦσαι[1] καθ' ἕκαστα,
καὶ λέγειν μετὰ κινδύνου πρὸς ἀπροσδοκήτους
διαβολάς. ὅθεν δ' ἡγοῦμαι σαφεστάτους τέ μοι
τοὺς λόγους ἔσεσθαι καὶ γνωρίμους ὑμῖν καὶ
δικαίους, ἐντεῦθεν ἄρξομαι, ἀπὸ τῶν περὶ τῆς
εἰρήνης λόγων καὶ τῆς αἱρέσεως τῆς πρεσβείας·
οὕτω γὰρ μάλιστα καὶ μεμνήσομαι, καὶ δυνή-
σομαι εἰπεῖν, καὶ ὑμεῖς μαθήσεσθε.

12 Ἅπαντας γὰρ ὑμᾶς οἶμαι τοῦτό γε αὐτοὺς[2]
μνημονεύειν, ὅθ' οἱ πρέσβεις οἱ τῶν Εὐβοέων,
ἐπειδὴ περὶ τῆς πρὸς αὐτοὺς εἰρήνης τῷ δήμῳ
διελέχθησαν, εἶπον, ὅτι καὶ Φίλιππος αὐτοὺς
κελεύσειεν ὑμῖν ἀπαγγεῖλαι ὅτι βούλεται διαλύσασθαι πρὸς ὑμᾶς καὶ εἰρήνην[3] ἄγειν. οὐ πολλῷ
δ' ὕστερον χρόνῳ Φρύνων ὁ Ῥαμνούσιος ἑάλω
ὑπὸ λῃστῶν ἐν ταῖς σπονδαῖς ταῖς Ὀλυμπιακαῖς,

---

[1] διαμνημονεῦσαι Weidner: the MSS. have τὰ λεχθέντα
before or after the verb.
[2] αὐτοὺς Herwerden: αὐτὸ MSS.
[3] εἰρήνην Baiter: τὴν εἰρήνην MSS.

destroyed the cities in Phocis, with having lost
you the Thracian coast, with having expelled from
his kingdom Cersobleptes, a friend and ally of the
city. And he undertook to liken me to Dionysius, the
tyrant of Sicily, and vehemently and with loud cries
he called upon you to be on your guard against me;
and he related the dream of the priestess in Sicily.[1]
Then, after all this exaggeration, he begrudged me
the credit even for what he had slanderously charged
me with accomplishing, and ascribed it all, not to
my words, but to the arms of Philip.

When now a man has shown such trickery and
effrontery, it is difficult even to remember every
single thing, and in the face of danger it is not easy
to answer unexpected slanders. But I will begin
with those events which I think will enable me to
make my presentation most clear and intelligible to
you, and fair; these events are the discussion that
took place concerning the peace, and the choice
of the ambassadors. In this way I shall best
remember his charges and best be able to speak
effectively, and you will be best instructed.

There is one thing, at any rate, which I think you
all yourselves remember: how the ambassadors from
Euboea, after they had discussed with our assembly
the question of our making peace with them, told
us that Philip also had asked them to report to you
that he wished to come to terms and be at peace
with you. Not long after this, Phrynon of Rhamnus
was captured by privateers, during the Olympian

---

[1] Neither the comparison with Dionysius nor the story of
the dream was retained by Demosthenes when he revised his
speech for publication.

ὡς αὐτὸς ᾐτιᾶτο· ἐπειδὴ δ' ἐπανῆλθε δεῦρο λυ-
τρωθείς, ἐδεῖτο ὑμῶν πρεσβευτὴν αὑτῷ πρὸς
Φίλιππον ἑλέσθαι, ἵνα, εἴ πως δύναιτο, ἀπολάβοι
τὰ λύτρα. πεισθέντες δ' ὑμεῖς εἵλεσθ' αὐτῷ
13 Κτησιφῶντα πρεσβευτήν. ἐπειδὴ δὲ ἐπανῆκε
δεῦρ' ἀπὸ τῆς πρεσβείας ὁ Κτησιφῶν, ἀπήγγειλε
πρὸς ὑμᾶς ὑπὲρ ὧν ἐπέμφθη, καὶ πρὸς τούτοις,
ὅτι φαίη Φίλιππος ἄκων μὲν πολεμῆσαι πρὸς
ὑμᾶς, βούλεσθαι δὲ καὶ νῦν ἀπαλλαγῆναι τοῦ
πολέμου. εἰπόντος δὲ ταῦτα τοῦ Κτησιφῶντος,
καὶ πολλήν τινα ἐξαγγείλαντος πρὸς τούτοις
φιλανθρωπίαν, καὶ τοῦ δήμου σφόδρα ἀποδεξαμένου καὶ τὸν Κτησιφῶντα ἐπαινέσαντος, ἀντει-
πόντος δ' οὐδενός, ἐνταῦθα ἤδη δίδωσι ψήφισμα
Φιλοκράτης ὁ Ἁγνούσιος, καὶ ὁ δῆμος ἅπας
ὁμογνωμονῶν ἐχειροτόνησεν, ἐξεῖναι Φιλίππῳ
δεῦρο κήρυκα[1] καὶ πρέσβεις πέμπειν ὑπὲρ εἰρήνης. πρότερον μὲν γὰρ καὶ αὐτὸ τοῦτ' ἐκωλύετο
ὑπό τινων, οἷς ἦν τοῦτ' ἐπιμελές, ὡς αὐτὸ τὸ
14 πρᾶγμα ἔδειξεν. γράφονται γὰρ οὗτοι παρανόμων τὸ ψήφισμα, Λυκῖνον ἐπὶ τὴν γραφὴν ἐπι-
γραψάμενοι, καὶ τίμημα ἑκατὸν τάλαντα. καὶ
μετὰ ταῦτ' εἰσῄει ἡ γραφὴ εἰς τὸ δικαστήριον,
ἀρρώστως δ' ἔχων ὁ Φιλοκράτης ἐκάλεσεν αὑτῷ
συνήγορον Δημοσθένην, ἀλλ' οὐκ ἐμέ. παρελθὼν
δ' ὁ μισοφίλιππος Δημοσθένης, κατέτριψε τὴν
ἡμέραν ἀπολογούμενος· καὶ τὸ τελευταῖον ἀπο-

κήρυκα Bekker : κήρυκας MSS.

---

[1] Shortly before the time for the Olympic festival in each
quadrennium, heralds were sent out by the Elean state to
carry to all Greeks the invitation to the festival and to pro-

truce, according to his own complaint.[1] Now when he had been ransomed and had come home, he asked you to choose an envoy to go to Philip in his behalf, in order that, if possible, he might recover his ransom money. You were persuaded, and chose Ctesiphon as envoy for him. When Ctesiphon returned from his mission, he first reported to you on the matters for which he was sent, and then in addition he said that Philip declared that he had gone to war with you against his own will, and that he wished, even now, to be rid of the war. When Ctesiphon had said this and had also told of the marked kindness of his reception, the people eagerly accepted his report and passed a vote of praise for Ctesiphon. Not a voice was raised in opposition. Then it was, and not till then, that Philocrates of Hagnus offered a motion, which was passed by unanimous vote of the people, that Philip be allowed to send to us a herald and ambassadors to treat for peace. For up to this time even that had been prevented by certain men who made it their business to do so, as the event itself proved. For they attacked the motion as unconstitutional,[2] subscribing the name of Lycinus to the indictment, in which they proposed a penalty of one hundred talents. When the case came to trial Philocrates was ill, and called as his advocate Demosthenes, not me. And Demosthenes the Philip-hater came to the platform and used up the day in his plea for the defence. Finally Philocrates was

claim a sacred truce between all warring Greek states. Phrynon claimed that Macedonian pirates had violated this truce.

[2] On the indictment for proposing an unconstitutional measure, see Speech III., Introduction.

φεύγει Φιλοκράτης, ὁ δὲ γραψάμενος τὸ πέμπτον
μέρος τῶν ψήφων οὐ μεταλαμβάνει. καὶ ταῦθ'
15 ὑμεῖς ἅπαντες ἴστε. ὑπὸ δὲ τοὺς αὐτοὺς καιροὺς
Ὄλυνθος ἑάλω, καὶ πολλοὶ τῶν ἡμετέρων ἐγκατε-
λήφθησαν πολιτῶν, ὧν ἦν Ἰατροκλῆς ὁ Ἐργοχά-
ρους ἀδελφὸς καὶ Εὐήρατος ὁ Στρομβίχου υἱός.
ὑπὲρ δὴ τούτων ἱκετηρίαν θέντες οἱ οἰκεῖοι ἐδέοντο
ὑμῶν ἐπιμέλειαν ποιήσασθαι. παρελθόντες δ'
αὐτοῖς συνηγόρουν Φιλοκράτης καὶ Δημοσθένης,
ἀλλ' οὐκ Αἰσχίνης. καὶ πέμπουσι πρεσβευτὴν
Ἀριστόδημον τὸν ὑποκριτὴν πρὸς Φίλιππον, διὰ
16 τὴν γνῶσιν καὶ φιλανθρωπίαν τῆς τέχνης. ὡς δ'
ἐπανήκων ἀπὸ τῆς πρεσβείας ὁ Ἀριστόδημος διά
τινας ἀσχολίας οὐ προσῄει πρὸς τὴν βουλήν,
ἀλλ' ἔφθασεν αὐτὸν Ἰατροκλῆς ἐλθὼν ἐκ Μακεδονίας ἀφεθεὶς ὑπὸ Φιλίππου ἄνευ λύτρων,[1] ἐνταῦθ' ἠγανάκτουν πολλοί, ὅτι τὴν πρεσβείαν οὐκ
ἀπήγγειλεν ὁ Ἀριστόδημος, τοὺς αὐτοὺς λόγους
ἀκούοντες τοῦ Ἰατροκλέους περὶ τοῦ Φιλίππου.
17 τελευταῖον δ' εἰσελθὼν[2] Δημοκράτης ὁ Ἀφιδναῖος
ἔπεισε τὴν βουλὴν ἀνακαλέσασθαι τὸν Ἀριστό-
δημον· εἰς δὲ τῶν βουλευτῶν ἦν Δημοσθένης ὁ
ἐμὸς κατήγορος. παρελθὼν δ' ὁ Ἀριστόδημος
πολλήν τινα εὔνοιαν ἀπήγγειλε τοῦ Φιλίππου
πρὸς τὴν πόλιν, καὶ προσέθηκεν ὅτι καὶ σύμ-
μαχος βούλοιτο τῇ πόλει γενέσθαι. καὶ ταῦτ'
οὐκ ἐν τῇ βουλῇ μόνον εἶπεν, ἀλλὰ καὶ ἐν τῷ
δήμῳ. κἀνταῦθ' οὐδὲν ἀντεῖπε Δημοσθένης,
ἀλλὰ καὶ στεφανῶσαι τὸν Ἀριστόδημον ἔγραψε.

---

[1] λύτρων Dobree : λύτρων γενόμενος αἰχμάλωτος MSS.
[2] εἰσελθὼν Weidner : the MSS. have εἰς τὴν βουλὴν before
or after εἰσελθὼν.

acquitted, and the prosecutor failed to receive the fifth part of the votes.[1] This is matter of common knowledge. Now about the same time Olynthus was taken, and many of our citizens were captured there, among them Iatrocles, brother of Ergochares, and Eueratus, son of Strombichus. Their families naturally made supplication in their behalf, and begged you to provide for them. Their spokesmen before the people were Philocrates and Demosthenes, not Aeschines. So Aristodemus the actor is sent as envoy to Philip, as being an acquaintance of his, and of a profession that naturally wins friends. But when Aristodemus returned from his mission, his report to the senate was delayed by certain business of his, and meanwhile Iatrocles came back from Macedonia, released by Philip without ransom. Then many people were angry with Aristodemus for having failed to make his report, for they heard from Iatrocles the same story about Philip.[2] Finally Democrates of Aphidna went before the senate and persuaded them to summon Aristodemus. One of the senators was Demosthenes, my accuser! Aristodemus appeared before them, reported Philip's great friendliness toward the city, and added this besides, that Philip even wished to become an ally of our state. This he said not only before the senate, but also at an assembly of the people. Here again Demosthenes spoke no word in opposition, but even moved that a crown be conferred on Aristodemus.

[1] A prosecutor who failed to receive one-fifth part of the votes of the jury was subject to a fine of 1,000 drachmas and disability to bring such a suit in the future.

[2] The same story that the Euboean ambassadors and Ctesiphon had brought, that Philip was ready to discuss peace.

18 Ῥηθέντων δὲ τούτων, ψήφισμα ἔγραψεν ὁ
Φιλοκράτης ἑλέσθαι πρέσβεις πρὸς Φίλιππον
ἄνδρας δέκα, οἵτινες διαλέξονται Φιλίππῳ περὶ
εἰρήνης καὶ τῶν κοινῇ συμφερόντων Ἀθηναίοις
καὶ Φιλίππῳ. χειροτονουμένων δὲ τῶν δέκα
πρέσβεων, ἐγὼ μὲν προεβλήθην ὑπὸ Ναυσικλέους,
Δημοσθένης δ᾽ ὑπ᾽ αὐτοῦ Φιλοκράτους, ὁ νυνὶ
19 Φιλοκράτους κατηγορῶν. οὕτω δ᾽ ἦν πρόθυμος
εἰς τὰ πράγματα, ὥστε ἐν τῇ βουλῇ γράφει, ἵνα
ἀζήμιος ὢν ἡμῖν ὁ Ἀριστόδημος συμπρεσβεύῃ,
ἑλέσθαι πρέσβεις ἐπὶ τὰς πόλεις ἐν αἷς ἔδει τὸν
Ἀριστόδημον ἀγωνίζεσθαι, οἵτινες ὑπὲρ αὐτοῦ
παραιτήσονται τὰς ζημίας. καὶ ὅτι ταῦτ᾽ ἐστὶν
ἀληθῆ, λαβέ μοι τὰ ψηφίσματα, καὶ τὴν ἐκμαρ-
τυρίαν ἀνάγνωθι τὴν Ἀριστοδήμου, καὶ κάλει
πρὸς οὓς ἐξεμαρτύρησεν, ἵν᾽ εἰδῶσιν οἱ δικασταί,
τίς ὁ Φιλοκράτους ἑταῖρος, καὶ τίς ὁ τὰς δωρεὰς
Ἀριστοδήμῳ φάσκων πείσειν δοῦναι τὸν δῆμον.

ΨΗΦΙΣΜΑΤΑ. ΕΚΜΑΡΤΥΡΙΑ[1]

20 Ἡ μὲν τοίνυν ἐξ ἀρχῆς ἔνστασις τῶν ὅλων
πραγμάτων ἐγένετο οὐ δι᾽ ἐμοῦ, ἀλλὰ διὰ Δημοσθένους καὶ Φιλοκράτους· ἐν δὲ τῇ πρεσβείᾳ
συσσιτεῖν ἡμῖν ἐσπούδασεν, οὐκ ἐμὲ πείσας, ἀλλὰ
τοὺς μετ᾽ ἐμοῦ, Ἀγλαοκρέοντα τὸν Τενέδιον, ὃν ἐκ
τῶν συμμάχων εἵλεσθε, καὶ Ἰατροκλέα. ἐν δὲ
τῇ πορείᾳ παρακελεύεσθαί με φησὶν αὐτῷ, ὅπως
τὸ θηρίον κοινῇ φυλάξομεν, τὸν Φιλοκράτην,
πρᾶγμα λέγων πεπλασμένον. πῶς γὰρ ἂν ἐγὼ
Δημοσθένην ἐπὶ Φιλοκράτην παρεκάλουν, ὃν

[1] ΨΗΦΙΣΜΑΤΑ. ΕΚΜΑΡΤΥΡΙΑ Blass: the MSS. have ψήφισμα and ἐκμαρτυρίαι or μαρτυρία.

Next Philocrates moved that ten ambassadors be
chosen to go to Philip and discuss with him both the
question of peace and the common interests of the
Athenians and Philip. At the election of the ten
ambassadors I was nominated by Nausicles, but Philocrates himself nominated Demosthenes—Demosthenes, the man who now accuses Philocrates. And
so eager was Demosthenes for the business, that in
order to make it possible for Aristodemus to be a
member of our embassy without loss to himself, he
moved in council that we elect envoys to go to the
cities in which Aristodemus was under contract to
act, and beg in his behalf the cancelling of his for-
feitures. To prove the truth of this [*to the Clerk of
the Court*] take, if you please, the decrees, and read
the deposition of Aristodemus, and call the witnesses
before whom the deposition was made, in order that
the jury may know who was the good friend of Philocrates, and who it was that promised to persuade
the people to bestow the rewards on Aristodemus.

THE DECREES. THE DEPOSITION

The whole affair, therefore, from the beginning
originated not with me, but with Demosthenes and
Philocrates. And on the embassy he was eager to
belong to our mess—not with my consent, but with
that of my companions, Aglaocreon of Tenedos,
whom you chose to represent the allies, and Iatrocles.
And he asserts that on the journey I urged him to
join me in guarding against the beast—meaning
Philocrates. But the whole story was a fabrica-
tion; for how could I have urged Demosthenes
against Philocrates, when I knew that he had

ἤδειν συνειπόντα μὲν Φιλοκράτει, ὅτ᾽ ἦν ἡ τῶι
παρανόμων γραφή, προβληθέντα δ᾽ εἰς τὴν πρε-
21 σβείαν ὑπὸ Φιλοκράτους; πρὸς δὲ τούτοις οὐκ ἐν
τοιούτοις ἦμεν λόγοις,[1] ἀλλ᾽ ὅλην τὴν πορείαν
ἠναγκαζόμεθα Δημοσθένην ὑπομένειν ἀφόρητον
καὶ βαρὺν ἄνθρωπον· ὃς διασκοπούντων ἡμῶν ὅ
τι χρὴ λέγειν,[2] καὶ Κίμωνος εἰπόντος ὅτι φοβοῖτο
μὴ δικαιολογούμενος περιγένοιτο ἡμῶν ὁ Φίλιππος, πηγὰς δὴ λόγων ἐπηγγέλλετο,[3] καὶ περὶ τῶν
δικαίων τῶν ὑπὲρ Ἀμφιπόλεως καὶ τῆς ἀρχῆς τοῦ
πολέμου τοιαῦτα ἐρεῖν ἔφη, ὥστε ἀπορράψειν τὸ
Φιλίππου στόμα ὁλοσχοίνῳ ἀβρόχῳ, καὶ πείσειν
Ἀθηναίους μὲν καταδέξασθαι Λεωσθένην, Φίλιππον δ᾽ Ἀθηναίοις Ἀμφίπολιν ἀποδοῦναι.

22 Ἵνα δὲ μὴ μακρολογῶ τὴν τούτου διεξιὼν
ὑπερηφανίαν, ὡς τάχιστα ἥκομεν εἰς Μακεδονίαν,
συνετάξαμεν πρὸς [4] ἡμᾶς αὐτούς, ὅταν προσίω-
μεν Φιλίππῳ, τὸν πρεσβύτατον πρῶτον [5] λέγειν
καὶ τοὺς λοιποὺς καθ᾽ ἡλικίαν· ἐτύγχανε δ᾽ ἡμῶν
νεώτατος ὤν, ὡς ἔφη, Δημοσθένης. ἐπειδὴ δὲ
εἰσεκλήθημεν,—καὶ τούτοις ἤδη μοι σφόδρα προσέχετε τὸν νοῦν· ἐντεῦθεν γὰρ κατόψεσθε τἀνθρώπου [6] φθόνον ὑπερβάλλοντα καὶ δεινὴν δειλίαν
ἅμα καὶ κακοήθειαν, καὶ τοιαύτας ἐπιβουλὰς κατ᾽

---

[1] λόγοις Baiter : λόγοις οἱ συμπρέσβεις MSS.

[2] λέγειν Taylor : λέγειν ἡμᾶς (or ὑμᾶς) τῶν συμπρέσβεων (or πρέσβεων) MSS.

[3] ἐπηγγέλλετο Taylor : before ἐπηγγέλλετο the MSS. have ἔχειν ἀφθόνους or ἀφθόνους ἔχειν.

[4] πρὸς added by Reiske.

[5] τὸν πρεσβύτατον πρῶτον Herwerden : τοὺς πρεσβυτάτους πρώτους MSS.

[6] τἀνθρώπου Markland : ἀνθρώπου MSS.

been Philocrates' advocate in the suit against the
legality of his motion, and that he had been nominated to the embassy by Philocrates? Moreover, this
was not the sort of conversation in which we were
engaged, but all the way we were forced to put up
with Demosthenes' odious and insufferable ways.
When we were discussing what should be said, and
when Cimon remarked that he was afraid Philip
would get the better of us in arguing his claims,
Demosthenes promised fountains of oratory, and said
that he was going to make such a speech about our
claims to Amphipolis and the origin of the war that
he would sew up Philip's mouth with an unsoaked
rush,[1] and he would persuade the Athenians to permit Leosthenes to return home,[2] and Philip to restore
Amphipolis to Athens.

But not to describe at length the overweening
self-confidence of this fellow, as soon as we were
come to Macedonia, we arranged among ourselves
that at our audience with Philip the eldest should
speak first, and the rest in the order of age. Now it
happened that the youngest man of us was, according
to his own assertion, Demosthenes. When we were
summoned—and pray now give especial attention to
this, for here you shall see the exceeding enviousness
of the man, and his strange cowardice and meanness
too, and such plottings against men who were his

---

[1] The job would be so easy that he would not have to stop
to soak the rush fibre and make it pliable. A proverbial
expression.

[2] Leosthenes was an Athenian orator and general, who
had been condemned to death in 361 because of the failure
of his campaign in the northern waters; he was now in exile
in Macedonia. The recovery of Amphipolis would mollify
the anger of the Athenians against him.

ἀνδρῶν συσσίτων καὶ συμπρέσβεων, ἃς οὐδ' ἂν
κατὰ τῶν ἐχθίστων τις εἰκῆ ποιήσαιτο. τοὺς γὰρ
τῆς πόλεως ἅλας καὶ τὴν δημοσίαν τράπεζαν περὶ
πλείστου δή φησι ποιεῖσθαι, οὐκ ὢν ἐπιχώριος,
23 εἰρήσεται γάρ, οὐδ' ἐγγενής. ἡμεῖς δέ, οἷς ἱερὰ
καὶ τάφοι προγόνων ὑπάρχουσιν ἐν τῇ πατρίδι,
καὶ διατριβαὶ καὶ συνήθειαι μεθ' ὑμῶν ἐλευθέριοι,
καὶ γάμοι κατὰ τοὺς νόμους καὶ κηδεσταὶ καὶ
τέκνα, Ἀθήνησι μὲν ἦμεν ἄξιοι τῆς ὑμετέρας
πίστεως, οὐ γὰρ ἄν ποτε ἡμᾶς εἵλεσθε, ἐλθόντες
δ' εἰς Μακεδονίαν ἐξαίφνης ἐγενόμεθα προδόται.
ὁ δὲ οὐδὲν ἄπρατον ἔχων μέρος τοῦ σώματος,[1] ὡς
ὢν Ἀριστείδης,[2] ὁ δίκαιος ἐπικαλούμενος, δυσχε-
ραίνει καὶ καταπτύει δωροδοκίας.
24 Ἀκούσατε δὴ τούς τε ἡμετέρους λόγους, οὓς
εἴπομεν ὑπὲρ ὑμῶν, καὶ πάλιν οὓς τὸ μέγα ὄφελος
τῆς πόλεως εἴρηκε Δημοσθένης, ἵν' ἐφεξῆς καὶ
κατὰ μικρὸν πρὸς ἕκαστα τῶν κατηγορημένων
ἀπολογήσωμαι. ἐπαινῶ δ' εἰς ὑπερβολὴν ὑμᾶς,
ὦ ἄνδρες δικασταί, ὅτι σιγῇ καὶ δικαίως ἡμῶν
ἀκούετε· ὥστε, ἐάν τι μὴ λύσω τῶν κατηγορημένων, οὐχ ὑμᾶς, ἀλλ' ἐμαυτὸν αἰτιάσομαι.

[1] Many MSS. add οὐδ' ὅθεν τὴν φωνὴν προΐεται (cp. § 88):
Blass brackets.
[2] Ἀριστείδης ὁ τοὺς φόρους τάξας τοῖς Ἕλλησιν MSS., Blass:
Scheibe and Weidner omit ὁ . . . Ἕλλησιν, as adapted from
iii. 258.

-----

[1] See Demosthenes xix. 189 ff. Aeschines had protested
that Demosthenes, in attacking his fellow-ambassadors on
their return from Macedonia, was violating the common
decencies of life, which demanded that men who had sat
at table together should treat one another as friends.

own fellow ambassadors and his messmates as one would hardly enter into even against his bitterest enemies. For you remember he says[1] it is the salt of the city and the table of the state for which he has most regard—he, who is no citizen born—for I will out with it!—nor akin to us.[2] But we, who have shrines and family tombs in our native land, and such life and intercourse with you as belong to free men, and lawful marriage, with its offspring and connections, we while at Athens were worthy of your confidence, or you would never have chosen us, but when we had come to Macedonia we all at once turned traitors! But the man who has not one member of his body left unsold, posing as a second Aristeides "the Just," is displeased, and spits on us, as takers of bribes.

Hear now the pleas that we made in your behalf, and again those which stand to the credit of Demosthenes, that great benefactor of the state, in order that I may answer one after another and in full detail each one of his accusations. But I commend you exceedingly, gentlemen of the jury, that in silence and with fairness you are listening to us. If, therefore, I fail to refute any one of his accusations, I shall have myself, not you, to blame.

[1] Demosthenes replied that the table and the salt, even in the case of the prytanes and other high officials who ate together at a common official table, gave no immunity to the wrong-doer; his fellow-officials were free to bring him to punishment. If the public table of the prytanes did not protect the guilty from attack by his fellow-officers, the table and the salt of the group of ambassadors should be no protection to Aeschines against Demosthenes' attack.

[2] In the *Speech against Ctesiphon*, 171 f., Aeschines declares that the maternal grandmother of Demosthenes was a Scythian.

25 Ἐπειδὴ γὰρ οἱ πρεσβύτεροι ταῖς ἡλικίαις ὑπὲρ
τῆς πρεσβείας εἰρήκεσαν, καὶ καθῆκεν εἰς ἡμᾶς ὁ
λόγος, τὰ μὲν καθ' ἕκαστα τῶν ἐκεῖ ῥηθέντων ὑπ'
ἐμοῦ, καὶ τοὺς πρὸς ταῦτα Φιλίππου [1] λόγους, ἐν
τῷ δήμῳ σαφῶς ἀπήγγειλα πρὸς ἅπαντας Ἀθηναίους, νυνὶ δὲ πειράσομαι διὰ κεφαλαίων ὑμᾶς
26 ὑπομιμνήσκειν. πρῶτον μὲν γὰρ πρὸς αὐτὸν
διεξῆλθον τὴν πατρικὴν εὔνοιαν καὶ τὰς εὐεργεσίας ἃς ὑμεῖς ὑπήρξατε Ἀμύντᾳ τῷ Φιλίππου
πατρί, οὐδὲν παραλείπων, ἀλλ' ἐφεξῆς ἅπαντα
ὑπομιμνήσκων, δεύτερον δέ, ὧν αὐτὸς ἦν μάρτυς
εὖ παθών. Ἀμύντου μὲν [2] γὰρ νεωστὶ τετελευ-
τηκότος καὶ Ἀλεξάνδρου τοῦ πρεσβυτάτου τῶν
ἀδελφῶν, Περδίκκου δὲ καὶ Φιλίππου παίδων
ὄντων, Εὐρυδίκης δὲ τῆς μητρὸς αὐτῶν προδεδο-
27 μένης ὑπὸ τῶν δοκούντων εἶναι [3] φίλων, Παυσανίου
δ' ἐπὶ τὴν ἀρχὴν [4] κατιόντος, φυγάδος μὲν ὄντος,
τῷ καιρῷ δ' ἰσχύοντος, πολλῶν δ' αὐτῷ συμ-
πραττόντων, ἔχοντος δὲ Ἑλληνικὴν δύναμιν, εἰλη-
φότος δὲ Ἀνθεμοῦντα καὶ Θέρμαν καὶ Στρέψαν
καὶ ἄλλ' ἄττα χωρία, Μακεδόνων δὲ οὐχ ὁμο-
νοούντων, ἀλλὰ τῶν πλείστων τὰ Παυσανίου
φρονούντων, ἐπὶ τῶν καιρῶν τούτων ἐχειροτόνησαν
Ἀθηναῖοι στρατηγὸν ἐπ' Ἀμφίπολιν Ἰφικράτην,
Ἀμφιπολιτῶν αὐτῶν ἐχόντων τότε τὴν πόλιν καὶ
28 τὴν χώραν καρπουμένων. ἀφικομένου δ' εἰς τοὺς
τόπους Ἰφικράτους μετ' ὀλίγων τὸ πρῶτον νεῶν,

---

[1] Φιλίππου Weidner : before Φιλίππου the MSS. have
λεχθέντας ὑπὸ or ῥηθέντας ὑπὸ.

[2] μὲν added by Franke from an ancient quotation of the
passage.

[3] εἶναι Cobet : the MSS. have αὐτῆς or αὐτοῖς before εἶναι.

[4] ἀρχὴν Cobet : ἀρχὴν αὐτῶν MSS.

So when the older men had spoken on the object of our mission, our turn came.[1] All that I said there and Philip's reply, I reported fully in your assembly in the presence of all the citizens, but I will try to recall it to you now in a summary way. In the first place, I described to him our traditional friendship and your generous services to Amyntas, the father of Philip, recalling them all one after another, and omitting nothing. Secondly, I reminded him of services of which he himself had been both witness and recipient. For shortly after the death of Amyntas, and of Alexander, the eldest of the brothers, while Perdiccas and Philip were still children, when their mother Eurydice had been betrayed by those who professed to be their friends, and when Pausanias was coming back to contend for the throne,[2] an exile then, but favoured by opportunity and the support of many of the people, and bringing a Greek force with him, and when he had already seized Anthemon, Therma, Strepsa, and certain other places, at a time when the Macedonians were not united, but most of them favoured Pausanias: at this crisis the Athenians elected Iphicrates as their general to go against Amphipolis—for at that time the people of Amphipolis were holding their city themselves and enjoying the products of the land. When Iphicrates had come into this region—with a few ships at first,

---

[1] The turn of Aeschines and Demosthenes as the youngest of the ambassadors.

[2] Amyntas, king of Macedonia, left three sons, Alexander, Perdiccas, and Philip. Alexander succeeded his father, but after a short reign he was assassinated. His mother Eurydice with her paramour Ptolemaeus took the throne. Her power was threatened by Pausanias, a member of a rival princely house.

ἐπὶ κατασκοπῇ μᾶλλον τῶν πραγμάτων ἢ πολιορ-
κίᾳ τῆς πόλεως, ἐνταῦθα, ἔφην ἐγώ, μετεπέμψατο
αὐτὸν Εὐρυδίκη ἡ μήτηρ ἡ σή, καὶ ὥς γε δὴ
λέγουσιν οἱ παρόντες πάντες, Περδίκκαν μὲν τὸν
ἀδελφὸν τὸν σὸν καταστήσασα εἰς τὰς χεῖρας τὰς
Ἰφικράτους, σὲ δὲ εἰς τὰ γόνατα τὰ ἐκείνου θεῖσα
παιδίον ὄντα, εἶπεν ὅτι " Ἀμύντας ὁ πατὴρ τῶν
παιδίων τούτων, ὅτ᾽ ἔζη, υἱὸν ἐποιήσατό σε, τῇ δὲ
Ἀθηναίων πόλει οἰκείως ἐχρήσατο, ὥστε συμβαίνει σοι καὶ ἰδίᾳ τῶν παίδων τούτων γεγενῆσθαι
29 ἀδελφῷ, καὶ δημοσίᾳ φίλῳ ἡμῖν εἶναι."   καὶ
μετὰ ταῦτα ἤδη δέησιν ἰσχυρὰν ἐποιεῖτο καὶ ὑπὲρ
ὑμῶν καὶ ὑπὲρ αὐτῆς καὶ ὑπὲρ τῆς ἀρχῆς καὶ
ὅλως ὑπὲρ τῆς σωτηρίας.   ἀκούσας δὲ ταῦτα
Ἰφικράτης ἐξήλασε Παυσανίαν ἐκ Μακεδονίας,
καὶ τὴν δυναστείαν ὑμῖν ἔσωσε. καὶ μετὰ ταῦτα
εἶπον περὶ Πτολεμαίου, ὃς ἦν ἐπίτροπος καθεστηκὼς τῶν πραγμάτων, ὡς ἀχάριστον καὶ δεινὸν
ἔργον διεπράξατο, διδάσκων ὅτι πρῶτον μὲν ὑπὲρ
Ἀμφιπόλεως ἀντέπραττε τῇ πόλει, καὶ πρὸς
Θηβαίους διαφερομένων Ἀθηναίων συμμαχίαν
ἐποιήσατο, καὶ πάλιν ὡς Περδίκκας εἰς τὴν ἀρχὴν
καταστὰς ὑπὲρ Ἀμφιπόλεως ἐπολέμησε τῇ πόλει.
30 καὶ τὴν ὑμετέραν ἠδικημένων ὅμως φιλανθρωπίαν
διεξῄειν, λέγων ὅτι κρατοῦντες τῷ πολέμῳ Περδίκκαν Καλλισθένους ἡγουμένου,[1] ἀνοχὰς πρὸς
αὐτὸν ἐποιήσασθε, ἀεί τινος προσδοκῶντες τῶν
δικαίων τεύξεσθαι.   καὶ τὴν διαβολὴν ταύτην

---

[1] ἡγουμένου Baiter : ἡγουμένου Ἀθηναίων or Ἀθηναίων ἡγουμένου MSS.

---

[1] Amyntas, hard pressed by his Illyrian and Thessalian
neighbours, had at one time been driven from his throne by

for the purpose of examining into the situation rather than of laying siege to the city—"Then," said I, "your mother Eurydice sent for him, and according to the testimony of all who were present, she put your brother Perdiccas into the arms of Iphicrates, and set you upon his knees—for you were a little boy—and said, 'Amyntas, the father of these little children, when he was alive, made you his son,[1] and enjoyed the friendship of the city of Athens; we have a right therefore to consider you in your private capacity a brother of these boys, and in your public capacity a friend to us.' After this she at once began to make earnest entreaty in your behalf and in her own, and for the maintenance of the throne—in a word for full protection. When Iphicrates had heard all this, he drove Pausanias out of Macedonia and preserved the dynasty for you." Next I spoke about Ptolemaeus, who had been made regent, telling what an ungrateful and outrageous thing he had done: I explained how in the first place he continually worked against our city in the interest of Amphipolis, and when we were in controversy with the Thebans, made alliance with them; and then how Perdiccas, when he came to the throne, fought for Amphipolis against our city. And I showed that, wronged as you were, you maintained your friendly attitude; for I told how, when you had conquered Perdiccas in the war, under the generalship of Callisthenes, you made a truce with him, ever expecting to receive some just return. And I tried to remove the ill feeling

a rival prince. After two years he was restored to power by the help of Sparta and Athens. It is conjectured that this was the occasion of his adoption of the Athenian Iphicrates, one of the most capable leaders of mercenary troops.

ἐπειρώμην λύειν, διδάσκων ὅτι Καλλισθένην ὁ
δῆμος ἀπέκτεινεν, οὐ διὰ τὰς πρὸς Περδίκκαν
ἀνοχάς, ἀλλὰ δι᾽ ἑτέρας αἰτίας. καὶ πάλιν οὐκ
ὤκνουν κατ᾽ αὐτοῦ λέγειν Φιλίππου, ἐπιτιμῶν ὅτι
τὴν ἐκδοχὴν ἐποιήσατο τοῦ[1] πρὸς τὴν πόλιν
31 πολέμου. καὶ πάντων ὧν εἴποιμι μάρτυρας τὰς
ἐκείνων ἐπιστολὰς παρειχόμην καὶ τὰ ψηφίσματα
τοῦ δήμου καὶ τὰς Καλλισθένους ἀνοχάς. περὶ
μὲν οὖν τῆς ἐξ ἀρχῆς κτήσεως τῆς χώρας, καὶ
τῶν καλουμένων Ἐννέα ὁδῶν, καὶ περὶ τῶν Θη-
σέως παίδων, ὧν Ἀκάμας λέγεται φερνὴν ἐπὶ τῇ
γυναικὶ λαβεῖν τὴν χώραν ταύτην, τότε μὲν ἥρ-
μοττέ τε λέγειν καὶ ἐρρήθη ὡς ἐνεδέχετο ἀκριβέ-
στατα, νυνὶ δὲ ἴσως ἀνάγκη συντέμνειν τοὺς
λόγους· ἃ δὲ ἦν τῶν σημείων οὐκ ἐν τοῖς ἀρχαίοις
μύθοις, ἀλλ᾽ ἐφ᾽ ἡμῶν γεγενημένα, καὶ[2] τού-
32 των ἐπεμνήσθην. συμμαχίας γὰρ Λακεδαιμονίων καὶ τῶν ἄλλων Ἑλλήνων συνελθούσης,
εἷς ὧν τούτων Ἀμύντας ὁ Φιλίππου πατὴρ καὶ
πέμπων σύνεδρον καὶ τῆς καθ᾽ αὑτὸν ψήφου
κύριος ὤν, ἐψηφίσατο Ἀμφίπολιν τὴν Ἀθηναίων
συνεξαιρεῖν μετὰ τῶν ἄλλων Ἑλλήνων Ἀθηναίοις.
καὶ τούτων τὸ κοινὸν δόγμα τῶν Ἑλλήνων καὶ
τοὺς ψηφισαμένους ἐκ τῶν δημοσίων γραμμάτων
33 μάρτυρας παρειχόμην. "Ὧν δὲ Ἀμύντας ἀπέστη[3]
ἐναντίον τῶν Ἑλλήνων ἁπάντων οὐ μόνον λόγοις,
ἀλλὰ καὶ ψήφῳ, τούτων," ἔφην ἐγώ, "σὲ τὸν ἐξ
ἐκείνου γεγενημένον οὐκ ἔστι δίκαιον ἀντιποιεῖ-
σθαι. εἰ δ᾽ ἀντιποιῇ κατὰ πόλεμον λαβὼν εἰκότως

---

[1] τοῦ . . . πόλιν Blass : τοῦ after πόλιν MSS.
[2] καὶ added by Franke.
[3] ἀπέστη Baiter : ἀπέστη ὁ Φιλίππου πατήρ MSS.

that was connected with this affair by showing that it was not the truce with Perdiccas that led the people to put Callisthenes to death, but other causes. And again I did not hesitate to complain of Philip himself, blaming him for having taken up in his turn the war against our state. As proof of all my statements, I offered the letters of the persons in question, the decrees of the people, and Callisthenes' treaty of truce. Now the facts about our original acquisition both of the district and of the place called Ennea Hodoi,[1] and the story of the sons of Theseus, one of whom, Acamas, is said to have received this district as the dowry of his wife—all this was fitting to the occasion then, and was given with the utmost exactness, but now I suppose I must be brief; but those proofs which rested, not on the ancient legends, but on occurrences of our own time, these also I called to mind. For at a congress[2] of the Lacedaemonian allies and the other Greeks, in which Amyntas, the father of Philip, being entitled to a seat, was represented by a delegate whose vote was absolutely under his control, he joined the other Greeks in voting to help Athens to recover possession of Amphipolis. As proof of this I presented from the public records the resolution of the Greek congress and the names of those who voted. "Now," said I, "a claim which Amyntas renounced in the presence of all the Greeks, and that not by words alone, but by his vote, that claim you his son have no right to advance. But if you argue that it is right for you to keep the place because you took it in war,

---

[1] Ennea Hodoi ("Nine Roads") was the old name of the place colonized by the Athenians in 436 under the name of Amphipolis.   [2] The "Congress of Sparta," 371 B.C.

ἔχειν, εἰ μὲν πρὸς ἡμᾶς πολεμήσας δοριάλωτον τὴν πόλιν εἷλες, κυρίως ἔχεις τῷ τοῦ πολέμου νόμῳ κτησάμενος· εἰ δ᾽ Ἀμφιπολίτας ἀφείλου τὴν Ἀθηναίων πόλιν, οὐχὶ τἀκείνων ἔχεις, ἀλλὰ τὴν Ἀθηναίων χώραν."

34 Ῥηθέντων δὲ καὶ τούτων καὶ ἑτέρων λόγων, ἤδη καθῆκεν εἰς Δημοσθένην τὸ τῆς πρεσβείας μέρος, καὶ πάντες προσεῖχον ὡς ὑπερβολάς τινας δυνάμεως ἀκουσόμενοι λόγων· καὶ γὰρ πρὸς αὐτὸν τὸν Φίλιππον, ὡς ἦν ὕστερον ἀκούειν, καὶ πρὸς τοὺς ἑταίρους ἐξήγγελτο[1] ἡ τῶν ἐπαγγελιῶν ὑπερβολή. οὕτω δὲ ἁπάντων διακειμένων πρὸς τὴν ἀκρόασιν, φθέγγεται τὸ θηρίον τοῦτο προοίμιον σκοτεινόν τι καὶ τεθνηκὸς δειλίᾳ, καὶ μικρὸν προαγαγὼν ἄνω τῶν πραγμάτων, ἐξαίφνης ἐσίγησε καὶ διηπορήθη,

35 τελευτῶν δὲ ἐκπίπτει ἐκ τοῦ λόγου. ἰδὼν δὲ αὐτὸν ὁ Φίλιππος ὡς διέκειτο, θαρρεῖν τε παρεκελεύετο καὶ μὴ νομίζειν, ὥσπερ ἐν τοῖς θεάτροις, διὰ τοῦτό[2] τι πεπονθέναι, ἀλλ᾽ ἡσυχῇ καὶ κατὰ μικρὸν ἀναμιμνῄσκεσθαι, καὶ λέγειν ὡς προείλετο. ὁ δ᾽ ὡς ἅπαξ ἐταράχθη καὶ τῶν γεγραμμένων διεσφάλη, οὐδ᾽ ἀναλαβεῖν αὐτὸν ἐδυνήθη, ἀλλὰ καὶ πάλιν ἐπιχειρήσας[3] ταυτὸν ἔπαθεν. ὡς δ᾽ ἦν σιωπή, μεταστῆναι ἡμᾶς ὁ κῆρυξ ἐκέλευσεν.

---

[1] ἐξήγγελτο Bekker : ἐξηγγέλλετο or ἐξηγγέλθη MSS. The MSS. have αὐτοῦ before or after the verb : Blass omits.
[2] τοῦτο Stephanus : τοῦτο οἴεσθαι MSS.
[3] ἐπιχειρήσας Weidner : the MSS. have λέγειν before or after ἐπιχειρήσας.

---

[1] Amphipolis was founded as a colony of Athens in 436, and became one of the most important cities on the northern coast. The Spartans seized it early in the Peloponnesian war, and held it till the close of the war. They then

if it is true that it was a war against us in which you took the city, you do hold it justly, by right of conquest; but if it was from the Amphipolitans that you took a city which belonged to the Athenians, it is not the property of the Amphipolitans that you are holding, but territory of Athens." [1]

Now when I had said this and more beside, at last came Demosthenes' turn to speak. All were intent, expecting to hear a masterpiece of eloquence. For, as we learned afterwards, his extravagant boasting had been reported to Philip and his court. So when all were thus prepared to listen, this creature mouthed forth a proem—an obscure sort of thing and as dead as fright could make it; and getting on a little way into the subject he suddenly stopped speaking and stood helpless; finally he collapsed completely. Philip saw his plight and bade him take courage, and not to think, as though he were an actor on the stage, that his collapse was an irreparable calamity, but to keep cool and try gradually to recall his speech, and speak it off as he had prepared it. But he, having been once upset, and having forgotten what he had written, was unable to recover himself; nay, on making a second attempt, he broke down again. Silence followed; then the herald bade us withdraw.

renounced their claim to it, but the people of the city themselves refused to return to Athenian allegiance. Repeated expeditions were sent out by the Athenians to retake the city, but without success. One of Philip's first acts was to seize Amphipolis. It was claimed at Athens that he had promised, if given a free hand, to restore the place to Athens; but this he refused to do, and so began the first war between Athens and Philip. The Athenian claim to the city was therefore one of the most important matters to be presented by the ambassadors whose mission Aeschines is here describing.

THE SPEECHES OF AESCHINES

36 Ἐπειδὴ δ' ἐφ' ἡμῶν αὐτῶν[1] ἐγενόμεθα, σφόδρα[2] σκυθρωπάσας ὁ χρηστὸς οὑτοσὶ Δημοσθένης ἀπολωλεκέναι με ἔφη τὴν πόλιν καὶ τοὺς συμμάχους. ἐκπλαγέντος δὲ οὐκ ἐμοῦ μόνου, ἀλλὰ καὶ τῶν συμπρέσβεων ἁπάντων, καὶ τὴν αἰτίαν πυνθανομένων δι' ἣν ταῦτ' εἶπεν, ἤρετό με εἰ τῶν Ἀθήνησι πραγμάτων ἐπιλέλησμαι, καὶ τὸν δῆμον καταπεπονημένον καὶ σφόδρα ἐπιθυμοῦντα εἰρήνης εἰ μὴ 37 μέμνημαι. "Ἦ μέγα φρονεῖς," ἔφη, "ἐπὶ ταῖς ἐψηφισμέναις μὲν πεντήκοντα ναυσίν, οὐδέποτε δὲ πληρωθησομέναις; οὕτω γὰρ ἠρέθικας Φίλιππον καὶ τοιαῦτα εἴρηκας, ἐξ ὧν οὐκ εἰρήνη γένοιτ' ἂν ἐκ πολέμου, ἀλλ' ἐξ εἰρήνης πόλεμος ἀκήρυκτος." ἀρχομένου δ' ἐμοῦ πρὸς ταῦτα ἀντιλέγειν, ἐκάλουν ἡμᾶς οἱ ὑπηρέται.[3]

38 Ὡς δ' εἰσήλθομεν καὶ ἐκαθεζόμεθα, ἐξ ἀρχῆς πρὸς ἕκαστον τῶν εἰρημένων ἐνεχείρει τι λέγειν ὁ Φίλιππος, πλείστην δὲ εἰκότως ἐποιήσατο διατριβὴν πρὸς τοὺς ἐμοὺς λόγους· ἴσως γὰρ οὐδὲν τῶν ἐνόντων εἰπεῖν, ὥς γε οἶμαι, παρέλιπον· καὶ πολλάκις μου τοὔνομα ἐν τοῖς λόγοις ὠνόμαζε· πρὸς δὲ Δημοσθένην τὸν οὕτω καταγελάστως ἀπαλλάξαντα οὐδ' ὑπὲρ ἑνὸς οἶμαι διελέχθη. τοῦτο δὲ ἦν 39 ἄρα ἀγχόνη καὶ λύπη τούτῳ. ἐπειδὴ δὲ κατέστρεψεν εἰς φιλανθρωπίαν τοὺς λόγους, καὶ τὸ συκοφάντημα ὃ προειρήκει κατ' ἐμοῦ πρὸς τοὺς συμπρέσβεις οὗτος, ὡς ἐσομένου πολέμου καὶ διαφορᾶς αἰτίου, διέπιπτεν αὐτῷ, ἐνταῦθα ἤδη καὶ παντελῶς ἐξιστάμενος αὐτοῦ καταφανὴς ἦν,

---

[1] αὐτῶν Baiter and Sauppe : αὐτῶν οἱ συμπρέσβεις MSS.
[2] σφόδρα Weidner : σφόδρα πάνυ MSS.
[3] ὑπηρέται Blass : ὑπηρέται οἱ τοῦ Φιλίππου MSS.

Now when we were by ourselves, our worthy colleague Demosthenes put on an exceedingly sour face and declared that I had ruined the city and the allies. And when not only I, but all the rest of the ambassadors were amazed, and asked him his reason for saying that, he asked me if I had forgotten the situation at Athens, and if I did not remember that the people were worn out and exceedingly anxious for peace. "Or does your confidence rest," said he, "on those fifty ships that have been voted but are never going to be manned? You have so exasperated Philip by the speech you have made that the effect of it could not possibly be to make peace out of war, but implacable war out of peace!" I was just beginning to answer him, when the attendants summoned us.

When we had come in and taken our seats, Philip began at the beginning and undertook to make some sort of answer to every argument which we had advanced. Naturally he dwelt especially on my argument, for I think I may fairly say that I had omitted nothing that could be said; and again and again he mentioned my name in the course of his argument. But in reply to Demosthenes, who had made such a laughing-stock of himself, not one word was said on a single point, I believe. And you may be sure that this was pain and anguish to him. But when Philip turned to expressions of friendship, and the bottom dropped out of the slander which this Demosthenes had previously uttered against me before our fellow ambassadors, that I was going to be the cause of disagreement and war, then indeed it was plain to see that he was altogether beside

ὥστε καὶ κληθέντων ἡμῶν ἐπὶ ξένια δεινῶς
ἀσχημονεῖν.

40 Ἀφορμώντων δ᾽ ἡμῶν οἴκαδε ἐκ τῆς πρεσβείας,
ἐξαίφνης κατὰ τὴν ὁδὸν παραδόξως ὡς[1] φιλανθρώπως πρὸς ἕκαστον διελέγετο. ὅ τι μὲν οὖν
ποτ᾽ ἦν ὁ κέρκωψ ἢ τὸ καλούμενον παιπάλημα ἢ
τὸ παλίμβολον ἢ τὰ τοιαῦτα ῥήματα, οὐκ ᾔδειν
πρότερον· νυνὶ δ᾽ ἐξηγητὴν τοῦτον λαβὼν τῆς
41 ἁπάσης κακοηθείας μεμάθηκα. διαλαμβάνων γὰρ
ἕκαστον ἡμῶν ἐν μέρει, τῷ μὲν ἔρανον συστήσειν
ἐπηγγέλλετο καὶ βοηθήσειν τοῖς ἰδίοις, τὸν δὲ εἰς
στρατηγίαν καταστήσειν· ἐμοὶ δὲ παρακολουθῶν
καὶ τὴν φύσιν μακαρίζων καὶ τοὺς λόγους οὓς
εἶπον ἐγκωμιάζων πολὺς ἦν τοῖς ἐπαίνοις καὶ
ἐπαχθής. συνδειπνούντων δ᾽ ἡμῶν ἁπάντων ἐν
Λαρίσῃ, αὑτὸν μὲν ἔσκωπτε καὶ τὴν ἀπορίαν τὴν
ἐν τῷ λόγῳ συμβᾶσαν ἑαυτῷ, τὸν δὲ Φίλιππον
τῶν ὑπὸ τὸν ἥλιον ἀνθρώπων ἔφη πάντων εἶναι
42 δεινότατον. συναποφηναμένου δὲ κἀμοῦ τι τοιοῦτον, ὡς καὶ μνημονικῶς εἴποι πρὸς τὰ παρ᾽ ἡμῶν
ῥηθέντα, Κτησιφῶντος δέ, ὅσπερ ἦν ἡμῶν πρεσβύτατος, ὑπερβολήν τινα ἑαυτοῦ παλαιότητος
καὶ πλήθους ἐτῶν εἰπόντος, καὶ προσθέντος, ὡς ἐν
τοσούτῳ χρόνῳ[2] οὐ πώποτ᾽ οὕτως ἡδὺν οὐδ᾽ ἐπα-
φρόδιτον ἄνθρωπον ἑωρακὼς εἴη, ἀνακροτήσας ὁ
43 Σίσυφος ὅδε τὰς χεῖρας, "Ταῦτα μέντοι," ἔφη, "ὦ
Κτησιφῶν, οὔτ᾽ ἂν σὺ πρὸς τὸν δῆμον εἴποις, οὔτ᾽
ἂν οὗτος," ἐμὲ δὴ λέγων, "τολμήσειεν εἰπεῖν πρὸς
Ἀθηναίους, ὡς ὁ Φίλιππος δεινὸς εἰπεῖν καὶ μνη-

---

[1] ὡς Cobet : καὶ MSS.
[2] χρόνῳ Cobet : χρόνῳ καὶ βίῳ MSS.

himself, so that even when we were invited to dinner he behaved with shameful rudeness.

When we set out on our return home after completing our mission, suddenly he began talking to each of us on the way in a surprisingly friendly manner. Why, up to that time I had never so much as known the meaning of words like " kerkops," or the so-called " paipalema," or " palimbolon " ; [1] but now after acquiring him as expounder of the mysteries of all rascality, I am fully instructed. And he would take each of us in turn to one side, and to one he would promise to open a subscription to help him in his private difficulties, and to another that he would get him elected general. As for me, he followed me about, congratulating me on my ability and praising my speech ; so lavish was he in his compliments that I became sick and tired of him. And when we were all dining together at Larisa, he made fun of himself and the embarrassment which had come upon him in his speech, and he declared that Philip was the most wonderful man under the sun. When I had added my testimony, saying something like this, that Philip had shown excellent memory in his reply to what we had said, and when Ctesiphon, who was the oldest of us, speaking of his own advanced age and the number of his years, added that in all his many years he had never looked upon so charming and lovable a man, then this Sisyphus [2] here clapped his hands and said, " But, Ctesiphon, it will never do for you to tell the people that, nor would our friend here," meaning me, " venture to say to the Athenians that Philip is a man of good

[1] We are as ignorant of the particular shades of vulgarity and rascality conveyed by these words as Aeschines says he was before his initiation.   [2] A proverbial name for a cheat.

μονικός.” ἀναισθήτως δὲ ἡμῶν ἐχόντων καὶ τὴν
ἐπιβουλὴν οὐ προορωμένων, ἣν αὐτίκα ἀκούσεσθε,
εἰς συνθήκην τινὰ ἡμᾶς κατέκλησεν ὑπὲρ τοῦ
ταῦτ' ἐρεῖν πρὸς ὑμᾶς. ἐμοῦ δὲ καὶ δέησιν ἰσχυρὰν ἐδεήθη μὴ παραλιπεῖν, ἀλλ' εἰπεῖν, ὡς ὑπὲρ
Ἀμφιπόλεώς τι καὶ Δημοσθένης εἴποι.

44   Μέχρι μὲν οὖν τούτων οἱ συμπρέσβεις εἰσί μοι
μάρτυρες, οὓς προπηλακίζων οὗτος καὶ διαβάλλων
ἐν τῇ κατηγορίᾳ διατετέλεκε· τῶν δ' ἐπὶ τοῦ
βήματος παρ' ὑμῖν λόγων ὑμεῖς ἀκηκόατε, ὥστε
οὐκ ἐνέσται μοι ψεύδεσθαι. δέομαι δὲ ὑμῶν προσ-
επιπονῆσαι ἀκούοντας καὶ τὴν λοιπὴν διήγησιν.
ὅτι μὲν γὰρ ἕκαστος ὑμῶν ποθεῖ τὰ περὶ Κερσοβλέπτην ἀκούειν καὶ τὰς περὶ Φωκέων αἰτίας,
σαφῶς οἶδα, καὶ πρὸς ταῦτα σπεύδω· ἀλλ' ἐὰν μὴ
τὰ πρὸ τούτων ἀκούσητε, οὐδ' ἐκείνοις ὁμοίως
παρακολουθήσετε. ἐὰν δ' ἐμοὶ τῷ κινδυνεύοντι
εἰπεῖν δῶτε ὡς βούλομαι, καὶ σῶταί με, εἰ μηδὲν
ἀδικῶ, δυνήσεσθε, ἱκανὰς εἰληφότες ἀφορμάς, καὶ
θεάσεσθε ἐκ τῶν ὁμολογουμένων καὶ τἀντιλεγό-
μενα.

45   Ὡς γὰρ δεῦρ' ἤλθομεν καὶ πρὸς τὴν βουλὴν ἐπὶ
κεφαλαίων τὴν πρεσβείαν ἀπηγγείλαμεν, καὶ τὴν
ἐπιστολὴν ἀπέδομεν τὴν παρὰ Φιλίππου, ἐπαινέτης ἦν ἡμῶν Δημοσθένης πρὸς τοὺς συμβουλευτάς,[1] καὶ τὴν Ἑστίαν ἐπώμοσε τὴν βουλαίαν
συγχαίρειν τῇ πόλει, ὅτι τοιούτους ἄνδρας ἐπὶ

---

[1] τοὺς συμβουλευτάς Blass : τοὺς βουλεύοντας or τοὺς αὐτοὺς
συμβουλευτάς MSS.

---

[1] Demosthenes dared them to do it ; they accepted the
challenge and wagered that they would.

memory and great eloquence." And we innocently, not foreseeing the trick of which you shall hear presently, allowed him to bind us in a sort of agreement that we would say this to you.[1] And he begged me earnestly not to fail to tell how Demosthenes also said something in support of our claim to Amphipolis.

Now up to this point I am supported by the testimony of my colleagues in the embassy, whom he has reviled and slandered from beginning to end of his accusation. But his words on the platform in your presence you yourselves have heard; so it will not be possible for me to misrepresent them. And I beg of you to continue to hear patiently the rest of my narrative. I do not forget that each of you is anxious to hear the story of Cersobleptes and the charges made about the Phocians, and I am eager to get to those subjects; but you will not be as well able to follow them unless you shall first hear all that preceded. And if, in my peril, you allow me to speak as I wish, you will be able to save me, if I am innocent, and that on good and sufficient grounds; and you will also have before you the facts that are acknowledged as you proceed to examine the points that are in dispute.

On our return, then, after we had rendered to the senate a brief report of our mission and had delivered the letter from Philip, Demosthenes praised us to his colleagues in the senate, and he swore by Hestia, goddess of the senate,[2] that he congratulated the city on having sent such men on the embassy,

[2] The hearth of the Prytaneum, the headquarters of the standing committee of the senate, was regarded as the common hearth of the state; a statue of Hestia was in this hall, and in the senate-house was an altar of that goddess.

τὴν πρεσβείαν ἐξέπεμψεν, οἳ καὶ τῇ πίστει καὶ
46 λέγοντες[1] ἦσαν ἄξιοι τῆς πόλεως. ὑπὲρ ἐμοῦ δὲ
εἶπέ τι τοιοῦτον, ὡς οὐ ψευσαίμην τὰς τῶν ἑλο-
μένων με ἐπὶ τὴν πρεσβείαν ἐλπίδας. τέλος δὲ
πάντων· ἔγραψε γὰρ ἡμᾶς στεφανῶσαι θαλλοῦ
στεφάνῳ ἕκαστον εὐνοίας ἕνεκα τῆς εἰς τὸν δῆμον,
καὶ καλέσαι ἐπὶ δεῖπνον εἰς τὸ πρυτανεῖον εἰς
αὔριον. ὅτι δ' οὐδὲν ψεῦδος εἴρηκα πρὸς ὑμᾶς,
λαβέτω μοι τὸ ψήφισμα ὁ γραμματεύς, καὶ τὰς
τῶν συμπρέσβεων μαρτυρίας ἀναγνώτω.

ΨΗΦΙΣΜΑ.   ΜΑΡΤΥΡΙΑΙ

47 Ἐπειδὴ τοίνυν ἀπηγγέλλομεν τὴν πρεσβείαν ἐν
τῷ δήμῳ, εἶπε παρελθὼν πρῶτος ἡμῶν[2] Κτησιφῶν
ἄλλους τέ τινας λόγους καὶ τοὺς πρὸς Δημοσθένην
αὐτῷ συγκειμένους ἐρεῖ, περί τε τῆς ἐντεύξεως
τῆς Φιλίππου καὶ τῆς ἰδέας αὐτοῦ καὶ τῆς ἐν τοῖς
πότοις ἐπιδεξιότητος. καὶ μετὰ τοῦτον Φιλοκράτους εἰπόντος μικρὰ καὶ Δερκύλου, παρῆλθον
48 ἐγώ. ἐπειδὴ δὲ τὴν ἄλλην διεξῆλθον πρεσβείαν,
ἀπήντησα καὶ πρὸς τὸν λόγον ὃν ἐν τοῖς συμπρέ-
σβεσι διωμολογησάμην, εἰπὼν ὅτι καὶ μνημονικῶς
καὶ δυνατῶς ὁ Φίλιππος εἴποι· καὶ τὴν δέησιν
οὐκ ἐπελαθόμην τὴν Δημοσθένους, ὅτι ταχθείη
λέγειν, ἐάν τι παραλίπωμεν ἡμεῖς, ὑπὲρ Ἀμφι-
49 πόλεως. ἐφ' ἅπασι δ' ἡμῖν ἀνίσταται τελευταῖος
Δημοσθένης, καὶ τερατευσάμενος, ὥσπερ εἴωθε, τῷ
σχήματι καὶ τρίψας τὴν κεφαλήν, ὁρῶν ἐπιση-

---

[1] καὶ τῇ πίστει καὶ λέγοντες Blass: καὶ τοῖς λόγοις καὶ τῇ
πίστει λέγοντες MSS.
[2] πρῶτος ἡμῶν Weidner: the MSS. have διὰ τὴν ἡλικίαν
before or after these words.

men who in honesty and eloquence were worthy of the state. In referring to me he said something like this: that I had not disappointed the hopes of those who elected me to the embassy. And to cap it all he moved that each of us be crowned with a garland of wild olive because of our loyalty to the people, and that we be invited to dine on the morrow in the Prytaneum. To prove that I have spoken to you nothing but the truth, please let the clerk take the decree, and let him read the testimony of my colleagues in the embassy.

THE DECREE. THE TESTIMONY

Now when we presented the report of our embassy before the assembly, Ctesiphon came forward first and spoke, including in his account the points that he was to make according to his agreement with Demosthenes, I mean about Philip's social accomplishments, his personal appearance, and his doughty deeds at the cups. Next Philocrates and Dercylus spoke briefly; then I came forward. After giving an account of our mission in general, I went on to say, according to the agreement with my colleagues on the embassy, that Philip showed both memory and eloquence when he spoke. And I did not forget what Demosthenes had asked me to mention, namely, that we had agreed that he was to speak about Amphipolis, in case any point should have been passed over by the rest of us. After we had spoken, last of all Demosthenes arose, and with that imposing air of his, and rubbing his forehead, when he saw that the people approved my

μαινόμενον τὸν δῆμον καὶ ἀποδεδεγμένον[1] τοὺς
παρ' ἐμοῦ λόγους, ἀμφοτέρων ἔφη θαυμάζειν, καὶ
τῶν ἀκουόντων καὶ τῶν πρεσβευσάντων, ὅταν
παρέντες τὸν χρόνον, οἱ μὲν τὸν τοῦ βουλεύεσθαι,
οἱ δὲ τὸν τοῦ συμβουλεύειν, ἀποδιατρίβωσι τὴν
ὑπερόριον λαλιὰν ἀγαπῶντες ἐν τοῖς οἰκείοις πρά-
γμασιν· οὐδὲν γὰρ εἶναι ῥᾷον ἢ πρεσβείαν ἀπαγ-
50 γεῖλαι. "Βούλομαι δ' ὑμῖν" ἔφη "καὶ ἐπιδεῖξαι,
ὡς δεῖ τὸ πρᾶγμα γίγνεσθαι." ἅμα δ' ἐκέλευσεν
ἀναγνωσθῆναι τὸ ψήφισμα τοῦ δήμου. ἀναγνωσθέντος δὲ εἶπεν, ὅτι "Κατὰ τοῦτο ἐξεπέμφθημεν,
καὶ ταῦτα ἐπράττομεν ἃ ἐνταυθοῖ γέγραπται.
λαβὲ δή μοι καὶ τὴν ἐπιστολὴν ἣν ἥκομεν παρὰ
Φιλίππου φέροντες." ἐπειδὴ δὲ ἀνεγνώσθη, "'Ἀπέ-
χετε" ἔφη "τὴν ἀπόκρισιν, καὶ λοιπὸν ὑμῖν ἐστι
βουλεύσασθαι."

51 Θορυβησάντων δ' ἐπ' αὐτῷ τῶν μέν, ὡς δεινός
τις εἴη καὶ σύντομος, τῶν δὲ πλειόνων, ὡς πονηρὸς
καὶ φθονερός, "Σκέψασθε δὲ" ἔφη "ὡς συντόμως
καὶ τἆλλα πάντα ἀπαγγελῶ. ἐδόκει δεινὸς[2] εἶναι
λέγειν Αἰσχίνῃ Φίλιππος, ἀλλ' οὐκ ἐμοί, ἀλλ' εἴ
τις αὐτοῦ τὴν τύχην περιελὼν ἑτέρῳ περιθείη, οὐκ
52 ἂν πολύ τι καταδεὴς εἴη. ἐδόκει Κτησιφῶντι τὴν
ὄψιν λαμπρὸς εἶναι, ἐμοὶ δ' οὐ χείρων Ἀριστόδημος ὁ ὑποκριτής," παρῆν δ' ἡμῖν καὶ συνεπρέ-
σβευε. "μνημονικόν τις αὐτόν φησιν εἶναι· καὶ
γὰρ ἕτεροι. πιεῖν[3] δεινὸς ἦν· Φιλοκράτης ὁ μεθ'
ἡμῶν δεινότερος. λόγον τίς φησιν ἐμοὶ καταλιπεῖν ὑπὲρ Ἀμφιπόλεως· ἀλλ' οὔτ' ἂν ὑμῖν ὁ

---

[1] ἀποδεδεγμένον Scaliger : δεδεγμένον MSS.
[2] δεινὸς Auger : μνημονικὸς καὶ δεινὸς MSS.
[3] πιεῖν Cobet : συμπιεῖν MSS. cp. § 112.

report and were satisfied with it, he said that he was amazed at both parties, as well the listeners as the ambassadors, for they were carelessly wasting time — the listeners wasting the time for taking counsel, the ambassadors the time for giving it, all of them amusing themselves with foreign gossip, when they ought to be giving attention to our own affairs; for nothing, he said, was easier than to render account of an embassy. "I wish," said he, "to show you how the thing ought to be done." As he said this he called for the reading of the decree of the people. When it had been read he said, "This is the decree according to which we were sent out; what stands written here, we did. Now, if you please, take the letter that we have brought from Philip." When this had been read he said, "You have your answer; it remains for you to deliberate."

The people shouted, some applauding his forceful brevity, but more of them rebuking his abominable jealousy. Then he went on and said, "See how briefly I will report all the rest. To Aeschines Philip seemed to be eloquent, but not to me; nay, if one should strip off his luck and clothe another with it, this other would be almost his equal. To Ctesiphon he seemed to be brilliant in person, but to me not superior to Aristodemus the actor" (he was one of us on the embassy). "One man says he has a great memory; so have others. 'He was a wonderful drinker'; our Philocrates could beat him. One says that it was left to me to speak about our claim to Amphipolis; but neither to you nor to me would this

53 ῥήτωρ οὗτος οὔτ' ἂν ἐμοὶ λόγου μεταδοίη. ταυτὶ
μὲν οὖν" ἔφη "λῆρός ἐστιν· ἐγὼ δὲ ψήφισμα
γράψω καὶ τῷ κήρυκι σπείσασθαι τῷ παρὰ Φιλίππου ἥκοντι, καὶ τοῖς μέλλουσι παρ' αὐτοῦ
δεῦρο ἰέναι πρέσβεσι, καὶ τοὺς πρυτάνεις, ἐπειδὰν
ἥκωσιν οἱ πρέσβεις, ἐκκλησίαν ἐπὶ δύο ἡμέρας
ποιεῖν μὴ μόνον ὑπὲρ εἰρήνης, ἀλλὰ καὶ περὶ συμμαχίας, καὶ τοὺς πρέσβεις ἡμᾶς, εἰ δοκοῦμεν ἄξιοι
εἶναι, ἐπαινέσαι καὶ καλέσαι ἐπὶ δεῖπνον εἰς τὸ
54 πρυτανεῖον εἰς αὔριον." ὅτι δ' ἀληθῆ λέγω, λαβέ
μοι τὰ ψηφίσματα, ἵνα εἰδῆτε, ὦ ἄνδρες δικασταί,
καὶ τὴν ἀνωμαλίαν αὐτοῦ καὶ τὸν φθόνον, καὶ τὴν
τῶν πραγμάτων μετὰ Φιλοκράτους κοινωνίαν, καὶ
τὸ ἦθος, ὡς ἐπίβουλον καὶ ἄπιστον. κάλει δέ
μοι καὶ τοὺς συμπρέσβεις, καὶ τὰς μαρτυρίας
αὐτῶν ἀνάγνωθι.[1]

ΨΗΦΙΣΜΑΤΑ

55 Οὐ τοίνυν μόνον ταῦτα ἔγραψεν, ἀλλὰ καὶ
μετὰ ταῦτα ἐν τῇ βουλῇ θέαν εἰς τὰ Διονύσια
κατανεῖμαι τοῖς πρέσβεσιν, ἐπειδὰν ἥκωσι, τοῖς
Φιλίππου. λέγε καὶ τοῦτο τὸ ψήφισμα.

ΨΗΦΙΣΜΑ

[1] ἀνάγνωθι Taylor: the MSS. add καὶ τὰ ψηφίσματα τὰ
Δημοσθένους.

---

[1] It had been expected that the ambassadors of Philip
would arrive in time to take up their business before the

orator be capable of yielding a moment of his time. All this talk of theirs," said he, "is sheer nonsense. But for my part, I am going to move that safe conduct be granted both for the herald who has come from Philip, and for the ambassadors who are to come here from him; also I shall move that on the arrival of the ambassadors the prytanes call a meeting of the assembly for two successive days to consider not only the question of peace, but the question of an alliance also; and finally, that if we, the members of the embassy, are thought to deserve the honour, a vote of thanks be passed, and an invitation be given us to dine to-morrow in the prytaneum." As proof of the truth of what I say, (*to the Clerk*) take, if you please, the decrees, that you, gentlemen of the jury, may know how crooked he is and how jealous, and how completely he and Philocrates were in partnership in the whole affair; and that you may know his character—how treacherous and faithless. Call also my colleagues in the embassy, if you please, and read their testimony.

DECREES

Moreover, he not only made these motions, but afterwards he moved in the senate to assign seats in the theatre for the Dionysia to the ambassadors of Philip when they should arrive.[1]   Read this decree also.

DECREE

Great Dionysia; the delay in their arrival necessitated postponing the business until after the festival, a period of about a week.

THE SPEECHES OF AESCHINES

Ἀνάγνωθι δὴ καὶ τὴν τῶν συμπρέσβεων μαρτυρίαν, ἵν᾽ εἰδῆτε, ὦ ἄνδρες Ἀθηναῖοι, ὅτι Δημοσθένης οὐχ ὑπὲρ τῆς πόλεως εἰπεῖν δύναται, ἀλλ᾽
ἐπὶ τοὺς συσσίτους καὶ ὁμοσπόνδους μελετᾷ.

ΜΑΡΤΥΡΙΑ

56 Τὴν μὲν τοίνυν κοινωνίαν τῶν περὶ τῆς εἰρήνης
πράξεων οὐκ ἐμὴν καὶ Φιλοκράτους, ἀλλὰ Δημοσθένους καὶ Φιλοκράτους εὑρίσκετε, καὶ τὰς
πίστεις τῶν εἰρημένων ἱκανὰς ὑμῖν οἶμαι παρε-
σχῆσθαι· τῶν μὲν γὰρ ἀπηγγελμένων ὑμεῖς ἐστέ
μοι μάρτυρες, τῶν δ᾽ ἐν Μακεδονίᾳ ῥηθέντων καὶ
τῶν κατὰ τὴν πορείαν ἡμῖν συμβάντων τοὺς
συμπρέσβεις ὑμῖν μάρτυρας παρεσχόμην. τῆς δὲ
ὑπὸ Δημοσθένους ἀρτίως εἰρημένης κατηγορίας
ἠκούσατε καὶ μέμνησθε, ἧς τὴν ἀρχὴν ἐποιήσατο
ἀπὸ τῆς δημηγορίας ἣν εἶπον ἐγὼ περὶ τῆς
57 εἰρήνης. πάντα δὲ ἐν τῷ μέρει τούτῳ τῆς κατηγορίας ἐψευσμένος, ἐπὶ τῷ καιρῷ τούτῳ δεινῶς
ἐσχετλίασε. τοὺς γὰρ λόγους τούτους ἐναντίον
φησὶ τῶν πρέσβεων λέγεσθαι οὓς ἔπεμψαν πρὸς
ὑμᾶς οἱ Ἕλληνες μεταπεμφθέντες ὑπὸ τοῦ δήμου,
ἵνα κοινῇ καὶ πολεμοῖεν, εἰ δέοι, Φιλίππῳ,[1] καὶ
τῆς εἰρήνης, εἰ τοῦτο εἶναι δοκοίη συμφέρον,
μετέχοιεν. σκέψασθε δὴ πράγματος μεγάλου
κλοπὴν καὶ δεινὴν ἀναισχυντίαν τἀνθρώπου.[2]
58 τῶν γὰρ πρεσβειῶν, ἃς[3] ἐξεπέμψατε εἰς τὴν
Ἑλλάδα ἔτι τοῦ πολέμου τοῦ πρὸς Φίλιππον ὑμῖν
ἐνεστηκότος, οἱ μὲν χρόνοι τῆς αἱρέσεως[4] καὶ τὰ

---

[1] Φιλίππῳ Weidner : Φιλίππῳ μετὰ Ἀθηναίων MSS.
[2] τἀνθρώπου Markland : ἀνθρώπου MSS.
[3] πρεσβειῶν ἃς Dobree : πρέσβεων οὓς MSS.
[4] αἱρέσεως Dobree : αἱρέσεως ὅτε ἐξεπέμφθησαν MSS.

Now read also the testimony of my colleagues in the embassy, that you may know, fellow citizens, that when it is a question of speaking in the city's behalf, Demosthenes is helpless, but against those who have broken bread with him and shared in the same libations, he is a practised orator.

TESTIMONY

You find, therefore, that it was not Philocrates and I who entered into partnership in the negotiations for the peace, but Philocrates and Demosthenes. And I think that the proofs which I have presented to you in confirmation of what I have said, are sufficient. For as to the report we made, you yourselves are my witnesses; but I have presented to you my colleagues in the embassy as witnesses of what was said in Macedonia and of what took place in the course of our journey. But you heard and remember the accusation which Demosthenes made a few moments ago. He began with the speech which I made in the assembly on the question of the peace. And, utterly untruthful in this part of his accusation, he complained bitterly about the occasion of that speech, saying that it was delivered in the presence of the ambassadors whom the Greeks had sent to you; for you had invited them in order that if you must go on with the war, they might join you against Philip, and that if peace should seem the better policy, they might participate in the peace. Now see the man's deceit in a momentous matter, and his outrageous shamelessness. For in the public archives you have the record of the dates when you chose the several embassies which you sent out into Hellas, when the

τῶν πρεσβευσάντων ὀνόματα ἐν τοῖς δημοσίοις
ἀναγέγραπται γράμμασι, τὰ δὲ σώματά ἐστιν
αὐτῶν οὐκ ἐν Μακεδονίᾳ, ἀλλ᾽ Ἀθήνησι· ταῖς δὲ
ξενικαῖς πρεσβείαις ἡ βουλὴ τὰς εἰς τὸν δῆμον
προσόδους προβουλεύει· οὗτος δ᾽ ἐφεστάναι τὰς
59 ἀπὸ τῶν Ἑλλήνων φησὶ πρεσβείας. παρελθὼν
τοίνυν, Δημόσθενες, ἐπὶ τὸ βῆμα τοῦτο ἐν τῷ ἐμῷ
λόγῳ, εἰπὲ πόλεως ἧστινος βούλει τῶν Ἑλληνί-
δων τοὔνομα ἐξ ἧς ἀφῖχθαι τότε φῂς τοὺς πρέ-
σβεις· καὶ τὰ προβουλεύματα αὐτῶν ἐκ τοῦ βουλευτηρίου δὸς ἀναγνῶναι, καὶ τοὺς Ἀθηναίων
κάλει πρέσβεις, οὓς ἐξέπεμψαν ἐπὶ τὰς πόλεις,
μάρτυρας. κἂν παρεῖναι καὶ μὴ ἀποδημεῖν, ὅτε
ἡ πόλις τὴν εἰρήνην ἐποιεῖτο, μαρτυρήσωσιν, ἢ
τὰς πρὸς τὴν βουλὴν αὐτῶν προσόδους καὶ τὰ
ψηφίσματα ἃν παράσχῃ ἐν ᾧ σὺ φῂς ὄντα χρόνῳ,
καταβαίνω καὶ θανάτου τιμῶμαι.

60 Ἀνάγνωθι δὴ καὶ τὸ τῶν συμμάχων δόγμα τί
λέγει, ἐν ᾧ διαρρήδην γέγραπται, ἐπειδὴ βουλεύ-
εται ὁ δῆμος ὁ Ἀθηναίων ὑπὲρ εἰρήνης πρὸς
Φίλιππον, οἱ δὲ πρέσβεις οὔπω πάρεισιν, οὓς
ἐξέπεμψεν ὁ δῆμος εἰς τὴν Ἑλλάδα παρακαλῶν
τὰς πόλεις ὑπὲρ τῆς ἐλευθερίας τῶν Ἑλλήνων,
δεδόχθαι τοῖς συμμάχοις, ἐπειδὰν ἐπιδημήσωσιν
οἱ πρέσβεις καὶ τὰς πρεσβείας ἀπαγγείλωσιν
Ἀθηναίοις καὶ τοῖς συμμάχοις, προγράψαι τοὺς
πρυτάνεις ἐκκλησίας δύο κατὰ τὸν νόμον, ἐν δὲ

war between you and Philip was still in progress, and
also the names of the ambassadors; and the men
themselves are not in Macedonia, but here in Athens.
Now for embassies from foreign states an opportunity
to address the assembly of the people is always provided by a decree of the senate. Now he says that
the ambassadors from the states of Hellas were
present. Come forward, then, Demosthenes, to this
platform while I have the floor, and mention the
name of any city of Hellas you choose from which
you say the ambassadors had at that time arrived.
And give us to read the senatorial decrees concerning
them from the records in the senate-house, and call
as witnesses the ambassadors whom the Athenians
had sent out to the various cities. If they testify
that they had returned and were not still abroad at
the time when the city was concluding the peace, or
if you offer in evidence any audience of theirs before
the senate, and the corresponding decrees dated at
the time of which you speak, I leave the platform
and declare myself deserving of death.

Now read also what is said in the decree of the
allies,[1] in which it stands expressly written, "Whereas
the people of the Athenians are deliberating with
regard to peace with Philip, and whereas the ambassadors have not yet returned whom the people sent
out into Hellas summoning the cities in behalf of
the freedom of the Hellenic states, be it decreed by
the allies that as soon as the ambassadors return and
make their report to the Athenians and their allies,
the prytanes shall call two meetings of the assembly
of the people according to law, and that in these

[1] A decree of the confederate synod, sitting in Athens.
The states referred to in the preceding paragraph were
outside this Athenian league.

ταύταις βουλεύσασθαι περὶ τῆς εἰρήνης 'Αθη-
ναίους· ὅ τι δ' ἂν ψηφίσηται [1] ὁ δῆμος, τοῦτ'
εἶναι κοινὸν δόγμα τῶν συμμάχων. ἀνάγνωθι δή
μοι τὸ τῶν συνέδρων δόγμα.

ΔΟΓΜΑ ΣΥΝΕΔΡΩΝ

61 Παρανάγνωθι δή μοι καὶ τὸ Δημοσθένους ψήφισμα, ἐν ᾧ κελεύει τοὺς πρυτάνεις μετὰ τὰ
Διονύσια τὰ ἐν ἄστει καὶ τὴν ἐν Διονύσου ἐκκλησίαν προγράψαι δύο ἐκκλησίας, τὴν μὲν τῇ ὀγδόῃ
ἐπὶ δέκα, τὴν δὲ τῇ ἐνάτῃ,[2] ὁρίζων τὸν χρόνον καὶ
προϋφαιρῶν τὰς ἐκκλησίας, πρὶν ἐπιδημῆσαι τοὺς
ἀπὸ τῶν Ἑλλήνων πρέσβεις. καὶ τὸ μὲν τῶν
συμμάχων δόγμα κελεύει, ᾧ συνειπεῖν καὶ ἐγὼ
ὁμολογῶ, ὑπὲρ εἰρήνης μόνον ὑμᾶς βουλεύσασθαι,
Δημοσθένης δὲ καὶ περὶ συμμαχίας κελεύει. λέγε
αὐτοῖς τὸ ψήφισμα.

ΨΗΦΙΣΜΑ

62 Τῶν μὲν ψηφισμάτων ἀμφοτέρων ἀκηκόατε,[3]
ὑφ' ὧν ἐξελέγχεται Δημοσθένης τὰς ἀποδημούσας
πρεσβείας ἐπιδημεῖν φάσκων, καὶ βουλομένων
ὑμῶν ἀκροάσασθαι, τὸ τῶν συμμάχων ἄκυρον
πεποιηκὼς δόγμα. οἱ μὲν γὰρ ἀπεφήναντο ἀναμεῖναι [4] τὰς Ἑλληνικὰς πρεσβείας, Δημοσθένης

---

[1] ψηφίσηται Cobet : βουλεύσηται MSS.
[2] ἐνάτῃ Cobet : ἐνάτῃ ἐπὶ δέκα MSS.
[3] The MSS. have ᾧ Ἀθηναῖοι before or after the verb : Weidner omits.
[4] ἀναμεῖναι Cobet : the MSS. have ἀναμεῖναι τὴν πόλιν (one has τῇ πόλει).

meetings the Athenians shall deliberate on the question of peace; and whatever the people shall decide, be it voted that this decision stand as the common vote of the allies." (*To the Clerk.*) Now please read the decree of the synod.

DECREE OF THE SYNOD

Now in contrast with this, read, if you please, the decree moved by Demosthenes, in which he orders the prytanes, after the celebration of the City Dionysia and the session of the assembly in the precinct of Dionysus,[1] to call two meetings of the assembly, the one on the eighteenth, the other on the nineteenth; for in thus fixing the dates, he saw to it that the meetings of your assembly should be held before the ambassadors from the states of Hellas should have arrived. Moreover, the decree of the allies, which I acknowledge I also supported, prescribes that you deliberate concerning peace—nothing more; but Demosthenes prescribes the subject of an alliance also. Read them the decree.

DECREE

You have heard both decrees; by them Demosthenes is convicted of saying that the ambassadors were here, when they were still abroad, and of having made void the decree of the allies, when you wished to comply with it. For it was their judgment that we should wait for the ambassadors from the other states of Hellas; but Demosthenes is responsible for having prevented your

---

[1] A meeting regularly held at the close of the City Dionysia to act on any matters growing out of the conduct of the festival.

δὲ οὐ λόγῳ μόνον κεκώλυκε περιμεῖναι, ὁ πάντων
αἴσχιστα καὶ τάχιστα μετατιθέμενος, ἀλλ' ἔργῳ
καὶ ψηφίσματι, προστάξας ἤδη βεβουλεῦσθαι.

63   Εἴρηκε δὲ ὡς ἐν τῇ προτέρᾳ τῶν ἐκκλησιῶν
δημηγορήσαντος Φιλοκράτους, ὕστερον ἀναβὰς
ἐγὼ κατεμεμψάμην ἣν εἰσηγεῖτο ἐκεῖνος εἰρήνην,
αἰσχρὰν καὶ τῆς πόλεως ἀναξίαν εἶναι φάσκων, τῇ
δ' ὑστεραίᾳ πάλιν[1] ὡς συναγορεύοιμι τῷ Φιλοκράτει, καὶ τὴν ἐκκλησίαν εὐημερήσας οἰχοίμην[2]
φέρων, πείθων ὑμᾶς μὴ προσέχειν τοῖς τὰς μάχας
καὶ τὰ τῶν προγόνων λέγουσι τρόπαια, μηδὲ τοῖς
64 Ἕλλησι βοηθεῖν. ὅτι δ' οὐ ψευδῆ μόνον κατη-
γόρηκεν, ἀλλὰ καὶ ἀδύνατα γενέσθαι, μίαν μὲν
αὐτὸς καθ' αὑτοῦ[3] μαρτυρίαν μαρτυρήσει, ἑτέραν
δὲ πάντες Ἀθηναῖοι καὶ ὑμεῖς ἀναμιμνησκόμενοι,
τρίτην δὲ ἡ τῆς αἰτίας ἀπιθανότης, τετάρτην δὲ
ἀνὴρ ἀξιόλογος, εἰς τῶν πολιτευομένων, Ἀμύντωρ,
ᾧ ψήφισμα[4] ἐπεδείξατο Δημοσθένης καὶ ἀνε-
κοινοῦτο, εἰ δῷ τῷ γραμματεῖ, οὐχ ὑπεναντία,[5]
65 ἀλλὰ ταὐτὰ[6] γεγραφὼς Φιλοκράτει.   καί μοι
λαβὲ τὸ ψήφισμα καὶ ἀνάγνωθι τὸ Δημοσθένους,
ἐν ᾧ φαίνεται γεγραφώς, τῇ μὲν προτέρᾳ τῶν
ἐκκλησιῶν συμβουλεύειν τὸν βουλόμενον, τῇ δ'
ὑστέρᾳ τοὺς προέδρους ἐπιψηφίζειν τὰς γνώμας,
λόγον δὲ μὴ προτιθέναι, ἐν ᾗ[7] μέ φησιν αὐτὸς
Φιλοκράτει συνειπεῖν.

---

[1] πάλιν Cobet : πάλιν ἡμέρᾳ MSS.
[2] οἰχοίμην Blass : ᾠχόμην MSS.
[3] αὑτοῦ Cobet : αὐτοῦ Δημοσθένης MSS.
[4] ψήφισμα Blass : τὸ ψήφισμα MSS.
[5] ὑπεναντία Blass : ὑπεναντίαν or ὑπεναντίον MSS.
[6] ταὐτὰ Blass : ταὐτὸν MSS.
[7] ᾗ Bekker : ᾧ MSS.

waiting for them, not only by his words, most shamelessly shifty of all men, but by his act and his decree, in which he required us to make our decision immediately.

But he has said that at the first of the two meetings of the assembly, after Philocrates had spoken, I then arose and found fault with the resolution for peace which he had introduced, calling it disgraceful and unworthy of the city; but that again on the next day I spoke in support of Philocrates, and succeeded in sweeping the assembly off its feet, persuading you to pay no attention to those who talked of our fathers' battles and trophies, and not to aid the Greeks. But that what he has laid to my charge is not only false, but a thing that could not have happened, he himself shall furnish one proof, a witness against himself; another proof all the Athenians shall furnish, and your own memory; a third, the incredibility of the charge; and the fourth, a man of repute, who is active in public affairs, Amyntor, to whom Demosthenes exhibited the draft of a decree, asking him whether he should advise him to hand it to the clerk, a decree not contrary in its provisions to that of Philocrates, but identical with it. Now, if you please, take and read the decree of Demosthenes,[1] in which you will see that he has prescribed that in the first of the two meetings of the assembly all who wish shall take part in the discussion, but that on the next day the presiding officers shall put the question to vote, without giving opportunity for debate—the day on which he asserts that I supported Philocrates in the discussion.

[1] This is not the draft of a decree just spoken of, but that decree in which Demosthenes had provided for the two meetings of the assembly.

ΨΗΦΙΣΜΑ

66 Οὐκοῦν τὰ μὲν ψηφίσματα, ὡς ἐξ ἀρχῆς
ἐγράφη, μένει, οἱ δὲ τῶν συκοφαντῶν λόγοι πρὸς
τοὺς ἐφ᾽ ἡμέραν καιροὺς λέγονται. ποιεῖ δέ μου
τὴν δημηγορίαν ὁ μὲν κατήγορος διαιρετήν, τὸ
ψήφισμα δὲ καὶ τἀληθὲς μίαν· λόγον γὰρ μὴ
προτιθέντων[1] εἰς τὴν ὑστέραν ἐκκλησίαν τῶν
προέδρων,[2] οὐκ ἐνῆν εἰπεῖν. τί δ᾽ ἂν καὶ βουλόμενος, εἴπερ ταὐτὰ Φιλοκράτει προειλόμην, κατηγόρουν μὲν πρὸς τοὺς αὐτοὺς ἀκροατὰς τῇ προ-
τεραίᾳ, μίαν δὲ νύκτα διαλιπὼν συνηγόρουν;
πότερα ὡς αὐτὸς εὐδοξήσων, ἢ ὡς ἐκεῖνον ὠφε-
λήσων; ἀλλ᾽ οὐκ ἐνῆν οὐδέτερα[3] ἐξενέγκασθαι,
ἀλλ᾽ ὑπὸ πάντων μὲν μισεῖσθαι, περαίνειν δὲ
μηδέν.

67 Κάλει δέ μοι καὶ Ἀμύντορα Ἑρχιέα, καὶ τὴν
μαρτυρίαν ἀνάγνωθι. ὃν δὲ τρόπον γέγραπται,
προδιελθεῖν ὑμῖν βούλομαι. μαρτυρεῖ Ἀμύντωρ
Αἰσχίνῃ, ὅτε ἐβουλεύετο ὁ δῆμος περὶ τῆς συμμαχίας τῆς πρὸς Φίλιππον κατὰ τὸ Δημοσθένους
ψήφισμα, ἐν τῇ ὑστέρᾳ τῶν δυοῖν ἐκκλησιῶν, ὅτε
οὐκ ἐξῆν δημηγορεῖν, ἀλλὰ τὰ περὶ τῆς εἰρήνης

68 καὶ συμμαχίας ψηφίσματα ἐπεψηφίζετο, ἐν
ταύτῃ τῇ ἐκκλησίᾳ Δημοσθένην ἐπιδείξασθαι
παρακαθήμενον ψήφισμα[4] ἑαυτῷ, ἐφ᾽ ᾧ ἐπεγέ-
γραπτο τὸ[5] Δημοσθένους ὄνομα, καὶ ἀνακοινοῦσθαι

---

[1] λόγον . . . προτιθέντων Cobet : λόγων . . . προτεθέντων MSS.
[2] προέδρων Cobet : προέδρων κωλυόντων MSS.
[3] οὐδέτερα Sakorraphos : ἀμφότερα MSS.
[4] The MSS. have ψήφισμα γεγραμμένον : Blass brackets
γεγραμμένον.
[5] τὸ added by Markland.

You see that the decrees stand as they were originally written, whereas the words of rascals are spoken to fit the day and the occasion. My accuser makes two speeches out of my plea before the assembly, but the decree and the truth make it one. For if the presiding officers gave no opportunity for discussion in the second meeting, it is impossible that I spoke then. And if my policy was the same as that of Philocrates, what motive could I have had for opposing on the first day, and then after an interval of a single night, in the presence of the same listeners, for supporting? Did I expect to gain honour for myself, or did I hope to help Philocrates? I could have done neither, but would have got myself hated by all, and could have accomplished nothing.

But please call Amyntor of the deme Herchia and read his testimony. First, however, I wish to go over its contents with you: Amyntor in support of Aeschines testifies that when the people were deliberating on the subject of the alliance with Philip, according to the decree of Demosthenes, in the second meeting of the assembly, when no opportunity was given to address the people, but when the decrees concerning the peace and alliance were being put to vote, at that meeting Demosthenes was sitting by the side of the witness, and showed him a decree, over which the name of Demosthenes stood written;

αὐτὸν αὑτῷ, εἰ δῷ¹ τοῖς προέδροις ἐπιψηφίσαι,²
καὶ εἶναι, ἐφ' οἷς τὴν εἰρήνην καὶ τὴν συμμαχίαν
ἔγραψε ποιεῖσθαι, ἐπὶ τοῖς αὐτοῖς ἐφ' οἷσπερ
καὶ Φιλοκράτης ἐγεγράφει. κάλει δέ μοι Ἀμύντορα Ἐρχιέα, καὶ ἐκκλήτευε, ἐὰν μὴ θέλῃ δευρὶ
παρεῖναι.

MΑΡΤΥΡΙΑ

69 Τῆς μὲν μαρτυρίας ἀκηκόατε, ὦ ἄνδρες Ἀθη-
ναῖοι· σκοπεῖτε δὴ πότερα ὑμῖν δοκεῖ Δημοσθένης
ἐμοῦ κατηγορηκέναι, ἢ τοὐναντίον αὐτὸς αὑτοῦ
ἐπὶ τῷ ἐμῷ ὀνόματι. ἐπειδὴ δὲ καὶ τὴν δημηγορίαν μου διαβάλλει, καὶ τοὺς εἰρημένους λόγους
ἐπὶ τὰ χείρω διεξέρχεται, οὔτ' ἂν ἀποδραίην, οὔτ'
ἂν τῶν τότ' εἰρημένων οὐδὲν ἀρνησαίμην, οὔτ'
αἰσχύνομαι ἐπ' αὐτοῖς, ἀλλὰ καὶ φιλοτιμοῦμαι.

70 Βούλομαι δ' ὑμᾶς καὶ τοὺς καιροὺς ὑπομνῆσαι,
ἐν οἷς ἐβουλεύεσθε. τὴν μὲν γὰρ ἀρχὴν ἐποιησάμεθα τοῦ πολέμου ὑπὲρ Ἀμφιπόλεως, συνέβαινε δ' ἡμῶν τὸν στρατηγὸν ἐν τῷ πολέμῳ
ἑβδομήκοντα μὲν καὶ πέντε πόλεις συμμαχίδας
ἀποβεβληκέναι, ἃς ἐκτήσατο Τιμόθεος ὁ Κόνωνος
καὶ κατέστησεν εἰς τὸ συνέδριον· (προῄρημαι γὰρ
παρρησιάσασθαι, καὶ ἐλευθέρως ἅμα καὶ τἀληθῆ
εἰπὼν σῴζεσθαι· ἐὰν δὲ ἄλλως πως γιγνώσκητε,
καταχρήσασθέ μοι· οὐ γὰρ ἂν ὑποστειλαίμην·)

¹ δῷ Markland : δῷ τῷ γραμματεῖ MSS.
² τοῖς προέδροις ἐπιψηφίσαι Blass (ἐπιψηφίσαι Markland) :
ἐπιψηφίσασθαι τοῖς προέδροις MSS.

and that he consulted him as to whether he should hand it to the presiding officers to put to vote; this decree contained the terms on which Demosthenes moved that peace and alliance be made, and these terms were identical with the terms which Philocrates had moved. Now, if you please, call Amyntor of the deme Herchia; if he does not come hither voluntarily, serve summons upon him.

TESTIMONY

You have heard the testimony, fellow citizens. Consider whether you conclude that it is I whom Demosthenes has accused, or whether on the contrary he has accused himself in my name. But since he also misrepresents the speech that I made, and puts a false construction on what was said, I have no disposition to run away, or to deny a word that was then spoken; I am not ashamed of what I said; on the contrary, I am proud of it.

But I wish also to recall to you the time and circumstances of your deliberations. We went to war in the first place over the question of Amphipolis. In the course of the war our general succeeded in losing seventy-five allied cities,[1] which Timotheus, the son of Conon, had won over and made members of the synod—I am determined, as you see, to speak right out, and to seek safety in frank and truthful speaking; if you are otherwise minded, do what you will with me; I cannot prevaricate—and a hundred

---

[1] Aeschines chooses to speak as though the war with Philip were one and the same with the other, contemporaneous war, in which a large part of the Athenian allies broke off from the naval league.

71 ἑκατὸν δὲ καὶ πεντήκοντα τριήρεις λαβόντα ἐκ
τῶν νεωρίων μὴ κατακεκομικέναι, καὶ ταῦτα ὑμῖν
ἐν τοῖς ἀγῶσιν ἀεὶ τοῖς Χάρητος οἱ κατήγοροι
δεικνύουσι, χίλια δὲ καὶ πεντακόσια τάλαντα οὐκ
εἰς στρατιώτας, ἀλλ' εἰς ἡγεμόνων ἀλαζονείας
ἀνηλωκέναι, Δηιάρην τε καὶ Δηίπυρον καὶ Πολυ-
φόντην, δραπέτας ἀνθρώπους ἐκ τῆς Ἑλλάδος
συνειλεγμένους, καὶ χωρὶς εἰς τοὺς περὶ τὸ βῆμα
καὶ τὴν ἐκκλησίαν μισθοφόρους, οἳ τοὺς μὲν
ταλαιπώρους νησιώτας καθ' ἕκαστον ἐνιαυτὸν
ἑξήκοντα τάλαντα εἰσέπραττον σύνταξιν, κατή-
γον δὲ τὰ πλοῖα καὶ τοὺς Ἕλληνας ἐκ τῆς
72 κοινῆς θαλάττης. ἀντὶ δὲ ἀξιώματος καὶ τῆς
τῶν Ἑλλήνων ἡγεμονίας, ἡ πόλις ἡμῶν τῆς [1]
Μυοννήσου καὶ τῆς τῶν λῃστῶν δόξης ἀνεπίμ-
πλατο· Φίλιππος δὲ ὁρμηθεὶς ἐκ Μακεδονίας,
οὐκέθ' ὑπὲρ Ἀμφιπόλεως πρὸς ἡμᾶς ἠγωνίζετο,
ἀλλ' ἤδη περὶ Λήμνου καὶ Ἴμβρου καὶ Σκύρου,
τῶν ἡμετέρων κτημάτων· ἐξέλειπον [2] δὲ Χερρόνησον ἡμῶν οἱ πολῖται, τὴν οὖσαν ὁμολογουμένως
Ἀθηναίων· πλείους δὲ ἐκκλησίας συγκλήτους
ἠναγκάζεσθε ἐκκλησιάζειν μετὰ φόβου καὶ θορύ-
73 βου, ἢ τὰς τεταγμένας ἐκ τῶν νόμων· οὕτω δ' ἦν
σφαλερὰ καὶ ἐπικίνδυνα τὰ πράγματα, ὥστε
ἠναγκάσθη γράψαι ψήφισμα Κηφισοφῶν ὁ Παιανιεύς, εἷς τῶν φίλων καὶ ἑταίρων τῶν Χάρητος,
ἐκπλεῖν τὴν ταχίστην Ἀντίοχον τὸν ἐπὶ τῶν
ὑπηρετικῶν, καὶ ζητεῖν τὸν στρατηγὸν τὸν ἐπὶ τῇ
δυνάμει τεταγμένον, κἂν ἐντύχῃ που, φράζειν ὅτι
θαυμάζει ὁ δῆμος ὁ Ἀθηναίων, εἰ Φίλιππος μὲν

---

[1] τῆς added by Bremi.
[2] ἐξέλειπον Stephanus : ἐξέλιπον MSS.

and fifty triremes which he took from the dockyards
he failed to bring back, a story which the accusers of
Chares are never tired of telling you in the courts;
and he spent fifteen hundred talents, not upon his
troops, but upon his tricky officers, a Deiares, a Deipyrus, a Polyphontes, vagabonds collected from all
Hellas (to say nothing of the wages of his hirelings
on the bema and in the popular assembly), who were
exacting from the wretched islanders a contribution
of sixty talents a year, and seizing merchant ships
and Greek citizens on the high seas. And instead
of respect and the hegemony of Hellas, Athens
had a name that stank like a nest of Myonnesian [1]
pirates. And Philip from his base in Macedonia was
no longer contending with us for Amphipolis, but
already for Lemnos, Imbros, and Scyros, our own
possessions, while our citizens were abandoning the
Chersonese, the undisputed property of Athens. And
the special meetings of the assembly which you were
forced to hold, in fear and tumult, were more in
number than the regular meetings. The situation
was so precarious and dangerous that Cephisophon
of Paeania, one of the friends and companions of
Chares, was compelled to make the motion that Antiochus, who commanded the dispatch boats, should
sail immediately and hunt up the general who had
been put in charge of our forces, and in case he
should happen to find him anywhere, should tell him
that the people of Athens were astonished to learn
that Philip was on the way to the Chersonese,

---

[1] Μυοννῆσος, *Mouse-island*, was a little island off the coast
of Thessaly, notorious as a nest of pirates.

THE SPEECHES OF AESCHINES

ἐπὶ Χερρόνησον τὴν Ἀθηναίων πορεύεται, Ἀθηναῖοι δὲ οὐδὲ τὸν στρατηγὸν ἴσασιν οὐδὲ τὴν
δύναμιν ἣν ἐξέπεμψαν, ὅπου ἐστίν. ὅτι δ' ἀληθῆ
λέγω, ἀκούσατε τοῦ ψηφίσματος, καὶ ἀναμνήσθητε τοῦ πολέμου, καὶ τὴν εἰρήνην τοὺς τῶν
ὅπλων ἡγεμόνας, ἀλλὰ μὴ τοὺς πρέσβεις, ἀπαι-
τεῖτε.

ΨΗΦΙΣΜΑ

74   Οἱ μὲν καιροὶ τῆς πόλεως τοιοῦτοι, ἐν οἷς οἱ περὶ
τῆς εἰρήνης ἐγίγνοντο λόγοι· ἀνιστάμενοι δὲ οἱ
συντεταγμένοι ῥήτορες, περὶ μὲν τῆς σωτηρίας τῆς
πόλεως οὐδ' ἐνεχείρουν λέγειν, ἀποβλέπειν δὲ εἰς
τὰ προπύλαια τῆς ἀκροπόλεως ἐκέλευον ὑμᾶς, καὶ
τῆς ἐν Σαλαμῖνι ναυμαχίας [1] μεμνῆσθαι, καὶ τῶν
75   τάφων τῶν προγόνων καὶ τῶν τροπαίων. ἐγὼ δὲ
ἁπάντων μὲν τούτων ἔφην δεῖν μεμνῆσθαι, μιμεῖσθαι μέντοι τὰς τῶν προγόνων εὐβουλίας, τὰ δὲ
ἁμαρτήματα αὐτῶν καὶ τὴν ἄκαιρον φιλονικίαν [2]
φυλάττεσθαι, τὴν μὲν ἐν Πλαταιαῖς πεζομαχίαν, [3]
καὶ τοὺς ἀγῶνας τοὺς περὶ Σαλαμῖνα, καὶ τὴν ἐν
Μαραθῶνι μάχην, καὶ τὴν ἐπ' Ἀρτεμισίῳ ναυμαχίαν, καὶ τὴν Τολμίδου ζηλοῦν στρατηγίαν
κελεύων, ὃς χιλίους ἔχων ἐπιλέκτους Ἀθηναίων,
διὰ μέσης Πελοποννήσου πολεμίας οὔσης ἀδεῶς
76   διεξῄει, τὴν δ' εἰς Σικελίαν στρατείαν φυλάττεσθαι, ἣν ἐξέπεμψαν Λεοντίνοις βοηθήσοντες, τῶν
πολεμίων ἐμβεβληκότων εἰς τὴν χώραν ἡμῶν καὶ
Δεκελείας ἐπιτετειχισμένης, καὶ τὴν τελευταίαν

---

[1] ναυμαχίας Cobet : the MSS. have πρὸς τὸν Πέρσην before
or after ναυμαχίας.
[2] φιλονικίαν Cobet : φιλονεικίαν MSS.
[3] πεζομαχίαν Cobet : πρὸς τοὺς Πέρσας πεζομαχίαν MSS.

Athenian territory, while as to the general and the force which they themselves had sent out, the Athenians did not even know what had become of them. To prove that I am speaking the truth, hear the decree and recall the facts of the war, and then charge the peace, not to the ambassadors, but to the commanders of our arms.

DECREE

Such was the situation of the city, such the circumstances under which the debate on the peace took place. But the popular speakers arose and with one consent ignored the question of the safety of the state, but called on you to gaze at the Propylaea of the Acropolis, and remember the battle of Salamis, and the tombs and trophies of our forefathers. I replied that we must indeed remember all these, but must imitate the wisdom of our forefathers, and beware of their mistakes and their unseasonable jealousies; I urged that we should emulate the battle that we fought at Plataea, the struggles off the shores of Salamis, the battles of Marathon and Artemisium, and the generalship of Tolmides, who with a thousand picked men of the Athenians fearlessly marched straight through the Peloponnesus, the enemy's country. But I urged that we should take warning from the Sicilian expedition, which was sent out to help the people of Leontini, at a time when the enemy were already in our own territory and Deceleia was fortified against us; and that

ἀβουλίαν,[1] ὅθ' ἡττημένοι τῷ πολέμῳ, προκαλου-
μένων αὐτοὺς Λακεδαιμονίων εἰρήνην ἄγειν ἔχοντας
πρὸς τῇ Ἀττικῇ Λῆμνον καὶ Ἴμβρον καὶ Σκῦρον
καὶ δημοκρατουμένους κατὰ τοὺς νόμους, τούτων
μὲν οὐδὲν ἤθελον ποιεῖν, πολεμεῖν δὲ προῃροῦντο
οὐ δυνάμενοι, Κλεοφῶν δὲ ὁ λυροποιός, ὃν πολλοὶ
δεδεμένον ἐν πέδαις ἐμνημόνευον, παρεγγραφεὶς
αἰσχρῶς πολίτης καὶ διεφθαρκὼς νομῇ χρημάτων
τὸν δῆμον, ἀποκόψειν ἠπείλει μαχαίρᾳ τὸν τρά-
77 χηλον, εἴ τις εἰρήνης μνησθήσεται· τελευτῶντες
δὲ εἰς τοῦτο τὴν πόλιν προήγαγον, ὥστε ἀγαπη-
τῶς τὴν εἰρήνην ποιήσασθαι, ἀποστάντας πάντων
καὶ τὰ τείχη καθελόντας, καὶ παραδεξαμένους
φρουρὰν καὶ Λακεδαιμόνιον ἁρμοστήν, καὶ τῆς
δημοκρατίας τοῖς τριάκοντα ἀφεμένους, οἳ χιλίους
καὶ πεντακοσίους τῶν πολιτῶν ἀκρίτους ἀπέκτειναν. τὴν μὲν τοιαύτην ἀβουλίαν ὁμολογῶ
παραγγέλλειν φυλάττεσθαι, τὰ δ' ὀλίγῳ πρότερον
εἰρημένα μιμεῖσθαι. οὐ γὰρ παρὰ τῶν ἀλλοτρίων,
ἀλλὰ παρὰ τοῦ πάντων οἰκειοτάτου ταῦτα ἐπυν-
78 θανόμην. Ἀτρόμητος γὰρ ὁ πατὴρ ὁ ἡμέτερος,
ὃν σὺ λοιδορεῖς οὔτ' εἰδὼς οὔτ' ἐπιδὼν τῆς ἑαυτοῦ
ἡλικίας ὅστις ἦν, καὶ ταῦτα, ὦ Δημόσθενες, ἐκ
τῶν νομάδων Σκυθῶν τὸ πρὸς μητρὸς ὢν γένος,
ἔφυγε μὲν ἐπὶ τῶν τριάκοντα, συγκατήγαγε δὲ τὸν
δῆμον· καὶ ὁ τῆς μητρὸς τῆς ἡμετέρας ἀδελφός,
θεῖος δὲ ἡμέτερος, Κλεόβουλος ὁ Γλαύκου τοῦ

---

[1] ἀβουλίαν Baiter : ἀβουλίαν φυλάξασθαι MSS.

final act of folly, when, outmatched in the war, and offered terms of peace by the Lacedaemonians, with the agreement that we should hold not only Attica, but Lemnos, Imbros, and Scyros also, and retain the constitutional democracy, the people would have none of it, but chose to go on with a war that was beyond their powers. And Cleophon, the lyre-maker, whom many remembered as a slave in fetters, who had dishonourably and fraudulently got himself enrolled as a citizen, and had corrupted the people by distribution of money,[1] threatened to take his knife and slit the throat of any man who should make mention of peace. Finally they brought the city to such a pass that she was glad to make peace, giving up everything, tearing down her walls, receiving a garrison and a Lacedaemonian governor, and surrendering the democracy to the Thirty, who put fifteen hundred citizens to death without a trial. I admit that I urged that we should guard against such folly as that, and imitate the conduct shortly before described. For it was from no stranger that I heard that story, but from him who is nearest of all men to me. For Atrometus our father, whom you slander, though you do not know him and never saw what a man he was in his prime—you, Demosthenes, a descendant through your mother of the nomad Scythians!—our father went into exile in the time of the Thirty, and later helped to restore the democracy; while our mother's brother, our uncle Cleobulus, the son of

---

[1] Aristotle (*Constitution of Athens*, xxviii.) tells us that it was Cleophon who introduced the two-obol donation from the treasury to provide a free seat in the theatre for every citizen who applied for it. This was the beginning of the Theorika, recognised in the time of Aeschines as one of the greatest abuses in the democracy.

Ἀχαρνέως υἱός, μετὰ Δημαινέτου τοῦ Βουζύγου συγκατεναυμάχησε Χείλωνα τὸν Λακεδαιμονίων ναύαρχον· ὥστε οἰκεῖά μοι καὶ συνήθη τὰ τῆς πόλεως ἀτυχήματα εἶναι τοῖς ὠσὶν ἀκούειν.

79 Ἐπιτιμᾷς δέ μοι καὶ τὴν ἐν τοῖς μυρίοις ἐν Ἀρκαδίᾳ δημηγορίαν καὶ πρεσβείαν, καὶ μεταβεβλῆσθαί με φής, αὐτὸς ὢν ἀνδραποδώδης καὶ μόνον οὐκ ἐστιγμένος αὐτόμολος. ἐγὼ δ᾿ ἐν μὲν τῷ πολέμῳ συνίστην, καθ᾿ ὅσον ἦν δυνατός, Ἀρκάδας καὶ τοὺς ἄλλους Ἕλληνας ἐπὶ Φίλιππον· οὐδενὸς δ᾿ ἀνθρώπων ἐπικουροῦντος τῇ πόλει, ἀλλὰ τῶν μὲν περιορώντων ὅ τι συμβήσεται, τῶν δὲ συνεπιστρατευόντων, τῶν δ᾿ ἐν τῇ πόλει ῥητόρων χορηγὸν ταῖς καθ᾿ ἡμέραν δαπάναις τὸν πόλεμον ποιουμένων, ὁμολογῶ συμβουλεῦσαι τῷ δήμῳ διαλύσασθαι πρὸς Φίλιππον καὶ τὴν εἰρήνην συνθέσθαι, ἣν σὺ νομίζεις νῦν αἰσχράν, ὁ[1] οὐδὲ πώποθ᾿ ἁψάμενος ὅπλων, ἐγὼ δὲ ταύτην εἶναι πολλῷ φημι καλλίω τοῦ πολέμου.

80 Χρὴ δέ, ὦ ἄνδρες Ἀθηναῖοι, τοὺς μὲν πρέσβεις θεωρεῖν πρὸς τὸν καιρὸν καθ᾿ ὃν ἐπρέσβευον, τοὺς δὲ στρατηγοὺς πρὸς τὰς δυνάμεις ὧν ἡγοῦντο. καὶ γὰρ τὰς εἰκόνας ἵστατε, καὶ τὰς προεδρίας καὶ τοὺς στεφάνους καὶ τὰς ἐν πρυτανείῳ σιτήσεις δίδοτε, οὐ τοῖς τὴν εἰρήνην ἀπαγγείλασιν, ἀλλὰ τοῖς τὴν μάχην νικήσασιν. εἰ δ᾿ ἔσονται

---

[1] ὁ added by Cobet.

Glaucus of the deme Acharnae, was with Demaenetus of the family of the Buzygae, when he won
the naval victory over Cheilon the Lacedaemonian
admiral. The sufferings of the city were therefore
a household word with us, familiar to my ears.

But you find fault with my service as ambassador
to Arcadia and my speech before the Ten Thousand [1]
there, and you say that I have changed sides—yourself more slave than freeman, all but branded as a
runaway! So long as the war lasted, I tried so far
as in me lay to unite the Arcadians and the rest of
Hellas against Philip. But when no man came to
the help of our city, but some were waiting to see
what was going to happen, and others were taking
the field against us, while the politicians in our own
city were using the war to subsidize the extravagance
of their daily life,[2] I acknowledge that I advised
the people to come to terms with Philip, and to
make the peace, which you, Demosthenes, now hold
disgraceful, you who never had a weapon of war in
your hands—but which I declare to be much more
honourable than the war.

You ought, fellow citizens, to judge your ambassadors in the light of the crisis in which they served;
your generals, in the light of the forces which they
commanded. For you set up your statues and you
give your seats of honour and your crowns and your
dinners in the Prytaneum, not to those who have
brought you tidings of peace, but to those who have
been victorious in battle. But if the responsibility

---

[1] The national assembly of the Arcadians. Aeschines appeared before them in 348 in the attempt to counteract the
work of Philip's agents among them.

[2] For this use of χορηγόν see the note on § 240 (χορηγεῖς) of
the Speech against Ctesiphon.

τῶν πολέμων αἱ μὲν εὔθυναι τῶν πρέσβεων, αἱ δὲ
δωρεαὶ τῶν στρατηγῶν, ἀσπόνδους καὶ ἀκηρύ-
κτους τοὺς πολέμους ποιήσετε· οὐδεὶς γὰρ ἐθελήσει
πρεσβεύειν.

81 Περὶ δὲ Κερσοβλέπτου καὶ Φωκέων καὶ τῶν
ἄλλων ἃ πρὸς τούτοις διαβέβλημαι, ὑπόλοιπον
εἰπεῖν. ἐγὼ γάρ, ὦ ἄνδρες Ἀθηναῖοι, καὶ ἐν τῇ
προτέρᾳ καὶ ἐν τῇ ὑστέρᾳ πρεσβείᾳ, ἃ μὲν εἶδον,
ὡς εἶδον, ὑμῖν ἀπήγγελλον, ἃ δ᾽ ἤκουσα, ὡς
ἤκουσα. τίνα οὖν ἦν ἑκάτερα τούτων, ἅ τε εἶδον
ἅ τε ἤκουσα περὶ Κερσοβλέπτου; εἶδον μὲν ἐγὼ
καὶ οἱ συμπρέσβεις ἅπαντες ὁμηρεύοντα τὸν υἱὸν
τὸν Κερσοβλέπτου παρὰ Φιλίππῳ· καὶ ἔτι καὶ
82 νῦν τοῦθ᾽ οὕτως ἔχει. συνέβαινε δέ, ὅτε τὴν προτέραν ἐπρεσβεύομεν πρεσβείαν, ἐμοὶ μὲν μετὰ
τῶν συμπρέσβεων ἀπιέναι δεῦρο, Φιλίππῳ δ᾽ ἐπὶ
Θρᾴκην ἐξιέναι, πρὸς δ᾽ ἡμᾶς ὡμολογηκέναι, ἕως
ἂν ὑμεῖς περὶ τῆς εἰρήνης βουλεύσησθε, μὴ ἐπι-
βήσεσθαι μεθ᾽ ὅπλων Χερρονήσου. ἐν ἐκείνῃ μὲν
οὖν τῇ ἡμέρᾳ ᾗ ὑμεῖς ἐψηφίσασθε τὴν εἰρήνην,
οὐδεμία μνεία ἐγένετο περὶ Κερσοβλέπτου· ἤδη
δὲ ἡμῶν κεχειροτονημένων ἐπὶ τοὺς ὅρκους, οὔπω
δὲ ἀπηρκότων ἐπὶ τὴν ὑστέραν πρεσβείαν, ἐκκλησία γίγνεται, ἐν ᾗ Δημοσθένης ὁ νυνὶ κατηγορῶν
83 ἐμοῦ λαγχάνει προεδρεύειν. ἐν δὲ ταύτῃ τῇ ἐκκλησίᾳ Κριτόβουλος ὁ Λαμψακηνὸς εἶπε παρελθών, ὅτι πέμψειε μὲν αὐτὸν Κερσοβλέπτης, ἀξιοίη[1]

---

[1] ἀξιοίη Franke : ἀξιοῖ MSS.

for the wars is to be laid upon the ambassadors, while the generals are to receive the rewards, the wars you wage will know neither truce nor herald of peace, for no man will be willing to be your ambassador.

Now it remains for me to speak of Cersobleptes and the Phocians, as well as the other matters in which I have been slandered. For, fellow citizens, both on the first and on the second embassy I reported to you what I saw, as I saw it; what I heard, as I heard it. What was it then in either case: what was it that I saw and what was it that I heard about Cersobleptes? I, as well as all my colleagues in the embassy, saw the son of Cersobleptes a hostage at Philip's court; and this is still the case. Now it happened on the occasion of our first embassy, that at the moment when I was leaving for home with the rest of the ambassadors, Philip was setting out for Thrace; but we had his promise that while you were deliberating concerning peace, he would not set foot on the Chersonese with an armed force. Now on that day when you voted the peace, no mention was made of Cersobleptes. But after we had already been elected to receive the oaths,[1] before we had set forth on the second embassy, an assembly was held, the presidency of which fell by lot to Demosthenes,[2] who is now accusing me. In that assembly Critobulus of Lampsacus came forward and said that Cersobleptes had sent him, and he demanded that he should be

---

[1] The same ambassadors who had negotiated the preliminaries of the peace were appointed to go back to Macedonia and receive the ratification of the peace by Philip and his allies.

[2] A board of nine senators presided over the meetings of the assembly; one member of the board was chosen by lot as chief presiding officer for the day.

THE SPEECHES OF AESCHINES

δὲ ἀποδοῦναι τοὺς ὅρκους τοῖς Φιλίππου πρέσβεσι, καὶ συναναγραφῆναι Κερσοβλέπτην ἐν τοῖς ὑμετέροις συμμάχοις. ῥηθέντων δὲ τῶν λόγων τούτων, Ἀλεξίμαχος ὁ Πήληξ δίδωσιν ἀναγνῶναι ψήφισμα τοῖς προέδροις, ἐν ᾧ ἐγέγραπτο ἀποδοῦναι τοὺς ὅρκους Φιλίππῳ μετὰ τῶν ἄλλων

84 συμμάχων τὸν ἥκοντα παρὰ Κερσοβλέπτου. ἀναγνωσθέντος δὲ τοῦ ψηφίσματος, καὶ ταῦτα οἶμαι πάντας ὑμᾶς μνημονεύειν, ἀναστὰς ἐκ τῶν προέδρων Δημοσθένης οὐκ ἔφη τὸ ψήφισμα ἐπιψηφιεῖν, οὐδὲ λύσειν τὴν πρὸς Φίλιππον εἰρήνην, οὐδὲ γιγνώσκειν τῶν συμμάχων τοὺς ὥσπερ συνεφαπτομένους τοῖς σπένδουσι τῶν ἱερῶν· ἀποδοθῆναι γὰρ περὶ τούτων ἑτέραν ἐκκλησίαν. βοώντων δὲ ὑμῶν καὶ τοὺς προέδρους ἐπὶ τὸ βῆμα καλούντων, οὕτως ἄκοντος αὐτοῦ τὸ ψή-

85 φισμα ἐπεψηφίσθη. ὅτι δ' ἀληθῆ λέγω, κάλει μοι τὸν γράψαντα τὸ ψήφισμα Ἀλεξίμαχον καὶ τοὺς συμπροέδρους τοὺς Δημοσθένους, καὶ τὴν μαρτυρίαν ἀνάγνωθι.

ΜΑΡΤΥΡΙΑ

Ὁ μὲν τοίνυν ἐπιδακρύσας ἀρτίως ἐνταυθοῖ Δημοσθένης μνησθεὶς Κερσοβλέπτου, φαίνεται τῆς συμμαχίας ἐκκλήων αὐτόν. ὡς δ' ἡ παροῦσα ἐκκλησία διελύθη, ἐξώρκιζον τοὺς συμμάχους οἱ τοῦ

---

[1] The peace that had just been negotiated was to be between Philip and his allies, and Athens and her allies. By the allies of Athens were meant the members of the Athenian naval league, whose synod, sitting at Athens, had ratified in advance whatever action the Athenian people might take as to the peace. Cersobleptes was not a member of this league,

allowed to give his oath to the ambassadors of Philip, and that Cersobleptes be enrolled among your allies.[1] When he had thus spoken, Aleximachus of the deme Pelex handed to the presiding officers a motion to be read, in which it was written that the representative of Cersobleptes be permitted to join the other allies in giving the oath to Philip. When the motion had been read—I think you all remember this—Demosthenes arose from among the presiding officers and refused to put the motion to vote, saying that he would not bring to naught the peace with Philip, and that he did not recognize the sort of allies who joined only in time, as it were, to help in pouring the peace libations; for they had had their opportunity at an earlier session of the assembly. But you shouted and called the board of presidents to the platform, and so against his will the motion was put to vote. To prove that I am speaking the truth, please call Aleximachus, the author of the motion, and the men who served with Demosthenes on the board of presidents, and read their testimony.

TESTIMONY

You see, therefore, that Demosthenes, who just now burst into tears here at mention of Cersobleptes, tried to shut him out of the alliance. Now on the adjournment of that session of the assembly, Philip's

but sought to be admitted at the last moment, in order to gain the protection of the peace. Demosthenes, feeling that his admission would endanger the success of the negotiations for peace, attempted to prevent his admission, by insisting on the irregularity of the procedure ; Cersobleptes should have presented his credentials to the senate and obtained from them a resolution advising the assembly to hear his plea ; and this should have been done at an earlier meeting.

Φιλίππου πρέσβεις ἐν τῷ στρατηγίῳ τῷ ὑμετέρῳ.
86 τετόλμηκε δὲ πρὸς ὑμᾶς εἰπεῖν ὁ κατήγορος, ὡς
ἀπὸ τῶν ἱερῶν ἐγὼ Κριτόβουλον ἀπήλασα τὸν πρεσβευτὴν τὸν παρὰ Κερσοβλέπτου, παρόντων μὲν
τῶν συμμάχων, ἐψηφισμένου δὲ τοῦ δήμου, παρακαθημένων δὲ τῶν στρατηγῶν, πόθεν τοσαύτην
ῥώμην λαβών; ἢ πῶς ἂν τὸ πρᾶγμα ἐσιγήθη; εἰ
δ᾽ ἄρα ἐγὼ ἐτόλμων τοῦτο ποιεῖν, ἐπέτρεψας ἄν,
ὦ Δημόσθενες, καὶ οὐκ ἐνέπλησας βοῆς καὶ κραυγῆς τὴν ἀγοράν, ὁρῶν με, ὡς ἔφησθ᾽ [1] ἀρτίως,
ὠθοῦντα ἀπὸ τῶν ἱερῶν τὸν πρεσβευτήν; καλείτω
δέ μοι τοὺς στρατηγοὺς ὁ κῆρυξ καὶ τοὺς συνέδρους τῶν συμμάχων, καὶ τὰς μαρτυρίας αὐτῶν
ἀκούσατε.

MAPTYPIAI

87   Οὐκ οὖν δεινόν, ὦ ἄνδρες Ἀθηναῖοι, εἴ τις κατ᾽
ἀνδρὸς πολίτου, οὐχ ἑαυτοῦ, ἀλλ᾽ ὑμετέρου, τοῦτο
γὰρ προδιορθοῦμαι, τολμᾷ τηλικαῦτα καταψεύ-
δεσθαι, κινδυνεύοντος ὑπὲρ τοῦ σώματος; ἢ πῶς
οὐκ εἰκότως οἱ πατέρες ἡμῶν ἐν ταῖς φονικαῖς
δίκαις ταῖς [2] ἐπὶ Παλλαδίῳ κατέδειξαν, τέμνον-
τα τὰ τόμια τὸν νικῶντα [3] τῇ ψήφῳ ἐξορκίζε-
σθαι, καὶ τοῦτο ὑμῖν πάτριόν ἐστιν ἔτι καὶ νῦν,
τἀληθῆ καὶ τὰ δίκαια ἐψηφίσθαι [4] τῶν δικαστῶν
ὅσοι τὴν ψῆφον ἤνεγκαν αὐτῷ, καὶ ψεῦδος μηδὲν
εἰρηκέναι, εἰ δὲ μή, ἐξώλη αὐτὸν εἶναι ἐπαρᾶσθαι
καὶ τὴν οἰκίαν τὴν αὐτοῦ, τοῖς δὲ δικασταῖς εὔχε-
σθαι πολλὰ καὶ ἀγαθὰ εἶναι; καὶ μάλα ὀρθῶς
88 καὶ πολιτικῶς, ὦ ἄνδρες Ἀθηναῖοι· εἰ γὰρ μηδεὶς

---

[1] ἔφησθ᾽ Franke : ἔφης MSS.   [2] ταῖς added by Scaliger.
[3] τὸν νικῶντα Scaliger : τοὺς νικῶντας MSS.
[4] ἐψηφίσθαι Scaliger : ψηφίζεσθαι (or ἐψηφίσθη) MSS.

ambassadors proceeded to administer the oaths to
your allies in your army-building. And my accuser
has dared to tell you that it was I who drove Critobulus, Cersobleptes' ambassador, from the ceremony
—in the presence of the allies, under the eyes of the
generals, after the people had voted as they did!
Where did I get all that power? How could the
thing have been hushed up? If I had really dared
to undertake such a thing, would you have suffered
it, Demosthenes? Would you not have filled the
market-place with your shouts and screams, if you
had seen me, as you just now said you did, thrust-
ing the ambassador away from the ceremony? But
please let the herald call the generals and the representatives of the allies, and do you hear their
testimony.

TESTIMONY

Is it not, therefore, an outrage, gentlemen, if one
dares utter such lies about a man who is his own—
no, I hasten to correct myself, not his own, but
your—fellow citizen, when he is in peril of his life?
Wisely, indeed, did our fathers prescribe that, in
the trials for bloodshed which are held at the Pal-
ladion,[1] the one who wins his case must cut in pieces
the sacrificial flesh, and take a solemn oath (and
the custom of your fathers is in force to this day),
affirming that those jurors who have voted on his side
have voted what is true and right, and that he himself has spoken no falsehood; and he calls down
destruction upon himself and his household, if this
be not true, and prays for many blessings for the
jurors. A right provision, fellow citizens, and worthy
of a democracy. For if no one of you would wil-

---

[1] This court was for cases of unintentional homicide.

ἂν ὑμῶν ἑαυτὸν ἀναπλῆσαι φόνου δικαίου βούλοιτο, ἢ που ἀδίκου γε φυλάξαιτ' ἄν, τὴν ψυχὴν
ἢ τὴν οὐσίαν ἢ τὴν ἐπιτιμίαν τινὸς ἀφελόμενος,
ἐξ ὧν αὐτοὺς ἀνῃρήκασί τινες, οἱ δὲ καὶ δημοσίᾳ
ἐτελεύτησαν. ἆρ' οὖν, ὦ ἄνδρες Ἀθηναῖοι, δοίητ'
ἄν μοι συγγνώμην, εἰ κίναιδον αὐτὸν προσειπὼν
καὶ μὴ καθαρεύοντα τῷ σώματι, μηδ' ὅθεν τὴν
φωνὴν ἀφίησιν, ἔπειτα τὸ λοιπὸν μέρος τοῦ κατη-
γορήματος τοῦ περὶ Κερσοβλέπτην ἐπ' αὐτοφώρῳ
δείξαιμι ψεῦδος ὄν;

89 Κάλλιστον γὰρ οἶμαι πρᾶγμα καὶ χρησιμώ-
τατον τοῖς διαβαλλομένοις παρ' ὑμῖν γίγνεται·
καὶ γὰρ τοὺς χρόνους καὶ τὰ ψηφίσματα καὶ τοὺς
ἐπιψηφίσαντας ἐν τοῖς δημοσίοις γράμμασι τὸν
ἅπαντα χρόνον φυλάττετε. εἴρηκε δὲ οὗτος πρὸς
ὑμᾶς, παρὰ τοῦτο διαφθαρῆναι τὰ Κερσοβλέπτου
πράγματα, ὅτι τῆς πρεσβείας ὢν ἡγεμὼν ἐγὼ καὶ
κατευημερηκὼς παρ' ὑμῖν, αὐτοῦ κελεύοντος εἰς
Θρᾴκην ἡμᾶς ἰέναι Κερσοβλέπτου πολιορκουμέ-
νου, καὶ διαμαρτύρασθαι Φιλίππῳ ταῦτα μὴ
ποιεῖν, οὐκ ἠθέλησα, ἀλλ' ἐκαθήμην ἐν Ὠρεῷ,
καὶ οἱ συμπρέσβεις, προξενίας κατασκευαζόμενοι.

90 ἀκούσατε δὴ τῆς Χάρητος ἐπιστολῆς, ἣν ἐπέ-
στειλε τότε τῷ δήμῳ, ὅτι Κερσοβλέπτης ἀπολώ-
λεκε τὴν ἀρχὴν καὶ Ἱερὸν ὄρος κατείληφε Φίλιππος Ἐλαφηβολιῶνος μηνὸς ἑβδόμῃ[1] φθίνοντος·
Δημοσθένης δ' ἐν τῷ δήμῳ προήδρευε τούτου τοῦ
μηνός, εἷς ὢν τῶν πρέσβεων, ἕκτῃ[1] φθίνοντος.

---

[1] ἑβδόμῃ . . . ἕκτῃ Spengel : ἕκτῃ . . . ἑβδόμῃ MSS. *cp.*
iii. 73.

---

[1] Athenian citizens were employed by foreign states to
represent their interests at Athens and aid their citizens

lingly defile himself with justifiable bloodshed, surely he would guard against that which was unjustifiable, such as robbing a man of life or property or civil rights—such acts as have caused some men to kill themselves, others to be put to death by decree of the state. Will you then, fellow citizens, pardon me, if I call him a lewd rascal, unclean of body, even to the place whence his voice issues forth, and if I go on to prove that the rest of his accusation about Cersobleptes is false on the face of it?

You have a practice which in my judgment is most excellent and most useful to those in your midst who are the victims of slander: you preserve for all time in the public archives your decrees, together with their dates and the names of the officials who put them to vote. Now this man has told you that what ruined the cause of Cersobleptes was this: that when Demosthenes urged that we should go to Thrace, where Cersobleptes was being besieged, and should solemnly call on Philip to cease doing this thing, I, as leader of the ambassadors and influential with you, refused, and sat down in Oreus, I and the rest of the ambassadors, busy with getting foreign consulships for ourselves.[1] Hear now the letter which Chares sent to the people at the time, saying that Cersobleptes had lost his kingdom and that Philip had taken Hieron Oros[2] on the twenty-fourth of Elaphebolion. And it was Demosthenes, one of the ambassadors, who was presiding in the assembly here on the twenty-fifth of that month.

there. Demosthenes asserted that the ambassadors were intent on getting such appointments for themselves.

[2] This was an important post on the Thracian coast, and had been held by an Athenian garrison, in the interest of Cersobleptes.

ΕΠΙΣΤΟΛΗ

91 Οὐ μόνον τοίνυν διετρίψαμεν τὰς λοιπὰς ἡμέρας
τοῦ μηνός, ἀλλὰ Μουνιχιῶνος ἐξωρμήσαμεν. καὶ
τούτου τὴν βουλὴν μάρτυρα ὑμῖν παρέξομαι·
ἔστι γὰρ αὐτῆς ψήφισμα, ὃ κελεύει ἀπιέναι τοὺς
πρέσβεις ἐπὶ τοὺς ὅρκους. καί μοι λέγε τὸ τῆς
βουλῆς ψήφισμα.

ΨΗΦΙΣΜΑ

Παρανάγνωθι δὴ καὶ τὸν χρόνον, ὅστις ἦν.

ΧΡΟΝΟΣ

92 Ἀκούετε ὅτι Μουνιχιῶνος ἐψηφίσθη τρίτῃ
ἱσταμένου. ὁ δὲ Κερσοβλέπτης πόσαις πρότερον
ἡμέραις ἀπώλεσε τὴν ἀρχὴν πρὶν ἐμὲ ἀπιέναι;
ὡς φησι Χάρης ὁ στρατηγός,[1] τοῦ προτέρου μηνός,
εἴπερ Ἐλαφηβολιών ἐστι Μουνιχιῶνος πρότερος.
ἐδυνάμην ἂν οὖν ἐγὼ σῶσαι Κερσοβλέπτην, ὃς
πρὶν ἐμὲ ἐξορμᾶν οἴκοθεν ἀπωλώλει· ἔπειτα
οἴεσθέ τι τοῦτον ἀληθὲς εἰρηκέναι ἢ περὶ τῶν ἐν
Μακεδονίᾳ πραχθέντων ἢ περὶ τῶν ἐν Θετταλίᾳ,
ὃς τοῦ βουλευτηρίου καὶ τῶν δημοσίων γραμμάτωι
καὶ τοῦ χρόνου καὶ τῶν ἐκκλησιῶν καταψεύδεται;
93 καὶ τὸν Κερσοβλέπτην Ἀθήνησι μὲν ἔκσπονδον
ἐποίεις,[2] ἐν Ὠρεῷ δ᾽ ἠλέεις; καὶ νῦν μὲν δωροδοκίας κατηγορεῖς, πρότερον δ᾽ ὑπέμεινας τὴν
ἐπιβολὴν τῆς βουλῆς τῆς ἐξ Ἀρείου πάγου, οὐκ
ἐπεξιὼν τῇ τοῦ τραύματος γραφῇ, ἣν ἐγράψω
Δημομέλην τὸν Παιανιέα, ἀνεψιὸν ὄντα, ἐπιτεμὼν

---

[1] στρατηγός Baiter : στρατηγὸς καὶ ἡ ἐπιστολή MSS.
[2] ἐποίεις Weidner : ἐποίεις πρόεδρος ὤν MSS.

Now not only did we delay all the rest of that month, but it was Munichion[1] when we set out. As witness of this I will present the senate, for there is a decree of theirs which commands the ambassadors to set out in order to receive the oaths. Please read the decree of the senate.

Now read also the date of the decree.

You hear that the decree was passed on the third of Munichion. How many days before I set out was it that Cersobleptes lost his kingdom? According to Chares the general it occurred the month before —that is, if Elaphebolion is the month next before Munichion! Was it, then, in my power to save Cersobleptes, who was lost before I set out from home? And now do you imagine that there is one word of truth in his account of what was done in Macedonia or of what was done in Thessaly, when he gives the lie to the senate-house and the public archives, and falsifies the date and the meetings of the assembly? And is it true, Demosthenes, that you at Athens tried to exclude Cersobleptes from the treaty, but pitied him when you got to Oreus? And do you to-day accuse me of having taken bribes, you who were once fined by the Senate of the Areopagus for not prosecuting your suit for assault, that time when you indicted your cousin Demomeles of Paeania for the cut on your head that you gave yourself with your own

[1] The next month after Elaphebolion.

229

τὴν σαυτοῦ κεφαλήν; καὶ σεμνολογεῖ[1] ὡς[2] οὐκ
εἰδόσι τούτοις ὅτι Δημοσθένους υἱὸς εἶ νόθος τοῦ
μαχαιροποιοῦ;

94 Ἐπεχείρησας δ᾿ εἰπεῖν, ὡς καὶ τὴν ἐπὶ τοὺς
Ἀμφικτύονας πρεσβείαν ἐξομοσάμενος παρεπρέ-
σβευσα, καὶ ψήφισμα τὸ μὲν ἀνέγνως, τὸ δὲ
ὑπερέβης. ἐγὼ δ᾿ αἱρεθεὶς πρεσβευτὴς ἐπὶ τοὺς
Ἀμφικτύονας, ἀρρώστως δ᾿ ἔχων, καὶ μετὰ πολλῆς
προθυμίας ἀπαγγέλλων ἀφ᾿ ἧς ἧκον πρεσβείας
πρὸς ὑμᾶς, τὴν μὲν πρεσβείαν οὐκ ἐξωμοσάμην,
ἀλλ᾿ ὑπεσχόμην πρεσβεύσειν, ἐὰν ὦ δυνατός,
πρὸς δὲ τὴν βουλὴν ἀπιόντων τῶν συμπρέσβεων
τὸν ἀδελφὸν τὸν ἐμαυτοῦ καὶ τὸν ἀδελφιδοῦν καὶ
95 τὸν ἰατρὸν ἔπεμψα, οὐκ ἐξομουμένους· οὐδὲ γὰρ ὁ
νόμος ἐᾷ τὰς ἐκ τοῦ δήμου χειροτονίας ἐν τῇ
βουλῇ ἐξόμνυσθαι· ἀλλὰ τὴν ἀρρωστίαν μου
δηλώσοντας.

---

[1] σεμνολογεῖ Cobet : σεμνολογεῖς MSS.
[2] ὡς Stephanus : ἡμῖν ὡς MSS.

---

[1] The reference is to a family quarrel which grew out of
the suit of the young Demosthenes against his guardians.

[2] A bastard in the sense that his mother was of a Scythian
family, and so debarred from legitimate Athenian wedlock.
See on § 22.

[3] The embassy was strictly to Philip, but as it was to deal
largely with Amphictyonic business in the hands of Philip
and allies of his who were in control of Amphictyonic affairs,
Aeschines can speak of it as "to the Amphictyons."

[4] The reference is to events after the return of the second
embassy. After their report was accepted, a third embassy
was appointed to go to Philip, extending the peace and
alliance to his descendants, and declaring that if the Phocians

hand?[1]   And do you put on airs before these jurymen, as though they did not know that you are the
bastard son of Demosthenes the cutler?[2]

But you undertook to say that I at first refused to
serve on the embassy to the Amphictyons,[3] and later
went on the embassy and was guilty of misconduct,
and you read the one decree and suppressed the
other.[4] I was, indeed, chosen one of the ambassadors
to the Amphictyons, and even as I had shown myself
zealous in reporting to you the embassy from which
I had returned, so now, although I was in poor
health, I did not refuse the new mission, but promised to serve, if I should have the strength.   But
as the ambassadors were on the point of setting out,
I sent my brother and his son with my physician
to the senate, not to decline service for me (for the
law does not permit men who have been elected by
the assembly to decline before the senate), but
merely to testify to my illness.

would not submit to the Amphictyons, the Athenians would
take the field against them.   Most of the men appointed on
this third embassy had served on the other two.   Demosthenes was nominated, but he refused to serve.   Aeschines
was elected, but finally on the plea of illness he was excused
by the senate, and his brother was appointed to take his
place.   The embassy had gone only as far as Euboea when
they received the news that the Phocians had surrendered
to Philip; they therefore immediately returned to Athens.
The Athenians now reappointed the same men, including
Aeschines, to go to meet Philip.   Aeschines, now recovered
in health, went on this fourth embassy.   Demosthenes (xix.
126) falsely declares that he went without having been
elected.   For the whole story from Demosthenes' standpoint,
see Demosthenes, *On the Embassy*, §§ 121-133.   In § 172,
Demosthenes betrays the fact that there really was a re-
election for the fourth embassy, and so confirms Aeschines'
statement.

Ἐπειδὴ δὲ οἱ συμπρέσβεις πυθόμενοι τὰ περὶ τοὺς Φωκέας συμβάντα ἀνέστρεψαν, γενομένης ἐκκλησίας ἤδη παρὼν καὶ δυνάμενος τῷ σώματι, προσαναγκάζοντος τοῦ δήμου μηδὲν ἧττον πρεσβεύειν ἡμᾶς τοὺς ἐξ ἀρχῆς αἱρεθέντας ἅπαντας, 96 ἀψευδεῖν πρὸς Ἀθηναίους ᾤμην δεῖν. καὶ ταύτης τῆς πρεσβείας οὐ κατηγορεῖς μου διδόντος τὰς εὐθύνας, ἀλλ᾽ ἐπὶ ταύτην[1] ἥκεις τὴν ἐπὶ τοὺς ὅρκους, ὑπὲρ ἧς ἐγὼ σαφῶς καὶ δικαίως ἀπολογήσομαι. σοὶ μὲν γὰρ ἁρμόττει καὶ πᾶσι τοῖς ψευδομένοις μεταφέρειν τοὺς χρόνους, ἐμοὶ δ᾽ ἐφεξῆς λέγειν, ἀναλαβόντι τὴν ἀρχὴν τοῦ λόγου ἀπὸ τῆς πορείας τῆς ἐπὶ τοὺς ὅρκους.[2]

97 Πρῶτον μὲν γὰρ δέκα πρέσβεων ὄντων, ἐνδεκάτου δὲ τοῦ συμπεμφθέντος ἡμῖν ἀπὸ τῶν συμμάχων, οὐδεὶς αὐτῷ συσσιτεῖν, ὅτ᾽ ἐξῆμεν ἐπὶ τὴν ὑστέραν πρεσβείαν, ἤθελεν, οὐδὲ[3] ἐν ταῖς ὁδοῖς, ὅπου δυνατὸν ἦν, εἰς ταὐτὸν πανδοκεῖον καταλύειν, ὁρῶντες αὐτὸν ἐν τῇ προτέρᾳ πρεσβείᾳ πᾶσιν 98 αὐτοῖς ἐπιβεβουλευκότα. περὶ μὲν οὖν τῆς ἐπὶ Θρᾴκης ὁδοῦ οὐκ ἐγένετο μνεία· οὔτε[4] γὰρ τὸ ψήφισμα τοῦθ᾽ ἡμῖν προσέταττεν, ἀλλ᾽ ἀπολαβεῖν μόνον τοὺς ὅρκους καὶ ἄλλ᾽ ἄττα, οὔτ᾽ ἐλθόντας πράττειν οὐδὲν ἐνεδέχετο, τῶν περὶ Κερσοβλέπτην ἤδη γεγενημένων, ὡς ἀρτίως ἠκούσατε,

---

[1] ταύτην Bekker : ταύτην τὴν πρεσβείαν MSS.
[2] ὅρκους Bekker : ὅρκους καὶ τῆς πρεσβείας MSS.
[3] οὐδὲ Bekker : οὔτε MSS.
[4] οὔτε Bekker : οὐδὲ MSS.

---

[1] That is, Aeschines felt that he ought now to say frankly that his health was such that he could not decline the service.

When now the ambassadors had been informed of the fate of the Phocians, they returned, and a meeting of the assembly was held. I had by this time recovered and was present. When the people insisted that we who had been originally elected should all go on with the embassy in spite of what had happened, I thought it my duty to speak the truth to the Athenians.[1] And when I rendered account of my service on that embassy, you, Demosthenes, preferred no charge, but you proceed against my conduct on this embassy, the embassy that was appointed to receive the oaths. As to this I will make a clear and just defence. For it serves you, as it does all liars, to confuse the dates, but it serves me to give the events in their order, beginning with our journey to receive the oaths.[2]

In the first place, of the ten ambassadors (or rather eleven, counting the representative of the allies, who was with us) not one was willing to mess with Demosthenes, when we set out on the second embassy, nor even to lodge at the same inn with him as we journeyed, whenever it could be avoided, for they had seen how he had plotted against them all on the previous embassy. Now not a word was said about making the journey along the Thracian coast;[3] for the decree did not prescribe any such journey, but simply that we should receive the oaths and transact certain other business, nor could we have accomplished anything if we had gone, for Cersobleptes' fate had already been decided, as you heard a moment ago; for there is not a word of

[2] Aeschines returns to the story of the second embassy.
[3] The journey which Demosthenes, in the speech for the prosecution, had said ought to have been made in order to forestall Philip's conquests there.

οὔθ' οὗτος οὐδὲν ἀληθὲς εἶπεν, ἀλλὰ ψεύδεται καὶ κατηγορεῖν οὐδὲν ἀληθὲς ἔχων τερατεύεται.

99 Συνηκολούθουν δ' αὐτῷ ἄνθρωποι δύο στρωματόδεσμα φέροντες· ἐν δὲ τῷ ἑτέρῳ τούτων, ὡς αὐτὸς ἔφη, τάλαντον ἐνῆν ἀργυρίου. ὥστε τοὺς συμπρέσβεις ἀναμιμνῄσκεσθαι τὰς ἀρχαίας ἐπωνυμίας αὐτοῦ· ἐν παισὶ μὲν γὰρ ὢν ἐκλήθη δι' αἰσχρουργίαν τινὰ καὶ κιναιδίαν Βάταλος, ἐκ παίδων δὲ ἀπαλλαττόμενος καὶ δεκαταλάντους δίκας ἑκάστῳ τῶν ἐπιτρόπων λαγχάνων, Ἀργᾶς,[1] ἀνὴρ δὲ γενόμενος προσείληφε τὴν τῶν πονηρῶν κοινὴν
100 ἐπωνυμίαν, συκοφάντης. ἐπορεύετο δὲ λυσόμενος τοὺς αἰχμαλώτους, ὡς ἔφη, καὶ πρὸς ὑμᾶς ἀρτίως εἴρηκεν, εἰδὼς μὲν Φίλιππον ἐν τῷ πολέμῳ οὐδένα πώποτε Ἀθηναίων λύτρα πραξάμενον, ἀκούων δὲ τῶν ἐκείνου φίλων ἁπάντων, ὅτι καὶ τοὺς λοιπούς, ἐὰν εἰρήνη γένηται, ἀφήσει, πολλῶν δ' ἠτυχηκότων τάλαντον φέρων, ἑνὸς ἀνδρός, οὐδὲ τούτου λίαν εὐπόρου, ἱκανὰ λύτρα.
101 Ὡς δ' ἦμεν ἐν Μακεδονίᾳ καὶ συνήλθομεν εἰς ταὐτόν, καὶ Φίλιππον ἐκ Θρᾴκης παρόντα κατειλήφεμεν, ἀνεγνώσθη μὲν τὸ ψήφισμα καθ' ὃ ἐπρεσβεύομεν, καὶ τὰ προστεταγμένα ἡμῖν πρὸς τῷ τοὺς ὅρκους ἀπολαβεῖν συνηριθμούμεθα· ὡς δὲ οὐδεὶς ὑπὲρ τῶν μεγίστων ἐμέμνητο, ἀλλὰ περὶ πραγμάτων ἐλαττόνων τὴν διατριβὴν ἐποι-

---

[1] Ἀργᾶς Blass : Ἀργᾶς ἐκλήθη MSS.

---

[1] " Batalos " has been thought to mean " stammerer," or perhaps " mamma-baby " (see Aeschines, i. §§ 126 and 131), but that explanation would hardly fit this passage. We really have no knowledge as to the derivation of the word. " Argas " was the name of a venomous snake.

truth in what he has said, but, at a loss for any true charge, he resorts to these prodigious lies.

On the journey two attendants followed him, carrying sacks of bedding; in one of the sacks, he assured us, was a talent of silver; so that his colleagues were reminded of those old nicknames of his; for the boys used to call him "Batalos," he was so vulgar and obscene; then when he was growing out of boyhood and was bringing against his guardians big lawsuits of ten talents each, he was called "Argas"; [1] now, grown to manhood, he has got also the name that we apply to rascals in general, "Blackmailer." And he was going with the intention of ransoming the captives, [2] as he said, and as he has just now told you, although he knew that at no time during the war had Philip exacted ransom-money for any Athenian, and although he had heard all Philip's friends say that he would release the rest also, if peace should be made. And he was carrying one talent for many unfortunates— sufficient ransom for one man, and not a very well-to-do man at that!

But when we reached Macedonia and found Philip returned from Thrace, we held a meeting; [3] the decree under which we were acting was read, and we went over the instructions that had been given us in addition to the business of receiving the oaths. But finding that no one mentioned the subjects that were most important, and all were dwelling on minor

---

[2] The Athenian citizens who had been captured at the fall of Olynthus, and were now in slavery in Macedonia.

[3] This was a private meeting of the Athenian ambassadors to discuss what they should say to Philip at the coming audience.

οὖντο, εἶπον ἐγὼ λόγους, οὓς ἀναγκαῖόν ἐστι πρὸς
102 ὑμᾶς ῥηθῆναι. καὶ πρὸς τῶν θεῶν, ὦ ἄνδρες
Ἀθηναῖοι, ὥσπερ καὶ τῆς κατηγορίας ἠκούσατε
ὡς αὐτὸς ὁ κατήγορος ἐβούλετο εἰπεῖν, οὕτω καὶ
τῆς ἀπολογίας εὐτάκτως ἀκούσατε, καὶ τὸν αὐτόν
μοι τρόπον διαμείνατε, ὅνπερ ἐξ ἀρχῆς ἐν τοῖς
προειρημένοις ἤδη λόγοις ἠκροᾶσθε. ὅπερ γὰρ
καὶ ἀρτίως ὑπεθέμην, ὦ ἄνδρες Ἀθηναῖοι, εἶπον
συνειλεγμένων τῶν πρέσβεων, ὅτι μοι δοκοῖεν
τὸ μέγιστον πρόσταγμα τοῦ δήμου δεινῶς ἀγνοεῖν.
103 "Τὸ μὲν γὰρ τοὺς ὅρκους ἀπολαβεῖν, καὶ περὶ
τῶν ἄλλων διαλεχθῆναι, καὶ περὶ τῶν αἰχμαλώ-
των εἰπεῖν, κἂν εἰ τοὺς ὑπηρέτας ἔπεμψεν ἡ πόλις
περιθεῖσα πίστιν αὐτοῖς, ἅπαντ' ἂν πραχθῆναι
νομίζω· τὸ δὲ ὑπὲρ τῶν ὅλων ὀρθῶς βουλεύσασθαι, ὅσα καθ' ἡμᾶς ἐστιν ἢ Φίλιππον, τοῦτο
ἤδη ἔργον ἐστὶ πρέσβεων φρονίμων. λέγω δέ," ἔφην
ἐγώ, "περὶ τῆς εἰς Πύλας στρατείας, ἣν ὁρᾶτε
οὖσαν ἐν παρασκευῇ. ὅτι δὲ οὐ κακῶς στοχά-
ζομαι περὶ τοῦ πράγματος, μεγάλα τούτων ὑμῖν
104 σημεῖα δείξω. πάρεισι μὲν γὰρ Θηβαίων, ἥκουσι
δὲ Λακεδαιμονίων πρέσβεις, ἀφίγμεθα δ' ἡμεῖς
ἔχοντες τοῦ δήμου ψήφισμα, ἐν ᾧ γέγραπται
'Πράττειν δὲ τοὺς πρέσβεις καὶ ἄλλ' ὅ τι ἂν
δύνωνται ἀγαθόν·' ἅπαντες δὲ οἱ Ἕλληνες πρὸς
τὸ μέλλον ἔσεσθαι βλέπουσιν. εἰ μὲν οὖν ἡγεῖτο
ὁ δῆμος αὐτῷ καλῶς ἔχειν ἐξενεγκεῖν μετὰ παρ-

---

[1] The supreme question of the hour was the settlement of
the long continued Phocian war. Whether Phocis was to be
defeated and Thebes given a dangerous increase of power
depended in large measure on what action Philip and the

matters, I spoke words which I must repeat to you.
And in heaven's name, gentlemen, even as you allowed my accuser to speak as he himself chose, pray
so continue to listen quietly to the defence also, in
the same manner in which from the beginning you
have listened during all my speech thus far. Well,
as I just now intimated, fellow citizens, at the meeting of the ambassadors I said that it seemed to me
that we were strangely ignoring the most important
matter that the people had entrusted to us. "The
reception of the oaths, the discussion of the other
questions, and the talk about the prisoners, all that
sort of thing could have been done, I think, if the
city had entrusted it to some of its petty servants
and sent them. But to reach a right solution of the
supreme question, so far as that is in our power or
Philip's,[1] this is now a task for wise ambassadors. I
mean," said I, "the question of the expedition to
Thermopylae, which you see in course of preparation.
That I am not wide of the mark in this matter, I
will show you by weighty considerations. For ambassadors from Thebes are here, ambassadors from
Lacedaemonia have arrived, and here are we with a
decree of the people in which it stands written,
'The ambassadors shall also negotiate concerning
any other good thing that may be within their
power.' All Hellas is watching to see what is going
to happen. If now our people had thought it wise
to speak out plainly to Philip, bidding him strip the

Athenians should decide to take, either jointly or severally.
The Athenians had been unable to persuade Philip's ambassadors to include the Phocians among the states to be protected by the peace, but it was hoped that these ambassadors
from Athens would be able to persuade Philip himself to
favour Phocis as against Thebes.

ρησίας¹ πρὸς Φίλιππον, Θηβαίων μὲν περιελεῖν
τὴν ὕβριν, Βοιωτῶν δὲ ἀναστῆσαι τὰ τείχη, ταῦτ'
ἂν ἠξίωσεν ἐν τῷ ψηφίσματι· νῦν δὲ αὐτοῖς μὲν
κατέλιπον τὴν εἰς τὸ ἀφανὲς ἀναφοράν, ἂν μὴ
πείθωσιν, ἐν ἡμῖν δὲ ἀποκινδυνεύειν ᾠήθησαν δεῖν.
105 δεῖ δὴ τοὺς πρὸς τὰ κοινὰ φιλοτιμουμένους μὴ
κατέχειν μὲν ἑτέρων χώραν πρέσβεων, οὓς ἐξῆν
πέμπειν ἀνθ' ἡμῶν Ἀθηναίους, λυτοὺς δὲ τὰς
πρὸς Θηβαίους ἀπεχθείας φεύγειν, ὧν εἷς ὢν
Ἐπαμεινώνδας,² οὐχ ὑποπτήξας τὸ τῶν Ἀθηναίων
ἀξίωμα, εἶπε διαρρήδην ἐν τῷ πλήθει τῶν Θηβαίων,
ὡς δεῖ τὰ τῆς Ἀθηναίων ἀκροπόλεως προπύλαια
μετενεγκεῖν εἰς τὴν προστασίαν τῆς Καδμείας."
106 ταῦτα δ' ἐμοῦ μεταξὺ λέγοντος, ἀναβοᾷ παμμέγεθες
Δημοσθένης, ὡς ἴσασι πάντες οἱ συμπρέσβεις·³ καὶ
γὰρ πρὸς τοῖς ἄλλοις κακοῖς βοιωτιάζει. ἦν δ' οὖν
παρ' αὐτοῦ τοιαυτὶ τὰ λεγόμενα· "Ἄνθρωπος⁴
οὑτοσὶ ταραχῆς καὶ τόλμης ἐστὶ μεστός· ἐγὼ δὲ
ὁμολογῶ μαλακὸς εἶναι καὶ τὰ δεινὰ πόρρωθεν
δεδιέναι, ἀπαγορεύω μέντοι μὴ συνταράττειν ἡμᾶς
πρὸς ἀλλήλας τὰς πόλεις, τὸ μὴ πολυπραγμονεῖν
ἡμᾶς τοὺς πρέσβεις μηδέν, τοῦτ' ἀγαθὸν ὑπολαμ-
107 βάνων εἶναι. πορεύεται Φίλιππος εἰς Πύλας, ἐγὼ
δὲ ἐγκαλύπτομαι. οὐδείς με τῶν ὅπλων ἕνεκα τῶν
Φιλίππου κρινεῖ, ἀλλ' ὧν ἂν εἴπω τι μὴ δέον,
ἢ πράξω τι τῶν μὴ προστεταγμένων." πέρας δὲ
τοῦ πράγματος, ἐψηφίσαντο οἱ συμπρέσβεις,
κατ' ἄνδρα ἐπερωτώμενοι ἕκαστον⁵ ἡμῶν ὅ τι

---

¹ παρρησίας Markland : παρρησίας ἐν τῷ ψηφίσματι MSS.
² Ἐπαμεινώνδας Dobree : Ἐπαμεινώνδας στρατηγός MSS.
³ συμπρέσβεις Cobet : συμπρέσβεις ἡμῶν MSS.
⁴ ἄνθρωπος Sauppe : ἄνθρωπος MSS.
⁵ ἐπερωτώμενοι ἕκαστον Cobet : ἐπερωτώμενος ἕκαστος MSS.

Thebans of their insolence, and rebuild the walls of the Boeotian towns,[1] they would have asked this of him in the decree. But as it is, by the obscurity of their language they left open a way of retreat for themselves, in case they should fail to persuade him, and they thought best to take the risk in our persons. Men, therefore, who are ambitious to serve the state must not assume the function of other ambassadors whom the Athenians could have sent instead of us, and at the same time, on their own initiative, try to avoid stirring up the hostility of the Thebans. Epameinondas was a Theban, and he did not cower before the fame of the Athenians, but spoke right out in the Theban assembly, saying that they must remove the propylaea of the Acropolis of Athens and set it up at the entrance to the Cadmeia." As I was in the midst of these words, Demosthenes protested with a loud voice, as all our colleagues know, for on top of all his other crimes he is for the Boeotians. At any rate words like these came from him : "This fellow is full of quarrelsomeness and rashness. For myself, I confess that I am timid, that I fear danger from afar, but I protest against embroiling the cities one with another; I hold it to be the wise course that we ambassadors refrain from meddlesome conduct. Philip is setting out for Thermopylae; I cover my eyes. No man is going to call me to account for the wars of Philip, but for what I say that I ought not to say, or what I do that I was not instructed to do." The upshot of the matter was that the ambassadors, when asked for their opinion man by man, voted that each of us should say what he thought

[1] The small towns of Boeotia which had been subjugated by Thebes, and were now supporting the Phocians in the hope of regaining their independence.

νομίζοι¹ συμφέρειν, τοῦτο λέγειν. ὅτι δ' ἀληθῆ
λέγω, κάλει μοι τοὺς συμπρέσβεις καὶ τὴν μαρτυρίαν αὐτῶν λέγε.

MAPTYPIA

108 Ἐπειδὴ τοίνυν, ὦ ἄνδρες Ἀθηναῖοι, συνελέγησαν μὲν εἰς Πέλλαν αἱ πρεσβεῖαι, παρῆν δὲ ὁ
Φίλιππος, καὶ τοὺς Ἀθηναίων πρέσβεις ὁ κῆρυξ
ἐκάλει, πρῶτον μὲν παρῆμεν οὐ καθ' ἡλικίαν,
ὥσπερ ἐν τῇ προτέρᾳ πρεσβείᾳ, ὃ παρά τισιν
εὐδοκίμει καὶ κόσμος εἶναι τῆς πόλεως ἐφαίνετο,
ἀλλὰ κατὰ τὴν Δημοσθένους ἀναισχυντίαν. φάσκων γὰρ νεώτατος εἶναι πάντων, τὴν τάξιν τοῦ
πρῶτος λέγειν οὐκ ἂν ἔφη παραλιπεῖν, οὐδ'
ἐπιτρέψειν τινί, αἰνιττόμενος εἰς ἐμέ, προκαταλα-
βόντα τὰ Φιλίππου ὦτα τοῖς ἄλλοις λόγον μὴ
καταλιπεῖν.

109 Ἀρξάμενος δὲ τοῦ λέγειν,² πρῶτον διαβολήν
τινα ὑπειπὼν κατὰ τῶν συμπρέσβεων, ὡς οὐχ
ἅπαντες ὑπὲρ τῶν αὐτῶν οὐδ' ὅμοιοι ταῖς δόξαις
ἥκοιμεν, διεξῄει τὰς ὑπηρεσίας τὰς ὑπηργμένας
εἰς Φίλιππον αὐτῷ, πρώτην μὲν τὴν τῷ³ ψηφίσματι τῷ Φιλοκράτους συνηγορίαν, ὅτε ἔφευγε
παρανόμων ἐξεῖναι γράψας Φιλίππῳ πρέσβεις
πρὸς Ἀθηναίους ὑπὲρ εἰρήνης πέμπειν· δεύτερον
δὲ ὑπανέγνω τὸ ψήφισμα ὃ γεγραφὼς αὐτὸς ἦν,
σπείσασθαι τῷ κήρυκι καὶ τῇ παρὰ Φιλίππου
πρεσβείᾳ, τρίτον δὲ τὸ περὶ τοῦ βουλεύσασθαι
110 τὸν δῆμον ὑπὲρ εἰρήνης ἐν τακταῖς ἡμέραις. καὶ
προσέθηκέ τι τοιοῦτον ἐνθύμημα τῷ λόγῳ, ὅτι

¹ νομίζοι Markland : νομίζει MSS.
² λέγειν Sauppe : πρῶτος λέγειν or λέγειν πρῶτος MSS.
³ τὴν τῷ H Wolf : τὴν ἐν τῷ MSS.

was to our interests. To show that I speak the truth, please call my colleagues and read their testimony.

TESTIMONY

Accordingly, fellow citizens, when the ambassadors were assembled at Pella, and Philip had arrived, and the herald called the ambassadors of the Athenians, we came forward, not in the order of age, as in the former embassy—a procedure which found favour with some, and which seemed to be in accord with the orderly way of our city [1]—but in the way that was dictated by the effrontery of Demosthenes. For he said that he was the youngest of all, but declared that he could not yield the position of first speaker, and would not permit a certain person—hinting at me—to take possession of Philip's ears and leave the rest no chance to speak.

He began his speech with certain slanderous allusions to his colleagues, to the effect that not all of us had come with the same end in view, nor were we all of one mind; and then he proceeded to review his own previous services to Philip: first, his defence of Philocrates' motion, when Philocrates, having moved that Philip be permitted to send ambassadors to the Athenians to discuss peace, was defendant on the charge of having made an unconstitutional proposal; secondly, he read the motion of which Demosthenes himself was author, to grant safe conduct to the herald and ambassadors from Philip; and thirdly, the motion that restricted the people's discussion of peace to appointed days. To the account he added a conclusion like this: that

[1] The Athenian "way" in such matters is described in Aeschines iii. § 2.

πρῶτος ἐπιστομίσαι τοὺς τὴν εἰρήνην ἐκκλῄοντας,
οὐ τοῖς λόγοις, ἀλλὰ τοῖς χρόνοις. ἔπειθ' ἕτερον
ἐπήγετο ψήφισμα, τὸ καὶ περὶ συμμαχίας βουλεύσασθαι τὸν δῆμον, καὶ μετὰ ταῦτ' ἤδη τὸ περὶ
τῆς προεδρίας τῆς εἰς τὰ Διονύσια τοῖς πρέσβεσι
111 τοῖς Φιλίππου ψήφισμα. καὶ προσέθηκε τὴν
ἐπιμέλειαν τὴν αὑτοῦ καὶ προσκεφαλαίων θέσιν
καὶ φυλακάς τινας καὶ ἀγρυπνίας διὰ τοὺς φθο-
νοῦντας καὶ βουλομένους εἰς τὴν αὑτοῦ φιλοτιμίαν
ὑβρίσαι, καὶ τά γε δὴ καταγέλαστα παντελῶς,
ἐφ' οἷς οἱ συμπρέσβεις ἐνεκαλύψαντο, ὡς ἐξένισε
τοὺς πρέσβεις τοὺς Φιλίππου, ὡς ἐμισθώσατ'
αὐτοῖς, ὅτ' ἀπῄεσαν, ὀρεικὰ ζεύγη καὶ συμπαρῄει
ἐφ' ἵππου, οὐ καταδὺς εἰς τὸ σκότος, ὥσπερ ἕτεροί
τινες, ἀλλὰ φανερῶς ἐπιδεικνύμενος τὴν τῶν
112 πραγμάτων θεραπείαν. ἐκεῖνα δ' ἤδη καὶ σφόδρα
διωρθοῦτο· "Οὐκ εἶπον, ὡς καλὸς εἶ· γυνὴ γὰρ
τῶν ὄντων ἐστὶ κάλλιστον· οὐδ' ὡς δεινὸς πιεῖν,[1]
σπογγιᾶς τὸν ἔπαινον ὑπολαμβάνων τοῦτον εἶναι·
οὐδ' ὡς μνημονικός, σοφιστοῦ τὰ τοιαῦτα νομίζων
ἐργολαβοῦντος ἐγκώμια εἶναι." ἵνα δὲ μὴ μακρολογῶ, τοιαῦτ' ἦν ἃ ἔλεγε παρόντων τῶν πρέσβεων
ὡς ἔπος εἰπεῖν ἐξ ἁπάσης τῆς Ἑλλάδος, ἐφ' οἷς
γέλωτες οὐχ οἱ τυχόντες ἐγίγνοντο.

113 Ἐπειδὴ δέ ποτ' ἐπαύσατο καὶ σιωπὴ ἐγένετο,
ἠναγκαζόμην ἐγὼ λέγειν μετὰ τοιαύτην ἀπαιδευ-

---

[1] πιεῖν Cobet : συμπιεῖν MSS.

he had been the first to put a curb on those who were trying to block the peace; that he had done this, not by his words, but by fixing the dates. Then he brought up another motion, the one which provided that the people should discuss an alliance also; then, after that, the motion about assigning the front seats at the Dionysia to Philip's ambassadors. He alluded also to the special attention he had shown them: the placing of cushions, and certain watchings and vigils of the night, caused by men who were jealous of him and wished to bring insult upon his honourable name! And that utterly absurd story, whereat his colleagues covered their faces for shame, how he gave a dinner to the ambassadors of Philip; and how when they set out for home he hired for them some teams of mules, and escorted them on horseback. For he did not hide in the dark, as certain others do, but made an exhibition of his fawning conduct. And finally he carefully corrected those other statements:[1] "I did not say that you are beautiful, for a woman is the most beautiful of all beings; nor that you are a wonderful drinker, for that is a compliment for a sponge, in my opinion; nor that you have a remarkable memory, for I think such praise belongs to the professional sophist." But not to prolong the story, he said such things in the presence of the ambassadors from almost the whole of Hellas, that laughter arose such as you seldom hear.

But when at last he stopped and there was silence, I was forced to speak—after such an exhibition of

---

[1] The statements that his colleagues had made to the assembly on their return from the first embassy, as related in §§ 47 and 52.

σίαν καὶ κολακείας αἰσχρᾶς ὑπερβολήν. καὶ
μικρὰ μὲν[1] προεῖπον ἐξ ἀνάγκης πρὸς τὴν προ-
ειρημένην κατὰ τῶν συμπρέσβεων ὑπ' αὐτοῦ
διαβολήν, λέγων ὅτι πέμψειαν ἡμᾶς Ἀθηναῖοι
πρέσβεις οὐκ ἀπολογησομένους ἐν Μακεδονίᾳ
περὶ ἡμῶν αὐτῶν, ἀλλ' οἴκοθεν ἐκ τοῦ βίου
114 δεδοκιμασμένους ἀξίους τῆς πόλεως εἶναι. βραχέα
δ' ὑπὲρ τῶν ὅρκων εἰπών, ἐφ' οὓς ἥκομεν,[2] καὶ
περὶ τῶν ἄλλων ἃ προσετάξατε ὑμεῖς, διεξῄειν· ὁ
γὰρ περιττὸς κἂν τοῖς λόγοις δεινὸς Δημοσθένης
οὐδενὸς τῶν ἀναγκαίων ἐμνήσθη· καὶ δὴ καὶ περὶ
τῆς εἰς Πύλας στρατείας εἶπον καὶ περὶ τῶν
ἱερῶν καὶ περὶ Δελφῶν καὶ περὶ τῶν Ἀμφικτυόνων, καὶ μάλιστα μὲν Φίλιππον ἠξίουν μὴ μεθ'
ὅπλων, ἀλλὰ μετὰ ψήφου καὶ κρίσεως τἀκεῖ
καθιστάναι, εἰ δ' ἄρα μὴ δυνατὸν εἴη, (τοῦτο δ'
ἦν πρόδηλον· τὸ γὰρ στρατόπεδον παρῆν καὶ
συνήθροιστο·) εἶπον, ὅτι τὸν μέλλοντα ὑπὲρ
Ἑλληνικῶν ἱερῶν βουλεύεσθαι πολλὴν προσήκει
πρόνοιαν ὑπὲρ εὐσεβείας ἔχειν, καὶ τοῖς περὶ τῶν
πατρίων ἐγχειροῦσι διδάσκειν προσέχειν τὸν νοῦν.
115 ἅμα δ' ἐξ ἀρχῆς διεξῆλθον τὴν κτίσιν τοῦ ἱεροῦ
καὶ τὴν πρώτην σύνοδον γενομένην τῶν Ἀμφικτυόνων, καὶ τοὺς ὅρκους αὐτῶν ἀνέγνων, ἐν οἷς
ἔνορκον ἦν τοῖς ἀρχαίοις, μηδεμίαν πόλιν τῶν
Ἀμφικτυονίδων ἀνάστατον ποιήσειν, μηδ' ὑδάτων
ναματιαίων εἴρξειν μήτ' ἐν πολέμῳ μήτ' ἐν εἰρήνῃ,
ἐὰν δέ τις ταῦτα παραβῇ, στρατεύσειν ἐπὶ τοῦτον
καὶ τὰς πόλεις ἀναστήσειν, καὶ ἐάν τις ἢ συλᾷ τὰ
τοῦ θεοῦ, ἢ συνειδῇ τι, ἢ βουλεύσῃ τι κατὰ τῶν

---

[1] μὲν added by Bekker.
[2] ἥκομεν Cobet: ἥκομεν ἀποληψόμενοι MSS.

ill-breeding and such excess of shameful flattery. Necessarily, by way of preface, I made a brief reply to his insinuations against his colleagues, saying that the Athenians had sent us as ambassadors, not to offer apologies in Macedonia for ourselves, but as men adjudged by our life at home to be worthy of our city. Then after speaking briefly on the subject of the oaths for which we had come, I reviewed the other matters that you had entrusted to us. For the eminent Demosthenes, for all his exceeding eloquence, had not mentioned a single essential point. And in particular I spoke about the expedition to Thermopylae, and about the holy places, and Delphi, and the Amphictyons. I called on Philip to settle matters there, preferably not with arms, but with vote and verdict; but if that should be impossible (it was already evident that it was, for the army was collected and on the spot), I said that he who was on the point of deciding the fate of the holy places of our nation ought to give careful thought to the question of piety, and to give attention to those who undertook to give instruction as to our traditions. At the same time I reviewed from the beginning the story of the founding of the shrine, and of the first synod of the Amphictyons that was ever held; and I read their oaths, in which the men of ancient times swore that they would raze no city of the Amphictyonic states, nor shut them off from flowing water either in war or in peace; that if anyone should violate this oath, they would march against such an one and raze his cities;[1] and if anyone should violate the shrine of the god or be accessory to such violation, or make any plot against the

---

[1] The city that has violated its Amphictyonic oath can no longer claim the protection of that oath.

ἱερῶν, τιμωρήσειν καὶ χειρὶ καὶ ποδὶ καὶ φωνῇ
καὶ πάσῃ δυνάμει· καὶ προσῆν τῷ ὅρκῳ ἀρὰ
116 ἰσχυρά. τούτων δὲ ἀναγνωσθέντων ἀπεφηνάμην, ὅτι ἐμοὶ δοκεῖ δίκαιον εἶναι μὴ περιορᾶν
κατεσκαμμένας τὰς ἐν Βοιωτοῖς πόλεις. ὅτι δ'
ἦσαν Ἀμφικτυονίδες καὶ ἔνορκοι, κατηριθμησάμην
ἔθνη δώδεκα τὰ μετέχοντα τοῦ ἱεροῦ, Θετταλούς,
Βοιωτούς, οὐ Θηβαίους μόνους, Δωριάς, Ἴωνας,
Περραιβούς, Μάγνητας, Δόλοπας,¹ Λοκρούς, Οἰ-
ταίους, Φθιώτας, Μαλιέας, Φωκέας. καὶ τούτων ἔδειξα ἕκαστον ἔθνος ἰσόψηφον γιγνόμενον,
τὸ μέγιστον τῷ ἐλαχίστῳ, τὸν ἥκοντα ἐκ Δωρίου
καὶ Κυτινίου ἴσον δυνάμενον Λακεδαιμονίοις, δύο
γὰρ ψήφους ἕκαστον φέρει ἔθνος, πάλιν ἐκ τῶν
Ἰώνων τὸν Ἐρετριᾶ καὶ Πριηνέα τοῖς Ἀθηναίοις,
καὶ τοὺς ἄλλους κατὰ ταῦτα.

117 Τὴν μὲν οὖν ἀρχὴν τῆς στρατείας ταύτης ὁσίαν
καὶ δικαίαν ἀπεφηνάμην εἶναι· συλλεγέντων δὲ
τῶν Ἀμφικτυόνων εἰς τὸ ἱερὸν καὶ τυχόντων
σωτηρίας καὶ ψήφου, τοὺς αἰτίους τῆς ἐξ ἀρχῆς
καταλήψεως τοῦ ἱεροῦ δίκης ἠξίουν τυχεῖν, μὴ
τὰς πατρίδας αὐτῶν, ἀλλ' αὐτοὺς τοὺς χειρουργή-
σαντας καὶ βουλεύσαντας, τὰς δὲ πόλεις παρε-
χούσας εἰς κρίσιν τοὺς ἀδικήσαντας ἀζημίους
εἶναι. "Εἰ δ' ἐπεξελθὼν δυνάμει βεβαιώσεις
τὰ Θηβαίων ἀδικήματα, παρ' ὧν μὲν βοηθεῖς οὐκ

¹ Δόλοπας added by Tittmann.

---

¹ See on § 104.
² The Council had been unable to meet while the Phocians
were holding the shrine. Aeschines would have Philip's
army occupy Delphi, and so restore the Amphictyons to
their rights.

holy places, they would punish him with hand and foot and voice, and all their power. To the oath was added a mighty curse. When I had read all this, I solemnly declared that in my opinion it was not right that we should overlook the fact that the cities in Boeotia were lying in ruins.[1] To prove that they were Amphictyonic cities and thus protected by the oaths, I enumerated twelve tribes which shared the shrine: the Thessalians, Boeotians (not the Thebans only), Dorians, Ionians, Perrhaebi, Magnetes, Dolopians, Locrians, Oetaeans, Phthiotians, Malians, and Phocians. And I showed that each of these tribes has an equal vote, the greatest equal to the least: that the delegate from Dorion and Cytinion has equal authority with the Lacedaemonian delegates, for each tribe casts two votes; again, that of the Ionian delegates those from Eretria and Priene have equal authority with those from Athens; and the rest in the same way.

Now I showed that the motive of this expedition was righteous and just; but I said that the Amphictyonic Council ought to be convened at the temple, receiving protection and freedom to vote,[2] and that those individuals who were originally responsible for the seizure of the shrine ought to be punished—not their cities, but the individuals who had plotted and carried out the deed; and that those cities which surrendered the wrongdoers for trial ought to be held guiltless. "But if you take the field and with your forces confirm the wrongdoing of the Thebans,[3] you will receive no gratitude from those whom you

[3] If Philip should help the Thebans to subdue the Phocians, the confirmation of Theban control over the Boeotian cities would naturally follow, as it did in the event.

ἀπολήψῃ χάριν· οὐ γὰρ ἂν δύναιο αὐτοὺς τηλικαῦτα εὐεργετῆσαι, ἡλίκα ᾿Αθηναῖοι πρότερον, ὧν
οὐ μέμνηνται· οὓς δ᾽ ἐγκαταλείψεις, ἀδικήσεις,
χρήσῃ δ᾽ ἐχθροῖς μείζοσιν, ἀλλ᾽ οὐ φίλοις."

118 ῞Ινα δὲ μὴ διατρίβω τοὺς ἐκεῖ λόγους ῥηθέντας
νυνὶ πρὸς ὑμᾶς ἀκριβῶς διεξιών, ἐν κεφαλαίῳ
περὶ πάντων εἰπὼν παύσομαι. ἡ μὲν τύχη καὶ
Φίλιππος ἦσαν τῶν ἔργων κύριοι, ἐγὼ δὲ τῆς
εἰς ὑμᾶς εὐνοίας καὶ τῶν λόγων. παρ᾽ ἐμοῦ μὲν
οὖν ἐρρήθη τὰ δίκαια καὶ τὰ συμφέροντα ὑμῖν,
ἀπέβη δὲ οὐχ ὡς ἡμεῖς ηὐχόμεθα, ἀλλ᾽ ὡς Φίλιππος ἔπραξε. πότερον οὖν ὁ μηδὲν προθυμηθεὶς
ἐργάσασθαι ἀγαθὸν δίκαιός ἐστιν εὐδοξεῖν, ἢ ὁ
μηδὲν ὧν ἦν δυνατὸς ἐλλιπών;[1] ἐν δὲ τῷ παρόντι
νυνὶ πολλὰ διὰ τὸν καιρὸν παραλείπω.

119 Εἶπε δέ, ὡς ἐψευδολόγουν φάσκων ὀλίγων
ἡμερῶν τὰς Θήβας ἔσεσθαι ταπεινάς, καὶ τοὺς
Εὐβοέας ὡς ἐφόβουν, προάγων εἰς ἐλπίδας κενὰς[2]
ὑμᾶς. ὃ δὲ ποιεῖ, καταμάθετε, ὦ ἄνδρες ᾿Αθηναῖοι.
ἐγὼ γὰρ παρὰ Φιλίππῳ μὲν ὢν ἠξίωσα, πρὸς δ᾽
ὑμᾶς ἥκων ἀπήγγελλον, ὅτι τὰς Θήβας Βοιωτίαν
δίκαιον ἡγοίμην εἶναι, καὶ μὴ τὴν Βοιωτίαν Θήβας. τοῦτο οὐκ ἀπαγγεῖλαι, ἀλλ᾽ ὑποσχέσθαι

120 μέ φησιν. ἔλεγον δὲ πρὸς ὑμᾶς, ὅτι Κλεοχάρης
ὁ Χαλκιδεὺς θαυμάζειν ὑμῶν καὶ Φιλίππου φαίη
τὴν ἐξαίφνης ὁμόνοιαν, ἄλλως τε καὶ[3] προστετα-
γμένον ἡμῖν, πράττειν ἀγαθὸν ὅ τι ἂν δυνώμεθα·[4]
τοὺς γὰρ μικροπολίτας, ὥσπερ αὐτός, φοβεῖν τὰ

---

[1] ἐλλιπών Hamaker : ἐλλείπων MSS.
[2] κενὰς Markland : τινὰς MSS.
[3] ἄλλως τε καὶ Blass : ὡς καὶ τὸ or καὶ τὸ MSS.
[4] δυνώμεθα Weidner : δυνάμεθα ἐν τῷ ψηφίσματι MSS.

help, for you could not possibly do them so great a service as the Athenians once did, and they have no memory for that; while you will be wronging those whom you leave in the lurch, and will find them, not your friends in the future, but all the more your enemies.''

But not to waste time in reciting to you now precisely what was spoken there, I will content myself with this brief summary of it all. Fortune and Philip were masters of the issue, but I, of loyalty to you and of the words spoken. My words were words of justice, and they were spoken in your interest; the issue was not according to our prayer, but according to Philip's acts. Who, therefore, is it that deserves your approval? Is it the man who showed no desire to do any good thing whatever, or the man who left undone nothing that was in his power? But I now pass over many things for lack of time.

He said that I deceived you by saying that within a few days Thebes would be humbled; and that I told about the Euboeans, how I had frightened them, and that I led you on into empty hopes. But, fellow citizens, let me tell you what it is that he is doing. While I was with Philip I demanded—and when I returned to you I reported that I thought it right— that Thebes should be Boeotian, and not Boeotia, Theban. He asserts, not that I reported this, but that I promised it. And I told you that Cleochares of Chalcis said that he was surprised at the sudden agreement between you and Philip, especially when we had been instructed "to negotiate concerning any good thing that should be within our power.'' For he said the people of the small states, like him-

τῶν μειζόνων ἀπόρρητα. ταῦτα οὐ διηγήσασθαί
με φησίν, ἀλλ' ἐπηγγέλθαι τὴν Εὔβοιαν παραδώσειν. ἐγὼ δὲ ὑπειλήφειν δεῖν τὴν πόλιν τὴν
ὑπὲρ τῶν ὅλων μέλλουσαν βουλεύεσθαι μηδενὸς
λόγου Ἑλληνικοῦ ἀνήκοον εἶναι.

121 Διέβαλλε δέ, κἀκεῖνον διαιρούμενος τὸν λόγον,
ὡς ἀπαγγέλλειν τἀληθῆ βουλόμενος, ὑπ' ἐμοῦ καὶ
Φιλοκράτους κωλυθείη. ἐγὼ δ' ὑμᾶς ἡδέως ἂν
ἐροίμην, εἴ τις πώποτε Ἀθηναίων πρεσβευτὴς
ἐκπεμφθείς, ἐφ' οἷς πεπρέσβευκε κεκώλυται πρὸς
τὸν δῆμον ἀπαγγέλλειν, καὶ ταῦτα παθὼν καὶ
ἀτιμασθεὶς ὑπὸ τῶν συμπρέσβεων, τούτους
ἔγραψ'[1] ἂν ἐπαινέσαι καὶ καλέσαι ἐπὶ δεῖπνον.
Δημοσθένης τοίνυν ἥκων ἀπὸ τῆς ὑστέρας πρεσβείας, ἐν ᾗ φησι τὰ τῶν Ἑλλήνων πράγματα ἀνα-
τραπῆναι, οὐκ ἐν τῷ ψηφίσματι μόνον ἡμᾶς
122 ἐπῄνει, ἀλλ' ἀπαγγείλαντος πρὸς τὸν δῆμον
ἐμοῦ τοὺς περὶ τῶν Ἀμφικτυόνων λόγους καὶ
Βοιωτῶν, οὐχ ὥσπερ νῦν συντέμνοντος οὐδ' ἐπει-
γομένου, ἀλλ' ὡς ἐδυνάμην κατὰ ῥῆμα ἀκριβέ-
στατα, καὶ τοῦ δήμου σφόδρα ἀποδεχομένου,
παρακληθεὶς ὑπ' ἐμοῦ μετὰ τῶν ἄλλων συμπρέσβεων καὶ ἐρωτώμενος,[2] εἰ τἀληθῆ καὶ ταὐτὰ
ἀπαγγέλλω πρὸς Ἀθηναίους ἅπερ πρὸς Φίλιππον
εἶπον, πάντων μαρτυρούντων καὶ ἐπαινούντων με
τῶν συμπρέσβεων, ἐπαναστὰς ἐπὶ πᾶσιν οὐκ ἔφη
με, ὥσπερ ἐκεῖ,[3] οὕτως ἐν τῷ παρόντι λέγειν, ἀλλ'
ἐκεῖ διπλασίῳ[4] ἄμεινον. καὶ τούτων ὑμεῖς οἱ τὴν
123 ψῆφον μέλλοντες φέρειν ἐστέ μοι μάρτυρες. καί-

---

[1] ἔγραψ' ἂν the editor : ἔγραψεν MSS.
[2] ἐρωτώμενος Cobet : διερωτώμενος MSS.
[3] After ἐκεῖ the MSS. have εἶπον : Blass brackets εἶπον.
[4] διπλασίῳ Bekker : διπλασίως MSS.

self, were afraid of the secret diplomacy of the greater. Demosthenes asserts, not that I related this fact, but that I promised to hand over Euboea! But I had supposed that when the city was about to deliberate on matters of supreme importance, no statement from any Hellenic source ought to be ignored.

But he falsely declared that when he wished to report the truth, he was hindered by me, together with Philocrates—for he divided the responsibility in that case also. Now I should like to ask you this: Has any ambassador sent out from Athens ever been prevented from presenting to the people an official report of his conduct? And if one had suffered such treatment and had been repudiated by his colleagues, would he ever have made a motion that they be given a vote of thanks and invited to dinner? But Demosthenes on his return from the second embassy, in which he says that the cause of Hellas was ruined, moved the vote of thanks in his decree; and not only that, but when I had reported to the people what I had said about the Amphictyons and Boeotians, not briefly and rapidly as now, but as nearly word for word as possible, and when the people heartily applauded, I called upon him together with the other ambassadors, and asked them whether my report was true, and identical with what I had said to Philip; and when all my colleagues had testified and praised me, after them all Demosthenes arose and said: No, I had not to-day been speaking as I spoke there, but that I spoke twice as well there. You who are going to give the verdict are my witnesses of this. And yet what better

τοι τίς ἂν αὐτῷ καλλίων καιρὸς ἐγένετο, ἢ τότ'
ἐξελέγχειν εὐθύς, εἴ τι τὴν πόλιν ἐξηπάτων; φὴς
γάρ με ἐν μὲν τῇ προτέρᾳ πρεσβείᾳ λαθεῖν σαυτὸν συνεστηκότα ἐπὶ τὴν πόλιν, ἐν δὲ τῇ ὑστέρᾳ
αἰσθέσθαι, ἐν ᾗ συναγορεύων μοι φαίνῃ. κἀκείνης
μὲν ἅμα κατηγορῶν οὐ φῂς κατηγορεῖν, τῆς δ' ἐπὶ
τοὺς ὅρκους κατηγορεῖς. καίτοι εἰ τὴν εἰρήνην
ψέγεις, σὺ καὶ τὴν συμμαχίαν ἔγραψας· καὶ
Φίλιππος εἴ τι τὴν πόλιν ἐξηπάτα, διὰ τοῦτο
ἐψεύδετο, ὅπως τῆς εἰρήνης ἥπερ [1] συνέφερεν
αὐτῷ τύχοι. οὐκοῦν ἡ μὲν προτέρα πρεσβεία τὸν
καιρὸν τοῦτον εἶχεν, ἡ δ' ὑστέρα ἐπὶ πεπραγμέ-
νοις ἐγίγνετο.

124   Τίνες οὖν ἦσαν αἱ ἀπάται, ταῦτα γὰρ τοῦ γόη-
τος ἀνθρώπου, ἐξ ὧν εἴρηκε λογίσασθε. εἰσπλεῖν
μέ φησιν ἐν μονοξύλῳ πλοίῳ κατὰ τὸν Λοιδίαν [2]
ποταμὸν τῆς νυκτὸς ὡς Φίλιππον, καὶ τὴν ἐπιστολὴν τὴν δεῦρο ἐλθοῦσαν Φιλίππῳ γράψαι. ὁ
μὲν γὰρ Λεωσθένης, ὁ φεύγων ἐνθένδε διὰ τοὺς
συκοφάντας, οὐ δυνατὸς ἦν ἐπιδεξίως ἐπιστολὴν
γράψαι, ὃν οὐκ ὀκνοῦσί τινες ἀποφαίνεσθαι μετὰ
Καλλίστρατον τὸν Ἀφιδναῖον τῶν ἄλλων μά-
125   λιστα εἰπεῖν δύνασθαι· οὐδ' αὐτὸς ὁ Φίλιππος,
πρὸς ὃν ἀντειπεῖν Δημοσθένης ὑπὲρ ὑμῶν οὐκ
ἠδυνήθη· οὐδ' ὁ Βυζάντιος Πύθων, ἄνθρωπος ἐπὶ
τῷ [3] γράφειν μέγα φρονῶν· ἀλλ' ὡς ἔοικε τὸ πρᾶγμα ἐμοῦ προσεδεῖτο. καὶ λέγεις μὲν ὅτι Φιλίππῳ
μεθ' ἡμέραν πολλάκις μόνος μόνῳ διελεγόμην,
αἰτιᾷ δὲ εἰσπλεῖν με νύκτωρ κατὰ τὸν ποταμόν·

---

[1] ἥπερ H. Wolf : εἴπερ (or εἴ τι) MSS.
[2] Λοιδίαν Reiske (Harpocration) : Λυδίαν MSS.
[3] ἐπὶ τῷ H. Wolf : περὶ τὸ MSS.

opportunity could he have had to convict me than to do it then and there, if I was in any wise deceiving the city? You say, Demosthenes, that while I was in a conspiracy against the city in the first embassy, you were not aware of it, but that on the second you found it out—the embassy in which we find you testifying to my services! And while accusing me for my conduct on the first embassy, you at the same time deny that you accuse me, and direct your accusations against the embassy that was sent to take the oaths. And yet if it is the peace you find fault with, it was you who moved to add the alliance to it. And if Philip did at any point deceive the city, his deception had to do with the peace, for he was manœuvring for the precise form of peace that would serve his own advantage. But it was the earlier embassy that offered the opportunity to accomplish this; the second took place after the thing was already done.

How he has deceived you—deceit is ever the mark of the charlatan—see from his own words. He says that I went down the Loedias river to Philip in a canoe by night, and that I wrote for Philip the letter which came to you. For Leosthenes, who had been exiled from Athens through the work of blackmailers, was not competent to write a clever letter—a man whom some do not hesitate to rank next to Callistratus of Aphidna as an able orator! and Philip himself was not competent, against whom Demosthenes was not able to hold his own when he tried to speak in your behalf! nor Python of Byzantium, a man who takes pride in his ability as a writer! but, as it seems, the thing required my help too! And you say that time and again I had private interviews with Philip in the daytime, but you accuse me of paddling down the

126 οὕτω νυκτερινῆς ἐπιστολῆς τὸ πρᾶγμα ἐδεῖτο. ὅτι
δ' οὐδὲν ἀληθὲς λέγεις, ἥκουσι μὲν μαρτυρήσοντες
μεθ' ὧν συνεσίτουν, 'Αγλαοκρέων ὁ Τενέδιος καὶ
'Ιατροκλῆς ὁ Πασιφῶντος, μεθ' ὧν ἑξῆς ἅπαντα
τὸν χρόνον τὰς νύκτας ἀνεπαυόμην, οἳ συνίσασίν
μοι μηδεμίαν πώποτε ἀπ' αὐτῶν νύκτα ἀπογενο-
μένῳ, μηδὲ μέρος νυκτός· ἄγομεν δὲ καὶ τοὺς οἰκέτας καὶ παραδίδομεν εἰς βάσανον. καὶ τὸν μὲν
λόγον, εἰ συγχωρεῖ[1] ὁ κατήγορος, καταλύω· παρέ-
σται δὲ ὁ δημόσιος καὶ βασανιεῖ ἐναντίον ὑμῶν,
ἂν κελεύητε. ἐνδέχεται δὲ τὸ λοιπὸν μέρος τῆς
ἡμέρας ταῦτα πρᾶξαι· πρὸς ἕνδεκα γὰρ ἀμφορέας
127 ἐν διαμεμετρημένῃ τῇ ἡμέρᾳ κρίνομαι. κἂν φῶσιν
ἀπόκοιτόν με τουτωνὶ πώποτε τῶν συσσίτων[2]
γεγονέναι, μὴ φείσησθέ μου, ὦ ἄνδρες 'Αθηναῖοι,
ἀλλ' ἀναστάντες ἀποκτείνατε. ἐὰν δ' ἐξελεγχθῇς
ψευδόμενος, Δημόσθενες, τοιαύτην δίκην δός· ὁμο-
λόγησον ἀνδρόγυνος εἶναι καὶ μὴ ἐλεύθερος ἐναντίον τούτων. κάλει μοι τοὺς οἰκέτας δεῦρο ἐπὶ
τὸ βῆμα, καὶ τὴν τῶν συμπρέσβεων ἀναγίγνωσκε
μαρτυρίαν.

ΜΑΡΤΥΡΙΑ.   ΠΡΟΚΛΗΣΙΣ

128 'Επειδὴ τοίνυν οὐ δέχεται τὴν πρόκλησιν, οὐδ'
ἄν φησιν ἐν βασάνοις ἀνδραπόδων γενέσθαι, λαβέ
μοι τὴν ἐπιστολὴν ταύτην, ἣν ὁ Φίλιππος ἔπεμψε.
δῆλον γὰρ ὅτι μεγάλα τὴν πόλιν παραλογίζεται,
δι' ἣν ἠγρυπνοῦμεν γράφοντες.

---

[1] συγχωρεῖ Scholiast : συγχωρήσει MSS.
[2] συσσίτων Baiter : συσσίτων βασανιζόμενοι MSS.

---

[1] Slave testimony was accepted in the Athenian courts
only when it was given, or offered, under torture.

river in the night—the need of a midnight letter
was so urgent! But there is no truth in your story,
as those who messed with me have come to testify—
Aglaocreon of Tenedos and Iatrocles the son of Pasi-
phon, with whom I slept every night during the
whole time, from beginning to end; they know that
I was never away from them a single night, nor any
part of a night. We present also our slaves and
offer them for torture;[1] and I offer to interrupt my
speech if the prosecution agree. The officer shall
come in and administer the torture in your presence,
gentlemen of the jury, if you so order. There is still
time enough to do it, for in the apportionment of
the day eleven jars of water have been assigned to
my defence.[2] If the slaves testify that I ever slept
away from these messmates of mine, spare me not,
fellow citizens, but rise up and kill me. But if you,
Demosthenes, shall be convicted of lying, let this be
your penalty—to confess in this presence that you
are a hermaphrodite, and no free man. Please summon the slaves to the platform here, and read the
testimony of my colleagues.

TESTIMONY. CHALLENGE

Since now he does not accept the challenge, saying
that he would not rest his case on the testimony of
tortured slaves, please take this letter, which Philip
sent. For a letter that kept us busy writing all
night long must obviously be full of clever deception
of the city.

[2] A definite time, measured by the water-clock, or
clepsydra, was assigned to each side. How long a time
would be occupied by the running of one amphora of water
through the clepsydra, we have no means of knowing.

ΕΠΙΣΤΟΛΗ

129 Ἀκούετε, ὦ ἄνδρες, ὅτι "τοὺς ὅρκους ἀποδέ-
δωκα," φησί, "τοῖς ὑμετέροις πρέσβεσι," καὶ τῶν
συμμάχων τῶν ἑαυτοῦ τοὺς παραγενομένους κατ᾽
ὄνομα γέγραφε, καὶ αὐτοὺς καὶ τὰς πόλεις αὐτῶν,
τοὺς δ᾽ ὑστερήσαντας τῶν συμμάχων ἀποστελεῖν
φησι πρὸς ὑμᾶς. ταῦτ᾽ οὖν οὐκ ἂν οἴεσθε δύνασθαι γράψαι Φίλιππον μεθ᾽ ἡμέραν ἄνευ ἐμοῦ;

130 Ἀλλ᾽ ἔμοιγε νὴ τοὺς θεοὺς οὗτος[1] δοκεῖ τοῦτο
μόνον λογίζεσθαι, ὅπως μεταξὺ λέγων εὐδοκιμή-
σει· εἰ δὲ μικρὸν ἐπισχὼν δόξει πονηρότατος τῶν
Ἑλλήνων εἶναι, οὐδὲ μικρὸν φροντίζειν.[2] τί γὰρ
ἄν τις τοιούτῳ πιστεύσειεν ἀνθρώπῳ, ὃς ἐγκεχεί-
ρηκε λέγειν ὡς Φίλιππος, οὐ τοῖς αὐτοῦ στρατη-
γήμασιν, ἀλλὰ ταῖς ἐμαῖς δημηγορίαις, εἴσω
Πυλῶν παρῆλθε; καὶ λογισμόν τινα ἡμερῶν
συνηριθμεῖτο πρὸς ὑμᾶς, ἐν αἷς ἐγὼ μὲν ἀπήγγελλον τὴν πρεσβείαν, οἱ δὲ Φαλαίκου τοῦ Φωκέων τυράννου δρομοκήρυκες τἀνθένδε ἐκεῖσε
διήγγελλον, πιστεύσαντες δὲ οἱ Φωκεῖς ἐμοὶ εἴσω
Πυλῶν αὐτὸν παρεδέξαντο καὶ τὰς πόλεις τὰς
αὑτῶν παρέδοσαν.

131 Ταῦτα μὲν οὖν ὁ κατήγορος μεμηχάνηται, τὰ δ᾽
ἐν Φωκεῦσι διεφθάρη πράγματα πρῶτον μὲν διὰ
τὴν τύχην, ἣ πάντων ἐστὶ κυρία, ἔπειτα διὰ τὸ
μῆκος τοῦ χρόνου καὶ τὸν δεκέτη πόλεμον. τὸ
γὰρ αὐτὸ ηὔξησέ τε τῶν ἐν Φωκεῦσι τυράννων
τὰ πράγματα καὶ καθεῖλε· κατέστησαν μὲν γὰρ
εἰς τὴν ἀρχὴν τολμήσαντες τῶν ἱερῶν χρημάτων

---

[1] οὗτος Blass : οὑτοσὶ MSS.
φροντίζειν Dobree : φροντίζει MSS.

LETTER

You hear, gentlemen, what he wrote: "I gave my oath to your ambassadors"; and he has written the names of those of his allies who were present, both the names of the representatives themselves and of their states; and he says he will send to you those of his allies who were not there in time. Does it seem to you that it would have been beyond Philip's ability to write that in the daytime, and without my help?

But, by heaven, the only thing, apparently, that this man Demosthenes cares about, is to win applause while he is on the platform; but whether or not a little later he will be considered the greatest scoundrel in Hellas, for that he appears to care not a whit. For how could one put any faith in a man who has undertaken to maintain that it was not Philip's generalship, but my speeches, that enabled Philip to get this side Thermopylae! And he gave you a sort of reckoning and enumeration of the days during which, while I was making my report on the embassy, the couriers of Phalaecus, the Phocian tyrant, were reporting to him how matters stood in Athens, while the Phocians, putting their trust in me, admitted Philip this side Thermopylae, and surrendered their own cities to him.

Now all this is the invention of my accuser. It was fortune, first of all, that ruined the Phocians, and she is mistress of all things; and secondly, it was the long continuance of the ten years' war. For the same thing that built up the power of the tyrants in Phocis, destroyed it also: they established themselves in power by daring to lay hands on the

ἄψασθαι, καὶ διὰ ξένων τὰς πολιτείας μετέστησαν, κατελύθησαν δ' ἀπορίᾳ χρημάτων, ἐπειδὴ
132 κατεμισθοφόρησαν τὰ ὑπάρχοντα. τρίτον δ' αὐτοὺς καθεῖλεν ἡ τοῖς ἀπορουμένοις στρατοπέδοις
συνήθως παρακολουθοῦσα στάσις, τέταρτον δ' ἡ
Φαλαίκου περὶ τῶν μελλόντων ἔσεσθαι πραγμάτων ἄγνοια. ἡ μὲν γὰρ Θετταλῶν καὶ Φιλίππου
στρατεία πρόδηλος ἦν, οὐ πολλῷ δὲ χρόνῳ πρότερον πρὶν τὴν πρὸς ὑμᾶς εἰρήνην γενέσθαι,
πρέσβεις πρὸς ὑμᾶς ἦλθον ἐκ Φωκέων, βοηθεῖν
αὐτοῖς κελεύοντες, καὶ ἐπαγγελλόμενοι παραδώσειν Ἀλπωνὸν καὶ Θρόνιον καὶ Νίκαιαν, τὰ τῶν
133 παρόδων τῶν εἰς Πύλας χωρία κύρια. ψηφισα-
μένων δ' ὑμῶν παραδοῦναι Προξένῳ τῷ στρατηγῷ
τοὺς Φωκέας ταῦτα τὰ χωρία, καὶ πεντήκοντα
πληροῦν τριήρεις, καὶ τοὺς μέχρι τετταράκοντα
ἐτῶν[1] ἐξιέναι, ἀντὶ τοῦ παραδοῦναι τὰ χωρία
Προξένῳ, ἔδησαν οἱ τύραννοι τοὺς πρέσβεις τοὺς
ἐπηγγελμένους[2] ὑμῖν παραδώσειν τὰ φυλακτήρια,
καὶ τοῖς σπονδοφόροις τοῖς τὰς μυστηριώτιδας
σπονδὰς ἐπαγγέλλουσι μόνοι τῶν Ἑλλήνων Φωκεῖς οὐκ ἐσπείσαντο. καὶ πάλιν Ἀρχιδάμου
τοῦ Λάκωνος παραλαμβάνειν ὄντος ἑτοίμου τὰ
χωρία καὶ φυλάττειν, οὐκ ἐπείσθησαν, ἀλλ'
ἀπεκρίναντο αὐτῷ τὰ τῆς Σπάρτης δεινὰ δεδιέναι
134 καὶ μὴ τὰ παρ' αὑτοῖς.[3] κἀνταῦθα οὔπω διελέ-
λυσθε Φιλίππῳ, ἀλλ' ἐν τῇ αὐτῇ ἡμέρᾳ περί τε
τῆς εἰρήνης ἐβουλεύεσθε, καὶ τῆς ἐπιστολῆς
ἠκούετε τῆς Προξένου, ὅτι Φωκεῖς οὐ παραδεδώ-

---

[1] ἐτῶν Blass : ἔτη γεγονότας MSS.
[2] ἐπηγγελμένους Hamaker : ἐπαγγελλομένους or ἐπαγγειλα-
μένους MSS.   [3] αὑτοῖς Markland : αὐτοῖς MSS.

treasures of the shrine, and by the use of mercenaries they put down the free governments; and it
was lack of funds that caused their overthrow, when
they had spent all their resources on these mercenaries. The third cause of their ruin was mutiny, such
as usually attends armies which are poorly supplied
with funds. The fourth cause was Phalaecus' in-
ability to foresee the future. For it was plain that
the Thessalians and Philip were going to take the
field; and shortly before the peace with you was concluded, ambassadors came to you from the Phocians,
urging you to help them, and offering to hand over to
you Alponus, Thronion, and Nicaea, the posts which
controlled the roads to Thermopylae. But when
you had passed a decree that the Phocians should
hand over these posts to your general Proxenus, and
that you should man fifty triremes, and that all
citizens up to the age of forty years should take
part in the expedition, then instead of surrendering
the posts to Proxenus, the tyrants arrested those
ambassadors of their own who had offered to hand
over the garrison posts to you; and when your
heralds carried the proclamation of the sacred truce
of the Mysteries,[1] the Phocians alone in all Hellas
refused to recognize the truce. Again, when Archi-
damus the Laconian was ready to take over those
posts and guard them, the Phocians refused his offer,
answering him that it was the danger from Sparta
that they feared, not the danger at home. That was
before you had come to terms with Philip; but on
the very day when you were discussing the question
of the peace, the letter of Proxenus was read to

---

[1] A provision for the safe conduct of all Greeks who
wished to attend the celebration of the lesser Eleusinian
Mysteries, which took place in Attica in the spring.

κασιν αὐτῷ τὰ χωρία, καὶ οἱ τὰ μυστήρια ἐπαγ-
γέλλοντες¹ μόνους τῶν ἄλλων Ἑλλήνων ἀπέ-
φαινον² Φωκέας οὐ δεδεγμένους τὰς σπονδάς,
ἀλλὰ καὶ τοὺς δεῦρο ἐληλυθότας πρέσβεις δεδε-
κότας. ὅτι δὲ ἀληθῆ λέγω, κάλει μοι τοὺς σπον-
δοφόρους, καὶ τοὺς παρὰ Προξένου τοῦ στρατηγοῦ
πρεσβεύσαντας εἰς Φωκέας, Καλλικράτην καὶ
Μεταγένην, καὶ τῆς ἐπιστολῆς ἀκούσατε τῆς
Προξένου.

MARTYΡIAI.   EΠIΣTOΛH

135   Ἀκούετε, ὦ ἄνδρες Ἀθηναῖοι, τῶν χρόνων παρ-
αναγιγνωσκομένων ἐκ τῶν δημοσίων γραμμάτων,
καὶ τῶν μαρτύρων ὑμῖν προσδιαμαρτυρούντων,³
ὅτι πρὶν ἐμὲ χειροτονηθῆναι πρεσβευτήν, Φάλαικος ὁ τῶν Φωκέων τύραννος ἡμῖν μὲν καὶ Λακεδαιμονίοις ἠπίστει, Φιλίππῳ δ' ἐπίστευεν.

136   Ἀλλ' οὗτος μόνος τὸ συμβησόμενον ἠγνόει;
ὑμεῖς δὲ αὐτοὶ δημοσίᾳ πῶς διέκεισθε; οὐ πάντες
προσεδοκᾶτε Φίλιππον ταπεινώσειν Θηβαίους,
ὁρῶντά τ'⁴ αὐτῶν τὴν θρασύτητα, καὶ τῷ⁵ μὴ
βούλεσθαι δύναμιν ἀνθρώπων ἀπίστων ἐπαυξῆσαι;⁶ Λακεδαιμόνιοι δὲ οὐ μεθ' ἡμῶν τἀναντία
Θηβαίοις ἐπρέσβευον, καὶ τελευτῶντες προσέ-
κρουον φανερῶς ἐν Μακεδονίᾳ καὶ διηπείλουντο;⁷
αὐτοὶ δὲ οὐκ ἠπόρουν καὶ ἐφοβοῦντο οἱ τῶν Θηβαίων πρέσβεις; Θετταλοὶ δὲ οὐ κατεγέλων τῶν

---

¹ ἐπαγγέλλοντες Baiter and Sauppe : ἀπαγγέλλοντες MSS.
² ἀπέφαινον Blass : ἀπέφηναν MSS.
³ προσδιαμαρτυρούντων Hamaker : προσδιαμαρτυρησάντων
MSS.   ⁴ τ' added by Dobree.   ⁵ τῷ H. Wolf : τὸ MSS.
⁶ ἐπαυξῆσαι Sauppe : ἐπασκῆσαι MSS.
⁷ διηπειλοῦντο Cobet : διηπείλουν MSS. After διηπείλουν the
MSS. have τοῖς τῶν Θηβαίων πρέσβεσιν, which Blass brackets.

you, in which he said that the Phocians had failed
to hand over the posts to him; and on the same day
the heralds of the Mysteries reported to you that
the Phocians alone in all Hellas had refused the
sacred truce, and had, furthermore, arrested the
ambassadors who had been here. To prove that I
am speaking the truth, please call the heralds of the
truce, and the envoys Callicrates and Metagenes,
whom Proxenus our general sent to the Phocians,
and let the letter of Proxenus be read.

TESTIMONY. LETTER

The dates, fellow citizens, taken from the public
archives, have been read and compared in your
hearing, and you have heard the witnesses, who
further testify that before I was elected ambassador,
Phalaecus the Phocian tyrant distrusted us and
the Lacedaemonians as well, but put his trust in
Philip.

But was Phalaecus the only one who failed to
discern what the outcome was going to be? How
stood public opinion here? Were you not yourselves
all expecting that Philip was going to humble the
Thebans, when he saw their audacity, and because
he was unwilling to increase the power of men
whom he could not trust? And did not the Lacedaemonians take part with us in the negotiations
against the Thebans, and did they not finally come
into open collision with them in Macedonia and
threaten them? Were not the Theban ambassadors
themselves perplexed and alarmed? And did not
the Thessalians laugh at all the rest and say that the

ἄλλων, ὑπὲρ αὐτῶν φάσκοντες τὴν στρατείαν
137 εἶναι; τῶν δ᾽ ἑταίρων τινὲς τῶν Φιλίππου οὐ
διαρρήδην πρός τινας ἡμῶν ἔλεγον ὅτι τὰς ἐν
Βοιωτοῖς πόλεις κατοικιεῖ Φίλιππος; Θηβαῖοι δ᾽
οὐκ ἐξεληλύθεσαν πανδημεί, ἀπιστοῦντες τοῖς
πράγμασιν; ὑμῖν δὲ ταῦθ᾽ ὁρῶν οὐκ ἔπεμψεν
ἐπιστολὴν ὁ Φίλιππος, ἐξιέναι πάσῃ τῇ δυνάμει
βοηθήσοντας τοῖς δικαίοις; οἱ δὲ νῦν πολεμικοὶ καὶ
τὴν εἰρήνην ἀνανδρίαν καλοῦντες, οὐ διεκώλυσαν
ὑμᾶς ἐξελθεῖν εἰρήνης καὶ συμμαχίας γεγενημένης,[1]
δεδιέναι φάσκοντες μὴ τοὺς στρατιώτας ὑμῶν
138 ὁμήρους λάβῃ Φίλιππος; πότερον οὖν ἐγὼ τοὺς
προγόνους ἐκώλυσα τὸν δῆμον μιμεῖσθαι, ἢ σὺ
καὶ οἱ μετὰ σοῦ συνεστηκότες ἐπὶ τὰ κοινά; καὶ
πότερον ἦν ἀσφαλεστέρα καὶ καλλίων Ἀθηναίοις
ἡ ἔξοδος, ἡνίκα ἤκμαζον μὲν[2] τῇ μανίᾳ Φωκεῖς,
ἐπολέμουν δὲ Φιλίππῳ, εἶχον δὲ Ἀλπωνὸν καὶ
Νίκαιαν, οὔπω παραδόντος Φαλαίκου Μακεδόσι,
τὰς σπονδὰς δὲ οἷς ἐμέλλομεν βοηθεῖν τὰς μυστηριώτιδας οὐκ ἐδέχοντο, Θηβαίους δ᾽ ὄπισθεν
κατελείπομεν,[3] ἢ μεταπεμπομένου μὲν Φιλίππου,
ὅρκων δ᾽ ἡμῖν καὶ συμμαχίας γεγενημένης, Θετταλῶν δὲ καὶ τῶν ἄλλων Ἀμφικτυόνων στρατευόν-
139 των; οὐ πολλῷ καλλίων οὗτος ἦν ὁ καιρὸς
ἐκείνου, ἐν ᾧ διὰ τὴν σὴν ἀνανδρίαν καὶ ἅμα
φθόνον ἐσκευαγώγησαν ἐκ τῶν ἀγρῶν Ἀθηναῖοι,

---

[1] γεγενημένης Weidner : ὑμῖν (or ἡμῖν) γεγενημένης or
γεγενημένης ὑμῖν MSS. [2] μὲν Dobree : ἐν MSS.
[3] κατελείπομεν Bekker : κατελίπομεν MSS.

expedition was for their own benefit? Did not some of Philip's companions say explicitly to some of us that Philip was going to re-establish the cities in Boeotia? Had not the Thebans already, suspicious of the situation, called out all their reserves and taken the field? And did not Philip, when he saw this, send a letter to you calling upon you to come out with all your forces in defence of the cause of justice? As for those who are now for war, and who call peace cowardice, did they not prevent your going out, in spite of the fact that peace and alliance had been made with Philip? Did they not say that they were afraid he would take your soldiers as hostages? Was it I, therefore, who prevented the people from imitating our forefathers, or was it you, Demosthenes, and those who were in conspiracy with you against the common good? And was it a safer and more honourable course for the Athenians to take the field at a time when the Phocians were at the height of their madness and at war with Philip, with Alponus and Nicaea in their possession—for Phalaecus had not yet surrendered these posts to the Macedonians —and when those whom we were proposing to aid would not accept the truce for the Mysteries, and when we were leaving the Thebans in our rear: or after Philip had invited us, when we had already received his oaths and had an alliance with him, and when the Thessalians and the other Amphictyons were taking part in the expedition? Was not the latter opportunity far better than the former? But at this later time, thanks to the combination of cowardice and envy in you, Demosthenes, the Athenians brought in their property from the fields, when

πρεσβεύοντος ἐμοῦ τὴν τρίτην ἤδη πρεσβείαν
τὴν[1] ἐπὶ τὸ κοινὸν τῶν Ἀμφικτυόνων, ἐφ᾽ ἣν
τολμᾷς με λέγειν ὡς οὐ χειροτονηθεὶς ᾠχόμην,
ἐχθρὸς δ᾽ ὢν οὐδέπω[2] καὶ τήμερον ἠθέληκάς με
εἰσαγγεῖλαι παραπρεσβεύσασθαι; οὐ γὰρ δὴ
φθονεῖς γέ μοι τῶν εἰς τὸ σῶμα τιμημάτων.

140   Τοιγάρτοι Θηβαίων μὲν παρακαθημένων καὶ
δεομένων, τῆς δ᾽ ἡμετέρας πόλεως διὰ σὲ τεθο-
ρυβημένης καὶ τῶν Ἀθηναίων ὁπλιτῶν οὐ παρόντων, Θετταλῶν δὲ Θηβαίοις προσθεμένων διὰ τὴν
ὑμετέραν ἀβουλίαν καὶ τὴν πρὸς Φωκέας ἔχθραν,
ἣ προὐπῆρχε Θετταλοῖς ἐκ παλαιῶν χρόνων, ὅτε
αὐτῶν τοὺς ὁμήρους λαβόντες Φωκεῖς κατηλόησαν,
Φαλαίκου δὲ πρὶν ἐμὲ ἐλθεῖν καὶ Στέφανον καὶ
Δερκύλον καὶ τοὺς ἄλλους[3] πρέσβεις ἀπεληλυ-
141   θότος ὑποσπόνδου, Ὀρχομενίων δὲ περιφόβων
ὄντων καὶ σπονδὰς τοῖς σώμασιν αἰτησάντων,
ὥστε ἀπελθεῖν ἐκ τῆς Βοιωτίας, παρεστηκότων
μὲν τῶν Θηβαίων πρέσβεων, ὑπολειπομένης δ᾽
ἔχθρας φανερᾶς Φιλίππῳ πρὸς Θηβαίους καὶ
Θετταλούς, τότε ἀπώλοντο αἱ πράξεις οὐ δι᾽ ἐμέ,
ἀλλὰ διὰ τὴν σὴν προδοσίαν καὶ τὴν πρὸς Θηβαίους προξενίαν. μεγάλα δ᾽ οἶμαι τούτων ἔργῳ[4]

---

[1] τὴν added by Franke.   [2] οὐδέπω Blass : οὔπω MSS.
[3] ἄλλους Blass : Ἀμφικτύονας MSS.
[4] ἔργῳ Blass : ἐγὼ MSS.

---

[1] See on § 94. This was, strictly speaking, the fourth
embassy; but as it was appointed to do what had been
entrusted to the third, and was made up of the same men,
Aeschines speaks of it as the third.

[2] The ambassadors to Philip, while not formally accredited
to negotiate with the Amphictyonic Council, which Philip

I was already absent on the third embassy,[1] and appearing before the assembly of the Amphictyons[2]—that embassy on which you dare to say that I set out without having been elected, although, enemy as you are to me, you have never to this day been willing to prosecute me as having wrongly served on it ; and we may safely assume that this is not because you begrudge me bodily pains and penalties.

When, therefore, the Thebans were besieging him with their importunities, and our city was in confusion, thanks to you, and the Athenian hoplites were not with him;[3] when the influence of the Thessalians had been added to that of the Thebans, thanks to your shortsightedness and because of the hostility to the Phocians which the Thessalians had inherited from that ancient time when Phocians seized and flogged the Thessalian hostages ; and when, before my coming and that of Stephanus, Dercylus, and the rest of the ambassadors, Phalaecus had already made terms and departed ; when the people of Orchomenus were in exceeding fear, and had begged for peace, on condition that their lives should be spared and they be allowed to go forth from Boeotia ;[4] when the Theban ambassadors were standing by, and when it was plain that Philip was threatened with the hostility of the Thebans and Thessalians : then it was that the cause was lost—not from any fault of mine, but thanks to your treachery, Demosthenes, and your hired service to Thebes. Of this I think I can furnish important

had called together to act on the punishment of the Phocians, were present at Delphi during their meeting, and Aeschines addressed the Council. See § 142.

[3] See § 137.

[4] Orchomenus was one of the towns referred to in § 104.

142 σημεῖα ἐπιδείξειν. εἰ γάρ τι τούτων ἀληθὲς ἦν ὧν
σὺ λέγεις, κατηγόρουν ἄν μου Βοιωτῶν καὶ Φωκέων
οἱ φεύγοντες, ὧν τοὺς μὲν ἐξεβεβλήκειν, τοὺς δ᾽
ἐκώλυσα κατελθεῖν· νῦν δ᾽ οὐχὶ τὰ συμβάντα
λογιζόμενοι, ἀλλὰ τὴν εὔνοιαν τὴν ἐμὴν ἀπο-
δεχόμενοι, συλλεγέντες οἱ φεύγοντες Βοιωτῶν
ᾕρηνταί μοι συνηγόρους, ἥκουσι δ᾽ ἀπὸ τῶν ἐν
Φωκεῦσι πόλεων πρέσβεις, οὓς ἐγὼ τὴν τρίτην
πρεσβείαν τὴν [1] ἐπὶ τοὺς Ἀμφικτύονας πρεσβεύων
ἔσωσα, Οἰταίων ἐγχειρούντων λέγειν ὡς δεῖ τοὺς
ἡβῶντας ὠθεῖν κατὰ τοῦ κρημνοῦ, καὶ παρήγαγον
εἰς τοὺς Ἀμφικτύονας, ὥστε ἀπολογίας τυχεῖν.
ὁ μὲν γὰρ Φάλαικος [2] ὑπόσπονδος ἀφεῖτο, οἱ δὲ
ἀναίτιοι ἀποθνῄσκειν ἔμελλον, συναγορεύοντος
143 δ᾽ ἐμοῦ διεσώθησαν. ὅτι δ᾽ ἀληθῆ λέγω, κάλει
μοι Μνάσωνα τὸν Φωκέα καὶ τοὺς συμπρέσβεις,
καὶ τοὺς ἀπὸ τῆς τῶν Βοιωτῶν φυγῆς ᾑρημένους.
ἀνάβηθι δεῦρο, Λίπαρε καὶ Πυθίων, καὶ τὴν αὐτὴν
ἀπόδοτέ μοι χάριν εἰς τὴν τοῦ σώματος σωτηρίαν,
ἥνπερ ἐγὼ ὑμῖν.

ΣΥΝΗΓΟΡΙΑ ΒΟΙΩΤΩΝ ΚΑΙ ΦΩΚΕΩΝ

Πῶς οὖν οὐκ ἂν δεινὰ πάθοιμι, εἰ κατηγοροῦντος
μὲν Δημοσθένους τοῦ Θηβαίων προξένου καὶ
πονηροτάτου τῶν Ἑλλήνων, συναγορευόντων δέ
μοι Φωκέων καὶ Βοιωτῶν ἁλοίην;

144 Ἐτόλμησε δ᾽ εἰπεῖν ὡς ἐγὼ τοῖς ἐμαυτοῦ λόγοις

[1] τὴν added by Franke.
[2] Φάλαικος Dobree : Φάλαικος τύραννος (or ὁ τύραννος) MSS.

confirmation from what has actually happened. For if there were any truth in these assertions of yours, the Boeotian fugitives, for whose expulsion I was responsible, and the Phocian exiles, whose restoration I prevented, would be accusing me now. But as a matter of fact they ignore the misfortunes that have come upon them, and satisfied with my loyalty to them, the Boeotian exiles have held a meeting and chosen men to speak in my behalf; and from the towns of Phocis have come ambassadors whose lives I saved when I was representing you before the Amphictyons on the third embassy; for when the representatives from Oetaea went so far as to say that they ought to cast the grown men over the cliffs, I brought the Phocians into the assembly of the Amphictyons and secured a hearing for them. For Phalaecus had made terms for himself and gone, and those who were guiltless were on the point of being put to death; but I pleaded for them, and their lives were spared. To prove that I speak the truth, please call Mnason the Phocian and those who have come with him, and call the delegates chosen by the Boeotian exiles. Come up to the platform, Liparus and Pythion, and do me the same service for the saving of my life that I did for you.

PLEA OF THE BOEOTIANS AND PHOCIANS

Would it not, then, be monstrous treatment for me if I should be convicted when my accuser is Demosthenes, the paid servant of Thebes and the wickedest man in Hellas, while my advocates are Phocians and Boeotians?

But he dared to say that I am tripped up by my

περιπίπτω. φησὶ γάρ με εἰπεῖν, ὅτ᾽ ἔκρινον
Τίμαρχον, ὅτι πάντες κατ᾽ αὐτοῦ τὴν τῆς πορνείας
φήμην παρειλήφασι, τὸν δ᾽ Ἡσίοδον ποιητὴν
ἀγαθὸν ὄντα λέγειν,

φήμη δ᾽ οὔτις πάμπαν ἀπόλλυται, ἥντινα λαοὶ
πολλοὶ φημίξωσι·[1] θεός νυ τίς ἐστι καὶ αὐτή.

τὴν δ᾽ αὐτὴν ταύτην θεὸν ἥκειν νῦν κατηγοροῦσαν
ἐμοῦ· πάντας γὰρ λέγειν ὡς χρήματα ἔχω παρὰ
145 Φιλίππου. εὖ δ᾽ ἴστε, ὦ ἄνδρες Ἀθηναῖοι, ὅτι
πλεῖστον διαφέρει φήμη καὶ συκοφαντία. φήμη
μὲν γὰρ οὐ κοινωνεῖ διαβολῇ, διαβολὴ δὲ ἀδελφόν
ἐστι συκοφαντίᾳ.[2] διοριῶ δ᾽ αὐτῶν ἑκάτερον ἐγὼ
σαφῶς. φήμη μέν ἐστιν, ὅταν τὸ πλῆθος τῶν
πολιτῶν αὐτόματον ἐκ μηδεμιᾶς προφάσεως λέγῃ
τινὰ ὡς γεγενημένην πρᾶξιν· συκοφαντία δ᾽ ἐστίν,
ὅταν πρὸς τοὺς πολλοὺς εἷς ἀνὴρ αἰτίαν ἐμβαλών,
ἔν τε ταῖς ἐκκλησίαις ἁπάσαις πρός τε τὴν βουλὴν
διαβάλλῃ τινά. καὶ τῇ μὲν φήμῃ δημοσίᾳ θύομεν
ὡς θεῷ, τῶν δὲ συκοφαντῶν ὡς κακούργων δημοσίᾳ προβολὰς ποιούμεθα. μὴ οὖν σύναγε εἰς
ταὐτὸν τὰ κάλλιστα τοῖς αἰσχίστοις.

146 Ἐπὶ πολλοῖς μὲν οὖν ἔγωγε τῶν κατηγορημένων
ἠγανάκτησα, μάλιστα δὲ ἡνίκα ᾐτιᾶτό με εἶναι
προδότην· ἅμα γὰρ ταῖς αἰτίαις ταύταις φανῆναί
με ἔδει θηριώδη καὶ τὴν ψυχὴν ἄστοργον καὶ
πολλοῖς ἑτέροις πρότερον ἁμαρτήμασι ἔνοχον.
τοῦ μὲν οὖν ἐμοῦ βίου καὶ τῆς καθ᾽ ἡμέραν διαίτης

---

[1] φημίξωσι Baiter and Sauppe. Here and in i. 129 the
MSS. have varying forms of the verb (so in the MSS. of
Hesiod).

[2] συκοφαντίᾳ Herwerden : συκοφαντία or καὶ συκοφαντία
MSS.

own words. For he says[1] that when I was prosecuting Timarchus I said that his lewdness was a
matter of common report, and that Hesiod, a good
poet, says, "But Common Report dies never, the
voice that tongues of many men do utter. She also
is divine."[2] He says that this same god comes now
and accuses me, for everybody says, according to
him, that I have got money from Philip. But be
assured, fellow citizens, there is the greatest difference between common report and slander. For
common report has no affinity with malice, but malice
is slander's own sister. I will define each of them
specifically : it is a case of common report when the
mass of the people, on their own impulse and for
no reason that they can give, say that a certain event
has taken place ; but it is slander when one person,
insinuating an accusation in the minds of the people,
calumniates a man in all the meetings of the assembly and before the senate. To Common Report
we offer public sacrifice, as to a god, but the slanderer
we prosecute, in the name of the people, as a
scoundrel. Do not, therefore, join together the
most honourable and the most shameful things.

At many of his charges I was indeed angry, but
most of all when he accused me of being a traitor.
For to bring such charges as those was to hold me
up to public view as a brute, without natural affection, and chargeable in the past with many other
sins. Now of my daily life and conduct I think you

---

[1] Demosthenes, *On the Embassy*, §§ 243 f.
[2] Aeschines, *Against Timarchus*, § 129.

ὑμᾶς δοκιμαστὰς ἱκανοὺς εἶναι νομίζω· ἃ δ' ἐστὶ
τοῖς μὲν πολλοῖς ἀσύνοπτα, τοῖς δὲ χρηστοῖς τὰς
ψυχὰς μέγιστα, τούτων ὑμῖν τὰ πλεῖστα καὶ
καλῶς ἔχοντα ἐκ τῶν νόμων ὁρᾶν ἀναβιβῶμαι,
ἵν' εἰδῆτε τὰς ἐμὰς παρακαταθήκας, ἃς οἴκοι κατα-
147 λιπὼν εἰς Μακεδονίαν ἐπρέσβευσα. σὺ μὲν γάρ,[1]
Δημόσθενες, ταῦτα ἐπλάσω ἐπ' ἐμέ, ἐγὼ δ' ὡς
ἐπαιδεύθην καὶ δικαίως ἐξηγήσομαι. οὑτοσὶ μέν
ἐστί μοι πατὴρ Ἀτρόμητος, σχεδὸν πρεσβύτατος
τῶν πολιτῶν· ἔτη γὰρ ἤδη βεβίωκεν ἐνενήκοντα
καὶ τέτταρα· συμβέβηκε δὲ αὐτῷ νέῳ μὲν ὄντι,
πρὶν τὴν οὐσίαν ἀπολέσαι διὰ τὸν πόλεμον,
ἀθλεῖν τῷ σώματι, ἐκπεσόντι δὲ ὑπὸ τῶν τριάκοντα στρατεύεσθαι μὲν ἐν τῇ Ἀσίᾳ, ἀριστεύειν
δ' ἐν τοῖς κινδύνοις, εἶναι δ' ἐκ φατρίας τὸ γένος
ᾗ τῶν αὐτῶν βωμῶν Ἐτεοβουτάδαις μετέχει, ὅθεν
ἡ τῆς Ἀθηνᾶς τῆς Πολιάδος ἐστὶν ἱέρεια, συγ-
κατάγειν δὲ τὸν δῆμον, ὥσπερ καὶ ὀλίγῳ πρότερον
εἶπον.

148   Ἐλευθέρους δέ μοι συμβέβηκεν εἶναι καὶ τοὺς
πρὸς μητρὸς ἅπαντας, ᾗ νῦν ἐμοὶ πρὸ τῶν ὀφθαλμῶν προφαίνεται φοβουμένη περὶ τῆς ἐμῆς
σωτηρίας καὶ διηπορημένη. καίτοι, Δημόσθενες,
ἡ μὲν ἐμὴ μήτηρ ἔφυγε μετὰ τοῦ ἀνδρὸς[2] εἰς Κό-
ρινθον καὶ μετέσχε τῶν πολιτικῶν κακῶν· σὺ δὲ
ὁ[3] ἀμφισβητῶν ἀνὴρ εἶναι, οὐ γὰρ ἂν τολμήσαιμι εἰπεῖν ὡς ἀνὴρ εἶ, ἐγράφης λιποταξίου, καὶ

---

[1] μὲν γάρ Franke : μὲν or μὲν οὖν MSS.
[2] τοῦ ἀνδρὸς Cobet : τοῦ αὐτῆς ἀνδρὸς (or τοῦ ἀνδρὸς αὐτῆς)
MSS.   [3] ὁ added by Bekker.

are competent judges. But facts that escape the public eye, yet are of greatest importance in the opinion of men of character, I will bring into court as my witnesses—facts very many in number and to my credit in the eyes of the law—in order that seeing them you may know what pledges I left at home when I set out for Macedonia on the embassy. For you, Demosthenes, fabricated these charges against me, but I will tell my story, as I was taught to do from childhood, truthfully. Yonder is my father, Atrometus; there are few older men among all the citizens, for he is now ninety-four years old. When he was a young man, before the war destroyed his property, he was so fortunate as to be an athlete; banished by the Thirty, he served as a soldier in Asia, and in danger he showed himself a man; by birth he was of the phratry[1] that uses the same altars as the Eteobutadae, from whom the priestess of Athena Polias comes; and he helped in the restoration of the democracy, as I said a little while ago.[2]

It is my good fortune, too, that all the members of my mother's family are free-born citizens; and to-day I see her here before my eyes in anxiety and fear for my safety. And yet, Demosthenes, this mother of mine went out to Corinth an exile, with her husband, and shared the disasters of the democracy; but you, who claim to be a man—that you really are a man I should not venture to say—you were once indicted for desertion, and you saved

---

[1] Each of the four Athenian tribes was divided into three phratries. Under the democracy these groups of families had only religious functions. Each phratry had its own place of worship.   [2] See § 78.

τὸν γραψάμενον Νικόδημον τὸν Ἀφιδναῖον χρήμασι πείσας ἐσώθης, ὃν ὕστερον μετὰ Ἀριστάρχου συναπέκτεινας, καὶ οὐ καθαρὸς ὢν εἰς τὴν
149 ἀγορὰν ἐμβάλλεις. Φιλοχάρης δ' οὑτοσί, ὁ πρεσβύτατος ἀδελφὸς ἡμῶν, οὐκ ἀγεννεῖς διατριβάς,
ὡς σὺ βλασφημεῖς,¹ ἀλλ' ἐν γυμνασίοις διατρί-
βων, καὶ μετὰ Ἰφικράτους συνεστρατευμένος, καὶ
συνεχῶς ἔτος ἤδη τουτὶ τρίτον στρατηγῶν, ἥκει
δεησόμενος ὑμῶν ἐμὲ σῶσαι. Ἀφόβητος δ' οὑτοσί, ὁ νεώτατος ἡμῶν ἀδελφός, πεπρεσβευκὼς
μὲν ὑπὲρ ὑμῶν ἀξίως τῆς πόλεως πρὸς τὸν
Περσῶν βασιλέα, καλῶς δὲ καὶ δικαίως τῶν
ὑμετέρων προσόδων ἐπιμεληθείς, ὅτε αὐτὸν ἐπὶ
τὴν κοινὴν διοίκησιν εἵλεσθε, καὶ πεπαιδοποιη-
μένος κατὰ τοὺς νόμους, ἀλλ' οὐ Κνωσίωνι τὴν
ἑαυτοῦ γυναῖκα παρακατακλίνων, ὥσπερ σύ,
πάρεστι καταφρονῶν τῶν σῶν λοιδοριῶν· τὸ
γὰρ ψευδὲς ὄνειδος οὐ περαιτέρω τῆς ἀκοῆς
150 ἀφικνεῖται. ἐτόλμησας δὲ καὶ περὶ τῶν ἐμῶν
κηδεστῶν εἰπεῖν· οὕτως ἀναιδὴς καὶ πόρρωθεν
ἀχάριστος εἶ, ὃς Φιλόδημον τὸν Φίλωνος πατέρα καὶ Ἐπικράτους οὐκ ἀγαπᾷς οὐδὲ προσ-
κυνεῖς, δι' ὃν εἰς τοὺς δημότας ἐνεγράφης, ὡς

---

¹ βλασφημεῖς Cobet : the MSS. have ἔχων after βλασφημεῖς
(or after ἀγεννεῖς).

---

[1] In the spring of 348 Demosthenes was serving on an
expedition sent out to Euboea. On the approach of the
Great Dionysia he was obliged to return to the city to serve
as choragus, a burden which he had previously volunteered
to take upon himself, at heavy cost. Personal enemies of
his brought, but did not prosecute, a charge of desertion in
the field.

yourself by buying off the man who indicted you,
Nicodemus of Aphidna, whom afterward you helped
Aristarchus to destroy;[1] wherefore you are polluted,
and have no right to be invading the market-place.[2]
Philochares yonder, our eldest brother, a man not of
ignoble pursuits, as you slanderously assert,[3] but a
frequenter of.the gymnasia, a one-time comrade of
Iphicrates in the field, and a general now for the
past three years, has come to beg you to save me.
Our youngest brother, too, Aphobetus yonder, who
as ambassador to the king of Persia has served
you to the credit of the city, who administered your
revenues honestly and well when you called him to
the department of the treasury, who has gotten him
children lawfully—not by putting his wife in Cnosion's
bed, as you, Demosthenes, did yours—he also is here,
despite your slanders; for defamation goes no further
than the ears. But you dared to speak about my wife's
family also—so shameless you are and so inherently
thankless, you that have neither affection nor respect
for Philodemus,[4] the father of Philon and Epicrates,
the man by whose good offices you were enrolled
among the men of your deme, as the elder Paeanians

The murder of Nicodemus by Aristarchus, a young friend
of Demosthenes, was a notorious case, but the attempts of
Demosthenes' enemies to connect him with it were entirely
unsuccessful. See Aeschines, *Against Timarchus*, § 172.

[2] A man under indictment for murder was not allowed
access to the market-place, for contact with a murderer
would pollute innocent men.

[3] For Demosthenes' taunts as to the brothers of Aeschines
and those of his wife, see his speech *On the Embassy*, §§ 237
and 287.　　　[4] See § 152.

ἴσασιν οἱ πρεσβύτεροι Παιανιέων. ἐκπέπληγμαι
δέ, εἰ σὺ λοιδορεῖν Φίλωνα τολμᾷς, καὶ ταῦτα ἐν
τοῖς ἐπιεικεστάτοις Ἀθηναίων, οἳ δεῦρο εἰσελη-
λύθασι δικάσοντες ἕνεκα τοῦ βελτίστου τῆς πόλεως, καὶ μᾶλλον προσέχουσι τοῖς βίοις ἡμῶν ἢ
151 τοῖς λόγοις. πότερα γὰρ ἂν προσδοκᾷς αὐτοὺς
εὔξασθαι μυρίους ὁπλίτας ὁμοίους Φίλωνι γενέσθαι, καὶ τὰ σώματα οὕτω διακειμένους καὶ τὴν
ψυχὴν οὕτω σώφρονας, ἢ τρισμυρίους κιναίδους
οἵους περ σύ; καὶ τὴν Ἐπικράτους εὐαγωγίαν,
τοῦ Φίλωνος ἀδελφοῦ, ἐπανάγεις εἰς ὀνείδη. καὶ
τίς αὐτὸν εἶδε πώποτε ἀσχημονήσαντα, ἢ μεθ᾽
ἡμέραν, ὡς σὺ φῄς, ἐν τῇ πομπῇ τῶν Διονυσίων,
ἢ νύκτωρ; οὐ γὰρ ἂν τοῦτό γ᾽ εἴποις, ὡς ἔλαθεν·
152 οὐ γὰρ ἠγνοεῖτο. ἐμοὶ δέ, ὦ ἄνδρες, ἐκ τῆς Φιλο-
δήμου θυγατρὸς καὶ Φίλωνος ἀδελφῆς καὶ Ἐπικράτους τρεῖς παῖδές εἰσι, μία μὲν θυγάτηρ, δύο
δὲ υἱεῖς· οὓς ἐγὼ δεῦρο ἥκω μετὰ τῶν ἄλλων
κομίζων, ἑνὸς ἐρωτήματος ἕνεκα καὶ τεκμηρίου
πρὸς τοὺς δικαστάς, ὃ νῦν δὴ ἐρήσομαι. ἐρωτῶ
γάρ, ὦ ἄνδρες Ἀθηναῖοι, εἰ δοκῶ ἂν ὑμῖν πρὸς
τῇ πατρίδι καὶ τῇ τῶν φίλων συνηθείᾳ καὶ ἱερῶν
καὶ τάφων πατρῴων μετουσίᾳ τουτουσὶ τοὺς πάντων ἀνθρώπων ἐμοὶ φιλτάτους προδοῦναι Φιλίππῳ, καὶ περὶ πλείονος τὴν ἐκείνου φιλίαν τῆς
τούτων σωτηρίας ποιήσασθαι. ποίᾳ κρατηθεὶς
ἡδονῇ; ἢ τί πώποτε ἄσχημον ἕνεκα χρημάτων

---

[1] Aeschines insinuates that only by some extraordinary
favouritism could Demosthenes, with his strain of Scythian
blood, ever have been recognised as an Athenian of pure

know.[1] But I am amazed if you dare slander Philon, and that, too, in the presence of the most reputable men of Athens, who, having come in here to render their verdict for the best interest of the state, are thinking more about the lives we have lived than what we say. Which think you would they pray heaven to give them, ten thousand hoplites like Philon, so fit in body and so sound of heart, or thrice ten thousand lewd weaklings like you? You try to bring into contempt the good breeding of Epicrates, Philon's brother; but who ever saw him behaving in an indecent manner, either by day in the Dionysiac procession, as you assert, or by night?[2] For you certainly could never say that he was unobserved, for he was no stranger. And I myself, gentlemen, have three children, one daughter and two sons, by the daughter of Philodemus, the sister of Philon and Epicrates; and I have brought them into court with the others for the sake of asking one question and presenting one piece of evidence to the jury. This question I will now put to you; for I ask, fellow citizens, whether you believe that I would have betrayed to Philip, not only my country, my personal friendships, and my rights in the shrines and tombs of my fathers, but also these children, the dearest of mankind to me. Do you believe that I would have held his friendship more precious than the safety of these children? By what lust have you seen me conquered? What unworthy act have I ever

blood, and so enrolled in the citizen-list when he came to manhood.

[2] In the passage referred to (Demosthenes, xix. 287) Demosthenes calls Epicrates by a nick-name, Cyrebion, and charges him with taking part in the Dionysiac revels without a mask.

THE SPEECHES OF AESCHINES

πράξας; οὐ γὰρ ἡ Μακεδονία κακοὺς ἢ χρηστοὺς
ποιεῖ, ἀλλ' ἡ φύσις· οὐδ' ἐσμὲν ἕτεροί τινες
ἥκοντες ἀπὸ τῆς πρεσβείας, ἀλλ' οἵους ὑμεῖς
ἐξεπέμψατε.

153 Συμπέπλεγμαι δ' ἐν τῇ πολιτείᾳ καθ' ὑπερβολὴν ἀνθρώπῳ γόητι καὶ πονηρῷ, ὃς οὐδ' ἂν
ἄκων ἀληθὲς οὐδὲν εἴποι. ἡγεῖται δέ, ὅταν τι
ψεύδηται, τῶν λόγων ὅρκος κατὰ τῶν ἀναισχύν-
των ὀφθαλμῶν, καὶ τὰ μὴ¹ γεγενημένα οὐ
μόνον ὡς ἔστι λέγει, ἀλλὰ καὶ τὴν ἡμέραν ἐν ᾗ
φησι γενέσθαι· καὶ προστίθησίν τινος ὄνομα
πλασάμενος, ὡς ἔτυχε παρών, μιμούμενος τοὺς
τἀληθῆ λέγοντας. ἐν δὲ εὐτυχοῦμεν οἱ μηδὲν
ἀδικοῦντες, ὅτι πρὸς τῇ τερατείᾳ τοῦ τρόπου καὶ
τῇ τῶν ὀνομάτων συνθέσει νοῦν οὐκ ἔχει. σκέψασθε γὰρ ἀφροσύνην ἅμα καὶ ἀπαιδευσίαν
τἀνθρώπου,² ὃς τοιοῦτον ἐπλάσατο³ τὸ περὶ τὴν
Ὀλυνθίαν γυναῖκα ψεῦδος κατ' ἐμοῦ, ἐφ' ᾧ
μεταξὺ λέγων ὑφ' ὑμῶν ἐξερρίφη· τὸν γὰρ πλεῖστον ἀφεστηκότα τῶν τοιούτων πρὸς τοὺς εἰδότας
154 διέβαλλε. σκέψασθε δέ, ὡς πόρρωθεν ἐπὶ τὴν
αἰτίαν ταύτην παρεσκευάζετο. ἔστι γάρ τις ἐπι-
δημῶν εἰς τὴν πόλιν⁴ Ἀριστοφάνης Ὀλύνθιος·
τούτῳ συσταθεὶς ὑπό τινων καὶ πυθόμενος ὡς
εἰπεῖν δύναται, ὑπερεκθεραπεύσας αὐτὸν καὶ προσ-
αγαγόμενος, ἔπειθεν ἐμοῦ τὰ ψευδῆ καταμαρτυ-
ρεῖν πρὸς ὑμᾶς, κἂν παρελθὼν ἐθελήσῃ σχετλιά-

---

¹ μὴ added by Casaubon.
² τἀνθρώπου Markland : ἀνθρώπου MSS.
³ ἐπλάσατο Cobet : ἔπλασε MSS.
⁴ εἰς τὴν πόλιν Markland : ἡμῶν εἰς τὴν πόλιν MSS. (one has
ἐν τῇ πόλει ἡμῶν).

done for money? It is not Macedon that makes men
good or bad, but their own inborn nature; and we
have not come back from the embassy changed men,
but the same men that you yourselves sent out.

But in public affairs I have become exceedingly
entangled with a cheat and rascal, who not even by
accident can speak a truthful word. No: when he
is lying, first comes an oath by his shameless eyes,
and things that never happened he not only presents
as facts, but he even tells the day on which they
occurred; and he invents the name of some one who
happened to be there, and adds that too, imitating
men who speak the truth. But we who are innocent
are fortunate in one thing, that he has no intelligence with which to supplement the trickery of his
character and his knack of putting words together.
For think what a combination of folly and ignorance
there must be in the man who could invent such a
lie against me as that about the Olynthian woman,[1]
such a lie that you shut him up in the midst of his
speech. For he was slandering a man who is the
farthest removed from any such conduct, and that in
the presence of men who know. But see how far
back his preparations for this accusation go. For
there is a certain Olynthian living here, Aristophanes
by name. Demosthenes was introduced to him by
some one, and having found out that he is an able
speaker, paid extravagant court to him and won his
confidence; this accomplished, he tried to persuade
him to give false testimony against me before you,

[1] See § 4, note.

THE SPEECHES OF AESCHINES

σαι καὶ λέγειν ὡς εἰς οἰκείαν αὐτοῦ γυναῖκα[1]
αἰχμάλωτον γεγενημένην πεπαρῴνηκα, πεντακοσίας μὲν ἤδη δραχμὰς ὑπισχνεῖτο αὐτῷ δώσειν,
πεντακοσίας δ' ἑτέρας, ἐπειδὰν καταμαρτυρήσῃ.
155 ὁ δ' αὐτῷ ἀπεκρίνατο, ὡς αὐτὸς διηγεῖτο, ὅτι τῆς
μὲν φυγῆς καὶ τῆς παρούσης ἀπορίας αὐτῷ οὐ
κακῶς, ἀλλ' ὡς οἷόν τε ἄριστα στοχάζοιτο, τοῦ δὲ
τρόπου πλεῖστον εἴη διημαρτηκώς· οὐδὲν γὰρ ἂν
τοιοῦτον πρᾶξαι. ὅτι δὲ ἀληθῆ λέγω, αὐτὸν
Ἀριστοφάνην μαρτυροῦντα παρέξομαι. κάλει
μοι Ἀριστοφάνην Ὀλύνθιον, καὶ τὴν μαρτυρίαν
ἀναγίγνωσκε, καὶ τοὺς ἀκηκοότας αὐτοῦ καὶ πρὸς
ἐμὲ ἀγγείλαντας, Δερκύλον Αὐτοκλέους Ἁγνού-
σιον καὶ Ἀριστείδην Εὐφιλήτου Κηφισιέα.

MΑΡΤΥΡΙΑΙ

156 Τῶν μὲν μαρτύρων διομνυμένων καὶ μαρτυρούντων ἀκούετε· τὰς δ' ἀνοσίους ταύτας τῶν λόγων
τέχνας, ἃς οὗτος πρὸς τοὺς νέους ἐπαγγέλλεται
καὶ κέχρηται νυνὶ κατ' ἐμοῦ, ἆρα μέμνησθε, ὡς
ἐπιδακρύσας καὶ τὴν Ἑλλάδα κατοδυράμενος, καὶ
Σάτυρον τὸν κωμικὸν ὑποκριτὴν προσεπαινέσας,
ὅτι ξένους τινὰς ἑαυτοῦ αἰχμαλώτους σκάπτοντας
ἐν τῷ Φιλίππου ἀμπελουργείῳ καὶ δεδεμένους
157 παρὰ πότον[2] ἐξῃτήσατο παρὰ Φιλίππου, ταῦθ'
ὑποθεὶς ἐπεῖπεν ἐντεινάμενος ταύτην τὴν ὀξεῖαν
καὶ ἀνόσιον φωνήν, ὡς δεινόν, εἰ ὁ μὲν τοὺς Κα-
ρίωνας καὶ Ξανθίας ὑποκρινόμενος οὕτως εὐγενὴς

[1] γυναῖκα Reiske : γυναῖκα καὶ MSS.
[2] παρὰ πότον Blass (Harpocration, Photius, Suidas) : παρὰ
τὸν πότον MSS.

278

promising, namely, to give him five hundred drachmas on the spot, if he would consent to come into court and complain of me, and say that I was guilty of drunken abuse of a woman of his family, who had been taken captive; and he promised to pay him five hundred more when he should have given the testimony. But Aristophanes answered him, as he himself told the story, that so far as his exile and present need were concerned, Demosthenes' aim had not been wide of the mark—indeed no aim could have been closer—but that he had entirely misjudged his character; for he could do nothing of the sort. I will offer Aristophanes himself to testify to the truth of what I say. Please call Aristophanes the Olynthian, and read his testimony, and call those who heard his story and reported it to me—Dercylus, of the deme Hagnus, the son of Autocles, and Aristeides of Cephisia, the son of Euphiletus.

TESTIMONY

You hear the sworn testimony. But these wicked arts of rhetoric, which Demosthenes offers to teach our youth, and has now employed against me, his tears and groans for Hellas, and his praise of Satyrus the comic actor, because over the cups he begged of Philip the release of certain friends of his who were captives in chains, digging in Philip's vineyard—you remember, do you not, how after this preface he lifted up that shrill and abominable voice of his and cried out, " How outrageous that when a man whose business it is to act the parts of a Carion or of a Xanthias [1] showed himself so noble and generous,

---

[1] Satyrus, the comic actor, would often take slave parts, for which Carion and Xanthias were among the traditional names.

καὶ μεγαλόψυχος γένοιτο, ἐγὼ δ' ὁ τῆς μεγίστης
σύμβουλος πόλεως, ὁ τοὺς μυρίους Ἀρκάδων νου-
θετῶν, οὐ κατάσχοιμι τὴν ὕβριν, ἀλλὰ παραθερ-
μανθείς, ὅθ' ἡμᾶς εἰστία Ξενόδοκος τῶν ἑταίρων
τις τῶν Φιλίππου, ἕλκοιμι τῶν τριχῶν καὶ λαβὼν
158 ῥυτῆρα μαστιγοίην αἰχμάλωτον γυναῖκα. οὐκοῦν
εἰ ὑμεῖς αὐτῷ ἐπιστεύσατε, ἢ Ἀριστοφάνης μου
συγκατεψεύσατο, ἐπ' αἰσχραῖς αἰτίαις ἀπωλόμην
ἄν.[1] ἐάσετε οὖν τὸ τοιοῦτον αὐτοῦ[2] προστρό-
παιον, μὴ γὰρ δὴ τῆς πόλεώς γε, ἐν[3] ὑμῖν ἀνα-
στρέφεσθαι; καὶ τὴν μὲν ἐκκλησίαν καθαίρετε, ἐν
δὲ τοῖς ψηφίσμασι διὰ τούτου τὰς εὐχὰς ποιήσεσθε, καὶ στρατιὰν ἢ πεζὴν ἢ ναυτικὴν ἐκπέμ-
ψετε; καὶ μὴν ὅ γε Ἡσίοδος λέγει,

πολλάκι τοι ξύμπασα πόλις κακοῦ ἀνδρὸς
ἀπηύρα,
ὅς κεν ἀλιτραίνῃ καὶ ἀτάσθαλα μηχανάαται.

159 Ἐν δὲ πρὸς τοῖς εἰρημένοις εἰπεῖν ἔτι βούλομαι. εἰ γάρ πού τις ἔστι κακία κατ' ἀνθρώπους,
ἃν μὴ πρωτεύοντα περὶ ταύτην ἀποδείξω Δημοσθένην, θανάτου τιμῶμαι. ἀλλ' οἶμαι πολλὰ
καὶ χαλεπὰ παρακολουθεῖ τῷ κρινομένῳ, καὶ
μετακαλεῖ τὴν ψυχὴν ἀπὸ τῆς ὀργῆς ὁ κίνδυνος
ἐπὶ τοὺς ὑπὲρ τῆς σωτηρίας λόγους, καὶ διαλο-
γισμὸν παρίστησι, μή τι παραλίπῃ τῶν κατηγορημένων. ὥστε ἅμα μὲν ὑμᾶς, ἅμα δὲ ἐμαυτὸν εἰς ἀνάμνησιν τῶν κατηγορημένων ἀγαγεῖν
160 βούλομαι. σκοπεῖτε γὰρ δὴ καθ' ἕκαστον, ὦ

---

[1] ἀπωλόμην ἄν Cobet : ἀδίκως ἀπωλόμην ἄν or ἀπωλόμην ἂν
ἀδίκως MSS.
[2] τὸ τοιοῦτον αὐτοῦ Blass : αὐτὸν τοιοῦτον or αὐτὸν τοιοῦτον
αὐτοῦ MSS.   [3] γε, ἐν Dobree : ὥστε ἐν or ὡς, ἐν MSS.

Aeschines, the counsellor of the greatest city, the adviser of the Ten Thousand of Arcadia, did not restrain his insolence, but in drunken heat, when Xenodocus, one of the picked corps of Philip, was entertaining us, seized a captive woman by the hair, and took a strap and flogged her!" If you had believed him, or Aristophanes had helped him out in his lies against me, I should have been destroyed under shameful accusations. Will you therefore harbour longer in your midst guilt that is so fraught with doom to itself—God grant it be not to the city!—and will you, who purify your assembly,[1] offer the prayers that are contained in your decrees on motion of this man, as you send your troops out by land or sea? You know the words of Hesiod:

"Ofttimes whole peoples suffer from one man
    Whose deeds are sinful and whose purpose base."[2]

One thing more I wish to add to what I have said: if there is anywhere among mankind any form of wickedness in which I fail to show that Demosthenes is preëminent, let my death be your verdict. But I think many difficulties attend a defendant: his danger calls his mind away from his anger, to the search for such arguments as shall secure his safety, and it causes him earnest thought lest he overlook some one of the accusations which have been brought against him. I therefore invite you, and at the same time myself, to recall the accusations. Consider, then, one by one, fellow citizens, the possible

[1] The Athenian assembly was regularly opened with a sacrifice of purification and prayer. *cp.* Aeschines, i. 23.
[2] *Works and Days*, 240 f.

ἄνδρες Ἀθηναῖοι, ποῖον ἐγὼ ψήφισμα γράψας
κρίνομαι, ἢ ποῖον νόμον λύσας, ἢ ποῖον γενέσθαι
κωλύσας, ἢ τίνας ὑπὲρ τῆς πόλεως συνθήκας
ποιησάμενος, ἢ τί τῶν δεδογμένων περὶ τῆς εἰρήνης ἀπαλείψας, ἢ τί τῶν μὴ δοξάντων ὑμῖν προσ-
161 γράψας. οὐκ ἤρεσκέ τισι τῶν ῥητόρων ἡ εἰρήνη·
ἔπειτα οὐ τότε ἀντιλέγειν αὐτοὺς ἐχρῆν, ἀλλὰ μὴ
νῦν ἐμὲ κρίνειν; ἐπλούτουν τινὲς ἐκ τοῦ πολέμου,
ἀπὸ τῶν ὑμετέρων εἰσφορῶν καὶ τῶν δημοσίων
προσόδων, νῦν δὲ πέπαυνται· εἰρήνη γὰρ ἀργίαν
οὐ τρέφει· ἔπειτα οἱ μὲν οὐκ ἀδικούμενοι, ἀλλ'
ἀδικοῦντες τὴν πόλιν, τιμωρήσονται τὸν προστάντα
τῆς εἰρήνης, οἱ δ' ὠφελούμενοι τοὺς χρησίμους
162 εἰς τὰ κοινὰ γενομένους [1] ἐγκαταλείψετε; συνῇδον γὰρ τοὺς παιᾶνας Φιλίππῳ, κατεσκαμμένων
τῶν ἐν Φωκεῦσι πόλεων, ὥς φησιν ὁ κατήγορος.
καὶ ποίῳ δύναιτ' ἄν τις τεκμηρίῳ τοῦτο σαφῶς
ἐπιδεῖξαι; ἐκλήθην μὲν γὰρ ἐπὶ τὰ ξένια μετὰ
τῶν συμπρέσβεων, ἦσαν δ' οἱ κλητοὶ καὶ συνδει-
πνοῦντες σὺν ταῖς ἀπὸ τῶν Ἑλλήνων πρεσβείαις
οὐκ ἐλάττους ἢ διακόσιοι. ἐν δὲ τούτοις ὡς ἔοικεν
ἐγὼ διαφανὴς ἦν οὐχ ὑποσιγῶν, ἀλλὰ συνᾴδων,
ὥς φησι Δημοσθένης, οὔτ' αὐτὸς παρών, οὔτε τῶν
ἐκεῖ παρόντων οὐδένα παρασχόμενος μάρτυρα.
163 καὶ τῷ [2] δῆλος ἦν, εἰ μή γε ὥσπερ ἐν τοῖς χοροῖς
προῆδον; οὐκοῦν εἰ μὲν ἐσίγων, ψευδῆ μου κατη-

---

[1] γενομένους Markland : γινομένους MSS.
[2] τῷ Cobet : τῷ γε MSS.

grounds for my prosecution: What decree have I proposed, what law have I repealed, what law have I kept from being passed, what covenant have I made in the name of the city, what vote as to the peace have I annulled, what have I added to the terms of peace that you did not vote? The peace failed to please some of our public men. Then ought they not to have opposed it at the time, instead of putting me on trial now? Certain men who were getting rich out of the war from your war-taxes and the revenues of the state, have now been stopped; for peace does not feed laziness. Shall those, then, who are not wronged, but are themselves wronging the city, punish the man who was sponsor for the peace,[1] and will you, who are benefited by it, leave in the lurch men who have proved themselves useful to the commonwealth? Yes, my accuser says, because I joined Philip in singing paeans when the cities of Phocis had been razed.[2] What evidence could be sufficient to prove that charge? I was, indeed, invited to receive the ordinary courtesies, as were my colleagues in the embassy. Those who were invited and were present at the banquet, including the ambassadors from other Hellenic states, were not less than two hundred. And so it seems that among all these I was conspicuous, not by my silence, but by joining in the singing—for Demosthenes says so, who was not there himself, and presents no witness from among those who were. Who would have noticed me, unless I was a sort of precentor and led the chorus? Therefore if I was silent, your charge

---

[1] Philocrates, the prime mover in the peace, had already gone into banishment, afraid to stand trial.

[2] Demosthenes, xix. 128.

γορεῖς· εἰ δὲ ὀρθῆς ἡμῖν τῆς πατρίδος οὔσης, καὶ
τῶν πολιτῶν κοινῇ μηδὲν ἀτυχούντων, συνῇδον
μετὰ τῶν ἄλλων πρέσβεων τὸν παιᾶνα, ἡνίκα ὁ
θεὸς μὲν ἐτιμᾶτο, Ἀθηναῖοι δὲ μηδὲν ἡδόξουν,
εὐσέβουν, ἀλλ᾿ οὐκ ἠδίκουν, καὶ δικαίως ἂν σω-
ζοίμην. ἔπειτα ἐγὼ μὲν διὰ ταῦτα ἀνηλεής τις [1]
εἰμὶ ἄνθρωπος, σὺ δὲ εὐσεβὴς ὁ τῶν ὁμοσπόνδων
καὶ συσσίτων κατήγορος;

164 Ὠνείδισας δέ μοι καὶ πολιτείας ἐμπληξίαν,
εἰ πεπρέσβευκα πρὸς Φίλιππον, πρότερον παρακαλῶν [2] ἐπ᾿ ἐκεῖνον τοὺς Ἕλληνας. καίτοι ταύτην,
εἰ βούλει, τὴν κατηγορίαν καὶ τῶν ἄλλων Ἀθηναίων δημοσίᾳ κατηγορήσεις. ἐπολεμεῖτε Λακεδαιμονίοις, καὶ μετὰ τὴν ἐν Λεύκτροις συμφορὰν
τοῖς αὐτοῖς ἐβοηθεῖτε· κατηγάγετε εἰς τὴν πατρίδα
φεύγοντας Θηβαίους, καὶ πάλιν τούτοις ἐμαχέ-
σασθε ἐν Μαντινείᾳ· ἐπολεμήσατε Ἐρετριεῦσι καὶ
Θεμίσωνι, καὶ πάλιν αὐτοὺς ἐσώσατε. καὶ μυρίοις
ἄλλοις ἤδη τῶν Ἑλλήνων οὕτω κέχρησθε· τοῖς
γὰρ καιροῖς συμπεριφέρεσθαι ἀνάγκη πρὸς τὸ
165 κράτιστον καὶ τὸν ἄνδρα καὶ τὴν πόλιν. τὸν δὲ
ἀγαθὸν σύμβουλον τί χρὴ ποιεῖν; οὐ τῇ πόλει
πρὸς τὸ παρὸν τὰ βέλτιστα συμβουλεύειν; τὸν
δὲ πονηρὸν κατήγορον τί; [3] οὐ τοὺς καιροὺς
ἀποκρυπτόμενον τῆς πράξεως κατηγορεῖν; τὸν δὲ
ἐκ φύσεως προδότην πῶς χρὴ θεωρεῖν; ἆρά γε
οὐχ ὡς σὺ τοῖς ἐντυγχάνουσι καὶ πιστεύσασι
κέχρησαι, λόγους εἰς δικαστήρια γράφοντα μισθοῦ,

---

[1] ἀνηλεής τις Dobree : ἀνηλέητος or ἀνηλέητός τις MSS.
[2] πεπρέσβευκα . . . παρακαλῶν Hamaker : πεπρεσβευκὼς . . .
παρεκάλουν MSS.
[3] τί Hamaker : τί χρὴ λέγειν MSS.

is false; but if, with our fatherland safe and no harm done to my fellow citizens, I joined the other ambassadors in singing the paean when the god was being magnified and the Athenians in no wise dishonoured, I was doing a pious act and no wrong, and I should justly be acquitted. Am I, forsooth, because of this to be considered as a man who knows no pity, but you a saint, you, the accuser of men who have shared your bread and cup?

But you have also reproached me with inconsistency in my political action, in that I have served as ambassador to Philip, when I had previously been summoning the Greeks to oppose him.[1] And yet, if you choose, you may bring this charge against the rest of the Athenian people as a body. You, gentlemen, once fought the Lacedaemonians, and then after their misfortune at Leuctra you aided the same people. You once restored Theban exiles to their country, and again you fought against them at Mantineia. You fought against Themison and the Eretrians, and again you saved them. And you have before now treated countless others of the Hellenes in the same way. For in order to attain the highest good the individual, and the state as well, is obliged to change front with changing circumstances. But what is the good counsellor to do? Is he not to give the state the counsel that is best in view of each present situation? And what shall the rascally accuser say? Is he not to conceal the occasion and condemn the act? And the born traitor—how shall we recognize him? Will he not imitate you, Demosthenes, in his treatment of those whom chance throws in his way and who have trusted him? Will he not take pay for writing speeches for them to deliver in the courts, and then

[1] See Demosthenes, xix. 9 ff.

τούτους ἐκφέρειν τοῖς ἀντιδίκοις; ἔγραψας λόγον
Φορμίωνι τῷ τραπεζίτῃ χρήματα λαβών· τοῦτον
ἐξήνεγκας Ἀπολλοδώρῳ τῷ περὶ τοῦ σώματος
166 κρίνοντι Φορμίωνα. εἰσῆλθες εἰς εὐδαιμονοῦσαν
οἰκίαν τὴν Ἀριστάρχου τοῦ Μόσχου· ταύτην
ἀπώλεσας. προὔλαβες τρία τάλαντα παρ᾽ Ἀριστάρχου φεύγοντος· τοῦτον τὰ τῆς φυγῆς ἐφόδια
ἀπεστέρησας, οὐκ αἰσχυνθεὶς τὴν φήμην ἣν
προσεποιήσω, ζηλωτὴς εἶναι τῆς ἡλικίας τοῦ
μειρακίου. οὐ γὰρ δὴ τῇ γε ἀληθείᾳ· οὐ γὰρ
προσδέχεται δίκαιος ἔρως πονηρίαν. ταῦτ᾽ ἐστὶν
ὁ προδότης καὶ τὰ τούτοις ὅμοια.

167 Ἐμνήσθη δέ που περὶ στρατείας, καὶ τὸν καλὸν
στρατιώτην ἐμὲ ὠνόμασεν. ἐγὼ δὲ οὐχ ἕνεκα τῆς
τούτου βλασφημίας, ἀλλὰ τοῦ παρόντος κινδύνου
προνοούμενος, καὶ περὶ τούτων ἀνεπίφθονον λέγειν
εἶναί μοι νομίζω· ποῦ γὰρ ἢ πότε αὐτῶν ἢ πρὸς
τίνας, παραλιπὼν τήνδε τὴν ἡμέραν, μνησθήσομαι; ἐκ παίδων μὲν γὰρ ἀπαλλαγεὶς περίπολος
τῆς χώρας ταύτης ἐγενόμην δύ᾽ ἔτη, καὶ τούτων
ὑμῖν τοὺς συνεφήβους καὶ τοὺς ἄρχοντας[1] ἡμῶν
168 μάρτυρας παρέξομαι· πρώτην δ᾽ ἐξελθὼν στρατείαν τὴν ἐν τοῖς μέρεσι καλουμένην, καὶ συμ-
παραπέμπων μετὰ τῶν ἡλικιωτῶν καὶ τῶν

---

[1] ἄρχοντας Bekker : συνάρχοντας MSS.

---

[1] cp. iii. 173.
[2] The occasion was the murder of Nicodemus by Aristarchus. See § 148, note.
[3] The young Athenian citizen, coming of legal age at
eighteen, was required to serve two years in the cadet corps,
stationed the first year at the Peiraeus, and on frontier posts
the second.

reveal the contents of these speeches to their
opponents?[1] You wrote a speech for the banker
Phormion and were paid for it: this speech you
communicated to Apollodorus, who was bringing a
capital charge against Phormion. You entered a
happy home, that of Aristarchus the son of Moschus;
you ruined it. You received three talents from Aristarchus in trust as he was on the point of going into
exile;[2] you cheated him out of the money that was
to have aided him in his flight, and were not ashamed
of the reputation to which you laid claim, that of
being a wooer of the young man's bodily charms—an
absurd story, of course, for genuine love has no place
for rascality. That conduct, and conduct like that,
defines the traitor.

But he spoke, I believe, about service in the field,
and named me "the fine soldier." But I think, in
view of my present peril rather than of his slander, I
may without offence speak of these matters also. For
where, or when, or to whom, shall I speak of them,
if I let this day go by? As soon as I passed out of
boyhood I became one of the frontier guards of this
land for two years.[3] As witnesses to this statement,
I will call my fellow cadets and our officers. My first
experience in the field was in what is called "division
service,"[4] when I was with the other men of my age

---

[4] When citizens were called out for military service, if it
was not necessary to call the whole body of reserves, the men
of some specified age were called, e.g. all between the ages of
twenty and thirty, or twenty and forty (cp. § 133). Since
the names of the men of a given age were kept in the register
under the name of the Archon Eponymos in whose year
they came of age, such a levy was called στρατεία ἐν τοῖς
ἐπωνύμοις. If only a part of such an age-group was called
out, it was called a division levy (στρατεία ἐν τοῖς μέρεσιν).

Ἀλκιβιάδου ξένων τὴν εἰς Φλειοῦντα παραπομ-
πήν, κινδύνου συμβάντος ἡμῖν περὶ τὴν Νεμεάδα
καλουμένην χαράδραν, οὕτως ἠγωνισάμην, ὥστε
ὑπὸ τῶν ἡγεμόνων ἐπαινεῖσθαι· καὶ τὰς ἄλλας
τὰς ἐκ διαδοχῆς ἐξόδους τὰς ἐν τοῖς ἐπωνύμοις καὶ
169 τοῖς μέρεσιν ἐξῆλθον, καὶ τὴν ἐν Μαντινείᾳ
μάχην συνεμαχεσάμην οὐκ αἰσχρῶς οὐδ᾽ ἀναξίως
τῆς πόλεως, καὶ τὰς εἰς Εὔβοιαν στρατείας
ἐστρατευσάμην, καὶ τὴν ἐν Ταμύναις μάχην ἐν
τοῖς ἐπιλέκτοις οὕτως ἐκινδύνευσα, ὥστε κἀκεῖ
στεφανωθῆναι καὶ δεῦρο ἥκων πάλιν ὑπὸ τοῦ
δήμου, τήν τε νίκην τῆς πόλεως ἀπαγγείλας, καὶ
Τεμενίδου τοῦ τῆς Πανδιονίδος ταξιάρχου καὶ
συμπρεσβεύσαντος ἀπὸ στρατοπέδου μοι δευρὶ [1]
περὶ τὸν γενόμενον κίνδυνον οἷος ἦν ἀπαγγείλαντος.
170 Ὅτι δὲ ἀληθῆ λέγω, λαβέ μοι τοῦτο τὸ ψήφισμα, καὶ κάλει τὸν Τεμενίδην καὶ τοὺς συν-
εστρατευμένους μοι τὰς ὑπὲρ τῆς πόλεως στρατείας
καὶ Φωκίωνα τὸν στρατηγόν, μήπω συνήγορον,
ἂν [2] τούτοις συνδοκῇ, ἀλλ᾽ ὑπεύθυνον τῷ συκοφάντῃ μάρτυρα, ἐὰν ψεύδηται.

ΨΗΦΙΣΜΑ. ΜΑΡΤΥΡΙΑΙ

171 Ἀπαγγείλας τοίνυν πρῶτος τὴν τῆς πόλεως
νίκην ὑμῖν καὶ τὴν τῶν παίδων τῶν ὑμετέρων

---

[1] δευρὶ Sauppe : δευρὶ καὶ MSS.
[2] ἂν Blass : ἂν μὴ MSS.

---

[1] In 363 B.C. See Xenophon, *Hellenica*, VII. ii. 17 ff.
[2] In 357 and 349/8.

and the mercenary troops of Alcibiades, who convoyed the provision train to Phleius. We fell into danger near the place known as the Nemean ravine, and I so fought as to win the praise of my officers.[1] I also served on the other expeditions in succession, whether we were called out by age-groups or by divisions. I fought in the battle of Mantineia, not without honour to myself or credit to the city. I took part in the expeditions to Euboea,[2] and at the battle of Tamynae[3] as a member of the picked corps I so bore myself in danger that I received a wreath of honour then and there, and another at the hands of the people on my arrival home; for I brought the news of the Athenian victory, and Temenides, taxiarch[4] of the tribe Pandionis, who was despatched with me from camp, told here how I had borne myself in the face of the danger that befell us.

But to prove that I am speaking the truth, please take this decree, and call Temenides and those who were my comrades in the expedition in the service of the city, and call Phocion, the general, not yet to plead for me,[5] if it please the jury, but as a witness who cannot speak falsely without exposing himself to the libellous attacks of my prosecutor.

DECREE. TESTIMONY

Since, then, it was I who brought you the first news of the victory of the city and the success of your

---

[3] The critical engagement of the second of the expeditions to Euboea.

[4] Each of the ten taxiarchs commanded the hoplites of a single tribe.

[5] Phocion will later be called to support the prayer of the defence for acquittal.

THE SPEECHES OF AESCHINES

κατόρθωσιν, πρώτην ταύτην ὑμᾶς ἀπαιτῶ χάριν,
τὴν τοῦ σώματος σωτηρίαν, οὐ μισόδημος ὤν,
ὥς φησιν ὁ κατήγορος, ἀλλὰ μισοπόνηρος, οὐδὲ
τοὺς Δημοσθένους ὑμᾶς οὐκ[1] ἐῶν προγόνους
μιμεῖσθαι, οὐ γὰρ εἰσίν, ἀλλὰ τῶν καλῶν καὶ
τῇ πόλει σωτηρίων βουλευμάτων ζηλωτὰς εἶναι
παρακαλῶν. νῦν δ' αὐτὰ πόρρωθεν ἀρξάμενος
μικρῷ δίειμι σαφέστερον.

172   Πρότερον ἡ πόλις ἡμῶν εὐδόξησε μετὰ τὴν ἐν
Σαλαμῖνι ναυμαχίαν,[2] καὶ τῶν τειχῶν ὑπὸ τῶν
βαρβάρων πεπτωκότων, εἰρήνης δ' ὑπαρχούσης
πρὸς Λακεδαιμονίους, διέμεινεν ἡμῖν τὸ τῆς δημοκρατίας πολίτευμα. συνταραχθέντες δὲ ὑπό
τινων, καὶ καταστάντες πρὸς Λακεδαιμονίους εἰς
πόλεμον, πολλὰ καὶ παθόντες κακὰ καὶ ποιήσαντες, Μιλτιάδου τοῦ Κίμωνος προκηρυκευσα-
μένου πρὸς Λακεδαιμονίους, ὄντος προξένου,
σπονδὰς[3] πεντηκονταετεῖς ἐποιησάμεθα, ἐχρη-
173   σάμεθα δὲ ἔτη τριακαίδεκα. ἐν δὲ τούτῳ τῷ
χρόνῳ ἐτειχίσαμεν μὲν[4] τὸν Πειραιᾶ καὶ τὸ
βόρειον τεῖχος ᾠκοδομήσαμεν, ἑκατὸν δὲ τριήρεις
πρὸς ταῖς ὑπαρχούσαις ἐναυπηγησάμεθα, τρια-

---

[1] ὑμᾶς οὐκ Reiske : the MSS. have οὔ. οὐκ or οὖ οὐκ or ὑμᾶς.
[2] ναυμαχίαν Cobet : ναυμαχίαν πρὸς τὸν Πέρσην MSS. cp. § 74.
[3] σπονδὰς Hamaker : σπονδὰς τοῦ πολέμου MSS.
[4] μὲν added by Bekker.

---

[1] See Demosthenes, xix. 16.
[2] Aeschines has taken the historical review which he gives
in §§ 172–176 from the speech of Andocides, *On the Peace
with the Lacedaemonians*, §§ 3 ff., condensing, and changing
the phraseology at will, and changing the application of the
facts which he cites. This sketch as given by Andocides is

sons, I ask of you this as my first reward, the saving
of my life. For I am not a hater of the democracy,
as my accuser asserts, but a hater of wickedness;
and I am not one who forbids your "imitating the
forefathers" of Demosthenes[1]—for he has none—
but one who calls upon you to emulate those policies
which are noble and salutary to the state. Those
policies I will now review somewhat more specifically,
beginning with early times.

In former days, after the battle of Salamis, our
city stood in high repute, and although our walls had
been thrown down by the barbarians, yet so long as
we had peace with the Lacedaemonians we preserved
our democratic form of government.[2] But when
certain men had stirred up trouble and finally caused
us to become involved in war with the Lacedaemonians, then, after we had suffered and inflicted
many losses, Miltiades, the son of Cimon, who was
proxenus[3] of the Lacedaemonians, negotiated with
them, and we made a truce for fifty years, and kept it
thirteen years.[4] During this period we fortified the
Peiraeus and built the north wall; we added one
hundred new triremes to our fleet; we also equipped

characterised by Eduard Meyer (*Forschungen zur Alten
Geschichte*, ii. 132 ff.) as a caricature of the actual course of
events, valuable only as a convincing proof of the untrust-
worthiness of oral tradition, and of the rapidity and certainty
with which confusion and error as to historical facts develop,
even in the mind of a contemporary who has had a prominent
part in the events.

[3] The proxenus was a citizen who was employed by a
foreign state to represent its interests in his own state.

[4] This was in fact a five years' truce negotiated by Cimon,
the son of Miltiades, in 450 B.C. The truce lasted, not
thirteen years, but less than five. The fortification of the
Peiraeus belongs more than a quarter of a century earlier.

κοσίους δ᾽ ἱππέας προσκατεσκευασάμεθα, καὶ
τριακοσίους Σκύθας ἐπριάμεθα, καὶ τὴν δημοκρατίαν βεβαίως εἴχομεν.

Παρεμπεσόντων δ᾽ εἰς τὴν πολιτείαν ἡμῶν οὐκ
ἐλευθέρων ἀνθρώπων καὶ τοῖς τρόποις οὐ μεισα-
τρίων, πάλιν πρὸς Λακεδαιμονίους δι᾽ [1] Αἰγινήτας
174 εἰς πόλεμον κατέστημεν, κἀνταῦθα οὐκ ὀλίγα
βλαβέντες, τῆς μὲν εἰρήνης ἐπεθυμήσαμεν, Ἀνδο-
κίδην δ᾽ ἐκπέμψαντες πρὸς τοὺς Λακεδαιμονίους
καὶ τοὺς συμπρέσβεις, εἰρήνην ἔτη τριάκοντα
ἠγάγομεν, ἣ τὸν δῆμον ὑψηλὸν ἦρεν· χίλια μὲν
γὰρ τάλαντα ἀνηνέγκαμεν νομίσματος εἰς τὴν
ἀκρόπολιν, ἑκατὸν δὲ τριήρεις ἑτέρας ἐναυπηγησάμεθα καὶ νεωσοίκους ᾠκοδομήσαμεν, χιλίους
δὲ καὶ διακοσίους ἱππέας κατεστήσαμεν καὶ
τοξότας ἑτέρους τοσούτους, καὶ τὸ μακρὸν τεῖχος
τὸ νότιον ἐτειχίσθη, καὶ τὸν δῆμον οὐδεὶς ἐνεχείρησε καταλῦσαι.

175 Πάλιν δὲ εἰς πόλεμον διὰ Μεγαρέας πεισθέντες
καταστῆναι, καὶ τὴν χώραν τμηθῆναι [2] προέμενοι
καὶ πολλῶν ἀγαθῶν στερηθέντες, εἰρήνης ἐδεήθη-
μεν, καὶ ἐποιησάμεθα διὰ Νικίου τοῦ Νικηράτου.
καὶ πάλιν ἐν τῷ χρόνῳ τούτῳ ἑπτακισχίλια
τάλαντα ἀνηνέγκαμεν εἰς τὴν ἀκρόπολιν διὰ τὴν
εἰρήνην ταύτην, τριήρεις δ᾽ ἐκτησάμεθα πλωίμους

[1] Λακεδαιμονίους δι᾽ added by Weidner.
[2] τμηθῆναι Blass, from Andoc. § 8 : νεμηθῆναι MSS.

---

[1] A corps of bowmen, Scythian slaves, owned by the state and used as city police.
[2] The war with Aegina ended before the above-mentioned truce began.

three hundred cavalrymen and bought three hundred Scythians;[1] and we held the democratic constitution unshaken.

But meanwhile men who were neither free by birth nor of fit character had intruded into our body politic, and finally we became involved in war again with the Lacedaemonians, this time because of the Aeginetans.[2] In this war we received no small injury, and became desirous of peace. We therefore sent Andocides and other ambassadors to the Lacedaemonians and negotiated a peace, which we kept for thirty years.[3] This peace brought the democracy to the height of its prosperity. For we deposited on the Acropolis a thousand talents of coined money; we built one hundred additional triremes, and constructed dockyards; we formed a corps of twelve hundred cavalry and a new force of as many bowmen, and the southern long wall was built; and no man undertook to overthrow the democratic constitution.

But again we were persuaded to go to war, now because of the Megarians.[4] Having given up our land to be ravaged, and suffering great privations, we longed for peace, and finally concluded it through Nicias, the son of Niceratus.[5] In the period that followed we again deposited treasure in the Acropolis, seven thousand talents, thanks to this peace, and we acquired triremes, seaworthy and fully equipped, no

[3] The thirty years' peace was in fact made in 446/5, and was kept only fifteen years.
[4] The beginning of the Peloponnesian war, 431 B.C.
[5] The "Peace of Nicias" was negotiated in 421, but its terms were only partially fulfilled from the beginning, and very soon the war was in full operation again. Andocides places in this period, which he falsely assumes to be one of peace, events that belong to the Periclean period.

καὶ ἐντελεῖς οὐκ ἐλάττους ἢ τριακοσίας, φόρος δ'
ἡμῖν κατ' ἐνιαυτὸν προσῄει πλέον ἢ χίλια καὶ
διακόσια τάλαντα, καὶ Χερρόνησον καὶ Νάξον
καὶ Εὔβοιαν εἴχομεν, πλείστας δ' ἀποικίας ἐν τοῖς
176 χρόνοις τούτοις ἀπεστείλαμεν. καὶ τοσαῦτ' ἔχοντες τἀγαθά, πάλιν πόλεμον¹ πρὸς Λακεδαιμονίους
ἐξηνέγκαμεν πεισθέντες ὑπ' Ἀργείων, καὶ τελευτῶντες ἐκ τῆς τῶν ῥητόρων ἀψιμαχίας εἰς φρουρὰν τῆς πόλεως καὶ τοὺς τετρακοσίους καὶ τοὺς
ἀσεβεῖς τριάκοντα ἐνεπέσομεν, οὐκ εἰρήνην ποιη-
σάμενοι, ἀλλ' ἐκ προσταγμάτων ἠναγκασμένοι.
πάλιν δὲ σωφρόνως πολιτευθέντες, καὶ τοῦ δήμου
κατελθόντος ἀπὸ Φυλῆς, Ἀρχίνου καὶ Θρασυ-
βούλου προστάντων τοῦ δήμου, καὶ τὸ μὴ μνη-
σικακεῖν πρὸς ἀλλήλους ἔνορκον ἡμῖν κατα-
στησάντων, ὅθεν σοφωτάτην ἅπαντες τὴν πόλιν
177 ἡγήσαντο εἶναι, κἀνταῦθα ἀναφύντος τοῦ δήμου
καὶ πάλιν ἐξ ἀρχῆς ἰσχύσαντος, ἄνθρωποι
παρέγγραπτοι γεγενημένοι πολῖται, καὶ τὸ νοσοῦν
τῆς πόλεως ἀεὶ προσαγόμενοι, καὶ πόλεμον ἐκ
πολέμου πολιτευόμενοι, ἐν μὲν εἰρήνῃ τὰ δεινὰ τῷ
λόγῳ προορώμενοι, καὶ τὰς ψυχὰς τὰς φιλοτί-
μους καὶ λίαν ὀξείας ἐρεθίζοντες, ἐν δὲ τοῖς πολέμοις ὅπλων οὐχ ἁπτόμενοι, ἐξετασταὶ δὲ καὶ
ἀποστολεῖς γιγνόμενοι, παιδοποιούμενοι δὲ ἐξ

¹ πόλεμον Markland : πόλεμον δι' Ἀργείους MSS.

---

¹ Athens entered into alliance with Argos, Mantineia, and
Elis in 420. This immediately reopened the war with the
Lacedaemonians.
² The oligarchy of the Four Hundred was the result of the
revolution of 411 B.C. The rule of the Thirty Tyrants followed the surrender of the city at the close of the Pelopon-

fewer than three hundred in number; a yearly tribute of more than twelve hundred talents came in
to us; we held the Chersonese, Naxos, and Euboea,
and in these years we sent out a host of colonies.
Though the blessings we were enjoying were so
great, we again brought war against the Lacedaemonians, persuaded by the Argives; [1] and at last, in
consequence of the eagerness of our public men for
war, we sank so low as to see a Spartan garrison in
our city, and the Four Hundred, and the impious
Thirty; [2] and it was not the making of peace that
caused this, [3] but we were forced by orders laid upon
us.   But when again a moderate government had
been established, and the exiled democracy had
come back from Phyle, [4] with Archinus and Thrasybulus as the leaders of the popular party, we took the
solemn oath with one another " to forgive and forget "—an act which, in the judgment of all men, won
for our state the reputation of the highest wisdom.
The democracy then took on new life and vigour.
But now men who have been illegally registered as
citizens, constantly attaching to themselves whatever element in the city is corrupt, and following
a policy of war after war, in peace ever prophesying
danger, and so working on ambitious and over-
excitable minds, yet when war comes never touching
arms themselves, but getting into office as auditors
and naval commissioners—men whose mistresses are
the mothers of their offspring, and whose slanderous

nesian war. The Thirty were supported by a Spartan
garrison (404-403).

[3] The setting up of the Thirty was dictated by Sparta.

[4] Phyle, a post on the Boeotian frontier, was the rallying
point of the band of exiles who began the movement for the
expulsion of the Thirty.

ἑταιρῶν, ἄτιμοι δ' ἐκ συκοφαντίας, εἰς τοὺς
ἐσχάτους κινδύνους[1] τὴν πόλιν καθιστᾶσι, τὸ[2]
μὲν τῆς δημοκρατίας ὄνομα οὐ τοῖς ἤθεσιν, ἀλλὰ
τῇ κολακείᾳ θεραπεύοντες, καταλύοντες δὲ τὴν
εἰρήνην, ἐξ ἧς ἡ δημοκρατία σῴζεται, συναγωνι-
ζόμενοι δὲ τοῖς πολέμοις, ἐξ ὧν ὁ δῆμος κατα-
λύεται.

178 Οὗτοι νῦν ἐπ' ἐμὲ συστραφέντες ἥκουσι, καὶ
φασὶ μὲν τὸν Φίλιππον τὴν εἰρήνην πρίασθαι,
καὶ προλαβεῖν ἡμῶν ἐν ταῖς συνθήκαις ἅπαντα,
ἣν δ' αὐτὸς εὗρεν εἰρήνην αὑτῷ συμφέρουσαν,
ταύτην παραβεβηκέναι. ἐμὲ δ' οὐχ ὡς πρεσβευτὴν κρίνουσιν, ἀλλ' ὡς ἐγγυητὴν Φιλίππου καὶ
τῆς εἰρήνης· καὶ τὸν τῶν λόγων κύριον τὰς τῶν
ἔργων προσδοκίας ἀπαιτοῦσι. τὸν αὐτὸν δὲ ἐν
μὲν τοῖς ψηφίσμασιν ἐπαινέτην ἐπιδείκνυμι, ἐν δὲ
τῷ δικαστηρίῳ κατηγόρῳ κέχρημαι. δέκατος δ'
αὐτὸς πρεσβεύσας, μόνος τὰς εὐθύνας δίδωμι.

179 Κἀμοὶ[3] συνδεησόμενοι πάρεισιν ὑμῶν πατὴρ
μέν, οὗ τὰς τοῦ γήρως ἐλπίδας μὴ ἀφέλησθε,
ἀδελφοὶ δέ, οἳ διαζυγέντες ἐμοῦ ζῆν οὐκ ἂν προ-
έλοιντο, κηδεσταὶ δὲ καὶ ταυτὶ τὰ μικρὰ παιδία
καὶ τοὺς μὲν[4] κινδύνους οὔπω συνιέντα, ἐλεινὰ δέ,
εἴ τι συμβήσεται ἡμῖν παθεῖν. ὑπὲρ ὧν ἐγὼ
δέομαι καὶ ἱκετεύω πολλὴν πρόνοιαν[5] ποιήσασθαι,

---

[1] κινδύνους Baiter and Sauppe : the MSS. have ἡμῶν before κινδύνους or after πόλιν.
[2] τὸ Bekker : καὶ τὸ MSS.
[3] κἀμοὶ Hamaker : κἀμοὶ μὲν οἱ MSS.
[4] τοὺς μὲν Blass : the MSS. have μὲν after μικρὰ or after ταυτὶ (one MS. omits).
[5] πρόνοιαν Blass (Aldus) : the MSS. have ὑμᾶς, ἡμῖν, or ἡμῶν before πρόνοιαν, or ἡμῖν or ἡμῶν after πρόνοιαν.

tongues ought to disfranchise them—these men are bringing the state into extreme peril, fostering the name of democracy, not by their character, but by their flatteries, trying to put an end to the peace, wherein lies the safety of the democracy, and in every way fomenting war, the destroyer of popular government.

These are the men who now are making a concerted attack on me; they say that Philip bought the peace, that he overreached us at every point in the articles of agreement, and that the peace which he contrived for his own interests, he himself has violated. And they put me on trial, not as an ambassador, but as a surety for Philip and the peace; the man who had nothing but words under his control they call to account for deeds—deeds that existed only in their own imagination. And the very man whom I exhibit to you as my eulogist in the public decrees, I have found as my accuser in the court-room. And although I was but one of ten ambassadors, I alone am made to give account.

To plead with you in my behalf are present my father, whom I beg of you not to rob of the hopes of his old age; my brothers, who would have no desire for life if I should be torn from them; my connections by marriage; and these little children, who do not yet realize their danger, but are to be pitied if disaster fall on us. For them I beg and beseech you to take earnest thought, and not to give them over into the

THE SPEECHES OF AESCHINES

καὶ μὴ τοῖς ἐχθροῖς αὐτοὺς μηδ' ἀνάνδρῳ καὶ
γυναικείῳ τὴν ὀργὴν ἀνθρώπῳ παραδοῦναι.

180   Παρακαλῶ δὲ καὶ ἱκετεύω σῶσαί με πρῶτον
μὲν τοὺς θεούς, δεύτερον δ' ὑμᾶς τοὺς τῆς ψήφου
κυρίους, οἷς ἐγὼ πρὸς ἕκαστον τῶν κατηγορημένων εἰς μνήμην εἶναι τὴν ἐμὴν ἀπολελόγημαι,
καὶ δέομαι σῶσαί με καὶ μὴ τῷ λογογράφῳ καὶ
Σκύθῃ παραδοῦναι, ὅσοι μὲν ὑμῶν πατέρες εἰσὶ
παίδων ἢ νεωτέρους ἀδελφοὺς περὶ πολλοῦ ποιεῖσθε, ἀναμνησθέντες, ὅτι τὴν τῆς σωφροσύνης
παράκλησιν διὰ τῆς περὶ Τίμαρχον κρίσεως
181 ἀειμνήστως παρακέκληκα, τοὺς δ' ἄλλους ἅπαντας,
οἷς ἐμαυτὸν ἄλυπον παρέσχημαι, τὴν μὲν τύχην
ἰδιώτης ὢν καὶ τοῖς μετρίοις ὑμῶν ὅμοιος, ἐν δὲ
τοῖς πολιτικοῖς ἀγῶσι μόνος τῶν ἄλλων ἐφ' ὑμᾶς
οὐ συνεστηκώς, αἰτῶ παρ' ὑμῶν τὴν σωτηρίαν,
μετὰ πάσης εὐνοίας τῇ πόλει πεπρεσβευκώς, καὶ
μόνος ὑπομείνας τὸν τῶν συκοφαντῶν θόρυβον,
ὃν ἤδη πολλοὶ τῶν τὰς ψυχὰς ἐν τοῖς πολέμοις
λαμπρῶν οὐχ ὑπέστησαν.   οὐ γὰρ ὁ θάνατος
182 δεινόν, ἀλλ' ἡ περὶ τὴν τελευτὴν ὕβρις.[1]   πῶς δὲ
οὐκ οἰκτρὸν ἰδεῖν ἐχθροῦ πρόσωπον ἐπεγγελῶντος,
καὶ τοῖς ὠσὶ τῶν ὀνειδῶν ἀκοῦσαι; ἀλλ' ὅμως
τετόλμηται· δέδοται τὸ σῶμα τῷ κινδύνῳ.   παρ'
ὑμῖν ἐτράφην, ἐν ταῖς ὑμετέραις διατριβαῖς βε-
βίωκα.   οὐδεὶς ὑμῶν διὰ τὰς ἐμὰς ἡδονὰς κάκιον
οἰκεῖ, οὐδὲ ἐστέρηται τῆς πατρίδος κατηγόρου
τυχών,[2] ὅτ' ἦσαν αἱ διαψηφίσεις, οὐδ' ὑπεύθυνος
ὢν ἀρχῆς ἐκινδύνευσεν.

<hr/>

[1] ὕβρις Cobet : ὕβρις φοβερά MSS.
[2] τυχὼν Benseler : the MSS. have ἐν τοῖς δήμοις after τυχὼν
or after οἰκεῖ.

hands of our enemies, or of a creature who is no man—no better in spirit than a woman.

And first of all I pray and beseech the gods to save me, and then I beseech you, who hold the verdict in your hands, before whom I have defended myself against every one of the accusations, to the best of my recollection; I beg you to save me, and not give me over to the hands of the rhetorician and the Scythian. You who are fathers of children or have younger brothers whom you hold dear, remember that to me they are indebted for a warning which they will not forget, admonished to live chastely through my prosecution of Timarchus. And all the rest of you, toward whom I have conducted myself without offence, in fortune a plain citizen, a decent man like any one of you, and the only man who in the strife of politics has refused to join in conspiracy against you, upon you I call to save me. With all loyalty I have served the city as her ambassador, alone subjected to the clamour of the slanderers, which before now many a man conspicuously brave in war has not had the courage to face; for it is not death that men dread, but a dishonoured end. Is he not indeed to be pitied who must look into the sneering face of an enemy, and hear with his ears his insults? But nevertheless I have taken the risk, I have exposed my body to the peril. Among you I grew up, your ways have been my ways. No home of yours is the worse for my pleasures; no man has been deprived of his fatherland by accusation of mine at any revision of the citizen-lists, nor has come into peril when rendering account of his administration of an office.

183 Μικρὰ δ' ἔτι[1] εἰπὼν ἤδη καταβαίνω. ἐγὼ γάρ, ὦ ἄνδρες Ἀθηναῖοι, τοῦ μὲν μηδὲν ἀδικεῖν ὑμᾶς κύριος ἦν, τοῦ δὲ μὴ ἔχειν αἰτίαν ἡ τύχη, ἢ συνεκλήρωσέ με ἀνθρώπῳ συκοφάντῃ καὶ[2] βαρβάρῳ, ὃς οὔτε ἱερῶν οὔτε σπονδῶν οὔτε τραπέζης φροντίσας, ἀλλὰ τοὺς εἰς τὸν μέλλοντα αὐτῷ χρόνον ἀντεροῦντας ἐκφοβῶν, ἥκει ψευδῆ συντάξας καθ' ἡμῶν κατηγορίαν. ἐὰν οὖν ἐθελήσητε σῴζειν τοὺς τῆς εἰρήνης καὶ τῆς ὑμετέρας ἀδείας συναγωνιστάς, πολλοὺς βοηθοὺς λήψεται τὸ τῆς πόλεως συμφέρον καὶ κινδυνεύειν ὑπὲρ ὑμῶν ἑτοίμους.

184 Παρακαλῶ δὲ Εὔβουλον μὲν ἐκ τῶν πολιτικῶν καὶ σωφρόνων ἀνδρῶν συνήγορον, Φωκίωνα δ' ἐκ τῶν στρατηγῶν, ἅμα δὲ καὶ δικαιοσύνῃ διενηνοχότα πάντων, ἐκ δὲ τῶν φίλων καὶ τῶν ἡλικιωτῶν τῶν ἐμαυτοῦ Ναυσικλέα καὶ τοὺς ἄλλους ἅπαντας, οἷστισιν ἐγὼ κέχρημαι καὶ τῶν αὐτῶν ἐπιτηδευμάτων μετέσχηκα.

Ὁ μὲν οὖν ἐμὸς λόγος εἴρηται, τὸ δὲ σῶμα ἤδη τουτὶ παραδίδωσιν ὑμῖν καὶ ἐγὼ καὶ ὁ νόμος.

---

[1] ἔτι added by Cobet.   [2] καὶ added by Dobree.

A word more and I have done. One thing was in my power, fellow citizens : to do you no wrong. But to be free from accusation, that was a thing which depended upon fortune, and fortune cast my lot with a slanderer, a barbarian, who cared not for sacrifices nor libations nor the breaking of bread together ; nay, to frighten all who in time to come might oppose him, he has fabricated a false charge against us and come in here. If, therefore, you are willing to save those who have laboured together with you for peace and for your security, the common good will find champions in abundance, ready to face danger in your behalf.

To endorse my plea I now call Eubulus as a representative of the statesmen and all honourable citizens, and Phocion as a representative of the generals, preëminent also among us all as a man of upright character. From among my friends and associates I call Nausicles, and all the others with whom I have associated and whose pursuits I have shared.

My speech is finished. This my body I, and the law, now commit to your hands.

III.—AGAINST CTESIPHON

Introduction

On receipt of the news of the defeat at Chaeronea
the Athenians made hasty and temporary repairs of
their fortifications. After the unexpectedly favourable peace terms offered by Philip had released them
from the fear of an immediate attack, they determined to undertake the mere thorough repair of the
walls. The work was apportioned to the several
tribes. Demosthenes was elected by the members
of his tribe to superintend the repairs assigned to
them, covering the important section around the Peiraeus. The sum of nearly ten talents was entrusted
to him for this work. Finding this sum insufficient
for the repairs that were needed, Demosthenes added
three talents of his own money, as a gift to the city.
His friend Ctesiphon saw now a happy occasion for
obtaining from the people an expression of their ap-
preciation of the services that Demosthenes had
performed in the long struggle against Macedon, of
their continued confidence in him even in defeat,
and of their love for the lost cause. Ctesiphon therefore carried a motion in the senate that at the coming
Dionysia, when the great theatre would be filled with
Athenian citizens and visitors from other Greek
states, a golden crown should be publicly bestowed

305

on Demosthenes, with a proclamation attesting his
lifelong devotion to the state. When the proposal
came to the assembly of the people for ratification,
Aeschines attacked the motion as illegal.[1] The effect
of this was to defer action on the motion and to
send the case thus instituted by Aeschines to the
law courts.[2] For reasons which we do not know,
the trial of the case was delayed for six years, but in
330 it came into court.

Aeschines based his indictment of Ctesiphon on
three charges : first, he cited a provision of the constitution which forbade crowning a public officer until
after the expiration of his term of office, and the
approval of his record by the official Board of Auditors. But at the time when Ctesiphon moved the
crown, Demosthenes was a commissioner of his tribe
for the repair of walls, and at the same time Superintendent of the Festival Fund, one of the most
important financial offices of the city. Secondly, the
constitution prescribed that crowns bestowed by the
city be proclaimed and received at a meeting of the
popular assembly held on the Pnyx. But Ctesiphon's
motion was that Demosthenes be crowned in the
theatre, on the occasion of the presentation of the
new tragedies. On both of these points Aeschines
had a strong case, probably a safe one, though it may
well be that the laws cited had fallen into neglect.
But to have won his case on these technical points

[1] The Athenian constitution consisted of the original code
of Solon, together with the whole body of laws ($\nu\acute{o}\mu o\iota$) which
in course of time had modified or enlarged it. It was illegal
to propose any resolution ($\psi\acute{\eta}\phi\iota\sigma\mu a$) which contravened this
constitution.

[2] For a full account of the Athenian procedure in such
cases, see Goodwin, *Demosthenes de Corona*, pp. 316-327.

only would not have satisfied Aeschines; it would have been a victory over Ctesiphon only; merely to have prevented the proposed crowning of Demosthenes would not have been enough to gratify Aeschines' hatred of the man who had put him on trial thirteen years before for treason. He therefore frankly declared that his main contention was that Ctesiphon was guilty of proposing to insert a false statement in a decree of the people, for his motion asserted that Demosthenes had always been a patriotic and useful citizen. This was the real issue, and it made the contest one of political life and death to the two men.

The time when the case came to trial was favourable to Aeschines. The Theban uprising against Alexander had been put down and the city destroyed, Alexander's expedition into Asia was at the height of its success, and finally the Spartan revolt against Macedon had just been ended by the prompt action of the Macedonian regent. A refusal of the Athenian people to honour Demosthenes at this time would be viewed at court as a declaration of Athenian submission to the new order in Greece. But Aeschines had failed to appreciate the hold of Demosthenes on the mass of the people, the undiminished power of his oratory, and the popular grief for the loss of the imperial position which the men of an earlier day had won and handed down to their descendants. The jury were unmoved by Aeschines' shrewd and bitter attacks upon Demosthenes as a man who had led Athens to defeat, and regardless of the strength of his technical case against Ctesiphon's motion, they gave an overwhelming verdict for the lost cause of Greek liberty and its foremost champion.

III.—ΚΑΤΑ ΚΤΗΣΙΦΩΝΤΟΣ

Τὴν μὲν παρασκευὴν ὁρᾶτε, ὦ ἄνδρες Ἀθηναῖοι,
καὶ τὴν παράταξιν ὅση γεγένηται, καὶ τὰς κατὰ
τὴν ἀγορὰν δεήσεις, αἷς κέχρηνταί τινες ὑπὲρ
τοῦ τὰ μέτρια καὶ συνήθη μὴ γίγνεσθαι ἐν τῇ
πόλει· ἐγὼ δὲ πεπιστευκὼς ἥκω πρῶτον μὲν τοῖς
θεοῖς, ἔπειτα[1] τοῖς νόμοις καὶ ὑμῖν, ἡγούμενος
οὐδεμίαν παρασκευὴν μεῖζον ἰσχύειν παρ' ὑμῖν
τῶν νόμων καὶ τῶν δικαίων.

2 Ἐβουλόμην μὲν οὖν, ὦ ἄνδρες Ἀθηναῖοι, καὶ
τὴν βουλὴν τοὺς πεντακοσίους καὶ τὰς ἐκκλησίας
ὑπὸ τῶν ἐφεστηκότων ὀρθῶς διοικεῖσθαι, καὶ τοὺς
νόμους οὓς ἐνομοθέτησεν ὁ Σόλων περὶ τῆς τῶν
ῥητόρων εὐκοσμίας ἰσχύειν, ἵνα ἐξῆν πρῶτον μὲν
τῷ πρεσβυτάτῳ τῶν πολιτῶν, ὥσπερ οἱ νόμοι
προστάττουσι, σωφρόνως ἐπὶ τὸ βῆμα παρελθόντι
ἄνευ θορύβου καὶ ταραχῆς ἐξ ἐμπειρίας τὰ βέλτιστα τῇ πόλει συμβουλεύειν, δεύτερον δ' ἤδη
καὶ τῶν ἄλλων πολιτῶν τὸν βουλόμενον καθ'
ἡλικίαν χωρὶς καὶ ἐν μέρει περὶ ἑκάστου γνώμην
ἀποφαίνεσθαι· οὕτω γὰρ ἄν μοι δοκεῖ ἥ τε πόλις
ἄριστα διοικεῖσθαι, αἵ τε κρίσεις ἐλάχισται
γίγνεσθαι.

3 Ἐπειδὴ δὲ πάντα τὰ πρότερον ὡμολογημένα
καλῶς ἔχειν νυνὶ καταλέλυνται, καὶ γράφουσί τε

---

[1] ἔπειτα Stephanus : ἔπειτα δεύτερον or δεύτερον δὲ MSS.

III.—AGAINST CTESIPHON

You see, fellow citizens, how certain persons have been making their preparations for this case: how they have mustered their forces, and how they have gone begging up and down the market place, in the attempt to prevent the fair and orderly course of justice in the state. But I have come trusting first in the gods, then in the laws and in you, believing that with you no scheming preparation can override law and justice.

I could wish, indeed, fellow citizens, that the Senate of Five Hundred and the assemblies of the people were properly conducted by those who preside over them, and the laws enforced which Solon enacted to secure orderly conduct on the part of public speakers; for then it would be permitted to the oldest citizen, as the law prescribes, to come forward to the platform first, with dignity, and, uninterrupted by shouting and tumult, out of his experience to advise for the good of the state; and it would then be permitted to all other citizens who wished, one by one in turn, in order of age, to express their opinion on every question; for so, I think, the state would be best governed, and least litigation would arise.

But now all our standards of orderly procedure have been set aside; there are men who do not

τινὲς ῥᾳδίως παρανόμους γνώμας, καὶ ταύτας[1]
ἕτεροι τινες[2] ἐπιψηφίζουσιν, οὐκ ἐκ τοῦ δικαιο-
τάτου τρόπου λαχόντες προεδρεύειν, ἀλλ' ἐκ
παρασκευῆς καθεζόμενοι, ἂν δέ τις τῶν ἄλλων
βουλευτῶν ὄντως λάχῃ προεδρεύειν,[3] καὶ τὰς
ὑμετέρας χειροτονίας ὀρθῶς ἀναγορεύῃ, τοῦτον
οἱ τὴν πολιτείαν οὐκέτι κοινήν, ἀλλ' ἰδίαν αὑτῶν
ἡγούμενοι, ἀπειλοῦσιν εἰσαγγελεῖν, καταδουλού-
μενοι τοὺς ἰδιώτας καὶ δυναστείας ἑαυτοῖς περι-
4 ποιούμενοι, καὶ τὰς κρίσεις τὰς μὲν ἐκ τῶν νόμων
καταλελύκασι, τὰς δ' ἐκ τῶν ψηφισμάτων μετ'
ὀργῆς κρίνουσι, σεσίγηται μὲν τὸ κάλλιστον
καὶ σωφρονέστατον κήρυγμα τῶν ἐν τῇ πόλει·
"Τίς ἀγορεύειν βούλεται τῶν ὑπὲρ πεντήκοντα
ἔτη γεγονότων;" καὶ πάλιν ἐν μέρει τῶν ἄλλων
Ἀθηναίων. τῆς δὲ τῶν ῥητόρων ἀκοσμίας οὐκέτι
κρατεῖν δύνανται οὔθ' οἱ νόμοι οὔθ' οἱ πρυτάνεις
οὔθ' οἱ πρόεδροι οὔθ' ἡ προεδρεύουσα φυλή, τὸ
δέκατον μέρος τῆς πόλεως.

5 Τούτων δ' ἐχόντων οὕτως, καὶ τῶν καιρῶν
ὄντων τῇ πόλει τοιούτων ὁποίους τινὰς αὐτοὺς
ὑμεῖς ὑπολαμβάνετε εἶναι, ἓν ὑπολείπεται μέρος
τῆς πολιτείας, εἴ τι κἀγὼ τυγχάνω γιγνώσκων,
αἱ τῶν παρανόμων γραφαί. εἰ δὲ καὶ ταύτας
καταλύσετε ἢ τοῖς καταλύουσιν ἐπιτρέψετε, προ-

---

[1] ταύτας Cobet : ταῦτα MSS.
[2] τινες Westermann : τινες τὰ ψηφίσματα MSS.
[3] λάχῃ προεδρεύειν Westermann : λάχῃ κληρούμενος προεδρεύειν MSS.

hesitate to make illegal motions, and other men who are ready to put these motions to the vote—not men who have been chosen by right and lawful allotment to preside, but men who hold the position by trickery ; and if any other senator does actually obtain the presidency by lot, and does honestly declare your votes, he is threatened with impeachment by men who no longer regard citizenship as a common right, but as their own private perquisite ; men who are making slaves of the common people, and arrogating lordship to themselves; men who have set aside the lawful processes of the courts, and carry their verdicts in the assembly by appeal to passion.[1] The result of all this is that we have ceased to hear that wisest and most judicious of all the proclamations to which the city was once accustomed, "Who of the men above fifty years of age wishes to address the people," and then who of the other Athenians in turn. The disorder of the public men can no longer be controlled by the laws, nor by the prytanes, nor by the presiding officers, nor by the presiding tribe, the tenth part of the city.[2]

Under such circumstances, and in a political situation the gravity of which you yourselves understand, only one part of the constitution is left to us—if I too may lay claim to some discernment—the suits against illegal motions. But if you shall annul these also, or give way to those who are trying to annul them, I warn you that before you know it

---

[1] The popular leaders, confident in their ability to carry the popular assembly by appeal to the passions of the masses, bring cases there in the form of impeachments, etc., which ought to go to the courts, to be decided under the laws.

[2] See i. 33 and note.

λέγω ὑμῖν, ὅτι λήσετε κατὰ μικρὸν τῆς πολιτείας
τισὶ παραχωρήσαντες.

6 Εὖ γὰρ ἴστε, ὦ ἄνδρες Ἀθηναῖοι, ὅτι τρεῖς
εἰσὶ πολιτεῖαι παρὰ πᾶσιν ἀνθρώποις, τυραννὶς
καὶ ὀλιγαρχία καὶ δημοκρατία· διοικοῦνται δ'
αἱ μὲν τυραννίδες καὶ ὀλιγαρχίαι τοῖς τρόποις
τῶν ἐφεστηκότων, αἱ δὲ πόλεις αἱ δημοκρατούμεναι τοῖς νόμοις τοῖς κειμένοις. μηδεὶς οὖν
ὑμῶν τοῦτ' ἀγνοείτω, ἀλλὰ σαφῶς ἕκαστος ἐπι-
στάσθω, ὅτι ὅταν εἰσίῃ εἰς δικαστήριον γραφὴν
παρανόμων δικάσων, ἐν ταύτῃ τῇ ἡμέρᾳ μέλλει
τὴν ψῆφον φέρειν περὶ τῆς ἑαυτοῦ παρρησίας.
διόπερ καὶ ὁ νομοθέτης τοῦτο πρῶτον ἔταξεν ἐν
τῷ τῶν δικαστῶν ὅρκῳ, "Ψηφιοῦμαι κατὰ τοὺς
νόμους," ἐκεῖνό γε εὖ εἰδώς, ὅτι ἂν διατηρη-
θῶσιν οἱ νόμοι τῇ πόλει, σῴζεται καὶ ἡ δημο-
7 κρατία. ἃ χρὴ διαμνημονεύοντας ὑμᾶς μισεῖν
τοὺς τὰ παράνομα γράφοντας, καὶ μηδὲν ἡγεῖσθαι μικρὸν εἶναι τῶν τοιούτων ἀδικημάτων, ἀλλ'
ἕκαστον ὑπερμέγεθες, καὶ τοῦθ' ὑμῶν τὸ δίκαιον
μηδένα ἐᾶν[1] ἀνθρώπων ἐξαιρεῖσθαι, μήτε τὰς
τῶν στρατηγῶν συνηγορίας, οἳ ἐπὶ πολὺν ἤδη
χρόνον συνεργοῦντές τισι τῶν ῥητόρων λυμαί-
νονται τὴν πολιτείαν, μήτε τὰς τῶν ξένων δεήσεις,
οὓς ἀναβιβαζόμενοί τινες ἐκφεύγουσιν ἐκ τῶν
δικαστηρίων, παράνομον πολιτείαν πολιτευόμενοι·
ἀλλ' ὥσπερ ἂν ὑμῶν ἕκαστος αἰσχυνθείη τὴν
τάξιν λιπεῖν ἣν ἂν ταχθῇ ἐν τῷ πολέμῳ, οὕτω
καὶ νῦν αἰσχύνθητε ἐκλιπεῖν τὴν τάξιν ἣν τέταχθε
ὑπὸ τῶν νόμων φύλακες τῆς δημοκρατίας τήνδε
τὴν ἡμέραν.

[1] ἐᾶν added by Askew.

you will step by step have surrendered your rights to a faction.

There are, as you know, fellow-citizens, three forms of government in the world: tyranny, oligarchy, and democracy. Tyrannies and oligarchies are administered according to the tempers of their lords, but democratic states according to their own established laws. Let no man among you forget this, but let each bear distinctly in mind that when he enters a court-room to sit as juror in a suit against an illegal motion, on that day he is to cast his vote for or against his own freedom of speech. This is why the lawgiver placed first in the jurors' oath these words, "I will vote according to the laws." For he well knew that if the laws are faithfully upheld for the state, the democracy also is preserved. This you ought always to remember, and to hate those who make illegal motions, and to hold no such offence as trivial, but every one as serious indeed. And you ought to let no man rob you of this right of yours, whether through the intercession of the generals, who by their cooperation with certain public men have this long time been outraging the constitution, or through petitions of foreigners, whom some bring in here, and so escape the courts, when their whole political career has been in defiance of the laws. But as each man of you would be ashamed to desert the post to which he had been assigned in war, so now you should be ashamed to desert the post to which the laws have called you, sentinels, guarding the democracy this day.

8 Κἀκεῖνο δὲ χρὴ διαμνημονεύειν, ὅτι νυνὶ πάντες
οἱ πολῖται παρακαταθέμενοι τὴν πόλιν ὑμῖν καὶ
τὴν πολιτείαν διαπιστεύσαντες, οἱ μὲν πάρεισι
καὶ ἐπακούουσι τῆσδε τῆς κρίσεως, οἱ δὲ ἄπεισιν
ἐπὶ τῶν ἰδίων ἔργων· οὓς αἰσχυνόμενοι καὶ τῶν
ὅρκων οὓς ὠμόσατε, μεμνημένοι καὶ τῶν νόμων,
ἐὰν ἐξελέγξω Κτησιφῶντα καὶ παράνομα γεγραφότα καὶ ψευδῆ καὶ ἀσύμφορα τῇ πόλει, λύετε,
ὦ ἄνδρες Ἀθηναῖοι, τὰς παρανόμους γνώμας,
βεβαιοῦτε τῇ πόλει τὴν δημοκρατίαν, κολάζετε
τοὺς ὑπεναντίως τοῖς νόμοις καὶ τῷ συμφέροντι
τῷ ὑμετέρῳ πολιτευομένους. κἂν ταύτην ἔχοντες
τὴν διάνοιαν ἀκούητε τῶν μελλόντων ῥηθήσεσθαι
λόγων, εὖ οἶδ' ὅτι καὶ δίκαια καὶ εὔορκα καὶ
συμφέροντα ὑμῖν αὐτοῖς ψηφιεῖσθε καὶ πάσῃ τῇ
πόλει.

9 Περὶ μὲν οὖν τῆς ὅλης κατηγορίας μετρίως μοι
ἐλπίζω προειρῆσθαι· περὶ δὲ αὐτῶν τῶν νόμων οἳ
κεῖνται περὶ τῶν ὑπευθύνων, παρ' οὓς τὸ ψήφισμα τυγχάνει γεγραφὼς Κτησιφῶν, διὰ βραχέων εἰπεῖν βούλομαι.

Ἐν γὰρ τοῖς ἔμπροσθεν χρόνοις ἄρχοντές τινες
τὰς μεγίστας ἀρχὰς καὶ τὰς προσόδους διοικοῦντες,
καὶ δωροδοκοῦντες περὶ ἕκαστα τούτων, προσλαμ-
βάνοντες τούς τε ἐκ τοῦ βουλευτηρίου ῥήτορας
καὶ τοὺς ἐκ τοῦ δήμου, πόρρωθεν προκατελάμ-
βανον τὰς εὐθύνας ἐπαίνοις καὶ κηρύγμασιν, ὥστ'
ἐν ταῖς εὐθύναις[1] εἰς τὴν μεγίστην μὲν ἀπορίαν
ἀφικνεῖσθαι τοὺς κατηγόρους, πολὺ δὲ ἔτι μᾶλλον
10 τοὺς δικαστάς. πολλοὶ γὰρ πάνυ τῶν ὑπευθύνων,

[1] εὐθύναις Weidner : εὐθύναις τῶν ἀρχῶν (or τῶν ἀρχόντων)
MSS.

And another thing you have to remember: to-day your fellow citizens as a body have put the city and the constitution into your hands as a solemn trust. Some of them are present, listening to this case; others are absent, busy with their personal affairs. Respect them therefore, and remember the oaths which you have sworn, and the laws; and if I convict Ctesiphon of having made a motion that is illegal, false, and injurious to the state, annul the illegal motion, fellow citizens; confirm the democratic government for our state; punish those whose policies are opposed to the laws and to your interests. If in this spirit you listen to the words which are about to be spoken, I am sure that your verdict will be just, faithful to your oath, and salutary alike to yourselves and to the commonwealth.

I hope now that what I have said is a sufficient introduction to my complaint as a whole; but I wish to speak briefly about the laws themselves which govern the rendering of account by public officers, the laws which are in fact violated by Ctesiphon's resolution.

In former times certain men who held the highest offices and administered the revenues—yes, and betrayed their every trust for money—would attach to themselves the public speakers of the senate-house and the assembly, and thus anticipate their day of accounting long in advance, with votes of thanks and with proclamations. The result was that when the time came for them to render their account, those who had charges to prefer fell into very great embarrassment, and this was even more the case with the jurors. For great numbers of those who were

ἐπ' αὐτοφώρῳ κλέπται τῶν δημοσίων χρημάτων
ὄντες ἐξελεγχόμενοι, διεφύγγανον ἐκ τῶν δικαστηρίων, εἰκότως· ἠσχύνοντο γὰρ οἶμαι οἱ δικασταί, εἰ φανήσεται ὁ αὐτὸς ἀνὴρ ἐν τῇ αὐτῇ
πόλει, πρώην [1] μέν ποτε ἀναγορευόμενος ἐν τοῖς
ἀγῶσιν, ὅτι στεφανοῦται ἀρετῆς ἕνεκα καὶ δικαιοσύνης ὑπὸ τοῦ δήμου χρυσῷ στεφάνῳ, ὁ δὲ
αὐτὸς ἀνὴρ μικρὸν ἐπισχὼν ἔξεισιν ἐκ τοῦ δικαστηρίου κλοπῆς ἕνεκα τὰς εὐθύνας ὠφληκώς·
ὥστε ἠναγκάζοντο τὴν ψῆφον φέρειν οἱ δικασταί,
11 οὐ περὶ τοῦ παρόντος ἀδικήματος, ἀλλ' ὑπὲρ τῆς
αἰσχύνης τοῦ δήμου.

Κατιδὼν δή [2] τις ταῦτα νομοθέτης τίθησι νόμον
καὶ μάλα καλῶς ἔχοντα, διαρρήδην [3] ἀπαγορεύ-
οντα τοὺς ὑπευθύνους μὴ στεφανοῦν. καὶ ταῦτα
οὕτως εὖ προκατειληφότος τοῦ νομοθέτου, εὕ-
ρηνται κρείττονες λόγοι τῶν νόμων, οὓς εἰ μή τις
ὑμῖν ἐρεῖ, λήσετε ἐξαπατηθέντες. τούτων γὰρ [4]
τῶν τοὺς ὑπευθύνους στεφανούντων παρὰ τοὺς
νόμους οἱ μὲν φύσει μέτριοί εἰσιν, εἰ δή τις ἐστὶ
μέτριος τῶν τὰ παράνομα γραφόντων, ἀλλ' οὖν
προβάλλονταί γέ τι πρὸ τῆς αἰσχύνης. προσγράφουσι [5] γὰρ πρὸς τὰ ψηφίσματα στεφανοῦν τὸν
ὑπεύθυνον "ἐπειδὰν λόγον καὶ εὐθύνας τῆς ἀρχῆς
12 δῷ." καὶ ἡ μὲν πόλις τὸ ἴσον ἀδίκημα ἀδικεῖται·
προκαταλαμβάνονται γὰρ ἐπαίνοις καὶ στεφάνοις

---

[1] πόλει, πρώην Cobet : after πόλει the MSS. have τυχὸν δὲ
καὶ ἐν τῷ αὐτῷ ἐνιαυτῷ.
[2] δή Blass (from an ancient quotation, Walz, *Rh.* iv. 512) :
δέ MSS. *cp.* § 44.
[3] διαρρήδην Cobet : τὸν διαρρήδην MSS.
[4] γὰρ Cobet : γάρ τινες MSS.
[5] προσγράφουσι Dobree : προσεγγράφουσι MSS.

subject to audit, though they were caught in the very act of stealing the public funds, went out from the court-room acquitted. And no wonder! For the jurors were ashamed, I imagine, to see the same man in the same city one day proclaimed at the festival as crowned by the people with a golden crown because of his virtue and justice, and then a little later to see the same man come out of the auditors' court convicted of theft. And so the jurors were forced to render, not the verdict that fitted the actual crime, but one that would avert the shame of the people.

Now some statesman who had observed this situation caused a law to be passed—and a most excellent law it is—which expressly forbids crowning men before they have passed their final accounting. And yet in spite of this wise provision of the framer of the law, forms of statement have been invented which circumvent the laws; and unless you are warned of them you will be taken unawares and deceived. For among those men who contrary to the laws crown officers who have not yet submitted their accounts, some, who at heart are orderly citizens—if any one is really orderly who proposes illegal measures—at any rate some do make an attempt to cloak their shame; for they add to their decrees the proviso that the man who is subject to audit shall be crowned "after he shall have rendered account and submitted to audit of his office." The injury to the state is indeed no less, for the hearings for accounting are prejudiced by previous votes of thanks and crowns; but the man who makes

THE SPEECHES OF AESCHINES

αἱ εὔθυναι· ὁ δὲ τὸ ψήφισμα γράφων ἐνδείκνυται
τοῖς ἀκούουσιν, ὅτι γέγραφε μὲν παράνομα, αἰ-
σχύνεται δὲ ἐφ' οἷς ἡμάρτηκε. Κτησιφῶν δέ, ὦ
ἄνδρες Ἀθηναῖοι, ὑπερπηδήσας τὸν νόμον τὸν
περὶ τῶν ὑπευθύνων κείμενον, καὶ τὴν πρόφασιν
ἣν ἀρτίως προεῖπον ὑμῖν ἀνελών, πρὶν λόγον πρὶν
εὐθύνας δοῦναι γέγραφε μεταξὺ Δημοσθένην ἄρχοντα στεφανοῦν.

13 Λέξουσι δέ, ὦ ἄνδρες Ἀθηναῖοι, καὶ ἕτερόν
τινα λόγον ὑπεναντίον τῷ ἀρτίως εἰρημένῳ, ὡς
ἄρα, ὅσα τις αἱρετὸς ὢν πράττει κατὰ ψήφισμα,
οὐκ ἔστι ταῦτα ἀρχή, ἀλλ' ἐπιμέλειά τις καὶ
διακονία· ἀρχὰς δὲ φήσουσιν ἐκείνας εἶναι ἃς οἱ
θεσμοθέται ἀποκληροῦσιν ἐν τῷ Θησείῳ, κἀκείνας
ἃς ὁ δῆμος χειροτονεῖ ἐν ἀρχαιρεσίαις, στρατηγοὺς
καὶ ἱππάρχους καὶ τὰς μετὰ τούτων ἀρχάς, τὰ δ'
ἄλλα πάντα πραγματείας προστεταγμένας κατὰ
ψήφισμα.

14 Ἐγὼ δὲ πρὸς τοὺς λόγους τοὺς τούτων νόμον
ὑμέτερον παρέξομαι, ὃν ὑμεῖς ἐνομοθετήσατε
λύσειν ἡγούμενοι τὰς τοιαύτας προφάσεις, ἐν ᾧ
διαρρήδην γέγραπται, "τὰς χειροτονητάς," φησίν,
"ἀρχάς," ἁπάσας ἑνὶ περιλαβὼν ὀνόματι,[1] καὶ
προσειπὼν ἀρχὰς ἁπάσας εἶναι ἃς ὁ δῆμος χειροτονεῖ, "καὶ τοὺς ἐπιστάτας," φησί, "τῶν δημοσίων ἔργων·" ἔστι δὲ ὁ Δημοσθένης τειχοποιός,
ἐπιστάτης τοῦ μεγίστου τῶν ἔργων· "καὶ πάντας
ὅσοι διαχειρίζουσί τι τῶν τῆς πόλεως πλέον ἢ
τριάκονθ' ἡμέρας, καὶ ὅσοι λαμβάνουσιν ἡγεμονίας

[1] ὀνόματι Westermann : ὀνόματι ὁ νομοθέτης MSS.

318

the motion does show to the hearers that while he has made an illegal motion, he is ashamed of the wrong thing that he has done. But Ctesiphon, fellow citizens, overleaping the law that governs those who are subject to audit, and not deigning to resort to the pretext of which I have just spoken, has moved that before the accounting, before the auditing, you crown Demosthenes—in the midst of his term of office.

But, fellow citizens, in opposition to the statement of the case which I have just presented, they will urge a different argument; for they will say, forsooth, that whatever a man is called on to do under special enactment, this is not an "office," but a sort of "commission" and "public service"; and they will say that "offices" are those to which the Thesmothetae appoint men by lot in the Theseum, and those which are filled by popular election (the offices of general, cavalry commander, and associated offices); but that all others are "employment under special enactment."

Well, to their arguments I will oppose your law, a law which you yourselves passed in the expectation of silencing such pretexts; for it expressly says "the elective offices," including all in a single phrase, calling everything which is filled by popular election an "office," and specifying "the superintendents of public works." But Demosthenes is in charge of the construction of walls, superintendent of the greatest of the works; "and all who have charge of any business of the state for more than thirty days, and all to whom is given the presidency of a court";

δικαστηρίων·" οἱ δὲ τῶν ἔργων ἐπιστάται πάντες
ἡγεμονίᾳ χρῶνται δικαστηρίου.

15 Τί τούτους κελεύει ποιεῖν; οὐ διακονεῖν, ἀλλ'
" ἄρχειν δοκιμασθέντας ἐν τῷ δικαστηρίῳ,"
ἐπειδὴ καὶ αἱ κληρωταὶ ἀρχαὶ οὐκ ἀδοκίμαστοι,
ἀλλὰ δοκιμασθεῖσαι ἄρχουσι, " καὶ λόγον¹ ἐγγράφειν πρὸς τὸν γραμματέα καὶ τοὺς λογιστάς,"
καθάπερ καὶ τὰς ἄλλας ἀρχάς.² ὅτι δὲ ἀληθῆ
λέγω, τοὺς νόμους ὑμῖν αὐτοὺς ἀναγνώσεται.

NOMOI

16 "Οταν τοίνυν, ὦ ἄνδρες Ἀθηναῖοι, ἃς ὁ νομοθέτης ἀρχὰς ὀνομάζει, οὗτοι προσαγορεύωσι πραγματείας καὶ ἐπιμελείας, ὑμέτερον ἔργον ἐστὶν
ἀπομνημονεύειν καὶ ἀντιτάττειν τὸν νόμον πρὸς
τὴν τούτων ἀναίδειαν, καὶ ὑποβάλλειν αὐτοῖς, ὅτι
οὐ προσδέχεσθε κακοῦργον σοφιστήν, οἰόμενον
ῥήμασι τοὺς νόμους ἀναιρήσειν, ἀλλ' ὅσῳ ἄν τις
ἄμεινον λέγῃ παράνομα γεγραφώς, τοσούτῳ μεί-
ζονος ὀργῆς τεύξεται. χρὴ γάρ, ὦ ἄνδρες Ἀθηναῖοι, τὸ αὐτὸ φθέγγεσθαι τὸν ῥήτορα καὶ τὸν
νόμον· ὅταν δὲ ἑτέραν μὲν φωνὴν ἀφιῇ ὁ νόμος,
ἑτέραν δὲ ὁ ῥήτωρ, τῷ τοῦ νόμου δικαίῳ χρὴ διδόναι τὴν ψῆφον, οὐ τῇ τοῦ λέγοντος ἀναισχυντίᾳ.

17 Πρὸς δὲ δὴ τὸν ἄφυκτον λόγον, ὅν φησι Δημοσθένης, βραχέα βούλομαι προειπεῖν. λέξει γὰρ

¹ λόγον Reiske : λόγον καὶ εὐθύνας MSS.
² ἀρχάς Franke : ἀρχὰς κελεύει MSS.

---

¹ It was a principle of the Athenian legal system that
litigation arising within the sphere of any executive department should come before a court presided over by the head
of that department.

but every superintendent of public works holds the presidency of a court.[1]

What is it that the law commands these men to do? Not to "serve," but "after approval by the court [2] to hold office" (for even the officers who are selected by lot are not exempt from the scrutiny, but hold their office only after approval); "and to submit their accounts before the clerk and board of auditors," precisely as other officers are required to do. As proof of the truth of my statement, the laws themselves shall be read to you.

THE LAWS

When, therefore, fellow citizens, what the lawgiver names "offices," they call "employments" and "commissions," it is your duty to remember the law, and to set it against their shamelessness, and to remind them that you refuse to accept a rascally sophist, who expects to destroy the laws with phrases; but that when a man has made an illegal motion, the more cleverly he talks, the more angry will he find you. For by right, fellow citizens, the orator and the law ought to speak the same language; but when the law utters one voice and the orator another, you ought to give your vote to the just demand of the law, not to the shamelessness of the speaker.

But now to "the irrefutable argument," as Demosthenes calls it, I wish to reply briefly in advance.

---

[2] All incoming officials were required to pass a formal "scrutiny" (δοκιμασία) before entering upon office. In the case of most officials this was conducted before a court. Aeschines mentions this preliminary scrutiny here because it would naturally follow that any person who had to pass the official scrutiny before entering on his work would have to pass the official accounting on laying it down.

οὗτος· "Τειχοποιός εἰμι· ὁμολογῶ· ἀλλ' ἐπιδέ-
δωκα τῇ πόλει μνᾶς ἑκατόν, καὶ τὸ ἔργον μεῖζον
ἐξείργασμαι. τίνος οὖν εἰμι ὑπεύθυνος; εἰ μή τις
ἐστὶν εὐνοίας εὔθυνα." πρὸς δὴ ταύτην τὴν πρόφασιν ἀκούσατέ μου λέγοντος καὶ δίκαια καὶ ὑμῖν
συμφέροντα.

Ἐν γὰρ ταύτῃ τῇ πόλει, οὕτως ἀρχαίᾳ οὔσῃ
καὶ τηλικαύτῃ τὸ μέγεθος, οὐδείς ἐστιν ἀνυπεύ-
θυνος τῶν καὶ ὁπωσοῦν πρὸς τὰ κοινὰ προσελη-
18 λυθότων. διδάξω δ' ὑμᾶς πρῶτον ἐπὶ τῶν παραδό-
ξων. οἷον τοὺς ἱερέας καὶ τὰς ἱερείας ὑπευθύνους
εἶναι κελεύει ὁ νόμος, καὶ συλλήβδην ἅπαντας καὶ
χωρὶς ἑκάστους κατὰ σῶμα, τοὺς τὰ γέρα μόνον
λαμβάνοντας καὶ τὰς εὐχὰς ὑπὲρ ὑμῶν πρὸς τοὺς
θεοὺς εὐχομένους, καὶ οὐ μόνον ἰδίᾳ, ἀλλὰ καὶ
κοινῇ τὰ γένη, Εὐμολπίδας καὶ Κήρυκας καὶ τοὺς
ἄλλους ἅπαντας.

19 Πάλιν τοὺς τριηράρχους ὑπευθύνους εἶναι
κελεύει ὁ νόμος, οὐ τὰ κοινὰ διαχειρίσαντας, οὐδ'
ἀπὸ τῶν ὑμετέρων[1] πολλὰ μὲν ὑφαιρουμένους,
βραχέα δὲ κατατιθέντας, οὐδ' ἐπιδιδόναι μὲν[2]
φάσκοντας, ἀποδιδόντας δὲ ὑμῖν τὰ ὑμέτερα, ἀλλ'
ὁμολογουμένως τὰς πατρῴας οὐσίας εἰς τὴν πρὸς
ὑμᾶς ἀνηλωκότας φιλοτιμίαν.

Οὐ τοίνυν μόνοι οἱ τριήραρχοι, ἀλλὰ καὶ τὰ
μέγιστα τῶν ἐν τῇ πόλει συνεδρίων ὑπὸ τὴν τῶν
20 δικαστηρίων ἔρχεται ψῆφον. πρῶτον μὲν γὰρ
τὴν βουλὴν τὴν ἐν Ἀρείῳ πάγῳ ἐγγράφειν πρὸς
τοὺς λογιστὰς ὁ νόμος κελεύει λόγον καὶ εὐθύνας
διδόναι, καὶ τὴν ἐκεῖ σκυθρωπὸν καὶ τῶν μεγίστων

---

[1] ὑμετέρων Bake : ὑμετέρων προσόδων MSS.
[2] οὐδ' ἐπιδιδόναι μὲν Blass : ἐπιδιδόναι δὲ MSS.

322

For he will say, " I am in charge of the construction of walls; I admit it; but I have made a present of a hundred minas to the state, and I have carried out the work on a larger scale than was prescribed; what then is it that you want to audit? unless a man's patriotism is to be audited!" Now to this pretext hear my answer, true to the facts and beneficial to you.

In this city, so ancient and so great, no man is free from the audit who has held any public trust. I will first cite cases where this would be least expected. For example, the law directs that priests and priestesses be subject to audit, all collectively, and each severally and individually—persons who receive perquisites only, and whose occupation is to pray to heaven for you; and they are made accountable not only separately, but whole priestly families together, the Eumolpidae, the Ceryces, and all the rest.

Again, the law directs that the trierarchs be subject to audit, though they have had no public funds in their hands, and though they are not men who filch large sums from your treasury and pay out small ones, and not men who claim to be making donations when they are only paying back what is your own, but men who are acknowledged by all to have spent their family fortunes in their ambition to serve you.

Furthermore, not the trierarchs alone, but also the highest bodies in the state, come under the verdict of the courts of audit. For, first, the Senate of the Areopagus is required by the law to file its accounts with the Board of Auditors and to submit to their examination; yes, even those men, who sit with solemn aspect yonder as the court of highest

κυρίαν¹ ἄγει² ὑπὸ τὴν ὑμετέραν ψῆφον. οὐκ
ἄρα στεφανωθήσεται ἡ βουλὴ ἡ ἐξ Ἀρείου πάγου; οὐδὲ γὰρ πάτριον αὐτοῖς.³ οὐκ ἄρα φιλοτι-
μοῦνται; πάνυ γε, ἀλλ᾽ οὐκ ἀγαπῶσιν, ἐάν τις
παρ᾽ αὐτοῖς μὴ ἀδικῇ, ἀλλ᾽ ἐάν τις ἐξαμαρτάνῃ,
κολάζουσιν· οἱ δὲ ὑμέτεροι ῥήτορες τρυφῶσι.
πάλιν τὴν βουλὴν τοὺς πεντακοσίους ὑπεύθυνον
21 πεποίηκεν ὁ νομοθέτης. καὶ οὕτως ἰσχυρῶς ἀπι-
στεῖ τοῖς ὑπευθύνοις, ὥστ᾽ εὐθὺς ἀρχόμενος τῶν
νόμων,⁴ "'Ἀρχὴν ὑπεύθυνον," φησί, "μὴ ἀποδημεῖν" "'Ὦ Ἡράκλεις," ὑπολάβοι ἄν τις, "ὅτι
ἦρξα, μὴ ἀποδημήσω;" ἵνα γε μὴ προλαβὼν χρήματα τῆς πόλεως ἢ πράξεις δρασμῷ χρήσῃ. πάλιν
ὑπεύθυνον οὐκ ἐᾷ τὴν οὐσίαν καθιεροῦν, οὐδὲ
ἀνάθημα ἀναθεῖναι, οὐδ᾽ ἐκποίητον γενέσθαι, οὐδὲ
διαθέσθαι τὰ ἑαυτοῦ, οὐδ᾽ ἄλλα πολλά· ἑνὶ δὲ
λόγῳ ἐνεχυράζει τὰς οὐσίας ὁ νομοθέτης τὰς τῶν
ὑπευθύνων, ἕως ἂν λόγον ἀποδῶσι τῇ πόλει.
22 "Ναί, ἀλλ᾽ ἔστι τις ἄνθρωπος ὃς οὔτ᾽ εἴληφεν
οὐδὲν τῶν δημοσίων οὔτ᾽ ἀνήλωκε, προσῆλθε δὲ
πρός τι τῶν κοινῶν." καὶ τοῦτον ἀποφέρειν
κελεύει λόγον πρὸς τοὺς λογιστάς. "Καὶ πῶς
ὅ γε μηδὲν λαβὼν μηδ᾽ ἀναλώσας ἀποίσει λόγον
τῇ πόλει;" αὐτὸς ὑποβάλλει καὶ διδάσκει ὁ νόμος

¹ τὴν . . . σκυθρωπὸν . . . κυρίαν Reiske: the MSS. have
τῶν . . . σκυθρωπῶν . . . κύριον or omit all between διδόναι and
ὑπό.   ² ἄγει H. Wolf: ἄγειν MSS.
³ αὐτοῖς Weidner: ἐστιν αὐτοῖς or αὐτοῖς ἐστιν MSS.
⁴ νόμων Cobet: νόμων λέγει MSS.

competence, are brought under your verdict. Shall the Senate of the Areopagus, then, receive no crown? They shall not, for such is not the tradition of our fathers. Have they, then, no love of honour? Indeed they have! They so love honour that they are not satisfied with merely keeping free from guilt, but they punish their members even for mistakes. But your politicians are pampered. Further, the lawgiver has made the Senate of Five Hundred subject to audit. And so deep is his distrust of those who are subject to audit, that he says at the very beginning of the laws, "The officer who has not yet submitted his accounts shall not leave the country." "Heracles!" some one may answer, "because I held an office may I not leave the country?" No, for fear you may make profit of the public money or the public acts, and then run away. Furthermore, the man who is subject to audit is not allowed to consecrate his property, or to make a votive offering, or to receive adoption,[1] or to dispose of his property by will; and he is under many other prohibitions. In a word, the lawgiver holds under attachment the property of all who are subject to audit, until their accounts shall have been audited. "Yes, but there is a man who has received no public funds and spent none, but has simply had something to do with administrative matters." He too is commanded to render account to the auditors. "And how shall the man who has received nothing and spent nothing render account to the state?" The law itself suggests and teaches

---

[1] An official who caused himself to be adopted into some family poorer than his own might thus diminish the security which the state would hold in case of his misconduct in office.

ἃ χρὴ γράφειν· κελεύει γὰρ αὐτὸ τοῦτο ἐγγράφειν, ὅτι "Οὔτ' ἔλαβον οὐδὲν τῶν τῆς πόλεως
οὔτ' ἀνήλωσα." ἀνυπεύθυνον δὲ καὶ ἀζήτητον
καὶ ἀνεξέταστον οὐδέν ἐστι τῶν ἐν τῇ πόλει.
ὅτι δὲ ἀληθῆ λέγω, αὐτῶν ἀκούσατε τῶν νόμων.

ΝΟΜΟΙ

23 "Οταν τοίνυν μάλιστα θρασύνηται Δημοσθένης,
λέγων ὡς διὰ τὴν ἐπίδοσιν οὐκ ἔστιν ὑπεύθυνος,
ἐκεῖνο αὐτῷ ὑποβάλλετε· Οὐκ οὖν ἐχρῆν σε,
ὦ Δημόσθενες, ἐᾶσαι τὸν τῶν λογιστῶν κήρυκα
κηρύξαι τὸ πάτριον καὶ ἔννομον κήρυγμα τοῦτο,
"Τίς βούλεται κατηγορεῖν;" ἔασον ἀμφισβητῆσαί
σοι τὸν βουλόμενον τῶν πολιτῶν, ὡς οὐκ ἐπέ-
δωκας, ἀλλ' ἀπὸ πολλῶν ὧν ἔχεις εἰς τὴν τῶν
τειχῶν οἰκοδομίαν μικρὰ κατέθηκας, δέκα τάλαντα
εἰς ταῦτα τῆς[1] πόλεως εἰληφώς. μὴ ἅρπαζε τὴν
φιλοτιμίαν, μηδὲ ἐξαιροῦ τῶν δικαστῶν τὰς ψήφους ἐκ τῶν χειρῶν, μηδ' ἔμπροσθεν τῶν νόμων,
ἀλλ' ὕστερος πολιτεύου. ταῦτα γὰρ ὀρθοῖ τὴν
δημοκρατίαν.

24 Πρὸς μὲν οὖν τὰς κενὰς[2] προφάσεις ἃς οὗτοι
προφασιοῦνται, μέχρι δεῦρο εἰρήσθω μοι· ὅτι δὲ
ὄντως ἦν ὑπεύθυνος ὁ Δημοσθένης, ὅθ' οὗτος
εἰσήνεγκε τὸ ψήφισμα, ἄρχων μὲν τὴν ἐπὶ τὸ
θεωρικὸν[3] ἀρχήν, ἄρχων δὲ τὴν τῶν τειχοποιῶν,
οὐδετέρας δέ πω τῶν ἀρχῶν τούτων λόγον ὑμῖν

---

[1] τῆς Blass : ἐκ τῆς MSS.
[2] κενὰς Stephanus : κοινὰς MSS.
[3] τὸ θεωρικὸν Blass, comparing Aristotle, Πολ. Ἀθ. 43, 1
and 47, 2 : τῷ θεωρικῷ MSS.

what he is to write; for it commands him to file precisely this statement, "I have neither received nor spent any public funds." There is nothing in all the state that is exempt from audit, investigation, and examination. As proof of what I say, hear the laws themselves.

THE LAWS

So when Demosthenes at the height of his impudence shall say that because the money was a gift he is not subject to audit, suggest this to him: Was it not, then, your duty, Demosthenes, to allow the herald of the Board of Auditors to make this proclamation, sanctioned by law and custom, "Who wishes to prefer charges?" Let any citizen who wishes have the opportunity to claim that you have given nothing, but that from the large sums under your control you have spent a mere trifle on the repair of the walls, whereas you have received ten talents from the city for this work. Do not grab honour; do not snatch the jurors' ballots from their hands; do not in your political career go before the laws, but follow them. For so is the democracy upheld.

As an answer then to the empty pretexts that they will bring forward, let what I have said suffice. But that Demosthenes was in fact subject to audit at the time when the defendant made his motion, since he held the office of Superintendent of the Theoric Fund [1] as well as the office of Commissioner for the Repair of Walls, and at that time had not rendered

---

[1] In time of peace all surplus revenue went into the festival fund (τὸ θεωρικόν), from which donations were made to the citizens on festival days. The fund was administered by an elective board of commissioners.

οὐδ' εὐθύνας δεδωκώς, ταῦτ' ἤδη πειράσομαι ὑμᾶς
διδάσκειν ἐκ τῶν δημοσίων γραμμάτων. καί μοι
ἀνάγνωθι, ἐπὶ τίνος ἄρχοντος καὶ ποίου μηνὸς καὶ
ἐν τίνι ἡμέρᾳ καὶ ἐν ποίᾳ ἐκκλησίᾳ ἐχειροτονήθη
Δημοσθένης τὴν ἀρχὴν τὴν ἐπὶ τὸ θεωρικόν.[1]

ΔΙΑΛΟΓΙΣΜΟΣ ΤΩΝ ΗΜΕΡΩΝ

Οὐκοῦν εἰ μηδὲν ἔτι περαιτέρω[2] δείξαιμι,
δικαίως ἂν ἁλίσκοιτο Κτησιφῶν· αἱρεῖ γὰρ αὐτὸν
οὐχ ἡ κατηγορία ἡ ἐμή, ἀλλὰ τὰ δημόσια γράμματα.

25 Πρότερον μὲν τοίνυν, ὦ ἄνδρες Ἀθηναῖοι, ἀντι-
γραφεὺς ἦν χειροτονητὸς τῇ πόλει, ὃς καθ' ἑκάστην
πρυτανείαν ἀπελογίζετο τὰς προσόδους τῷ δήμῳ·
διὰ δὲ τὴν πρὸς Εὔβουλον γενομένην πίστιν ὑμῖν
οἱ ἐπὶ τὸ θεωρικὸν κεχειροτονημένοι ἦρχον μέν,
πρὶν ἢ τὸν Ἡγήμονος νόμον γενέσθαι, τὴν τοῦ
ἀντιγραφέως ἀρχήν, ἦρχον δὲ τὴν τῶν ἀποδεκτῶν,
καὶ νεωρίων ἦρχον,[3] καὶ σκευοθήκην ᾠκοδόμουν,
ἦσαν δὲ καὶ ὁδοποιοί, καὶ σχεδὸν τὴν ὅλην διοί-
26 κησιν εἶχον τῆς πόλεως. καὶ οὐ κατηγορῶν αὐτῶν
οὐδ' ἐπιτιμῶν λέγω, ἀλλ' ἐκεῖνο ὑμῖν ἐνδείξασθαι
βουλόμενος,[4] ὅτι ὁ μὲν νομοθέτης, ἐάν τις μιᾶς
ἀρχῆς τῆς ἐλαχίστης ὑπεύθυνος ᾖ, τοῦτον οὐκ
ἐᾷ, πρὶν ἂν λόγον[5] καὶ εὐθύνας δῷ, στεφανοῦν,
Κτησιφῶν δὲ[6] Δημοσθένην τὸν συλλήβδην ἁπάσας
τὰς Ἀθήνησιν ἀρχὰς ἄρχοντα οὐκ ὤκνησε γράψαι
στεφανῶσαι.

[1] τὸ θεωρικόν Blass : τῷ θεωρικῷ or τῶν θεωρικῶν MSS.
[2] περαιτέρω Weidner : τούτου περαιτέρω or περαιτέρω τούτου
MSS.   [3] νεωρίων ἦρχον Kaibel : νεωρίων ἀρχήν MSS.
[4] βουλόμενος Cobet : βούλομαι MSS.

to you his account and reckoning for either office, this I will now try to show you from the public records. Read, if you please, in what archonship and in what month and on what day and in what assembly Demosthenes was elected a Superintendent of the Theoric Fund.

ENUMERATION OF THE DAYS

If now I should prove nothing beyond this, Ctesiphon would be justly convicted, for it is not my complaint that convicts him, but the public records.

In earlier times, fellow citizens, the city used to elect a Comptroller of the Treasury, who every prytany made to the people a report of the revenues. But because of the trust which you placed in Eubulus, those who were elected Superintendents of the Theoric Fund held (until the law of Hegemon was passed) the office of Comptroller of the Treasury and the office of Receiver of Moneys; they also controlled the dockyards, had charge of the naval arsenal that was building, and were Superintendents of Streets; almost the whole administration of the state was in their hands. I say this, not to accuse or blame them, but because I wish to show you this: that while the lawgiver, in case any one is subject to audit for a single office—though it be the least— does not permit him to be crowned until he has rendered his account and submitted to audit, Ctesiphon did not hesitate to move to crown Demosthenes, who was holding all the offices in Athens at once.

---

⁵ λόγον Scheibe : λόγους MSS.
⁶ Κτησιφῶν δὲ Blass : ὁ δὲ Κτησιφῶν MSS.

27 Ὡς τοίνυν καὶ τὴν τῶν τειχοποιῶν ἀρχὴν ἦρχεν,
ὅθ᾽ οὗτος τὸ ψήφισμα ἔγραψε, καὶ τὰ δημόσια
χρήματα διεχείριζε, καὶ ἐπιβολὰς ἐπέβαλλε,
καθάπερ οἱ ἄλλοι ἄρχοντες, καὶ δικαστηρίων
ἡγεμονίας ἐλάμβανε, τούτων ὑμῖν αὐτὸν Δημοσθένην μάρτυρα[1] παρέξομαι. ἐπὶ γὰρ Χαιρώνδου
ἄρχοντος, Θαργηλιῶνος μηνὸς δευτέρᾳ φθίνοντος,
ἐκκλησίας οὔσης ἔγραψε Δημοσθένης ἀγορὰν
ποιῆσαι τῶν φυλῶν Σκιροφοριῶνος δευτέρᾳ ἱσταμένου καὶ τρίτῃ, καὶ ἐπέταξεν ἐν τῷ ψηφίσματι
ἑκάστης τῶν φυλῶν ἑλέσθαι τοὺς ἐπιμελησομένους
τῶν ἔργων ἐπὶ τὰ τείχη καὶ ταμίας, καὶ μάλα
ὀρθῶς, ἵν᾽ ἡ πόλις ἔχοι ὑπεύθυνα σώματα παρ᾽
ὧν ἔμελλε τῶν ἀνηλωμένων λόγον ἀπολήψεσθαι.
καί μοι λέγε τὸ ψήφισμα.[2]

ΨΗΦΙΣΜΑ[3]

28 Ναί, ἀλλ᾽ ἀντιδιαπλέκει πρὸς τοῦτο εὐθὺς
λέγων ὡς οὔτ᾽ ἔλαχε τειχοποιὸς οὔτ᾽ ἐχειροτονήθη
ὑπὸ τοῦ δήμου. καὶ περὶ τούτου Δημοσθένης μὲν
καὶ Κτησιφῶν πολὺν ποιήσονται λόγον· ὁ δέ γε
νόμος βραχὺς καὶ σαφὴς καὶ ταχὺ λύων τὰς
τούτων τέχνας. μικρὰ δὲ ὑμῖν ὑπὲρ αὐτῶν πρῶ-
29 τον προειπεῖν βούλομαι. ἔστι γάρ, ὦ ἄνδρες Ἀθηναῖοι, τῶν περὶ τὰς ἀρχὰς εἴδη τρία, ὧν ἓν μὲν
καὶ πᾶσι φανερώτατον οἱ κληρωτοὶ καὶ οἱ χειρο-
τονητοὶ ἄρχοντες, δεύτερον δὲ ὅσοι τι διαχειρίζουσι
τῶν τῆς πόλεως ὑπὲρ τριάκοντα ἡμέρας καὶ οἱ

---

[1] Δημοσθένην μάρτυρα Hamaker : Δημοσθένην μάρτυρα καὶ
Κτησιφῶντα or Δημοσθένην καὶ Κτησιφῶντα μάρτυρας MSS.

[2] τὸ ψήφισμα Franke : τὰ ψηφίσματα MSS.

[3] ΨΗΦΙΣΜΑ Franke : the MSS. have the plural, or omit
the title.

Furthermore I will present to you Demosthenes himself as witness to the fact that at the time when Ctesiphon made his motion, Demosthenes was holding the office of Commissioner for the Repair of Walls, and so was handling public funds, imposing fines like the other magistrates, and privileged to preside in court.[1] For in the archonship of Chaerondas, on the last day but one of Thargelion,[2] Demosthenes made a motion in the assembly that on the second and third days of Skirophorion assemblies of the tribes be held ; and he directed in his decree that men be chosen from each tribe as superintendents and treasurers for the work upon the walls ; and very properly, that the city might have responsible persons upon whom to call for an accounting of the money spent. Please read the decree.

DECREE

Yes, but he immediately tries to wriggle out of this by saying that it was not the people who elected him, or appointed him by lot, as Commissioner of Walls. On this point Demosthenes and Ctesiphon will argue at length. But the law is brief and clear and it makes short work of their devices. I wish first to speak to you briefly about this. There are, fellow citizens, three classes of public officers. The first and most obvious class are all who are appointed by lot or by election ; the second class are those who administer some public business for more than thirty

---

[1] See on § 14.
[2] The spring of 337, nine months after the battle of Chaeronea. Skirophorion was the next month after Thargelion.

τῶν δημοσίων ἔργων ἐπιστάται, τρίτον δ' ἐν τῷ
νόμῳ γέγραπται, καὶ εἴ τινες ἄλλοι [1] ἡγεμονίας
δικαστηρίων λαμβάνουσι, "καὶ τούτους ἄρχειν
30 δοκιμασθέντας." ἐπειδὰν δ' ἀφέλῃ τις τοὺς ὑπὸ
τοῦ δήμου κεχειροτονημένους καὶ τοὺς κληρωτοὺς
ἄρχοντας, καταλείπονται οὓς αἱ φυλαὶ καὶ αἱ
τριττύες καὶ οἱ δῆμοι ἐξ ἑαυτῶν αἱροῦνται τὰ
δημόσια χρήματα διαχειρίζειν.[2] τοῦτο δὲ γίγνεται,
ὅταν, ὥσπερ νῦν, ἐπιταχθῇ τι ταῖς φυλαῖς, ἢ
τάφρους ἐξεργάζεσθαι ἢ τριήρεις ναυπηγεῖσθαι.
ὅτι δὲ ἀληθῆ λέγω, ἐξ αὐτῶν τῶν νόμων μαθήσεσθε.

NOMOI

31 Ἀναμνήσθητε δὴ τοὺς προειρημένους λόγους,
ὅτι ὁ μὲν νομοθέτης τοὺς ἐκ τῶν φυλῶν ἄρχειν
κελεύει δοκιμασθέντας ἐν τῷ δικαστηρίῳ, ἡ δὲ
Πανδιονὶς φυλὴ ἄρχοντα καὶ τειχοποιὸν ἀπέδειξε
Δημοσθένην, ὃς ἐκ τῆς διοικήσεως εἰς ταῦτα ἔχει
μικροῦ δεῖν δέκα τάλαντα, ἕτερος δ' ἀπαγορεύει
νόμος ἀρχὴν ὑπεύθυνον μὴ στεφανοῦν, ὑμεῖς δὲ
ὀμωμόκατε κατὰ τοὺς νόμους ψηφιεῖσθαι, ὁ δὲ
ῥήτωρ γέγραφε τὸν ὑπεύθυνον στεφανοῦν, οὐ
προσθεὶς "ἐπειδὰν δῷ λόγον καὶ εὐθύνας," ἐγὼ
δὲ ἐξελέγχω τὸ παράνομον μάρτυρας ἅμα τοὺς
νόμους καὶ τὰ ψηφίσματα καὶ τοὺς ἀντιδίκους

---

[1] ἄλλοι Cobet: ἄλλοι αἱρετοὶ MSS.
[2] διαχειρίζειν Scheibe: διαχειρίζειν τούτους αἱρετοὺς ἄρχοντας
εἶναι MSS.

days, and the Commissioners of Public Works; but third it stands written in the law that if any others receive presidencies of courts,[1] they also shall "hold office on passing their scrutiny." Now when you subtract those officials who are chosen by popular election and those appointed by lot, there remain those whom the tribes, the trittyes,[2] and the demes appoint from among their own number to administer public funds. This happens when, as in the present case, some work is assigned to the several tribes, like the digging of trenches or the building of triremes. That what I say is true, you shall learn from the laws themselves.

THE LAWS

Recall now what has been said: the lawgiver directs that after approval in court[3] those appointed by the tribes shall "hold office"; but the tribe Pandionis appointed Demosthenes an "officer," a Builder of Walls; and he has received for this work from the general treasury nearly ten talents. Another law forbids crowning an official before he has rendered his accounts, and you have sworn to vote according to the laws; but yonder politician has moved to crown the man who has not yet rendered his accounts, and he has not added "when he shall have rendered account and submitted to audit"; and I convict him of the unlawful act, bringing as my witnesses the laws, the decrees, and the

[1] See on § 14.

[2] A trittys was a third of a tribe, and was composed of a group of adjoining demes. The division was recognized for certain administrative purposes.

[3] The court for the scrutiny of incoming officers. See on § 15.

παρεχόμενος. πῶς οὖν ἄν τις περιφανέστερον
ἐπιδείξειεν ἄνθρωπον παράνομα γεγραφότα;

32 Ὡς τοίνυν καὶ τὴν ἀνάρρησιν τοῦ στεφάνου
παρανόμως ἐν τῷ ψηφίσματι κελεύει γίγνεσθαι,
καὶ τοῦθ᾽ ὑμᾶς διδάξω. ὁ γὰρ νόμος διαρρήδην
κελεύει, ἐὰν μέν τινα στεφανοῖ ἡ βουλή, ἐν τῷ
βουλευτηρίῳ ἀνακηρύττεσθαι, ἐὰν δὲ ὁ δῆμος, ἐν
τῇ ἐκκλησίᾳ, "ἄλλοθι δὲ μηδαμοῦ." καί μοι
λέγε τὸν νόμον.

NOMOΣ

33 Οὗτος ὁ νόμος, ὦ ἄνδρες Ἀθηναῖοι, καὶ μάλα
καλῶς ἔχει. οὐ γὰρ οἶμαι ᾤετο δεῖν ὁ νομοθέτης
τὸν ῥήτορα σεμνύνεσθαι πρὸς τοὺς ἔξωθεν, ἀλλ᾽
ἀγαπᾶν ἐν αὐτῇ τῇ πόλει τιμώμενον ὑπὸ τοῦ
δήμου, καὶ μὴ ἐργολαβεῖν ἐν τοῖς κηρύγμασιν.
ὁ μὲν οὖν νομοθέτης οὕτως· ὁ δὲ Κτησιφῶν πῶς;
ἀναγίγνωσκε τὸ ψήφισμα.

ΨΗΦΙΣΜΑ

34 Ἀκούετε, ὦ ἄνδρες Ἀθηναῖοι, ὅτι ὁ μὲν νομοθέτης κελεύει ἐν τῷ δήμῳ ἐν Πυκνὶ τῇ ἐκκλησίᾳ
ἀνακηρύττειν τὸν ὑπὸ τοῦ δήμου στεφανούμενον,
"ἄλλοθι δὲ μηδαμοῦ," Κτησιφῶν δὲ ἐν τῷ θεάτρῳ,
οὐ τοὺς νόμους μόνον ὑπερβάς, ἀλλὰ καὶ τὸν
τόπον μετενεγκών, οὐδὲ ἐκκλησιαζόντων Ἀθηναίων, ἀλλὰ τραγῳδῶν γιγνομένων, οὐδ᾽ ἐναντίον
τοῦ δήμου, ἀλλ᾽ ἐναντίον τῶν Ἑλλήνων, ἵν᾽ ἡμῖν
συνειδῶσιν οἷον ἄνδρα τιμῶμεν.

35 Οὕτω τοίνυν περιφανῶς παράνομα γεγραφώς,
παραταχθεὶς μετὰ Δημοσθένους ἐποίσει τέχνας

defendants. How could one more clearly prove that a man has made an unlawful motion?

Furthermore, I will show you that the proclamation of the crown, as proposed in his decree, is to be made in an illegal manner. For the law expressly commands that if the Senate confer a crown, the crown shall be proclaimed in the senate-house, and if the people confer it, in the assembly, "and nowhere else." Read me the law.

LAW

This, fellow citizens, is an excellent law. For it seems that it was the idea of the lawgiver that the public man ought not to be thinking of outsiders as he receives his honours, but to be well content with honour received in the city itself and from the people; and that he ought not to treat such proclamations as a source of revenue. So thought the lawgiver. But Ctesiphon how? Read his decree.

DECREE

You hear, fellow citizens, how the lawgiver commands that the man who is crowned by the people be proclaimed among the people, on the Pnyx, at a meeting of the assembly, "and nowhere else"; but Ctesiphon, in the theatre—not only overriding the laws but also changing the place; not when the Athenians are in assembly, but when tragedies are being performed; not in the presence of the people, but in the presence of the Hellenes, that they also may know what sort of man we honour.

Having, then, made a motion that is so manifestly illegal, he will call Demosthenes as his ally and bring up the artifices of rhetoric for the assault on the laws.

τοῖς νόμοις· ἃς ἐγὼ δηλώσω καὶ προερῶ ὑμῖν,
ἵνα μὴ λάθητε ἐξαπατηθέντες.

Οὗτοι γάρ, ὡς μὲν οὐκ ἀπαγορεύουσιν οἱ νόμοι
τὸν ὑπὸ τοῦ δήμου στεφανούμενον μὴ κηρύττειν
ἔξω τῆς ἐκκλησίας, οὐχ ἕξουσι λέγειν, οἴσουσι δὲ
εἰς τὴν ἀπολογίαν τὸν Διονυσιακὸν νόμον, καὶ
χρήσονται τοῦ νόμου μέρει τινὶ κλέπτοντες τὴν
36 ἀκρόασιν ὑμῶν, καὶ παρέξονται νόμον οὐδὲν
προσήκοντα τῇδε τῇ γραφῇ, καὶ λέξουσιν ὡς εἰσὶ
τῇ πόλει δύο νόμοι κείμενοι περὶ τῶν κηρυγμάτων,
εἷς μέν, ὃν νῦν ἐγὼ παρέχομαι, διαρρήδην ἀπα-
γορεύων τὸν ὑπὸ τοῦ δήμου στεφανούμενον μὴ
κηρύττεσθαι ἔξω τῆς ἐκκλησίας, ἕτερον δ᾽ εἶναι
νόμον φήσουσιν ἐναντίον τούτῳ, τὸν δεδωκότα
ἐξουσίαν ποιεῖσθαι τὴν ἀνάρρησιν τοῦ στεφάνου
τραγῳδοῖς ἐν τῷ θεάτρῳ, "ἐὰν ψηφίσηται ὁ
δῆμος"· κατὰ δὴ τοῦτον τὸν νόμον φήσουσι
γεγραφέναι τὸν Κτησιφῶντα.

37 Ἐγὼ δὲ πρὸς τὰς τούτων τέχνας παρέξομαι
συνηγόρους τοὺς νόμους τοὺς ὑμετέρους, ὅπερ
διατελῶ σπουδάζων παρὰ πᾶσαν τὴν κατηγορίαν.
εἰ γὰρ τοῦτό ἐστιν ἀληθές, καὶ τοιοῦτον ἔθος
παραδέδυκεν ὑμῶν εἰς τὴν πολιτείαν, ὥστ᾽ ἀκύρους
νόμους ἐν τοῖς κυρίοις ἀναγεγράφθαι, καὶ δύο περὶ
μιᾶς πράξεως ὑπεναντίους ἀλλήλοις, τί ἂν ἔτι
ταύτην εἴποι τις εἶναι πολιτείαν,[1] ἐν ᾗ ταὐτὰ
προστάττουσιν οἱ νόμοι ποιεῖν καὶ μὴ ποιεῖν;
38 ἀλλ᾽ οὐκ ἔχει ταῦθ᾽ οὕτως· μήθ᾽ ὑμεῖς ποτε εἰς
τοσαύτην ἀταξίαν τῶν νόμων προβαίνητε, οὔτε
ἠμέληται περὶ τῶν τοιούτων τῷ νομοθέτῃ τῷ
τὴν δημοκρατίαν καταστήσαντι, ἀλλὰ διαρρήδην

πολιτείαν Poutsma : τὴν πολιτείαν MSS.

These tricks I will reveal and of these I will fore-warn you, lest you be taken unawares and deceived.

They will not be able to deny that the laws forbid the man who is crowned by the people to be pro-claimed outside the assembly, but they will present for their defence the Dionysiac law, and will use a certain portion of the law, cheating your ears. For they will offer a law that has nothing to do with this case, and will say that the city has two laws govern-ing proclamations: one, the law that I now offer in evidence, which expressly forbids the man who is crowned by the people to be proclaimed outside the assembly; but they will say that there is another law, contradictory to this, and that that law has given authority for the proclamation of the crown at the time of the tragedies in the theatre, "if the people vote." And so they will say that it is in accordance with that law that Ctesiphon has made his motion.

Now against their tricks I will introduce your own laws as my advocates, as indeed I earnestly try to do throughout this whole prosecution. For if what they say is true, and such a custom has crept into your government that invalid laws stand written among the valid, and that there exist two laws con-cerning one and the same action, which contradict each other, how could any man longer call this a "government," if in it the laws command to do and not to do one and the same thing? But that is not the case. May you never reach the point where your laws are in such disorder as that! Nor was the law-giver who established the democracy guilty of such

προστέτακται τοῖς θεσμοθέταις καθ᾽ ἕκαστον
ἐνιαυτὸν διορθοῦν ἐν τῷ δήμῳ τοὺς νόμους, ἀκριβῶς ἐξετάσαντας καὶ σκεψαμένους, εἴ τις ἀναγέγραπται νόμος ἐναντίος ἑτέρῳ νόμῳ, ἢ ἄκυρος
ἐν τοῖς κυρίοις, ἢ εἴ που εἰσὶ νόμοι πλείους ἑνὸς
39 ἀναγεγραμμένοι περὶ ἑκάστης πράξεως. κἄν τι
τοιοῦτον εὑρίσκωσιν, ἀναγεγραφότας ἐν σανίσιν
ἐκτιθέναι κελεύει πρόσθεν τῶν ἐπωνύμων, τοὺς δὲ
πρυτάνεις ποιεῖν ἐκκλησίαν ἐπιγράψαντας νομοθέταις,[1] τὸν δ᾽ ἐπιστάτην τῶν προέδρων διαχειρο-
τονίαν διδόναι[2] τοὺς μὲν[3] ἀναιρεῖν τῶν νόμων,
τοὺς δὲ καταλείπειν, ὅπως ἂν εἷς ᾖ νόμος καὶ μὴ
πλείους περὶ ἑκάστης πράξεως. καί μοι λέγε
τοὺς νόμους.

NOMOI

40 Εἰ τοίνυν, ὦ ἄνδρες Ἀθηναῖοι, ἀληθὴς ἦν ὁ
παρὰ τούτων λόγος, καὶ ἦσαν δύο κείμενοι νόμοι
περὶ τῶν κηρυγμάτων, ἐξ ἀνάγκης οἶμαι τῶν μὲν
θεσμοθετῶν ἐξευρόντων, τῶν δὲ πρυτάνεων ἀπο-
δόντων τοῖς νομοθέταις ἀνῄρητ᾽ ἂν ὁ ἕτερος τῶν

[1] νομοθέταις Dobree : νομοθέτας MSS.
[2] διδόναι Schöll : διδόναι τῷ δήμῳ MSS.
[3] τοὺς μὲν Kaibel : καὶ τοὺς μὲν MSS.

---

[1] The Thesmothetae were the six lower archons. They
had general supervision of all the courts, and particular
control of numerous specified cases.

[2] The regular place for posting many of the public notices
was in front of the statues of the ten heroes for whom the
tribes were named. The statues stood on the Agora, near
the senate-house and the Tholos.

neglect; he has expressly laid upon the Thesmothetae[1] the duty of making an annual revision of the laws in the presence of the people, prescribing sharp investigation and examination, in order to determine whether any law stands written which contradicts another law, or an invalid law stands among the valid, or whether more laws than one stand written to govern each action. And if they find such a thing, they are required to write it out and post it on bulletins in front of the Eponymi;[2] and the prytanes are required to call a meeting of the assembly, writing at the head of the call, "For Nomothetae";[3] and the chairman of the presiding officers must submit to vote[4] the question of the removal of one set of laws and the retention of the other, in order that for each action there may be one law and no more. Please read the laws.

LAWS

If now, fellow citizens, what they assert were true, and two laws had been in force governing proclamations, I think the Thesmothetae would necessarily have searched them out, and the prytanes would have referred them to the Nomothetae, and one or the other of the two laws would have been repealed, either

---

[3] The Nomothetae were a special commission, chosen by lot from among the jurors of the year, to whom were referred with power all proposed changes in the fundamental laws ($\nu\acute{o}\mu o\iota$) or additions to them.

[4] The people having approved the proposition to appoint Nomothetae, and that body having been duly constituted, and having heard the arguments on either side, the presiding officer of the Nomothetae finally put to vote the question of the retention of the laws in their old form, or the adoption of the changes proposed ($\delta\iota\alpha\chi\epsilon\iota\rho\sigma\tau\sigma\nu\acute{\iota}\alpha$).

νόμων, ἤτοι ὁ τὴν ἐξουσίαν δεδωκὼς ἀνειπεῖν ἢ ὁ
ἀπαγορεύων· ὁπότε δὲ μηδὲν τούτων γεγένηται,
φανερῶς δή που ἐξελέγχονται οὐ μόνον ψευδῆ
λέγοντες, ἀλλὰ καὶ παντελῶς ἀδύνατα γενέσθαι.

41 Ὅθεν δὲ τὸ ψεῦδος τοῦτο ἐπιφέρουσιν, ἐγὼ
διδάξω ὑμᾶς, προειπὼν ὧν ἕνεκα οἱ νόμοι ἐτέθησαν
οἱ περὶ τῶν ἐν τῷ θεάτρῳ κηρυγμάτων. γιγνομένων γὰρ τῶν ἐν ἄστει τραγῳδῶν ἀνεκήρυττόν
τινες, οὐ πείσαντες τὸν δῆμον, οἱ μὲν ὅτι στεφανοῦνται ὑπὸ τῶν φυλετῶν, ἕτεροι δ' ὅτι[1] ὑπὸ τῶν
δημοτῶν· ἄλλοι δέ τινες ὑποκηρυξάμενοι τοὺς
αὑτῶν οἰκέτας ἀφίεσαν ἐλευθέρους,[2] μάρτυρας[3]
42 τοὺς Ἕλληνας ποιούμενοι. ὃ δ' ἦν ἐπιφθονώτατον,
προξενίας εὑρημένοι τινὲς ἐν ταῖς ἔξω πόλεσι,
διεπράττοντο ἀναγορεύεσθαι ὅτι στεφανοῖ αὐτοὺς
ὁ δῆμος, εἰ οὕτω τύχοι, ὁ τῶν Ῥοδίων ἢ Χίων ἢ
καί τινος ἄλλης πόλεως, ἀρετῆς ἕνεκα καὶ ἀνδραγαθίας. καὶ ταῦτ' ἔπραττον, οὐχ ὥσπερ οἱ ὑπὸ
τῆς βουλῆς τῆς ὑμετέρας στεφανούμενοι ἢ ὑπὸ τοῦ
δήμου, πείσαντες ὑμᾶς καὶ μετὰ ψηφίσματος, πολλὴν χάριν καταθέμενοι, ἀλλ' αὐτοὶ προελόμενοι,
43 ἄνευ δόγματος ὑμετέρου. ἐκ δὲ τούτου τοῦ τρόπου
συνέβαινε τοὺς μὲν θεατὰς καὶ τοὺς χορηγοὺς καὶ
τοὺς ἀγωνιστὰς ἐνοχλεῖσθαι, τοὺς δὲ ἀνακηρυττο-
μένους ἐν τῷ θεάτρῳ μείζοσι τιμαῖς τιμᾶσθαι τῶν
ὑπὸ τοῦ δήμου στεφανουμένων. τοῖς μὲν γὰρ
ἀπεδέδεικτο τόπος ἡ ἐκκλησία, ἐν ᾗ χρῆν στεφανοῦσθαι, καὶ ἀπείρητο ἄλλοθι μηδαμοῦ κηρύτ-

---

[1] ὅτι added by Cobet.
[2] ἐλευθέρους Cobet : ἀπελευθέρους MSS.
[3] μάρτυρας Cobet : the MSS. have τῆς ἀπελευθερίας after
μάρτυρας or after Ἕλληνας.

the law that gave authority for the proclamation, or the law that forbade it. But seeing that no such thing has been done, surely what they say is demonstrated to be, not only false, but absolutely impossible.

But I will show you where they get this false assertion. First, however, I will tell the reason why the laws governing the proclamations in the theatre were enacted. It frequently happened that at the performance of the tragedies in the city proclamations were made without authorization of the people, now that this or that man was crowned by his tribe, now that others were crowned by the men of their deme, while other men by the voice of the herald manumitted their household slaves, and made all Hellas their witness; and, most invidious of all, certain men who had secured positions as agents of foreign states managed to have proclaimed that they were crowned —it might be by the people of Rhodes, or of Chios, or of some other state—in recognition of their merit and uprightness. And this they did, not like those who were crowned by your senate or by the people, by first obtaining your consent and by your decree, and after establishing large claims upon your gratitude, but themselves reaching out after the honour with no authorization from you. The result of this practice was that the spectators, the choregi, and the actors alike were discommoded, and that those who were crowned in the theatre received greater honours than those whom the people crowned. For the latter had a place prescribed where they must receive their crown, the assembly of the people, and proclamation "anywhere else" was forbidden; but

τεσθαι· οἱ δὲ ἀνηγορεύοντο ἐναντίον¹ ἁπάντων
τῶν Ἑλλήνων· κἀκεῖνοι μὲν μετὰ ψηφίσματος,
πείσαντες ὑμᾶς, οὗτοι δ' ἄνευ ψηφίσματος.

44 Συνιδὼν δή τις ταῦτα νομοθέτης, τίθησι νόμον
οὐδὲν ἐπικοινωνοῦντα τῷ περὶ τῶν ὑπὸ τοῦ δήμου
στεφανουμένων νόμῳ, οὔτε λύσας ἐκεῖνον· οὐδὲ
γὰρ ἡ ἐκκλησία ἠνωχλεῖτο, ἀλλὰ τὸ θέατρον· οὔτ'
ἐναντίον τοῖς πρότερον κειμένοις νόμοις τιθείς· οὐ
γὰρ ἔξεστιν· ἀλλὰ περὶ τῶν ἄνευ ψηφίσματος
ὑμετέρου στεφανουμένων ὑπὸ τῶν φυλετῶν καὶ
δημοτῶν, καὶ περὶ τῶν τοὺς οἰκέτας ἀπελευθε-
ρούντων, καὶ περὶ τῶν ξενικῶν στεφάνων, καὶ
διαρρήδην ἀπαγορεύει μήτ' οἰκέτην ἀπελευθεροῦν
ἐν τῷ θεάτρῳ, μήθ' ὑπὸ τῶν φυλετῶν ἢ δημοτῶν
ἀναγορεύεσθαι στεφανούμενον, "μήθ' ὑπ' ἄλλου,"
φησί, "μηδενός, ἢ ἄτιμον εἶναι τὸν κήρυκα.

45 Ὅταν οὖν ἀποδείξῃ τοῖς μὲν ὑπὸ τῆς βουλῆς
στεφανουμένοις τὸ² βουλευτήριον ἀναρρηθῆναι,
τοῖς δ' ὑπὸ τοῦ δήμου³ τὴν⁴ ἐκκλησίαν, τοῖς δ'
ὑπὸ τῶν δημοτῶν καὶ φυλετῶν ἀπείπῃ μὴ κηρύτ-
-τεσθαι τοῖς τραγῳδοῖς, ἵνα μηδεὶς ἐρανίζων στεφάνους καὶ κηρύγματα ψευδῆ φιλοτιμίαν κτᾶται,
προσαπείπῃ δ' ἐν τῷ νόμῳ μηδ' ὑπὸ ἄλλου
μηδενὸς ἀνακηρύττεσθαι, ἀπούσης βουλῆς καὶ
δήμου καὶ φυλετῶν καὶ δημοτῶν,—ὅταν δέ τις
ταῦτα ἀφέλῃ, τί τὸ καταλειπόμενόν ἐστι πλὴν οἱ
ξενικοὶ στέφανοι ;

46 Ὅτι δ' ἀληθῆ λέγω, σημεῖον ὑμῖν μέγα τούτου

¹ ἐναντίον Cobet : ἐνώπιον MSS.
² τὸ Usener : εἰς τὸ MSS.
³ δήμου . . . δημοτῶν Cobet : after each of these words the
MSS. have στεφανουμένοις.
⁴ τὴν Usener : εἰς τὴν MSS.

the others were proclaimed in the presence of all the Hellenes; the one class with your consent, by your decree; the other, without decree.

Now some legislator, seeing this, caused a law to be enacted which has nothing to do with the law concerning those who are crowned by our people, and did not supersede it. For it was not the assembly that was being disturbed, but the theatre; and he was not enacting a law contradictory to the previously existing laws, for that may not be done; but a law governing those who, without your decree, are crowned by their tribe or deme, and governing the freeing of slaves, and also the foreign crowns. He expressly forbids the manumission of a slave in the theatre, or the proclamation of a crown by the tribe or deme, "or by any one else," he says, "and the herald who disobeys shall lose his civic rights."

When, therefore, the lawgiver designates, for those who are crowned by the senate, the senate-house as the place of proclamation, and, for those who are crowned by the people, the assembly, and when he forbids those who are crowned by the demes or tribes to be proclaimed at the tragedies—that no one may try to get spurious honour by begging crowns and proclamations, and when in the law he further forbids proclamation being made by any one else, senate, people, tribe, and deme being thus eliminated—when one takes these away, what is it that is left except the foreign crowns?

For the truth of my assertion I will show you a

ἐξ αὐτῶν τῶν νόμων ἐπιδείξω. αὐτὸν γὰρ τὸν
χρυσοῦν στέφανον, ὃς ἂν ἐν τῷ θεάτρῳ τῷ ἐν
ἄστει ἀναρρηθῇ, ἱερὸν εἶναι τῆς Ἀθηνᾶς ὁ νόμος
κελεύει, ἀφελόμενος τὸν στεφανούμενον. καίτοι
τίς ἂν ὑμῶν τολμήσειε τοσαύτην ἀνελευθερίαν
καταγνῶναι τοῦ δήμου τοῦ Ἀθηναίων; μὴ γὰρ
ὅτι πόλις, ἀλλ᾽ οὐδ᾽ ἂν ἰδιώτης οὐδὲ εἷς οὕτως
ἀγεννὴς γένοιτο, ὥστε ὃν αὐτὸς ἔδωκε στέφανον
ἅμα ἀνακηρύττειν καὶ ἀφαιρεῖσθαι.[1] ἀλλ᾽ οἶμαι
διὰ τὸ ξενικὸν εἶναι τὸν στέφανον καὶ ἡ κα-
θιέρωσις γίγνεται, ἵνα μηδεὶς ἀλλοτρίαν εὔνοιαν
περὶ πλείονος ποιούμενος τῆς πατρίδος χείρων
47 γένηται τὴν ψυχήν. ἀλλ᾽ οὐκ ἐκεῖνον τὸν ἐν
τῇ ἐκκλησίᾳ ἀναρρηθέντα στέφανον οὐδεὶς κα-
θιεροῖ, ἀλλ᾽ ἔξεστι κεκτῆσθαι, ἵνα μὴ μόνον
αὐτός, ἀλλὰ καὶ οἱ ἐξ ἐκείνου, ἔχοντες ἐν τῇ
οἰκίᾳ τὸ ὑπόμνημα, μηδέποτε κακοὶ τὴν ψυχὴν
εἰς τὸν δῆμον γίγνωνται. καὶ διὰ τοῦτο προσέθηκεν ὁ νομοθέτης μὴ κηρύττεσθαι τὸν ἀλλότριον
στέφανον ἐν τῷ θεάτρῳ, "ἐὰν μὴ ψηφίσηται ὁ
δῆμος," ἵν᾽ ἡ πόλις ἡ βουλομένη τινὰ τῶν ὑμετέρων στεφανοῦν πρέσβεις πέμψασα δεηθῇ τοῦ
δήμου, καὶ ὁ[2] κηρυττόμενος μείζω χάριν εἰδῇ τῶν
στεφανούντων ὑμῖν,[3] ὅτι κηρύξαι ἐπετρέψατε.
ὅτι δ᾽ ἀληθῆ λέγω, τῶν νόμων αὐτῶν ἀκούσατε.

NOMOI

48 Ἐπειδὰν τοίνυν ἐξαπατῶντες ὑμᾶς λέγωσιν ὡς
προσγέγραπται ἐν τῷ νόμῳ ἐξεῖναι στεφανοῦν,
"ἐὰν ψηφίσηται ὁ δῆμος," ἀπομνημονεύετε αὐτοῖς

---

[1] ἀφαιρεῖσθαι Weidner : ἀφαιρεῖσθαι καὶ καθιεροῦν MSS.
[2] καὶ ὁ Halm : ἵνα MSS.
[3] ὑμῖν H. Wolf : ὑμῖν ἢ τοῖς στεφανοῦσιν MSS.

strong argument derived from the laws themselves. For the golden crown itself which is proclaimed in the city theatre the law takes from the man who is crowned, and commands that it be dedicated to Athena. And yet who among you would dare to charge the Athenian people with such illiberality? For certainly no state, nay, not even a private person —not one—would be so mean as to proclaim a crown and at the same moment demand back the gift which he himself had made. But I think it is because the crown is the gift of foreigners that the dedication is made, lest any one set a higher value upon the gratitude of a foreign state than upon that of his own country, and so become corrupted. But the other crown, the crown that is proclaimed in the assembly, no one dedicates, but he is permitted to keep it, that not only he, but also his descendants, having the memorial in their house, may never become disloyal to the democracy. And the reason why the lawgiver also forbade the proclamation of the foreign crown in the theatre "unless the people vote," is this: he would have the state that wishes to crown any one of your citizens send ambassadors and ask permission of the people, for so he who is proclaimed will be more grateful to you for permitting the proclamation than to those who confer the crown. But to show that my statements are true, hear the laws themselves.

LAWS

When, therefore, they try to deceive you, and say that it is added in the law that the bestowal of the crown is permitted "if the people vote," do not

ὑποβάλλειν· Ναί, εἴ γε σέ τις ἄλλη πόλις στε-
φανοῖ· εἰ δὲ ὁ δῆμος ὁ Ἀθηναίων, ἀποδέδεικταί
σοι τόπος ὅπου δεῖ τοῦτο γίγνεσθαι, ἀπείρηταί
σοι ἔξω τῆς ἐκκλησίας μὴ κηρύττεσθαι. τὸ γὰρ
"ἄλλοθι δὲ μηδαμοῦ" ὅ τι ἐστίν, ὅλην τὴν
ἡμέραν λέγε· οὐ γὰρ ἀποδείξεις ὡς ἔννομα γέγραφεν.

49 Ἔστι δὲ ὑπόλοιπόν μοι μέρος τῆς κατηγορίας
ἐφ' ᾧ μάλιστα σπουδάζω· τοῦτο δέ ἐστιν ἡ πρό-
φασις δι' ἣν αὐτὸν ἀξιοῖ στεφανοῦσθαι. λέγει
γὰρ οὕτως ἐν τῷ ψηφίσματι· "Καὶ τὸν κήρυκα
ἀναγορεύειν ἐν τῷ θεάτρῳ πρὸς τοὺς Ἕλληνας,
ὅτι στεφανοῖ αὐτὸν ὁ δῆμος ὁ Ἀθηναίων[1] ἀρετῆς
ἕνεκα καὶ ἀνδραγαθίας," καὶ τὸ μέγιστον· "ὅτι
διατελεῖ καὶ λέγων καὶ πράττων τὰ ἄριστα τῷ
50 δήμῳ." ἁπλοῦς δὴ παντάπασιν ὁ μετὰ ταῦτα
ἡμῖν λόγος γίγνεται, καὶ ὑμῖν ἀκούσασι κρῖναι
εὐμαθής· δεῖ γὰρ δή που τὸν μὲν κατηγοροῦντα
ἐμὲ τοῦθ' ὑμῖν ἐπιδεικνύναι, ὡς εἰσὶν οἱ κατὰ
Δημοσθένους ἔπαινοι ψευδεῖς, καὶ ὡς οὔτ' ἤρξατο
"λέγειν τὰ βέλτιστα," οὔτε νῦν "διατελεῖ πράττων τὰ συμφέροντα τῷ δήμῳ." κἂν τοῦτ' ἐπιδείξω,
δικαίως δή που τὴν γραφὴν ἁλώσεται Κτησιφῶν·
ἅπαντες γὰρ ἀπαγορεύουσιν οἱ νόμοι μηδένα
ψευδῆ γράμματα ἐγγράφειν ἐν τοῖς δημοσίοις
ψηφίσμασι. τῷ δ' ἀπολογουμένῳ τοὐναντίον
τούτου δεικτέον ἐστίν. ὑμεῖς δ' ἡμῖν ἔσεσθε τῶν
λόγων κριταί.

51 Ἔχει δ' οὕτως. ἐγὼ τὸν μὲν ἴδιον[2] βίον τὸν
Δημοσθένους ἐξετάζειν μακροτέρου λόγου ἔργον

---

[1] ὁ Ἀθηναίων Weidner : ὁ τῶν Ἀθηναίων MSS.
[2] ἴδιον added by Herwerden.

forget to suggest to them, Yes, if it is another state that is crowning you; but if it is the Athenian people, a place is designated for you where the ceremony must be performed; it is forbidden you to be crowned outside the assembly. For you may spend the whole day in explaining the meaning of the words "and nowhere else"; you will never show that his motion is lawful.

But that part of my accusation remains upon which I lay greatest stress: the pretext upon which he claims that the crown is deserved. It reads thus in his motion: "And the herald shall proclaim in the theatre in the presence of the Hellenes that the Athenian people crown him for his merit and uprightness," and that monstrous assertion, "because he continually speaks and does what is best for the people." You see how entirely simple the remainder of our argument becomes, and how easy for you, my hearers, to weigh. For it is obviously incumbent upon me, the complainant, to show this to you, that the praise given to Demosthenes is false, and that he never began to "speak what was best," nor now "continues to do what is good for the people." If I show this, then Ctesiphon will doubtless lose his case, and justly; for all the laws forbid inserting falsehoods in the decrees of the people. But the defence must show the opposite of this. And you are to be the judges of our pleas.

The case is this: To review the private life of Demosthenes would, in my opinion, demand too long

ἡγοῦμαι. τί γὰρ δεῖ νῦν ταῦτα λέγειν, ἢ τὰ περὶ
τὴν τοῦ τραύματος γραφὴν αὐτῷ συμβεβηκότα,
ὅτ᾽ ἐγράψατο εἰς Ἄρειον πάγον Δημομέλην τὸν
Παιανιέα, ἀνεψιὸν ὄντα ἑαυτῷ, καὶ τὴν τῆς κεφα-
λῆς ἐπιτομήν· ἢ τὰ περὶ τὴν Κηφισοδότου στρατηγίαν καὶ τὸν τῶν νεῶν ἔκπλουν τὸν εἰς Ἑλλήσ-
52 ποντον, ὅτε εἷς ὢν τῶν τριηράρχων Δημοσθένης,
καὶ περιάγων τὸν στρατηγὸν ἐπὶ τῆς νεώς, καὶ
συσσιτῶν καὶ συνθύων καὶ συσπένδων, τούτων [1]
ἀξιωθεὶς διὰ τὸ πατρικὸς αὐτῷ φίλος εἶναι, οὐκ
ὤκνησεν ἀπ᾽ εἰσαγγελίας αὐτοῦ κρινομένου περὶ
θανάτου κατήγορος γενέσθαι· καὶ ταῦτα δὴ [2] τὰ
περὶ Μειδίαν καὶ τοὺς κονδύλους, οὓς ἔλαβεν ἐν
τῇ ὀρχήστρᾳ χορηγὸς ὤν, καὶ ὡς ἀπέδοτο τριάκοντα μνῶν ἅμα τήν τε εἰς αὑτὸν ὕβριν καὶ τὴν
τοῦ δήμου καταχειροτονίαν, ἣν ἐν Διονύσου κατε-
53 χειροτόνησε Μειδίου. ταῦτα μὲν οὖν μοι δοκῶ
καὶ τἆλλα τὰ τούτοις ὅμοια ὑπερβήσεσθαι, οὐ
προδιδοὺς ὑμᾶς οὐδὲ τὸν ἀγῶνα καταχαριζόμενος,
ἀλλ᾽ ἐκεῖνο φοβούμενος, μή μοι παρ᾽ ὑμῶν ἀπαν-
τήσῃ τὸ δοκεῖν ἀληθῆ μὲν [3] λέγειν, ἀρχαῖα δὲ καὶ
λίαν ὁμολογούμενα. καίτοι, ὦ Κτησιφῶν, ὅτῳ τὰ
μέγιστα τῶν αἰσχρῶν οὕτως ἐστὶ πιστὰ καὶ γνώριμα τοῖς ἀκούουσιν, ὥστε τὸν κατήγορον μὴ
δοκεῖν ψευδῆ λέγειν, ἀλλὰ παλαιὰ καὶ λίαν προ-

---

[1] τούτων Halm : καὶ τούτων MSS.
[2] δὴ Cobet : ἤδη MSS.
[3] ἀληθῆ μὲν Cobet : μὲν ἀληθῆ MSS.

---

[1] See ii. 93.
[2] Meidias was a rich and domineering man, who had conceived a bitter hatred for Demosthenes in the course of the
suits against Demosthenes' guardians. When Demosthenes

a speech. And why need I tell it all now? the story of what happened to him in the matter of the suit over the wound, when he summoned his own cousin, Demomeles of Paeania, before the Areopagus;[1] and the cut on his head; or the story of the generalship of Cephisodotus, and the naval expedition to the Hellespont, when Demosthenes as one of the trierarchs carried the general on his ship, and shared his table, his sacrifices, and his libations; and how after he had been thus honoured because the general was an old friend of his father's, he did not hesitate, when the general was impeached, and was on trial for his life, to become one of his accusers; or, again, that story about Meidias and the blow of the fist that Demosthenes got when he was choregus, in the orchestra, and how for thirty minas he sold both the insult to himself and the vote of censure that the people had passed against Meidias in the theatre of Dionysus.[2] Now these incidents and all the others like them I think it is best to pass over; not that I would betray you, gentlemen of the jury, or politely yield this case to him, but because I fear that I shall encounter in you the feeling that, while all this is true, it is an old story, admitted by everybody. And yet, Ctesiphon, when a man's utter shame is so credible to the hearers and so notorious that his accuser seems, not to be speaking what is false, but what is stale, and what everybody admits

was serving as choregus, Meidias, meeting him in the orchestra, in the presence of the spectators, struck him in the face. The people, at a meeting held in the theatre at the close of the festival, passed a vote of censure against Meidias, and Demosthenes instituted a suit in the courts; but finally, probably for worthy political reasons, he compromised the case.

ὡμολογημένα, πότερα αὐτὸν δεῖ χρυσῷ στεφάνῳ
στεφανωθῆναι, ἢ ψέγεσθαι; καὶ σὲ τὸν ψευδῆ καὶ
παράνομα τολμῶντα γράφειν πότερα χρὴ καταφρονεῖν τῶν δικαστηρίων, ἢ δίκην τῇ πόλει δοῦναι;

54   Περὶ δὲ τῶν δημοσίων ἀδικημάτων πειράσομαι
σαφέστερον εἰπεῖν.   καὶ γὰρ πυνθάνομαι μέλλειν
Δημοσθένην, ἐπειδὰν αὐτοῖς ὁ λόγος ἀποδοθῇ,
καταριθμεῖσθαι πρὸς ὑμᾶς, ὡς ἄρα τῇ πόλει τέτ-
ταρες ἤδη γεγένηνται καιροί, ἐν οἷς αὐτὸς πεπολί-
τευται.   ὧν ἕνα μὲν καὶ πρῶτον, ὡς ἔγωγε ἀκούω,
καταλογίζεται ἐκεῖνον τὸν χρόνον ἐν ᾧ πρὸς Φίλιππον ὑπὲρ Ἀμφιπόλεως ἐπολεμοῦμεν· τοῦτον
δ' ἀφορίζεται τῇ γενομένῃ εἰρήνῃ καὶ συμμαχίᾳ
ἣν Φιλοκράτης ὁ Ἁγνούσιος ἔγραψε καὶ αὐτὸς
55 οὗτος μετ' ἐκείνου, ὡς ἐγὼ δείξω.   δεύτερον δέ φησι
καιρὸν γενέσθαι, ὃν ἤγομεν χρόνον τὴν εἰρήνην,
δηλονότι μέχρι τῆς ἡμέρας ἐκείνης ἐν ᾗ καταλύσας
τὴν ὑπάρχουσαν εἰρήνην τῇ πόλει, ὁ αὐτὸς οὗτος
ῥήτωρ ἔγραψε τὸν πόλεμον· τρίτον δὲ ὃν ἐπολε-
μοῦμεν χρόνον μέχρι τῶν ἐν[1] Χαιρωνείᾳ, τέταρτον
δὲ τὸν νῦν παρόντα καιρόν.   ταῦτα δὲ καταριθ-
μησάμενος, ὡς ἀκούω, μέλλει με παρακαλεῖν καὶ
ἐπερωτᾶν, ὁποίου τούτων τῶν τεττάρων αὐτοῦ
καιρῶν κατηγορῶ, καὶ πότε αὐτὸν οὐ τὰ βέλτιστά
φημι τῷ δήμῳ πεπολιτεῦσθαι· κἂν μὴ θέλω
ἀποκρίνασθαι, ἀλλ' ἐγκαλύπτωμαι καὶ ἀποδιδρά-
σκω, ἐκκαλύψειν μέ φησι προσελθὼν καὶ ἄξειν
ἐπὶ τὸ βῆμα καὶ ἀναγκάσειν ἀποκρίνασθαι.

56   Ἵν' οὖν μήθ' οὗτος ἰσχυρίζηται ὑμεῖς τε προειδ-
δῆτε ἐγώ τε ἀποκρίνωμαι, ἐναντίον σοι τῶν δικα-

---

[1] τῶν ἐν Cobet: τῆς ἀτυχίας τῶν ἐν or τῆς ἀτυχίας τῆς ἐν
MSS.

at the outset, ought that man to be crowned with a golden crown, or ought he to be censured? And you, who had the effrontery to make your false and unlawful motion, ought you to despise the courts, or ought you to give satisfaction to the city?

But concerning the crimes of his public life I will try to speak more explicitly. For I understand that when the defence are given opportunity to speak, Demosthenes will enumerate to you four periods in the history of the city as the periods of his own political activity.[1] One of them, and the first, as I hear, he reckons as the time of our war with Philip over Amphipolis. He marks this off by the peace and alliance that were made on motion of Philocrates of Hagnus, and with the coöperation of Demosthenes himself, as I shall show. And he says that the second period was the time while we kept the peace, doubtless up to that day on which this same orator put an end to the existing peace, by himself introducing the motion for war; and the third period, the period of war, up to the events of Chaeronea; and the fourth, the present period. When he has enumerated these, he intends, as I hear, to call me forward and ask me to tell him for which of these four periods I accuse him, and when it is that I say that his policy has not been for the best interests of the people. And if I refuse to answer, and cover my face and run away, he says he will come and uncover me and lead me to the platform, and force me to answer.

In order, then, that he may lose his confidence, and that you may be instructed in advance, and that I

---

[1] In fact, Demosthenes made no such division.

στῶν, Δημόσθενες, καὶ τῶν ἄλλων πολιτῶν, ὅσοι
δὴ [1] ἔξωθεν περιεστᾶσι, καὶ τῶν Ἑλλήνων, ὅσοις
ἐπιμελὲς γέγονεν ἐπακούειν [2] τῆσδε τῆς κρίσεως·
ὁρῶ δὲ οὐκ ὀλίγους παρόντας, ἀλλ' ὅσους οὐδεὶς
πώποτε μέμνηται πρὸς ἀγῶνα δημόσιον παρα-
γενομένους· ἀποκρίνομαι, ὅτι ἁπάντων τῶν τετ-
57 τάρων καιρῶν κατηγορῶ σου ὅσους [3] διαιρῇ, κἂν
οἵ τε θεοὶ θέλωσι καὶ οἱ δικασταὶ ἐξ ἴσου ἡμῶν
ἀκούσωσι κἀγὼ δύνωμαι ἀπομνημονεῦσαι ἅ σοι
σύνοιδα, πάνυ προσδοκῶ ἐπιδείξειν τοῖς δικασταῖς
τῆς μὲν σωτηρίας τῇ πόλει τοὺς θεοὺς αἰτίους
γεγενημένους καὶ τοὺς φιλανθρώπως καὶ μετρίως
τοῖς τῆς πόλεως πράγμασι χρησαμένους, τῶν δὲ
ἀτυχημάτων ἁπάντων Δημοσθένην.[4] καὶ χρή-
σομαι τῇ τοῦ λόγου τάξει ταύτῃ ᾗ τοῦτον πυνθάνομαι μέλλειν,[5] λέξω δὲ πρῶτον περὶ τοῦ πρώτου
καιροῦ, καὶ δεύτερον περὶ τοῦ δευτέρου, καὶ τρίτον
περὶ τοῦ ἐφεξῆς, καὶ τέταρτον περὶ τῶν νυνὶ
καθεστηκότων πραγμάτων. καὶ δὴ ἐπανάγω
ἐμαυτὸν ἐπὶ τὴν εἰρήνην ἣν σὺ καὶ Φιλοκράτης
ἐγράψατε.

58   Ὑμῖν γὰρ ἐξεγένετ' ἄν, ὦ ἄνδρες Ἀθηναῖοι, τὴν
προτέραν ἐκείνην εἰρήνην ποιήσασθαι μετὰ κοινοῦ
συνεδρίου τῶν Ἑλλήνων, εἴ τινες ὑμᾶς εἴασαν
περιμεῖναι τὰς πρεσβείας ἃς ἦτε ἐκπεπομφότες
κατ' ἐκεῖνον τὸν καιρὸν εἰς τὴν Ἑλλάδα, παρακαλ-

---

[1] δὴ Blass : the MSS. have δὲ or τε, or omit.
[2] ἐπακούειν Markland : ὑπακούειν MSS.
[3] ὅσους Weidner : οὓς σὺ MSS.
[4] Δημοσθένην Taylor : the MSS. have αἴτιον γεγενημένον
or γεγενημένον αἴτιον after Δημοσθένην.
[5] μέλλειν Weidner : μέλλειν ποιεῖσθαι or ποιεῖσθαι μέλλειν
MSS.

may reply, in the presence of the jury, Demosthenes, and of all the other citizens who are standing there outside the bar, and of all the other Greeks who have taken the trouble to listen to this case—and I see that not a few are here, more in fact than have ever attended a public trial within the memory of any man—I answer you that for all the four periods which you enumerate I accuse you. And if the gods permit, and the jurors give us an impartial hearing, and I am able to call to mind all that I know about you, I confidently expect to show to the jury that for the safety of the city it is the gods who are responsible, and the men who in the crisis have treated the city with humanity and moderation;[1] but for all our misfortunes, Demosthenes. The order of my treatment shall be that which I understand he will follow; and I will speak first concerning the first period, second concerning the second, third concerning the next, and fourth concerning the present situation. So now I address myself to the peace which you and Philocrates formally proposed.

You could have made that former peace,[2] fellow citizens, supported by the joint action of a congress of the Greek states, if certain men had allowed you to wait for the return of the embassies which at that crisis you had sent out among the Greeks, with the

---

[1] The reference is to the unexpected moderation shown by both Philip and Alexander in their treatment of Athens, when they had the city entirely in their power, after her persistent efforts against them.

[2] "That former peace" is the Peace of Philocrates, 346 B.C., so distinguished from the peace existing at the time of this speech.

οὖντες ἐπὶ Φίλιππον,[1] καὶ προϊόντος τοῦ χρόνου
παρ' ἑκόντων τῶν Ἑλλήνων ἀπολαβεῖν τὴν ἡγε-
μονίαν· καὶ τούτων ἀπεστερήθητε διὰ Δημοσθένην
καὶ Φιλοκράτην καὶ τὰς τούτων δωροδοκίας, ἃς
ἐδωροδόκησαν συστάντες ἐπὶ τὸ δημόσιον τὸ
ὑμέτερον.

59   Εἰ δέ τισιν ὑμῶν ἐξαίφνης ἀκούσασιν ἀπιστό-
τερος προσπέπτωκεν ὁ τοιοῦτος λόγος, ἐκείνως
τὴν ὑπόλοιπον ποιήσασθε ἀκρόασιν. ὥσπερ ὅταν
περὶ χρημάτων ἀνηλωμένων διὰ πολλοῦ χρόνου
καθεζώμεθα ἐπὶ τοὺς λογισμούς, ἐρχόμεθα δή
που ἐνίοτε ψευδεῖς οἴκοθεν δόξας ἔχοντες·[2] ἀλλ'
ὅμως ἐπειδὰν ὁ λογισμὸς συγκεφαλαιωθῇ, οὐδείς
ἐστιν[3] οὕτω δύσκολος τὴν φύσιν, ὅστις οὐκ ἀπέρ-
χεται τοῦτο ὁμολογήσας ἀληθὲς εἶναι, ὅ τι ἂν ὁ
60 λογισμὸς αἱρῇ· οὕτω καὶ νῦν τὴν ἀκρόασιν ποιήσασθε. εἴ τινες ὑμῶν ἐκ τῶν ἔμπροσθεν χρόνων
ἥκουσιν οἴκοθεν τοιαύτην ἔχοντες τὴν δόξαν, ὡς
ἄρα ὁ Δημοσθένης οὐδὲν πώποτε εἴρηκεν ὑπὲρ
Φιλίππου συστὰς μετὰ Φιλοκράτους,—ὅστις οὕτω
διάκειται, μήτ' ἀπογνώτω μηδὲν μήτε καταγνώτω
πρὶν ἂν[4] ἀκούσῃ· οὐ γὰρ δίκαιον. ἀλλ' ἐάν,
ἐμοῦ διὰ βραχέων[5] ὑπομιμνήσκοντος τοὺς καιροὺς
καὶ τὰ ψηφίσματα παρεχομένου ἃ μετὰ Φιλοκράτους ἔγραψε Δημοσθένης, αὐτὸς[6] ὁ τῆς ἀληθείας λογισμὸς καταλάβῃ[7] τὸν Δημοσθένην
πλείω μὲν γεγραφότα ψηφίσματα Φιλοκράτους

---

[1] Φίλιππον Dobree : Φίλιππον μετασχεῖν Ἑλληνικοῦ συνεδρίου
MSS.
[2] ἔχοντες Sauppe : ἔχοντες κατὰ τὸν λογισμὸν or κατὰ τῶν
λογισμῶν MSS.
[3] ἐστιν Blass : the MSS. have ὑμῶν or ἡμῶν before or after
ἐστιν.   [4] ἂν added by Reisig.

call to join you against Philip ; and in the course of time the Greeks would of their own accord have accepted your hegemony again. Of this you were deprived, thanks to Demosthenes and Philocrates, and the bribes which they took in their conspiracy against the common weal.

But if such a statement as I have just made, falling suddenly on your ears, is too incredible to some of you, permit me to suggest how you ought to listen to the rest of my argument : When we take our seats to audit the accounts of expenditures which extend back a long time, it doubtless some-times happens that we come from home with a false impression ; nevertheless, when the accounts have been balanced, no man is so stubborn as to refuse, before he leaves the room, to assent to that conclusion, whatever it may be, which the figures themselves establish. I ask you to give a similar hearing now. If some of you have come from home with the opinion, formed in the past, that of course Demosthenes has never in conspiracy with Philocrates said a word in Philip's interest—if any man of you is under such impression, let him decide nothing either way, aye or no, until he has heard ; for that would not be fair. But if, as I briefly recall the dates, and cite the resolutions which Demosthenes moved in coöperation with Philo-crates, the truthful audit of the facts shall convict Demosthenes of having moved more resolutions than Philocrates concerning the original peace and alliance,

---

⁵ After βραχέων the MSS. have ἀκούσητε or ἀκούσαντε or ἀκούσαντες : Blass brackets.

⁶ Before αὐτὸς the MSS. have ἐὰν : Blass brackets.

⁷ καταλάβῃ Franke : ἐγκαταλαμβάνῃ MSS.

61 περὶ τῆς ἐξ ἀρχῆς εἰρήνης καὶ συμμαχίας, καθ'
ὑπερβολὴν δὲ αἰσχύνης κεκολακευκότα Φίλιππον
καὶ τοὺς παρ' ἐκείνου πρέσβεις,[1] αἴτιον δὲ γεγονότα τῷ δήμῳ τοῦ μὴ μετὰ κοινοῦ συνεδρίου
τῶν Ἑλλήνων ποιήσασθαι τὴν εἰρήνην, ἔκδοτον
δὲ πεποιηκότα Φιλίππῳ Κερσοβλέπτην τὸν
Θρᾴκης βασιλέα, ἄνδρα φίλον καὶ σύμμαχον τῇ
πόλει,—ἐὰν ταῦθ' ὑμῖν σαφῶς ἐπιδείξω, δεήσομαι
ὑμῶν μετρίαν δέησιν· ἐπινεύσατέ μοι πρὸς θεῶν
τὸν πρῶτον τῶν τεττάρων καιρῶν μὴ καλῶς αὐτὸν πεπολιτεῦσθαι. λέξω δὲ ὅθεν μάλιστα παρακολουθήσετε.

62 Ἔγραψε Φιλοκράτης ἐξεῖναι Φιλίππῳ δεῦρο
κήρυκα καὶ πρέσβεις πέμπειν περὶ εἰρήνης. τοῦτο
τὸ ψήφισμα ἐγράφη παρανόμων. ἦκον οἱ τῆς
κρίσεως χρόνοι· κατηγόρει μὲν Λυκῖνος ὁ γραψάμενος, ἀπελογεῖτο δὲ Φιλοκράτης, συναπελογεῖτο
δὲ Δημοσθένης· ἀπέφυγε Φιλοκράτης. μετὰ ταῦτα ἐπῄει[2] Θεμιστοκλῆς ἄρχων· ἐνταῦθ' εἰσέρ-
χεται βουλευτὴς[3] Δημοσθένης, οὔτε λαχὼν οὔτ'
ἐπιλαχών, ἀλλ' ἐκ παρασκευῆς πριάμενος, ἵν' εἰς
ὑποδοχὴν ἅπαντα καὶ λέγοι καὶ πράττοι Φιλο-
63 κράτει, ὡς αὐτὸ ἔδειξε τὸ ἔργον. νικᾷ γὰρ ἕτερον
ψήφισμα Φιλοκράτης, ἐν ᾧ κελεύει ἑλέσθαι δέκα
πρέσβεις, οἵτινες ἀφικόμενοι ὡς Φίλιππον ἀξιώ-
σουσιν αὐτὸν δεῦρο πρέσβεις αὐτοκράτορας ἀπο-

---

[1] καὶ . . . πρέσβεις H. Wolf: after πρέσβεις many MSS. have
οὐκ ἀναμείναντα; those of one group have καὶ οὐκ ἀναμείναντα
τοὺς πρέσβεις.
[2] ἐπῄει Weidner : ἐπῄει χρόνος MSS.
[3] After βουλευτὴς the MSS. have εἰς τὸ βουλευτήριον : Blass
brackets.

and of having flattered Philip and his ambassadors
with a shamelessness which was beyond measure,
and of being responsible to the people for the failure
to secure the concurrence of a general congress of
the Greek states in the making of the peace, and
of having betrayed to Philip Cersobleptes, king of
Thrace, a friend and ally of our city—if I shall
clearly demonstrate all this to you, I shall make of
you this modest request : in God's name agree with
me, that in the first of his four periods his policies
have not been those of a good citizen. I will speak
in a way that will enable you to follow me most
easily.

Philocrates made a motion[1] that we permit Philip
to send to us a herald and ambassadors to treat
concerning peace. This motion was attacked in the
courts as illegal. The time of the trial came.
Lycinus, who had indicted him, spoke for the prosecution ; Philocrates made answer for himself, and
Demosthenes spoke in his behalf;[2] Philocrates was
cleared. After this came the archonship of Themistocles.[3] Now Demosthenes came in as senator, not
drawn by the lot either as a member of the senate
or as a substitute, but through intrigue and bribery ;
the purpose of it was to enable him to support Philocrates in every way, by word and deed, as the event
itself made evident. For now Philocrates carries
a second resolution, providing for the election of ten
ambassadors, who shall go to Philip and ask him to

---

[1] In 348 B.C.
[2] In the Speech on the Embassy (§ 14) Aeschines says that
Philocrates was ill, and called in Demosthenes as his advocate (συνήγορος). Probably Philocrates made only a brief
and formal answer in court, and left the real defence to
Demosthenes.   [3] Beginning in midsummer, 347 B.C.

στέλλειν ὑπὲρ εἰρήνης. τούτων εἷς ἦν Δημοσθένης.
κἀκεῖθεν ἐπανήκων ἐπαινέτης ἦν τῆς εἰρήνης, καὶ
ταὐτὰ τοῖς ἄλλοις πρέσβεσιν ἀπήγγελλε, καὶ
μόνος τῶν βουλευτῶν ἔγραψε σπείσασθαι τῷ κήρυκι τῷ ἀπὸ Φιλίππου καὶ τοῖς πρέσβεσιν, ἀκόλουθα γράφων Φιλοκράτει· ὁ μέν γε τὴν ἐξουσίαν
δέδωκε τοῦ δεῦρο κήρυκα καὶ πρέσβεις πέμπεσθαι,
ὁ δὲ τῇ πρεσβείᾳ σπένδεται.

64 Τὰ δὲ μετὰ ταῦτα ἤδη μοι σφόδρα προσέχετε
τὸν νοῦν. ἐπράττετο γὰρ οὐ πρὸς τοὺς ἄλλους
πρέσβεις, τοὺς πολλὰ συκοφαντηθέντας ὕστερον
ἐκ μεταβολῆς ὑπὸ Δημοσθένους, ἀλλὰ πρὸς Φιλοκράτην καὶ Δημοσθένην, εἰκότως, τοὺς ἅμα μὲν
πρεσβεύοντας, ἅμα δὲ τὰ ψηφίσματα γράφοντας,
πρῶτον μὲν ὅπως μὴ περιμενεῖτε[1] τοὺς πρέσβεις
οὓς ἦτε ἐκπεπομφότες παρακαλοῦντας[2] ἐπὶ Φίλιππον, ἵνα μὴ μετὰ τῶν Ἑλλήνων, ἀλλ' ἰδίᾳ
65 ποιήσαισθε[3] τὴν εἰρήνην· δεύτερον δ' ὅπως μὴ
μόνον εἰρήνην, ἀλλὰ καὶ συμμαχίαν εἶναι ψηφιεῖσθε πρὸς Φίλιππον, ἵνα, εἴ τινες προσέχοιεν τῷ
πλήθει τῷ ὑμετέρῳ, εἰς τὴν ἐσχάτην ἐμπέσοιεν
ἀθυμίαν, ὁρῶντες ὑμᾶς αὐτοὺς μὲν παρακαλοῦντας
ἐπὶ τὸν πόλεμον, οἴκοι δὲ μὴ μόνον εἰρήνην, ἀλλὰ
καὶ συμμαχίαν ἐψηφισμένους ποιεῖσθαι· τρίτον
δὲ ὅπως Κερσοβλέπτης ὁ Θρᾴκης βασιλεὺς μὴ
ἔσται ἔνορκος, μηδὲ[4] μετέσται τῆς συμμαχίας καὶ
τῆς εἰρήνης αὐτῷ. παρηγγέλλετο δ' ἐπ' αὐτὸν
66 ἤδη στρατεία. καὶ ταῦθ' ὁ μὲν ἐξωνούμενος οὐκ

---

[1] περιμενεῖτε Stephanus : περιμείνητε MSS.
[2] παρακαλοῦντας Markland : παρακαλοῦντες MSS.
[3] ποιήσαισθε Bekker : ποιήσησθε MSS.
[4] μηδὲ Bekker : μήτε MSS.

send hither plenipotentiaries to negotiate peace. Of these ambassadors one was Demosthenes. On his return, Demosthenes was a eulogist of the peace, he agreed with the other ambassadors in their report, and he alone of the senators moved to give safe-conduct to Philip's herald and ambassadors; and in this motion he was in accord with Philocrates, for the one had given permission to send a herald and ambassadors hither, the other gave safe-conduct to the embassy.

As to what followed, I beg you now to pay especial attention. For negotiations were entered into—not with the other ambassadors, who were slandered again and again by Demosthenes after he had changed face, but with Philocrates and Demosthenes (naturally, for they were at once ambassadors and authors of the motions)—first, that you should not wait for the ambassadors whom you had sent out with your summons against Philip, for they wished you to make the peace, not together with the Greeks, but by yourselves; secondly, that you should vote, not only for peace, but also for alliance with Philip, in order that any states which were taking note of what the Athenian democracy was doing might fall into utter discouragement on seeing that, while you were summoning them to war, you had at home voted to make both peace and an alliance; and thirdly, that Cersobleptes, king of Thrace, should not be included in the oaths, nor share the alliance and peace—indeed, an expedition was already being levied against him. Now the man who was buying

ἠδίκει, πρὸ γὰρ τῶν ὅρκων καὶ τῶν συνθηκῶν
ἀνεμέσητον ἦν αὐτῷ πράττειν τὰ συμφέροντα, οἱ
δ' ἀποδόμενοι καὶ κατακοινωνήσαντες τὰ τῆς πόλεως ἰσχυρὰ μεγάλης ὀργῆς ἦσαν ἄξιοι. ὁ γὰρ
μισαλέξανδρος νυνὶ φάσκων εἶναι, καὶ τότε μισοφίλιππος, Δημοσθένης, ὁ τὴν ξενίαν ἐμοὶ προφέ-
ρων τὴν Ἀλεξάνδρου, γράφει ψήφισμα, τοὺς
67 καιροὺς τῆς πόλεως ὑφαιρούμενος, ἐκκλησίαν
ποιεῖν τοὺς πρυτάνεις τῇ ὀγδόῃ ἱσταμένου τοῦ
Ἐλαφηβολιῶνος μηνός, ὅτ' ἦν τῷ Ἀσκληπιῷ ἡ
θυσία καὶ ὁ προαγών, ἐν τῇ ἱερᾷ ἡμέρᾳ, ὃ πρότερον οὐδεὶς μέμνηται γεγονός, τίνα πρόφασιν
ποιησάμενος; "'Ίνα," φησίν, " ἐὰν παρῶσιν ἤδη
οἱ Φιλίππου πρέσβεις, βουλεύσηται ὁ δῆμος ὡς
τάχιστα περὶ τῶν πρὸς Φίλιππον," τοῖς οὔπω
παροῦσι πρέσβεσι προκαταλαμβάνων τὴν ἐκκλησίαν, καὶ τοὺς χρόνους ὑμῶν ὑποτεμνόμενος καὶ
τὸ πρᾶγμα κατασπεύδων, ἵνα μὴ μετὰ τῶν ἄλλων
Ἑλλήνων, ἐπανελθόντων τῶν ὑμετέρων πρέσβεων,
ἀλλὰ μόνοι ποιήσησθε τὴν εἰρήνην.

68 Μετὰ ταῦτα, ὦ ἄνδρες Ἀθηναῖοι, ἧκον οἱ
Φιλίππου πρέσβεις· οἱ δὲ ὑμέτεροι [1] ἀπεδήμουν,
παρακαλοῦντες τοὺς Ἕλληνας ἐπὶ Φίλιππον.
ἐνταῦθ' ἕτερον νικᾷ ψήφισμα Δημοσθένης, ἐν ᾧ

---

[1] ὑμέτεροι Blass : ἡμέτεροι MSS.

---

[1] The Great Dionysia, April 5th, 346 B.C.

such services was doing no wrong, for before the oaths had been taken and the agreements entered into, he could not be blamed for negotiating to his own advantage; but the men who sold, who admitted Philip into partnership in the control of the strongholds of the state, were deserving of your great indignation. For the man who now shouts, "Down with Alexander!" and in those days, "Down with Philip!" the man who throws in my face the friendship of Alexander, this man Demosthenes, stole away the opportunities of the city by making the motion that the prytanes call an assembly for the eighth day of Elaphebolion, the day of the sacrifice to Asclepius, and the introductory day of the festival [1]—the sacred day!—a thing that no man remembers ever to have been done before. And what was his pretext? "In order," he says, "that if Philip's ambassadors shall by that time have arrived, the people may most speedily deliberate on their relations with Philip." He thus appropriates the assembly for the ambassadors in advance, before their arrival, cutting short your time, and hurrying on the whole business; and this was in order that you might make the peace, not in coöperation with the other Greeks, on the return of your ambassadors,[2] but alone.

After this, fellow citizens, Philip's ambassadors arrived;[3] but yours were absent, summoning the Greeks against Philip. Thereupon Demosthenes carries another resolution, in which he provides that

[2] The ambassadors who had been sent out to call other Greek states to unite against Philip (§ 58).

[3] It seems that Philip's ambassadors did not arrive in time for the discussion appointed for the 8th; but they were in Athens during at least a part of the Dionysia (§ 76).

γράφει μὴ μόνον ὑπὲρ εἰρήνης, ἀλλὰ καὶ περὶ
συμμαχίας βουλεύσασθαι, μὴ περιμείναντας τοὺς
πρέσβεις τοὺς ὑμετέρους, ἀλλ' εὐθὺς μετὰ τὰ
Διονύσια τὰ ἐν ἄστει, τῇ ὀγδόῃ καὶ ἐνάτῃ ἐπὶ δέκα.
ὅτι δ' ἀληθῆ λέγω, τῶν ψηφισμάτων ἀκούσατε.

ΨΗΦΙΣΜΑΤΑ

69 Ἐπειδὴ τοίνυν, ὦ ἄνδρες Ἀθηναῖοι, παρεληλύ-
θει τὰ Διονύσια, ἐγίγνοντο δὲ αἱ ἐκκλησίαι, ἐν [1]
τῇ προτέρᾳ τῶν ἐκκλησιῶν [2] ἀνεγνώσθη δόγμα
κοινὸν τῶν συμμάχων, οὗ τὰ κεφάλαια διὰ βραχέων ἐγὼ προερῶ. πρῶτον μὲν γὰρ ἔγραψαν
ὑπὲρ εἰρήνης ὑμᾶς μόνον βουλεύσασθαι, τὸ δὲ τῆς
συμμαχίας ὄνομα ὑπερέβησαν, οὐκ ἐπιλελησμέ-
νοι, ἀλλὰ καὶ τὴν εἰρήνην ἀναγκαιοτέραν ἢ καλλίω ὑπολαμβάνοντες εἶναι· ἔπειτα ἀπήντησαν
ὀρθῶς ἰασόμενοι τὸ Δημοσθένους δωροδόκημα,
70 καὶ προσέγραψαν [3] ἐξεῖναι τῷ βουλομένῳ τῶν
Ἑλλήνων ἐν τρισὶ μησὶν εἰς τὴν αὐτὴν στήλην
ἀναγράφεσθαι μετ' Ἀθηναίων καὶ μετέχειν τῶν
ὅρκων καὶ τῶν συνθηκῶν, δύο τὰ μέγιστα προ-
καταλαμβάνοντες, πρῶτον μὲν τὸν χρόνον τὸν τῆς
τριμήνου ταῖς τῶν Ἑλλήνων πρεσβείαις ἱκανὸν
παραγενέσθαι κατασκευάζοντες, ἔπειτα τὴν τῶν
Ἑλλήνων εὔνοιαν τῇ πόλει μετὰ κοινοῦ συνεδρίου

[1] ἐν Bake : ἐν δὲ MSS.
[2] ἐκκλησιῶν Taylor : after ἐκκλησιῶν or after δόγμα the
MSS. have τῇ ὀγδόῃ ἐπὶ δέκα.
[3] After προσέγραψαν the MSS. have ἐν τῷ δόγματι : Blass
brackets.

we take counsel, not only regarding peace, but on the subject of an alliance also; and that we should do this without waiting for your ambassadors to return, but immediately after the City Dionysia, on the 18th and 19th of the month. As proof of the truth of what I say, hear the resolutions.

RESOLUTIONS

When now, fellow citizens, the Dionysia were past and the assemblies took place, in the first assembly a resolution of the synod of the allies was read,[1] the substance of which I will give briefly before having it read to you. First, they provided only that you should take counsel regarding peace, and omitted the word "alliance"—and that not inadvertently, but because they looked upon even the peace as necessary, rather than honourable; secondly, they met Demosthenes' bribery with a well-chosen remedy, by adding in their resolution that any Greek state that wished should be permitted within the space of three months to have its name inscribed with the Athenians on the same stone, and to share the oaths and agreements. In this way they were taking two precautions, and those of the greatest importance; for first, they provided the period of three months, a sufficient time for the ambassadors of the Greek states to arrive; and secondly, they sought to secure to the city the good-will of the Greeks, by the provision for a general congress, in order that in case the

---

[1] At this time Athens was at the head of a small league, all that was left of the great maritime league begun in 378, but largely broken up by the league war of 357–55. It was the synod of this league, sitting at Athens, which passed the resolution cited. The resolution empowered Athens in advance to act in behalf of the league.

THE SPEECHES OF AESCHINES

κτώμενοι, ἵν' εἰ παραβαίνοιντο αἱ συνθῆκαι, μὴ
μόνοι μηδ' ἀπαράσκευοι πολεμήσαιμεν, ὃ¹ νῦν
ἡμῖν παθεῖν συνέβη διὰ Δημοσθένην. ὅτι δ'
ἀληθῆ λέγω, ἐξ αὐτοῦ τοῦ δόγματος ἀκούσαντες
μαθήσεσθε.

ΔΟΓΜΑ ΣΥΜΜΑΧΩΝ

71 Τούτῳ τῷ δόγματι συνειπεῖν ὁμολογῶ, καὶ
πάντες οἱ ἐν τῇ προτέρᾳ τῶν ἐκκλησιῶν δημηγο-
ροῦντες· καὶ ὁ δῆμος ἀπῆλθε τοιοῦτόν τι ὑπειληφώς,² ὡς ἔσται μὲν ἡ εἰρήνη (περὶ δὲ συμμαχίας
οὐκ ἄμεινον εἴη διὰ τὴν τῶν Ἑλλήνων παράκλησιν βουλεύσασθαι), ἔσται δὲ κοινῇ μετὰ τῶν
Ἑλλήνων ἁπάντων. νὺξ ἐν μέσῳ, καὶ παρῆμεν
τῇ ὑστεραίᾳ εἰς τὴν ἐκκλησίαν. ἐνταῦθα δὴ
προκαταλαβὼν Δημοσθένης τὸ βῆμα, οὐδενὶ τῶν
ἄλλων παραλιπὼν λόγον, οὐδὲν ὄφελος ἔφη τῶν
χθὲς εἰρημένων εἶναι λόγων, εἰ ταῦθ' οἱ Φιλίππου
μὴ συμπεισθήσονται πρέσβεις, οὐδὲ γιγνώσκειν
72 ἔφη τὴν εἰρήνην ἀπούσης συμμαχίας. οὐ γὰρ
ἔφη δεῖν, καὶ γὰρ τὸ ῥῆμα μέμνημαι ὡς εἶπε, διὰ
τὴν ἀηδίαν τοῦ λέγοντος ἅμα καὶ τοῦ ὀνόματος,
"ἀπορρῆξαι" τῆς εἰρήνης τὴν συμμαχίαν, οὐδὲ
τὰ τῶν Ἑλλήνων ἀναμένειν μελλήματα, ἀλλ'
ἢ πολεμεῖν αὐτούς, ἢ τὴν εἰρήνην ἰδίᾳ ποιεῖσθαι.
καὶ τελευτῶν ἐπὶ τὸ βῆμα παρακαλέσας Ἀντί-
πατρον ἐρώτημά τι ἠρώτα, προειπὼν μὲν ἃ ἐρή-
σεται, προδιδάξας δὲ ἃ χρὴ κατὰ τῆς πόλεως
ἀποκρίνασθαι. καὶ τέλος ταῦτ' ἐνίκα, τῷ μὲν

---

¹ ὃ Cobet : ἃ MSS.
² τοιοῦτόν τι ὑπειληφώς Weidner (cp. i. 49): τοιαύτην τινὰ
δόξαν εἰληφώς (or ὑπειληφώς) MSS.

agreements should be violated, we might not enter upon the war unprepared and alone—the misfortune that actually came upon us, thanks to Demosthenes. Now that what I say is true, you shall learn by hearing the resolution itself.

THE RESOLUTION OF THE ALLIES

I acknowledge that I supported this resolution, as did all who spoke in the first of the two assemblies; and the people left the assembly with substantially this supposition, that peace would be made (that, however, it was better not to discuss an alliance, because of our summons to the Greeks), and that the peace would be shared by all the Greeks. Night intervened. We came the next day to the assembly. Then it was that Demosthenes, hastening to get possession of the platform, and leaving no other man an opportunity to speak, said that the propositions of yesterday were utterly useless unless Philip's ambassadors could be persuaded to assent to them. He further said that he could not conceive of peace without alliance. For he said we must not—I remember the expression he used, for the word was as odious as the man—he said we must not "rip off" the alliance from the peace, nor wait for the slow decisions of the other Greeks, but we must either fight ourselves, or by ourselves make the peace. And finally he called Antipater [1] to the platform, and proceeded to ask him a certain question—he had previously told him what he was going to ask, and had instructed him what he was to answer, to the injury of the state. Finally this thing prevailed, Demosthenes

---

[1] One of Philip's ambassadors.

λόγῳ προσβιασαμένου¹ Δημοσθένους, τὸ δὲ
73 ψήφισμα γράψαντος Φιλοκράτους. ὃ δὲ ἦν ὑπόλοιπον αὐτοῖς, Κερσοβλέπτην καὶ τὸν ἐπὶ Θρᾴκης
τόπον ἔκδοτον ποιῆσαι, καὶ τοῦτ' ἔπραξαν ἕκτῃ
φθίνοντος τοῦ Ἐλαφηβολιῶνος, πρὶν ἐπὶ τὴν
ὑστέραν ἀπαίρειν πρεσβείαν τὴν ἐπὶ τοὺς ὅρκους
Δημοσθένην· ὁ γὰρ μισαλέξανδρος καὶ μισοφίλιππος ἡμῖν οὑτοσὶ ῥήτωρ δὶς ἐπρέσβευσεν εἰς
Μακεδονίαν, ἐξὸν μηδὲ ἅπαξ, ὁ νυνὶ κελεύων τῶν
Μακεδόνων καταπτύειν. εἰς δὲ τὴν ἐκκλησίαν
τὴν τῇ ἕκτῃ προκαθεζόμενος βουλευτὴς ὢν ἐκ
παρασκευῆς, ἔκδοτον Κερσοβλέπτην μετὰ Φιλο-
74 κράτους ἐποίησε. λανθάνει γὰρ ὁ μὲν Φιλοκράτης
ἐν ψηφίσματι μετὰ τῶν ἄλλων² παρεγγράψας,
ὁ δ' ἐπιψηφίσας, Δημοσθένης,³ " Ἀποδοῦναι δὲ
τοὺς ὅρκους τοῖς πρέσβεσι τοῖς παρὰ Φιλίππου
ἐν τῇδε τῇ ἡμέρᾳ τοὺς συνέδρους τῶν συμμάχων."
παρὰ δὲ Κερσοβλέπτου σύνεδρος οὐκ ἐκάθητο·
γράψας δὲ τοὺς συνεδρεύοντας ὀμνύναι, τὸν
Κερσοβλέπτην οὐ συνεδρεύοντα ἐξέκλεισε τῶν
75 ὅρκων. ὅτι δ' ἀληθῆ λέγω, ἀνάγνωθί μοι, τίς
ἦν ὁ ταῦτα γράψας, καὶ τίς ὁ⁴ ἐπιψηφίσας.⁵

ΨΗΦΙΣΜΑ

Καλόν, ὦ ἄνδρες Ἀθηναῖοι, καλὸν ἡ τῶν δημοσίων γραμμάτων φυλακή· ἀκίνητον γάρ ἐστι,
καὶ οὐ συμμεταπίπτει τοῖς αὐτομολοῦσιν ἐν τῇ

---

¹ προσβιασαμένου Reiske : προβιασαμένου MSS.
² ἄλλων Blass : ἄλλων γραμμάτων MSS.
³ Δημοσθένης Markland : the MSS. add ἐν ᾧ γέγραπται.
⁴ After ὁ the MSS. have ταῦτα : Blass brackets.
⁵ ἐπιψηφίσας Franke : ἐπιψηφίσας πρόεδρος MSS.

forcing you to it by his talk, and Philocrates moving the resolution. One thing remained now for them to do—to betray Cersobleptes and the Thracian coast. This they accomplished on the 25th of Elaphebolion, before Demosthenes set out on the second embassy, the embassy for the ratification of the oaths (for this orator of ours, this man who shouts "Down with Alexander!" and "Down with Philip!" has twice been an ambassador to Macedonia, when he need not have gone once—the man who now bids you spit on the Macedonians). Presiding over the assembly on the 25th, for he had gained a seat in the senate by intrigue,[1] he, with the help of Philocrates, betrayed Cersobleptes; for Philocrates unobserved slipped this clause in among the provisions of his resolution, and Demosthenes put it to the vote, that "The members of the synod of the allies do on this day give their oaths to the ambassadors from Philip." But no representative of Cersobleptes had a seat in the synod; and so in providing that those who were sitting in the synod should give oath, he excluded Cersobleptes from the oaths, for he had no place in the synod.[2] As proof that I am speaking the truth, read, if you please, who it was that made this motion, and who it was that put it to vote.

THE RESOLUTION

An excellent thing, fellow citizens, an excellent thing is the preservation of the public acts. For the record remains undisturbed, and does not shift sides with political turncoats, but whenever the

---

[1] The presiding officer of the assembly was a senator, chosen by lot for the day. [2] *cp.* ii. §§ 81-86.

πολιτείᾳ, ἀλλ' ἀπέδωκε τῷ δήμῳ, ὁπόταν βού-
ληται, συνιδεῖν τοὺς πάλαι μὲν πονηρούς, ἐκ
μεταβολῆς δ' ἀξιοῦντας εἶναι χρηστούς.

76 'Υπόλοιπον δ' ἐστί μοι τὴν κολακείαν διεξελθεῖν. Δημοσθένης γάρ, ὦ ἄνδρες 'Αθηναῖοι,
ἐνιαυτὸν βουλεύσας, οὐδεμίαν πώποτε φανήσεται
πρεσβείαν εἰς προεδρίαν καλέσας, ἀλλὰ τότε
μόνον καὶ πρῶτον·[1] καὶ προσκεφάλαια ἔθηκε,
καὶ φοινικίδας περιεπέτασε, καὶ ἅμα τῇ ἡμέρᾳ
ἡγεῖτο τοῖς πρέσβεσιν εἰς τὸ θέατρον, ὥστε καὶ
συρίττεσθαι διὰ τὴν ἀσχημοσύνην καὶ κολακείαν. καὶ ὅτ' ἀπῄεσαν,[2] ἐμισθώσατο αὐτοῖς τρία
ζεύγη ὀρεικὰ καὶ τοὺς πρέσβεις προὔπεμψεν εἰς
Θήβας, καταγέλαστον τὴν πόλιν ποιῶν. ἵνα δ'
ἐπὶ τῆς ὑποθέσεως μείνω, λαβέ μοι τὸ ψήφισμα
τὸ περὶ τῆς προεδρίας.

ΨΗΦΙΣΜΑ

77 Οὗτος τοίνυν, ὦ ἄνδρες 'Αθηναῖοι, ὁ τηλικοῦτος
τὸ μέγεθος κόλαξ, πρῶτος διὰ τῶν κατασκόπων
τῶν παρὰ Χαριδήμου πυθόμενος τὴν Φιλίππου
τελευτήν, τῶν μὲν θεῶν συμπλάσας ἑαυτῷ ἐνύπνιον κατεψεύσατο, ὡς οὐ παρὰ Χαριδήμου τὸ
πρᾶγμα πεπυσμένος, ἀλλὰ παρὰ τοῦ Διὸς καὶ
τῆς 'Αθηνᾶς, οὓς μεθ' ἡμέραν ἐπιορκῶν νύκτωρ
φησὶν ἑαυτῷ διαλέγεσθαι καὶ τὰ μέλλοντα ἔσεσθαι
προλέγειν, ἑβδόμην δ' ἡμέραν τῆς θυγατρὸς αὐτῷ
τετελευτηκυίας, πρὶν πενθῆσαι καὶ τὰ νομιζόμενα
ποιῆσαι, στεφανωσάμενος καὶ λευκὴν ἐσθῆτα

---

[1] πρῶτον the editor : πρῶτον πρέσβεις εἰς προεδρίαν ἐκάλεσε
MSS.
[2] ἀπῄεσαν Taylor : ἀπῄεσαν εἰς Θήβας MSS.

people desire, it gives them opportunity to discern who have been rascals of old, but have now changed face and claim to be honourable men.

It remains for me to describe his flattery. For Demosthenes, fellow citizens, was senator for a year, yet he will be found never to have invited any other embassy to the seat of honour [1]—nay, that was the first and the only time; and he placed cushions and spread rugs; and at daybreak he came escorting the ambassadors into the theatre, so that he was actually hissed for his unseemly flattery. And when they set out on their return journey, he hired for them three span of mules, and escorted the ambassadors as far as Thebes, making the city ridiculous. But that I may not wander from my subject, please take the resolution concerning the seats of honour.

RESOLUTION

Now this man it was, fellow citizens, this past master of flattery, who, when informed through scouts of Charidemus [2] that Philip was dead, before any one else had received the news, made up a vision for himself and lied about the gods, pretending that he had received the news, not from Charidemus, but from Zeus and Athena, the gods by whose name he perjures himself by day, and who then converse with him in the night, as he says, and tell him of things to come. And though it was but the seventh day after the death of his daughter, and though the ceremonies of mourning were not yet completed, he put a garland on his head and white raiment on his body, and there he

---

[1] In the Theatre of Dionysus.

[2] Charidemus was a mercenary general, then serving Athens in the north.

THE SPEECHES OF AESCHINES

λαβὼν ἐβουθύτει καὶ παρενόμει, τὴν μόνην ὁ
δείλαιος καὶ πρώτην αὐτὸν πατέρα προσειποῦ-
78 σαν ἀπολέσας. καὶ οὐ τὸ δυστύχημα ὀνειδίζω,
ἀλλὰ τὸν τρόπον ἐξετάζω. ὁ γὰρ μισότεκνος καὶ
πατὴρ πονηρὸς οὐκ ἄν ποτε γένοιτο δημαγωγὸς
χρηστός, οὐδὲ ὁ τὰ φίλτατα καὶ οἰκειότατα
σώματα μὴ στέργων οὐδέποθ᾿ ὑμᾶς περὶ πολλοῦ
ποιήσεται τοὺς ἀλλοτρίους, οὐδέ γε ὁ ἰδίᾳ πονηρὸς
ἄν ποτε γένοιτο δημοσίᾳ χρηστός, οὐδ᾿ ὅστις ἐστὶν
οἴκοι φαῦλος, οὐδέποτ᾿ ἦν ἐν Μακεδονίᾳ καλὸς
κἀγαθός· οὐ γὰρ τὸν τρόπον, ἀλλὰ τὸν τόπον
μετήλλαξεν.

79 Πόθεν οὖν ἐπὶ τὴν μεταβολὴν ἦλθε τῶν πραγμάτων, οὗτος γάρ ἐστιν ὁ δεύτερος καιρός, καὶ τί
ποτ᾿ ἐστὶ τὸ αἴτιον, ὅτι Φιλοκράτης μὲν ἀπὸ
τῶν αὐτῶν πολιτευμάτων Δημοσθένει φυγὰς ἀπ᾿
εἰσαγγελίας γεγένηται, Δημοσθένης δὲ ἐπέστη
τῶν ἄλλων κατήγορος, καὶ πόθεν ποθ᾿ ὑμᾶς εἰς
τὴν ἀτυχίαν ὁ μιαρὸς ἄνθρωπος ἐμβέβληκε, ταῦτ᾿
80 ἤδη διαφερόντως ἄξιόν ἐστιν ἀκοῦσαι. ὡς γὰρ
τάχιστα εἴσω Πυλῶν Φίλιππος παρῆλθε, καὶ τάς
τε ἐν Φωκεῦσι πόλεις παραδόξως ἀναστάτους
ἐποίησε, Θηβαίους τε,[1] ὡς τόθ᾿ ὑμῖν ἐδόκει, περαιτέρω τοῦ καιροῦ καὶ τοῦ ὑμετέρου συμφέροντος
ἰσχυροὺς κατεσκεύασεν, ὑμεῖς τε ἐκ τῶν ἀγρῶν
φοβηθέντες ἐσκευαγωγήσατε, ἐν ταῖς μεγίσταις
δ᾿ ἦσαν αἰτίαις οἱ πρέσβεις οἱ τὴν εἰρήνην
πρεσβεύσαντες, πολὺ δὲ τῶν ἄλλων διαφερόντως
Φιλοκράτης καὶ Δημοσθένης, διὰ τὸ μὴ μόνον
πρεσβεύειν, ἀλλὰ καὶ τὰ ψηφίσματα γεγραφέναι,

[1] τε Blass : δὲ MSS.

stood making thank-offerings, violating all decency—
miserable man, who had lost the first and only one
who ever called him "father"! Not that I reproach him for his misfortune, but I am probing
his character. For the man who hates his child and
is a bad father could never become a safe guide to
the people; the man who does not cherish the persons who are nearest and dearest to him, will never
care much about you, who are not his kinsmen; the
man who is wicked in his private relations would
never be found trustworthy in public affairs; and
the man who is base at home was never a good and
honourable man in Macedonia, for by his journey he
changed his position, not his disposition.

Now how it was that he came to reverse his
policies (for this is the second period),[1] and what is
the reason that policies identical with those of Demosthenes led to the impeachment and exile of
Philocrates,[2] while Demosthenes suddenly stood
forth as accuser of the rest, and how it is that the
pestilential fellow has plunged you into misfortune,
this you ought now especially to hear. For as soon as
Philip had come this side Thermopylae, and contrary
to all expectation had destroyed the cities of Phocis,
and strengthened the Thebans beyond what was
seasonable and advantageous for you, as you then
thought, and when you in alarm had brought in your
movable property from the country districts, and the
ambassadors who had negotiated the peace were
under the gravest accusation—Philocrates and Demosthenes far beyond all the rest, because they not
only had been ambassadors, but were also the authors

[1] See § 55.
[2] Philocrates was indicted by Hypereides in 343 B.C., and
went into exile without standing trial.

81 συνέβη τε ἐν τοῖς αὐτοῖς χρόνοις διαφέρεσθαί τι
Δημοσθένην καὶ Φιλοκράτην σχεδὸν ὑπὲρ τούτων
ὑπὲρ ὧν καὶ ὑμεῖς ὑπωπτεύσατε·[1] τοιαύτης[2] ἐμ-
πιπτούσης ταραχῆς, μετὰ τῶν συμφύτων αὐτῷ
νοσημάτων ἤδη τὰ μετὰ ταῦτα ἐβουλεύετο, μετὰ
δειλίας καὶ τῆς πρὸς Φιλοκράτην ὑπὲρ τῆς δωροδοκίας ζηλοτυπίας, καὶ ἡγήσατο, εἰ τῶν συμ-
πρεσβευόντων καὶ τοῦ Φιλίππου κατήγορος ἀνα-
φανείη, τὸν μὲν Φιλοκράτην προδήλως ἀπολεῖσθαι,
τοὺς δὲ ἄλλους συμπρέσβεις κινδυνεύσειν, αὐτὸς
δ' εὐδοκιμήσειν, καὶ προδότης ὢν τῶν φίλων καὶ
πονηρός, πιστὸς τῷ δήμῳ φανήσεσθαι.

82   Κατιδόντες δ' αὐτὸν οἱ τῇ τῆς πόλεως προσπο-
λεμοῦντες ἡσυχίᾳ, ἅσμενοι παρεκάλουν ἐπὶ τὸ
βῆμα, τὸν μόνον ἀδωροδόκητον ὀνομάζοντες τῇ
πόλει· ὁ δὲ παριὼν ἀρχὰς αὐτοῖς ἐνεδίδου πολέμου
καὶ ταραχῆς. οὗτός ἐστιν, ὦ ἄνδρες Ἀθηναῖοι,
ὁ πρῶτος ἐξευρὼν Σέρριον τεῖχος καὶ Δορίσκον
καὶ Ἐργίσκην καὶ Μυρτίσκην καὶ Γάνος καὶ
Γανιάδα,[3] χωρία ὧν οὐδὲ τὰ ὀνόματα ᾔδεμεν
πρότερον. καὶ εἰς τοῦτο φέρων περιέστησε τὰ
πράγματα, ὥστ' εἰ μὲν μὴ πέμποι πρέσβεις
Φίλιππος, καταφρονεῖν αὐτὸν ἔφη τῆς πόλεως,
εἰ δὲ πέμποι, κατασκόπους πέμπειν, ἀλλ' οὐ
83 πρέσβεις. εἰ δὲ ἐπιτρέπειν ἐθέλοι πόλει τινὶ ἴσῃ

---

[1] ὑπωπτεύσατε the editor : αὐτοὺς ὑπωπτεύσατε διενεχθῆναι
MSS.
[2] τοιαύτης Taylor : τοιαύτης δὲ MSS. cp. § 149 and ii. 157.
[3] Γανιάδα Franke (Harpocration): Γανίδα MSS.

---

[1] Demosthenes, in xviii. 27, mentions Serrhium, Myrtenus,
and Ergisca. Aeschines, in his ridicule of the little places,
seems to be making jingles of their names, coining Myrtisca

of the resolutions, and when it happened at the same time that Demosthenes and Philocrates had a falling out—you were able to guess the reasons without much difficulty—when all this disturbance had arisen, then Demosthenes proceeded to take counsel as to his future course, consulting his own innate corruption, his cowardice, and his jealousy of Philocrates' bribes; and he came to the conclusion that if he should step forward as the accuser of his colleagues on the embassy and of Philip, Philocrates would surely be ruined, his other colleagues would be put in jeopardy, and he himself would gain favour, and—scoundrel and traitor to his friends—would appear to be a faithful servant of the people.

Now when the men who are always the foes of public tranquillity caught sight of him, they were delighted, and repeatedly called him to the platform, and named him our sole and only incorruptible citizen; and he as often came forward and furnished them with the sources of disturbance and war. He it is, fellow citizens, who first discovered Serrhium-Teichus and Doriscus and Ergisca and Myrtisca and Ganus and Ganias;[1] for before that we did not even know the names of these places. And he put such forced and perverse interpretation upon what was done, that, if Philip did not send ambassadors, Demosthenes said that Philip was treating the city with contempt; and if he did send them, that he was sending spies, not ambassadors; and if Philip was willing to refer our differences to some state as

out of Myrtenus, to rhyme with Ergisca, and inventing Ganias to go with Ganus.
Demosthenes claimed that Philip, by occupying these posts before he signed the peace treaty, made his control of Thrace secure. See Demosthenes, xviii. 32.

καὶ ὁμοίᾳ περὶ τῶν ἐγκλημάτων, οὐκ εἶναι κριτὴν
ἴσον ἡμῖν ἔφη καὶ Φιλίππῳ. Ἁλόννησον ἐδίδου·
ὁ δ᾽ ἀπηγόρευε μὴ λαμβάνειν, "εἰ δίδωσιν, ἀλλὰ
μὴ ἀποδίδωσι," περὶ συλλαβῶν διαφερόμενος. καὶ
τὸ τελευταῖον στεφανώσας τοὺς μετὰ Ἀριστοδήμου εἰς Θετταλίαν καὶ Μαγνησίαν παρὰ τὰς τῆς
εἰρήνης συνθήκας πρεσβεύσαντας, τὴν μὲν εἰρήνην
διέλυσε, τὴν δὲ συμφορὰν καὶ τὸν πόλεμον κατεσκεύασεν.

84 Ναί, ἀλλὰ χαλκοῖς καὶ ἀδαμαντίνοις τείχεσιν,
ὡς αὐτός φησι, τὴν χώραν ἡμῶν ἐτείχισε, τῇ τῶν
Εὐβοέων καὶ Θηβαίων συμμαχίᾳ. ἀλλά, ὦ
ἄνδρες Ἀθηναῖοι, περὶ ταῦτα καὶ μέγιστα ἠδικήθητε
καὶ μάλιστα ἠγνοήκατε. σπεύδων δ᾽ εἰπεῖν περὶ
τῆς θαυμαστῆς συμμαχίας τῆς τῶν Θηβαίων, ἵν᾽
ἐφεξῆς λέγω, περὶ τῶν Εὐβοέων πρῶτον μνησθήσομαι.

85 Ὑμεῖς γάρ, ὦ ἄνδρες Ἀθηναῖοι, πολλὰ καὶ
μεγάλα ἠδικημένοι ὑπὸ Μνησάρχου τοῦ Χαλκι-
δέως, τοῦ Καλλίου καὶ Ταυροσθένους πατρός, οὓς
οὗτος νυνὶ μισθὸν λαβὼν Ἀθηναίους εἶναι τολμᾷ
γράφειν, καὶ πάλιν ὑπὸ Θεμίσωνος τοῦ Ἐρετριέως,
ὃς ἡμῶν εἰρήνης οὔσης Ὠρωπὸν ἀφείλετο, τούτων
ἑκόντες ἐπιλαθόμενοι, ἐπειδὴ διέβησαν εἰς Εὔβοιαν
Θηβαῖοι καταδουλώσασθαι τὰς πόλεις πειρώμενοι,
ἐν πέντε ἡμέραις ἐβοηθήσατε αὐτοῖς καὶ ναυσὶ
καὶ πεζῇ δυνάμει, καὶ πρὶν τριάκονθ᾽ ἡμέρας
διελθεῖν ὑποσπόνδους Θηβαίους ἀφήκατε, κύριοι
τῆς Εὐβοίας γενόμενοι, καὶ τάς τε πόλεις αὐτὰς

---

[1] The anti-Macedonian party refused to accept the island
unless Philip would admit that he had been holding it

an equal and impartial arbiter, he said that between Philip and us there was no impartial arbiter. Philip offered to give us Halonnesus; Demosthenes forbade us to accept it if he "gave it," instead of "giving it back," quarrelling over syllables.[1] And finally, by bestowing crowns of honour on the embassy which Aristodemus led to Thessaly and Magnesia contrary to the provisions of the peace, he violated the peace and prepared the final disaster and the war.

Yes, but with walls of brass and steel, as he himself says, he fortified our land, by the alliance with Euboea and Thebes. Nay, fellow citizens, it is just here that you have been most wronged and most deceived. But eager as I am to speak about that wonderful alliance with Thebes, I will speak first about the Euboeans, that I may follow the events in their order.

You, fellow citizens, had suffered many serious injuries at the hands of Mnesarchus of Chalcis, father of Callias and Taurosthenes, men whom Demosthenes now for gold dares to propose for enrolment as Athenian citizens; and again at the hands of Themison of Eretria, who in time of peace robbed us of Oropus; but you were willing to overlook these wrongs, and when the Thebans had crossed over into Euboea in an attempt to enslave its cities,[2] in five days you went to their rescue with fleet and troops, and before thirty days had passed you brought the Thebans to terms and sent them home; and being now yourselves in complete control of Euboea, you

---

wrongfully, and so was "giving it back," not "giving it" (ἀποδίδωσι—δίδωσιν).

[2] In 357 B.C. two groups of Euboean cities were at war one with the other; one group having called in the Thebans, the other group, led by Eretria, appealed to Athens for help.

καὶ τὰς πολιτείας ἀπέδοτε ὀρθῶς καὶ δικαίως τοῖς
παρακαταθεμένοις, οὐχ ἡγούμενοι δίκαιον εἶναι
τὴν ὀργὴν ἀπομνημονεύειν ἐν τῷ πιστευθῆναι.

86 Καὶ τηλικαῦθ' ὑφ' ὑμῶν εὖ πεπονθότες οἱ
Χαλκιδεῖς οὐ τὰς ὁμοίας ὑμῖν ἀπέδοσαν,[1] ἀλλ'
ἐπειδὴ[2] διέβητε εἰς Εὔβοιαν Πλουτάρχῳ βοηθήσοντες, τοὺς μὲν πρώτους χρόνους ἀλλ' οὖν
προσεποιοῦνθ' ὑμῖν εἶναι φίλοι, ἐπειδὴ δὲ τάχιστα
εἰς Ταμύνας παρήλθομεν, καὶ τὸ Κοτύλαιον
ὀνομαζόμενον ὄρος ὑπερεβάλομεν, ἐνταῦθα Καλλίας ὁ Χαλκιδεύς, ὃν Δημοσθένης μισθαρνῶν
87 ἐνεκωμίαζεν, ὁρῶν τὸ στρατόπεδον τὸ τῆς πόλεως
εἰς δεινὰς δυσχωρίας κατακεκλημένον, ὅθεν μὴ
νικήσασι μάχην οὐκ ἦν ἀναχώρησις, οὐδὲ[3] βοηθείας ἐλπὶς οὔτ' ἐκ γῆς οὔτ' ἐκ θαλάττης, συνα-
γείρας ἐξ ἁπάσης τῆς Εὐβοίας στρατόπεδον,
καὶ παρὰ Φιλίππου δύναμιν προσμεταπεμψά-
μενος, ὅ τ' ἀδελφὸς αὐτοῦ Ταυροσθένης, ὁ νυνὶ
πάντας δεξιούμενος καὶ προσγελῶν, τοὺς Φωκικοὺς
ξένους διαβιβάσας, ἦλθον ἐφ' ἡμᾶς ὡς ἀναιρή-
88 σοντες. καὶ εἰ μὴ πρῶτον μὲν θεῶν τις ἔσωσε τὸ
στρατόπεδον, ἔπειθ' οἱ στρατιῶται οἱ ὑμέτεροι
καὶ οἱ πεζοὶ καὶ οἱ ἱππεῖς ἄνδρες ἐγένοντο ἀγαθοί,
καὶ παρὰ τὸν ἱππόδρομον τὸν ἐν Ταμύναις ἐκ
παρατάξεως μάχῃ κρατήσαντες ὑποσπόνδους ἀφεῖ-
σαν τοὺς πολεμίους, ἐκινδύνευσεν ἂν ἡ πόλις

---

[1] ἀπέδοσαν Cobet : ἀπέδοσαν χάριτας MSS.
[2] ἐπειδὴ Sauppe : ἐπειδὴ τάχιστα MSS.
[3] οὐδὲ Bekker : οὔτε MSS.

---

[1] The expedition of 357 B.C. had brought the pro-Athenian
element in Euboea into control ; but Philip was now en-

righteously and justly restored the cities themselves
and their constitutions to those who had entrusted
them to you; for you felt that it was not right to
cherish your anger, now that they had put faith in
you.

After receiving such benefits at your hands, the
Chalcidians did not requite you with like treatment,
but as soon as you had crossed over to Euboea to
help Plutarchus,[1] while at first they did pretend to
be friends to you, yet as soon as we had come to
Tamynae and had crossed the mountain called Cotylaeum, then Callias the Chalcidian, who had been
the object of Demosthenes' hired praises, seeing the
troops of our city shut up in a place which was difficult and dangerous, from which there was no with-
drawal unless we could win a battle, and where there
was no hope of succour from land or sea, collected
troops from all Euboea, and sent to Philip for rein-
forcements, while his brother, Taurosthenes, who
nowadays shakes hands with us all and smiles in our
faces, brought over the mercenaries from Phocis, and
together they came upon us to destroy us.[2] And had
not, in the first place, some god saved the army, and
had not then your soldiers, horse and foot, showed
themselves brave men, and conquered the enemy in
a pitched battle by the hippodrome at Tamynae,
and brought them to terms and sent them back, our
city would have been in danger of the greatest

couraging the anti-Athenian partisans, and supporting the
opponents of Plutarchus of Eretria. Plutarchus turned to
Athens for help. The date of the expedition is much disputed : Schaefer places it in 350 B.C., Grote in 349, and
Weil and Blass in 348.

[2] Aeschines speaks from vivid recollection, for he was a
member of the expedition. See Aeschines, ii. 169.

αἴσχιστα παθεῖν· οὐ γὰρ τὸ δυστυχῆσαι κατὰ
πόλεμον μέγιστόν ἐστι κακόν, ἀλλ' ὅταν τις πρὸς
ἀνταγωνιστὰς ἀναξίους [1] διακινδυνεύων ἀποτύχῃ,
διπλασίαν εἰκὸς εἶναι τὴν συμφοράν.

Ἀλλ' ὅμως ὑμεῖς τοιαῦτα πεπονθότες πάλιν
διελύσασθε πρὸς αὐτούς. τυχὼν δὲ συγγνώμης
89 παρ' ὑμῶν Καλλίας ὁ Χαλκιδεύς, μικρὸν διαλιπὼν χρόνον πάλιν ἧκε φερόμενος εἰς τὴν
ἑαυτοῦ φύσιν, Εὐβοϊκὸν μὲν τῷ λόγῳ συνέδριον
εἰς Χαλκίδα συνάγων, ἰσχυρὰν δὲ τὴν Εὔβοιαν
ἐφ' ὑμᾶς ἔργῳ κατασκευάζων,[2] ἐξαίρετον δ' αὑτῷ
τυραννίδα περιποιούμενος. κἀνταῦθα ἐλπίζων
συναγωνιστὴν Φίλιππον λήψεσθαι, ἀπῆλθεν
εἰς Μακεδονίαν καὶ περιῄει μετὰ Φιλίππου,
90 καὶ τῶν ἑταίρων εἷς ὠνομάζετο. ἀδικήσας δὲ
Φίλιππον κἀκεῖθεν ἀποδράς, ὑπέβαλεν ἑαυτὸν
φέρων Θηβαίοις. καταλιπὼν [3] δὲ κἀκείνους, καὶ
πλείους τραπόμενος τροπὰς τοῦ Εὐρίπου, παρ' ὃν
ᾤκει, εἰς μέσον πίπτει τῆς τε Θηβαίων ἔχθρας καὶ
τῆς Φιλίππου. ἀπορῶν δ' ὅ τι χρήσαιτο αὑτῷ,
καὶ παραγγελλομένης ἐπ' αὐτὸν ἤδη στρατείας,[4]
μίαν ἐλπίδα λοιπὴν κατεῖδε σωτηρίας, ἔνορκον
λαβεῖν τὸν Ἀθηναίων δῆμον, σύμμαχον ὀνο-
μασθέντα, βοηθήσειν, εἴ τις ἐπ' αὐτὸν ἴοι· ὃ
πρόδηλον ἦν ἐσόμενον, εἰ μὴ ὑμεῖς κωλύσετε.

91 Ταῦτα διανοηθείς, ἀποστέλλει δεῦρο πρέσβεις
Γλαυκέτην καὶ Ἐμπέδωνα καὶ Διόδωρον τὸν
δολιχοδρομήσαντα, φέροντας τῷ μὲν δήμῳ κενὰς

---

[1] ἀναξίους Weidner : ἑαυτοῦ ἀναξίους or ἀναξίους αὐτοῦ MSS.
[2] κατασκευάζων Blass : παρασκευάζων MSS.
[3] καταλιπὼν Franke : ἐγκαταλιπὼν MSS.
[4] στρατείας Stephanus : στρατιᾶς MSS.

disaster. For it is not ill fortune in war that is the greatest calamity, but when one hazards success against unworthy foes and then fails, the misfortune is naturally twofold.

But yet, even after such treatment as that, you became reconciled to them again; and Callias of Chalcis, obtaining pardon from you, soon made haste to return to his natural disposition, and tried ostensibly to assemble a Euboean congress at Chalcis, but in fact to strengthen Euboea thoroughly against you, and to win the position of tyrant as his own personal reward. Then, hoping to get Philip's help, he went to Macedonia, and travelled about with him, and was named a "comrade."[1] But having wronged Philip and run away from thence, he made haste to throw himself at the feet of the Thebans. Then abandoning them also, and making more twists and turns than the Euripus, by whose shores he used to live, he falls between the hatred of the Thebans and of Philip. At his wits' end what to do, when an expedition had already been called out against him, he saw one gleam of hope for safety left—to get the Athenian people solemnly bound, under the name of allies, to aid him if any one should attack, a thing that was sure to happen unless you should prevent it.

With this plan in view Callias sent ambassadors hither,[2] Glaucetes, Empedon, and Diodorus the long-distance runner, who brought to the people empty

---

[1] The "comrades" ('Εταῖροι), a body of Macedonian nobles, were the cavalry guards, the king's corps.
[2] This was in 342 B.C.

ἐλπίδας, Δημοσθένει δ' ἀργύριον καὶ τοῖς περὶ
τοῦτον. τρία δ' ἦν ἃ ἅμα ἐξεωνεῖτο, πρῶτον μὲν
μὴ διασφαλῆναι τῆς πρὸς ὑμᾶς συμμαχίας· οὐδὲν
γὰρ ἦν τὸ μέσον, εἰ μνησθεὶς τῶν προτέρων
ἀδικημάτων ὁ δῆμος μὴ προσδέξαιτο τὴν συμμαχίαν, ἀλλ' ὑπῆρχεν αὐτῷ ἢ φεύγειν ἐκ Χαλκίδος, ἢ τεθνάναι ἐγκαταληφθέντι· τηλικαῦται
δυνάμεις ἐπ' αὐτὸν ἐπεστράτευον, ἥ τε Φιλίππου
καὶ Θηβαίων. δεύτερον δ' ἦκον οἱ μισθοὶ τῷ
γράψοντι[1] τὴν συμμαχίαν ὑπὲρ τοῦ μὴ συνε-
δρεύειν Ἀθήνησι Χαλκιδέας, τρίτον δὲ ὥστε μὴ
92 τελεῖν συντάξεις. καὶ τούτων τῶν προαιρέσεων
οὐδεμιᾶς ἀπέτυχε Καλλίας, ἀλλ' ὁ μισοτύραννος
Δημοσθένης, ὡς αὐτὸς προσποιεῖται, ὅν φησι
Κτησιφῶν τὰ βέλτιστα λέγειν, ἀπέδοτο μὲν τοὺς
καιροὺς τοὺς τῆς πόλεως, ἔγραψε δ' ἐν τῇ συμμαχίᾳ βοηθεῖν ἡμᾶς Χαλκιδεῦσι, ῥῆμα μόνον
ἀντικαταλλαξάμενος ἀντὶ τούτων, εὐφημίας ἕνεκα
προσγράψας "Καὶ Χαλκιδέας βοηθεῖν, ἐάν τις ἴῃ
93 ἐπ' Ἀθηναίους·" τὰς δὲ συνεδρίας καὶ τὰς συντάξεις, ἐξ ὧν ἰσχύσειν ὁ πόλεμος ἔμελλεν, ἄρδην
ἀπέδοτο, καλλίστοις ὀνόμασιν αἰσχίστας πράξεις
γράφων, καὶ τῷ λόγῳ προσβιβάζων ὑμᾶς, τὰς
μὲν βοηθείας ὡς δεῖ τὴν πόλιν πρότερον ποιεῖσθαι
τοῖς ἀεὶ δεομένοις τῶν Ἑλλήνων, τὰς δὲ συμμαχίας ὑστέρας μετὰ τὰς εὐεργεσίας. ἵνα δ' εὖ

―――――――――――――――――
[1] γράψοντι Scheibe : γράψαντι MSS.

―――――――――――――――――
[1] Had the Euboeans come back into the naval alliance (see
§ 69, n.), they would have been on the same footing with
the other states that were subordinate to Athens, and would
have had to pay their share of the war-fund of the Athenian

hopes, but silver to Demosthenes and his following. And he was buying three things at once : first, to be assured of your alliance, for he had no alternative if the people, remembering his past crimes, should refuse the alliance, since one of two things was sure, that he would be banished from Chalcis, or be caught and put to death—such were the forces that were moving against him, the combined power of Philip and the Thebans ; and the second service for which the pay came to the man who was to move the alliance, was to provide that the Chalcidians should not sit in the synod at Athens ;[1] and the third was that they should pay no contributions to the league. Now in not one of these plans did Callias fail ; and Demosthenes, the tyrant-hater, as he pretends to be, who, Ctesiphon says, "speaks what is best,"[2] bartered away the opportunities of the city, and in his motion for the alliance provided that we were to aid the Chalcidians, stipulating in return for this a mere phrase ; for he added, to make it sound well, "The Chalcidians on their part are to bring aid if any one shall come against Athens" ; but the membership in the synod and the contributions of money, the sources of strength for the coming war, he sold completely, in fairest words proposing most shameful deeds, and leading you on by his talk, telling how our city must first furnish aid to any Greeks who might need it from time to time, but provide for their alliance afterward, after giving them aid. But that you may

league. As it was, they came into a special alliance with Athens herself, and as her equals.

[2] See Ctesiphon's motion for the crowning of Demosthenes, quoted in § 49.

εἰδῆτε ὅτι ἀληθῆ λέγω, λαβέ μοι τὴν Καλλίᾳ
γραφεῖσαν[1] συμμαχίαν. ἀνάγνωθι τὸ ψήφισμα.

ΨΗΦΙΣΜΑ

94 Οὔπω τοίνυν τοῦτ᾽ ἐστὶ δεινόν, εἰ καιροὶ τηλι-
κοῦτοι πεπραμένοι τυγχάνουσιν καὶ συνεδρίαι καὶ
συντάξεις, ἀλλὰ πολὺ τούτου δεινότερον φανήσεται ὃ μέλλω λέγειν. εἰς γὰρ τοῦτο προή-
χθη Καλλίας μὲν[2] ὕβρεως καὶ πλεονεξίας, Δημοσθένης δέ, ὃν ἐπαινεῖ Κτησιφῶν, δωροδοκίας,
ὥστε τὰς ἐξ Ὠρεοῦ συντάξεις καὶ τὰς ἐξ Ἐρετρίας, τὰ δέκα τάλαντα, ζώντων φρονούντων
βλεπόντων ἔλαθον ὑμῶν ὑφελόμενοι, καὶ τοὺς ἐκ
τῶν πόλεων τούτων συνέδρους παρ᾽ ὑμῶν μὲν
ἀνέστησαν, πάλιν δὲ εἰς Χαλκίδα καὶ τὸ καλούμενον Εὐβοϊκὸν συνέδριον συνήγαγον. ὃν δὲ τρόπον καὶ δι᾽ οἵων κακουργημάτων, ταῦτ᾽ ἤδη
ἄξιόν ἐστιν ἀκοῦσαι.

95 Ἀφικνεῖται γὰρ πρὸς ὑμᾶς οὐκέτι δι᾽ ἀγγέλων,
ἀλλ᾽ αὐτὸς ὁ Καλλίας, καὶ παρελθὼν εἰς τὴν ἐκκλησίαν λόγους διεξῆλθε κατεσκευασμένους ὑπὸ
Δημοσθένους. εἶπε γὰρ ὡς ἥκοι ἐκ Πελοποννήσου νεωστὶ σύνταγμα συντάξας εἰς ἑκατὸν ταλάντων πρόσοδον ἐπὶ Φίλιππον, καὶ διελογίζετο
ὅσον ἑκάστους ἔδει συντελεῖν, Ἀχαιοὺς μὲν πάντας καὶ Μεγαρέας ἑξήκοντα τάλαντα, τὰς δ᾽ ἐν
96 Εὐβοίᾳ πόλεις ἁπάσας τετταράκοντα· ἐκ δὲ τούτων τῶν χρημάτων ὑπάρξειν καὶ ναυτικὴν καὶ
πεζὴν δύναμιν· εἶναι δὲ πολλοὺς καὶ ἄλλους τῶν

---

[1] Καλλίᾳ γραφεῖσαν Blass : Καλλίου γραφὴν καὶ τὴν MSS.
[2] Καλλίας μὲν Hamaker : Καλλίας μὲν ὁ Χαλκιδεὺς MSS.

be sure that I am speaking the truth, please take the motion for the alliance proposed for the benefit of Callias. Read the resolution.

RESOLUTION

But this was only the beginning of outrage—this actual selling of such opportunities and accessions to the league and contributions of money; for that which I am about to relate was far worse, as you shall see. For Callias was led on to such a pitch of insolence and arrogance, and Demosthenes—whom Ctesiphon praises—to such a pitch of rapacity for bribes, that, while you still had life and sight and senses, they succeeded in stealing away from you the contributions of Oreus and Eretria, ten talents in all, and they detached from you the delegates from those cities, and carried them back to Chalcis, uniting them in the so-called Euboean Congress. But how they did it and by what crimes, it is high time for you to hear.

Callias, depending no longer on messengers, came himself to you,[1] and coming forward in your assembly repeated a speech that Demosthenes had prepared for him. He said that he had just come from the Peloponnesus, and that he had made arrangements for contributions which would yield a revenue of not less than one hundred talents for use against Philip; and he counted off what each state was to pay: the united Achaeans and the Megarians sixty talents, and the united cities in Euboea, forty. From this fund he said we could be sure of forces by land and sea, adding that there were many other Greeks who

---

[1] In the spring of 340 B.C.

Ἑλλήνων οὓς βούλεσθαι κοινωνεῖν τῆς συντά-
ξεως, ὥστε οὔτε χρημάτων οὔτε στρατιωτῶν
ἀπορίαν ἔσεσθαι. καὶ ταῦτα μὲν τὰ φανερά·
ἔφη δὲ καὶ πράξεις πράττειν ἑτέρας δι' ἀπορρή-
των, καὶ τούτων εἶναί τινας μάρτυρας τῶν ἡμετέρων πολιτῶν, καὶ τελευτῶν ὀνομαστὶ παρεκάλει
Δημοσθένην καὶ συνειπεῖν ἠξίου.

97   Ὁ δὲ σεμνῶς πάνυ παρελθών, τόν τε Καλ-
λίαν ὑπερεπῄνει, τό τε ἀπόρρητον προσεποιή-
σατο εἰδέναι· τὴν δ' ἐκ Πελοποννήσου πρεσβείαν
ἣν ἐπρέσβευσε, καὶ τὴν ἐξ Ἀκαρνανίας ἔφη
βούλεσθαι ὑμῖν ἀπαγγεῖλαι. ἦν δ' αὐτῷ κεφάλαιον τῶν λόγων, πάντας μὲν Πελοπον-
νησίους ὑπάρχειν, πάντας δ' Ἀκαρνᾶνας συντε-
ταγμένους ἐπὶ Φίλιππον ὑφ' ἑαυτοῦ, εἶναι δὲ τὸ
σύνταγμα χρημάτων μὲν εἰς ἑκατὸν νεῶν ταχυναυτουσῶν πληρώματα καὶ εἰς πεζοὺς στρα-
98   τιώτας μυρίους καὶ ἱππέας χιλίους, ὑπάρξειν δὲ
πρὸς τούτοις καὶ τὰς πολιτικὰς δυνάμεις, ἐκ
Πελοποννήσου μὲν πλέον ἢ δισχιλίους ὁπλίτας,
ἐξ Ἀκαρνανίας δὲ ἑτέρους τοσούτους· δεδόσθαι δὲ
ἁπάντων τούτων τὴν ἡγεμονίαν ὑμῖν· πραχθήσε-
σθαι δὲ ταῦτα οὐκ εἰς μακράν, ἀλλ' εἰς τὴν ἕκτην
ἐπὶ δέκα τοῦ Ἀνθεστηριῶνος μηνός· εἰρῆσθαι γὰρ
ἐν ταῖς πόλεσιν ὑφ' αὑτοῦ καὶ παρηγγέλθαι
πάντας ἥκειν συνεδρεύσοντας Ἀθήναζε εἰς τὴν
πανσέληνον. καὶ γὰρ τοῦτο ἄνθρωπος[1] ἴδιον
99   καὶ οὐ κοινὸν ποιεῖ. οἱ μὲν γὰρ ἄλλοι ἀλα-
ζόνες, ὅταν τι ψεύδωνται, ἀόριστα καὶ ἀσαφῆ
πειρῶνται λέγειν, φοβούμενοι τὸν ἔλεγχον· Δημοσθένης δ' ὅταν ἀλαζονεύηται, πρῶτον μὲν μεθ'

---

[1] ἄνθρωπος Markland : ἄνθρωπος or ἀνθρώπων MSS.

wished to share in contributing, so that there would
be no lack of money or men. So much was openly
told; but he said that he had also conducted other
negotiations in secret, and that certain of our citizens were witnesses of them; finally he called on
Demosthenes by name and bade him confirm his
statements.

Demosthenes came forward with a most solemn
air, praised Callias above measure, and pretended
to know the secret business; but he said that he
wished to report to you his own recent mission to
the Peloponnesus and Acarnania. The sum of what
he said was that all Peloponnesus could be counted
on, and that he had brought all the Acarnanians into
line against Philip; that the contributions of money
were sufficient to provide for the manning of one
hundred swift ships, and to employ ten thousand foot
soldiers and a thousand cavalry; and that in addition
to these forces the citizen troops would be ready,
from the Peloponnesus more than two thousand
hoplites, and as many more from Acarnania; that
the leadership of them all was given to you, and
that all this was going to be done, not after a long
interval, but by the 16th of Anthesterion;[1] for he
himself had given notice in the cities, and invited
all the delegates to come to Athens by the time of
the full moon to take part in a congress.[2] For this
is Demosthenes' personal and peculiar way of doing
things: other deceivers, when they are lying, try
to speak in vague and ambiguous terms, afraid of
being convicted; but Demosthenes, when he is
cheating you, first adds an oath to his lie, calling

---

[1] March 9, 340 B.C.

[2] Not the congress of the old maritime league, but of the
new confederation now being formed against Macedonia.

ὅρκου ψεύδεται, ἐξώλειαν ἐπαρώμενος ἑαυτῷ, δεύτερον δέ, ἃ εὖ οἶδεν οὐδέποτε ἐσόμενα, τολμᾷ
λέγειν εἰς ὁπότ' ἔσται, καὶ ὧν τὰ σώματα οὐχ
ἑώρακε, τούτων τὰ ὀνόματα λέγει, κλέπτων τὴν
ἀκρόασιν καὶ μιμούμενος τοὺς τἀληθῆ λέγοντας.
διὸ καὶ σφόδρα ἄξιός ἐστι μισεῖσθαι, ὅτι πονηρὸς
ὢν καὶ τὰ τῶν χρηστῶν σημεῖα διαφθείρει.

100 Ταῦτα δ' εἰπὼν δίδωσιν ἀναγνῶναι ψήφισμα
τῷ γραμματεῖ μακρότερον μὲν τῆς Ἰλιάδος, κενό-
τερον δὲ τῶν λόγων οὓς εἴωθε λέγειν, καὶ τοῦ βίου
ὃν βεβίωκε, μεστὸν δ' ἐλπίδων οὐκ ἐσομένων καὶ
στρατοπέδων οὐδέποτε συλλεγησομένων. ἀπαγαγὼν δ' ὑμᾶς ἄπωθεν ἀπὸ τοῦ κλέμματος καὶ
ἀνακρεμάσας ἀπὸ τῶν ἐλπίδων, ἐνταῦθ' ἤδη συ-
στρέψας γράφει,[1] ἑλέσθαι πρέσβεις εἰς Ἐρέτριαν,
οἵτινες δεήσονται τῶν Ἐρετριέων, πάνυ γὰρ ἔδει
δεηθῆναι, μηκέτι διδόναι τὴν σύνταξιν ὑμῖν, τὰ
πέντε τάλαντα, ἀλλὰ Καλλίᾳ, καὶ πάλιν ἑτέρους[2]
εἰς Ὠρεόν,[3] οἵτινες δεήσονται τὸν αὐτὸν Ἀθηναί-
101 οις καὶ φίλον καὶ ἐχθρὸν νομίζειν.[4] ἔπειτα ἀνα-
φαίνεται παρ' ἅπαντ' ὢν[5] ἐν τῷ ψηφίσματι πρὸς
τῷ κλέμματι, γράψας καὶ τὰ πέντε τάλαντα τοὺς
πρέσβεις ἀξιοῦν τοὺς Ὠρείτας μὴ ὑμῖν,[6] ἀλλὰ
Καλλίᾳ διδόναι. ὅτι δ' ἀληθῆ λέγω, ἀφελὼν τὸν
κόμπον καὶ τὰς τριήρεις καὶ τὴν ἀλαζονείαν ἀνά-

---

[1] γράφει Franke : after γράφει the MSS. have κελεύων or
καὶ κελεύει.
[2] ἑτέρους Franke : after ἑτέρους the MSS. have αἱρήσεται or
αἱρεῖσθαι.
[3] Ὠρεόν Franke : Ὠρεὸν πρὸς τοὺς Ὠρείτας πρέσβεις MSS.
[4] νομίζειν Taylor : νομίζειν εἶναι MSS.

down destruction on himself; and secondly, predicting an event that he knows will never happen, he dares to tell the date of it; and he tells the names of men, when he has never so much as seen their faces, deceiving your ears and imitating men who tell the truth. And this is, indeed, another reason why he richly deserves your hatred, that he is not only a scoundrel himself, but destroys your faith even in the signs and symbols of honesty.

But now when he had said this, he gave the clerk a resolution to read, longer than the Iliad, but more empty than the speeches that he is accustomed to deliver and the life that he has lived. Empty did I say? Nay, full—of hopes that were not to be realised and of armies that were never to be assembled. And leading you off out of sight of his fraud, and suspending you on hopes, at last he gathers all up in a motion that you choose ambassadors to go to Eretria and beg the Eretrians—of course it was necessary to beg!—no longer to pay their contribution of five talents to you,[1] but to Callias; and further, that you choose other ambassadors to go to Oreus to beg the people of that city to make common cause with the Athenians. Here again, in this resolution, you see how entirely absorbed he is in his thievery, for he also moves that your ambassadors ask the people of Oreus to give their five talents, not to you, but to Callias. But to prove that I am speaking the truth, read—leave out the grandiloquence and

[1] The contribution that they had formerly paid as members of the maritime league; but it was now some years since they had thus contributed.

⁵ παρ' ἅπαντ' ὦν Blass : περὶ ἁπάντων or περὶ πάντων MSS.
⁶ ὑμῖν Blass (Aldus) : ἡμῖν MSS.

γνῶθι· τοῦ κλέμματος[1] ἅψαι, ὃ ὑφείλετο ὁ μιαρὸς
καὶ ἀνόσιος ἄνθρωπος, ὅν φησι Κτησιφῶν ἐν τῷδε
τῷ ψηφίσματι διατελεῖν λέγοντα καὶ πράττοντα
τὰ ἄριστα τῷ δήμῳ τῷ[2] Ἀθηναίων.

ΨΗΦΙΣΜΑ

102 Οὐκοῦν τὰς μὲν τριήρεις καὶ τὴν πεζὴν στρατιὰν καὶ τὴν πανσέληνον καὶ τοὺς συνέδρους
λόγῳ ἠκούσατε, τὰς δὲ συντάξεις τῶν συμμάχων,
τὰ δέκα τάλαντα, ἔργῳ ἀπωλέσατε.

103 Ὑπόλοιπον δ᾽ εἰπεῖν ἐστί μοι, ὅτι λαβὼν τρία
τάλαντα μισθὸν τὴν γνώμην ταύτην ἔγραψε
Δημοσθένης, τάλαντον μὲν ἐκ Χαλκίδος παρὰ
Καλλίου, τάλαντον δ᾽ ἐξ Ἐρετρίας παρὰ Κλειτ-
άρχου τοῦ τυράννου, τάλαντον δὲ ἐξ Ὠρεοῦ, δι᾽ ὃ
καὶ καταφανὴς ἐγένετο, δημοκρατουμένων τῶν
Ὠρειτῶν καὶ πάντα πραττόντων μετὰ ψηφίσματος. ἐξανηλωμένοι γὰρ ἐν τῷ πολέμῳ καὶ
παντελῶς ἀπόρως διακείμενοι, πέμπουσι πρὸς
αὐτὸν Γνωσίδημον τὸν Χαριγένους υἱὸν τοῦ δυνα-
στεύσαντός ποτε ἐν Ὠρεῷ, δεησόμενον τὸ μὲν
τάλαντον ἀφεῖναι τῇ πόλει, ἐπαγγελούμενον[3] δ᾽

104 αὐτῷ χαλκῆν εἰκόνα σταθήσεσθαι ἐν Ὠρεῷ. ὁ
δὲ ἀπεκρίνατο τῷ Γνωσιδήμῳ, ὅτι ἐλάχιστα
χαλκοῦ δέοιτο,[4] τὸ δὲ τάλαντον διὰ τοῦ Καλλίου
εἰσέπραττεν. ἀναγκαζόμενοι δὲ οἱ Ὠρεῖται καὶ
οὐκ εὐποροῦντες, ὑπέθεσαν αὐτῷ τοῦ ταλάντου
τὰς δημοσίας προσόδους, καὶ τόκον ἤνεγκαν
Δημοσθένει τοῦ δωροδοκήματος δραχμὴν τοῦ

---

[1] τοῦ κλέμματος: the MSS. have καὶ τοῦ κλέμματος or καὶ
ἀπὸ τοῦ κλέμματος.
[2] δήμῳ τῷ Weidner: δήμῳ τῶν MSS.

the triremes and the pretence, and come to the trick
worked on us by the vile and wicked man, who,
according to Ctesiphon's motion which we are discussing, "constantly speaks and does what is best
for the people of Athens."

RESOLUTION

So then the triremes and the land forces and the
full moon and the congress were so much talk for
your ears, but the contributions of the allies, those
ten talents, were very real, and you lost them.

It remains for me to say that Demosthenes was
paid three talents for making this motion: a talent
from Chalcis, paid over by Callias, a talent from
Eretria, paid by the tyrant Cleitarchus, and a talent
from Oreus. And it was this last by means of which
he was found out; for the government of Oreus is a
democracy, and everything is done there by popular
vote. Now they, exhausted by the war and entirely
without means, sent to him Gnosidemus, son of
Charigenes, a man who had once been powerful in
Oreus, to ask him to release the city from paying the
talent, and to offer him a statue of bronze to be set
up in Oreus. But he replied to Gnosidemus that the
last thing that he was in need of was bronze, and he
tried to collect the talent through Callias. Now the
people of Oreus, pressed for payment and without
means, mortgaged to him the public revenues as
security for the talent, and paid Demosthenes interest
on the fruit of his bribery at the rate of a drachma

---

³ ἐπαγγελούμενον Stephanus : ἐπαγγελλόμενον MSS.
⁴ ἐλάχιστα χαλκοῦ δέοιτο Halm : ἐλαχίστου χαλκοῦ οὐδὲν
δέοιτο MSS.

105 μηνὸς τῆς μνᾶς, ἕως τὸ κεφάλαιον ἀπέδοσαν. καὶ
ταῦτ᾽ ἐπράχθη μετὰ ψηφίσματος τοῦ δήμου. ὅτι
δὲ ἀληθῆ λέγω, λαβέ μοι τὸ ψήφισμα τῶν
Ὠρειτῶν.

ΨΗΦΙΣΜΑ

Τοῦτ᾽ ἐστὶ τὸ ψήφισμα, ὦ ἄνδρες Ἀθηναῖοι,
αἰσχύνη μὲν τῆς πόλεως, ἔλεγχος δὲ οὐ μικρὸς
τῶν Δημοσθένους πολιτευμάτων, φανερὰ δὲ κατηγορία Κτησιφῶντος· τὸν γὰρ οὕτως αἰσχρῶς
δωροδοκοῦντα οὐκ ἔστιν ἄνδρα γεγονέναι ἀγαθόν,
δ¹ τετόλμηκεν οὗτος γράψαι.²

106 Ἐνταῦθ᾽ ἤδη τέτακται καὶ ὁ τρίτος τῶν καιρῶν,
μᾶλλον δ᾽ ὁ πάντων πικρότατος χρόνος, ἐν ᾧ Δημοσθένης ἀπώλεσε τὰς τῶν Ἑλλήνων καὶ τῆς
πόλεως πράξεις, ἀσεβήσας μὲν εἰς τὸ ἱερὸν τὸ ἐν
Δελφοῖς, ἄδικον δὲ καὶ οὐδαμῶς ἴσην τὴν πρὸς
Θηβαίους συμμαχίαν γράψας. ἄρξομαι δὲ ἀπὸ
τῶν εἰς τοὺς θεοὺς πλημμελημάτων³ λέγειν.

107 Ἔστι γάρ, ὦ ἄνδρες Ἀθηναῖοι, τὸ Κιρραῖον
ὠνομασμένον πεδίον καὶ λιμὴν ὁ νῦν ἐξάγιστος
καὶ ἐπάρατος ὠνομασμένος. ταύτην ποτὲ τὴν
χώραν κατῴκησαν Κιρραῖοι καὶ Κραγαλίδαι, γένη
παρανομώτατα, οἳ εἰς τὸ ἱερὸν τὸ ἐν Δελφοῖς καὶ
περὶ τὰ ἀναθήματα ἠσέβουν, ἐξημάρτανον δὲ καὶ
εἰς τοὺς Ἀμφικτύονας. ἀγανακτήσαντες δ᾽ ἐπὶ
τοῖς γιγνομένοις μάλιστα μέν, ὡς λέγονται, οἱ
πρόγονοι οἱ ὑμέτεροι, ἔπειτα καὶ οἱ ἄλλοι Ἀμφικτύονες, μαντείαν ἐμαντεύσαντο παρὰ τῷ θεῷ, τίνι

---

¹ δ Stephanus : ἃ MSS.
² γράψαι Weidner : the MSS. have ἐν τῷ ψηφίσματι before
or after γράψαι.

per month on the mina,[1] until they paid off the principal. This was done by vote of the people. To prove that what I am telling you is true, please take the decree of the people of Oreus.

This is the decree, fellow citizens, a disgrace to our city, no slight exposure of Demosthenes' policies, and a clear accusation against Ctesiphon as well. For the man who so shamelessly received bribes cannot have been the good man that Ctesiphon has dared to set forth.

I come now to the third period, or rather to that bitterest period of all, in which Demosthenes brought ruin upon our state and upon all Hellas by his impiety toward the shrine at Delphi, and by moving the alliance with Thebes—an unjust alliance and utterly unequal. But I will begin with his sins against the the gods.

There is, fellow citizens, a plain, called the plain of Cirrha, and a harbour, now known as "dedicate and accursed." This district was once inhabited by the Cirrhaeans and the Cragalidae, most lawless tribes, who repeatedly committed sacrilege against the shrine at Delphi and the votive offerings there, and who transgressed against the Amphictyons also. This conduct exasperated all the Amphictyons, and your ancestors most of all, it is said, and they sought at the shrine of the god an oracle to tell them with what penalty

---

[1] Twelve per cent. a year, an ordinary rate of interest.

---

[3] πλημμελημάτων Weidner : αὐτοῦ πλημμελημάτων or πλημμελημάτων αὐτοῦ MSS.

χρὴ τιμωρίᾳ τοὺς ἀνθρώπους τούτους μετελθεῖν.
108 καὶ αὐτοῖς ἀναιρεῖ ἡ Πυθία πολεμεῖν Κιρραίοις
καὶ Κραγαλίδαις πάντ' ἤματα καὶ πάσας νύκτας,
καὶ τὴν χώραν αὐτῶν ἐκπορθήσαντας καὶ αὐτοὺς
ἀνδραποδισαμένους ἀναθεῖναι τῷ Ἀπόλλωνι τῷ
Πυθίῳ καὶ τῇ Ἀρτέμιδι καὶ τῇ[1] Λητοῖ καὶ Ἀθηνᾷ
Προναίᾳ[2] ἐπὶ πάσῃ ἀεργίᾳ, καὶ ταύτην τὴν
χώραν μήτ' αὐτοὺς ἐργάζεσθαι μήτ' ἄλλον ἐᾶν.

Λαβόντες δὲ τὸν χρησμὸν τοῦτον οἱ Ἀμφικτύονες ἐψηφίσαντο Σόλωνος εἰπόντος Ἀθηναίου
τὴν γνώμην, ἀνδρὸς καὶ νομοθετῆσαι δυνατοῦ καὶ
περὶ ποίησιν καὶ φιλοσοφίαν διατετριφότος, ἐπιστρατεύειν ἐπὶ τοὺς ἐναγεῖς κατὰ τὴν μαντείαν
109 τοῦ θεοῦ· καὶ συναθροίσαντες δύναμιν πολλὴν τῶν
Ἀμφικτυόνων, ἐξηνδραποδίσαντο τοὺς ἀνθρώπους
καὶ τὸν λιμένα καὶ τὴν πόλιν αὐτῶν κατέσκαψαν
καὶ τὴν χώραν[3] καθιέρωσαν κατὰ τὴν μαντείαν.
καὶ ἐπὶ τούτοις ὅρκον ὤμοσαν ἰσχυρόν, μήτ'
αὐτοὶ τὴν ἱερὰν γῆν ἐργάσεσθαι μήτ' ἄλλῳ
ἐπιτρέψειν, ἀλλὰ βοηθήσειν τῷ θεῷ καὶ τῇ γῇ τῇ
ἱερᾷ καὶ χειρὶ καὶ ποδὶ καὶ φωνῇ[4] καὶ πάσῃ
110 δυνάμει. καὶ οὐκ ἀπέχρησεν αὐτοῖς τοῦτον τὸν
ὅρκον ὀμόσαι, ἀλλὰ καὶ προστροπὴν καὶ ἀρὰν
ἰσχυρὰν ὑπὲρ τούτων ἐποιήσαντο. γέγραπται
γὰρ οὕτως ἐν τῇ ἀρᾷ, "Εἴ τις τάδε," φησί, "παρα-
βαίνοι ἢ πόλις ἢ ἰδιώτης ἢ ἔθνος, ἐναγής," φησίν,
"ἔστω τοῦ Ἀπόλλωνος καὶ τῆς Ἀρτέμιδος καὶ

---

[1] τῇ added by Herwerden.
[2] Προναίᾳ Bekker : Προνοίᾳ MSS.   So in §§ 110 and 111.
[3] χώραν Markland : χώραν αὐτῶν MSS.
[4] καὶ φωνῇ added by Baiter and Sauppe.   cp. § 120 and ii.
115.

they should visit these men. The Pythia replied
that they must fight against the Cirrhaeans and the
Cragalidae day and night, utterly ravage their country,
enslave the inhabitants, and dedicate the land to the
Pythian Apollo and Artemis and Leto and Athena
Pronaea,[1] that for the future it lie entirely unculti-
vated ; that they must not till this land themselves
nor permit another.

Now when they had received this oracle, the
Amphictyons voted, on motion of Solon of Athens,
a man able as a law-giver and versed in poetry
and philosophy, to march against the accursed men
according to the oracle of the god. Collecting a great
force of the Amphictyons, they enslaved the men,
destroyed their harbour and city, and dedicated their
land, as the oracle had commanded. Moreover they
swore a mighty oath, that they would not themselves
till the sacred land nor let another till it, but that
they would go to the aid of the god and the sacred
land with hand and foot and voice, and all their might.
They were not content with taking this oath, but
they added an imprecation and a mighty curse concerning this ; for it stands thus written in the curse :
" If any one should violate this," it says, " whether
city or private man, or tribe, let them be under the
curse," it says, " of Apollo and Artemis and Leto and

[1] The MSS. read Προνοίᾳ, "Goddess of Forethought." But
undoubtedly the form in the ancient oracle was Προναίᾳ, a
name peculiar to the Athena of Delphi, and arising from
the fact that there she was the Athena of the "Fore-
temple" (προ-ναός), for her temple lay in front of that of
Apollo.

111 τῆς¹ Λητοῦς καὶ ᾿Αθηνᾶς Προναίας.'' ² καὶ
ἐπεύχεται αὐτοῖς μήτε γῆν καρποὺς φέρειν, μήτε
γυναῖκας τέκνα τίκτειν γονεῦσιν ἐοικότα, ἀλλὰ
τέρατα, μήτε βοσκήματα κατὰ φύσιν γονὰς
ποιεῖσθαι, ἧτταν δὲ αὐτοῖς εἶναι πολέμου καὶ
δικῶν καὶ ἀγορᾶς, καὶ ἐξώλεις εἶναι καὶ αὐτοὺς
καὶ οἰκίας καὶ γένος ἐκείνων. " Καὶ μήποτε,"
φησίν, "ὁσίως θύσειαν τῷ ᾿Απόλλωνι μηδὲ τῇ
᾿Αρτέμιδι μηδὲ τῇ Λητοῖ μηδ' ᾿Αθηνᾷ Προναίᾳ,
112 μηδὲ δέξαιντο αὐτοῖς τὰ ἱερά." ὅτι δ' ἀληθῆ λέγω,
ἀνάγνωθι τὴν τοῦ θεοῦ μαντείαν. ἀκούσατε τῆς
ἀρᾶς. ἀναμνήσθητε τῶν ὅρκων, οὓς ὑμῶν οἱ
πρόγονοι μετὰ τῶν ᾿Αμφικτυόνων συνώμοσαν.

MANTEIA

[Οὐ πρὶν τῆσδε πόληος ἐρείψετε πύργον
ἑλόντες,
πρίν γε θεοῦ τεμένει κυανώπιδος ᾿Αμφιτρίτης
κῦμα ποτικλύζῃ κελαδοῦν ἱεραῖσιν ἐπ' ἀκταῖς.]

OPKOI. APA

113 Ταύτης τῆς ἀρᾶς καὶ τῶν ὅρκων καὶ τῆς μαντείας ἀναγεγραμμένων ἔτι καὶ νῦν, οἱ Λοκροὶ οἱ
᾿Αμφισσεῖς, μᾶλλον δὲ οἱ προεστηκότες αὐτῶν,
ἄνδρες παρανομώτατοι, ἐπηργάζοντο τὸ πεδίον,
καὶ τὸν λιμένα τὸν ἐξάγιστον καὶ ἐπάρατον πάλιν
ἐτείχισαν καὶ συνῴκισαν, καὶ τέλη τοὺς κατα-
πλέοντας ἐξέλεγον, καὶ τῶν ἀφικνουμένων εἰς
Δελφοὺς πυλαγόρων ἐνίους χρήμασι διέφθειρον,
114 ὧν εἷς ἦν Δημοσθένης. χειροτονηθεὶς γὰρ ὑφ'

---

¹ τῆς added by Herwerden.
² For Προναίας and Προναίᾳ below, see on § 108.

Athena Pronaea." The curse goes on: That their
land bear no fruit; that their wives bear children
not like those who begat them, but monsters; that
their flocks yield not their natural increase; that defeat await them in camp and court and market-place,
and that they perish utterly, themselves, their houses,
their whole race; "And never," it says, "may they
offer pure sacrifice unto Apollo, nor to Artemis, nor
to Leto, nor to Athena Pronaea, and may the gods
refuse to accept their offerings." As a proof of this,
let the oracle of the god be read; hear the curse;
call to mind the oaths that your fathers swore
together with all the other Amphictyons.

THE ORACLE

[Ye may not hope to capture town nor tower,
Till dark-eyed Amphitrite's waves shall break
And roar against Apollo's sacred shore.[1]]

THE OATHS. THE CURSE

This curse, these oaths, and this oracle stand
recorded to this day; yet the Locrians of Amphissa,
or rather their leaders, most lawless of men, did
till the plain, and they rebuilt the walls of the
harbour that was dedicate and accursed, and settled
there and collected port-dues from those who sailed
into the harbour; and of the deputies[2] who came
to Delphi they corrupted some with money, one of
whom was Demosthenes. For after he had been

---

[1] The oracle given in the MSS. is evidently not the one
that Aeschines cited. Some ancient editor has inserted it,
finding it in Pausanias' account of these events (Pausan.
x. xxxvii. 6). [2] See on § 115

ὑμῶν πυλάγορος, λαμβάνει δισχιλίας δραχμὰς
παρὰ τῶν Ἀμφισσέων, τοῦ μηδεμίαν μνείαν
περὶ αὐτῶν ἐν τοῖς Ἀμφικτύοσι ποιεῖσθαι. διω-
μολογήθη δ᾽ αὐτῷ καὶ εἰς τὸν λοιπὸν χρόνον
ἀποστέλλεσθαι Ἀθήναζε τοῦ ἐνιαυτοῦ ἑκάστου
μνᾶς εἴκοσιν ἐκ τῶν ἐξαγίστων καὶ ἐπαράτων
χρημάτων, ἐφ᾽ ᾧτε βοηθήσει τοῖς Ἀμφισσεῦσιν
Ἀθήνησι κατὰ πάντα τρόπον· ὅθεν ἔτι μᾶλλον
ἢ πρότερον συμβέβηκεν αὐτῷ, ὅτου ἂν προσάψη-
ται, ἢ ἀνδρὸς [1] ἰδιώτου ἢ δυνάστου ἢ πόλεως
δημοκρατουμένης, τούτων ἑκάστους ἀνιάτοις συμφοραῖς περιβάλλειν.

115   Σκέψασθε δὴ τὸν δαίμονα καὶ τὴν τύχην,
ὅσῳ περιεγένετο τῆς τῶν Ἀμφισσέων ἀσεβείας.
ἐπὶ γὰρ Θεοφράστου ἄρχοντος, ἱερομνήμονος ὄντος
Διογνήτου Ἀναφλυστίου, πυλαγόρους ὑμεῖς εἵλεσθε Μειδίαν τε ἐκεῖνον τὸν Ἀναγυράσιον, ὃν
ἐβουλόμην ἂν πολλῶν ἕνεκα ζῆν, καὶ Θρασυκλέα
τὸν ἐξ Οἴου, καὶ τρίτον μετὰ τούτων ἐμέ. συνέβη
δ᾽ ἡμῖν ἀρτίως μὲν εἰς Δελφοὺς ἀφῖχθαι, παραχρῆμα δὲ τὸν ἱερομνήμονα Διόγνητον πυρέττειν·
τὸ δ᾽ αὐτὸ τοῦτο συνεπεπτώκει καὶ τῷ Μειδίᾳ.
116   οἱ δ᾽ ἄλλοι συνεκάθηντο Ἀμφικτύονες. ἐξηγγέλλετο δ᾽ ἡμῖν παρὰ τῶν βουλομένων εὔνοιαν
ἐνδείκνυσθαι τῇ πόλει, ὅτι οἱ Ἀμφισσεῖς ὑπο-
πεπτωκότες τότε καὶ δεινῶς θεραπεύοντες τοὺς
Θηβαίους εἰσέφερον δόγμα κατὰ τῆς ἡμετέρας

---

[1] ἢ ἀνδρὸς Blass : ἀνδρὸς or ἢ ἀνδρὸς ἢ MSS.

elected your deputy,[1] he received two thousand drachmas from the Amphissians, in return for which he was to see that no mention of them should be made in the assembly of the Amphictyons. And it was agreed with him that thereafter twenty minas of the accursed and abominable money should be sent to Athens to him yearly, on condition that he at Athens aid the Amphissians in every way. In consequence of this it has come to pass even more than before, that whatsoever he touches, be it private citizen, or ruler, or democratic state, becomes entangled, every one, in irreparable misfortune.

Now behold how providence and fortune triumphed over the impiety of the Amphissians. It was in the archonship of Theophrastus;[2] Diognetus of Anaphlystus was our hieromnemon; as pylagori[3] you elected Meidias of Anagyrus, whom you all remember —I wish for many reasons he were still living[4]—and Thrasycles of Oeum; I was the third. But it happened that we were no sooner come to Delphi than Diognetus, the hieromnemon, fell sick with fever; the same misfortune had befallen Meidias already. The other Amphictyons took their seats. Now it was reported to us by one and another who wished to show friendship to our city, that the Amphissians, who were at that time dominated by the Thebans and were their abject servants, were in the act of bringing in a resolution against our city, to the

---

[1] In 343 B.C.   [2] 340/39 B.C.

[3] The hieromnemon, selected annually by lot, was the official representative of the state in the Amphictyonic Council; the three pylagori were selected by vote as his advisers. The pylagori had the privilege of taking part in the debates of the Amphictyonic Council, but the vote of the state was cast by the hieromnemon.   [4] See on § 52.

πόλεως, πεντήκοντα ταλάντοις ζημιῶσαι τὸν δῆμον τὸν Ἀθηναίων, ὅτι χρυσᾶς ἀσπίδας ἀνέθεμεν
πρὸς τὸν καινὸν νεὼν πρὶν ἐξαρέσασθαι, καὶ
ἐπεγράψαμεν τὸ προσῆκον ἐπίγραμμα, "Ἀθηναῖοι
ἀπὸ Μήδων καὶ Θηβαίων, ὅτε τἀναντία τοῖς
Ἕλλησιν ἐμάχοντο."

Μεταπεμψάμενος δ' ἐμὲ ὁ ἱερομνήμων ἠξίου
εἰσελθεῖν εἰς τὸ συνέδριον καὶ εἰπεῖν τι πρὸς
τοὺς Ἀμφικτύονας ὑπὲρ τῆς πόλεως, καὶ αὐτὸν
117 οὕτω προῃρημένον. ἀρχομένου δέ μου λέγειν καὶ
προθυμότερόν πως εἰσεληλυθότος εἰς τὸ συνέδριον, τῶν ἄλλων πυλαγόρων μεθεστηκότων,
ἀναβοήσας τις τῶν Ἀμφισσέων, ἄνθρωπος ἀσελ-
γέστατος καὶ ὡς ἐμοὶ ἐφαίνετο οὐδεμιᾶς παιδείας
μετεσχηκώς, ἴσως δὲ καὶ δαιμονίου τινὸς ἐξαμαρτάνειν προαγομένου, "Ἀρχὴν δέ γε," ἔφη,
"ὦ ἄνδρες Ἕλληνες, εἰ ἐσωφρονεῖτε, οὐδ' ἂν
ὠνομάζετε τοὔνομα τοῦ δήμου τοῦ Ἀθηναίων
ἐν ταῖσδε ταῖς ἡμέραις, ἀλλ' ὡς ἐναγεῖς ἐξείργετ'
118 ἂν ἐκ τοῦ ἱεροῦ." ἅμα δὲ ἐμέμνητο τῆς τῶν
Φωκέων συμμαχίας, ἣν ὁ Κρωβύλος ἐκεῖνος
ἔγραψε, καὶ ἄλλα πολλὰ καὶ δυσχερῆ κατὰ τῆς
πόλεως διεξῄει, ἃ ἐγὼ οὔτε τότ' ἐκαρτέρουν ἀκούων,
οὔτε νῦν ἡδέως μέμνημαι αὐτῶν. ἀκούσας δὲ οὕτω
παρωξύνθην, ὡς οὐδεπώποτ' ἐν τῷ ἐμαυτοῦ βίῳ.

Καὶ τοὺς μὲν ἄλλους λόγους ὑπερβήσομαι·
ἐπῄει δ' οὖν μοι ἐπὶ τὴν γνώμην μνησθῆναι τῆς

---

¹ The temple of Apollo at Delphi had been seriously
injured by fire in 373 B.C. Repairs had been going on under
an inter-state commission. The work had been interrupted
by the Phocian war, but was at this time nearing completion.
The shields that the Athenians had caused to be re-hung

effect that the people of Athens be fined fifty talents, because we had affixed gilded shields to the new temple and dedicated them before the temple had been consecrated, and had written the appropriate inscription, "The Athenians, from the Medes and Thebans when they fought against Hellas." [1]

The hieromnemon sent for me and asked me to go into the council and speak to the Amphictyons in behalf of our city—indeed I had already determined of myself so to do.   When I had entered the council, perhaps a little too impetuously—the other pylagori had withdrawn [2]—and when I was just beginning to speak, one of the Amphissians, a scurrilous fellow, and, as I plainly saw, a man of no education whatever, but perhaps also led on to folly by some divine visitation, cried out, "O Greeks, if you were in your right mind, you would not have so much as named the name of the people of Athens in these sacred days, but you would have debarred them from the shrine, as men polluted." And at the same time he reminded them of your alliance with the Phocians, proposed by that man whom we used to call " Top-knot "; [3] and he went through a long list of vexatious charges against our city, which angered me almost beyond endurance as I listened to them then, and which it is no pleasure to recall now.   For as I listened, I was exasperated as never before in my life.

I will pass over the rest of what I said, but this occurred to me, to call attention to the impiety

were a part of the Athenian booty from the battle of Plataea.   For almost a century and a half they had been an eyesore to the Thebans.

[2] It would appear that the debate was over and the voting members, the hieromnemons, alone remained, when Aeschines rushed in and began to speak.   [3] See on i. 64.

τῶν Ἀμφισσέων περὶ τὴν γῆν τὴν ἱερὰν ἀσεβείας,
καὶ αὐτόθεν ἑστηκὼς ἐδείκνυον τοῖς Ἀμφικτύοσιν·
ὑπόκειται γὰρ τὸ Κιρραῖον πεδίον τῷ ἱερῷ καὶ
119 ἔστιν εὐσύνοπτον. "Ὁρᾶτε," ἔφην ἐγώ, "ὦ ἄνδρες Ἀμφικτύονες, ἐξειργασμένον τουτὶ τὸ πεδίον
ὑπὸ τῶν Ἀμφισσέων, καὶ κεραμεῖα ἐνῳκοδομημένα
καὶ αὔλια· ὁρᾶτε τοῖς ὀφθαλμοῖς τὸν ἐξάγιστον
καὶ ἐπάρατον λιμένα τετειχισμένον· ἴστε τούτους
αὐτοί, καὶ οὐδὲν ἑτέρων δεῖσθε μαρτύρων, τέλη
πεπρακότας[1] καὶ χρήματα λαμβάνοντας ἐκ τοῦ
ἱεροῦ λιμένος." ἅμα δὲ ἀναγιγνώσκειν ἐκέλευον
αὐτοῖς τὴν μαντείαν τοῦ θεοῦ, τὸν ὅρκον τῶν
προγόνων, τὴν ἀρὰν τὴν γενομένην, καὶ διωριζόμην
120 ὅτι "Ἐγὼ μὲν ὑπὲρ τοῦ δήμου τοῦ Ἀθηναίων καὶ
τοῦ σώματος καὶ τῶν τέκνων καὶ οἰκίας τῆς ἐμαυτοῦ βοηθῶ κατὰ τὸν ὅρκον καὶ τῷ θεῷ καὶ τῇ γῇ
τῇ ἱερᾷ καὶ χειρὶ καὶ ποδὶ καὶ φωνῇ καὶ πᾶσιν οἷς
δύναμαι, καὶ τὴν πόλιν τὴν ἡμετέραν τὰ πρὸς τοὺς
θεοὺς ἀφοσιῶ· ὑμεῖς δ' ὑπὲρ ὑμῶν αὐτῶν ἤδη
βουλεύεσθε. ἐνῆρκται μὲν τὰ κανᾶ, παρέστηκε
δὲ τὰ θύματα τοῖς βωμοῖς, μέλλετε δ' αἰτεῖν τοὺς
121 θεοὺς τἀγαθὰ καὶ κοινῇ καὶ ἰδίᾳ. σκοπεῖτε δή,
ποίᾳ φωνῇ, ποίᾳ ψυχῇ, ποίοις ὄμμασι, τίνα
τόλμαν κτησάμενοι τὰς ἱκετείας ποιήσεσθε, τούτους παρέντες ἀτιμωρήτους τοὺς ἐναγεῖς καὶ ταῖς
ἀραῖς ἐνόχους. οὐ γὰρ δι' αἰνιγμῶν, ἀλλ' ἐναργῶς
γέγραπται[2] κατά τε τῶν ἀσεβησάντων, ἃ χρὴ
παθεῖν αὐτούς, καὶ κατὰ τῶν ἐπιτρεψάντων, καὶ
τελευταῖον ἐν τῇ ἀρᾷ γέγραπται, 'Μηδ' ὁσίως,'

---

[1] πεπρακότας Hamaker : πεπραχότας MSS.
[2] γέγραπται : γέγραπται ἐν τῇ ἀρᾷ MSS. Blass brackets ἐν τῇ ἀρᾷ. See two lines below.

of the Amphissians in relation to the sacred land;
and from the very spot where I was standing I
pointed it out to the Amphictyons; for the plain of
Cirrha lies just below the shrine and is clearly visible.
"You see," I said, "O Amphictyons, the plain
yonder tilled by the Amphissians, and pottery works
and farm buildings erected there. You see with
your own eyes the dedicated and accursed harbour
walled again. You know of your own knowledge,
and have no need of other witness, how these men
have farmed out port-dues, and how they are making
money from the sacred harbour." At the same
time I called for the reading of the oracle of the
god, the oath of our fathers, and the curse that was
proclaimed. And I made this declaration: "I, in
behalf of the people of Athens, in my own behalf, and in behalf of my children and my house,
do come to the help of the god and the sacred
land according unto the oath, with hand and foot and
voice, and all my powers; and I purge our city of
this impiety. As for you, now make your own decision. The sacred baskets are prepared; the sacrificial victims stand ready at the altars; and you are
about to pray to the gods for blessings on state and
hearth. Consider then with what voice, with what
spirit, with what countenance, possessed of what
effrontery, you will make your supplications, if you
let go unpunished these men, who stand under the
ban of the curse. For not in riddles, but plainly
is written the penalty to be suffered by those
who have been guilty of impiety, and for those
who have permitted it; and the curse closes with
these words: 'May they who fail to punish them

φησί, ' θύσειαν οἱ μὴ τιμωροῦντες τῷ Ἀπόλλωνι
μηδὲ τῇ Ἀρτέμιδι μηδὲ τῇ Λητοῖ μηδ' Ἀθηνᾷ
Προναίᾳ,[1] μηδὲ δέξαιντο αὐτοῖς[2] τὰ ἱερά.'"

122   Ταῦτα[3] καὶ πρὸς τούτοις ἕτερα πολλὰ διε-
ξελθόντος ἐμοῦ, ἐπειδή ποτε ἀπηλλάγην καὶ
μετέστην ἐκ τοῦ συνεδρίου, κραυγὴ πολλὴ καὶ
θόρυβος ἦν τῶν Ἀμφικτυόνων, καὶ ὁ λόγος ἦν
οὐκέτι περὶ τῶν ἀσπίδων ἃς ἡμεῖς ἀνέθεμεν, ἀλλ'
ἤδη περὶ τῆς τῶν Ἀμφισσέων τιμωρίας. ἤδη
δὲ πόρρω τῆς ἡμέρας ὄν,[4] προελθὼν[5] ὁ κῆρυξ
ἀνεῖπε, Δελφῶν ὅσοι ἐπὶ διετὲς ἡβῶσι, καὶ δούλους καὶ ἐλευθέρους, ἥκειν αὔριον ἅμα τῇ ἡμέρᾳ
ἔχοντας ἅμας καὶ δικέλλας πρὸς τὸ Θυτεῖον
ἐκεῖ καλούμενον· καὶ πάλιν ὁ αὐτὸς κῆρυξ ἀνα-
γορεύει τοὺς ἱερομνήμονας καὶ τοὺς πυλαγόρους
ἅπαντας ἥκειν εἰς τὸν αὐτὸν τόπον βοηθήσοντας
τῷ θεῷ καὶ τῇ γῇ τῇ ἱερᾷ· "Ἥτις δ' ἂν μὴ παρῇ
πόλις, εἴρξεται τοῦ ἱεροῦ καὶ ἐναγὴς ἔσται καὶ τῇ
ἀρᾷ ἔνοχος.

123   Τῇ δὲ ὑστεραίᾳ ἥκομεν ἕωθεν εἰς τὸν προειρη-
μένον τόπον, καὶ κατέβημεν εἰς τὸ Κιρραῖον
πεδίον, καὶ τὸν λιμένα κατασκάψαντες καὶ τὰς
οἰκίας ἐμπρήσαντες ἀνεχωροῦμεν. ταῦτα δὲ ἡμῶν
πραττόντων οἱ Λοκροὶ οἱ Ἀμφισσεῖς, ἑξήκοντα
στάδια ἄπωθεν οἰκοῦντες Δελφῶν, ἦλθον ἐφ'
ἡμᾶς μεθ' ὅπλων πανδημεί· καὶ εἰ μὴ δρόμῳ
μόλις ἐξεφύγομεν εἰς Δελφούς, ἐκινδυνεύσαμεν
ἂν ἀπολέσθαι.

[1] Προναίᾳ. See on § 108.
[2] αὐτοῖς Dobree : αὐτῶν MSS.
[3] ταῦτα Reiske : τοιαῦτα MSS.
[4] ὄν Herwerden : οὔσης MSS.
[5] προελθὼν Markland : προσελθὼν MSS.

never offer pure sacrifice unto Apollo, nor to Artemis, nor to Leto, nor to Athena Pronaea, and may the gods refuse to accept their offerings.' "

These words I spoke, and many more. And when now I had finished and gone out from the council, there was great outcry and excitement among the Amphictyons, and nothing more was said about the shields that we had dedicated, but from now on the subject was the punishment of the Amphissians. As it was already late in the day, the herald came forward and made proclamation that all the men of Delphi who were of full age, slaves and free men alike, should come at daybreak on the morrow with shovels and mattocks to the place that is there called the Thyteion. And again the same herald proclaimed that all the hieromnemons and the pylagori should come to the same place to the aid of the god and the sacred land; "And whatever city shall fail to appear, shall be debarred from the shrine and shall be impure and under the curse."

The next morning we came to the designated spot, and descended to the Cirrhaean plain. And when we had despoiled the harbour and burned down the houses, we set out to return. But meanwhile the Locrians of Amphissa, who lived sixty stadia from Delphi, came against us, armed and in full force; and it was only by running that we barely got back to Delphi in safety, for we were in peril of our lives.

124 Τῇ δὲ ἐπιούσῃ ἡμέρᾳ Κόττυφος ὁ τὰς γνώμας
ἐπιψηφίζων ἐκκλησίαν ἐποίει τῶν Ἀμφικτυόνων·
ἐκκλησίαν γὰρ ὀνομάζουσιν, ὅταν τις μὴ μόνον
τοὺς πυλαγόρους καὶ τοὺς ἱερομνήμονας συγκα-
λέσῃ, ἀλλὰ καὶ τοὺς θύοντας καὶ τοὺς χρωμένους
τῷ θεῷ. ἐνταῦθ' ἤδη πολλαὶ μὲν τῶν Ἀμφισσέων
ἐγίγνοντο κατηγορίαι, πολὺς δ' ἔπαινος ἦν κατὰ
τῆς ἡμετέρας πόλεως· τέλος δὲ παντὸς τοῦ λόγου
ψηφίζονται ἥκειν τοὺς ἱερομνήμονας πρὸ τῆς
ἐπιούσης πυλαίας ἐν ῥητῷ χρόνῳ εἰς Πύλας,
ἔχοντας δόγμα καθ' ὅ τι δίκας δώσουσιν οἱ
Ἀμφισσεῖς ὑπὲρ ὧν εἰς τὸν θεὸν καὶ τὴν γῆν τὴν
ἱερὰν καὶ τοὺς Ἀμφικτύονας ἐξήμαρτον. ὅτι δὲ
ἀληθῆ λέγω, ἀναγνώσεται τὸ ψήφισμα ὑμῖν ὁ
γραμματεύς.

ΨΗΦΙΣΜΑ

125 Τοῦ δόγματος τούτου ἀποδοθέντος ὑφ' ἡμῶν ἐν
τῇ βουλῇ καὶ πάλιν ἐν τῇ ἐκκλησίᾳ, καὶ τὰς
πράξεις ἡμῶν ἀποδεξαμένου τοῦ δήμου, καὶ τῆς
πόλεως ἁπάσης προαιρουμένης εὐσεβεῖν, καὶ
Δημοσθένους ὑπὲρ τοῦ μεσεγγυήματος τοῦ ἐξ
Ἀμφίσσης ἀντιλέγοντος, καὶ ἐμοῦ φανερῶς ἐναντίον ὑμῶν ἐξελέγχοντος, ἐπειδὴ ἐκ τοῦ φανεροῦ
τὴν πόλιν ἄνθρωπος[1] οὐκ ἐδύνατο σφῆλαι, εἰσελθὼν εἰς τὸ βουλευτήριον καὶ μεταστησάμενος τοὺς
ἰδιώτας, ἐκφέρεται προβούλευμα εἰς τὴν ἐκκλησίαν, προσλαβὼν τὴν τοῦ γράψαντος ἀπειρίαν·

___

[1] ἄνθρωπος Markland : ἄνθρωπος MSS.

___

[1] Before the next regular meeting of the Amphictyonic
Council. The Council met twice a year, in spring and

Now on the next day Cottyphus, the presiding officer, called an "assembly" of the Amphictyons (they call it an "assembly" when not only the pylagori and hieromnemons are called together, but with them those who are sacrificing and consulting the god). Then immediately one charge after another was brought against the Amphissians, and our city was much praised. As the outcome of all that was said, they voted that before the next Pylaea[1] the hieromnemons should assemble at Thermopylae at a time designated, bringing with them a resolution for the punishment of the Amphissians for their sins against the god and the sacred land and the Amphictyons. As proof of what I say, the clerk shall read the decree to you.

DECREE

Now when we had reported this decree to our senate, and then to the assembly, and when the people had approved our acts, and the whole city was ready to choose the righteous course, and when Demosthenes had spoken in opposition—he was earning his retaining-fee from Amphissa—and when I had clearly convicted him in your presence, thereupon the fellow, unable to frustrate the city by open means, goes into the senate chamber, expels all listeners, and from the secret session brings out a bill to the assembly, taking advantage of the inexperience of the man who made the motion.[2]

autumn. They always assembled at Thermopylae, and proceeded thence to Delphi.

[2] Aeschines implies that Demosthenes drafted the motion in a form which gave it a very different effect from what was expected by the inexperienced senator through whom he had it presented to the senate

THE SPEECHES OF AESCHINES

126 τὸ δ' αὐτὸ τοῦτο καὶ ἐν τῇ ἐκκλησίᾳ διεπράξατο
ἐπιψηφισθῆναι καὶ γενέσθαι δήμου ψήφισμα,
ἐπ' ἀναστάσει τῆς ἐκκλησίας οὔσης,¹ ἀπελη-
λυθότος ἐμοῦ, οὐ γὰρ ἄν ποτε ἐπέτρεψα, καὶ τῶν
πολλῶν διαφειμένων· οὗ τὸ κεφάλαιόν ἐστι, "Τὸν
ἱερομνήμονα," φησί, "τὸν Ἀθηναίων καὶ τοὺς
πυλαγόρους τοὺς ἀεὶ πυλαγοροῦντας πορεύεσθαι
εἰς Πύλας καὶ εἰς Δελφοὺς ἐν τοῖς τεταγμένοις
χρόνοις ὑπὸ τῶν προγόνων," εὐπρεπῶς γε τῷ ὀνόματι, ἀλλὰ τῷ ἔργῳ αἰσχρῶς· κωλύει γὰρ εἰς τὸν
σύλλογον τὸν ἐν Πύλαις ἀπαντᾶν, ὃς ἐξ ἀνάγκης
πρὸ τοῦ καθήκοντος ἔμελλε χρόνου γίγνεσθαι.

127 καὶ πάλιν ἐν τῷ αὐτῷ ψηφίσματι πολὺ καὶ
σαφέστερον καὶ πικρότερον γράφει,² "Τὸν ἱερομνήμονα," φησί, "τὸν Ἀθηναίων καὶ τοὺς πυλαγόρους τοὺς ἀεὶ πυλαγοροῦντας μὴ μετέχειν τοῖς
ἐκεῖσε συλλεγομένοις μήτε λόγου μήτε ἔργου μήτε
δόγματος μήτε πράξεως μηδεμιᾶς." τὸ δὲ μὴ
μετέχειν τί ἐστι; πότερα τἀληθὲς εἴπω, ἢ τὸ
ἥδιστον ἀκοῦσαι; τἀληθὲς ἐρῶ· τὸ γὰρ ἀεὶ πρὸς
ἡδονὴν λεγόμενον οὑτωσὶ τὴν πόλιν διατέθηκεν.
οὐκ ἐᾷ μεμνῆσθαι τῶν ὅρκων, οὓς ἡμῶν ὤμοσαν
οἱ πρόγονοι, οὐδὲ τῆς ἀρᾶς, οὐδὲ τῆς τοῦ θεοῦ
μαντείας.

128 Ἡμεῖς μὲν οὖν, ὦ ἄνδρες Ἀθηναῖοι, κατεμείνα-
μεν διὰ τοῦτο τὸ ψήφισμα, οἱ δ' ἄλλοι Ἀμφικτύονες συνελέγησαν εἰς Πύλας πλὴν μιᾶς πόλεως,
ἧς ἐγὼ οὔτ' ἂν τοὔνομα εἴποιμι, μήθ' αἱ συμφοραὶ
παραπλήσιοι γένοιντο αὐτῆς μηδενὶ τῶν Ἑλλή-

¹ οὔσης added by Hamaker.
² γράφει Dobree : after γράφει the MSS. have πρόσταγμα or σύγγραμμα.

406

And he managed to have this same bill put to vote in the assembly and passed by the people, at the moment when the assembly was on the point of adjourning, when I had already left the place— for I would never have allowed it—and when most of the people had dispersed. Now the substance of the bill was this: "The hieromnemon of the Athenians," it says, "and the pylagori who are at the time in office, shall go to Thermopylae and Delphi at the times appointed by our fathers"; fine in sound, shameful in fact; for it prevents attendance on the special meeting at Thermopylae, which had to be held before the date of the regular meeting. Again in the same decree he writes much more explicitly and malignantly: "The hieromnemon of the Athenians," he says, "and the pylagori who are at the time in office, shall take no part with those assembled there, in word or deed or decree, or in any act whatsoever." But what does it mean to "take no part"? Shall I tell you the truth, or what is most agreeable for your ears? I will tell you the truth, for it is the universal habit of speaking to please you that has brought the city to such a pass. It means that you are forbidden to remember the oaths which our fathers swore, or the curse, or the oracle of the god.

And so, fellow citizens, we stayed at home because of this decree, while the other Amphictyons assembled at Thermopylae—all but one city, whose name I would not mention; I pray that misfortune like unto hers may come upon no city of Hellas.[1] And

---

[1] Thebes, like Athens, held aloof from the special meeting of the Amphictyons. The final result of Thebes' adoption of Demosthenes' anti-Macedonian policy was her annihilation by Alexander five years before this speech was delivered.

νων. καὶ συνελθόντες ἐψηφίσαντο ἐπιστρατεύειν
ἐπὶ τοὺς Ἀμφισσέας, καὶ στρατηγὸν εἵλοντο
Κόττυφον τὸν Φαρσάλιον τὸν τότε τὰς γνώμας
ἐπιψηφίζοντα, οὐκ ἐπιδημοῦντος ἐν Μακεδονίᾳ
Φιλίππου, οὐδ'[1] ἐν τῇ Ἑλλάδι παρόντος, ἀλλ'
ἐν Σκύθαις οὕτω μακρὰν ἀπόντος· ὃν αὐτίκα μάλα
τολμήσει λέγειν Δημοσθένης ὡς ἐγὼ ἐπὶ τοὺς
129 Ἕλληνας ἐπήγαγον. καὶ παρελθόντες τῇ πρώτῃ
στρατείᾳ καὶ μάλα μετρίως ἐχρήσαντο τοῖς
Ἀμφισσεῦσιν· ἀντὶ γὰρ τῶν μεγίστων ἀδικημάτων
χρήμασιν αὐτοὺς ἐζημίωσαν, καὶ ταῦτ' ἐν ῥητῷ
χρόνῳ προεῖπον τῷ θεῷ καταθεῖναι, καὶ τοὺς μὲν
ἐναγεῖς καὶ τῶν πεπραγμένων αἰτίους μετέστησαν,[2] τοὺς δὲ δι' εὐσέβειαν φεύγοντας κατήγαγον.
ἐπειδὴ δὲ οὔτε τὰ χρήματα ἐξέτινον τῷ θεῷ, τούς
τ' ἐναγεῖς κατήγαγον, καὶ τοὺς εὐσεβεῖς καὶ
κατελθόντας διὰ τῶν Ἀμφικτυόνων ἐξέβαλον,
οὕτως ἤδη τὴν δευτέραν στρατείαν[3] ἐποιήσαντο,
πολλῷ χρόνῳ ὕστερον, ἐπανεληλυθότος Φιλίππου
ἐκ τῆς ἐπὶ τοὺς Σκύθας στρατείας, τῶν μὲν θεῶν
τὴν ἡγεμονίαν τῆς εὐσεβείας ἡμῖν παραδεδωκότων,
τῆς δὲ Δημοσθένους δωροδοκίας ἐμποδὼν γεγενημένης.

130 Ἀλλ' οὐ προύλεγον, οὐ προεσήμαινον οἱ θεοὶ
φυλάξασθαι, μόνον γε οὐκ ἀνθρώπων φωνὰς
προσκτησάμενοι; οὐδεμίαν τοι πώποτε ἔγωγε
μᾶλλον πόλιν ἑώρακα ὑπὸ μὲν τῶν θεῶν σωζο-
μένην, ὑπὸ δὲ τῶν ῥητόρων ἐνίων ἀπολλυμένην.

---

[1] οὐδ' Schaefer : ἀλλ' οὐδ' MSS.
[2] μετέστησαν Cobet : μετεστήσαντο MSS.
[3] στρατείαν Sauppe : the MSS. have ἐπὶ τοὺς Ἀμφισσέας
before or after στρατείαν.

when they were assembled they voted to march against the Amphissians. As general they chose Cottyphus of Pharsalus, who was at the time president of the Amphictyons. Philip was not in Macedonia at that time, nor in Hellas, but in Scythia—so far away as that! And yet presently Demosthenes will dare to say that it was I who brought him against Hellas! Now when they had come through the pass[1] in the first expedition, they dealt very leniently with the Amphissians, for as penalty for their monstrous crimes, they laid a money fine upon them, and ordered them to pay it at the temple within a stated time ; and they removed the wicked men who were responsible for what had been done, and restored others, whose piety had forced them into exile. But when the Amphissians failed to pay the money to the god, and had restored the guilty men, and banished those righteous men who had been restored by the Amphictyons, under these circumstances at last the second campaign was made, a long time afterward, when Philip had now returned from his Scythian expedition. It was to us that the gods had offered the leadership in the deed of piety, but Demosthenes' taking of bribes had prevented us.

But did not the gods forewarn us, did they not admonish us, to be on our guard, all but speaking with human voice ? No city have I ever seen offered more constant protection by the gods, but more inevitably ruined by certain of its politicians. Was

---

[1] Aeschines is thinking especially of the Thessalian commander of the expedition and his northern contingents, who had to " come through " the Pass of Thermopylae.

οὐχ ἱκανὸν ἦν τὸ τοῖς μυστηρίοις φανὲν σημεῖον,[1]
ἡ τῶν μυστῶν τελευτή; οὐ περὶ τούτων Ἀμεινιά-
δης μὲν προύλεγεν εὐλαβεῖσθαι καὶ πέμπειν εἰς
Δελφοὺς ἐπερησομένους τὸν θεὸν ὅ τι χρὴ πράττειν, Δημοσθένης δὲ ἀντέλεγε, φιλιππίζειν τὴν
Πυθίαν φάσκων, ἀπαίδευτος ὢν καὶ ἀπολαύων
καὶ ἐμπιμπλάμενος τῆς δεδομένης ὑφ' ὑμῶν αὐτῷ
131 ἐξουσίας; οὐ τὸ τελευταῖον ἀθύτων καὶ ἀκαλλιε-
ρήτων ὄντων τῶν ἱερῶν ἐξέπεμψε τοὺς στρατιώτας
ἐπὶ τὸν πρόδηλον κίνδυνον; καίτοι πρώην γέ
ποτε ἀπετόλμα λέγειν ὅτι παρὰ τοῦτο Φίλιππος
οὐκ ἦλθεν ἡμῶν ἐπὶ τὴν χώραν, ὅτι οὐκ ἦν αὐτῷ
καλὰ τὰ ἱερά. τίνος οὖν σὺ ζημίας ἄξιος εἶ
τυχεῖν,[2] ὦ τῆς Ἑλλάδος ἀλειτήριε; εἰ γὰρ ὁ μὲν
κρατῶν οὐκ ἦλθεν εἰς τὴν τῶν κρατουμένων χώραν,
ὅτι οὐκ ἦν αὐτῷ καλὰ τὰ ἱερά, σὺ δ' οὐδὲν προ-
ειδὼς τῶν μελλόντων ἔσεσθαι, πρὶν καλλιερῆσαι
τοὺς στρατιώτας ἐξέπεμψας, πότερα στεφανοῦ-
σθαί σε δεῖ ἐπὶ ταῖς τῆς πόλεως ἀτυχίαις, ἢ
ὑπερωρίσθαι;

132   Τοιγάρτοι τί τῶν ἀνελπίστων καὶ ἀπροσδο-
κήτων ἐφ' ἡμῶν οὐ γέγονεν; οὐ γὰρ βίον γε
ἡμεῖς ἀνθρώπινον βεβιώκαμεν, ἀλλ' εἰς παραδο-
ξολογίαν τοῖς μεθ' ἡμᾶς[3] ἔφυμεν. οὐχ ὁ μὲν
τῶν Περσῶν βασιλεύς, ὁ τὸν Ἄθω διορύξας, ὁ

----

[1] σημεῖον Baiter : σημεῖον φυλάξασθαι MSS.

[2] σὺ . . . τυχεῖν Blass : the MSS. have εἰ σὺ ζημίας ἄξιος
τυχεῖν or ζημίας ἄξιος εἰ τυχεῖν.

[3] μεθ' ἡμᾶς Cobet : the MSS. have ἐσομένοις before or after
μεθ' ἡμᾶς.

----

[1] The Scholiast explains that certain celebrants were
seized by a shark as they were taking the sacred bath in the
sea at Eleusis.

not that portent sufficient which appeared at the Mysteries—the death of the celebrants? [1] In view of this did not Ameiniades warn you to be on your guard, and to send messengers to Delphi to inquire of the god what was to be done? And did not Demosthenes oppose, and say that the Pythia had gone over to Philip? Boor that he was, gorged with his feast of indulgence from you! And did he not at last from smouldering and ill-omened sacrifices send forth our troops into manifest danger? And yet it was but yesterday that he dared to assert that the reason why Philip did not advance against our country [2] was that the omens were not favourable to him. What punishment, then, do you deserve, you curse of Hellas! For if the conqueror refrained from entering the land of the conquered because the omens were not favourable to him, whereas you, ignorant of the future, sent out our troops before the omens were propitious, ought you to be receiving a crown for the misfortunes of the city, or to have been thrust already beyond her borders?

Wherefore what is there, strange and unexpected, that has not happened in our time! [3] For it is not the life of men we have lived, but we were born to be a tale of wonder to posterity. Is not the king of the Persians—he who channelled

[2] After Philip's overwhelming victory at Chaeronea it was a surprise to every one that he did not immediately press on and invade Attica.

[3] Athens and Thebes, in the old days god-fearing states of Hellas, have refused the service due the Delphic god, and have suffered every disaster; Philip, the barbarian, undertook the service of the god, and has received as his reward unheard-of power.

τὸν Ἑλλήσποντον ζεύξας, ὁ γῆν καὶ ὕδωρ τοὺς
Ἕλληνας αἰτῶν, ὁ τολμῶν ἐν ταῖς ἐπιστολαῖς
γράφειν, ὅτι δεσπότης ἐστὶν ἁπάντων ἀνθρώπων
ἀφ' ἡλίου ἀνιόντος μέχρι δυομένου, νῦν οὐ περὶ
τοῦ κύριος ἑτέρων εἶναι διαγωνίζεται, ἀλλ' ἤδη
περὶ τῆς τοῦ σώματος σωτηρίας; καὶ τοὺς αὐτοὺς
ὁρῶμεν τῆς τε δόξης ταύτης καὶ τῆς ἐπὶ τὸν
Πέρσην ἡγεμονίας ἠξιωμένους, οἳ καὶ τὸ ἐν Δελ-
133 φοῖς ἱερὸν ἠλευθέρωσαν; Θῆβαι δέ, Θῆβαι, πόλις
ἀστυγείτων, μεθ' ἡμέραν μίαν ἐκ μέσης τῆς Ἑλλάδος ἀνήρπασται, εἰ καὶ δικαίως, περὶ τῶν ὅλων
οὐκ ὀρθῶς βουλευσάμενοι, ἀλλὰ τήν γε θεοβλά-
βειαν καὶ τὴν ἀφροσύνην οὐκ ἀνθρωπίνως, ἀλλὰ
δαιμονίως κτησάμενοι. Λακεδαιμόνιοι δ' οἱ ταλαίπωροι, προσαψάμενοι μόνον τούτων τῶν πραγμάτων ἐξ ἀρχῆς περὶ τὴν τοῦ ἱεροῦ κατάληψιν, οἱ
τῶν Ἑλλήνων ποτὲ ἀξιοῦντες ἡγεμόνες εἶναι, νῦν
ὁμηρεύσοντες καὶ τῆς συμφορᾶς ἐπίδειξιν ποιη-
σόμενοι μέλλουσιν ὡς Ἀλέξανδρον ἀναπέμπεσθαι,
τοῦτο πεισόμενοι καὶ αὐτοὶ καὶ ἡ πατρίς, ὅ τι
ἂν ἐκείνῳ δόξῃ, καὶ ἐν τῇ τοῦ κρατοῦντος καὶ
προηδικημένου μετριότητι κριθησόμενοι.

134 Ἡ δ' ἡμετέρα πόλις, ἡ κοινὴ καταφυγὴ τῶν
Ἑλλήνων, πρὸς ἣν ἀφικνοῦντο πρότερον ἐκ τῆς
Ἑλλάδος αἱ πρεσβεῖαι, κατὰ πόλεις ἕκαστοι παρ'
ἡμῶν τὴν σωτηρίαν εὑρησόμενοι, νῦν οὐκέτι περὶ
τῆς τῶν Ἑλλήνων ἡγεμονίας ἀγωνίζεται, ἀλλ' ἤδη
περὶ τοῦ τῆς πατρίδος ἐδάφους. καὶ ταῦθ' ἡμῖν

---

[1] The Persian king was already dead when this speech was
delivered, but the news had not yet reached Athens.

[2] The seizure by the Phocians at the beginning of the
Phocian war.

Athos, he who bridged the Hellespont, he who demanded earth and water of the Greeks, he who dared to write in his letters that he was lord of all men from the rising of the sun unto its setting —is he not struggling now, no longer for lordship over others, but already for his life? [1] And do we not see this glory and the leadership against the Persians bestowed on the same men who liberated the temple of Delphi? But Thebes! Thebes, our neighbour, has in one day been swept from the midst of Hellas—even though justly, for her main policy was wrong, yet possessed by an infatuate blindness and folly that were not of men, but a divine visitation. And the wretched Lacedaemonians, who barely touched these acts at their beginning in connection with the seizure of the temple,[2] they who once claimed the right to lead the Greeks, are now about to be sent to Alexander to serve as hostages, and to make an exhibition of their misfortunes [3]—destined, themselves and their country, to suffer whatever may please him; their fate dependent on the mercy of the man who has conquered them after receiving unprovoked injury at their hands.

And our city, the common refuge of the Greeks, to which in former days used to come the embassies of all Hellas, each city in turn to find safety with us, our city is now no longer contending for the leadership of Hellas, but from this time on for the soil of the fatherland. And this has come upon us

---

[3] The Spartans had led an ill-advised revolt against the Macedonian overlordship, and had been completely defeated shortly before this speech was delivered. They were required to send fifty noble citizens as hostages to Alexander, who was now in Asia.

συμβέβηκεν ἐξ ὅτου Δημοσθένης πρὸς τὴν πολιτείαν προσελήλυθεν. εὖ γὰρ περὶ τῶν τοιούτων
Ἡσίοδος ὁ ποιητὴς ἀποφαίνεται. λέγει γάρ που,
παιδεύων τὰ πλήθη καὶ συμβουλεύων ταῖς πόλεσι
τοὺς πονηροὺς τῶν δημαγωγῶν μὴ προσδέχεσθαι·
135 λέξω δὲ κἀγὼ τὰ ἔπη· διὰ τοῦτο γὰρ οἶμαι παῖδας
ὄντας ἡμᾶς τὰς τῶν ποιητῶν γνώμας ἐκμανθάνειν,
ἵν' ἄνδρες ὄντες αὐταῖς χρώμεθα·

πολλάκι δὴ ξύμπασα πόλις κακοῦ ἀνδρὸς
ἀπηύρα,
ὅς κεν ἀλιτραίνῃ καὶ ἀτάσθαλα μητιάαται.
τοῖσιν δ' οὐρανόθεν μέγ' ἐπήγαγε πῆμα Κρονίων,
λιμὸν ὁμοῦ καὶ λοιμόν, ἀποφθινύθουσι δὲ λαοί·
ἢ τῶν γε στρατὸν εὐρὺν ἀπώλεσεν ἢ ὅ γε τεῖχος,
ἢ νέας ἐν πόντῳ ἀποτείνυται εὐρύοπα Ζεύς.

136 ἐὰν περιελόντες τοῦ ποιητοῦ τὸ μέτρον τὰς γνώμας
ἐξετάζητε, οἶμαι ὑμῖν δόξειν οὐ ποιήματα Ἡσιόδου
εἶναι, ἀλλὰ χρησμὸν εἰς τὴν Δημοσθένους πολι-
τείαν· καὶ γὰρ ναυτικὴ καὶ πεζῇ στρατιὰ καὶ
πόλεις ἄρδην εἰσὶν ἀνηρπασμέναι ἐκ τῆς τούτου
πολιτείας.

137 Ἀλλ' οἶμαι οὔτε Φρυνώνδας οὔτε Εὐρύβατος
οὔτ' ἄλλος οὐδεὶς πώποτε τῶν πάλαι πονηρῶν
τοιοῦτος μάγος καὶ γόης ἐγένετο, ὅς, ὦ γῆ καὶ
θεοὶ καὶ δαίμονες καὶ ἄνθρωποι, ὅσοι βούλεσθε
ἀκούειν τἀληθῆ, τολμᾷ λέγειν βλέπων εἰς τὰ
πρόσωπα τὰ ὑμέτερα, ὡς ἄρα Θηβαῖοι τὴν συμμαχίαν ὑμῖν ἐποιήσαντο οὐ διὰ τὸν καιρόν, οὐ διὰ
τὸν φόβον τὸν περιστάντα αὐτούς, οὐ διὰ τὴν
ὑμετέραν δόξαν, ἀλλὰ διὰ τὰς Δημοσθένους
138 δημηγορίας. καίτοι πολλὰς μὲν πρότερον πρε-

from the time when Demosthenes came into political leadership. Well does the poet Hesiod speak concerning such men; for he says somewhere, instructing the people and advising the cities not to take to themselves corrupt politicians—but I will myself recite the verses; for this is the reason, I think, that in our childhood we commit to memory the sentiments of the poets, that when we are men we may make use of them:

> Ofttimes whole peoples suffer from one man,
> Whose deeds are sinful, and whose purpose base.
> From heaven Cronion launches on their heads
> Dire woe of plague and famine joined ; and all
> The people waste away. Or else he smites
> Their wide-camped host, or wall. Or wrath of Zeus
> Far-thundering wrecks their ships upon the sea.[1]

If you disregard the poet's metre and examine only his thought, I think this will seem to you to be, not a poem of Hesiod, but an oracle directed against the politics of Demosthenes. For by his politics army and navy and peoples have been utterly destroyed.

I think that not Phrynondas and not Eurybatus, nor any other of the traitors of ancient times ever proved himself such a juggler and cheat as this man, who, oh earth and heaven, oh ye gods and men—if any men of you will listen to the truth—dares to look you in the face and say that Thebes actually made the alliance with you, not because of the crisis, not because of the fear that was impending over them, not because of your reputation, but because of Demosthenes' declamations! And yet in other days many

---

[1] Hesiod, *Works and Days*, 240 ff.; *cp.* Aeschines, ii. 158.

σβείας ἐπρέσβευσαν εἰς Θήβας οἱ μάλιστα οἰκείως
ἐκείνοις διακείμενοι, πρῶτος μὲν Θρασύβουλος
ὁ Κολλυτεύς, ἀνὴρ ἐν Θήβαις πιστευθεὶς ὡς
οὐδεὶς ἕτερος, πάλιν Θράσων ὁ Ἐρχιεύς, πρόξενος
139 ὢν Θηβαίοις, Λεωδάμας ὁ Ἀχαρνεύς, οὐχ ἧττον
Δημοσθένους λέγειν δυνάμενος, ἀλλ᾽ ἔμοιγε καὶ
ἡδίων, Ἀρχέδημος ὁ Πήληξ, καὶ δυνατὸς εἰπεῖν
καὶ πολλὰ κεκινδυνευκὼς ἐν τῇ πολιτείᾳ διὰ
Θηβαίους, Ἀριστοφῶν[1] ὁ Ἀζηνιεύς, πλεῖστον
χρόνον τὴν τοῦ βοιωτιάζειν ὑπομείνας αἰτίαν,
Πύρρανδρος ὁ Ἀναφλύστιος, ὃς ἔτι καὶ νῦν ζῇ.
ἀλλ᾽ ὅμως οὐδεὶς πώποτε αὐτοὺς ἐδυνήθη προ-
τρέψασθαι εἰς τὴν ὑμετέραν φιλίαν. τὸ δ᾽ αἴτιον
οἶδα μέν, λέγειν δ᾽ οὐδὲν δέομαι διὰ τὰς ἀτυχίας
140 αὐτῶν. ἀλλ᾽ οἶμαι, ἐπειδὴ Φίλιππος αὐτῶν
ἀφελόμενος Νίκαιαν Θετταλοῖς παρέδωκε, καὶ τὸν
πόλεμον, ὃν πρότερον ἐξήλασεν ἐκ τῆς χώρας τῆς
Βοιωτῶν, τοῦτον πάλιν τὸν αὐτὸν πόλεμον ἐπῆγε[2]
διὰ τῆς Φωκίδος ἐπ᾽ αὐτὰς τὰς Θήβας, καὶ τὸ
τελευταῖον Ἐλάτειαν καταλαβὼν ἐχαράκωσε καὶ
φρουρὰν εἰσήγαγεν, ἐνταῦθ᾽ ἤδη, ἐπεὶ τὸ δεινὸν
αὐτῶν ἥπτετο, μετεπέμψαντο Ἀθηναίους, καὶ
ὑμεῖς ἐξήλθετε καὶ εἰσῆτε εἰς τὰς Θήβας ἐν τοῖς
ὅπλοις διεσκευασμένοι, καὶ οἱ πεζοὶ καὶ οἱ ἱππεῖς,
πρὶν περὶ συμμαχίας μίαν μόνον συλλαβὴν

[1] Ἀριστοφῶν Bekker : δημαγωγὸς Ἀριστοφῶν MSS.
[2] ἐπῆγε Blass : ἐπήγαγε MSS.

---

[1] "It would be invidious to say that it was their pride
and steady malice, when their malice had been renounced
under duress, and their pride had had such a fatal fall."
(Simcox.)

[2] Nicaea was an important strategic post at the eastern
end of the Pass of Thermopylae.

men who had stood in the closest relations with the Thebans had gone on missions to them; first, Thrasybulus of Collytus, a man trusted in Thebes as no other ever was; again, Thrason of Erchia, proxenus of the Thebans; Leodamas of Acharnae, a speaker no less able than Demosthenes, and more to my taste; Archedemus of Pelekes, a powerful speaker, and one who had met many political dangers for the sake of the Thebans; Aristophon of Azenia, who had long been subject to the charge of having gone over to the Boeotians; Pyrrhandrus of Anaphlystus, who is still living. Yet no one of these was ever able to persuade them to be friends with you. And I know the reason, but because of the present misfortune of Thebes, I have no desire to speak it.[1] But, I think, when Philip had taken Nicaea[2] from them and given it to the Thessalians, and when he was now bringing back again upon Thebes herself through Phocis the same war that he had formerly driven from the borders of Boeotia,[3] and when finally he had seized Elateia and fortified and garrisoned it,[4] then, and not till then, it was, when the peril was laying hold on them, that they sent for the Athenians. You went out and were on the point of marching into Thebes under arms, horse and foot, before ever Demosthenes

[3] Aeschines represents the Amphissian war as virtually a resumption of the Phocian war; both were wars in behalf of the Delphic shrine, but the relation of Thebes to the two was very different.

[4] After passing through Thermopylae, Philip seized Elateia in northern Phocis and made it his base for the winter. It commanded the main road towards Thebes and Athens. For the Athenian feeling of the significance of its seizure, see the famous passage in the speech of Demosthenes, *On the Crown*, 168 ff.

141 γράψαι Δημοσθένην. ὁ δ' εἰσάγων ἦν ὑμᾶς εἰς
τὰς Θήβας καιρὸς καὶ φόβος καὶ χρεία συμμαχίας, ἀλλ' οὐ Δημοσθένης.

Ἐπεὶ περί γε ταύτας τὰς πράξεις τρία πάντων
μέγιστα Δημοσθένης εἰς ὑμᾶς ἐξημάρτηκε, πρῶτον
μέν, ὅτι Φιλίππου τῷ μὲν ὀνόματι πολεμοῦντος
ὑμῖν, τῷ δ' ἔργῳ πολὺ μᾶλλον μισοῦντος Θηβαίους, ὡς αὐτὰ τὰ πράγματα δεδήλωκε, καὶ τί
δεῖ τὰ πλείω λέγειν; ταῦτα μὲν τὰ τηλικαῦτα τὸ
μέγεθος ἀπεκρύψατο, προσποιησάμενος δὲ μέλλειν
τὴν συμμαχίαν γενήσεσθαι οὐ διὰ τοὺς καιρούς,

142 ἀλλὰ διὰ τὰς αὑτοῦ πρεσβείας, πρῶτον μὲν
συνέπεισε τὸν δῆμον μηκέτι βουλεύεσθαι ἐπὶ τίσι
δεῖ ποιεῖσθαι τὴν συμμαχίαν, ἀλλ' ἀγαπᾶν μόνον
εἰ γίγνεται, τοῦτο δὲ προλαβὼν ἔκδοτον μὲν τὴν
Βοιωτίαν ἅπασαν ἐποίησε Θηβαίοις, γράψας ἐν
τῷ ψηφίσματι, " Ἐάν τις ἀφιστῆται πόλις ἀπὸ
Θηβαίων, βοηθεῖν Ἀθηναίους Βοιωτοῖς τοῖς ἐν
Θήβαις," τοῖς ὀνόμασι κλέπτων καὶ μεταφέρων τὰ
πράγματα, ὥσπερ εἴωθεν, ὡς τοὺς Βοιωτοὺς ἔργῳ
κακῶς πάσχοντας τὴν τῶν ὀνομάτων σύνθεσιν
τῶν Δημοσθένους ἀγαπήσοντας, ἀλλ' οὐ μᾶλλον
ἐφ' οἷς κακῶς ἐπεπόνθεσαν ἀγανακτήσοντας·

143 δεύτερον δὲ τῶν εἰς τὸν πόλεμον ἀναλωμάτων
τὰ μὲν δύο μέρη ὑμῖν ἀνέθηκεν, οἷς ἦσαν ἀπω-
τέρω οἱ κίνδυνοι, τὸ δὲ τρίτον μέρος Θηβαίοις,
δωροδοκῶν ἐφ' ἑκάστοις τούτοις, καὶ τὴν ἡγεμονίαν
τὴν μὲν κατὰ θάλατταν ἐποίησε κοινήν, τὸ δ'
ἀνάλωμα ἴδιον ὑμέτερον, τὴν δὲ κατὰ γῆν, εἰ
μὴ δεῖ ληρεῖν, ἄρδην φέρων ἀνέθηκε Θηβαίοις,
ὥστε παρὰ τὸν γενόμενον πόλεμον μὴ κύριον
γενέσθαι Στρατοκλέα τὸν ὑμέτερον στρατηγὸν

had moved one single syllable about an alliance. What brought you into Thebes was the crisis and fear and need of alliance, not Demosthenes.

For in this whole affair Demosthenes is responsible to you for three most serious mistakes. The first was this: when Philip was nominally making war against you, but really was far more the enemy of Thebes, as the event itself has proved (why need I say more?), Demosthenes concealed these facts, which were so important, and pretending that the alliance was to be brought about, not through the crisis, but through his own negotiations, first he persuaded the people to give up all consideration of the terms of the alliance, and to count themselves fortunate if only it were made; and when he had gained this point he betrayed all Boeotia to the Thebans by writing in the decree, "If any city refuse to follow Thebes, the Athenians shall aid the Boeotians in Thebes,"[1] cheating with words and altering the facts, as he is wont to do; as though, forsooth, when the Boeotians should be suffering in fact, they would be content with Demosthenes' fine phrases, rather than indignant at the outrageous way in which they had been treated; and, secondly, he laid two thirds of the costs of the war upon you, whose danger was more remote, and only one third on the Thebans (in all this acting for bribes); and the leadership by sea he caused to be shared equally by both; but all the expenditure he laid upon you; and the leadership by land, if we are not to talk nonsense, he carried away bodily and handed it over to Thebes. The result was that in all the war that followed, Stratocles,

[1] The traditional policy of Athens had been to support the smaller Boeotian cities in their refusal to recognise Theban dominion over them.

βουλεύσασθαι περὶ τῆς τῶν στρατιωτῶν σωτη-
144 ρίας. καὶ ταῦτ' οὐκ ἐγὼ μὲν κατηγορῶ, ἕτεροι
δὲ παραλείπουσιν, ἀλλὰ κἀγὼ λέγω καὶ πάντες
ἐπιτιμῶσι καὶ ὑμεῖς σύνιστε—καὶ οὐκ ὀργίζεσθε.
ἐκεῖνο γὰρ πεπόνθατε πρὸς Δημοσθένην· συνεί-
θισθε ἤδη τἀδικήματα αὐτοῦ ἀκούειν, ὥστε οὐ
θαυμάζετε. δεῖ δὲ οὐχ οὕτως, ἀλλ' ἀγανακτεῖν
καὶ τιμωρεῖσθαι, εἰ χρὴ τὰ λοιπὰ τῇ πόλει καλῶς
ἔχειν.

145 Δεύτερον δὲ καὶ πολὺ τούτου μεῖζον ἀδίκημα
ἠδίκησεν, ὅτι τὸ βουλευτήριον τὸ τῆς πόλεως
καὶ τὴν δημοκρατίαν ἄρδην ἔλαθεν ὑφελόμενος,
καὶ μετήνεγκεν εἰς Θήβας εἰς τὴν Καδμείαν,
τὴν κοινωνίαν τῶν πράξεων τοῖς Βοιωτάρχαις
συνθέμενος· καὶ τηλικαύτην αὐτὸς αὑτῷ δυναστείαν κατεσκεύασεν, ὥστ' ἤδη παριὼν ἐπὶ
τὸ βῆμα πρεσβεύσειν μὲν ἔφη ὅποι ἂν αὐτῷ
146 δοκῇ, κἂν μὴ ὑμεῖς ἐκπέμπητε, εἰ δέ τις αὐτῷ
τῶν στρατηγῶν ἀντείποι, καταδουλούμενος τοὺς
ἄρχοντας καὶ συνεθίζων μηδὲν αὑτῷ ἀντιλέγειν,
διαδικασίαν ἔφη γράψειν τῷ βήματι πρὸς τὸ
στρατήγιον· πλείω γὰρ ὑμᾶς ἀγαθὰ ὑφ' ἑαυτοῦ
ἔφη ἀπὸ τοῦ βήματος πεπονθέναι ἢ ὑπὸ τῶν
στρατηγῶν ἐκ τοῦ στρατηγίου. μισθοφορῶν δ'
ἐν τῷ ξενικῷ κεναῖς χώραις, καὶ τὰ στρατιωτικὰ
χρήματα κλέπτων, καὶ τοὺς μυρίους ξένους ἐκ-
μισθώσας Ἀμφισσεῦσι, πολλὰ διαμαρτυρομένου

---

[1] In connection with their service as commanders of the
army and navy the generals had a considerable share in the
responsibility for foreign relations.

[2] The charge is that Demosthenes was in a conspiracy to
pad the rolls.

your general, had no authority to plan for the safety of his troops. And it is not true that in this I alone accuse, while others are silent; nay, I speak, all men blame him, you know the facts—and are not angry! For this is your experience as regards Demosthenes: you have so long been accustomed to hear of his crimes that they no longer surprise you. But it ought not so to be; you ought to be indignant, and to punish him, if the city is to prosper in the future.

But he was guilty of a second and far greater crime; for he stole the senate-house of the city and the democracy outright and carried them off to Thebes, to the Cadmeia, by his agreement with the Boeotarchs for joint control. And he contrived such domination for himself that now he came forward to the platform and declared that he was going as ambassador wherever he chose, whether you sent him or not; and, treating your magistrates as his slaves, and teaching them to raise no word of opposition against him, he declared that if any of the generals should oppose him,[1] he would bring suit to settle the claims of the speakers' platform as against those of the war office; for he said you owed more benefits to him from the platform than to the generals from the war office. And by drawing pay for empty places in the mercenary force,[2] by stealing the pay of the troops, and by hiring out those ten thousand mercenaries to the Amphissians[3] against my repeated protests and com-

---

[3] The administration, by detaching this large body of mercenaries and sending them to the immediate aid of the Amphissians, gave Philip the opportunity to sweep them away before meeting the army of the Athenians and Thebans at Chaeronea.

καὶ σχετλιάζοντος ἐν ταῖς ἐκκλησίαις ἐμοῦ,
προσέμειξε φέρων ἀναρπασθέντων τῶν ξένων
147 τὸν κίνδυνον ἀπαρασκεύῳ τῇ πόλει. τί γὰρ ἂν
οἴεσθε Φίλιππον ἐν τοῖς τότε καιροῖς εὔξασθαι;
οὐ χωρὶς μὲν πρὸς τὴν πολιτικὴν δύναμιν, χωρὶς
δ᾽ ἐν Ἀμφίσσῃ πρὸς τοὺς ξένους διαγωνίσασθαι,
ἀθύμους δὲ τοὺς Ἕλληνας λαβεῖν τηλικαύτης
πληγῆς προγεγενημένης; καὶ τηλικούτων κακῶν
αἴτιος γενόμενος, Δημοσθένης οὐκ ἀγαπᾷ εἰ μὴ
δίκην δέδωκεν, ἀλλ᾽ εἰ μὴ καὶ χρυσῷ στεφάνῳ
στεφανωθήσεται, ἀγανακτεῖ· οὐδ᾽ ἱκανόν ἐστιν
αὐτῷ ἐναντίον ὑμῶν κηρύττεσθαι, ἀλλ᾽ εἰ μὴ τῶν
Ἑλλήνων ἐναντίον ἀναρρηθήσεται, τοῦτ᾽ ἀγα-
νακτεῖ. οὕτως ὡς ἔοικε πονηρὰ φύσις, μεγάλης
ἐξουσίας ἐπιλαβομένη, δημοσίας ἀπεργάζεται
συμφοράς.
148 Τρίτον δὲ καὶ τῶν προειρημένων μέγιστόν ἐστιν
ὃ μέλλω λέγειν. Φιλίππου γὰρ οὐ καταφρονοῦντος τῶν Ἑλλήνων, οὐδ᾽ ἀγνοοῦντος, οὐ γὰρ ἦν
ἀσύνετος, ὅτι περὶ τῶν ὑπαρχόντων ἀγαθῶν ἐν
ἡμέρας μικρῷ μέρει διαγωνιεῖται, καὶ διὰ ταῦτα
βουλομένου ποιήσασθαι εἰρήνην καὶ πρεσβείας
ἀποστέλλειν μέλλοντος, καὶ τῶν ἀρχόντων τῶν
ἐν Θήβαις φοβουμένων τὸν ἐπιόντα κίνδυνον—
εἰκότως· οὐ γὰρ ῥήτωρ ἀστράτευτος καὶ λιπὼν
τὴν τάξιν αὐτοὺς ἐνουθέτησεν, ἀλλ᾽ ὁ Φωκικὸς
πόλεμος δεκέτης γεγονὼς ἀείμνηστον παιδείαν
149 αὐτοὺς ἐπαίδευσε—τούτων ἐχόντων οὕτως αἰσθόμενος Δημοσθένης, καὶ τοὺς Βοιωτάρχας ὑπο-
πτεύσας μέλλειν εἰρήνην ἰδίᾳ ποιεῖσθαι, χρυσίον
ἄνευ αὐτοῦ παρὰ Φιλίππου λαβόντας, ἀβίωτον
ἡγησάμενος εἶναι εἴ τινος ἀπολειφθήσεται δωρο-

plaints in the assembly—when the mercenaries had thus been carried off, he rushed the city all unprepared into the mist of peril. What, think you, would Philip have prayed for at that crisis? Would it not have been that he might in one place fight against the city's forces, and in another, in Amphissa, against the mercenaries, and thus close his hand upon the Greeks already discouraged by so great a disaster? And Demosthenes, who is responsible for such misfortunes as that, is not content with escaping punishment, but is miserable unless he shall be crowned with a golden crown! Nor is he satisfied that the crown shall be announced in your presence, but if it is not to be proclaimed before the Hellenes, he is miserable over that. So true it seems to be that a wicked nature, when it has laid hold on great license, works out public disaster.

But the third and greatest of the crimes that I have mentioned is that which I am about to describe. Philip did not despise the Greeks, and he was well aware (for he was not without understanding) that he was about to contend in a little fraction of a day for all that he possessed; for that reason he wished to make peace, and was on the point of sending envoys. The officials at Thebes also were frightened at the impending danger — naturally, for they had no run-away orator and deserter to advise them, but the ten years' Phocian war had taught them a lesson not to be forgotten. Now when Demosthenes saw that such was the situation, suspecting that the Boeotarchs were about to conclude a separate peace and get gold from Philip without his being in it, and thinking that life was not worth living if he was to be left out of any act

δοκίας, ἀναπηδήσας ἐν τῇ ἐκκλησίᾳ, οὐδενὸς
ἀνθρώπων λέγοντος οὔθ' ὡς δεῖ ποιεῖσθαι πρὸς
Φίλιππον εἰρήνην οὔθ' ὡς οὐ δεῖ, ἀλλ' ὡς ᾤετο
κήρυγμά τι τοῦτο[1] τοῖς Βοιωτάρχαις προκηρύττων
ἀναφέρειν αὐτῷ τὰ μέρη τῶν λημμάτων, διώμνυτο
150 τὴν Ἀθηνᾶν, ἣν ὡς ἔοικε Φειδίας ἐνεργολαβεῖν
ἠργάσατο καὶ ἐνεπιορκεῖν Δημοσθένει, ἦ μήν, εἴ
τις ἐρεῖ ὡς χρὴ πρὸς Φίλιππον εἰρήνην ποιήσασθαι, ἀπάξειν εἰς τὸ δεσμωτήριον ἐπιλαβόμενος
τῶν τριχῶν, ἀπομιμούμενος τὴν Κλεοφῶντος
πολιτείαν, ὃς ἐπὶ τοῦ πρὸς Λακεδαιμονίους πολέμου, ὡς λέγεται, τὴν πόλιν ἀπώλεσεν. ὡς δ' οὐ
προσεῖχον αὐτῷ οἱ ἄρχοντες οἱ ἐν ταῖς Θήβαις,
ἀλλὰ καὶ τοὺς στρατιώτας τοὺς ὑμετέρους πάλιν
ἀνέστρεψαν ἐξεληλυθότας, ἵνα βουλεύσησθε περὶ
151 τῆς εἰρήνης, ἐνταῦθ' ἤδη παντάπασιν ἔκφρων
ἐγένετο, καὶ παρελθὼν ἐπὶ τὸ βῆμα προδότας τῶν
Ἑλλήνων ἀπεκάλει τοὺς Βοιωτάρχας, καὶ γράψειν ἔφη ψήφισμα, ὁ τοῖς πολεμίοις οὐδεπώποτ'
ἀντιβλέψας, πέμπειν ὑμᾶς πρέσβεις εἰς Θήβας
αἰτήσοντας Θηβαίους δίοδον ἐπὶ Φίλιππον. ὑπεραισχυνθέντες δὲ οἱ ἐν Θήβαις ἄρχοντες, μὴ
δόξωσιν ὡς ἀληθῶς εἶναι προδόται τῶν Ἑλλήνων,
ἀπὸ μὲν τῆς εἰρήνης ἀπετράποντο, ἐπὶ δὲ τὴν
παράταξιν ὥρμησαν.
152   Ἔνθα δὴ καὶ τῶν ἀνδρῶν τῶν ἀγαθῶν ἄξιόν
ἐστιν ἐπιμνησθῆναι, οὓς οὗτος ἀθύτων καὶ ἀκαλ-
λιερήτων ὄντων τῶν ἱερῶν ἐκπέμψας ἐπὶ τὸν
πρόδηλον κίνδυνον, ἐτόλμησε τοῖς δραπέταις
ποσὶ καὶ λελοιπόσι τὴν τάξιν ἀναβὰς ἐπὶ τὸν

---

[1] κήρυγμά τι τοῦτο Blass : κηρύγματι τούτῳ or τοῦτο κήρυγμα
τι MSS.

of bribery, he jumped up in the assembly, when no man was saying a word either in favour of making peace with Philip or against it; and with the idea of serving a sort of notice on the Boeotarchs that they must turn over to him his share of the gain, he swore by Athena (whose statue, it seems, Pheidias wrought expressly that Demosthenes might have it to perjure himself by and to make profit of) that if any one should say that we ought to make peace with Philip, he would seize him by the hair and drag him to prison—in this imitating the politics of Cleophon, who, they tell us, in the time of the war against the Lacedaemonians, brought ruin to the state. But when the officials in Thebes would pay no attention to him, but even turned your soldiers back again when they had marched out, for they wished to give you an opportunity to deliberate concerning peace, then indeed he became frantic, and went forward to the platform and stigmatised the Boeotarchs as traitors to Hellas, and declared that he would move a decree—he, who never looked on the face of an enemy in arms!—that you should send ambassadors to Thebes to ask them to give you free passage through their country for the march against Philip. But the officials in Thebes, ashamed lest they should seem in reality to be traitors to Hellas, turned from the thought of peace, and threw themselves into the war.

Here indeed it is fitting that we should pay the tribute of memory to those brave men whom he, regardless of the smouldering and ill-omened sacrifices, sent forth into manifest danger—he who, when they had fallen, dared to set his cowardly and run-away

τάφον τὸν τῶν τελευτησάντων, ἐγκωμιάζειν τὴν
ἐκείνων ἀρετήν. ὦ πρὸς μὲν τὰ μεγάλα καὶ
σπουδαῖα τῶν ἔργων τῶν ἀνθρώπων ἀπάντων [1]
ἀχρηστότατε, πρὸς δὲ τὴν ἐν τοῖς λόγοις τόλμαν
θαυμασιώτατε, ἐπιχειρήσεις [2] αὐτίκα μάλα, βλέπων εἰς τὰ τούτων πρόσωπα, λέγειν ὡς δεῖ σε ἐπὶ
ταῖς τῆς πόλεως συμφοραῖς στεφανοῦσθαι; ἐὰν
δ' οὗτος λέγῃ, ὑμεῖς ὑπομενεῖτε, καὶ συναποθα-
νεῖται τοῖς τελευτήσασιν ὡς ἔοικε καὶ ἡ ὑμετέρα
153 μνήμη; γένεσθε δή μοι μικρὸν χρόνον τὴν διάνοιαν
μὴ ἐν τῷ δικαστηρίῳ, ἀλλ' ἐν τῷ θεάτρῳ, καὶ
νομίσαθ' ὁρᾶν προϊόντα τὸν κήρυκα καὶ τὴν ἐκ
τοῦ ψηφίσματος ἀνάρρησιν μέλλουσαν γίγνεσθαι,
καὶ λογίσασθε πότερ' οἴεσθε τοὺς οἰκείους τῶν
τελευτησάντων πλείω δάκρυα ἀφήσειν ἐπὶ ταῖς
τραγῳδίαις καὶ τοῖς ἡρωικοῖς πάθεσι τοῖς μετὰ
ταῦτ' ἐπεισιοῦσιν, ἢ ἐπὶ τῇ τῆς πόλεως ἀγνω-
154 μοσύνῃ. τίς γὰρ οὐκ ἂν ἀλγήσειεν ἄνθρωπος
Ἕλλην καὶ παιδευθεὶς ἐλευθερίως, [3] ἀναμνησθεὶς
ἐν τῷ θεάτρῳ ἐκεῖνό γε, εἰ μηδὲν ἕτερον, ὅτι ταύτῃ
ποτὲ τῇ ἡμέρᾳ μελλόντων ὥσπερ νυνὶ τῶν τραγῳδῶν γίγνεσθαι, ὅτ' εὐνομεῖτο μᾶλλον ἡ πόλις καὶ
βελτίοσι προστάταις ἐχρῆτο, προελθὼν ὁ κήρυξ
καὶ παραστησάμενος τοὺς ὀρφανοὺς ὧν οἱ πατέρες
ἦσαν ἐν τῷ πολέμῳ τετελευτηκότες, νεανίσκους
πανοπλίᾳ κεκοσμημένους, ἐκήρυττε τὸ κάλλιστον
κήρυγμα καὶ προτρεπτικώτατον πρὸς ἀρετήν, ὅτι
τούσδε τοὺς νεανίσκους, ὧν οἱ πατέρες ἐτελεύτησαν ἐν τῷ πολέμῳ ἄνδρες ἀγαθοὶ γενόμενοι, μέχρι

---

[1] τῶν ἀνθρώπων ἀπάντων the editor: πάντων ἀνθρώπων or
ἀπάντων ἀνθρώπων or τῶν ἀνθρώπων MSS.

[2] ἐπιχειρήσεις Reiske: ἐπιχειρήσειν ἐθέλεις or ἐπιχειρήσειν
ἐθελήσεις MSS.   [3] ἐλευθερίως Cobet: ἐλευθέρως MSS.

feet upon their tomb and eulogise the valour of the dead.[1] O man of all mankind most useless for great and serious deeds, but for boldness of words most wonderful, will you presently undertake to look this jury in the face and say that over the disasters of the city you must be crowned? And, gentlemen, if he does, will you endure it? Are we to believe that you and your memory are to die with the dead? I ask you to imagine for a little time that you are not in the court-room, but in the theatre, and to imagine that you see the herald coming forward to make the proclamation under the decree; consider whether you believe the relatives of the dead will shed more tears over the tragedies and the sufferings of the heroes soon afterward to be presented on the stage, or over the blindness of the city. For what Greek, nurtured in freedom, would not mourn as he sat in the theatre and recalled this, if nothing more, that once on this day, when as now the tragedies were about to be performed, in a time when the city had better customs and followed better leaders, the herald would come forward and place before you the orphans whose fathers had died in battle, young men clad in the panoply of war; and he would utter that proclamation so honourable and so incentive to valour: "These young men, whose fathers showed themselves brave men and died in war, have been

---

[1] Demosthenes was elected to pronounce the eulogy at the public funeral of those who fell at Chaeronea.

μὲν ἥβης ὁ δῆμος ἔτρεφε, νυνὶ δὲ καθοπλίσας
τῇδε τῇ πανοπλίᾳ, ἀφίησιν ἀγαθῇ τύχῃ τρέπεσθαι ἐπὶ τὰ ἑαυτῶν, καὶ καλεῖ εἰς προεδρίαν.
155 τότε μὲν ταῦτ' ἐκήρυττεν, ἀλλ' οὐ νῦν, ἀλλὰ
παραστησάμενος τὸν τῆς ὀρφανίας τοῖς παισὶν
αἴτιον, τί ποτ' ἀνερεῖ, ἢ τί φθέγξεται; καὶ γὰρ
ἐὰν αὐτὰ διεξίῃ τὰ ἐκ τοῦ ψηφίσματος προστά-
γματα, ἀλλ' οὐ τό γ' ἐκ τῆς ἀληθείας αἰσχρὸν
σιωπήσεται, ἀλλὰ τἀναντία δόξει τῇ τοῦ κήρυκος
φωνῇ φθέγγεσθαι, ὅτι τόνδε τὸν ἄνδρα, εἰ δὴ
καὶ οὗτος ἀνήρ, στεφανοῖ ὁ δῆμος ὁ Ἀθηναίων
ἀρετῆς ἕνεκα—τὸν κάκιστον, καὶ ἀνδραγαθίας
ἕνεκα—τὸν ἄνανδρον καὶ λελοιπότα τὴν τάξιν.
156 μὴ πρὸς Διὸς καὶ θεῶν, ἱκετεύω ὑμᾶς, ὦ ἄνδρες
Ἀθηναῖοι, μὴ τρόπαιον ἵστατε ἀφ' ὑμῶν αὐτῶν
ἐν τῇ τοῦ Διονύσου ὀρχήστρᾳ, μηδ' αἱρεῖτε παρα-
νοίας ἐναντίον τῶν Ἑλλήνων τὸν δῆμον τὸν Ἀθηναίων, μηδ' ὑπομιμνήσκετε τῶν ἀνιάτων καὶ
ἀνηκέστων κακῶν τοὺς ταλαιπώρους Θηβαίους,
οὓς φεύγοντας[1] διὰ τοῦτον ὑποδέδεχθε τῇ πόλει,
ὧν ἱερὰ καὶ τέκνα καὶ τάφους ἀπώλεσεν ἡ Δημοσθένους δωροδοκία καὶ τὸ βασιλικὸν χρυσίον·
157 ἀλλ' ἐπειδὴ τοῖς σώμασιν οὐ παρεγένεσθε, ἀλλὰ
ταῖς γε διανοίαις ἀποβλέψατ' αὐτῶν εἰς τὰς
συμφοράς, καὶ νομίσαθ' ὁρᾶν ἁλισκομένην τὴν
πόλιν, τειχῶν κατασκαφάς, ἐμπρήσεις οἰκιῶν,
ἀγομένας γυναῖκας καὶ παῖδας εἰς δουλείαν,
πρεσβύτας ἀνθρώπους, πρεσβύτιδας γυναῖκας
ὀψὲ μεταμανθάνοντας τὴν ἐλευθερίαν, κλαίοντας,
ἱκετεύοντας ὑμᾶς, ὀργιζομένους οὐ τοῖς τιμωρου-

---

[1] φεύγοντας Franke : φυγόντας MSS.

supported by the state until they have come of age ; and now, clad thus in full armour by their fellow citizens, they are sent out with the prayers of the city, to go each his way ; and they are invited to seats of honour in the theatre." This was the proclamation then, but not to-day. For when the herald has led forward the man who is responsible for making the children orphans, what will he proclaim ? What words will he utter ? For if he shall recite the mere dictates of the decree, yet the truth, ashamed, will refuse to be silent, and we shall seem to hear it crying out in words which contradict the voice of the herald, " This man, if man he can be called, the Athenian people crown, the basest—'for his virtue' ; and 'for his nobility'—the coward and deserter." No! by Zeus and the gods, do not, my fellow citizens, do not, I beseech you, set up in the orchestra of Dionysus a memorial of your own defeat; do not in the presence of the Greeks convict the Athenian people of having lost their reason ; do not remind the poor Thebans of their incurable and irreparable disasters, men who, exiled through Demosthenes' acts, found refuge with you, when their shrines and children and tombs had been destroyed by Demosthenes' taking of bribes and by the Persian gold.[1] But since you were not present in person, yet in imagination behold their disaster ; imagine that you see their city taken, the razing of their walls, the burning of their homes ; their women and children led into captivity ; their old men, their aged matrons, late in life learning to forget what freedom means ; weeping, supplicating you, angry not so much at

---

[1] Aeschines assumes that Demosthenes' opposition to Macedon was paid for by the king of Persia.

μένοις, ἀλλὰ τοῖς τούτων αἰτίοις, ἐπισκήπτοντας
μηδενὶ τρόπῳ τὸν τῆς Ἑλλάδος ἀλειτήριον στεφανοῦν, ἀλλὰ καὶ τὸν δαίμονα καὶ τὴν τύχην τὴν
συμπαρακολουθοῦσαν τῷ ἀνθρώπῳ φυλάξασθαι.
158 οὔτε πόλις γὰρ οὔτ' ἀνὴρ ἰδιώτης οὐδεὶς πώποτε
καλῶς ἀπήλλαξε Δημοσθένει συμβούλῳ χρησά-
μενος. ὑμεῖς δέ, ὦ ἄνδρες Ἀθηναῖοι, οὐκ αἰσχύνεσθε, εἰ ἐπὶ μὲν τοὺς πορθμέας τοὺς εἰς Σαλαμῖνα
πορθμεύοντας νόμον ἔθεσθε, ἐάν τις αὐτῶν ἄκων
ἐν τῷ πόρῳ πλοῖον ἀνατρέψῃ, τούτῳ μὴ ἐξεῖναι
πάλιν πορθμεῖ γενέσθαι, ἵνα μηδεὶς αὐτοσχεδιάζῃ
εἰς τὰ τῶν Ἑλλήνων σώματα, τὸν δὲ τὴν Ἑλλάδα
καὶ τὴν πόλιν ἄρδην ἀνατετροφότα, τοῦτον ἐάσετε
πάλιν ἀπευθύνειν τὰ κοινά;

159 Ἵνα δ' εἴπω καὶ περὶ τοῦ τετάρτου καιροῦ καὶ
τῶν νυνὶ καθεστηκότων πραγμάτων, ἐκεῖνο ὑμᾶς
ὑπομνῆσαι βούλομαι, ὅτι Δημοσθένης οὐ τὴν ἀπὸ
στρατοπέδου μόνον τάξιν ἔλιπεν, ἀλλὰ καὶ τὴν
ἐκ τῆς πόλεως, τριήρη προσλαβὼν ὑμῶν, καὶ τοὺς
Ἕλληνας ἀργυρολογήσας. καταγαγούσης δ' αὐτὸν εἰς τὴν πόλιν τῆς ἀπροσδοκήτου σωτηρίας,
τοὺς μὲν πρώτους χρόνους ὑπότρομος ἦν ἄνθρωπος,[1] καὶ παριὼν ἡμιθνὴς ἐπὶ τὸ βῆμα, εἰρηνο-
φύλακα ὑμᾶς αὐτὸν ἐκέλευε χειροτονεῖν· ὑμεῖς δὲ[2]
οὐδ' ἐπὶ τὰ ψηφίσματα εἴατε τὸ Δημοσθένους

---

[1] ἄνθρωπος Markland : ἄνθρωπος MSS.
[2] ὑμεῖς δὲ Taylor : ὑμεῖς δὲ κατὰ μὲν τοὺς πρώτους χρόνους
MSS. cp. the second line above.

those who are taking vengeance upon them, as at the men who are responsible for it all ; and calling on you by no means to crown the curse of Hellas, but rather to guard yourselves against the evil genius and the fate that ever pursue the man. For there is no city, there is no private man—not one— that has ever come off safe after following Demosthenes' counsel. You have passed a law, fellow citizens, governing the men who steer the boats across the strait to Salamis ; if one of them by accident overturns a boat in the strait, your law permits him no longer to be a ferryman, in order that no man may be careless of Greek lives ; are you not then ashamed if this man, who has utterly overturned the city and all Hellas, if this man is to be permitted again to pilot the ship of state ?

But that I may speak concerning the fourth period also, and the present situation, I wish to remind you of this fact, that Demosthenes not only deserted his post in the army, but his post in the city also ; for he took possession of one of your triremes and levied money upon the Greeks.[1] But when our unexpected safety[2] had brought him back to the city, during the first months the man was timid, and he came forward half-dead to the platform and urged you to elect him "preserver of the peace." But as for you, you would not even let resolutions that were passed bear the

---

[1] Demosthenes says (*On the Crown*, § 248) that after the battle of Chaeronea the measures that were taken for the defence of the city were by his motions, and that he was also elected grain-commissioner. He may well have made a hurried voyage to the allies to raise money and supplies for the emergency.

[2] Philip, contrary to Demosthenes' expectation, did not advance on Athens, and he offered moderate terms of peace.

ἐπιγράφειν ὄνομα, ἀλλὰ Ναυσικλεῖ τοῦτο προσ-
ετάττετε· νυνὶ δ' ἤδη καὶ στεφανοῦσθαι ἀξιοῖ.

160 Ἐπειδὴ δ' ἐτελεύτησε μὲν Φίλιππος, Ἀλέξανδρος δ' εἰς τὴν ἀρχὴν κατέστη, πάλιν αὖ τερατευόμενος ἱερὰ μὲν ἱδρύσατο Παυσανίου, εἰς αἰτίαν
δὲ εὐαγγελίων θυσίας τὴν βουλὴν κατέστησεν,
ἐπωνυμίαν δ' Ἀλεξάνδρῳ Μαργίτην ἐτίθετο,
ἀπετόλμα δὲ λέγειν ὡς οὐ κινηθήσεται ἐκ Μακε-
δονίας· ἀγαπᾶν γὰρ αὐτὸν [1] ἐν Πέλλῃ περιπα-
τοῦντα καὶ τὰ σπλάγχνα φυλάττοντα. καὶ ταυτὶ
λέγειν ἔφη οὐκ εἰκάζων, ἀλλ' ἀκριβῶς εἰδώς, ὅτι
αἵματός ἐστιν ἡ ἀρετὴ ὠνία, αὐτὸς οὐκ ἔχων αἷμα,
καὶ θεωρῶν τὸν Ἀλέξανδρον οὐκ ἐκ τῆς Ἀλεξάνδρου φύσεως, ἀλλ' ἐκ τῆς ἑαυτοῦ ἀνανδρίας.

161 ἤδη δ' ἐψηφισμένων Θετταλῶν ἐπιστρατεύειν ἐπὶ
τὴν ἡμετέραν πόλιν, καὶ τοῦ νεανίσκου τὸ πρῶτον
παροξυνθέντος εἰκότως, ἐπειδὴ περὶ Θήβας ἦν τὸ
στρατόπεδον, πρεσβευτὴς ὑφ' ὑμῶν χειροτονηθείς,
ἀποδρὰς ἐκ μέσου τοῦ Κιθαιρῶνος ἧκεν ὑπο-
στρέψας, οὔτ' ἐν εἰρήνῃ οὔτ' ἐν πολέμῳ χρήσιμον
ἑαυτὸν παρέχων. καὶ τὸ πάντων δεινότατον,
ὑμεῖς μὲν τοῦτον οὐ προὔδοτε, οὐδ' εἰάσατε κριθῆ-
ναι ἐν τῷ τῶν Ἑλλήνων συνεδρίῳ, οὗτος δ' ὑμᾶς
νυνὶ προδέδωκεν, εἴπερ ἀληθῆ ἐστιν ἃ λέγεται.

[1] αὐτὸν Blass : αὐτὸν ἔφη (or ἔφησε) MSS.

---

[1] Pausanias was the man who assassinated Philip.

[2] Margites was the name of a caricature of Achilles in a
poem that passed under the name of Homer. "Demosthenes
asserted, then, that Alexander, in his aspiration to be a
second Achilles, would never get farther than to become
a caricature of him." (Richardson.)

[3] Perhaps a sneer at Alexander's studies under Aristotle,
the "Peripatetic."

name of Demosthenes as the mover, but gave that honour to Nausicles. And yet, to-day, here is Demosthenes actually demanding a crown!

But when Philip was dead and Alexander had come to the throne, Demosthenes again put on prodigious airs and caused a shrine to be dedicated to Pausanias [1] and involved the senate in the charge of having offered sacrifice of thanksgiving as for good news. And he nicknamed Alexander " Margites " ; [2] and had the effrontery to say that Alexander would never stir out of Macedonia, for he was content, he said, to saunter around [3] in Pella, and keep watch over the omens ; and he said this statement was not based on conjecture, but on accurate knowledge, for valour was to be purchased at the price of blood. For Demosthenes, having no blood himself, formed his judgment of Alexander, not from Alexander's nature, but from his own cowardice. But when now the Thessalians had voted to march against our city, and the young Alexander was at first bitterly angry—naturally [4]— and when the army was near Thebes, Demosthenes, who had been elected ambassador by you, turned back when half-way across Cithaeron and came running home—useless in peace and war alike ! And worst of all : while you did not surrender him [5] nor allow him to be brought to trial in the synod of the Greeks, he has betrayed you now, if current report is true.

---

[4] Philip's death was immediately followed by revolutionary movements centring in Thebes and Athens. The reference here is to Alexander's sudden descent upon Thebes, with the Thessalians as his supporters.

[5] After the destruction of Thebes and the suppression of the revolt elsewhere, Alexander demanded the surrender of Demosthenes and other anti-Macedonian Athenian statesmen.

162 ὡς γάρ φασιν οἱ Πάραλοι καὶ οἱ πρεσβεύσαντες
πρὸς Ἀλέξανδρον, καὶ τὸ πρᾶγμα εἰκότως πιστεύε-
ται, ἔστι τις Ἀριστίων Πλαταϊκός, ὁ τοῦ
Ἀριστοβούλου τοῦ φαρμακοπώλου υἱός, εἴ τις
ἄρα καὶ ὑμῶν γιγνώσκει. οὗτός ποτε ὁ νεανίσκος
ἑτέρων τὴν ὄψιν διαφέρων γενόμενος ᾤκησε πολὺν
χρόνον ἐν τῇ Δημοσθένους οἰκίᾳ, ὅ τι δὲ πάσχων
ἢ πράττων, ἀμφίβολος ἡ αἰτία, καὶ τὸ πρᾶγμα
οὐδαμῶς εὔσχημον ἐμοὶ λέγειν. οὗτος, ὡς ἐγὼ
ἀκούω, ἠγνοημένος ὅστις ποτ' ἐστὶ καὶ πῶς βεβιωκώς, τὸν Ἀλέξανδρον ὑποτρέχει καὶ πλησιάζει
ἐκείνῳ. διὰ τούτου γράμματα πέμψας Δημοσθένης ὡς Ἀλέξανδρον, ἄδειάν τινα εὕρηται καὶ
καταλλαγάς, καὶ πολλὴν τὴν κολακείαν πεποίηται.

163 Ἐκεῖθεν δὲ θεωρήσατε ὡς ὅμοιόν ἐστι τὸ πρᾶγμα
τῇ αἰτίᾳ. εἰ γάρ τι τούτων ἐφρόνει Δημοσθένης
καὶ πολεμικῶς εἶχεν, ὥσπερ καὶ φησί, πρὸς Ἀλέξανδρον, τρεῖς αὐτῷ καιροὶ κάλλιστοι παραγεγό-
νασιν, ὧν οὐδενὶ φαίνεται κεχρημένος. εἷς μὲν ὁ
πρῶτος, ὅτ' εἰς τὴν ἀρχὴν οὐ πάλαι καθεστηκὼς
Ἀλέξανδρος, ἀκατασκεύων αὐτῷ τῶν ἰδίων ὄντων,
εἰς τὴν Ἀσίαν διέβη, ἤκμαζε δ' ὁ τῶν Περσῶν
βασιλεὺς καὶ ναυσὶ καὶ χρήμασι καὶ πεζῇ στρα-
τιᾷ, ἄσμενος δ' ἂν ἡμᾶς εἰς τὴν συμμαχίαν προσε-
δέξατο διὰ τοὺς ἐπιφερομένους ἑαυτῷ κινδύνους.
εἶπάς τινα ἐνταῦθα λόγον, Δημόσθενες, ἢ ἔγραψάς
τι ψήφισμα; βούλει σε θῶ φοβηθῆναι καὶ χρή-

---

[1] The citizen crew of the dispatch-ship Paralus.
[2] The " Plataean status " was that of foreigners (slaves in
some cases) who had received citizenship in return for services

434

For, as the people of the Paralus say,[1] and those who have been ambassadors to Alexander—and the story is sufficiently credible—there is one Aristion, a man of Plataean status,[2] son of Aristobulus the apothecary, known perhaps to some of you. This young man, distinguished for extraordinary beauty of person, once lived a long time in Demosthenes' house (what he used to do there or what was done to him, is a scandal that is in dispute, and the story is one that would be quite improper for me to repeat). Now I am told that this Aristion, his origin and personal history being unknown to the king, is worming himself into favour with Alexander and getting access to him. Through him Demosthenes has sent a letter to Alexander, and has secured a certain degree of immunity for himself, and reconciliation ; and he has carried his flattery to great lengths.

But see from the following how the facts tally with the charge. For if Demosthenes had been bent on war with Alexander, as he claims to have been, or had any thought of it, three of the best opportunities in the world have been offered to him, and, as you see, he has not seized one of them. One, the first, was when Alexander, newly come to the throne, and not yet fairly settled in his personal affairs, crossed into Asia. The king of Persia was at the height of his power then, with ships and money and troops, and he would gladly have received us into his alliance because of the dangers that were threatening him. But did you, Demosthenes, at that time say a word ? Did you move a decree ? Shall I assume that you

to the state. The status was named " Plataean " after those Plataean exiles who were made Athenian citizens after the destruction of Plataea in the fifth year of the Peloponnesian war.

σασθαι τῷ σαυτοῦ τρόπῳ; καίτοι ῥητορικὴν δει-
164 λίαν δημόσιος καιρὸς οὐκ ἀναμένει. ἀλλ' ἐπειδὴ
πάσῃ τῇ δυνάμει Δαρεῖος κατεβεβήκει, ὁ δ' Ἀλέξανδρος ἦν ἀπειλημμένος ἐν Κιλικίᾳ πάντων ἐνδεής,
ὡς ἔφησθα σύ, αὐτίκα μάλα δ' ἔμελλεν, ὡς ἦν ὁ
παρὰ σοῦ λόγος, συμπατηθήσεσθαι ὑπὸ τῆς Περ-
σικῆς ἵππου, τὴν δὲ σὴν ἀηδίαν ἡ πόλις οὐκ
ἐχώρει καὶ τὰς ἐπιστολὰς ἃς ἐξηρτημένος ἐκ τῶν
δακτύλων περιῄεις, ἐπιδεικνύων τισὶ τὸ ἐμὸν πρόσωπον ὡς ἐκπεπληγμένου καὶ ἀθυμοῦντος, καὶ
χρυσόκερων ἀποκαλῶν καὶ κατεστέφθαι φάσκων,
εἴ τι πταῖσμα συμβήσεται Ἀλεξάνδρῳ, οὐδ' ἐνταῦθα ἔπραξας οὐδέν, ἀλλ' εἴς τινα καιρὸν ἀνε-
βάλλου καλλίω.

165 Ὑπερβὰς τοίνυν ἅπαντα ταῦτα, ὑπὲρ τῶν νυνὶ
καθεστηκότων λέξω. Λακεδαιμόνιοι μὲν καὶ τὸ
ξενικὸν ἐπέτυχον μάχῃ, καὶ διέφθειραν τοὺς περὶ
Κόρραγον στρατιώτας, Ἠλεῖοι δ' αὐτοῖς συμμετε-
βάλοντο καὶ Ἀχαιοὶ πάντες πλὴν Πελληνέων,
καὶ Ἀρκαδία πᾶσα πλὴν Μεγάλης πόλεως, αὕτη
δὲ ἐπολιορκεῖτο καὶ καθ' ἑκάστην ἡμέραν ἐπίδοξος
ἦν ἁλῶναι, ὁ δ' Ἀλέξανδρος ἔξω τῆς ἄρκτου καὶ
τῆς οἰκουμένης ὀλίγου δεῖν πάσης μεθειστήκει, ὁ
δὲ Ἀντίπατρος πολὺν χρόνον συνῆγε στρατόπεδον,
τὸ δ' ἐσόμενον ἄδηλον ἦν. ἐνταῦθ' ἡμῖν ἀπόδειξιν

---

[1] The coast of Cilicia; the time referred to is that preceding the battle of Issus.

followed your natural disposition and were frightened? And yet the public opportunity waits not for the orator's fears. But when Darius was come down to the coast [1] with all his forces, and Alexander was shut up in Cilicia in extreme want, as you yourself said, and was, according to your statement, on the point of being trampled under the hoofs of the Persian horse, and when there was not room enough in the city to contain your odious demonstrations and the letters that you carried around, dangling them from your fingers, while you pointed to my face as showing my discouragement and consternation, and in anticipation of some mishap to Alexander you called me "gilded horn," and said the garland was already on my head, [2] not even then did you take one step, but deferred it all for some more favourable opportunity.

But I will pass over all this, and speak of the most recent events. The Lacedaemonians and their mercenary force had been successful in battle and had destroyed the forces of Corrhagus; [3] the Eleans and the Achaeans, all but the people of Pellene, had come over to them, and so had all Arcadia except Megalopolis, and that city was under siege and its capture was daily expected. Meanwhile Alexander had withdrawn to the uttermost regions of the North, almost beyond the borders of the inhabited world, and Antipater was slow in collecting an army; the whole outcome was uncertain. Pray set forth to us, Demos-

[2] The Greeks gilded the horns of cattle that were about to be sacrificed, and put garlands on their heads.

[3] Corrhagus was the Macedonian commander. The reference is to the Spartan revolt against Macedonia, which had been put down by Antipater shortly before the case of Aeschines against Ctesiphon came to trial.

ποίησαι, Δημόσθενες, τί ποτ᾽ ἦν ἃ ἔπραξας, ἢ τί
ποτ᾽ ἦν ἃ ἔλεγες· καὶ εἰ βούλει, παραχωρῶ σοι
166 τοῦ βήματος ἕως ἂν εἴπῃς. ἐπειδὴ δὲ σιγᾷς, ὅτι
μὲν ἀπορεῖς, συγγνώμην ἔχω σοι, ἃ δὲ τότ᾽ ἔλεγες,
ἐγὼ νυνὶ λέξω. οὐ μέμνησθε αὐτοῦ τὰ μιαρὰ καὶ
ἀπίθανα ῥήματα, ἃ πῶς ποθ᾽ ὑμεῖς, ὦ σιδηροῖ,
ἐκαρτερεῖτε ἀκροώμενοι; ὅτ᾽ ἔφη παρελθών· "᾽Αμ-
πελουργοῦσί τινες τὴν πόλιν, ἀνατετμήκασί τινες
τὰ κλήματα τὰ τοῦ δήμου, ὑποτέτμηται τὰ νεῦρα
τῶν πραγμάτων, φορμορραφούμεθα, ἐπὶ τὰ στενά
167 τινες πρῶτον ὥσπερ τὰς βελόνας διείρουσι." ταῦτα δὲ τί ἐστιν, ὦ κίναδος; ῥήματα ἢ θαύματα;
καὶ πάλιν ὅτε κύκλῳ περιδινῶν σεαυτὸν ἐπὶ τοῦ
βήματος ἔλεγες, ὡς ἀντιπράττων ᾽Αλεξάνδρῳ
"῾Ομολογῶ τὰ Λακωνικὰ συστῆσαι, ὁμολογῶ
Θετταλοὺς καὶ Περραιβοὺς ἀφιστάναι." σὺ Θετταλοὺς ἀφιστάναι; σὺ γὰρ ἂν κώμην ἀποστή-
σειας; σὺ γὰρ ἂν προσέλθοις μὴ ὅτι πρὸς πόλιν,
ἀλλὰ πρὸς οἰκίαν, ὅπου κίνδυνος πρόσεστιν; ἀλλ᾽
εἰ μέν που χρήματα ἀναλίσκεται, προσκαθιζήσει,
πρᾶξιν δὲ ἀνδρὸς οὐ πράξεις· ἐὰν δ᾽ αὐτόματόν τι
συμβῇ, προσποιήσῃ καὶ σαυτὸν ἐπὶ τὸ γεγενημένον ἐπιγράψεις· ἂν δ᾽ ἔλθῃ φόβος τις, ἀπο-
δράσῃ· ἂν δὲ θαρρήσωμεν, δωρεὰς αἰτήσεις καὶ
χρυσοῦς στεφάνους.[1]
168 Ναί, ἀλλὰ δημοτικός ἐστιν. ἂν μὲν τοίνυν πρὸς
τὴν εὐφημίαν αὐτοῦ τῶν λόγων ἀποβλέπητε, ἐξα-

---

[1] χρυσοῦς στεφάνους Weidner : χρυσοῖς στεφάνοις (or χρυσοῦς
στεφάνους) στεφανοῦσθαι (or ἀξιώσεις στεφανοῦσθαι) MSS.

thenes, what in the world there was that you did then, or what in the world there was that you said. I will yield the platform to you, if you wish, until you have told us. You are silent. I can well understand your embarrassment. But what you said then, I myself will tell now. Do you not remember, gentlemen, his disgusting and incredible words? Ye men of iron, how had you ever the endurance to listen to them! When he came forward and said, " Certain men are pruning the city, certain men have trimmed off the tendrils of the people, the sinews of the state have been cut, we are being matted and sewed up, certain men are first drawing us like needles into tight places." What are these things, you beast? Are they words or monstrosities? And again when you whirled around in a circle on the platform and said, pretending that you were working against Alexander, "I admit that I organized the Laconian uprising, I admit that I am bringing about the revolt of the Thessalians and the Perrhaebi." You cause a revolt of the Thessalians? What! Could you cause the revolt of a village? Would you actually approach —let us talk not about a city—would you actually approach a house, where there was danger? But if money is being paid out anywhere, you will lay siege to the place; a man's deed you will never do. If any good-fortune come of itself, you will lay claim to it, and sign your name to the thing after it has been done; but if any danger approach, you will run away; and then if we regain confidence, you will call for rewards and crowns of gold.

Yes, but he is a friend of the people! If now you attend only to the plausible sound of his words, you

πατηθήσεσθε, ὥσπερ καὶ πρότερον, ἐὰν δ' εἰς τὴν
φύσιν καὶ τὴν ἀλήθειαν, οὐκ ἐξαπατηθήσεσθε.
ἐκείνως δὲ ἀπολάβετε παρ' αὐτοῦ λόγον. ἐγὼ μὲν
μεθ' ὑμῶν λογιοῦμαι ἃ δεῖ ὑπάρξαι ἐν τῇ φύσει
τῷ δημοτικῷ ἀνδρὶ καὶ σώφρονι, καὶ πάλιν ἀντι-
θήσω ποῖόν τινα εἰκός ἐστι εἶναι τὸν ὀλιγαρχικὸν
ἄνθρωπον καὶ φαῦλον· ὑμεῖς δ' ἀντιθέντες ἑκάτερα
τούτων θεωρήσατ' αὐτόν, μὴ ὁποτέρου τοῦ λόγου,
ἀλλ' ὁποτέρου τοῦ βίου ἐστίν.

169   Οἶμαι τοίνυν ἅπαντας ἂν ὑμᾶς ὁμολογῆσαι τάδε
δεῖν ὑπάρξαι τῷ δημοτικῷ, πρῶτον μὲν ἐλεύθερον[1] εἶναι καὶ πρὸς πατρὸς καὶ πρὸς μητρός,
ἵνα μὴ διὰ τὴν περὶ τὸ γένος ἀτυχίαν δυσμενὴς ᾖ
τοῖς νόμοις, οἳ σῴζουσι τὴν δημοκρατίαν, δεύτερον
δ' ἀπὸ τῶν προγόνων εὐεργεσίαν τινὰ αὐτῷ πρὸς
τὸν δῆμον ὑπάρχειν, ἢ τό γ' ἀναγκαιότατον μηδεμίαν ἔχθραν, ἵνα μὴ βοηθῶν τοῖς τῶν προγόνων
ἀτυχήμασι κακῶς ἐπιχειρῇ ποιεῖν τὴν πόλιν.

170   τρίτον σώφρονα καὶ μέτριον χρὴ πεφυκέναι αὐτὸν
πρὸς τὴν καθ' ἡμέραν δίαιταν, ὅπως μὴ διὰ τὴν
ἀσέλγειαν τῆς δαπάνης δωροδοκῇ κατὰ τοῦ δήμου.
τέταρτον εὐγνώμονα καὶ δυνατὸν εἰπεῖν· καλὸν
γὰρ τὴν μὲν διάνοιαν προαιρεῖσθαι τὰ βέλτιστα,
τὴν δὲ παιδείαν τὴν τοῦ ῥήτορος καὶ τὸν λόγον
πείθειν τοὺς ἀκούοντας· εἰ δὲ μή, τήν γ' εὐγνωμοσύνην ἀεὶ προτακτέον τοῦ λόγου. πέμπτον ἀν-
δρεῖον εἶναι τὴν ψυχήν, ἵνα μὴ παρὰ τὰ δεινὰ καὶ
τοὺς κινδύνους ἐγκαταλίπῃ τὸν δῆμον. τὸν δ'
ὀλιγαρχικὸν πάντα δεῖ τἀναντία τούτων ἔχειν·

[1] ἐλεύθερον Weidner: αὐτὸν ἐλεύθερον or ἐλεύθερον αὐτὸν
MSS.

will be deceived as in the past; but if you look at his character and the truth, you will not be deceived. Call him to account in this way: with your help I will reckon up what ought to be the inborn qualities of the "friend of the people" and the orderly citizen; and over against them I will set down what manner of man one would expect the oligarch and the worthless man to be. And I ask you to compare the two and to see to which class he belongs—not by his professions, but by his life.

I think you would all acknowledge that the following qualities ought to be found in the "friend of the people": in the first place, he should be free-born, on both his father's and his mother's side, lest because of misfortune of birth he be disloyal to the laws that preserve the democracy. In the second place, he should have as a legacy from his ancestors some service which they have done to the democracy, or at the very least there must be no inherited enmity against it, lest in the attempt to avenge the misfortunes of his family he undertake to injure the city. Thirdly, he ought to be temperate and self-restrained in his daily life, lest to support his wanton extravagance he take bribes against the people. Fourthly, he ought to be a man of good judgment and an able speaker; for it is well that his discernment choose the wisest course, and his training in rhetoric and his eloquence persuade the hearers; but if he cannot have both, good judgment is always to be preferred to eloquence of speech. Fifthly, he ought to be a man of brave heart, that in danger and peril he may not desert the people. But the oligarch we should expect to have all the opposite qualities; why need

τί γὰρ δεῖ πάλιν διεξιέναι; σκέψασθε δή, τί
τούτων ὑπάρχει Δημοσθένει· ὁ δὲ λογισμὸς ἔστω
ἐπὶ πᾶσι δικαίοις.

171 Τούτῳ πατὴρ μὲν ἦν Δημοσθένης ὁ Παιανιεύς,
ἀνὴρ ἐλεύθερος· οὐ γὰρ δεῖ ψεύδεσθαι. τὰ δ' ἀπὸ
τῆς μητρὸς καὶ τοῦ πάππου τοῦ πρὸς μητρὸς πῶς
ἔχει αὐτῷ, ἐγὼ φράσω. Γύλων ἦν ἐκ Κεραμέων.
οὗτος προδοὺς τοῖς πολεμίοις Νύμφαιον τὸ ἐν τῷ
Πόντῳ, τότε τῆς πόλεως ἐχούσης τὸ χωρίον τοῦτο,
φυγὰς ἀπ' εἰσαγγελίας ἐκ τῆς πόλεως ἐγένετο,[1]
τὴν κρίσιν οὐχ ὑπομείνας, καὶ ἀφικνεῖται εἰς
Βόσπορον, κἀκεῖ λαμβάνει δωρεὰν παρὰ τῶν τυ-
172 ράννων τοὺς ὠνομασμένους Κήπους, καὶ γαμεῖ
γυναῖκα πλουσίαν μὲν νὴ Δία καὶ χρυσίον ἐπιφε-
ρομένην πολύ, Σκύθιν δὲ τὸ γένος, ἐξ ἧς αὐτῷ
γίγνονται θυγατέρες δύο, ἃς ἐκεῖνος δεῦρο μετὰ
πολλῶν χρημάτων ἀποστείλας, συνῴκισε τὴν μὲν
ἑτέραν ὁτῳδήποτε, ἵνα μὴ πολλοῖς ἀπεχθάνωμαι·
τὴν δ' ἑτέραν ἔγημε παριδὼν τοὺς τῆς πόλεως
νόμους Δημοσθένης ὁ Παιανιεύς, ἐξ ἧς ὑμῖν ὁ
περίεργος καὶ συκοφάντης γεγένηται.[2] οὐκοῦν
ἀπὸ μὲν τοῦ πάππου πολέμιος ἂν εἴη τῷ δήμῳ,
θάνατον γὰρ αὐτοῦ τῶν προγόνων κατέγνωτε, τὰ
δ' ἀπὸ τῆς μητρὸς Σκύθης, βάρβαρος ἑλληνίζων
τῇ φωνῇ· ὅθεν καὶ τὴν πονηρίαν οὐκ ἐπιχώριός
173 ἐστι. περὶ δὲ τὴν καθ' ἡμέρων δίαιταν τίς ἐστιν;

[1] ἐγένετο Bake : ἐγένετο θανάτου καταγνωσθέντος αὐτοῦ MSS.
[2] γεγένηται Weidner : Δημοσθένης γεγένηται or γεγένηται
Δημοσθένης MSS.

---

[1] Nymphaeum was a port of the Tauric Chersonese.
[2] The Cimmerian Bosporus; the chief city was Panti-
capeum, the modern Kertch.

I go over them again? Examine, then, and see what one of these qualities belongs to Demosthenes. And let the reckoning be made with all fairness.

His father was Demosthenes of Paeania, a free man, for there is no need of lying. But how the case stands as to his inheritance from his mother and his maternal grandfather, I will tell you. There was a certain Gylon of Cerameis. This man betrayed Nymphaeum in the Pontus to the enemy, for the place at that time belonged to our city.[1] He was impeached and became an exile from the city, not awaiting trial. He came to Bosporus [2] and there received as a present from the tyrants of the land a place called "the Gardens." Here he married a woman who was rich, I grant you, and brought him a big dowry, but a Scythian by blood. This wife bore him two daughters, whom he sent hither with plenty of money. One he married to a man whom I will not name—for I do not care to incur the enmity of many persons,— the other, in contempt of the laws of the city,[3] Demosthenes of Paeania took to wife. She it was who bore your busy-body and informer. From his grandfather, therefore, he would inherit enmity toward the people, for you condemned his ancestors to death; and by his mother's blood he would be a Scythian, a Greek-tongued barbarian—so that his knavery, too, is no product of our soil. But in daily

---

[3] In 451/0 Pericles carried a measure which excluded from citizenship all who could not show pure Athenian blood through both parents. By the close of the Peloponnesian war this restriction had fallen into neglect, and in 403 the restored democracy passed an enactment excluding from citizenship children born of a foreign mother after that date. If Demosthenes' mother was born of a Thracian mother and after 403 (neither fact is certain), she could not bear legitimate children to her Athenian husband.

ἐκ τριηράρχου λογογράφος ἀνεφάνη, καταγελάστως τὰ πατρῷα προέμενος· ἄπιστος δὲ καὶ περὶ
ταῦτα δόξας εἶναι καὶ τοὺς λόγους ἐκφέρων τοῖς
ἀντιδίκοις, ἀνεπήδησεν ἐπὶ τὸ βῆμα· πλεῖστον δ᾽
ἐκ τῆς πολιτείας εἰληφὼς ἀργύριον, ἐλάχιστα
περιεποιήσατο. νῦν μέντοι τὸ βασιλικὸν χρυσίον
ἐπικέκλυκε τὴν δαπάνην αὐτοῦ, ἔσται δ᾽ οὐδὲ τοῦθ᾽
ἱκανόν· οὐδεὶς γὰρ πώποτε πλοῦτος τρόπου πονη-
ροῦ περιεγένετο. καὶ τὸ κεφάλαιον, τὸν βίον οὐκ
ἐκ τῶν ἰδίων προσόδων πορίζεται, ἀλλ᾽ ἐκ τῶν
ὑμετέρων κινδύνων.

174   Περὶ δ᾽ εὐγνωμοσύνην καὶ λόγου δύναμιν πῶς
πέφυκε; δεινὸς λέγειν, κακὸς βιῶναι. οὕτω γὰρ
κέχρηται καὶ τῷ ἑαυτοῦ σώματι καὶ παιδοποιίᾳ,
ὥστ᾽ ἐμὲ μὴ βούλεσθαι λέγειν ἃ τούτῳ πέπρακται·
ἤδη γάρ ποτε εἶδον μισηθέντας τοὺς τὰ τῶν πλη-
σίον αἰσχρὰ λίαν σαφῶς λέγοντας. ἔπειτα τί
συμβαίνει τῇ πόλει; οἱ μὲν λόγοι καλοί, τὰ δ᾽
175 ἔργα φαῦλα. πρὸς δὲ ἀνδρείαν βραχύς μοι λεί-
πεται λόγος. εἰ μὲν γὰρ ἠρνεῖτο μὴ δειλὸς εἶναι,
ἢ ὑμεῖς μὴ συνῄδετε, διατριβὴν ὁ λόγος ἄν μοι
παρεῖχεν· ἐπειδὴ δὲ καὶ αὐτὸς ὁμολογεῖ ἐν ταῖς
ἐκκλησίαις, καὶ ὑμεῖς σύνιστε, λοιπὸν ὑπομνῆσαι
τοὺς περὶ τούτων κειμένους νόμους. ὁ γὰρ Σόλων
ὁ παλαιὸς νομοθέτης ἐν τοῖς αὐτοῖς ἐπιτιμίοις
ᾤετο δεῖν ἐνέχεσθαι τὸν ἀστράτευτον καὶ τὸν
λελοιπότα τὴν τάξιν καὶ τὸν δειλὸν ὁμοίως· εἰσὶ

life what is he? From being a trierarch he suddenly
came forward as a hired writer of speeches,[1] when he
had disreputably squandered his patrimony. But
when he had lost his reputation even in this profession, for he disclosed his clients' arguments to their
opponents, he vaulted on to the political platform.
And though he made enormous profits out of politics,
he laid up next to nothing. It is true that just now
the Persian's gold has floated his extravagance, but
even that will not suffice, for no wealth ever yet kept
up with a debauched character. And to sum it all up,
he supplies his wants, not from his private income,
but from your perils.

But as regards good judgment and power of speech,
how does it stand with him? Eloquent of speech,
infamous of life! For so licentious has been his
treatment of his own body that I prefer not to
describe his conduct; for before now I have seen
people hated who recount too exactly the sins of
their neighbours. Then again, what is the outcome
for the city? His words are fine, his acts worthless.
But as concerns his bravery little remains for me to
say. For if he denied that he is a coward, or if you
did not know it as well as he does himself, the
account of it would have detained me. But since
he admits it himself in the assembly, and you are
perfectly aware of it, it remains only to remind you
of the laws as to this matter. For Solon, the ancient
lawgiver, thought it necessary to apply the same
penalties to the coward as to the man who failed to
take the field or the man who deserted his post. For

[1] To be a trierarch implied that a man was in comfortable
circumstances. "He sank as a trierarch to rise as a petti-
fogger." (Simcox.)

γὰρ καὶ δειλίας γραφαί. καίτοι θαυμάσειεν ἄν
τις ὑμῶν, εἰ εἰσὶ φύσεως γραφαί. εἰσίν. τίνος
ἕνεκα; ἵν᾽ ἕκαστος ἡμῶν τὰς ἐκ τῶν νόμων ζημίας
φοβούμενος μᾶλλον ἢ τοὺς πολεμίους, ἀμείνων
176 ἀγωνιστὴς ὑπὲρ τῆς πατρίδος ὑπάρχῃ· ὁ μὲν τοίνυν νομοθέτης τὸν ἀστράτευτον καὶ τὸν δειλὸν καὶ
τὸν λιπόντα τὴν τάξιν ἔξω τῶν περιραντηρίων τῆς
ἀγορᾶς ἐξείργει, καὶ οὐκ ἐᾷ στεφανοῦσθαι, οὐδ᾽
εἰσιέναι εἰς τὰ ἱερὰ τὰ δημοτελῆ· σὺ δὲ τὸν ἀστε-
φάνωτον ἐκ τῶν νόμων κελεύεις ἡμᾶς στεφανοῦν,
καὶ τῷ σαυτοῦ ψηφίσματι τὸν οὐ προσήκοντα
εἰσκαλεῖς τοῖς τραγῳδοῖς εἰς τὴν ὀρχήστραν, εἰς
τὸ ἱερὸν τοῦ Διονύσου τὸν τὰ ἱερὰ διὰ δειλίαν
προδεδωκότα.

Ἵνα δὲ μὴ ἀποπλανῶ ὑμᾶς ἀπὸ τῆς ὑποθέσεως,
ἐκεῖνο μέμνησθε, ὅταν φῇ δημοτικὸς εἶναι· θεω-
ρεῖτ᾽ αὐτοῦ μὴ τὸν λόγον, ἀλλὰ τὸν βίον, καὶ
σκοπεῖτε μὴ τίς φησιν εἶναι, ἀλλὰ τίς ἐστιν.

177 Ἐπεὶ δὲ στεφάνων ἀνεμνήσθην καὶ δωρεῶν, ἕως
ἔτι μέμνημαι, προλέγω ὑμῖν, ὦ ἄνδρες Ἀθηναῖοι,
εἰ μὴ καταλύσετε τὰς ἀφθόνους ταύτας δωρεὰς
καὶ τοὺς εἰκῇ διδομένους στεφάνους, οὔθ᾽ οἱ τιμώ-
μενοι χάριν ὑμῖν εἴσονται, οὔτε τὰ τῆς πόλεως
πράγματα ἐπανορθωθήσεται· τοὺς μὲν γὰρ πονηροὺς οὐ μή ποτε βελτίους ποιήσετε, τοὺς δὲ
χρηστοὺς εἰς τὴν ἐσχάτην ἀθυμίαν ἐμβαλεῖτε.
ὅτι δ᾽ ἀληθῆ λέγω, μεγάλα τούτων οἶμαι σημεῖα
δείξειν ὑμῖν.

there are such things as indictments for cowardice. Some of you may indeed be surprised to know that there are indictments for inborn defects. There are. To what end? In order that each man of us, fearing the punishment of the laws more than he fears the enemy, may become a better champion of his country. Therefore the man who fails to take the field, and the coward, and the man who has deserted his post are excluded by the lawgiver from the purified precincts of the Agora, and may not be crowned, nor take part in the sacred rites of the people. But you, Ctesiphon, command us to crown the man who by command of the laws is uncrowned; and by your decree you invite into the orchestra at the time of the tragedies the man who has no right to enter, and into the shrine of Dionysus the man who has betrayed all our shrines through cowardice.

But that I may not lead you away from the subject, remember this when he says that he is the "friend of the people"; examine, not his speech, but his life; and consider, not who he says he is, but who he is.

I have mentioned crowns and rewards. Let me, fellow citizens, while I still have the matter in mind, warn you that unless you put a stop to these prodigal gifts and these crowns thoughtlessly bestowed, neither those who receive honours from you will be grateful, nor will the prosperity of the city be restored. For you will never in the world reform those who are bad, and the good you will plunge into extreme discouragement. But I will present proofs which I think will convince you that what I say is true.

178 Εἰ γάρ τις ὑμᾶς ἐρωτήσειε, πότερον ὑμῖν ἐνδο-
ξοτέρα δοκεῖ ἡ πόλις ἡμῶν εἶναι ἐπὶ τῶν νυνὶ
καιρῶν ἢ ἐπὶ τῶν προγόνων, ἅπαντες ἂν ὁμολογή-
σαιτε, ἐπὶ τῶν προγόνων. ἄνδρες δὲ πότερον τότε
ἀμείνους ἦσαν ἢ νυνί; τότε μὲν διαφέροντες, νυνὶ
δὲ πολλῷ καταδεέστεροι. δωρεαὶ δὲ καὶ στέφανοι
καὶ κηρύγματα καὶ σιτήσεις ἐν πρυτανείῳ πότερα
τότε ἦσαν πλείους ἢ νυνί; τότε μὲν ἦν σπάνια
τὰ καλὰ παρ' ἡμῖν, καὶ τὸ τῆς ἀρετῆς ὄνομα
τίμιον· νυνὶ δ' ἤδη καταπέπλυται τὸ πρᾶγμα, καὶ
τὸ στεφανοῦν ἐξ ἔθους, ἀλλ' οὐκ ἐκ προνοίας,
179 ποιεῖσθε. οὐκ οὖν ἄτοπον οὕτωσὶ διαλογιζομένοις,
τὰς μὲν δωρεὰς νυνὶ πλείους εἶναι, τὰ δὲ πράγματα τὰ τῆς πόλεως τότε μᾶλλον ἰσχύειν, καὶ
τοὺς ἄνδρας νῦν μὲν χείρους εἶναι, τότε δ' ἀμείνους; ἐγὼ δὲ τοῦθ' ὑμᾶς ἐπιχειρήσω διδάσκειν.
οἴεσθ' ἄν ποτε, ὦ ἄνδρες Ἀθηναῖοι, ἐθελῆσαί τινα
ἐπασκεῖν εἰς τὰ Ὀλύμπια, ἢ ἄλλον τινὰ τῶν
στεφανιτῶν ἀγώνων, παγκράτιον ἢ καὶ ἄλλο τι
τῶν βαρυτέρων ἄθλων, εἰ ὁ στέφανος ἐδίδοτο μὴ
τῷ κρατίστῳ, ἀλλὰ τῷ διαπραξαμένῳ· οὐδεὶς ἂν
180 ποτ' ἠθέλησεν.[1] νῦν δ' οἶμαι διὰ τὸ σπάνιον καὶ
τὸ περιμάχητον καὶ τὸ καλὸν καὶ τὸ ἀείμνηστον
ἐκ τῆς νίκης ἐθέλουσίν τινες τὰ σώματα παραθέμενοι[2] καὶ τὰς μεγίστας ταλαιπωρίας ὑπομείναντες διακινδυνεύειν. ὑπολάβετε τοίνυν ὑμᾶς
αὐτοὺς εἶναι ἀγωνοθέτας πολιτικῆς ἀρετῆς, κἀκεῖνο
ἐκλογίσασθε, ὅτι, ἐὰν μὲν τὰς δωρεὰς ὀλίγοις
καὶ ἀξίοις καὶ κατὰ τοὺς νόμους διδῶτε, πολλοὺς
ἀγωνιστὰς ἕξετε τῆς ἀρετῆς, ἂν δὲ τῷ βουλομένῳ

---

[1] ἠθέλησεν Weidner : ἠθέλησεν ἐπασκεῖν MSS.
[2] παραθέμενοι Herwerden : παρακαταθέμενοι MSS.

If any one should ask you whether our city seems to you more glorious in our own time or in the time of our fathers, you would all agree, in the time of our fathers. And were there better men then than now? Then, eminent men; but now, far inferior. But rewards and crowns and proclamations, and maintenance in the Prytaneum—were these things more common then than now? Then, honours were rare among us, and the name of virtue was itself an honour. But now the custom is already completely faded out, and you do the crowning as a matter of habit, not deliberately. Are you not therefore surprised, when you look at it in this light, that the rewards are now more numerous, but the city was then more prosperous? And that the men are now inferior, but were better then? I will try to explain this to you. Do you think, fellow citizens, that any man would ever have been willing to train for the pancratium or any other of the harder contests in the Olympic games, or any of the other games that confer a crown, if the crown were given, not to the best man, but to the man who had successfully intrigued for it? No man would ever have been willing. But as it is, because the reward is rare, I believe, and because of the competition and the honour, and the undying fame that victory brings, men are willing to risk their bodies, and at the cost of the most severe discipline to carry the struggle to the end. Imagine, therefore, that you yourselves are the officials presiding over a contest in political virtue, and consider this, that if you give the prizes to few men and worthy, and in obedience to the laws, you will find many men to compete in virtue's struggle; but if your gifts

449

καὶ τοῖς διαπραξαμένοις χαρίζησθε, καὶ τὰς
ἐπιεικεῖς φύσεις διαφθερεῖτε.

181 Ὅτι δὲ ὀρθῶς λέγω, ἔτι μικρῷ σαφέστερον
ὑμᾶς βούλομαι διδάξαι. πότερον ὑμῖν ἀμείνων
ἀνὴρ εἶναι δοκεῖ Θεμιστοκλῆς, ὁ στρατηγήσας
ὅτ᾽ ἐν τῇ περὶ Σαλαμῖνα ναυμαχίᾳ τὸν Πέρσην
ἐνικᾶτε, ἢ Δημοσθένης, ὁ νυνὶ τὴν τάξιν λιπών;
Μιλτιάδης δέ, ὁ τὴν ἐν Μαραθῶνι μάχην νικήσας,[1] ἢ οὗτος; ἔτι δ᾽ οἱ ἀπὸ Φυλῆς φεύγοντα
τὸν δῆμον καταγαγόντες; Ἀριστείδης δ᾽ ὁ δί-
καιος, ὁ τὴν ἀνόμοιον ἔχων ἐπωνυμίαν Δημο-
182 σθένει; ἀλλ᾽ ἔγωγε μὰ τοὺς θεοὺς τοὺς Ὀλυμπίους οὐδ᾽ ἐν ταῖς αὐταῖς ἡμέραις ἄξιον ἡγοῦμαι
μεμνῆσθαι τοῦ θηρίου τούτου κἀκείνων τῶν
ἀνδρῶν. ἐπιδειξάτω τοίνυν Δημοσθένης[2] εἴ που
γέγραπταί τινα τούτων τῶν ἀνδρῶν στεφανῶσαι.
ἀχάριστος ἄρ᾽ ἦν ὁ δῆμος; οὔκ, ἀλλὰ μεγαλό-
φρων, κἀκεῖνοί γε[3] τῆς πόλεως ἄξιοι· οὐ γὰρ
ᾤοντο δεῖν ἐν τοῖς γράμμασι τιμᾶσθαι, ἀλλ᾽
ἐν τῇ μνήμῃ τῶν εὖ πεπονθότων, ἢ ἀπ᾽ ἐκείνου
τοῦ χρόνου μέχρι τῆσδε τῆς ἡμέρας ἀθάνατος
οὖσα διαμένει. δωρεὰς δὲ τίνας ἐλάμβανον, ἄξιόν
ἐστι μνησθῆναι.

183 Ἦσάν τινες, ὦ ἄνδρες Ἀθηναῖοι, κατὰ τοὺς
τότε καιρούς, οἳ πολὺν πόνον ὑπομείναντες καὶ
μεγάλους κινδύνους ἐπὶ τῷ Στρυμόνι ποταμῷ
ἐνίκων μαχόμενοι Μήδους· οὗτοι δεῦρο ἀφικόμενοι
τὸν δῆμον ᾔτησαν δωρεάν, καὶ ἔδωκεν αὐτοῖς ὁ
δῆμος τιμὰς μεγάλας, ὡς τότ᾽ ἐδόκει, τρεῖς λιθίνους
Ἑρμᾶς στῆσαι ἐν τῇ στοᾷ τῇ τῶν Ἑρμῶν, ἐφ᾽

---

[1] νικήσας Weidner : τοὺς βαρβάρους νικήσας or νικήσας τοὺς
βαρβάρους MSS.

[2] Δημοσθένης Cobet : Δημοσθένης ἐν τῷ ἑαυτοῦ λόγῳ MSS.

are compliments to any man who seeks them and to those who intrigue for them, you will corrupt even honest minds.

How true this is, I wish to teach you a little more explicitly. Does it seem to you that Themistocles, who was general when you conquered the Persian in the battle of Salamis, was the better man, or Demosthenes, who the other day deserted his post? Miltiades, who won the battle of Marathon, or yonder man? Further—the men who brought back the exiled democracy from Phyle? And Aristeides "the Just," a title most unlike the name men give Demosthenes? But, by the Olympian gods, I think one ought not to name those men on the same day with this monster! Now let Demosthenes show if anywhere stands written an order to crown any one of those men. Was the democracy, then, ungrateful? No, but noble-minded, and those men were worthy of their city. For they thought that their honour should be conferred, not in written words, but in the memory of those whom they had served; and from that time until this day it abides, immortal. But what rewards they did receive, it is well to recall.

There were certain men in those days, fellow citizens, who endured much toil and underwent great dangers at the river Strymon, and conquered the Medes in battle. When they came home they asked the people for a reward, and the democracy gave them great honour, as it was then esteemed— permission to set up three stone Hermae in the Stoa of the Hermae, but on condition that they should

---

[3] κἀκεῖνοι γε Hamaker: the MSS. have κἀκεῖνοί γε οἱ μὴ (or οἱ μὴ οὕτω or εἰ μὴ) τετιμημένοι.

ᾦτε μὴ ἐπιγράφειν τὸ ὄνομα τὸ ἑαυτῶν, ἵνα μὴ
τῶν στρατηγῶν, ἀλλὰ τοῦ δήμου δοκῇ εἶναι τὸ
184 ἐπίγραμμα. ὅτι δ' ἀληθῆ λέγω, ἐξ αὐτῶν τῶν
ποιημάτων γνώσεσθε. ἐπιγέγραπται γὰρ ἐπὶ τῷ
μὲν πρώτῳ τῶν Ἑρμῶν·

ἦν ἄρα κἀκεῖνοι ταλακάρδιοι, οἵ ποτε Μήδων
    παισὶν ἐπ' Ἠϊόνι, Στρυμόνος ἀμφὶ ῥοάς,
λιμόν τ' αἴθωνα κρατερόν τ' ἐπάγοντες Ἄρηα
    πρῶτοι δυσμενέων εὗρον ἀμηχανίην.

ἐπὶ δὲ τῷ δευτέρῳ·

ἡγεμόνεσσι δὲ μισθὸν Ἀθηναῖοι τάδ' ἔδωκαν
    ἀντ' εὐεργεσίης καὶ μεγάλης ἀρετῆς.
μᾶλλόν τις τάδ' ἰδὼν καὶ ἐπεσσομένων ἐθελήσει
    ἀμφὶ ξυνοῖσι πράγμασι μόχθον ἔχειν.

185 ἐπὶ δὲ τῷ τρίτῳ ἐπιγέγραπται Ἑρμῇ·

ἔκ ποτε τῆσδε πόληος ἅμ' Ἀτρείδῃσι Μενεσθεὺς
    ἡγεῖτο ζάθεον Τρωικὸν ἂμ πεδίον,
ὅν ποθ' Ὅμηρος ἔφη Δαναῶν πύκα χαλκοχι-
        τώνων
    κοσμητῆρα μάχης ἔξοχον ἄνδρα μολεῖν.
οὕτως οὐδὲν ἀεικὲς Ἀθηναίοισι καλεῖσθαι
    κοσμητὰς πολέμου τ' ἀμφὶ καὶ ἠνορέης.

not inscribe their own names upon them, in order
that the inscription might not seem to be in honour
of the generals, but of the people. That this is
true, you shall learn from the verses themselves; for
on the first of the Hermae stands written :

" Brave men and daring were they who once by the
      city of Eion,
    Far off by Strymon's flood, fought with the sons
      of the Medes.
Fiery famine they made their ally, and Ares on-
      rushing ;
    So they found helpless a foe stranger till then
      to defeat."

and on the second :

" This, the reward of their labour, has Athens be-
      stowed on her leaders ;
    Token of duty well done, honour to valour
      supreme.
Whoso in years yet to be shall read these lines
      in the marble,
    Gladly will toil in his turn, giving his life for
      the state."

And on the third of the Hermae stands written :

" Once from this city Menestheus, summoned to join
      the Atreidae,
    Led forth an army to Troy, plain beloved of the
      gods.
Homer has sung of his fame, and has said that of
      all the mailed chieftains
    None could so shrewdly as he marshal the ranks
      for the fight.
Fittingly then shall the people of Athens be
      honoured, and called
    Marshals and leaders of war, heroes in combat
      of arms."

ἔστι που τὸ τῶν στρατηγῶν ὄνομα; οὐδαμοῦ,
ἀλλὰ τὸ τοῦ δήμου.

186   Προέλθετε δὴ τῇ διανοίᾳ καὶ εἰς τὴν στοὰν τὴν
ποικίλην· ἁπάντων γὰρ ἡμῖν τῶν καλῶν ἔργων
τὰ ὑπομνήματα ἐν τῇ ἀγορᾷ ἀνάκειται. τί οὖν
ἐστιν, ὦ ἄνδρες Ἀθηναῖοι, ὃ ἐγὼ λέγω; ἐνταῦθα
ἡ ἐν Μαραθῶνι μάχη γέγραπται. τίς οὖν ἦν ὁ
στρατηγός; οὑτωσὶ μὲν ἐρωτηθέντες ἅπαντες
ἀποκρίναισθε ἄν, ὅτι Μιλτιάδης· ἐκεῖ δὲ οὐκ
ἐπιγέγραπται. πῶς; οὐκ ᾔτησε ταύτην τὴν δωρεάν; ᾔτησεν, ἀλλ' ὁ δῆμος οὐκ ἔδωκεν, ἀλλ' ἀντὶ
τοῦ ὀνόματος συνεχώρησεν αὐτῷ γραφῆναι πρώ-
187   τῳ παρακαλοῦντι τοὺς στρατιώτας. ἐν τοίνυν τῷ
Μητρῴῳ[1] ἦν ἔδοτε δωρεὰν τοῖς ἀπὸ Φυλῆς φεύγοντα τὸν δῆμον καταγαγοῦσιν, ἔστιν ἰδεῖν. ἦν
μὲν γὰρ ὁ τὸ ψήφισμα νικήσας Ἀρχῖνος ὁ ἐκ
Κοίλης, εἷς τῶν καταγαγόντων τὸν δῆμον, ἔγραψε
δὲ πρῶτον μὲν αὐτοῖς εἰς θυσίαν καὶ ἀναθήματα
δοῦναι χιλίας δραχμάς, καὶ τοῦτ' ἔστιν ἔλαττον ἢ
δέκα δραχμαὶ κατ' ἄνδρα, ἔπειτα[2] στεφανῶσαι
θαλλοῦ στεφάνῳ αὐτῶν ἕκαστον, ἀλλ' οὐ χρυσῷ·
τότε μὲν γὰρ ἦν ὁ τοῦ θαλλοῦ στέφανος τίμιος,
νυνὶ δὲ καὶ ὁ χρυσοῦς καταπεφρόνηται. καὶ οὐδὲ
τοῦτο εἰκῆ πρᾶξαι κελεύει, ἀλλ' ἀκριβῶς τὴν
βουλὴν σκεψαμένην, ὅσοι αὐτῶν ἐπὶ Φυλῇ ἐπο-
λιορκήθησαν ὅτε Λακεδαιμόνιοι καὶ οἱ τριάκοντα
προσέβαλλον,[3] οὐχ ὅσοι τὴν τάξιν ἔλιπον ἐν
Χαιρωνείᾳ τῶν πολεμίων ἐπιόντων. ὅτι δ' ἀληθῆ
λέγω, ἀναγνώσεται ὑμῖν τὸ ψήφισμα.

---

[1] Μητρῴῳ Bake : Μητρῴῳ παρὰ τὸ βουλευτήριον MSS.
[2] ἔπειτα Cobet : ἔπειτα κελεύει MSS.
[3] προσέβαλλον Hamaker : προσέβαλλον τοῖς καταλαβοῦσι
Φυλήν MSS.

Is the name of the generals anywhere here?
Nowhere; only the name of the people.

And now pass on in imagination to the Stoa
Poecile[1]; for the memorials of all our noble deeds
stand dedicated in the Agora. What is it then,
fellow citizens, to which I refer? The battle of
Marathon is pictured there. Who then was the
general? If you were asked this question you
would all answer, "Miltiades." But his name is
not written there. Why? Did he not ask for this
reward? He did ask, but the people refused it; and
instead of his name they permitted that he should
be painted in the front rank, urging on his men.
Again, in the Metroön you may see the reward that
you gave to the band from Phyle, who brought the
people back from exile. For Archinus of Coele, one
of the men who brought back the people, was the
author of the resolution. He moved, first, to give
them for sacrifice and dedicatory offerings a thousand
drachmas, less than ten drachmas per man; then
that they be crowned each with a crown of olive
(not of gold, for then the crown of olive was prized,
but to-day even a crown of gold is held in disdain).
And not even this will he allow to be done carelessly,
but only after careful examination by the Senate, to
determine who of them actually stood siege at Phyle
when the Lacedaemonians and the Thirty made
their attack, not those who deserted their post—as
at Chaeroneia—in the face of the advancing enemy.
As proof of what I say, the clerk shall read the
resolution to you.

[1] The "Painted Colonnade," probably on the eastern side
of the Agora, was decorated with frescoes by some of the
greatest painters, depicting famous battles and victories in
the history of the city.

THE SPEECHES OF AESCHINES

188   Παρανάγνωθι δὴ καὶ ὃ γέγραφε Κτησιφῶν
Δημοσθένει τῷ τῶν μεγίστων αἰτίῳ κακῶν.

ΨΗΦΙΣΜΑ

Τούτῳ τῷ ψηφίσματι ἐξαλείφεται ἡ τῶν καταγαγόντων δωρεά. εἰ τοῦτ' ἔχει καλῶς, ἐκεῖνο
αἰσχρῶς· εἰ ἐκεῖνοι κατ' ἀξίαν ἐτιμήθησαν, οὗτος
ἀνάξιος ὢν στεφανοῦται.

189   Καίτοι πυνθάνομαί γ' αὐτὸν μέλλειν λέγειν, ὡς
οὐ δίκαια ποιῶ παραβάλλων αὐτῷ τὰ τῶν προγόνων ἔργα· οὐδὲ γὰρ Φιλάμμωνα [1] τὸν πύκτην
Ὀλυμπίασι στεφανωθῆναι νικήσαντα Γλαῦκον
τὸν παλαιὸν ἐκεῖνον,[2] ἀλλὰ τοὺς καθ' ἑαυτὸν
ἀγωνιστάς, ὥσπερ ὑμᾶς ἀγνοοῦντας ὅτι τοῖς μὲν
πύκταις ἐστὶν ὁ ἀγὼν πρὸς ἀλλήλους, τοῖς δ'
ἀξιοῦσι στεφανοῦσθαι πρὸς αὐτὴν τὴν ἀρετήν,
ἧς καὶ ἕνεκα στεφανοῦνται. δεῖ γὰρ τὸν κήρυκα
ἀψευδεῖν, ὅταν τὴν ἀνάρρησιν ἐν τῷ θεάτρῳ
ποιῆται πρὸς τοὺς Ἕλληνας. μὴ οὖν ἡμῖν, ὡς
Παταικίωνος ἄμεινον πεπολίτευσαι, διέξιθι, ἀλλ'
ἐφικόμενος τῆς ἀνδραγαθίας, οὕτω τὰς χάριτας
τὸν δῆμον ἀπαίτει.

190   Ἵνα δὲ μὴ ἀποπλανῶ ὑμᾶς ἀπὸ τῆς ὑποθέσεως,
ἀναγνώσεται ὑμῖν ὁ γραμματεὺς τὸ ἐπίγραμμα ὃ

---

[1] Φιλάμμωνα Cobet : the MSS. have φήσει or φασὶ or φησι
before Φιλάμμωνα.
[2] ἐκεῖνον Cobet : ἐκεῖνον πύκτην MSS.

RESOLUTION AS TO THE REWARD OF THE BAND FROM PHYLE

Now over against this read the resolution which Ctesiphon has proposed for Demosthenes, the man who is responsible for our greatest disasters.

THE RESOLUTION

By this resolution the reward of those who restored the democracy is annulled. If this resolution is good, the other was bad. If they were worthily honoured, this man is unworthy of the crown that is proposed.

And yet I am told that he intends to say that I am unfair in holding up his deeds for comparison with those of our fathers. For he will say that Philammon the boxer was crowned at Olympia, not as having defeated Glaucus, that famous man of ancient days, but because he beat the antagonists of his own time;[1] as though you did not know that in the case of boxers the contest is of one man against another, but for those who claim a crown, the standard is virtue itself; since it is for this that they are crowned. For the herald must not lie when he makes his proclamation in the theatre before the Greeks. Do not, then, recount to us how you have been a better citizen than Pataecion,[2] but first attain unto nobility of character, and then call on the people for their grateful acknowledgment.

But lest I lead you away from the subject, the clerk shall read to you the epigram that is inscribed

[1] The Scholiast puts Philammon's victory in 360 B.C.

[2] We are not reliably informed what notorious incapacity or scandalous conduct made Pataecion's name appropriate for this comparison. The audience evidently needed no explanation.

ἐπιγέγραπται τοῖς ἀπὸ Φυλῆς τὸν δῆμον καταγαγοῦσιν.

ΕΠΙΓΡΑΜΜΑ

Τούσδ' ἀρετῆς ἕνεκα στεφάνοις ἐγέραιρε πα-
λαίχθων
δῆμος Ἀθηναίων, οἵ ποτε τοὺς ἀδίκοις
θεσμοῖς ἄρξαντας πόλιος πρῶτοι καταπαύειν
ἦρξαν, κίνδυνον σώμασιν ἀράμενοι.

191 Ὅτι τοὺς παρὰ τοὺς νόμους ἄρξαντας κατέλυσαν, διὰ τοῦτ' αὐτούς φησιν ὁ ποιητὴς τιμηθῆναι.
ἔναυλον γὰρ ἦν ἔτι τότε πᾶσιν, ὅτι τηνικαῦτα ὁ
δῆμος κατελύθη, ἐπειδή τινες τὰς γραφὰς τῶν
παρανόμων ἀνεῖλον. καὶ γάρ τοι, ὡς ἐγὼ τοῦ
πατρὸς τοῦ ἐμαυτοῦ ἐπυνθανόμην, ὃς ἔτη βιοὺς
ἐνενήκοντα καὶ πέντε ἐτελεύτησεν, ἁπάντων μετα-
σχὼν τῶν πόνων τῇ πόλει, οὓς[1] πολλάκις πρὸς
ἐμὲ διεξῄει ἐπὶ σχολῆς· ἔφη γάρ, ὅτε ἀρτίως
κατεληλύθει ὁ δῆμος, εἴ τις εἰσίοι γραφὴ παρανόμων εἰς δικαστήριον, εἶναι ὅμοιον τὸ ὄνομα καὶ
τὸ ἔργον. τί γάρ ἐστιν ἀνοσιώτερον ἀνδρὸς
192 παράνομα λέγοντος καὶ πράττοντος; καὶ τὴν
ἀκρόασιν, ὡς ἐκεῖνος ἀπήγγελλεν, οὐ τὸν αὐτὸν
τρόπον ἐποιοῦντο ὥσπερ νῦν γίγνεται, ἀλλ' ἦσαν
πολὺ χαλεπώτεροι οἱ δικασταὶ τοῖς τὰ παράνομα
γράφουσιν αὐτοῦ τοῦ κατηγόρου, καὶ πολλάκις
ἀνεπόδιζον τὸν γραμματέα καὶ ἐκέλευον πάλιν

---

[1] οὓς Markland : ὃς MSS.

in honour of the band from Phyle, who restored the democracy.

EPIGRAM

"These men, noble of heart, hath the ancient
    Athenian people
    Crowned with an olive crown. First were they
      to oppose
Tyrants who knew not the laws, whose rule was
    the rule of injustice.
    Danger they met unafraid, pledging their lives
    to the cause."

Because they put down those who ruled unlawfully, for this cause the poet says they were honoured. For then it was still in the ears of all men that the democracy was overthrown only after certain men had put out of the way the provision for the indictment of men who propose illegal measures. Yes, as I have heard my own father say,[1] for he lived to be ninety-five years old, and had shared all the toils of the city, which he often described to me in his leisure hours—well, he said that in the early days of the re-established democracy, if any indictment for an illegal motion came into court, the word was as good as the deed.[2] For what is more wicked than the man who speaks and does what is unlawful? And in those days, so my father said, they gave no such hearing as is given now, but the jurors were far more severe toward the authors of illegal motions than was the accuser himself ; and it frequently happened that they made the clerk stop,

---

[1] "The form of the paragraph is lively and ungrammatical." (Simcox.)

[2] "Punish him" was no sooner said than done.

ἀναγιγνώσκειν τοὺς νόμους καὶ τὸ ψήφισμα, καὶ
ἡλίσκοντο οἱ τὰ παράνομα γράφοντες, οὐκ εἰ
πάντας παραπηδήσειαν τοὺς νόμους, ἀλλ' εἰ μίαν
μόνον συλλαβὴν παραλλάξειαν. τὸ δὲ νυνὶ
γιγνόμενον πρᾶγμα ὑπερκαταγέλαστόν ἐστιν· ὁ
μὲν γὰρ γραμματεὺς ἀναγιγνώσκει τὸ παράνομον,
οἱ δὲ δικασταὶ ὥσπερ ἐπῳδὴν ἢ ἀλλότριόν τι
πρᾶγμα ἀκροώμενοι, πρὸς ἑτέρῳ τινὶ τὴν γνώμην
ἔχουσιν.

193   Ἤδη δ' ἐκ τῶν τεχνῶν τῶν Δημοσθένους
αἰσχρὸν ἔθος ἐν τοῖς δικαστηρίοις παραδέδεχθε.[1]
μετενήνεκται γὰρ ὑμῖν[2] τὰ τῆς πόλεως δίκαια·
ὁ μὲν γὰρ κατήγορος ἀπολογεῖται, ὁ δὲ φεύγων
τὴν γραφὴν κατηγορεῖ, οἱ δὲ δικασταὶ ἐνίοτε ὧν
μέν εἰσι κριταὶ ἐπιλανθάνονται, ὧν δ' οὐκ εἰσί,[3]
περὶ τούτων ἀναγκάζονται τὴν ψῆφον φέρειν.
λέγει δὲ ὁ φεύγων, ἂν ἄρα ποθ' ἅψηται τοῦ
πράγματος, οὐκ ὡς ἔννομα γέγραφεν, ἀλλ' ὡς ἤδη
ποτὲ καὶ πρότερον ἕτερος τοιαῦτα γράψας ἀπέφυγεν. ἐφ' ᾧ καὶ νυνὶ μέγα φρονεῖν ἀκούω
194   Κτησιφῶντα. ἐτόλμα δ' ἐν ὑμῖν ποτε σεμνύνεσθαι
Ἀριστοφῶν ἐκεῖνος ὁ Ἀζηνιεὺς λέγων ὅτι γραφὰς
παρανόμων ἀπέφυγεν ἑβδομήκοντα καὶ πέντε.
ἀλλ' οὐχὶ Κέφαλος ὁ παλαιὸς ἐκεῖνος, ὁ δοκῶν
δημοτικώτατος γεγονέναι, οὐχ οὕτως, ἀλλ' ἐπὶ
τοῖς ἐναντίοις ἐφιλοτιμεῖτο, λέγων ὅτι πλεῖστα
πάντων γεγραφὼς ψηφίσματα, οὐδεμίαν πώποτε
γραφὴν πέφευγε παρανόμων, καλῶς οἶμαι σεμ-
νυνόμενος. ἐγράφοντο γὰρ ἀλλήλους παρανόμων

---

[1] παραδέδεχθε Cobet : παραδέχεσθε MSS.
[2] ὑμῖν Markland : ἡμῖν or ὑμῶν MSS.
[3] εἰσί Cobet : εἰσὶ δικασταί MSS.

and told him to read to them the laws and the motion a second time; and they convicted a man of making an illegal motion, not in case he had overleaped all the laws together, but if one syllable only was contravened. But the process as it is conducted nowadays is ridiculous. The clerk reads the statement of the illegality which is charged, and the jurors, as though hearing an incantation, or some matter which is no concern of theirs, are attending to something else.

And already as a result of the tricks of Demosthenes you have admitted a shameful custom into your courts; for you have allowed your legal procedure to become perverted: the accuser is on the defensive, and the defendant plays the part of accuser; and the jurors sometimes forget what they are to judge, and are forced to bring in a verdict on matters which were never committed to their decision; while the defendant, if by any chance he does touch on the question at issue, pleads, not that his motion was lawful, but that on some past occasion another man has made an equally unlawful motion and been acquitted; a plea in which I hear Ctesiphon now places great confidence. Once the famous Aristophon of Azenia dared in your presence to boast that he had been acquitted seventy-five times on charge of making illegal motions. Not so the venerable Cephalus, famous as the truest representative of democracy—not so, but he took pride in the very opposite fact, saying that although he had been the author of more measures than any other man, he had never once been indicted for an illegal motion; an honourable pride, I think. For indictments for illegal motions were in those times brought,

οὐ μόνον οἱ διαπολιτευόμενοι, ἀλλὰ καὶ οἱ φίλοι
τοὺς φίλους, εἴ τι ἐξαμαρτάνοιεν εἰς τὴν πόλιν.
195 ἐκεῖθεν δὲ τοῦτο γνώσεσθε. Ἀρχῖνος γὰρ ὁ ἐκ
Κοίλης ἐγράψατο παρανόμων Θρασύβουλον τὸν
Στειριέα γράψαντά τι παρὰ τοὺς νόμους, ἕνα
τῶν ἀπὸ Φυλῆς αὐτῷ συγκατελθόντων, καὶ
εἷλε, νεωστὶ γεγενημένων αὐτῷ τῶν εὐεργεσιῶν,
ἃς οὐχ ὑπελογίσαντο οἱ δικασταί· ἡγοῦντο γάρ,
ὥσπερ τότε αὐτοὺς φεύγοντας[1] Θρασύβουλος
κατήγαγεν, οὕτω νῦν μένοντας ἐξελαύνειν παρὰ
196 τοὺς νόμους γράφοντά τι. ἀλλ᾽ οὐ νῦν, ἀλλὰ
πᾶν τοὐναντίον γίγνεται· οἱ γὰρ ἀγαθοὶ στρα-
τηγοὶ ὑμῖν καὶ τῶν τὰς σιτήσεις τινὲς εὑρημένων
ἐν τῷ πρυτανείῳ ἐξαιτοῦνται τὰς γραφὰς τῶν
παρανόμων, οὓς ὑμεῖς ἀχαρίστους εἶναι δικαίως
ἂν ὑπολαμβάνοιτε· εἰ γάρ τις ἐν δημοκρατίᾳ
τετιμημένος, ἐν τοιαύτῃ πολιτείᾳ, ἣν οἱ θεοὶ
καὶ οἱ νόμοι σῴζουσι, τολμᾷ βοηθεῖν τοῖς παράνομα γράφουσι, καταλύει τὴν πολιτείαν ὑφ᾽ ἧς
τετίμηται.
197 Τίς οὖν ἀποδέδεικται λόγος ἀνδρὶ δικαίῳ
συνηγόρῳ, ἐγὼ λέξω. εἰς τρία μέρη διαιρεῖται
ἡ ἡμέρα, ὅταν εἰσίῃ γραφὴ παρανόμων εἰς τὸ
δικαστήριον. ἐγχεῖται γὰρ τὸ μὲν πρῶτον ὕδωρ
τῷ κατηγόρῳ καὶ τοῖς νόμοις καὶ τῇ δημοκρατίᾳ,
τὸ δὲ δεύτερον[2] τῷ τὴν γραφὴν φεύγοντι καὶ
τοῖς εἰς αὐτὸ τὸ πρᾶγμα λέγουσιν· ἐπειδὰν δὲ

---

[1] φεύγοντας Dobree : φεύγοντας ἀπὸ Φυλῆς MSS.
[2] δεύτερον Weidner : δεύτερον ὕδωρ MSS.

not only by political rivals against one another, but
by friend against friend, if one was responsible for
any error toward the state.   Yes, the following shall
serve as an illustration : Archinus of Coele brought
an indictment for an illegal motion against Thrasybulus of Steiria, one of his own companions in the
return from Phyle ; and he convicted him ; and
though his services were recent, the jurors did not
take them into account ; for they thought that, just
as Thrasybulus had brought them back from exile
then, so now when they had been restored, by
making a motion which was against the laws he
was driving them into exile again.   But it is not
so to-day ; the very opposite is done.   For your
worthy generals, and some of those who have received maintenance in the Prytaneum, beg men off
who have been indicted for illegal motions.[1]   But
you ought to regard them as ungrateful.   For if
any man who has been honoured in a democracy, a
government which owes its safety to the gods and
to the laws, dares to aid men who make illegal
motions, he is undermining the government from
which he received his honours.

But I will tell you what plea is in order from
the honest advocate.   When an indictment for an
illegal motion is tried in court, the day is divided
into three parts.   The first water is poured in[2]
for the accuser, the laws, and the democracy ; the
second water, for the defendant and those who
speak on the question at issue ; but when the

[1] The meaning is that these influential men come into
court and use their influence to secure the acquittal of
personal friends of theirs.
[2] Into the clepsydra, by which the time allowed to each
side was measured.   Cp. ii. 126 and note.

τῇ πρώτῃ ψήφῳ λυθῇ τὸ παράνομον, ἤδη τὸ
τρίτον ὕδωρ ἐγχεῖται τῇ τιμήσει καὶ τῷ μεγέθει
198 τῆς ὀργῆς τῆς ὑμετέρας. ὅστις μὲν οὖν ἐν τῇ
τιμήσει τὴν ψῆφον αἰτεῖ, τὴν ὀργὴν τὴν ὑμετέραν
παραιτεῖται· ὅστις δ᾽ ἐν τῷ πρώτῳ λόγῳ τὴν
ψῆφον αἰτεῖ, ὅρκον αἰτεῖ, νόμον αἰτεῖ, δημοκρατίαν
αἰτεῖ, ὧν οὔτε αἰτῆσαι οὐδὲν ὅσιον οὐδενί, οὔτ᾽
αἰτηθέντα ἑτέρῳ δοῦναι. κελεύσατε οὖν αὐτούς,
ἐάσαντας τὴν πρώτην ὑμᾶς ψῆφον κατὰ τοὺς
νόμους διενεγκεῖν, ἀπαντᾶν εἰς τὴν τίμησιν.

199 Ὅλως δ᾽ ἔγωγε, ὦ ἄνδρες Ἀθηναῖοι, ὀλίγου δέω
εἰπεῖν ὡς καὶ νόμον δεῖ τεθῆναι ἐπὶ ταῖς γραφαῖς
μόναις ταῖς τῶν [1] παρανόμων, μὴ ἐξεῖναι μήτε τῷ
κατηγόρῳ συνηγόρους παρασχέσθαι, μήτε τῷ τὴν
γραφὴν [2] φεύγοντι. οὐ γὰρ ἀόριστόν ἐστι τὸ
δίκαιον, ἀλλ᾽ ὡρισμένον τοῖς νόμοις τοῖς ὑμετέροις.
ὥσπερ γὰρ ἐν τῇ τεκτονικῇ, ὅταν εἰδέναι βουλώ-
μεθα τὸ ὀρθὸν καὶ τὸ μή, τὸν κανόνα προσφέρο-
200 μεν, ᾧ διαγιγνώσκεται, οὕτω καὶ ἐν ταῖς γραφαῖς
ταῖς τῶν παρανόμων παράκειται κανὼν τοῦ δικαίου
τουτὶ τὸ σανίδιον, τὸ [3] ψήφισμα καὶ οἱ παρα-
γεγραμμένοι νόμοι. ταῦτα συμφωνοῦντα ἀλλήλοις ἐπιδείξας κατάβαινε· καὶ τί δεῖ σε Δημοσθένην παρακαλεῖν; ὅταν δ᾽ ὑπερπηδήσας τὴν
δικαίαν ἀπολογίαν παρακαλῇς κακοῦργον ἄνθρω-

---

[1] ταῖς τῶν Weidner : τῶν (ταῖς in one) MSS.
[2] γραφὴν Weidner : γραφὴν τῶν παρανόμων MSS.
[3] τὸ Sauppe : καὶ τὸ MSS.

---

[1] The jurors balloted first on the question whether the
motion was illegal as charged. If they sustained the prosecution, both sides then argued the question of the nature
and extent of the penalty, after which the jurors cast a final
ballot, fixing the penalty.

question of illegality has been decided by the first ballot,[1] then the third water is poured in for the question of the penalty and the extent of your anger. Whoever therefore in the discussion on the penalty asks for your vote,[2] is begging you to mitigate your anger; but he who in the first speech asks for your vote is asking you to surrender your oath, to surrender the law, to surrender the democratic constitution—things which no man has a right to ask you to surrender, nor any man to grant another for his asking. Bid them, therefore, to allow you to cast your first ballot according to the laws, before they plead on the question of penalty.

In short, fellow citizens, for my part I am almost ready to say that we ought to pass a special law governing indictments for illegal motions, which shall forbid either accuser or defendant to call in advocates. For the question of right involved is not an indefinite one, but is defined by your own laws. For as in carpentry, when we wish to know what is straight and what is not, we apply the carpenters' rule, which serves as our standard, so in indictments for illegal motions there lies ready to our hand as a rule of justice this tablet, containing the measure proposed and the laws which it transgresses.[3] Show that these agree one with another, Ctesiphon, and then take your seat. Why need you call Demosthenes to your support? When you overleap the just defence and call forward a rascal

---

[2] The reference is still to the request of influential men who come into court to help their friends.

[3] The tablet is the bulletin-board which had been publicly posted in advance of the trial, containing the indictment, the motion which was attacked, and the laws which were alleged to be violated by the motion.

πον καὶ τεχνίτην λόγων, κλέπτεις τὴν ἀκρόασιν,
βλάπτεις τὴν πόλιν, καταλύεις τὴν δημοκρατίαν.

201 Τίς οὖν ἐστιν ἀποτροπὴ τῶν τοιούτων λόγων,
ἐγὼ προερῶ. ἐπειδὰν προελθὼν ἐνταυθοῖ Κτησιφῶν διεξέλθῃ πρὸς ὑμᾶς τοῦτο δὴ τὸ συντεταγ-
μένον αὐτῷ προοίμιον, ἔπειτ᾽ ἐνδιατρίβῃ καὶ μὴ
ἀπολογῆται, ὑπομνήσατ᾽ αὐτὸν ἀθορύβως, τὸ
σανίδιον λαβεῖν καὶ τοὺς νόμους τῷ ψηφίσματι
παραναγνῶναι. ἐὰν δὲ μὴ προσποιῆται ὑμῶν
ἀκούειν, μηδὲ ὑμεῖς ἐκείνου ἐθέλετε ἀκούειν· οὐ
γὰρ τῶν φευγόντων τὰς δικαίας ἀπολογίας εἰσελη-
λύθατε ἀκροασόμενοι, ἀλλὰ τῶν ἐθελόντων δικαίως
202 ἀπολογεῖσθαι. ἐὰν δ᾽ ὑπερπηδήσας τὴν δικαίαν
ἀπολογίαν παρακαλῇ Δημοσθένην, μάλιστα μὲν
μὴ προσδέχεσθε σοφιστὴν οἰόμενον ῥήμασι τοὺς
νόμους ἀναιρήσειν, μηδ᾽ ἐν ἀρετῇ τοῦθ᾽ ὑμῶν
μηδεὶς καταλογιζέσθω, ὃς ἂν ἐπανερομένου Κτησιφῶντος, εἰ καλέσῃ[1] Δημοσθένην, πρῶτος ἀνα-
βοήσῃ "Κάλει, κάλει." ἐπὶ σαυτὸν καλεῖς, ἐπὶ
τοὺς νόμους καλεῖς, ἐπὶ τὴν δημοκρατίαν καλεῖς.
ἂν δ᾽ ἄρα ὑμῖν δόξῃ ἀκούειν, ἀξιώσατε τὸν Δημοσθένην τὸν αὐτὸν τρόπον ἀπολογεῖσθαι ὅνπερ
κἀγὼ κατηγόρηκα. ἐγὼ δὲ πῶς κατηγόρηκα; ἵνα
καὶ ὑπομνήσω ὑμᾶς.

203 Οὔτε τὸν ἴδιον βίον τὸν Δημοσθένους πρότερον
διεξῆλθον, οὔτε τῶν δημοσίων ἀδικημάτων οὐδενὸς
πρότερον ἐμνήσθην, ἄφθονα δήπου καὶ πολλὰ

---

[1] καλέσῃ Bekker : καλεσει or καλεσεις or καλεσω MSS.

and a rhetorician, you cheat the ears of the jury, you injure the city, you undermine the democracy.

How you may avert speeches of that sort, fellow citizens, I will tell you. When Ctesiphon comes forward here and recites to you that introduction which has of course been composed for him,[1] and when he then tries to kill time, and makes no answer to the charge, suggest to him, quietly, that he take the tablet and read the laws and his resolution side by side. If he pretends that he does not hear you, then do you refuse to hear him. For you have not come here to listen to men who dodge an honest defence, but to those who are willing to defend themselves with justice. But if he shall overleap the just defence and call Demosthenes to the platform, the best course for you is to refuse to receive a sophist, who expects to overthrow the laws with words. And when Ctesiphon asks you if he shall call Demosthenes, let no man of you consider that he is doing a meritorious thing in being the first to cry, " Aye, call him, call him." Against yourself you are calling him, against the laws you are calling him, against the constitution you are calling him. But if after all you decide to listen, demand that Demosthenes make his defence in the same way in which I have made the accusation. In what way have I made the accusation? Let me recall it to you.

I did not at the beginning review the private life of Demosthenes, nor did I at the beginning call to mind a single one of his public crimes—though I

---

[1] Aeschines assumes that Ctesiphon's speech has been composed for him by Demosthenes, and that it will be a mere introduction to the real defence, which will follow from the lips of Demosthenes himself, speaking nominally as friendly supporter (συνήγορος) of Ctesiphon.

ἔχων, ἢ πάντων γ' ἂν εἴην ἀπορώτατος· ἀλλὰ
πρῶτον μὲν τοὺς νόμους ἐπέδειξα ἀπαγορεύοντας
μὴ στεφανοῦν τοὺς ὑπευθύνους, ἔπειτα τὸν ῥήτορα
ἐξήλεγξα γράψαντα Δημοσθένην ὑπεύθυνον ὄντα
στεφανοῦν οὐδὲν προβαλόμενον,[1] οὐδὲ προσγρά-
ψαντα " Ἐπειδὰν δῷ τὰς εὐθύνας," ἀλλὰ παντελῶς
καὶ ὑμῶν καὶ τῶν νόμων καταπεφρονηκότα· καὶ τὰς
ἐσομένας πρὸς ταῦτα προφάσεις εἶπον, ἃς ἀξιῶ καὶ
204 ὑμᾶς διαμνημονεύειν. δεύτερον δ' ὑμῖν διεξῆλθον
τοὺς περὶ τῶν κηρυγμάτων νόμους, ἐν οἷς διαρρήδην
ἀπείρηται τὸν ὑπὸ τοῦ δήμου στεφανούμενον μὴ
κηρύττεσθαι ἔξω τῆς ἐκκλησίας· ὁ δὲ ῥήτωρ ὁ
φεύγων τὴν γραφὴν οὐ τοὺς νόμους μόνον παρα-
βέβηκεν, ἀλλὰ καὶ τὸν καιρὸν τῆς ἀναρρήσεως
καὶ τὸν τόπον, κελεύων οὐκ ἐν τῇ ἐκκλησίᾳ, ἀλλ'
ἐν τῷ θεάτρῳ τὴν ἀνάρρησιν γίγνεσθαι, οὐδ' ἐκκλησιαζόντων Ἀθηναίων, ἀλλὰ μελλόντων τραγῳδῶν εἰσιέναι. ταῦτα δ' εἰπὼν μικρὰ μὲν περὶ τῶν
ἰδίων εἶπον, τὰ δὲ πλεῖστα περὶ τῶν δημοσίων
205 ἀδικημάτων. οὕτω δὴ καὶ τὸν Δημοσθένην ἀξιώσατε ἀπολογεῖσθαι, πρὸς τὸν τῶν ὑπευθύνων νόμον
πρῶτον, τὸν περὶ τῶν κηρυγμάτων δεύτερον, τρίτον
δὲ τὸ μέγιστον,[2] ὡς οὐδὲ ἀνάξιός ἐστι τῆς δωρεᾶς.
ἐὰν δ' ὑμῶν δέηται συγχωρῆσαι αὐτῷ περὶ τῆς
τάξεως τοῦ λόγου, κατεπαγγελλόμενος ὡς ἐπὶ τῇ
τελευτῇ τῆς ἀπολογίας λύσει τὸ παρανόμον, μὴ
συγχωρεῖτε, μηδ' ἀγνοεῖθ' ὅτι πάλαισμα τοῦτ'

---

[1] προβαλόμενον Stephanus : προβαλλόμενον MSS.
[2] μέγιστον λέγω MSS.: Blass brackets λέγω.

certainly had great abundance of material, or else I must be the most helpless of mortals—but first I exhibited the laws which forbid crowning men who have not yet rendered their accounts, and then I convicted the orator of having moved to crown Demosthenes before he had rendered account, and that too without inserting the qualifying proviso, "When he shall have rendered account," but in utter contempt of you and of your laws. And I told you what excuses they would offer for this, which I earnestly pray you to keep in mind. Secondly, I recited to you the laws which govern proclamations, in which it is expressly forbidden that when one is crowned by the people the proclamation shall be made in any other place than in the assembly. But the politician who is the defendant in this case has not only transgressed the laws, but the time of proclamation, and the place of it; for he orders the proclamation to be made, not in the assembly, but in the theatre, not when the Athenian assembly is in session, but when the tragedies are about to be performed. After saying this, I spoke briefly about his private life, but chiefly about his public crimes. I insist, therefore, that you demand the same order of defence from Demosthenes; first, let him defend himself against the law of accountability, secondly, against the law which governs proclamations, and thirdly, and most important, let him show also that he is not unworthy of the reward. But if he asks you to indulge him as to the order of his speech, and solemnly promises that at the close of his defence he will clear away the matter of illegality, do not yield to him, and do not forget that

ἔστι δικαστηρίου· οὐ γὰρ εἰσαῦθίς ποτε βούλοιτ᾽
ἂν πρὸς τὸ παράνομον ἀπολογεῖσθαι, ἀλλ᾽ οὐδὲν
ἔχων δίκαιον εἰπεῖν, ἑτέρων παρεμβολῇ πραγμάτων εἰς λήθην ὑμᾶς βούλεται τῆς κατηγορίας
206 ἐμβαλεῖν. ὥσπερ οὖν ἐν τοῖς γυμνικοῖς ἀγῶσιν
ὁρᾶτε τοὺς πύκτας περὶ τῆς στάσεως ἀλλήλοις
διαγωνιζομένους, οὕτω καὶ ὑμεῖς ὅλην τὴν ἡμέραν
ὑπὲρ τῆς πόλεως περὶ τῆς στάσεως¹ αὐτῷ τοῦ
λόγου μάχεσθε, καὶ μὴ ἐᾶτε αὐτὸν ἔξω τοῦ παρανόμου περιίστασθαι, ἀλλ᾽ ἐγκαθήμενοι καὶ ἐνε-
δρεύοντες ἐν τῇ ἀκροάσει, εἰσελαύνετε αὐτὸν εἰς
τοὺς τοῦ παρανόμου λόγους, καὶ τὰς ἐκτροπὰς
αὐτοῦ τῶν λόγων ἐπιτηρεῖτε.

207 Ἀλλ᾽ ἃ δὴ συμβήσεται ὑμῖν, ἐὰν τοῦτον τὸν
τρόπον τὴν ἀκρόασιν ποιήσησθε, ταῦθ᾽ ὑμῖν ἤδη
δίκαιός εἰμι προειπεῖν. ἐπεισάξει γὰρ τὸν γόητα
καὶ βαλλαντιοτόμον καὶ διατετμηκότα τὴν πολιτείαν. οὗτος κλάει μὲν ῥᾷον ἢ οἱ ἄλλοι γελῶσιν,
ἐπιορκεῖ δὲ πάντων προχειρότατα· οὐκ ἂν θαυμά-
σαιμι δέ, εἰ μεταβαλόμενος² τοῖς ἔξωθεν³ περιε-
στηκόσι λοιδορήσεται, φάσκων τοὺς μὲν ὀλιγαρ-
χικοὺς ὑπ᾽ αὐτῆς τῆς ἀληθείας διηριθμημένους
ἥκειν πρὸς τὸ τοῦ κατηγόρου βῆμα, τοὺς δὲ δημο-
208 τικοὺς πρὸς τὸ τοῦ φεύγοντος. ὅταν δὴ τὰ τοιαῦτα
λέγῃ, πρὸς μὲν τοὺς στασιαστικοὺς λόγους ἐκεῖνο
αὐτῷ ὑποβάλλετε· "Ὦ Δημόσθενες, εἰ ὅμοιοι
ἦσαν σοὶ οἱ ἀπὸ Φυλῆς φεύγοντα τὸν δῆμον κατα-

¹ στάσεως Faber : τάξεως MSS.
² μεταβαλόμενος Blass : μεταβαλλόμενος MSS.
³ ἔξωθεν Kleyn : ἔξω MSS.

this is an old trick of the court-room. For he would never of his own choice return to the defence against the illegality; but because he has nothing to say which is just, he seeks by the insertion of extraneous matters to plunge you into forgetfulness of the charge. As, therefore, in gymnastic contests you see the boxers contending with one another for position, so do you for the city's sake fight with him the whole day long for position as regards argument; and do not let him set his feet outside the bounds of the illegality charged, but watch him and lie in wait for him as you listen, drive him into discussion of the illegality, and look out for the twists and turns of his speech.

What, on the other hand, will surely be the result for you if you listen in the way that they propose, I ought now to forewarn you. For the defendant will call to his aid this juggler and cut-purse, a man who has torn the constitution to shreds. This man weeps more readily than other men laugh, and nothing is so easy for him as perjury. And I should not wonder if he should change his tactics and slander the listeners outside the bar, alleging that those whom truth herself has singled out and counted as oligarchs have come to the platform of the prosecution, but all the friends of the people to the platform of the defence.[1] Now when he talks like that, in answer to such appeals to faction, make this suggestion to him: "Demosthenes, if the men of Phyle, who brought back the people from exile, had

---

[1] In court, plaintiff and defendant had each a platform, where he sat with his intimate friends and supporters. It would appear from this passage that listeners who sympathised with either party grouped themselves near his platform.

γαγόντες, οὐκ ἂν ποθ᾽ ἡ δημοκρατία κατέστη. νῦν
δὲ ἐκεῖνοι μὲν μεγάλων κακῶν συμβάντων ἔσωσαν
τὴν πόλιν τὸ κάλλιστον ἐκ παιδείας ῥῆμα φθεγ-
ξάμενοι, ῾μὴ μνησικακεῖν᾽· σὺ δὲ ἑλκοποιεῖς, καὶ
μᾶλλόν σοι μέλει τῶν αὐθημερὸν λόγων, ἢ τῆς
σωτηρίας τῆς πόλεως."

"Ὅταν δ᾽ ἐπίορκος ὢν εἰς τὴν τῶν ὅρκων[1]
πίστιν καταφυγγάνῃ, ἐκεῖνο ἀπομνημονεύσατε
αὐτῷ, ὅτι τῷ πολλάκις μὲν ἐπιορκοῦντι, ἀεὶ
δὲ[2] μεθ᾽ ὅρκων ἀξιοῦντι πιστεύεσθαι, δυοῖν
θάτερον ὑπάρξαι δεῖ,[3] ἢ τοὺς θεοὺς καινούς, ἢ
209 τοὺς ἀκροατὰς μὴ τοὺς αὐτούς. περὶ δὲ τῶν
δακρύων καὶ τοῦ τόνου τῆς φωνῆς, ὅταν ὑμᾶς ἐπε-
ρωτᾷ· "Ποῖ καταφύγω, ἄνδρες Ἀθηναῖοι; περι-
εγράψατέ με· οὐκ ἔστιν ὅποι ἀναπτήσομαι,"
ἀνθυποβάλλετε αὐτῷ· "Ὁ δὲ δῆμος ὁ Ἀθηναίων
ποῖ καταφύγῃ, Δημόσθενες; πρὸς ποίαν συμμάχων παρασκευήν; πρὸς ποῖα χρήματα; τί προ-
βαλλόμενος ὑπὲρ τοῦ δήμου πεπολίτευσαι; ἃ μὲν
γὰρ ὑπὲρ σεαυτοῦ βεβούλευσαι, πάντες ὁρῶμεν.
ἐκλιπὼν μὲν τὸ ἄστυ οὐκ οἰκεῖς, ὡς δοκεῖς, ἐν
Πειραιεῖ, ἀλλ᾽ ἐξορμεῖς ἐκ τῆς πόλεως, ἐφόδια δὲ
πεπόρισαι τῇ σαυτοῦ ἀνανδρίᾳ τὸ βασιλικὸν χρυ-
210 σίον καὶ τὰ δημόσια δωροδοκήματα." ὅλως δὲ τί
τὰ δάκρυα; τίς ἡ κραυγή; τίς ὁ τόνος τῆς φωνῆς;
οὐχ ὁ μὲν τὴν γραφὴν φεύγων ἐστὶ Κτησιφῶν, ὁ

---

[1] τῶν ὅρκων Sakorraphos : ἀπὸ or διὰ τῶν ὅρκων MSS.
[2] ἀεὶ δὲ Dobree : ἀεὶ δὲ πρὸς τοὺς αὐτοὺς MSS.
[3] δεῖ Cobet : after δεῖ the MSS. have ὧν οὐδέτερόν ἐστ.
Δημοσθένει ὑπάρχον.

been like you, never had the democracy been re-
established. But as it was, they saved the city
out of great disasters, and gave utterance to those
words which are the fairest product of enlightened
minds, 'Forgive and forget.' But as for you, you
tear open old sores, and you care more for the
words of the moment than for the safety of the
state."

But when, perjurer that he is, he takes refuge in
the confidence which you place in oaths, remind
him of this, that when a man repeatedly perjures
himself, and yet is continually demanding to be
believed because of his oaths, one of two things
ought to be true, either the gods ought to be
new gods, or the hearers not the same. But in
answer to his tears and the straining of his voice
when he asks you, "Whither shall I flee, fellow
citizens? You have compassed me about, I have not
whither to take wings," suggest to him, " But the
Athenian people, Demosthenes, whither shall they
flee? What allies have been made ready to receive
them? What resources are prepared? What bul-
wark have you thrown up before the people by your
policies? For we all see what provision you have
made for yourself. You have left the upper city;
and the Peiraeus, as it seems, is not so much
your home, as an anchorage for you, off the city's
coast. And you have provided as means for your
cowardly flight, the King's gold and the fruits of your
political bribery." But, after all, why these tears?
Why all this noise? Why this straining of the voice?
Is it not Ctesiphon who is the defendant? Is not
the suit one in which the penalty is for the jury to

δ᾽ ἀγὼν οὐκ ἀτίμητος, σὺ δ᾽ οὔτε περὶ τοῦ σώματος
οὔτε περὶ τῆς ἐπιτιμίας οὔτε περὶ τῆς οὐσίας ἀγω-
νίζῃ; ἀλλὰ περὶ τίνος ἐστὶν αὐτῷ ἡ σπουδή; περὶ
χρυσῶν στεφάνων καὶ κηρυγμάτων ἐν τῷ θεάτρῳ
211 παρὰ τοὺς νόμους· ὃν ἐχρῆν, εἰ καὶ μανεὶς ὁ δῆμος
ἢ τῶν καθεστηκότων ἐπιλελησμένος, ἐπὶ τοιαύτης
ἀκαιρίας ἐβούλετο στεφανοῦν αὐτόν, παρελθόντα
εἰς τὴν ἐκκλησίαν εἰπεῖν· " Ἄνδρες Ἀθηναῖοι, τὸν
μὲν στέφανον δέχομαι, τὸν δὲ καιρὸν ἀποδοκιμάζω
ἐν ᾧ τὸ κήρυγμα γίγνεται· οὐ γὰρ δεῖ, ἐφ᾽ οἷς ἡ
πόλις ἐκείρατο,¹ ἐπὶ τούτοις ἐμὲ στεφανοῦσθαι."
ἀλλ᾽ οἶμαι ταῦτα μὲν ἂν εἴποι ἀνὴρ ὄντως βεβιω-
κὼς μετ᾽ ἀρετῆς· ἃ δὲ σὺ λέξεις, εἴποι ἂν κάθαρμα
212 ζηλοτυποῦν ἀρετήν. οὐ γὰρ δὴ μὰ τὸν Ἡρακλέα
τοῦτό γε ὑμῶν οὐδεὶς φοβήσεται, μὴ Δημοσθένης,
ἀνὴρ μεγαλόψυχος καὶ τὰ πολεμικὰ διαφέρων,
ἀποτυχὼν τῶν ἀριστείων ἐπανελθὼν οἴκαδε ἑαυτὸν διαχρήσηται· ὃς τοσοῦτον καταγελᾷ τῆς πρὸς
ὑμᾶς φιλοτιμίας, ὥστε τὴν μιαρὰν κεφαλὴν ταύτην καὶ ὑπεύθυνον, ἣν οὗτος παρὰ πάντας τοὺς
νόμους γέγραφε στεφανῶσαι, μυριάκις κατατέ-
τμηκε καὶ τούτων μισθοὺς εἴληφε τραύματος ἐκ
προνοίας γραφὰς γραφόμενος, καὶ κατακεκονδύ-
λισται, ὥστε αὐτὸν οἶμαι τὰ τῶν κονδύλων ἴχνη

---

¹ ἐκείρατο Weidner : ἐπένθησε καὶ ἐκείρατο or ἐκείρετο καὶ
ἐπένθησε MSS.

---

¹ ἀγῶνες ἀτίμητοι were those in which the penalty was
fixed by statute ; in ἀγῶνες τιμητοί the penalty was to be
determined in each case by the jury. Aeschines represents
the latter class of cases as involving less peril to the
defendant.

determine?[1] Is it not true that you are pleading
neither for your person nor for your citizenship nor
for your property? But what is this anxiety of his
about? About crowns of gold and proclamations
in the theatre—against the laws. Nay, but if the
people gone mad, or forgetful of the existing situation, had actually wished to crown him at a time so
unfitting, he ought to have come before the assembly
and said, "Fellow citizens, I accept the crown, but
I do not approve the time at which the proclamation is to be made. For events which have caused
our city to shear her head in mourning are no
fitting occasion for my head to receive a crown."
This I think a man would say whose life had been
one of genuine virtue. But the words which you,
Demosthenes, will speak, are the natural expression
of a worthless scoundrel, with whom virtue is a pretence. One thing at any rate is sure, by Heracles;
no one of you will feel any anxiety lest Demosthenes,
a man high-spirited and distinguished in war, will, if
he fails to receive the meed of valour, go back home
and make away with himself—he who so despises
honour in your eyes that on this pestilential and
accountable[2] head of his upon which Ctesiphon, in
defiance of all the laws, proposes that you set a
crown, he has inflicted a thousand gashes, and he
has made money out of his wounds by bringing suit[3]
for malicious assault. And on one occasion he got
such a smashing blow that I imagine he still carries

---

[2] The Greek word ὑπεύθυνον, here rendered "accountable,"
is the technical expression for the accountability of the
official who has not yet appeared before the board of
auditors.

[3] See ii. 93. The single case there referred to is, so far as
we know, the only pretext for Aeschines' "thousand gashes."

THE SPEECHES OF AESCHINES

τῶν Μειδίου ἔχειν ἔτι φανερά· ὁ γὰρ ἄνθρωπος οὐ
κεφαλήν, ἀλλὰ πρόσοδον κέκτηται.[1]

213 Περὶ δὲ Κτησιφῶντος τοῦ γράψαντος τὴν γνώμην βραχέα βούλομαι εἰπεῖν, τὰ δὲ πολλὰ ὑπερβήσομαι, ἵνα καὶ πεῖραν λάβω,[2] εἰ δύνασθε τοὺς
σφόδρα πονηρούς, κἂν μή τις προείπῃ, διαγιγνώ-
σκειν. ὃ δ᾽ ἐστὶ κοινὸν καὶ δίκαιον κατ᾽ ἀμφοτέρων αὐτῶν ἀπαγγεῖλαι πρὸς ὑμᾶς, τοῦτ᾽ ἐρῶ.
περιέρχονται γὰρ τὴν ἀγορὰν ἀληθεῖς κατ᾽ ἀλλήλων ἔχοντες δόξας καὶ λόγους οὐ ψευδεῖς λέγοντες.

214 ὁ μὲν γὰρ Κτησιφῶν οὐ τὸ καθ᾽ ἑαυτὸν φησι φοβεῖσθαι, ἐλπίζειν γὰρ δόξειν ἰδιώτης εἶναι, ἀλλὰ
τὴν τοῦ Δημοσθένους ἐν τῇ πολιτείᾳ δωροδοκίαν[3]
καὶ τὴν ἐμπληξίαν καὶ δειλίαν· ὁ δὲ Δημοσθένης
εἰς αὑτὸν μὲν ἀποβλέπων θαρρεῖν φησιν, τὴν δὲ
τοῦ Κτησιφῶντος πονηρίαν καὶ πορνοβοσκίαν
ἰσχυρῶς δεδιέναι. τοὺς δὴ κατεγνωκότας ἀλλήλων μηδαμῶς ὑμεῖς οἱ κοινοὶ κριταὶ τῶν ἐγκλημάτων ἀπολύσητε.

215 Περὶ δὲ τῶν εἰς ἐμαυτὸν λοιδοριῶν βραχέα βούλομαι προειπεῖν. πυνθάνομαι γὰρ λέξειν Δημοσθένην, ὡς ἡ πόλις ὑπ᾽ αὐτοῦ μὲν ὠφέληται πολλά,
ὑπ᾽ ἐμοῦ δὲ καταβέβλαπται, καὶ τὸν Φίλιππον
καὶ τὸν Ἀλέξανδρον καὶ τὰς ἀπὸ τούτων αἰτίας
ἀνοίσειν ἐπ᾽ ἐμέ. οὕτω δ᾽[4] ἐστὶν ὡς ἔοικε δεινὸς
δημιουργὸς λόγων, ὥστε οὐκ ἀποχρῇ αὐτῷ, εἴ τι
πεπολίτευμαι παρ᾽ ὑμῖν ἐγώ, ἢ εἴ τινας δημηγορίας

[1] Weidner accepts Westermann's brilliant conjecture, and writes οὐ πρόσωπον, ἀλλὰ πρόσοδον κέκτηται.
[2] καὶ πεῖραν λάβω Baiter and Sauppe: the MSS. have also ὑμῶν in varying position.
[3] δωροδοκίαν Hamaker: δωροδοκίαν φησὶ φοβεῖσθαι MSS.
[4] δ᾽ Blass: γάρ MSS.

476

the visible marks of Meidias' knuckles.[1] For it is not a head that the creature possesses, but an investment.

Now I wish to speak briefly about Ctesiphon, the author of the motion; and I will pass over the greater part of what might be said, for I should like to test your ability, even when no one cautions you, to discern those men who are utter rascals. I will speak only of what is common to the pair of them, and what I can honestly report to you concerning both. For the opinion that each of them has of the other is true, and the things that each, as he goes about the market-place, says of the other are no falsehoods. For Ctesiphon says he is not afraid so far as he himself is concerned, since he hopes it will appear that he is but a plain citizen, but that what he does fear is Demosthenes' corruption in his conduct of affairs, and his instability and cowardice. And Demosthenes says that when he looks at his own case only, he is confident, but that he is exceedingly anxious in view of Ctesiphon's wickedness and licentiousness! Well, when men have thus condemned one another, you, the common judges of both, must surely not acquit them of the crimes they charge.

I wish also to caution you in a few words as to the slanders which they will utter against me. For I learn that Demosthenes will say that the city has been greatly benefited by him, but damaged by me; and he will bring up against me Philip and Alexander, and the charges connected with them. And he is, as it seems, such a master-craftsman of words that he is not content to bring charges against whatever part I have taken in your political action, or

[1] See on § 52.

216 εἴρηκα, τούτων κατηγορεῖν, ἀλλὰ καὶ τὴν ἡσυχίαν
αὐτὴν τοῦ βίου διαβάλλει καὶ τῆς σιωπῆς μου
κατηγορεῖ, ἵνα μηδεὶς αὐτῷ τόπος ἀσυκοφάντητος
παραλείπηται, καὶ τὰς ἐν τοῖς γυμνασίοις μετὰ
τῶν νεωτέρων μου διατριβὰς καταμέμφεται, καὶ
κατὰ τῆσδε τῆς κρίσεως εὐθὺς ἀρχόμενος τοῦ λόγου φέρει τινὰ αἰτίαν, λέγων ὡς ἐγὼ τὴν γραφὴν
οὐχ ὑπὲρ τῆς πόλεως ἐγραψάμην, ἀλλ᾽ ἐνδεικνύ-
μενος Ἀλεξάνδρῳ διὰ τὴν πρὸς αὐτὸν ἔχθραν.

217 καὶ νὴ Δία, ὡς ἐγὼ πυνθάνομαι, μέλλει με ἀνερω-
τᾶν, διὰ τί τὸ μὲν κεφάλαιον αὐτοῦ τῆς πολιτείας
ψέγω, τὰ δὲ καθ᾽ ἕκαστον οὐκ ἐκώλυον οὐδ᾽ ἐγρα-
φόμην, ἀλλὰ διαλείπων καὶ πρὸς τὴν πολιτείαν
οὐ πυκνὰ προσιὼν ἀπήνεγκα τὴν γραφήν. ἐγὼ δὲ
οὔτε τὰς Δημοσθένους διατριβὰς ἐζήλωκα, οὔτ᾽
ἐπὶ ταῖς ἐμαυτοῦ αἰσχύνομαι, οὔτε τοὺς εἰρημένους
ἐν ὑμῖν λόγους ἐμαυτῷ ἀρρήτους ἂν[1] εἶναι βουλοίμην, οὔτε τὰ αὐτὰ τούτῳ δημηγορήσας δεξαί-

218 μην[2] ἂν ζῆν. τὴν δ᾽ ἐμὴν σιωπήν, ὦ Δημόσθενες,
ἡ τοῦ βίου μετριότης παρεσκεύασεν· ἀρκεῖ γάρ
μοι μικρά, καὶ μειζόνων αἰσχρῶς οὐκ ἐπιθυμῶ,
ὥστε καὶ σιωπῶ καὶ λέγω βουλευσάμενος, οὐκ
ἀναγκαζόμενος ὑπὸ τῆς ἐν τῇ φύσει δαπάνης. σὺ
δ᾽ οἶμαι λαβὼν μὲν σιγᾷς,[3] ἀναλώσας δὲ κέκραγας·
λέγεις δὲ οὐχ ὅταν σοι δοκῇ, οὐδ᾽ ἂν βούλῃ,[4] ἀλλ᾽
ὅταν οἱ μισθοδόται σοι προστάττωσιν· οὐκ αἰσχύνῃ δὲ ἀλαζονευόμενος, ἃ παραχρῆμα ἐξελέγχῃ

219 ψευδόμενος. ἀπηνέχθη γὰρ ἡ κατὰ τοῦδε τοῦ

---

[1] ἂν added by Bekker.
[2] δεξαίμην Blass : ἐδεξάμην MSS.
[3] σιγᾷς Cobet : σεσίγηκας MSS.
[4] ἂν βούλῃ Weidner : ἃ βούλει MSS.

whatever speeches I have delivered, but he actually attacks the very quietness of my life, and makes my silence an accusation, in order that no topic may be left untouched by his slanders. And he censures my frequenting of the gymnasia with the younger men.[1] And at the very beginning of his speech he demurs against this legal process, saying that I instituted the suit, not in behalf of the city, but as a manifesto to Alexander because he hates Demosthenes.[2] And, by Zeus, I understand that he proposes to ask me why I denounce his policy as a whole, but did not try to thwart it in detail, and did not prefer charges in the courts; and why I have brought suit at this late day without having steadily attacked his policy. But I have never in the past emulated the habits of Demosthenes, nor am I ashamed of my own, nor would I wish unsaid the words which I have spoken in your presence, nor would I care to live had my public speeches been like his. As to my silence, Demosthenes, it has been caused by the moderation of my life. For a little money suffices me, and I have no shameful lust for more. Both my silence and my speech are therefore the result of deliberation, not of the impulse of a spendthrift nature. But you, I think, are silent when you have gotten, and bawl aloud after you have spent; and you speak, not when your judgment approves, and not what you wish to speak, but whenever your pay-masters so order. And you are not ashamed of impostures in which you are instantly convicted of falsehood. For my

[1] No such charge as to Aeschines' relations with the young men is found in Demosthenes' published speech.

[2] No such point is made at the beginning of Demosthenes' published speech, nor explicitly in any other part of it.

ψηφίσματος γραφή, ἣν οὐχ ὑπὲρ τῆς πόλεως,
ἀλλ' ὑπὲρ τῆς πρὸς Ἀλέξανδρον ἐνδείξεώς με φῂς
ἀπενεγκεῖν, ἔτι Φιλίππου ζῶντος, πρὶν Ἀλέξανδρον εἰς τὴν ἀρχὴν καταστῆναι, οὔπω σοῦ τὸ περὶ
Παυσανίαν ἐνύπνιον ἑωρακότος, οὐδὲ πρὸς τὴν
Ἀθηνᾶν καὶ τὴν Ἥραν νύκτωρ διειλεγμένου. πῶς
ἂν οὖν ἐγὼ προενεδεικνύμην Ἀλεξάνδρῳ; εἴ γε μὴ
ταὐτὸν ἐνύπνιον ἐγὼ καὶ Δημοσθένης εἴδομεν.

220   Ἐπιτιμᾷς δέ μοι, εἰ μὴ συνεχῶς, ἀλλὰ διαλείπων, πρὸς τὸν δῆμον προσέρχομαι, καὶ τὴν ἀξίωσιν
ταύτην οἴει λανθάνειν μεταφέρων οὐκ ἐκ δημοκρατίας, ἀλλ' ἐξ ἑτέρας πολιτείας. ἐν μὲν γὰρ ταῖς
ὀλιγαρχίαις οὐχ ὁ βουλόμενος, ἀλλ' ὁ δυναστεύων
δημηγορεῖ,[1] ἐν δὲ ταῖς δημοκρατίαις ὁ βουλόμενος,
καὶ ὅταν αὐτῷ δοκῇ. καὶ τὸ μὲν διὰ χρόνου
λέγειν σημεῖόν ἐστιν ἐπὶ τῶν καιρῶν καὶ τοῦ
συμφέροντος ἀνδρὸς πολιτευομένου, τὸ δὲ μηδεμίαν παραλείπειν ἡμέραν ἐργαζομένου καὶ μισθαρ-
221   νοῦντος. ὑπὲρ δὲ τοῦ μήπω κεκρίσθαι ὑπ' ἐμοῦ,
μηδὲ τῶν ἀδικημάτων τιμωρίαν ὑποσχεῖν, ὅταν
καταφεύγῃς ἐπὶ τοὺς τοιούτους λόγους, ἢ τοὺς
ἀκούοντας ἐπιλήσμονας ὑπολαμβάνεις, ἢ σαυτὸν
παραλογίζῃ.

Τὰ μὲν γὰρ περὶ τοὺς Ἀμφισσέας ἠσεβη-
μένα σοι καὶ τὰ περὶ τὴν Εὔβοιαν δωροδοκηθέντα, ἐφ'[2] οἷς ὑπ' ἐμοῦ φανερῶς ἐξηλέγχου,
χρόνων ἐγγεγενημένων[3] ἴσως ἐλπίζεις τὸν δῆμον
222   ἀμνημονεῖν· τὰ δὲ περὶ τὰς τριήρεις καὶ τοὺς τρι-

---

[1] δημηγορεῖ Bekker : κατηγορεῖ MSS.
[2] ἐφ' οἷς Blass : ἐν οἷς MSS.
[3] χρόνων ἐγγεγενημένων placed before ἴσως by Dobree : after
δωροδοκηθέντα in the MSS.

suit against this motion, which you say I instituted, not in the city's behalf, but as a manifesto to Alexander, was instituted while Philip was still alive, before Alexander had come to the throne, before ever you had had that dream of yours about Pausanias, or ever had conversed with Athena and Hera in the night.[1] How then could I have been already making a manifesto to Alexander? Unless, indeed, I and Demosthenes had the same dream!

And you blame me if I come before the people, not constantly, but only at intervals. And you imagine that your hearers fail to detect you in thus making a demand which is no outgrowth of democracy, but borrowed from another form of government. For in oligarchies it is not he who wishes, but he who is in authority, that addresses the people; whereas in democracies he speaks who chooses, and whenever it seems to him good. And the fact that a man speaks only at intervals marks him as a man who takes part in politics because of the call of the hour, and for the common good; whereas to leave no day without its speech, is the mark of a man who is making a trade of it, and talking for pay. But as to your never having been brought to trial by me, and never having been punished for your crimes— when you take refuge in assertions like that, either you think that your hearers are forgetful, or you are deceiving yourself.

Your impiety in the case of the Amphissians[2] and your corruption in the Euboean affair,[3] of which you were clearly convicted by me, perhaps you hope the people have forgotten in the lapse of time; but what length of time could conceal your

---

[1] See § 77.   [2] See §§ 107 ff.   [3] See §§ 85 ff.

THE SPEECHES OF AESCHINES

ηράρχους ἁρπάγματα τίς ἂν ἀποκρύψαι χρόνος
δύναιτ' ἄν, ὅτε νομοθετήσας περὶ τῶν τριακοσίων,
καὶ σαυτὸν πείσας 'Αθηναίους ἐπιστάτην τάξαι
τοῦ ναυτικοῦ, ἐξηλέγχθης ὑπ' ἐμοῦ ἑξήκοντα καὶ
πέντε νεῶν ταχυναυτουσῶν τριηράρχους ὑφῃρη-
μένος, πλέον τῆς πόλεως ἀφανίζων ναυτικὸν ἢ ᾧ
ποτε¹ 'Αθηναῖοι τὴν ἐν Νάξῳ ναυμαχίαν Λακεδαι-
223 μονίους καὶ Πόλλιν ἐνίκησαν; οὕτω δὲ ταῖς αἰτίαις
ἐνέφραξας τὰς κατὰ σαυτοῦ τιμωρίας, ὥστε τὸν
κίνδυνον εἶναι μὴ σοὶ τῷ ἀδικήσαντι, ἀλλὰ τοῖς
ἐπεξιοῦσι, πολὺν μὲν τὸν 'Αλέξανδρον καὶ τὸν
Φίλιππον ἐν ταῖς διαβολαῖς φέρων, αἰτιώμενος δέ
τινας ἐμποδίζειν τοὺς τῆς πόλεως καιρούς, ἀεὶ τὸ
παρὸν λυμαινόμενος, τὸ δὲ μέλλον κατεπαγγελλόμενος. οὐ τὸ τελευταῖον εἰσαγγέλλεσθαι μέλλων
ὑπ' ἐμοῦ, τὴν 'Αναξίνου σύλληψιν τοῦ 'Ωρείτου
κατεσκεύασας, τοῦ τὰ ἀγοράσματα 'Ολυμπιάδι
224 ἀγοράζοντος; καὶ τὸν αὐτὸν ἄνδρα δὶς στρεβλώσας
τῇ σαυτοῦ χειρί, ἔγραψας αὐτὸν θανάτῳ ζημιῶσαι,
καὶ παρὰ τῷ αὐτῷ ἐν 'Ωρεῷ κατήγου, καὶ ᾧ²
ἀπὸ τῆς αὐτῆς τραπέζης ἔφαγες καὶ ἔπιες καὶ

¹ ᾧ ποτε Weidner: ὁπότε or ὅτε MSS.
² ᾧ added by Blass.

---

[1] The wealthy leaders of the property-groups on which
the burden of the trierarchy was laid.

[2] In 340 B.C. Demosthenes carried a reform of the naval
system, by which he compelled the richest citizens to con-
tribute to the support of the navy strictly in proportion to
their wealth. Under his system the number of individuals
contributing (the trierarchs) may well have been diminished,
but the number of the triremes was not lessened, their
efficiency was increased, and taxation was made equitable.
The matter is fully discussed in Demosthenes, *On the Crown*,
§§ 102-109

acts of plunder in the case of the triremes and the trierarchs? For when you had carried constitutional amendments as to the Three Hundred,[1] and had persuaded the Athenians to make you Commissioner of the Navy, you were convicted by me of having stolen away trierarchs from sixty-five swift ships,[2] making away with a greater naval force of the city than that with which the Athenians once defeated Pollis and the Lacedaemonians at Naxos.[3] And by your recriminations you so blocked the punishment which was your due that the danger came, not upon you, the wrong-doer, but upon those who attempted to proceed against you; for in your charges you everlastingly brought forward Alexander and Philip, and complained that certain persons were fettering the opportunities of the city—you who always ruin the opportunity of to-day, and guarantee that of to-morrow. And when at last you were on the point of being impeached by me, did you not contrive the arrest of Anaxinus of Oreus, who was making purchases for Olympias?[4] And you twice put to the torture with your own hand and moved to punish with death the same man in whose house you had been entertained at Oreus. The man with whom at the same table you had eaten and drunken and poured libations, the man

---

[3] In the battle of Naxos, 376 B.C., Chabrias with an Athenian fleet of 83 triremes defeated Pollis, who with a Lacedaemonian fleet of 65 ships was trying to cut off the Athenian grain ships.

[4] Demosthenes asserts (*On the Crown*, § 137) that Anaxinus had come as a spy of the Macedonians, and that Aeschines was caught in a secret interview with him. The purchases for Olympias, Philip's wife, may well have been a pretext for his visit to Athens.

ἔσπεισας, καὶ τὴν δεξιὰν ἐνέβαλες ἄνδρα φίλον
καὶ ξένον ποιούμενος, τοῦτον[1] ἀπέκτεινας. καὶ
περὶ τούτων ἐν ἅπασιν Ἀθηναίοις ἐξελεγχθεὶς ὑπ'
ἐμοῦ καὶ κληθεὶς ξενοκτόνος, οὐ τὸ ἀσέβημα ἠρ-
νήσω, ἀλλ' ἀπεκρίνω ἐφ' ᾧ ἀνεβόησεν ὁ δῆμος καὶ
ὅσοι ξένοι περιέστασαν τὴν ἐκκλησίαν· ἔφησθα
γὰρ τοὺς τῆς πόλεως ἅλας περὶ πλείονος ποιεῖσθαι
225 τῆς ξενικῆς τραπέζης. ἐπιστολὰς δὲ σιγῶ ψευδεῖς
καὶ κατασκόπων συλλήψεις καὶ βασάνους ἐπ'
αἰτίαις ἀγενήτοις, ὡς ἐμοῦ μετά τινων νεωτερίζειν[2] βουλομένου.

Ἔπειτα ἐπερωτᾶν με, ὡς ἐγὼ πυνθάνομαι,
μέλλει, τίς ἂν εἴη τοιοῦτος ἰατρός, ὅστις τῷ
νοσοῦντι μεταξὺ μὲν ἀσθενοῦντι μηδὲν συμβου-
λεύοι, τελευτήσαντος δὲ ἐλθὼν εἰς τὰ ἔνατα
διεξίοι πρὸς τοὺς οἰκείους ἃ ἐπιτηδεύσας ὑγιὴς ἂν
226 ἐγένετο. σαυτὸν δ' οὐκ ἀντερωτᾷς, τίς ἂν εἴη
δημαγωγὸς τοιοῦτος, ὅστις τὸν μὲν δῆμον θωπεῦ-
σαι δύναιτο, τοὺς δὲ καιροὺς ἐν οἷς ἦν σῴζεσθαι
τὴν πόλιν, ἀποδοῖτο, τοὺς δ' εὖ φρονοῦντας κωλύοι
διαβάλλων συμβουλεύειν, ἀποδρὰς δ' ἐκ τῶν
κινδύνων καὶ τὴν πόλιν ἀνηκέστοις συμφοραῖς
περιβαλὼν ἀξιοίη στεφανοῦσθαι ἐπ' ἀρετῇ, ἀγαθὸν μὲν πεποιηκὼς μηδέν, πάντων δὲ τῶν κακῶν
αἴτιος γεγονώς, ἐπερωτῴη δὲ τοὺς συκοφαντηθέντας ἐκ τῆς πολιτείας ἐπ' ἐκείνων τῶν καιρῶν ὅτ'
ἐνῆν σῴζεσθαι, διὰ τί αὐτὸν οὐκ ἐκώλυσαν ἐξα-
227 μαρτάνειν, ἀποκρύπτοιτο δὲ τὸ πάντων τελευταῖον,
ὅτι τῆς μάχης ἐπιγενομένης οὐκ ἐσχολάζομεν περὶ

---

[1] τοῦτον Cobet : καὶ τοῦτον MSS.
[2] νεωτερίζειν Weidner : the MSS. have ἐν τῇ πόλει before
or after νεωτερίζειν.

with whom you had clasped hands in token of friendship and hospitality, that man you put to death! When I convicted you of this in the presence of all Athens, and charged you with being the murderer of your host, you did not deny the impious crime, but gave an answer that called forth a cry of protest from the citizens and all the foreigners who were standing about the assembly. For you said that you held the city's salt as of more importance than the table of your foreign host. I say nothing of forged letters and the arrest of spies, and torture applied on groundless charges, on your assertion that I with certain persons was seeking a revolution.

Furthermore, he intends, as I learn, to ask me what kind of a physician he would be who should give no advice to his patient in the course of his illness, but after his death should come to the funeral and tell over to the relatives by what course of treatment the man might have been cured. But, Demosthenes, you fail to ask yourself in turn what kind of a statesman he would be who, having the power to cajole the people, should sell the opportunities for saving the city, and by his calumnies prevent patriots from giving advice; and when he had run away from danger and had entangled the city in misfortunes from which there was no escape, should demand that he be crowned for his virtue, when he had done no thing that was good, but was himself responsible for all the disasters; and should then ask those who had been driven out of public life by his slanders in those critical days when there was still a chance of safety, why they had not prevented his wrong doing; and should conceal the final fact of all, that after the battle we had no

τὴν σὴν εἶναι τιμωρίαν, ἀλλ' ὑπὲρ τῆς σωτηρίας
τῆς πόλεως ἐπρεσβεύομεν. ἐπειδὴ δὲ οὐκ ἀπέχρη
σοι δίκην μὴ δεδωκέναι, ἀλλὰ καὶ δωρεὰς ᾔτεις,[1]
καταγέλαστον ἐν τοῖς Ἕλλησι τὴν πόλιν ποιῶν,
ἐνταῦθ' ἐνέστην καὶ τὴν γραφὴν ἀπήνεγκα.

228 Καὶ νὴ τοὺς θεοὺς τοὺς Ὀλυμπίους, ὧν ἐγὼ
πυνθάνομαι Δημοσθένην λέξειν, ἐφ' ᾧ νυνὶ μέλλω
λέγειν ἀγανακτῶ μάλιστα. ἀφομοιοῖ γάρ μου
τὴν φύσιν ταῖς Σειρῆσιν.[2] καὶ γὰρ ὑπ' ἐκείνων
οὐ κηλεῖσθαί φησι τοὺς ἀκροωμένους, ἀλλ' ἀπόλ-
λυσθαι, διόπερ οὐδ' εὐδοκιμεῖν τὴν τῶν Σειρήνων
μουσικήν· καὶ δὴ καὶ τὴν τῶν ἐμῶν εὔροιαν[3]
λόγων καὶ τὴν φύσιν μου γεγενῆσθαι ἐπὶ βλάβῃ
τῶν ἀκουόντων. καίτοι τὸν λόγον τοῦτον ὅλως
μὲν ἔγωγε οὐδενὶ πρέπειν ἡγοῦμαι περὶ ἐμοῦ λέ-
γειν· τῆς γὰρ αἰτίας αἰσχρὸν τὸν αἰτιώμενόν ἐστι
229 τὸ ἔργον μὴ ἔχειν ἐπιδεῖξαι· εἰ δ' ἦν ἀναγκαῖον
ῥηθῆναι, οὐ Δημοσθένους ἦν ὁ λόγος, ἀλλ' ἀνδρὸς
στρατηγοῦ μεγάλα μὲν τὴν πόλιν ἀγάθ' εἰργασμένου,[4] λέγειν δὲ ἀδυνάτου καὶ τὴν τῶν ἀντιδίκων
διὰ τοῦτο ἐζηλωκότος φύσιν, ὅτι σύνοιδεν ἑαυτῷ
μὲν οὐδὲν ὧν διαπέπρακται δυναμένῳ φράσαι, τὸν
δὲ κατήγορον ὁρᾷ δυνάμενον καὶ τὰ μὴ πεπραγμένα ὑπ' αὐτοῦ παριστάνειν τοῖς ἀκούουσιν ὡς

___

[1] ᾔτεις Blass : αἰτεῖς MSS.
[2] ταῖς Σειρῆσιν Baiter : the MSS. have ὡς ἔοικε before or
after ταῖς Σειρῆσιν.
[3] εὔροιαν λόγων Blass : εὐπορίαν λόγων, λόγων εὐπορίαν,
λόγων ἀπορίαν, λόγων ἐμπειρίαν MSS.
[4] ἀγάθ' εἰργασμένου Herwerden : κατειργασμένου MSS.

time to attend to punishing you, but were engrossed
in negotiations for the safety of the city. But when,
not content with having escaped punishment, you
were actually calling for rewards, making the city
an object of ridicule in the eyes of all Hellas, then
I interposed and brought my indictment.

And, by the Olympian gods, of all the things
which I understand Demosthenes is going to say, I
am most indignant at what I am now about to tell
you. For he likens me in natural endowment to the
Sirens, saying that it was not charm that the Sirens
brought to those who listened to them, but destruction, and that therefore the Siren-song has no
good repute; and that in like manner the smooth
flow of my speech and my natural ability have
proved the ruin of those who have listened to me.[1]
And yet I think no man in the world is justified
in making such a statement about me. It is a
shame to accuse a man and not to be able to show
the ground for the accusation. But if the charge
really had to be made, it was not for Demosthenes
to make it, but for some general who, although he
had rendered distinguished services to the state,
was not gifted with the power of speech, and for
that reason was envious of the natural endowments
of his opponents in court, because he knew that
he had not the ability to describe one of all the
things he had accomplished, but saw in his accuser
a man able to set forth to the hearers in all detail
how he had himself administered things which had

---

[1] No such passage occurs in the published speech of Demosthenes. It is likely that he omitted it when he revised
his speech for publication.

διῴκηκεν. ὅταν δ' ἐξ ὀνομάτων συγκείμενος ἄνθρωπος, καὶ τούτων πικρῶν καὶ περιέργων, ἔπειτα
ἐπὶ τὴν ἁπλότητα καὶ τὰ ἔργα καταφεύγῃ, τίς ἂν
ἀνάσχοιτο; οὗ τὴν γλῶτταν ὥσπερ τῶν αὐλῶν
ἐάν τις ἀφέλῃ, τὸ λοιπὸν οὐδέν ἐστιν.

230   Θαυμάζω δ' ἔγωγε ὑμῶν, ὦ ἄνδρες Ἀθηναῖοι,
καὶ ζητῶ, πρὸς τί ἂν ἀποβλέψαντες ἀποψηφί-
σαισθε τὴν γραφήν. πότερον ὡς τὸ ψήφισμά
ἐστιν ἔννομον; ἀλλ' οὐδεμία πώποτε γνώμη
παρανομωτέρα γεγένηται. ἀλλ' ὡς ὁ τὸ ψήφισμα
γράψας οὐκ ἐπιτήδειός ἐστι δίκην δοῦναι; οὐκ ἄρ'
εἰσὶ παρ' ὑμῖν εὔθυναι βίου, εἰ τοῦτον ἀφήσετε.
ἐκεῖνο δ' οὐ λυπηρόν, εἰ πρότερον μὲν ἐνεπίμπλατο
ἡ ὀρχήστρα χρυσῶν στεφάνων, οἷς ὁ δῆμος ἐστε-
φανοῦτο ὑπὸ τῶν Ἑλλήνων,[1] ἐκ δὲ τῶν Δημοσθένους πολιτευμάτων ὑμεῖς μὲν ἀστεφάνωτοι καὶ
231   ἀκήρυκτοι γίγνεσθε, οὗτος δὲ κηρυχθήσεται; καὶ
εἰ μέν τις τῶν τραγικῶν ποιητῶν τῶν μετὰ ταῦτα
ἐπεισαγόντων ποιήσειεν ἐν τραγῳδίᾳ τὸν Θερσί-
την ὑπὸ τῶν Ἑλλήνων στεφανούμενον, οὐδεὶς ἂν
ὑμῶν ὑπομείνειεν, ὅτι φησὶν Ὅμηρος ἄνανδρον
αὐτὸν εἶναι καὶ συκοφάντην· αὐτοὶ δ' ὅταν τὸν
τοιοῦτον ἄνθρωπον στεφανῶτε, οὐκ ἂν[2] οἴεσθε ἐν
ταῖς τῶν Ἑλλήνων δόξαις συρίττεσθαι; οἱ μὲν
γὰρ πατέρες ὑμῶν τὰ μὲν ἔνδοξα καὶ λαμπρὰ τῶν
πραγμάτων ἀνετίθεσαν τῷ δήμῳ, τὰ δὲ ταπεινὰ
καὶ καταδεέστερα εἰς τοὺς ῥήτορας τοὺς φαύλους
ἔτρεπον· Κτησιφῶν δ' ὑμᾶς οἴεται δεῖν ἀφελόν-
τας τὴν ἀδοξίαν ἀπὸ Δημοσθένους περιθεῖναι τῷ

---

[1] Ἑλλήνων Halm : after Ἑλλήνων the MSS. have διὰ τὸ
ξενικοῖς στεφάνοις ταύτην ἀποδεδόσθαι τὴν ἡμέραν.
[2] ἂν added by Cobet.

not been done by him at all. But when a man who is made up of words, and those words bitter words and useless—when such a man takes refuge in "simplicity" and "the facts," who could have patience with him? If you treat him as you might a clarinet, and take out his tongue, you have nothing left!

But for my part I am surprised at you, fellow citizens, and I ask under what possible consideration you could refuse to sustain this indictment. On the ground that Ctesiphon's motion is lawful? Never was a more unlawful motion made. On the ground that he who moved the decree is not the sort of man to be punished? You give up the possibility of calling any man to account for his manner of life, if you let this man go. And is it not vexatious that whereas in former times the orchestra was piled with golden crowns with which the state was honoured by the Hellenes,[1] to-day in consequence of the policies of Demosthenes you the people go uncrowned and unproclaimed, but he is to be honoured by the voice of the herald? If any one of the tragic poets who are to bring on their plays after the crowning should in a tragedy represent Thersites as crowned by the Greeks, no one of you would tolerate it, for Homer says he was a coward and a slanderer; but when you yourselves crown such a man as this, think you not that you would be hissed by the voice of Hellas? Your fathers were wont to attribute to the people such deeds as were glorious and brilliant, but mean and unworthy acts they threw upon the incompetent politicians. But Ctesiphon thinks that you ought to take off from Demosthenes his ill-fame, and

[1] Crowns were frequently sent from one state to another in recognition of generous services.

232 δήμῳ. καὶ φατὲ μὲν εὐτυχεῖς εἶναι, ὡς καὶ ἐστὲ
καλῶς ποιοῦντες, ψηφιεῖσθε δ' ὑπὸ μὲν τῆς τύχης
ἐγκαταλελεῖφθαι, ὑπὸ Δημοσθένους δὲ εὖ πεπονθέναι; καὶ τὸ πάντων ἀτοπώτατον, ἐν τοῖς αὐτοῖς
δικαστηρίοις τοὺς μὲν τὰς τῶν δώρων γραφὰς
ἁλισκομένους ἀτιμοῦτε, ὃν δ' αὐτοὶ μισθοῦ πολι-
τευόμενον σύνιστε, στεφανώσετε; καὶ τοὺς μὲν
κριτὰς τοὺς ἐκ τῶν Διονυσίων, ἐὰν μὴ δικαίως
τοὺς κυκλίους χοροὺς κρίνωσι, ζημιοῦτε· αὐτοὶ δὲ
οὐ κυκλίων χορῶν κριταὶ καθεστηκότες, ἀλλὰ
νόμων καὶ πολιτικῆς ἀρετῆς, τὰς δωρεὰς οὐ κατὰ
τοὺς νόμους οὐδ' ὀλίγοις καὶ τοῖς ἀξίοις, ἀλλὰ τῷ
διαπραξαμένῳ δώσετε;

233 Ἔπειτ' ἔξεισιν ἐκ τοῦ δικαστηρίου ὁ τοιοῦτος
κριτὴς ἑαυτὸν μὲν ἀσθενῆ πεποιηκώς, ἰσχυρὸν δὲ
τὸν ῥήτορα. ἀνὴρ γὰρ ἰδιώτης ἐν πόλει δημο-
κρατουμένῃ νόμῳ καὶ ψήφῳ βασιλεύει· ὅταν δ'
ἑτέρῳ ταῦτα παραδῷ, καταλέλυκε τὴν αὐτὸς αὐτοῦ δυναστείαν. ἔπειθ' ὁ μὲν ὅρκος ὃν ὀμωμοκὼς
δικάζει, συμπαρακολουθῶν αὐτὸν λυπεῖ· δι' αὐτὸν γὰρ οἶμαι γέγονε τὸ ἁμάρτημα· ἡ δὲ χάρις
πρὸς ὃν ἐχαρίζετο ἄδηλος γεγένηται· ἡ γὰρ
ψῆφος ἀφανὴς φέρεται.

234 Δοκοῦμεν δ' ἔμοιγε, ὦ ἄνδρες Ἀθηναῖοι, ἀμφότερα καὶ κατορθοῦν καὶ παρακινδυνεύειν εἰς
τὴν πολιτείαν, οὐ σωφρονοῦντες. ὅτι μὲν γὰρ
ἐπὶ τῶν νυνὶ καιρῶν οἱ πολλοὶ τοῖς ὀλίγοις
προῖεσθε τὰ τῆς δημοκρατίας ἰσχυρά, οὐκ
ἐπαινῶ· ὅτι δ' οὐ γεγένηται φορὰ καθ' ἡμᾶς

crown the people with it. And while you assert
that you are favourites of fortune—as indeed you
are, thank heaven—will you declare by public resolution that you have been abandoned by fortune, but
blessed by Demosthenes? And—strangest of all—
in the same court-rooms do you disfranchise those
who are convicted of receiving bribes, and then yourselves propose to crown a man who, to your own
knowledge, has always been in politics for pay? If
the judges at the Dionysiac festival are not honest
in their award of the prize to the cyclic choruses,
you punish them; but do you yourselves, who are
sitting as judges, not of cyclic choruses, but of the
laws and of integrity in public life, do you propose
to bestow your rewards, not according to the laws,
and not upon the rare and deserving, but upon the
successful intriguer?

Furthermore, a juror who so acts will go out from
the court-room responsible for having made himself
weak and the politician strong. For in a democracy
the private citizen is a king by virtue of the constitution and his own vote; but when he hands these
over to another man, he has by his own act dethroned
himself. Still further, the oath that he has sworn
before taking his seat haunts him and troubles him,
for it was his oath, I think, that made him act a sin;
and his service is unknown to the man whom he
was trying to please, for the vote is cast in secret.

But it seems to me, fellow citizens, that the political situation, while fortunate, is also perilous; for we
are not wise. The fact that at the present time you,
the people, give over the mainstays of the democracy
to the few is to be deplored; but the fact that there
has not sprung up to our hurt a crop of politicians

THE SPEECHES OF AESCHINES

ῥητόρων πονηρῶν ἅμα καὶ τολμηρῶν, εὐτυχοῦμεν.
πρότερον μὲν γὰρ τοιαύτας φύσεις ἤνεγκε τὸ
δημόσιον, αἳ ῥᾳδίως οὕτω κατέλυσαν τὸν δῆμον·
ἔχαιρε γὰρ κολακευόμενος, ἔπειτ᾽ αὐτὸν οὐχ οὓς
ἐφοβεῖτο, ἀλλ᾽ οἷς ἑαυτὸν ἐνεχείριζε, κατέλυσαν·

235 ἔνιοι δὲ καὶ αὐτοὶ τῶν τριάκοντα ἐγένοντο, οἳ
πλείους ἢ χιλίους καὶ πεντακοσίους τῶν πολιτῶν
ἀκρίτους ἀπέκτειναν, πρὶν καὶ τὰς αἰτίας ἀκοῦσαι
ἐφ᾽ αἷς ἔμελλον ἀποθνῄσκειν, καὶ οὐδ᾽ ἐπὶ τὰς
ἐκφορὰς¹ τῶν τελευτησάντων εἴων τοὺς προσή-
κοντας παραγενέσθαι. οὐχ ὑφ᾽ ὑμῖν αὐτοῖς ἕξετε
τοὺς πολιτευομένους; οὐ ταπεινώσαντες ἀποπέμ-
ψετε τοὺς νῦν ἐπηρμένους; οὐ μεμνήσεσθ᾽² ὅτι
οὐδεὶς πώποτε ἐπέθετο πρότερον δήμου καταλύσει
πρὶν ἂν μεῖζον τῶν δικαστηρίων ἰσχύσῃ;

236 Ἡδέως δ᾽ ἂν ἔγωγε, ὦ ἄνδρες Ἀθηναῖοι, ἐναντίον ὑμῶν ἀναλογισαίμην πρὸς τὸν γράψαντα τὸ
ψήφισμα, διὰ ποίας εὐεργεσίας ἀξιοῖ Δημοσθένην
στεφανῶσαι. εἰ μὲν γὰρ λέξεις, ὅθεν τὴν ἀρχὴν
τοῦ ψηφίσματος ἐποιήσω, ὅτι τὰς τάφρους τὰς
περὶ τὰ τείχη καλῶς ἐτάφρευσε, θαυμάζω σου.
τοῦ γὰρ ταῦτ᾽ ἐξεργασθῆναι καλῶς τὸ γεγενῆσθαι
τούτων αἴτιον μείζω κατηγορίαν ἔχει· οὐ γὰρ
περιχαρακώσαντα χρὴ τὰ τείχη, οὐδὲ τάφους
δημοσίους³ ἀνελόντα τὸν ὀρθῶς πεπολιτευμένον

¹ τὰς ἐκφορὰς Weidner : τὰς ταφὰς καὶ ἐκφορὰς MSS.
² μεμνήσεσθ᾽ Cobet : μέμνησθ᾽ MSS.
³ τάφους δημοσίους Blass : ταφὰς δημοσίας or τὰς δημοσίας ταφὰς MSS.

---

¹ We learn from the orator Lycurgus (*Against Leocrates*, § 44) that in the haste to fortify the city immediately after Chaeronea the very tombs were made to yield stones, as

both corrupt and daring is a gift of fortune. For in former times the state did bring forth such characters, and they made short work of putting down the democracy. For the people loved to be flattered, and in consequence were overthrown, not by the men whom they feared, but by those in whose hands they had placed themselves. And some of them actually joined the Thirty, who killed more than fifteen hundred of the citizens without trial, before they had even heard the charges on which they were to be put to death, and who would not even allow the relatives to be present at the burial of the dead. Will you not hold the politicians under your control? Will you not humble and dismiss those who are now exultant? Will you not bear in mind that in the past no one has ever attempted the overthrow of the democracy until he has made himself stronger than the courts?

But I would like to reckon up in your presence, fellow citizens, with the author of this motion, the benefactions for which he calls on you to crown Demosthenes. For if, Ctesiphon, you propose to cite that which you made the beginning of your motion, that he did good work in excavating the trenches around the walls, I am astonished at you. For to have been responsible for the necessity of doing the work at all involves an accusation greater than is the credit for having done it well. Indeed, it is not for surrounding the walls with palisades, and not for tearing down the public tombs[1] that the

they had done in the hurried fortifying by Themistocles after the Persian wars (Thucydides, I. xciii. 1). Aeschines wrongly implies that these hurried emergency measures were a part of the work that was done later in a thorough manner under Demosthenes' direction.

δωρεὰς αἰτεῖν, ἀλλ' ἀγαθοῦ τινος αἴτιον γεγενη-
237 μένον τῇ πόλει. εἰ δὲ ἥξεις ἐπὶ τὸ δεύτερον μέρος
τοῦ ψηφίσματος, ἐν ᾧ τετόλμηκας γράφειν ὡς
ἔστιν ἀνὴρ ἀγαθός, καὶ "διατελεῖ λέγων καὶ πράττων τὰ ἄριστα τῷ δήμῳ τῷ Ἀθηναίων," ἀφελὼν
τὴν ἀλαζονείαν καὶ τὸν κόμπον τοῦ ψηφίσματος
ἅψαι τῶν ἔργων, ἐπίδειξον ἡμῖν ὅ τι λέγεις. τὰς
μὲν γὰρ περὶ τοὺς Ἀμφισσέας καὶ τοὺς Εὐβοέας
δωροδοκίας παραλείπω· ὅταν δὲ τῆς πρὸς Θηβαίους συμμαχίας τὰς αἰτίας ἀνατιθῇς Δημοσθένει,
τοὺς μὲν ἀγνοοῦντας ἐξαπατᾷς, τοὺς δ' εἰδότας
καὶ αἰσθανομένους ὑβρίζεις. ἀφελὼν γὰρ τὸν
καιρὸν καὶ τὴν δόξαν τὴν τούτων, δι' ἣν ἐγένετο ἡ
συμμαχία, λανθάνειν οἴει ἡμᾶς τὸ τῆς πόλεως
ἀξίωμα Δημοσθένει περιτιθείς.

238 Ἡλίκον δ' ἐστὶ τὸ ἀλαζόνευμα τοῦτο, ἐγὼ
πειράσομαι μεγάλῳ σημείῳ διδάξαι. ὁ γὰρ
τῶν Περσῶν βασιλεὺς οὐ πολλῷ χρόνῳ πρὸ
τῆς Ἀλεξάνδρου διαβάσεως εἰς τὴν Ἀσίαν κατέπεμψε τῷ δήμῳ καὶ μάλα ὑβριστικὴν καὶ βάρ-
βαρον ἐπιστολήν, ἐν ᾗ τά τε δὴ ἄλλα καὶ
μάλ' ἀπαιδεύτως διελέχθη, καὶ ἐπὶ τελευτῆς
ἐνέγραψεν,[1] "Ἐγώ," φησίν, "ὑμῖν χρυσίον οὐ
239 δώσω· μή με αἰτεῖτε· οὐ γὰρ λήψεσθε." οὗτος
μέντοι ὁ αὐτὸς ἐγκαταληφθεὶς ὑπὸ τῶν νυνὶ
παρόντων αὐτῷ κινδύνων, οὐκ αἰτούντων Ἀθηναίων, αὐτὸς ἑκὼν κατέπεμψε τριακόσια τάλαντα
τῷ δήμῳ, ἃ σωφρονῶν οὐκ ἐδέξατο. ὁ δὲ κομίζων
ἦν τὸ χρυσίον καιρὸς καὶ φόβος καὶ χρεία συμμάχων. τὸ δὲ αὐτὸ τοῦτο καὶ τὴν Θηβαίων
συμμαχίαν ἐξηργάσατο. σὺ δὲ τὸ μὲν τῶν

---

[1] ἐνέγραψεν Hamaker : ἐνέγραψεν ἐν τῇ ἐπιστολῇ MSS.

statesman of clean record ought to ask reward, but
for having been responsible for some good to the
city. But if you turn to the second part of your
decree, in which you have had the effrontery to
write that he is a good man, and "constantly speaks
and does what is best for the Athenian people," omit
the pretence and the bombast of your decree, and
take hold of the facts, and show us what you mean.
I pass by his corruption in the case of the Amphissians and Euboeans; but when you give Demosthenes
the credit for the alliance with Thebes, you deceive
the ignorant and insult the sensible and well informed. For in failing to mention the crisis and the
prestige of these your fellow citizens, which were
the real reasons why the alliance was made, you
think you prevent our seeing that you are crowning
Demosthenes with the credit which belongs to the
city.

How great is this imposture, I will try to show you
by a signal proof. Not long before Alexander crossed
over into Asia, the king of the Persians sent to our
people a most insolent and barbarous letter, in which
everything was expressed in the most ill-mannered
terms; and at the close he wrote, "I will not give
you gold; stop asking me for it; you will not get it."
But this same man, overtaken by the dangers which
are now upon him,[1] sent, not at the request of the
Athenians, but of his own accord, three hundred
talents to the people, which they were wise enough
to refuse. Now what brought the gold was the crisis,
and his fear, and his need of allies. And this same
thing it was that brought about the alliance with
Thebes. But you, Demosthenes, tire us out with

[1] See on § 132.

THE SPEECHES OF AESCHINES

Θηβαίων ὄνομα καὶ τὸ τῆς δυστυχεστάτης συμμαχίας ἐνοχλεῖς ἀεὶ λέγων, τὰ δ' ἑβδομήκοντα
τάλαντα ὑποσιωπᾷς, ἃ προλαβὼν τοῦ βασιλικοῦ
240 χρυσίου ἀπεστέρηκας. οὐ δι' ἔνδειαν χρημάτων
ἕνεκα μὲν πέντε ταλάντων οἱ ξένοι Θηβαίοις τὴν
ἄκραν οὐ παρέδοσαν; διὰ ἐννέα δὲ τάλαντα ἀργυρίου πάντων Ἀρκάδων ἐξεληλυθότων καὶ τῶν
ἡγεμόνων ἑτοίμων ὄντων βοηθεῖν, ἡ πρᾶξις οὐ
γεγένηται; σὺ δὲ πλουτεῖς καὶ ταῖς ἡδοναῖς ταῖς
σαυτοῦ χορηγεῖς. καὶ τὸ κεφάλαιον, τὸ μὲν
βασιλικὸν χρυσίον παρὰ τούτῳ, οἱ δὲ κίνδυνοι
παρ' ὑμῖν.

241 Ἄξιον δ' ἐστὶ καὶ τὴν ἀπαιδευσίαν αὐτῶν
θεωρῆσαι. εἰ γὰρ τολμήσει Κτησιφῶν μὲν Δημοσθένην παρακαλεῖν λέξοντα εἰς ὑμᾶς, οὗτος δ'
ἀναβὰς ἑαυτὸν ἐγκωμιάζειν,[1] βαρύτερον τῶν ἔργων ὧν πεπόνθαμεν τὸ ἀκρόαμα γίγνεται. ὅπου
γὰρ τοὺς[2] ὄντως ἄνδρας ἀγαθούς, οἷς πολλὰ καὶ
καλὰ σύνισμεν ἔργα, τοὺς καθ' ἑαυτῶν ἐπαίνους
ἐὰν λέγωσιν, οὐ φέρομεν, ὅταν[3] ἄνθρωπος αἰσχύνη

---

[1] ἐγκωμιάζειν Reiske : ἐγκωμιάσει (or ἐγκωμιάζει) MSS.
[2] τοὺς Gebauer : τοὺς μὲν MSS.
[3] ὅταν Markland : ὅταν δὲ MSS.

---

[1] It appears that when Athens refused the 300 talents
which had been brought from the king of Persia to help in
organising a revolt against Alexander, the Persian envoys
put at least a part of the gold into Demosthenes' hands, in
the expectation that he would use it in unofficial efforts
against Macedon.

[2] After Thebes revolted from Alexander, her citadel was
still held by a garrison of his mercenaries.

[3] This accusation is elaborated in Deinarchus' speech against
Demosthenes (§§ 18–21). He says that the Arcadians came

your everlasting talk of Thebes and of that most ill-starred alliance, while you are silent as to the seventy talents of the king's gold which you have seized and embezzled.[1] Was it not for lack of money, nay, for lack of five talents, that the mercenaries failed to deliver up the citadel to the Thebans?[2] And when all the Arcadians were mobilized and their leaders were ready to bring aid, did not the negotiations fail for want of nine talents of silver?[3] But you are a rich man, you serve as choregus[4]—to your own lusts. In a word, the king's gold stays with Demosthenes, the dangers, fellow citizens, with you.

But we may well consider their lack of good breeding also. For if Ctesiphon shall have the effrontery to call Demosthenes to the platform to speak to you,[5] and he to come forward and praise himself, that will be even harder for you to hear than his deeds were to bear. We refuse to listen even to honest men when they speak their own praises, though we know full well how many noble deeds they have done; who,

up as far as the Isthmus, and that their general offered their services for ten talents, but that Demosthenes refused to furnish the money to the Thebans, who were conducting the negotiations, and so the Arcadian general sold out to the Macedonians and led his troops home.

[4] The rich Athenian took his turn in serving the city as choregus, contributing to meet the expenses of some state-festival. Demosthenes, too, is a rich man of the choregus class, but all his contributions are to serve his own lusts.

[5] Although each party to a suit was required to plead his own cause, he might call on friends to supplement his plea. In some cases this supporting plea was in reality the main plea in the case, as it certainly was on this occasion. See on § 201.

τῆς πόλεως γεγονὼς ἑαυτὸν ἐγκωμιάζῃ, τίς ἂν τὰ
τοιαῦτα καρτερήσειεν ἀκούων;

242 Ἀπὸ μὲν οὖν τῆς ἀναισχύντου πραγματείας,
ἐὰν σωφρονῇς, ἀποστήσῃ, ποιήσῃ [1] δέ, ὦ Κτησιφῶν, διὰ σαυτοῦ τὴν ἀπολογίαν. οὐ γὰρ δή που
τοῦτό γε σκήψῃ, ὡς οὐ δυνατὸς εἶ λέγειν. καὶ γὰρ
ἂν ἄτοπόν σοι συμβαίνοι, εἰ πρώην μέν ποθ᾽ ὑπέμεινας πρεσβευτὴς ὡς Κλεοπάτραν τὴν Φιλίππου
θυγατέρα χειροτονεῖσθαι, συναχθεσθησόμενος ἐπὶ
τῇ τοῦ Μολοττῶν βασιλέως Ἀλεξάνδρου τελευτῇ, νυνὶ δὲ οὐ φήσεις δύνασθαι λέγειν. ἔπειτα
γυναῖκα μὲν ἀλλοτρίαν πενθοῦσαν δύνασαι παρα-
μυθεῖσθαι, γράψας δὲ μισθοῦ ψήφισμα οὐκ ἀπο-
243 λογήσῃ; ἢ τοιοῦτός ἐστιν ὃν γέγραφας στεφανοῦσθαι, οἷος μὴ γιγνώσκεσθαι ὑπὸ τῶν εὖ πεπονθότων, ἂν μή τις συνείπῃ; ἐπερώτησον δὴ τοὺς
δικαστάς, εἰ ἐγίγνωσκον Χαβρίαν καὶ Ἰφικράτην
καὶ Τιμόθεον, καὶ πυθοῦ παρ᾽ αὐτῶν, διὰ τί τὰς
δωρεὰς αὐτοῖς ἔδοσαν καὶ τὰς εἰκόνας ἔστησαν.
ἅπαντες γὰρ ἅμα ἀποκρινοῦνται, ὅτι Χαβρίᾳ μὲν
διὰ τὴν περὶ Νάξον ναυμαχίαν, Ἰφικράτει δὲ ὅτι
μόραν Λακεδαιμονίων ἀπέκτεινε, Τιμοθέῳ δὲ διὰ
τὸν περίπλουν τὸν εἰς Κέρκυραν, καὶ ἄλλοις, ὧν
ἑκάστῳ πολλὰ καὶ καλὰ κατὰ πόλεμον ἔργα πέ-
244 πρακται. Δημοσθένει δ᾽ ἀντερῶ διὰ τί; [2] ὅτι
δωροδόκος, ὅτι δειλός, ὅτι τὴν τάξιν ἔλιπε; καὶ
πότερον τοῦτον τιμήσετε, ἢ ὑμᾶς αὐτοὺς ἀτιμωρήτους ἐάσετε καὶ τοὺς ὑπὲρ ὑμῶν ἐν τῇ μάχῃ
τελευτήσαντας; οὓς νομίσαθ᾽ ὁρᾶν σχετλιάζοντας,

---

[1] ποιήσῃ Bekker : ποιήσαι MSS.
[2] διὰ τί Sauppe : διὰ τί δώσετε MSS.

then, could endure to listen when a man who has made himself a disgrace to the city lauds himself?

From such shameless business as that, Ctesiphon, you will therefore withdraw, if you are wise, and make your defence in your own person. For surely you will not put forth this excuse, that you have not the ability to speak. It was only the other day that you allowed yourself to be elected as envoy to Cleopatra, the daughter of Philip, to condole with her over the death of Alexander, king of the Molossians;[1] you would then be in a strange position to-day, if you should say that you have not the ability to speak. Have you, then, the ability to console a foreign woman in her grief, but when you have made a motion for pay, will you not speak in defence of it? Or is the man whom you have moved to crown so obscure a man as not to be known by those whom he has served, unless some one shall help you to describe him? Pray ask the jury whether they knew Chabrias and Iphicrates and Timotheus, and inquire why they gave them those rewards and set up their statues. All will answer with one voice, that they honoured Chabrias for the battle of Naxos, and Iphicrates because he destroyed a regiment of the Lacedaemonians, and Timotheus because of his voyage to Corcyra, and other men, each because of many a glorious deed in war. But ask them why Demosthenes is to be honoured. Because he is a taker of bribes? Because he is a coward? Because he deserted his post? And will you in reality be honouring him, or leaving unavenged yourselves and those who died for you in the battle? In imagination see them

[1] This Alexander, brother of Philip's wife Olympias, married Philip's daughter Cleopatra. He was killed in Italy in 330 B.C. in an expedition to aid the Tarentines.

εἰ οὗτος στεφανωθήσεται. καὶ γὰρ ἂν εἴη δεινόν,
ὦ ἄνδρες Ἀθηναῖοι, εἰ τὰ μὲν ξύλα καὶ τοὺς
λίθους καὶ τὸν σίδηρον, τὰ ἄφωνα καὶ τὰ ἀγνώ-
μονα, ἐάν τῳ ἐμπεσόντα ἀποκτείνῃ, ὑπερορίζομεν,
καὶ ἐάν τις αὑτὸν διαχρήσηται, τὴν χεῖρα τὴν
τοῦτο πράξασαν χωρὶς τοῦ σώματος θάπτομεν,
245 Δημοσθένην δέ, ὦ ἄνδρες Ἀθηναῖοι, τὸν γράψαντα μὲν τὴν πανυστάτην ἔξοδον, προδόντα δὲ
τοὺς στρατιώτας, τοῦτον ὑμεῖς τιμήσετε. οὐκοῦν
ὑβρίζονται μὲν οἱ τελευτήσαντες, ἀθυμότεροι δὲ
οἱ ζῶντες γίγνονται, ὁρῶντες τῆς ἀρετῆς ἆθλον
μὲν[1] τὸν θάνατον κείμενον, τὴν δὲ μνήμην ἐπι-
λείπουσαν· καὶ τὸ μέγιστον, ἐπερωτῶσιν ὑμᾶς
οἱ νεώτεροι, πρὸς ὁποῖον χρὴ παράδειγμα αὑτοὺς
246 τὸν βίον ποιεῖσθαι. εὖ γὰρ ἴστε, ὦ ἄνδρες Ἀθηναῖοι, ὅτι οὐχ αἱ παλαῖστραι οὐδὲ τὰ διδασκαλεῖα
οὐδ᾽ ἡ μουσικὴ μόνον παιδεύει τοὺς νέους, ἀλλὰ
πολὺ μᾶλλον τὰ δημόσια κηρύγματα. κηρύττεταί
τις ἐν τῷ θεάτρῳ, ὅτι στεφανοῦται ἀρετῆς ἕνεκα
καὶ ἀνδραγαθίας καὶ εὐνοίας, ἄνθρωπος ἀσχη-
μονῶν τῷ βίῳ καὶ βδελυρός· ὁ δέ γε νεώτερος
ταῦτ᾽ ἰδὼν διεφθάρη. δίκην τις δέδωκε πονηρὸς
καὶ πορνοβοσκός, ὥσπερ Κτησιφῶν· οἱ δέ γε
ἄλλοι πεπαίδευνται. τἀναντία τις ψηφισάμενος
τῶν καλῶν καὶ δικαίων, ἐπανελθὼν οἴκαδε παιδεύει τὸν υἱόν· ὁ δέ γε εἰκότως οὐ πείθεται, ἀλλὰ
τὸ νουθετεῖν ἐνοχλεῖν[2] ἤδη δικαίως ὀνομάζεται.
247 ὡς οὖν μὴ μόνον κρίνοντες, ἀλλὰ καὶ θεωρούμενοι,
οὕτω τὴν ψῆφον φέρετε, εἰς ἀπολογισμὸν τοῖς νῦν

---

[1] μὲν added by Blass.
[2] ἐνοχλεῖν Weidner: ἐνταῦθα ἐνοχλεῖν or ἐνοχλεῖν ἐνταῦθα
MSS.

expostulating against the crowning of this man. When sticks and stones and iron, voiceless and senseless things, fall on any one and kill him, we cast them beyond the borders,[1] and when a man kills himself, the hand that did the deed is buried apart from the body; how outrageous, then, fellow citizens, if Demosthenes, who made the motion for that final campaign, and then betrayed the soldiers, is to receive honour from you! So are the dead insulted, and the living are disheartened, when they see that death is the prize of valour, while the memory of it fades away. And, most important of all, the younger men inquire of you after what example they ought to shape their lives. For be assured, fellow citizens, it is not our wrestling halls or the schools or our system of liberal studies alone that educate the young, but far more our public proclamations. It is proclaimed in the theatre that one is crowned for virtue and nobility and patriotism, a man whose life is shameful and loathsome; a younger man, at sight of that, is corrupted. A man has been punished who is a rascal and libertine—like Ctesiphon; the rest have received instruction. A juror who has cast his vote against honour and justice goes home and proceeds to instruct his son; the boy refuses to obey, and with good reason, and he is surely justified thenceforth in calling exhortation vexation. Cast your vote, then, not only as men who are rendering a verdict, but also as men who are in the public eye, to be called to account by the citizens who, though

---

[1] This strange custom perpetuated the old feeling of the ceremonial impurity that rested on any man or thing that had shed human blood.

μὲν οὐ παροῦσι τῶν πολιτῶν, ἐπερησομένοις δὲ
ὑμᾶς τί ἐδικάζετε. εὖ γὰρ ἴστε, ὦ ἄνδρες Ἀθηναῖοι, ὅτι τοιαύτη δόξει ἡ πόλις εἶναι, ὁποῖός τις
ἂν ᾖ ὁ κηρυττόμενος· ἔστι δὲ ὄνειδος μὴ τοῖς
προγόνοις ὑμᾶς, ἀλλὰ τῇ Δημοσθένους ἀνανδρίᾳ,
προσεικασθῆναι.

Πῶς οὖν ἄν τις τὴν τοιαύτην αἰσχύνην ἐκφύ-
248 γοι; ἐὰν τοὺς προκαταλαμβάνοντας τὰ κοινὰ
καὶ φιλάνθρωπα τῶν ὀνομάτων, ἀπίστους δ᾽ [1]
ὄντας τοῖς ἤθεσι, φυλάξησθε. ἡ γὰρ εὔνοια
καὶ τὸ τῆς δημοκρατίας ὄνομα κεῖται μὲν ἐν
μέσῳ, φθάνουσι δ᾽ ἐπ᾽ αὐτὰ καταφεύγοντες τῷ
λόγῳ ὡς ἐπὶ τὸ πολὺ οἱ τοῖς ἔργοις πλεῖστον
249 ἀπέχοντες. ὅταν οὖν λάβητε ῥήτορα στεφάνων [2]
καὶ κηρυγμάτων ἐν τοῖς Ἕλλησιν ἐπιθυμοῦντα,
ἐπανάγειν αὐτὸν κελεύετε τὸν λόγον, ὥσπερ καὶ
τὰς βεβαιώσεις τῶν κτημάτων ὁ νόμος κελεύει
ποιεῖσθαι, εἰς βίον ἀξιόχρεων καὶ τρόπον σώφρονα. ὅτῳ δὲ ταῦτα μὴ μαρτυρεῖται, μὴ βεβαιοῦτε αὐτῷ τοὺς ἐπαίνους, καὶ τῆς δημοκρατίας
250 ἐπιμελήθητε ἤδη διαφευγούσης ὑμᾶς. ἢ οὐ δεινὸν
ὑμῖν εἶναι δοκεῖ, εἰ τὸ μὲν βουλευτήριον καὶ ὁ
δῆμος παρορᾶται, αἱ δ᾽ ἐπιστολαὶ καὶ αἱ πρεσβεῖαι ἀφικνοῦνται εἰς ἰδιωτικὰς οἰκίας, οὐ παρὰ
τῶν τυχόντων ἀνθρώπων, ἀλλὰ παρὰ τῶν πρω-
τευόντων ἐν τῇ Ἀσίᾳ καὶ τῇ Εὐρώπῃ; καὶ ἐφ᾽
οἷς ἐστιν ἐκ τῶν νόμων ζημία θάνατος, ταῦτά

---

[1] δ᾽ added by Blass.
[2] στεφάνων Benseler : ξενικῶν στεφάνων MSS.

they are not now present, will nevertheless ask you what your verdict was. For be assured, fellow citizens, men will hold the city to be of like character with the man who is proclaimed. And it is a reproach for you to be likened, not to your fathers, but to the cowardice of Demosthenes.

How then could you escape such disgrace? By guarding against those who arrogate to themselves the name of "patriot" and "benefactor," but are untrustworthy in character. For loyalty and the name of friend of the people are prizes which are offered to us all, but for the most part those persons are the first to take refuge in them in speech who are farthest from them in conduct. When, therefore, you find a politician coveting crowns and proclamations in the presence of the Greeks, bid him bring his argument back to the proof of a worthy life and a sound character, precisely as the law commands a man to give security for property.[1] But if he has no testimony to this, do not confirm to him the praises which he seeks; let your thought be for the democracy, which is already slipping through your hands. Does it not seem to you to be an outrage if the senate-house and the people are coming to be ignored, while the letters and ambassadors come to private houses, sent hither not by ordinary men, but by the first men of Asia and Europe? And deeds the legal penalty for which is death, these

---

[1] "Just as the law orders that a vendor should give a purchaser of property a security for the validity of his purchase, so should the orator be compelled to show that his conduct, for which the reward is claimed, is a sure and proper ground on which to grant it." (Gwatkin and Shuckburgh, *ad loc.*)

τινες οὐκ ἐξαρνοῦνται πράττειν, ἀλλ' ὁμολογοῦσιν
ἐν τῷ δήμῳ, καὶ τὰς ἐπιστολὰς ἀλλήλοις παρανα-
γιγνώσκουσιν· παρακελεύονται δ' οἱ μὲν [1] βλέπειν
εἰς τὰ ἑαυτῶν πρόσωπα ὡς φύλακες τῆς δημοκρατίας, ἕτεροι δ' αἰτοῦσι δωρεὰς ὡς σωτῆρες τῆς
251 πόλεως ὄντες. ὁ δὲ δῆμος ἐκ τῆς ἀθυμίας τῶν
συμβεβηκότων ὥσπερ παραγεγηρακὼς ἢ παρα-
νοίας ἑαλωκώς, αὐτὸ μόνον τοὔνομα τῆς δημοκρατίας περιποιεῖται, τῶν δ' ἔργων ἑτέροις παρα-
κεχώρηκεν. ἔπειτ' ἀπέρχεσθε ἐκ τῶν ἐκκλησιῶν
οὐ βουλευσάμενοι, ἀλλ' ὥσπερ ἐκ τῶν ἐράνων, τὰ
252 περιόντα νειμάμενοι. ὅτι δ' οὐ ληρῶ, ἐκεῖθεν τὸν
λόγον θεωρήσατε. ἐγένετό τις, ἄχθομαι δὲ πολλάκις μεμνημένος, ἀτυχίᾳ τῇ πόλει. ἐνταῦθ'
ἀνὴρ ἰδιώτης ἐκπλεῖν μόνον εἰς Σάμον ἐπιχειρήσας, ὡς προδότης τῆς πατρίδος αὐθημερὸν ὑπὸ
τῆς ἐξ Ἀρείου πάγου βουλῆς θανάτῳ ἐζημιώθη.
ἕτερος δ' ἐκπλεύσας ἰδιώτης εἰς Ῥόδον, ὅτι τὸν
φόβον ἀνάνδρως ἤνεγκε, πρώην ποτὲ εἰσηγ-
γέλθη, καὶ ἴσαι αἱ ψῆφοι αὐτῷ ἐγένοντο· εἰ δὲ
253 μία ψῆφος [2] μετέπεσεν, ὑπερώριστ' ἄν. [3] ἀντιθῶ-
μεν δὴ τὸ νυνὶ γιγνόμενον. ἀνὴρ ῥήτωρ, ὁ πάντων τῶν κακῶν αἴτιος, ἔλιπε μὲν τὴν ἀπὸ στρατοπέδου τάξιν, ἀπέδρα δ' ἐκ τῆς πόλεως· οὗτος
στεφανοῦσθαι ἀξιοῖ καὶ κηρύττεσθαι οἴεται δεῖν.
οὐκ ἀποπέμψεσθε τὸν ἄνθρωπον ὡς κοινὴν τῶν

---

[1] οἱ μὲν Sauppe : ὑμῖν οἱ μὲν or οἱ μὲν ὑμῖν MSS.
[2] ψῆφος Blass (Harpocration) : μόνον MSS.
[3] ὑπερώριστ' ἄν A. Schaefer : ὑπερώριστ' ἂν ἢ ἀπέθανεν MSS

deeds certain men do not deny, but acknowledge them before the people; and they read their letters to one another and compare them. And some of them bid you look into their faces as being guardians of the democracy, and others call for rewards as being saviours of the state. But the people, discouraged by what they have experienced, as though in very dotage or declared of unsound mind, lay claim only to the name of democracy, and have surrendered the substance to others. And so you go home from the meetings of your assembly, not as from a deliberative session, but as from some picnic, where you have been given the leavings as your share. To prove that this is not mere talk, consider my statement in the light of the following facts: There came—it pains me to call it to mind repeatedly—there came a certain disaster to the city. At that time a certain private citizen who merely undertook to sail to Samos was on the same day punished with death by the Senate of the Areopagus, as a traitor to his country. Another private citizen, who sailed away to Rhodes, was only the other day prosecuted, because he was a coward in the face of danger. The vote of the jury was a tie, and if a single vote had been changed, he would have been cast outside our borders.[1] Now with that let us compare what is taking place to-day. A politician, the man who is responsible for all our disasters, deserted his post in the field, and then ran away from the city:[2] this man is calling for a crown, and he thinks he must be proclaimed. Away

---

[1] This was Leocrates, who had ventured to return to Athens after eight years' absence. Lycurgus' speech for the prosecution has come down to us.

[2] See § 159 and note

Ἑλλήνων συμφοράν; ἢ συλλαβόντες ὡς λῃστὴν
τῶν πραγμάτων, ἐπ᾽ ὀνομάτων διὰ τῆς πολιτείας
πλέοντα, τιμωρήσεσθε;

254 Καὶ τὸν καιρὸν μέμνησθε, ἐν ᾧ τὴν ψῆφον
φέρετε. ἡμερῶν μὲν ὀλίγων μέλλει τὰ Πύθια
γίγνεσθαι καὶ τὸ συνέδριον τὸ τῶν Ἑλλήνων
συλλέγεσθαι· διαβέβληται δ᾽ ἡ πόλις ἐκ τῶν
Δημοσθένους πολιτευμάτων περὶ τοὺς νυνὶ και-
ρούς· δόξετε δέ, ἐὰν μὲν τοῦτον στεφανώσητε,
ὁμογνώμονες εἶναι τοῖς παραβαίνουσι τὴν κοινὴν
εἰρήνην, ἐὰν δὲ τοὐναντίον τούτου πράξητε, ἀπο-
λύσετε τὸν δῆμον τῶν αἰτιῶν.

255 Μὴ οὖν ὡς ὑπὲρ ἀλλοτρίας, ἀλλ᾽ ὡς ὑπὲρ
οἰκείας τῆς πόλεως βουλεύεσθε, καὶ τὰς φιλοτιμίας μὴ νέμετε, ἀλλὰ κρίνετε, καὶ τὰς δωρεὰς εἰς
βελτίω σώματα καὶ ἄνδρας ἀξιολογωτέρους ἀπό-
θεσθε, καὶ μὴ μόνον τοῖς ὠσίν, ἀλλὰ καὶ τοῖς
ὄμμασι διαβλέψαντες εἰς ὑμᾶς αὐτοὺς βουλεύ-
σασθε, τίνες ὑμῶν εἰσιν οἱ βοηθήσοντες Δημοσθένει, πότερον οἱ συγκυνηγέται, ἢ οἱ συγγυμνασταὶ
αὐτοῦ, ὅτ᾽ ἦν ἐν ἡλικίᾳ—ἀλλὰ μὰ τὸν Δία τὸν
Ὀλύμπιον οὐχ ὗς ἀγρίους κυνηγετῶν, οὐδὲ τῆς
τοῦ σώματος εὐεξίας ἐπιμελόμενος, ἀλλ᾽ ἐπασκῶν
τέχνας ἐπὶ τοὺς τὰς οὐσίας κεκτημένους διαγεγέ-
256 νηται—ἀλλ᾽ εἰς τὴν ἀλαζονείαν ἀποβλέψαντες,
ὅταν φῇ Βυζαντίους μὲν ἐκ τῶν χειρῶν πρεσβεύσας ἐξελέσθαι τῶν Φιλίππου, ἀποστῆσαι δὲ

---

[1] The recent revolt of Sparta against Macedonia and the
present brilliant success of Alexander in Asia made the
situation especially critical for Greece so far as any thought
of opposition to Macedon was still cherished. It might well

with the fellow, the curse of all Hellas! Nay, rather, seize and punish him, the pirate of politics, who sails on his craft of words over the sea of state.

And mark well the occasion on which you are casting your vote. A few days hence the Pythian games are to be celebrated and the synod of Hellas assembled. Our city is already the object of slander in consequence of the policies of Demosthenes in connection with the present critical situation.[1] If you crown him, you will seem to be in sympathy with those who violate the general peace, whereas if you do the opposite, you will free the people from these charges.

Deliberate, therefore, not as for some foreign state, but as for your own; treat your honours, not as favours to be bestowed, but as rewards of merit; reserve your crowns for better heads and more worthy men. Deliberate, not with the help of your ears alone, but with your eyes as well, looking sharply among yourselves to see who of your number they are who propose to aid Demosthenes; whether they are comrades of his youth in the hunting-field, or companions in the gymnasium—but no, by the Olympian Zeus, that cannot be, for his time has been spent, not in hunting wild boars, and not in cultivating vigour of body, but in practising his art of hunting down men of property. Yes, look at his imposture when he says that by his services as envoy he dragged Byzantium from Philip's hands, and caused the revolt of the Acarnanians, and carried

be expected that at the coming meeting of the Amphictyonic Council, or at a special synod of delegates from the Greek states held at the time of the Pythian games, complaint would be brought by the Macedonians against the Spartans and those who had encouraged them in breaking the peace.

Ἀκαρνᾶνας, ἐκπλῆξαι δὲ Θηβαίους δημηγορήσας·
οἴεται γὰρ ὑμᾶς εἰς τοσοῦτον εὐηθείας ἤδη προβε-
βηκέναι, ὥστε καὶ ταῦτα ἀναπεισθήσεσθαι, ὥσπερ Πειθὼ τρέφοντας, ἀλλ' οὐ συκοφάντην ἄνθρωπον ἐν τῇ πόλει.

257   Ὅταν δ' ἐπὶ τελευτῆς ἤδη τοῦ λόγου συνηγόρους τοὺς κοινωνοὺς τῶν δωροδοκημάτων αὐτῷ
παρακαλῇ, ὑπολαμβάνετε ὁρᾶν ἐπὶ τοῦ βήματος, οὗ νῦν ἕστηκὼς ἐγὼ λέγω, ἀντιπαρατε-
ταγμένους πρὸς τὴν τούτων ἀσέλγειαν τοὺς
τῆς πόλεως εὐεργέτας, Σόλωνα μὲν τὸν καλλίστοις νόμοις κοσμήσαντα τὴν δημοκρατίαν,
ἄνδρα φιλόσοφον καὶ νομοθέτην ἀγαθόν, σωφρόνως, ὡς προσῆκον[1] αὐτῷ, δεόμενον ὑμῶν μηδενὶ
τρόπῳ τοὺς Δημοσθένους λόγους περὶ πλείονος
258   ποιήσασθαι τῶν ὅρκων καὶ τῶν νόμων, Ἀριστείδην δὲ τὸν τοὺς φόρους τάξαντα τοῖς Ἕλλησιν,
οὗ τελευτήσαντος τὰς θυγατέρας ἐξέδωκεν ὁ δῆμος, σχετλιάζοντα ἐπὶ τῷ τῆς δικαιοσύνης προ-
πηλακισμῷ, καὶ ἐπερωτῶντα, εἰ οὐκ αἰσχύνεσθε,
εἰ οἱ μὲν πατέρες ὑμῶν Ἄρθμιον τὸν Ζελείτην
κομίσαντα εἰς τὴν Ἑλλάδα τὸ ἐκ Μήδων χρυσίον,
ἐπιδημήσαντα εἰς τὴν πόλιν, πρόξενον ὄντα τοῦ
δήμου τοῦ Ἀθηναίων, παρ' οὐδὲν μὲν ἦλθον ἀπο-
κτεῖναι, ἐξεκήρυξαν δ' ἐκ τῆς πόλεως καὶ ἐξ ἁπά-
259   σης ἧς ἄρχουσιν Ἀθηναῖοι, ὑμεῖς δὲ Δημοσθένην,
οὐ κομίσαντα τὸ ἐκ Μήδων χρυσίον, ἀλλὰ δωρο-
δοκήσαντα καὶ ἔτι καὶ νῦν κεκτημένον, χρυσῷ
στεφάνῳ μέλλετε στεφανοῦν. Θεμιστοκλέα δὲ
καὶ τοὺς ἐν Μαραθῶνι τελευτήσαντας καὶ τοὺς ἐν
Πλαταιαῖς καὶ αὐτοὺς τοὺς τάφους τοὺς τῶν

----
[1] προσῆκον Emperius : προσῆκεν MSS.

the Thebans away by his harangues. For he supposes
that you have by this time come to such a pitch of
folly that you will credit even this, as though it were
the goddess Persuasion that you have been nurturing
in your city, and not a slanderer !

But when at last at the close of his speech he
calls forward to support his cause the men who have
shared his bribes, imagine that on the platform
where now I am standing as I speak, you see,
drawn up in array against the lawlessness of these
men, the benefactors of the state : Solon, who
equipped the democracy with the best of laws, a
philosopher and a good lawgiver, begging you
soberly, as he naturally would, by no means to hold
the words of Demosthenes as more weighty than your
oaths and the laws ; and that man who assessed the
tribute of the Greeks, and whose daughters our people
dowered after his death, Aristeides, expressing his
indignation at this mockery of justice, and asking
you if you are not ashamed that whereas, when
Arthmius of Zeleia transported the gold of the
Medes into Hellas,[1] although he had once resided
in our city, and was proxenus of the Athenian
people, your fathers were all but ready to kill him,
and they warned him out of their city, and out
of all the territory under Athenian control, you now
propose to crown with a golden crown Demosthenes,
a man who has not indeed "transported" the gold of
the Medes, but has received it as a bribe, and keeps
it to this day. Think you not that Themistocles and
those who died at Marathon and at Plataea, and the
very sepulchres of your fathers, will groan aloud, if

---

[1] Arthmius was sent by Xerxes into the Peloponnesus.

προγόνων οὐκ οἴεσθε στενάξειν, εἰ ὁ μετὰ τῶν
βαρβάρων ὁμολογῶν τοῖς Ἕλλησιν ἀντιπράττειν
στεφανωθήσεται;

260   Ἐγὼ μὲν οὖν, ὦ γῆ καὶ ἥλιε καὶ ἀρετὴ καὶ σύν-
εσις καὶ παιδεία, ᾗ διαγιγνώσκομεν τὰ καλὰ καὶ
τὰ αἰσχρά, βεβοήθηκα καὶ εἴρηκα. καὶ εἰ μὲν
καλῶς καὶ ἀξίως τοῦ ἀδικήματος κατηγόρηκα,
εἶπον ὡς ἐβουλόμην, εἰ δὲ ἐνδεεστέρως, ὡς
ἐδυνάμην. ὑμεῖς δὲ καὶ ἐκ τῶν εἰρημένων λόγων
καὶ ἐκ τῶν παραλειπομένων αὐτοὶ τὰ δίκαια καὶ
τὰ συμφέροντα ὑπὲρ τῆς πόλεως ψηφίσασθε.

the man who admits that he has negotiated with the barbarians against the Greeks shall receive a crown ?

Be ye my witnesses, O Earth and Sun, and Virtue and Conscience, and Education, by which we distinguish the honourable and the base, that I have heard my country's call, and have spoken. If I have presented the accusations well and in a manner commensurate with the crime, I have spoken according to my desire ; if insufficiently, according to my ability. It remains for you, fellow citizens, in view both of what has been spoken and what is left unsaid, yourselves to give the verdict that is just and for the city's good.

INDEX

[References are to pages.]

INDEX

pression of the Lacedaemonian revolt, 413; the prosecution of Ctesiphon is not intended as a manifesto to Alexander, as Demosthenes asserts it to be, 479, 481; the friendship of Alexander is made a ground of accusation against Aeschines, 361, 477; Alexander's name is constantly in Demosthenes' mouth, 483; is hated by Demosthenes, according to Demosthenes' own words, 361; Demosthenes falsely asserts that he has been bent on war against Alexander, 435, 439; Demosthenes is now trying to ingratiate himself with Alexander, 435

Alexander, brother of Philip, 181 n.

Alexander, king of the Molossians, 499

Aleximachus, seeks to secure the inclusion of Cersobleptes among the allies of Athens, 223

Alponus, one of the strongholds commanding the approach to the pass of Thermopylae, 259, 263

Ambassadors, Athenian, sent out to summon the Greek states for common action with reference to Philip, 361

Ambassadors, Macedonian, at Athens, 361 n. 3

Ameiniades, the prophet, 411

Amphictyonic League, the: constituent states, 247; the oath of the league, 245; the first Synod, 247

Amphictyonic Council, the: times and places of meeting, 405 and n. 1, 407; delegates, 397 n. 3; brought under the control of Philip, 159; the fate of the Phocians rests in their hands, xii, 231 n. 3, 245, 247, 263 ff.; ancient decree against the Cirrhaeans and Cragalidae, 391–395, 401–403; war against the Amphissians in the time of Aeschines, xiv, 403–409

Amphipolis, relation to Athens, 181, 183, 185 ff., 186 n.; war between Athens and Philip for the control of Amphipolis, 211 f., 351

Amphissians, sacrilege of the, 395; services of Demosthenes retained, 395–397; complaint against Athens in the Amphictyonic Council, 397–399; their land raided by the members of the Council and others, 403; war with the Amphictyons and finally with Philip, xiv, 403–409

Amphisthenes, a witness in the case against Timarchus, 56

Amyntas, father of Philip, 181 ff.; relations with Athens, 183 and n.; recognised the claims of Athens to Amphipolis, 185

Amyntor, a witness as to Demosthenes' position on the Peace of Philocrates, 207–211

Anaxinus of Oreus, arrested by Demosthenes, 483 ff.

Andocides, the statesman: the peace of, 293; the so-called Herm of, 103; his sketch of Athenian history transcribed by Aeschines, 291–295

Andros, Timarchus' magistracy in, 87

Anthemon, a town in Macedonia, 181

Anticipation of opponent's arguments, 101 n. 1

Anticles, a patron of Timarchus, 47

Anticles, the stadium-runner, 127

Antiochus, commander of the Athenian dispatch-boats, 213

Antipater, ambassador from Philip, 365; regent of Macedonia, 437

Aphobetus, brother of Aeschines, viii, 273

Apollo, the Pythian, 393, 395, 403; temple at Delphi, 399

Apollodorus, suit against Phormion, 287

Arbitration, proposed by Philip, 373–375

Arcadia, visited by Aeschines early in the contest against Philip, 219 and n. 1, 281; failed to join the anti-Macedonian alliance in the Chaeronea campaign for lack of nine talents of money, 497; joined the Lacedaemonian revolt against Alexander, 437

Archedemus of Pelekes, an Athenian friend of Thebes, 417

514

INDEX

INDEX

exiles intercede for Aeschines, 267

Bosporus, the Cimmerian, 443

Boys, the lovers of, 107 ff.

Bribery, punishment for, 71–73

Byzantium, taken from the hands of Philip, 507

Cadmeia, the, citadel of Thebes, 239, 421

Callias of Chalcis: betrayed the Athenian army in Euboea, 377; was with Philip in Macedonia, 379; with the Thebans, then abandoned them, 379; formed Euboean congress at Chalcis, 379, 387; bribed Demosthenes to bring about Athenian alliance with Chalcis, 381; mission to the Peloponnesus, 383–385; report in the Athenian assembly, 383; secured pay for Demosthenes, 389; is proposed for Athenian citizenship by Demosthenes, 375

Callicrates, an Athenian envoy to the Phocians, 261

Callisthenes, an Athenian general, 183, 185

Callistratus, the orator, 253

Carion, a traditional name for a slave, in comedy, 279

Cedonides, a bestial companion of Timarchus, 47

Cephalus, the statesman, 461

Cephisodorus, a dissolute character, 127

Cephisodotus, an Athenian general, 349

Cephisophon, moves an investigation of naval operations, 213

Cepoi, in Bosporus, see " Gardens "

Cersobleptes, the Thracian king, expelled from his kingdom by Philip, 169; excluded from the Peace of Philocrates, 221–229, 359, 367–369

Ceryces, the, a priestly family of Athens, 323

Chabrias, the Athenian general, 499

Chaeronea, the battle of, 351, 455

Chalcis, ungrateful conduct toward Athens, 377; unequal alliance with Athens, 381–383;

made the seat of a Euboean congress, 379–383; paid one talent to Demosthenes for his services in bringing about the Athenian alliance, 389

Chares, the Athenian general in the North, 227–229; complaints against, 213

Charidemus, commander of mercenaries of Athens, 369

Cheilon, a Lacedaemonian admiral, defeated by the Athenians under Demaenetus (probably in the Corinthian war, 395–386 B.C.) 219

Chersonese, the, held by Athens in the time of her empire, 295; threatened by Philip, 213, 221

Children, laws to protect the morals of, 9–21

Choregus, laws prescribing the age of the, 11; metaphorical use of the term, 219 and n. 2

Cilicia, Alexander in, 437

Cimon, the truce of (450 B.C.), 291 n. 4

Cimon, a member of the first embassy to Philip, 177

Cirrha, the plain of, 391, 401; ancient curse against, 393–395; settled again by the Amphissians, 395; raided by the Amphictyons, 403

Cithaeron, Mount, 433

Citizen lists, Athenian, the revision of, 65

Citizenship, Athenian, restricted to people of pure blood, 443 n. 3

Cleaenetus, the chorus-master, 81

Cleitarchus, tyrant of Eretria, 389

Cleobulus, uncle of Aeschines, viii, 217–219

Cleochares, an ambassador from Chalcis to Philip, 249

Cleopatra, daughter of Philip, 499

Cleophon, the demagogue, 217 and n., 425

Clepsydra, the, to measure time allowance in court, 131 n. 1, 255 n., 463

Cnosion, alleged to be the father of Demosthenes' child, 273

Common Report (Φήμη), 103 ff., 269 ff.

Comptroller of the treasury, 329

INDEX

Comrades ('Εταῖροι) of Philip, 379 n.

Confederacy, the Second Athenian Naval, *see* Athenian Naval League

Congress of anti-Macedonian States called to meet in Athens (340 B.C.), 385

Congress of Sparta (371 B.C.), 185

Constitution, Athenian, revision of, 143 n., 306 n. 1, 339

Contracts for prostitution, 129 ff.

Corcyra, the voyage of Timotheus to (375 B.C.), 499

Corinth, Aeschines' mother an exile in, 271

Corrhagus, a Macedonian general, 437 and n. 2

Cottyphus of Pharsalus, president of the Amphictyonic Council, 405, 409; commander of troops against the Amphissians, 409

Cotylaeum, Mount, in Euboea, 377

Council of Elders at Sparta, 145 and n.

Courts, Athenian : presidency of, 319, 321 n., 333 ; Aeschines' criticism of procedure in, 143 ; pleas of supporting friends, 497 n. 5

Court-rooms, Athenian · the platforms, and the supporters of plaintiff and defendant, 471 and n. 1

Cragalidae, the, a tribe near Delphi, 391

Critias, a leader of the Thirty Tyrants, 139

Crito, son of Astyochus, beautiful of person, and a chaste lover, 125

Critobulus of Lampsacus, representative of Cersobleptes at Athens, 221, 225

" Crobylus," *see* " Hegesippus "

Cronion, *i.e.* Zeus, the Son of Cronos, 415

Crowns, former honours of the Athenian state, 489

Crowning of public officials at Athens : legal restrictions as to the time of crowning, 317 ; legal restrictions as to the place of crowning, 335 ; abuses of the custom, 315 ff. ; evasion of the restrictions as to time, 317–319

Crowning of the outgoing Senate, 90 n. 1

Ctesiphon, the friend of Demosthenes : moves that Demosthenes be crowned, xvi, 305 ; the substance of the motion, 335–337, 347, 381, 389 ; his motion, an act of effrontery to the state, 351 ; his mission to the daughter of Philip, 499 ; he is a rascal and libertine, 477, 501

Ctesiphon, a special envoy to Philip, 171 ; a member of the first embassy to Philip, 195

Cyclic choruses, 11, 491

Cyrebion, nickname of Epicrates, 275 n. 2

Cytinion, represented in the Amphictyonic League, 247

Darius, King of Persia, 413 n. 1, 437, 495

Deceleia, fortified by the Spartans against Athens in the Peloponnesian war, 215

Decrees, Athenian, distinguished from laws, 143 n. 1

Deiares, a mercenary commander in Athenian service, 213

Deipyrus, a mercenary commander in Athenian service, 213

Delphi : the shrine of Apollo, 391, 398 n. 1 ; the oracle, 411 ; *see also* " Amphictyonic Council " and " Pythia "

Delphians, the, summoned for a raid on the plain of Cirrha, 403

Demaenetus, an Athenian commander who defeated a Lacedaemonian fleet under Cheilon (probably in the Corinthian war, 395–386 B.C.), 219

Democracies, distinguished from autocracies and oligarchies, 7

Democracy, nature and protection of, 313 ; definition of the " Friend of the people," 441

Democrates, persuades the Senate to summon Aristodemus to report to them on his mission to Philip, 173

Demomeles, cousin of Demosthenes, 229, 349

INDEX

Demophilus, the author of a proposal to revise the citizen-lists, 71 and n.

Demosthenes of Paeania, the father of Demosthenes, the orator, 231, 443

Demosthenes, the orator: his father, 231, 443; of Scythian blood through his maternal grandmother, 179, 217, 225, 231 and n. 2, 291, 299, 301, 443; involved in quarrels with his cousin Demomeles, 229–231, 349; made capital of self-inflicted wounds, 475; became a hunter of rich youths, 137; his relations with Aristarchus, 137 ff.; was a teacher of rhetoric, 95 n. 2, 137 n., 139, 279; a hired writer of speeches, discredited by betraying the cause of his clients, 285–287, 445; served as trierarch on an expedition to the Hellespont, 349, 445; his relations with Cephisodotus, the general, 349; was choregus at the Dionysia of 348 B.C., 349; trouble with Meidias and insult by him in the theatre, 139 n. 1, 349 and n. 2, 475–477; served on the Euboean expedition of 348 B.C., 273 n. 1; enumeration of four periods of Demosthenes' political career, 351; favoured peace negotiations with Philip in 347 B.C., 158; spoke in behalf of Athenian captives in Macedonia, 173; aided Aristodemus in securing release from engagements, to enable him to go as an envoy to Philip, 175; moved a crown for Aristodemus as reward for his services in the interest of peace, 173; co-operated with Philocrates in all the preliminaries of the peace, 171, 177, 355–361, 367, 371; was nominated by Philocrates as a member of the embassy to Philip, 175; served on the first embassy, 175; boasted of what he would do in securing Athenian rights from Philip, 177; his failure at Philip's court, 177–191; his report of the first embassy, 195–

199; prepared the way for the coming of Philip's ambassadors, 199; his flattery of Philip's ambassadors, 243, 369; his part in the assembly which voted peace and alliance with Philip, 207, 365 ff.; his responsibility for the exclusion of Cersobleptes of Thrace from the peace, 223 ff., 367–369; his responsibility for the exclusion of many Greek states from the peace, 205 ff., 353–367; his service on the second embassy, 233 ff.; his speech before Philip, 241–243; his report of the second embassy, 231; he turns against Philocrates and the other members of the second embassy, 373; his charges against Aeschines in the matter of the second embassy, 159 ff.; his connection with Timarchus, 2 ff.; his defence of Timarchus, 77; during the period of peace he constantly foments trouble, 373–375; as delegate to the Amphictyonic Council in 343 B.C. he is corrupted by the Amphissians, and his services are retained by them, 395–397, 405; his dealings with Callias of Euboea, and his betrayal of Athenian interests, 375, 379; receives pay for his services to the Euboean cities, 389; refuses to accept a statue from the people of Oreus in place of his fee, 389; claims the credit of making the alliance with Euboea and with Thebes, 375; is not to be credited with the Theban alliance, 495; in the alliance with Thebes he made an unfair division of cost and of leadership, 419; he brought all Boeotia under control of Thebes, 419; by his trierarchal law he deprived the city of trierarchs for 65 ships, 483; assures the people that the Peloponnesus and Acarnania will give substantial help against Philip, 385; assumes a defiant attitude toward any restraint, 421; his un-

INDEX

righteous conduct in the whole matter of the sacrilege of the Amphissians and the war against them, 391–415; declares that the Pythia has gone over to the service of Philip, 411; betrays the cause of the allies by dividing their forces, 421; prevents reconciliation with Philip when that course is open and favoured by Thebes, 423; is Superintendent of the Theoric Fund in 337 B.C., 327; his services in the repair of the walls after the battle of Chaeronea, 305, 327, 331, 493; his eulogy over the citizens who fell at Chaeronea, 425, 427 n.; his flight from the city, 431, 505; is discredited with the people in the first months after the defeat, 431–433; announces the death of Philip, as revealed to him by the gods in a dream, 369, 481; his unseemly rejoicing over the assassination of Philip, 433; his ridicule of the young Alexander, 433; he neglects three excellent opportunities for action against Alexander, 435 ff.; he runs away from the embassy to Alexander, 433; is seeking through Aristion to curry favour with Alexander, 435; is constantly in readiness to take flight from the city, 473; has prepared Ctesiphon's speech for him, 467

The personal qualities of Demosthenes as portrayed by Aeschines: his nicknames, Batalus, 103, 235 and n., and Argas, 235; his effeminacy, 107, 235; his licentiousness, 445; his insincerity, 471; his own peculiar manner of lying, 385; he is a Sisyphus, 191; Ctesiphon's testimony to his instability and cowardice, 477; his contempt for the obligations of hospitality, 483; his lack of feeling at the death of his only child, 369–371; his cowardice in the field, 425, 445, 451, 455, 505; has made profit from padded army rolls, 421; speaks in public

only for money, 479; is now supported by Persian gold, 445, 497, 509; as a speaker, he is a tongue and nothing more, 489; his words and gestures are violent and uncouth, 425, 439; he is under the curse of heaven, 397; he is himself the curse of Hellas, 431

Dercylus, a member of the Athenian embassy to Philip, 195, 265; a witness for Aeschines, 279

Diodorus, ambassador from Callias of Chalcis, 379

Diognetus, Athenian Hieromnemon at Delphi, 397

Dionysia, the City, 205 and n., 361 and n. 1, 363, 491; seats of honour assigned to Philip's ambassadors, 199, 243; the occasion for the proposed crowning of Demosthenes, 305–307

Dionysia, the Rural, 125

Dionysiac Law, the, 337 ff.

Dionysiac procession, the, 39, 275

Dionysius, the Sicilian tyrant, 169

Dionysus, the precinct of, 447; session of the Athenian assembly here, 205 and n. 1, 349; the orchestra of Dionysus, 429

Diopeithes, an inefficient arbitrator, 55

Diophantes, "the Orphan," a prostitute, 127

Documents, read to the jury by clerk of the court, but not published with the speeches, 13 n.

Dolopians, the, members of the Amphictyonic League, 247

Dorians, the, members of the Amphictyonic League, 247

Dorion, represented in the Amphictyonic Council, 247

Doriscus, a Thracian town, 373 and n.

Draco, laws of, to protect the morals of children, 9 ff.

Eion, on the river Strymon, 453

Elateia, seizure and fortification of, by Philip, 417

Election, Athenian magistrates chosen by 93 n. 1, 319

519

INDEX

INDEX

INDEX

INDEX

INDEX

by Aeschines when their case is before the Amphictyonic Council, 267; have sent ambassadors to support Aeschines in his defence, 267; will be brought into the defence of Timarchus by Demosthenes, 141

Phocion, the general and statesman, xvi; witness to Aeschines' services in the Euboean expedition, 289; supports Aeschines in the case "On the Embassy," 301

Phoenix, the, of Euripides, 289

Phormion, Demosthenes' speech for, 287

Phrynon, a prisoner in Macedonia, 169; a member of the second embassy to Philip 167

Phrynondas, the traitor, 415

Phthiotians, the, members of the Amphictyonic League, 247

Phratries, Athenian, 271 n.

Phyle, the starting point of the democratic "return," 295, 463; the heroes of, 451, 455, 459

Physician, Demosthenes' illustration of the, and Aeschines' answer, 485 ff.

Pittalacus, a state-slave, patron of Timarchus, 49–57

Plataea, the battle of, 215, 509; Persian and Theban shields from, 398 and n. 1

Plataean status, the, 435 and n. 2

Plutarchus of Eretria, treachery of, toward Athens, 377 and n.

Pnyx, the assembly place of the Athenians, 355; buildings there, 69

Poenae, the, see "Furies"

Polemagenes, an Athenian known for his beauty of person, 125

Pollis, the Lacedaemonian admiral at the battle of Naxos, 483

Polyphontes, a mercenary officer, 213

Pontus, the, 443

Presidency of courts, the, 319 ff.

Presiding officers of the Athenian assembly, 31 and n. 3, 221 n. 2, 339, 367 and n.

Priests and priestesses, subject to accounting, 323

Procedure, orderly, in senate and assembly, 309

Procurers, Solon's laws against, 147

Pronaea, see Athena.

Prosecution, penalty for failure in, 131 n., 173 n. 1

Prostitutes, tax on, 97 ff.; "Timarchian prostitutes," 125

Prostitution, contracts for, 129 ff.; exclusion of the male prostitute from public life, 19; laws against prostitution of boys, 15 ff.

Proxenus, the office of, 226 n., 291 n. 3, 341

Proxenus, the Athenian general, 259 ff.

Prytanes, the, 199, 203, 205, 311, 339, 361

Prytaneum, maintenance in the, 449, 463; the hearth of the Prytaneum, 193 n. 2

Ptolemaeus, paramour of Philip's mother, 181 n. 2, 183

Public men (ῥήτορες), 26 n.

Purification ceremonial of the Athenian assemblies, 21–23

Pylagori, the, at Delphi, 397 n. 3

Pyrrhandrus, a speaker in the Athenian assembly, 71, 417

Pythia, the: ancient reply to the Amphictyons, 393; accused by Demosthenes of having gone over to Philip, 411

Pythian Apollo, 393

Pythian games, the, 507

Python, called to plead for Aeschines, 267

Python of Byzantium in the service of Philip, 253

Salamis, the statue of Solon at, 25; law as to the ferrymen in the straits, 431; the battle of, 215, 291, 451

Samos, Athenian colony in, 47

Satyrus, the actor, 279

Schools for boys, laws governing, 11 ff.

Scrutiny: of incoming officials (δοκιμασία), 26 n, 27 ff., 321 and n. 2; for the right to address the assembly, 27 ff., 68 n. 1

Scyros, possession of, offered to Athens in the Peloponnesian war,

INDEX

217; possession of, disputed by Philip, 213

Scythia, Philip in, 409

Scythian blood in Demosthenes, *see* " Demosthenes "

Senate of Five Hundred: subject to accounting, 325; usual testimonial for services, 90 n.; procedure in expulsion of members, 91 n.

Senate-house, 193 n. 2

Serrhium - Teichus, a Thracian stronghold, 373 and n.

Sicilian expedition, the, 215

Sirens, Demosthenes' illustration of the, 487

Sisyphus, Demosthenes so named by Aeschines, 191

Skirophorion, an Attic month, 331

Slaves, law against outrage of, 17; their services hired out, 79 n. suits in behalf of, 53 n.; excluded from the wrestling-schools, 111; forbidden to be lovers of free boys, 113

Socrates, the death of, 139

Solon, the Athenian lawgiver and philosopher, 509; his statue at Salamis, 25; the leader of the Amphictyons against the sacrilegious Cirrhaeans, 393; his laws to protect the morals of children, 9 ff.; laws governing the chastity of women, 147; laws punishing the coward, 445; laws to secure orderly conduct on the part of public speakers, 309

Spartan, *see* " Lacedaemonian "

Stephanus, an Athenian ambassador to Philip, 265

Stoa, the, of the Hermae, 451; the Stoa Poecile, 455

Strepsa, a town in Macedonia, 181

Strymon, the battle of the (475 B.C.), 451 ff.

Suits, two classes of, according as the penalty was prescribed by law or not, 474 n. 1

Summons to testify, refusal of, punished by law, 41 n.; summons to scrutiny of the right to address the assembly, 68 n. 1

Superintendent of the Theoric Fund, 327

Synod, the Confederate, decree as to peace, 203–205, 363 ff.; provision for giving their oath to the treaty, 367; Chalcis to be detached from, 381 and n. 1

Tamynae, the battle of, ix, 289, 377

Taurosthenes of Chalcis, 375–377

Teachers, laws governing the conduct of, 11 ff.

Temenides, an Athenian taxiarch, 289

Thanks, votes of: abuse of the custom, 315 ff.

Thargelion, an Attic month, 331

Theatre, the custom of making proclamations in the, 341–347; the old custom of introducing there the sons of men who had fallen in battle, 427 ff.; seats of honour, 369

Theban shields from the spoil of Plataea, 399

Thebes: inconsistent attitude of Athens toward, 239, 285; traditional hostility toward Athens, 417; attempt to enslave Euboea (357 B.C.), 375 and n. 2; anxiety as to Philip's action in the Phocian war, 261–265; strengthened by Philip after the destruction of the Phocian cities, 371; dominate the Amphictyons, 397; not represented at the meeting of the Amphictyonic Council which declares war on the Amphissians, 407; their alliance with Athens not to be credited to Demosthenes' persuasion, 375, 415 ff., 495, 509; given more than fair share of control in the alliance with Athens, 421; their officials inclined to come to terms with Philip, 423–425; their citadel held by Macedonian mercenaries, 496 n. 2; the approach of Alexander's army, 433; destroyed by Alexander, 407 n. 1; picture of its capture, 429; the citizens find refuge in Athens, 429; Aes-

526

INDEX

chines' lamentation for Thebes, 413. *See also* " Boeotia "
Themison of Eretria, 285, 375
Themistocles, the Athenian general, 167, 451, 509
Themistocles, archon 347/6 B.C., 357
Theodorus, the actor, ix
Theophrastus, archon 340/39 B.C., 397
Theoric Fund, the (τὸ θεωρικόν), 327
Therma, a town in Macedonia, 181
Thermopylae, the meeting-place of the Amphictyonic Council, 404 n. 1, 407; control of, in the Phocian war, 259; Philip's expedition to, 237–239, 245, 257–259, 371
Thersandrus, a bestial companion of Timarchus, 47
Thersites, the slanderer, 489
Theseum, the, 319
Theseus, the sons of, 185
Thesmothetae, the, 319, 339 and n. 1
Thessaly: member of the Amphictyonic League, 247; long-standing enmity toward the Phocians, 265; attitude toward Philip, 259–261, 265; receives Nicaea from Philip, 417; is ready to join Alexander in an expedition against Athens, 433; Demosthenes' negotiations, 439; embassy to Thessaly led by Aristodemus, 375
Thetis, the mother of Achilles, 117 ff.
Thirty Tyrants, the, 35, 217, 295, 493
Thrace, expedition of Philip against 221, 227, 235; its coast lost to Athens, 169, 367. *See also* " Cersobleptes "
Thrason, an Athenian statesman, 417
Thrasybulus of Collytus, an Athenian friend of the Thebans, 417
Thrasybulus of Steiria, leader of the restored democracy, 295, 463
Thrasycles, an Athenian Pylagorus, 397
Thrasyllus, the tomb of, 83

Thronion, a northern stronghold, 259
Thyteion, the, at Delphi, 403
Timarchian prostitutes, 125
Timarchus, son of Arizelus, xiii; the speech of Aeschines against, 1–155; the case against, 2 f.; unseemly conduct on the platform, 25; attack on the law providing for orderly conduct of the assembly, 31 ff.; in the house of Euthydicus, the physician, 35; goes to live in lewdness with Misgolas, 37–47; then with Anticles, 47; frequents the gaming-places, 47–49; goes to live in shame with Pittalacus, 49–51; thence to Hegesandrus, 51 ff., 77–79; is the laughing-stock of the assembly, 67–71; has wasted the large estate left by his father, 79–87; neglected his helpless uncle, 85; as auditor was a bribe-taker and black-mailer, 87; abused his magistracy in Andros, 87–89; as senator, conspired with Hegesandrus to rob the city, 89–93; as inspector of troops in Eretria was confessedly guilty of theft, 93; was guilty of blackmail in the case of Philotades, 93–95; is condemned by Common Report, 101–107
Timarchus, son of Teisias, a chaste youth, 125
Time allowance in Athenian courts, 130 n.
Timesitheus, the runner, known for his beauty of person, 125
Timomachus, the general, unfortunate connection with Hegesandrus, 49–51
Timotheus, the Athenian general, 211
Tolmides, an Athenian commander, 215
" Top-knot," nickname of Hegesippus, 55 n. 2, 61, 399
Treasurers, the ten, 89 n. 2
Trierarchs, subject to accounting, 323; their number changed by Demosthenes' revision of the law, 483 and n. 2

527

INDEX

THE LOEB CLASSICAL LIBRARY

VOLUMES ALREADY PUBLISHED

Latin Authors

AMMIANUS MARCELLINUS. Translated by J. C. Rolfe. 3 Vols.

APULEIUS: THE GOLDEN ASS (METAMORPHOSES). W. Adlington (1566). Revised by S. Gaselee.

ST. AUGUSTINE: CITY OF GOD. 7 Vols. Vol. I. G. E. McCracken. Vols. II and VII. W. M. Green. Vol. III. D. Wiesen. Vol. IV. P. Levine. Vol. V. E. M. Sanford and W. M. Green. Vol. VI. W. C. Greene.

ST. AUGUSTINE, CONFESSIONS OF. W. Watts (1631). 2 Vols.

ST. AUGUSTINE, SELECT LETTERS. J. H. Baxter.

AUSONIUS. H. G. Evelyn White. 2 Vols.

BEDE. J. E. King. 2 Vols.

BOETHIUS: TRACTS and DE CONSOLATIONE PHILOSOPHIAE. Rev. H. F. Stewart and E. K. Rand. Revised by S. J. Tester.

CAESAR: ALEXANDRIAN, AFRICAN and SPANISH WARS. A. G. Way.

CAESAR: CIVIL WARS. A. G. Peskett.

CAESAR: GALLIC WAR. H. J. Edwards.

CATO: DE RE RUSTICA. VARRO: DE RE RUSTICA. H. B. Ash and W. D. Hooper.

CATULLUS. F. W. Cornish. TIBULLUS. J. B. Postgate. PERVIGILIUM VENERIS. J. W. Mackail. Revised by G. P. Goold.

CELSUS: DE MEDICINA. W. G. Spencer. 3 Vols.

CICERO: BRUTUS and ORATOR. G. L. Hendrickson and H. M. Hubbell.

[CICERO]: AD HERENNIUM. H. Caplan.

CICERO: DE ORATORE, etc. 2 Vols. Vol. I. DE ORATORE, Books I and II. E. W. Sutton and H. Rackham. Vol. II. DE ORATORE, Book III. DE FATO; PARADOXA STOICORUM; DE PARTITIONE ORATORIA. H. Rackham.

CICERO: DE FINIBUS. H. Rackham.

CICERO: DE INVENTIONE, etc. H. M. Hubbell.

CICERO: DE NATURA DEORUM and ACADEMICA. H. Rackham.

CICERO: DE OFFICIIS. Walter Miller.

CICERO: DE RE PUBLICA and DE LEGIBUS. Clinton W. Keyes.

CICERO: DE SENECTUTE, DE AMICITIA, DE DIVINATIONE. W. A. Falconer.

CICERO: IN CATILINAM, PRO FLACCO, PRO MURENA, PRO SULLA. New version by C. Macdonald.

CICERO: LETTERS TO ATTICUS. E. O. Winstedt. 3 Vols.

CICERO: LETTERS TO HIS FRIENDS. W. Glynn Williams, M. Cary, M. Henderson. 4 Vols.

CICERO: PHILIPPICS. W. C. A. Ker.

CICERO: PRO ARCHIA, POST REDITUM, DE DOMO, DE HARUSPICUM RESPONSIS, PRO PLANCIO. N. H. Watts.

CICERO: PRO CAECINA, PRO LEGE MANILIA, PRO CLUENTIO, PRO RABIRIO. H. Grose Hodge.

CICERO: PRO CAELIO, DE PROVINCIIS CONSULARIBUS, PRO BALBO. R. Gardner.

CICERO: PRO MILONE, IN PISONEM, PRO SCAURO, PRO FONTEIO, PRO RABIRIO POSTUMO, PRO MARCELLO, PRO LIGARIO, PRO REGE DEIOTARO. N. H. Watts.

CICERO: PRO QUINCTIO, PRO ROSCIO AMERINO, PRO ROSCIO COMOEDO, CONTRA RULLUM. J. H. Freese.

CICERO: PRO SESTIO, IN VATINIUM. R. Gardner.

CICERO: TUSCULAN DISPUTATIONS. J. E. King.

CICERO: VERRINE ORATIONS. L. H. G. Greenwood. 2 Vols.

CLAUDIAN. M. Platnauer. 2 Vols.

COLUMELLA: DE RE RUSTICA. DE ARBORIBUS. H. B. Ash, E. S. Forster and E. Heffner. 3 Vols.

CURTIUS, Q.: HISTORY OF ALEXANDER. J. C. Rolfe. 2 Vols.

FLORUS. E. S. Forster.

FRONTINUS: STRATAGEMS and AQUEDUCTS. C. E. Bennett and M. B. McElwain.

FRONTO: CORRESPONDENCE. C. R. Haines. 2 Vols.

GELLIUS. J. C. Rolfe. 3 Vols.

HORACE: ODES and EPODES. C. E. Bennett.

HORACE: SATIRES, EPISTLES, ARS POETICA. H. R. Fairclough.

JEROME: SELECTED LETTERS. F. A. Wright.

JUVENAL and PERSIUS. G. G. Ramsay.

LIVY. B. O. Foster, F. G. Moore, Evan T. Sage, and A. C. Schlesinger and R. M. Geer (General Index). 14 Vols.

LUCAN. J. D. Duff.

LUCRETIUS. W. H. D. Rouse. Revised by M. F. Smith.

MANILIUS. G. P. Goold.

MARTIAL. W. C. A. Ker. 2 Vols. Revised by E. H. Warmington.

MINOR LATIN POETS: from PUBLILIUS SYRUS to RUTILIUS NAMATIANUS, including GRATTIUS, CALPURNIUS SICULUS, NEMESIANUS, AVIANUS and others, with " Aetna " and the " Phoenix." J. Wight Duff and Arnold M. Duff. 2 Vols.

MINUCIUS FELIX. Cf. TERTULLIAN.

2

NEPOS, CORNELIUS. J. C. Rolfe.

OVID: THE ART OF LOVE and OTHER POEMS. J. H. Mosley. Revised by G. P. Goold.

OVID: FASTI. Sir James G. Frazer. Revised by G. P. Goold.

OVID: HEROIDES and AMORES. Grant Showerman. Revised by G. P. Goold.

OVID: METAMORPHOSES. F. J. Miller. 2 Vols. Revised by G. P. Goold.

OVID: TRISTIA and EX PONTO. A. L. Wheeler. Revised by G. P. Goold.

PERSIUS. Cf. JUVENAL.

PERVIGILIUM VENERIS. Cf. CATULLUS.

PETRONIUS. M. Heseltine. SENECA: APOCOLOCYNTOSIS. W. H. D. Rouse. Revised by E. H. Warmington.

PHAEDRUS and BABRIUS (Greek). B. E. Perry.

PLAUTUS. Paul Nixon. 5 Vols.

PLINY: LETTERS, PANEGYRICUS. Betty Radice. 2 Vols.

PLINY: NATURAL HISTORY. 10 Vols. Vols. I–V and IX. H. Rackham. VI.–VIII. W. H. S. Jones. X. D. E. Eichholz.

PROPERTIUS. H. E. Butler.

PRUDENTIUS. H. J. Thomson. 2 Vols.

QUINTILIAN. H. E. Butler. 4 Vols.

REMAINS OF OLD LATIN. E. H. Warmington. 4 Vols. Vol. I. (ENNIUS AND CAECILIUS) Vol. II. (LIVIUS, NAEVIUS PACUVIUS, ACCIUS) Vol. III. (LUCILIUS and LAWS OF XII TABLES) Vol. IV. (ARCHAIC INSCRIPTIONS)

RES GESTAE DIVI AUGUSTI. Cf. VELLEIUS PATERCULUS.

SALLUST. J. C. Rolfe.

SCRIPTORES HISTORIAE AUGUSTAE. D. Magie. 3 Vols.

SENECA, THE ELDER: CONTROVERSIAE, SUASORIAE. M. Winterbottom. 2 Vols.

SENECA: APOCOLOCYNTOSIS. Cf. PETRONIUS.

SENECA: EPISTULAE MORALES. R. M. Gummere. 3 Vols.

SENECA: MORAL ESSAYS. J. W. Basore. 3 Vols.

SENECA: TRAGEDIES. F. J. Miller. 2 Vols.

SENECA: NATURALES QUAESTIONES. T. H. Corcoran. 2 Vols.

SIDONIUS: POEMS and LETTERS. W. B. Anderson. 2 Vols.

SILIUS ITALICUS. J. D. Duff. 2 Vols.

STATIUS. J. H. Mozley. 2 Vols.

SUETONIUS. J. C. Rolfe. 2 Vols.

TACITUS: DIALOGUS. Sir Wm. Peterson. AGRICOLA and GERMANIA. Maurice Hutton. Revised by M. Winterbottom, R. M. Ogilvie, E. H. Warmington.

TACITUS: HISTORIES and ANNALS. C. H. Moore and J. Jackson. 4 Vols.

3

TERENCE. John Sargeaunt. 2 Vols.

TERTULLIAN: APOLOGIA and DE SPECTACULIS. T. R. Glover. MINUCIUS FELIX. G. H. Rendall.

TIBULLUS. Cf. CATULLUS.

VALERIUS FLACCUS. J. H. Mozley.

VARRO: DE LINGUA LATINA. R. G. Kent. 2 Vols.

VELLEIUS PATERCULUS and RES GESTAE DIVI AUGUSTI. F. W. Shipley.

VIRGIL. H. R. Fairclough. 2 Vols.

VITRUVIUS: DE ARCHITECTURA. F. Granger. 2 Vols.

Greek Authors

ACHILLES TATIUS. S. Gaselee.

AELIAN: ON THE NATURE OF ANIMALS. A. F. Scholfield. 3 Vols.

AENEAS TACTICUS. ASCLEPIODOTUS and ONASANDER. The Illinois Greek Club.

AESCHINES. C. D. Adams.

AESCHYLUS. H. Weir Smyth. 2 Vols.

ALCIPHRON, AELIAN, PHILOSTRATUS: LETTERS. A. R. Benner and F. H. Fobes.

ANDOCIDES, ANTIPHON. Cf. MINOR ATTIC ORATORS.

APOLLODORUS. Sir James G. Frazer. 2 Vols.

APOLLONIUS RHODIUS. R. C. Seaton.

APOSTOLIC FATHERS. Kirsopp Lake. 2 Vols.

APPIAN: ROMAN HISTORY. Horace White. 4 Vols.

ARATUS. Cf. CALLIMACHUS.

ARISTIDES: ORATIONS. C. A. Behr.

ARISTOPHANES. Benjamin Bickley Rogers. 3 Vols. Verse trans.

ARISTOTLE: ART OF RHETORIC. J. H. Freese.

ARISTOTLE: ATHENIAN CONSTITUTION, EUDEMIAN ETHICS, VICES AND VIRTUES. H. Rackham.

ARISTOTLE: GENERATION OF ANIMALS. A. L. Peck.

ARISTOTLE: HISTORIA ANIMALIUM. A. L. Peck. Vols. I.–II.

ARISTOTLE: METAPHYSICS. H. Tredennick. 2 Vols.

ARISTOTLE: METEOROLOGICA. H. D. P. Lee.

ARISTOTLE: MINOR WORKS. W. S. Hett. On Colours, On Things Heard, On Physiognomies, On Plants, On Marvellous Things Heard, Mechanical Problems, On Indivisible Lines, On Situations and Names of Winds, On Melissus, Xenophanes, and Gorgias.

ARISTOTLE: NICOMACHEAN ETHICS. H. Rackham.

4

ARISTOTLE: OECONOMICA and MAGNA MORALIA. G. C. Armstrong (with METAPHYSICS, Vol. II).

ARISTOTLE: ON THE HEAVENS. W. K. C. Guthrie.

ARISTOTLE: ON THE SOUL, PARVA NATURALIA, ON BREATH. W. S. Hett.

ARISTOTLE: CATEGORIES, ON INTERPRETATION, PRIOR ANALYTICS. H. P. Cooke and H. Tredennick.

ARISTOTLE: POSTERIOR ANALYTICS, TOPICS. H. Tredennick and E. S. Forster.

ARISTOTLE: ON SOPHISTICAL REFUTATIONS.
On Coming to be and Passing Away, On the Cosmos. E. S. Forster and D. J. Furley.

ARISTOTLE: PARTS OF ANIMALS. A. L. Peck; MOTION AND PROGRESSION OF ANIMALS. E. S. Forster.

ARISTOTLE: PHYSICS. Rev. P. Wicksteed and F. M. Cornford. 2 Vols.

ARISTOTLE: POETICS and LONGINUS. W. Hamilton Fyfe; DEMETRIUS ON STYLE. W. Rhys Roberts.

ARISTOTLE: POLITICS. H. Rackham.

ARISTOTLE: PROBLEMS. W. S. Hett. 2 Vols.

ARISTOTLE: RHETORICA AD ALEXANDRUM (with PROBLEMS. Vol. II). H. Rackham.

ARRIAN: HISTORY OF ALEXANDER and INDICA. Rev. E. Iliffe Robson. 2 Vols. New version P. Brunt.

ATHENAEUS: DEIPNOSOPHISTAE. C. B. Gulick. 7 Vols.

BABRIUS AND PHAEDRUS (Latin). B. E. Perry.

ST. BASIL: LETTERS. R. J. Deferrari. 4 Vols.

CALLIMACHUS: FRAGMENTS. C. A. Trypanis. MUSAEUS: HERO AND LEANDER. T. Gelzer and C. Whitman.

CALLIMACHUS, Hymns and Epigrams, and LYCOPHRON. A. W. Mair; ARATUS. G. R. Mair.

CLEMENT OF ALEXANDRIA. Rev. G. W. Butterworth.

COLLUTHUS. Cf. OPPIAN.

DAPHNIS AND CHLOE. Thornley's Translation revised by J. M. Edmonds: and PARTHENIUS. S. Gaselee.

DEMOSTHENES I.: OLYNTHIACS, PHILIPPICS and MINOR ORATIONS I.–XVII. and XX. J. H. Vince.

DEMOSTHENES II.: DE CORONA and DE FALSA LEGATIONE. C. A. Vince and J. H. Vince.

DEMOSTHENES III.: MEIDIAS, ANDROTION, ARISTOCRATES, TIMOCRATES and ARISTOGEITON I. and II. J. H. Vince.

DEMOSTHENES IV.–VI: PRIVATE ORATIONS and IN NEAERAM. A. T. Murray.

DEMOSTHENES VII: FUNERAL SPEECH, EROTIC ESSAY, EXORDIA and LETTERS. N. W. and N. J. DeWitt.

DIO CASSIUS: ROMAN HISTORY. E. Cary. 9 Vols.

5

DIO CHRYSOSTOM. J. W. Cohoon and H. Lamar Crosby. 5 Vols.

DIODORUS SICULUS. 12 Vols. Vols. I.–VI. C. H. Oldfather. Vol. VII. C. L. Sherman. Vol. VIII. C. B. Welles. Vols. IX. and X. R. M. Geer. Vol. XI. F. Walton. Vol. XII. F. Walton. General Index. R. M. Geer.

DIOGENES LAERTIUS. R. D. Hicks. 2 Vols. New Introduction by H. S. Long.

DIONYSIUS OF HALICARNASSUS: ROMAN ANTIQUITIES. Spelman's translation revised by E. Cary. 7 Vols.

DIONYSIUS OF HALICARNASSUS: CRITICAL ESSAYS. S. Usher. 2 Vols.

EPICTETUS. W. A. Oldfather. 2 Vols.

EURIPIDES. A. S. Way. 4 Vols. Verse trans.

EUSEBIUS: ECCLESIASTICAL HISTORY. Kirsopp Lake and J. E. L. Oulton. 2 Vols.

GALEN: ON THE NATURAL FACULTIES. A. J. Brock.

GREEK ANTHOLOGY. W. R. Paton. 5 Vols.

GREEK BUCOLIC POETS (THEOCRITUS, BION, MOSCHUS). J. M. Edmonds.

GREEK ELEGY AND IAMBUS with the ANACREONTEA. J. M. Edmonds. 2 Vols.

GREEK LYRIC. D. A. Campbell. 4 Vols. Vols. I and II.

GREEK MATHEMATICAL WORKS. Ivor Thomas. 2 Vols.

HERODAS. Cf. THEOPHRASTUS: CHARACTERS.

HERODIAN. C. R. Whittaker. 2 Vols.

HERODOTUS. A. D. Godley. 4 Vols.

HESIOD AND THE HOMERIC HYMNS. H. G. Evelyn White.

HIPPOCRATES and the FRAGMENTS OF HERACLEITUS. W. H. S. Jones and E. T. Withington. 7 Vols. Vols. I.–VI.

HOMER: ILIAD. A. T. Murray. 2 Vols.

HOMER: ODYSSEY. A. T. Murray. 2 Vols.

ISAEUS. E. W. Forster.

ISOCRATES. George Norlin and LaRue Van Hook. 3 Vols.

[ST. JOHN DAMASCENE]: BARLAAM AND IOASAPH. Rev. G. R. Woodward, Harold Mattingly and D. M. Lang.

JOSEPHUS. 10 Vols. Vols. I.–IV. H. Thackeray. Vol. V. H. Thackeray and R. Marcus. Vols. VI.–VII. R. Marcus. Vol. VIII. R. Marcus and Allen Wikgren. Vols. IX.–X. L. H. Feldman.

JULIAN. Wilmer Cave Wright. 3 Vols.

LIBANIUS. A. F. Norman. 2 Vols. Vols. I.–II.

LUCIAN. 8 Vols. Vols. I.–V. A. M. Harmon. Vol. VI. K. Kilburn. Vols. VII.–VIII. M. D. Macleod.

LYCOPHRON. Cf. CALLIMACHUS.

Lyra Graeca, III J. M. Edmonds. (Vols. I. and II. have been replaced by Greek Lyric I. and II.

Lysias. W. R. M. Lamb.

Manetho. W. G. Waddell.

Marcus Aurelius. C. R. Haines.

Menander. W. G. Arnott. 3 Vols. Vol. I.

Minor Attic Orators (Antiphon, Andocides, Lycurgus, Demades, Dinarchus, Hyperides). K. J. Maidment and J. O. Burtt. 2 Vols.

Musaeus: Hero and Leander. Cf. Callimachus.

Nonnos: Dionysiaca. W. H. D. Rouse. 3 Vols.

Oppian, Colluthus, Tryphiodorus. A. W. Mair.

Papyri. Non-Literary Selections. A. S. Hunt and C. C. Edgar. 2 Vols. Literary Selections (Poetry). D. L. Page.

Parthenius. Cf. Daphnis and Chloe.

Pausanias: Description of Greece. W. H. S. Jones. 4 Vols. and Companion Vol. arranged by R. E. Wycherley.

Philo. 10 Vols. Vols. I.–V. F. H. Colson and Rev. G. H. Whitaker. Vols. VI.–IX. F. H. Colson. Vol. X. F. H. Colson and the Rev. J. W. Earp.

Philo: two supplementary Vols. (*Translation only.*) Ralph Marcus.

Philostratus: The Life of Apollonius of Tyana. F. C. Conybeare. 2 Vols.

Philostratus: Imagines; Callistratus: Descriptions. A. Fairbanks.

Philostratus and Eunapius: Lives of the Sophists. Wilmer Cave Wright.

Pindar. Sir J. E. Sandys.

Plato: Charmides, Alcibiades, Hipparchus, The Lovers, Theages, Minos and Epinomis. W. R. M. Lamb.

Plato: Cratylus, Parmenides, Greater Hippias, Lesser Hippias. H. N. Fowler.

Plato: Euthyphro, Apology, Crito, Phaedo, Phaedrus, H. N. Fowler.

Plato: Laches, Protagoras, Meno, Euthydemus. W. R. M. Lamb.

Plato: Laws. Rev. R. G. Bury. 2 Vols.

Plato: Lysis, Symposium, Gorgias. W. R. M. Lamb.

Plato: Republic. Paul Shorey. 2. Vols.

Plato: Statesman, Philebus. H. N. Fowler; Ion. W. R. M. Lamb.

Plato: Theaetetus and Sophist. H. N. Fowler.

Plato: Timaeus, Critias, Cleitophon, Menexenus, Epistulae. Rev. R. G. Bury.

7

PLOTINUS: A. H. Armstrong. 7 Vols.

PLUTARCH: MORALIA. 16 Vols. Vols I.–V. F. C. Babbitt. Vol. VI. W. C. Helmbold. Vols. VII. and XIV. P. H. De Lacy and B. Einarson. Vol. VIII. P. A. Clement and H. B. Hoffleit. Vol. IX. E. L. Minar, Jr., F. H. Sandbach, W. C. Helmbold. Vol. X. H. N. Fowler. Vol. XI. L. Pearson and F. H. Sandbach. Vol. XII. H. Cherniss and W. C. Helmbold. Vol. XIII 1–2. H. Cherniss. Vol. XV. F. H. Sandbach.

PLUTARCH: THE PARALLEL LIVES. B. Perrin. 11 Vols.

POLYBIUS. W. R. Paton. 6 Vols.

PROCOPIUS. H. B. Dewing. 7 Vols.

PTOLEMY: TETRABIBLOS. F. E. Robbins.

QUINTUS SMYRNAEUS. A. S. Way. Verse trans.

SEXTUS EMPIRICUS. Rev. R. G. Bury. 4 Vols.

SOPHOCLES. F. Storr. 2 Vols. Verse trans.

STRABO: GEOGRAPHY. Horace L. Jones. 8 Vols.

THEOCRITUS. Cf. GREEK BUCOLIC POETS.

THEOPHRASTUS: CHARACTERS. J. M. Edmonds. HERODAS. etc. A. D. Knox.

THEOPHRASTUS: ENQUIRY INTO PLANTS. Sir Arthur Hort, Bart. 2 Vols.

THEOPHRASTUS: DE CAUSIS PLANTARUM. G. K. K. Link and B. Einarson. 3 Vols. Vol. I.

THUCYDIDES. C. F. Smith. 4 Vols.

TRYPHIODORUS. Cf. OPPIAN.

XENOPHON: CYROPAEDIA. Walter Miller. 2 Vols.

XENOPHON: HELLENICA. C. L. Brownson. 2 Vols.

XENOPHON: ANABASIS. C. L. Brownson.

XENOPHON: MEMORABILIA and OECONOMICUS. E. C. Marchant, SYMPOSIUM and APOLOGY. O. J. Todd.

XENOPHON: SCRIPTA MINORA. E. C. Marchant. CONSTITUTION OF THE ATHENIANS. G. W. Bowersock.